Governing
States
and Localities

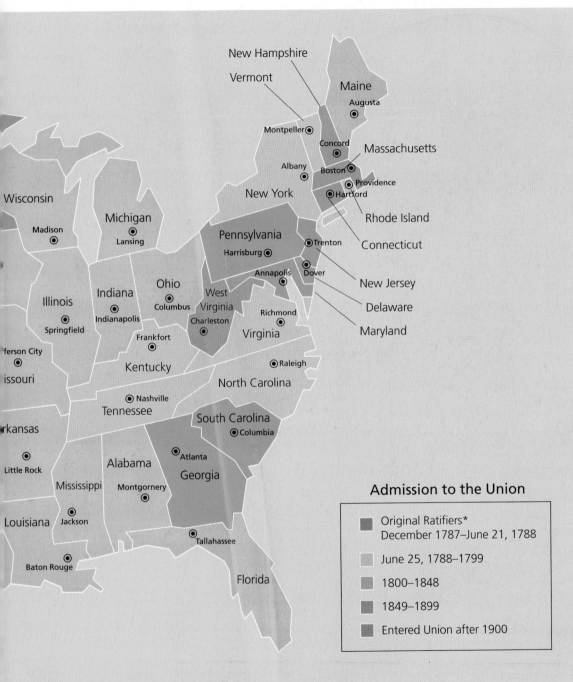

New Hampshire

Vermont

Maine

Augusta ◉

Montpeller ◉

Concord ◉

Massachusetts

Albany ◉

Boston ◉

Providence ◉

Hartford ◉

Rhode Island

New York

Connecticut

Wisconsin

Michigan

Madison ◉

Lansing ◉

Pennsylvania

Trenton ◉

New Jersey

Harrisburg ◉

Annapolis ◉

Dover ◉

Delaware

Illinois

Indiana

Ohio

West Virginia

Richmond ◉

Maryland

Columbus ◉

Indianapolis ◉

Charleston ◉

Springfield ◉

Virginia

Frankfort ◉

fferson City ◉

Kentucky

Raleigh ◉

issouri

North Carolina

rkansas

Nashville ◉

Tennessee

South Carolina

Columbia ◉

Little Rock ◉

Alabama

Atlanta ◉

Georgia

Mississippi

Montgornery ◉

Louisiana

Jackson ◉

Tallahassee ◉

Baton Rouge ◉

Florida

Admission to the Union

■ Original Ratifiers*
December 1787–June 21, 1788

■ June 25, 1788–1799

■ 1800–1848

■ 1849–1899

■ Entered Union after 1900

Source: Bruce Wetterau, *Desk Reference on the States* (Washington, D.C.: CQ Press), 1999: 8–10.

* Until these first nine states ratified the Constitution, it technically was not in effect.

Governing
States
Third Edition # and Localities

Kevin B. Smith, University of Nebraska–Lincoln

Alan Greenblatt

Michele Mariani Vaughn, Pew Center on the States

CQ PRESS

A Division of SAGE
Washington, D.C.

CQ Press
2300 N Street, NW, Suite 800
Washington, DC 20037

Phone, 202-729-1900; toll-free, 1-866-427-7737 (1-866-4CQ-PRESS)

Web: www.cqpress.com

Cover design: Anne Kerns, Anne Likes Red, Inc.
Interior design: Naylor Design Inc.
Composition: C&M Digitals (P) Ltd.

Editorial/political cartoons:
Copyright by Bill Mauldin (1962). Courtesy of Bill Mauldin Estate LLC: 154
© Jeff Parker, Florida Today, and PoliticalCartoons.com: 296

Historic Alabama voter registration materials: 154–155
Courtesy of the Civil Rights Movement Veterans Web site (www.crmvet.org).

Cartograms: 11, 18, 21, 115
International Mapping Associates

Image credits:
Alamy: 419, 512
AP Images: 3, 12, 29, 49, 92, 95, 135, 146, 159, 172, 223, 229, 239, 250, 273, 279, 286, 319, 329, 374, 379, 384, 413, 437, 455, 465, 489, 495, 527, 548, 556, 569, 601, 606, 623
Corbis: 120, 177, 446, 574
Courtesy of Hon. John A. Fritchey: 265
Courtesy of the Library of Congress: 73, 338, 400, 538
Courtesy of nationalatlas.gov: 251
Courtesy of Steve Barrett: 214
Getty Images: 6, 23, 38, 67, 101, 188, 325, 405, 565, 591, 626, 630
Reuters: 106, 219, 516, 530

♾ The paper used in this publication exceeds the requirements of the American National Standard for Information Sciences—Permanence of Paper for Printed Library Materials, ANSI Z39.48-1992.

Printed and bound in Canada

14 13 12 11 10   1 2 3 4 5

Library of Congress Cataloging-in-Publication Data

Smith, Kevin B.
Governing states and localities / Kevin B. Smith, Alan Greenblatt, Michele Mariani Vaughn.—3rd ed.
    p. cm.
Includes bibliographical references and index.
ISBN 978-1-60426-728-0 (alk. paper)
   1. State governments—United States—Textbooks. 2. Local government—United States—Textbooks. 3. Comparative government—Textbooks. I. Greenblatt, Alan. II. Vaughn, Michele Mariani. III. Title.

JK2408.S57 2011
320.473—dc22

2010020561

For my parents, Phyllis and Jerry Greenblatt, with thanks

For my parents, Ron and Ginnie Mariani

Brief Contents

134 Chapter Five

Political
Attitudes and
Participation:
Venting and
Voting

176 Chapter Six

Parties and
Interest Groups:
Elephants,
Donkeys, and
Cash Cows

222 Chapter Seven

Legislatures:
The Art of
Herding Cats

272 Chapter Eight

Governors and
Executives:
There Is No
Such Thing as
Absolute Power

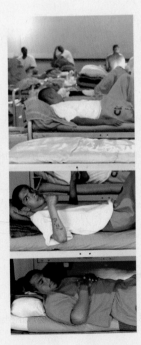

Contents

Chapter 1   **2**
Introduction to State and Local Government: They Tax Dogs in West Virginia, Don't They?

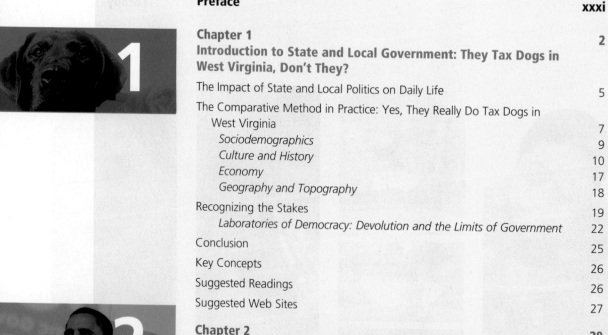

Chapter 2   **28**
Federalism: The Power Plan

Chapter 3
Constitutions: Operating Instructions

Chapter 10

Bureaucracy: What Nobody Wants but Everybody Needs 378

Chapter 11

Local Government: Function Follows Form 412

Chapter 12   454
Metropolitics: The Hole Problem of Government

Chapter 13   488
Education: Reading, Writing, and Regulation

Tables, Figures, and Maps

Tables

Figures

Maps

Boxed Features

Chapter 15: Health and Welfare

Chapter 16: Environment and Climate Change

About the Authors

Kevin B. Smith is professor of political science at the University of Nebraska–Lincoln. He is the author of *The Public Policy Theory Primer* and numerous scholarly articles on state politics and policy, and is the longtime editor of CQ Press's annual *State and Local Government* reader. He is also a former associate editor of *State Politics & Policy Quarterly*. Prior to becoming an academic, he covered state and local politics as a newspaper reporter.

Alan Greenblatt has been writing about politics and government in Washington and the states for nearly two decades. As a reporter for *Congressional Quarterly*, he won the National Press Club's Sandy Hume award for political journalism. While on staff at *Governing* magazine, he covered many issues of concern to state and local governments, such as budgets, taxes, and higher education. Along the way, he has written about politics and culture for numerous other outlets, including the *New York Times*, the *Washington Post*, and NPR.org.

Michele Mariani Vaughn is a project manager for the Pew Center on the States, a division of The Pew Charitable Trusts, where her research focuses on issues related to states' fiscal health, economic competitiveness, and government performance. Prior to joining Pew, she was a reporter and editor for magazines, including *Governing*, where she was nominated for a National Magazine Award.

Preface

The primary goal of this third edition of *Governing States and Localities* is to offer a comprehensive introduction to state and local governments and to do it with a difference. This book is a unique collaboration between academic and professional writers that rests on a foundation of academic scholarship, more than a decade of experience teaching undergraduates about state and local governments, and the insight and experience of journalists who cover state and local politics.

Like its predecessors, this third edition of *Governing States & Localities* aims to provide a fresh and contemporary perspective on state and local politics in terms of coverage and content as well as in the look and feel of the book. The text deliberately follows a news magazine's crisp news-writing style, and the book employs magazine-quality, full-color layout and design. Our intent is to deliver a text that meets the highest academic and pedagogical standards while remaining engaging and easily accessible to undergraduates.

This third edition of the textbook contains a number of significant updates and revisions. This includes an entirely new chapter on environmental policy (chapter 16), which examines the expanding role of states and localities in dealing with issues ranging from global warming to renewable energy. It also includes a special focus on the impact of the Great Recession on states and localities. The toughest economic environment since the Great Depression has reshaped intergovernmental relations, placed constraints on policymaking, prompted grassroots participatory movements like the Tea Party movement, and triggered a wide-ranging reexamination of what governments can or should do. To reflect the enormous changes that the Great Recession is bringing to state and local government, we have not only thoroughly updated the chapter on government finances but placed it earlier in the book so it can better serve as a basis for helping students understand how economics is changing the way governments do business. To help provide even more focus on this topical theme, we have introduced a new series of feature boxes, centered on the theme of "States under Stress," that are designed to highlight and explain some of these changes. In addition, all chapters have been revised substantially, with the content updated whenever possible to reflect the latest issues, trends, and political changes, including:

- An analysis of the results of the most recent legislative and gubernatorial elections
- Discussions of the most important state supreme court decisions and constitutional debates
- The key changes in campaign and elections regulations
- An in-depth examination of recent events and issues that have impacted (and in some cases transformed) states and localities

Although these represent significant revisions, the current edition retains the pedagogical philosophy of the comparative method. This approach compares similar units of analysis to explain *why* differences exist. As scholars know well, state and local governments make excellent units of analysis for comparison because they operate within a single political system. The similarities and differences that mark their institutional structures, laws and regulations, political cultures, histories, demographics, economies, and geographies mean that they make exciting laboratories for asking and answering important questions about politics and government. Put simply, their differences make a difference.

The appeal of exploring state and local government through comparison is not just that it makes for good political science. It is also a great way to engage students because it gives undergraduates an accessible, practical, and systematic way to understand politics and policy in the real world. Students learn that even such seemingly personal concerns as why their tuition is so darned high are not just relevant to their particular situation and educational institution but also are fundamental to the interaction of that institution with its state's political culture, economy, history, and tax structure and even to the school's geographical and demographical position within the state and region. Using the comparative method, this book gives students the resources they need to ask and answer such questions themselves.

Key Features

This book includes a number of elements designed to showcase and promote its main themes. A set of chapter-opening questions engages student interest and prompts students to look systematically for answers using the comparative method. The idea is not simply to spoon-feed the answers to students but, rather, to demonstrate how the comparative method can be used to explore and explain questions about politics and policy.

Following the comparative questions, each chapter moves on to an opening vignette modeled after a lead in a news magazine article—a compelling story that segues naturally into the broader themes of the chapter. Many of these vignettes (as well as many of the feature boxes) represent original reporting.

The feature boxes in each chapter also emphasize and reinforce the comparative theme:

- "A Difference That Makes a Difference" boxes provide clear examples of how variation among states and localities can be used to explain a wide range of political and policy phenomena. These pieces detail the ways in which the institutions, regulations, political culture, demographics, and other factors of a particular state shape its constitution, the way its political parties function, how its citizens tend to vote, how it allocates its financial resources, and why its courts are structured the way they are, to name a few.
- "Local Focus" boxes spotlight the ways localities function independently of the states and show how they are both constrained and empowered by intergovernmental ties. From battles to wrest control of their budgets from the state to constitutional restrictions on how they can tax and spend, the topics addressed in these boxes showcase the rich variety that exists in these nearly 87,000 substate entities.
- "Policy in Practice" boxes demonstrate how different states and localities have interpreted and implemented the legislation handed down from higher levels of government and the consequences of these decisions. Gubernatorial policy innovators in Wisconsin and Maryland, the surprising effects of new e-government tools, and the political and policy challenges involved in tuition hikes are just some of the issues addressed.
- "States under Stress" boxes demonstrate how the Great Recession is reshaping how state and local governments operate. The issues addressed in these boxes include power shifting toward the federal government, the scramble for federal stimulus dollars, and the weakened negotiating stand of public-sector labor unions.

Another key feature that serves the comparative theme is the design and use of graphics and tables. Nearly thirty full-color fifty-state maps, including four unique cartograms, provide a visual representation of and an intuitively easy way to grasp the differences among states and localities, whether these differences are the sizes of the state economies, the party-affiliation requirements for voting in direct primaries, the methods of judicial selection, or state incarceration rates. Similarly, more than sixty tables and figures emphasize how states and localities differ and what these differences mean to politics and policy. State rankings of voter turnout rates, state-by-state data on per-pupil educational spending, recent regional murder rates, and many other features support comparisons made in the text.

To help students assimilate content and review for tests, each chapter includes a set of highlighted key concepts. These terms are defined in the margins near the place where they are introduced and are compiled into a list at the end of each chapter with corresponding page numbers. We've also placed expanded and updated lists of Web links and lists of suggested readings, both with brief annotations, at the end of each chapter. A comprehensive glossary of key terms precedes the book's index.

Organization of the Book

The book is organized so that each chapter logically builds on previous chapters. The first chapter (subtitled "They Tax Dogs in West Virginia, Don't They?") is essentially a persuasive essay that lays the conceptual groundwork for the book. Its aim is to convince students that state and local politics are important to their day-to-day lives and to their futures as professionals and as citizens. That is, it makes the case for why students should care about state and local politics. Along the way, it introduces the advantages of the comparative method as a systematic way to explore this subject. In introducing the book's approach, the chapter provides the basic context for studying state and local governments, especially the differences in economics, culture, demographics, and geography that drive policy and politics at the regional level.

The next two chapters cover federalism and state constitutions. These chapters provide a basic understanding of what state and local governments are and what powers, responsibilities, and roles they have within the political system of the United States, as well as a sense of how they legally can make different political and policy choices.

Chapter 4 examines the finances of state and local governments. The economy has become *the* unifying focus of government during the past couple of years. All the key revenue streams for states and localities—income, sales, and property taxes—were affected by the Great Recession. While revenues contracted, the demand for state and local services, if anything, increased. This basic imbalance between revenues and expenditures has had an enormous impact on what states and localities can do and has shifted power toward the federal government. This chapter gives students a fundamental sense of the revenues and expenditures of state and local governments and their central importance to virtually everything government does.

Chapter 5 examines political participation with an eye to helping students understand how citizens connect to the core policymaking institutions of government. Chapters 6–10 are separate treatments of those core institutions: parties and interest groups, legislatures, governors and executives, courts, and the bureaucracy. There is special emphasis in each chapter on how variations in the structure, powers, and responsibilities of these institutions have real-life implications for citizens of states and localities.

Chapters 11 and 12 focus on local government. Chapter 11 concentrates on laying out the basic structure, authority, and responsibilities of local government. Chapter 12 examines the relations among local governments from a regional perspective. The final four chapters are devoted to specific policy areas—education, crime and punishment, health and welfare, and the environment—that represent a selection of the most critical policy functions of state and local governments.

Ancillaries

We are pleased to offer an updated and significantly expanded suite of high-quality, classroom-ready instructor and student ancillaries to accompany the book. Written by Lori Riverstone-Newell of Illinois State University and Ralph Durham of Kennesaw State University, the ancillaries are specifically tailored to the third edition of *Governing States and Localities*.

A set of downloadable instructor's resources is available free to adopters, including a comprehensive test bank of more than six hundred true/false, multiple-choice, fill-in-the-blank, and short-answer questions. Available in a number of formats, this test bank also can be used with *Respondus*—a flexible and easy-to-use test-generation software that allows professors to build, customize, and even integrate exams into course management platforms.

In addition, instructors will find more than two hundred PowerPoint lecture slides tailored to the text. These slides carefully detail the core concepts of each chapter, underscoring the book's comparative principles.

An Instructor's Manual with clear chapter summaries, downloadable lecture outlines, points for discussion, and sample syllabi for the course is included as well. Instructors have access to a full suite of .jpg and .ppt format files of all of the tables, figures, and maps in the book. These can be used to create additional PowerPoint slides or transparency masters when covering comparative data in the classroom or in discussion groups. In addition, these visuals can be imported into exams.

A host of new and improved student resources can be found on the book's Web site at http://college.cqpress.com/govstateandlocal, including chapter summaries with clear chapter objectives and a set of self-testing study questions, nearly three hundred self-grading comprehensive quiz questions, a set of flashcards for review of key concepts, and a set of annotated links to important state and local Web sites.

Students and instructors alike will find *Governing* magazine's Web site especially useful for further research and in-class discussion. To help instructors bring the latest word from the states and localities into their classrooms, adopters may receive a free semester-long subscription to *Governing* magazine.

Acknowledgments

A lot of effort and dedication go into the making of a textbook like this, only a fraction of which is contributed by those whose names end up on the cover.

To Dwain Smith, Charisse Kiino, Julie Nemer, and Lorna Notsch, the editorial team at CQ Press responsible for much of what happened from game plan to actualization, a single word: Thanks! The word is miserly compensation for their work, effort, and dedication, and in no way makes up for all the trouble we caused. Nonetheless, our thanks are most sincerely meant (again). We heartily thank our many reviewers, past and present, for their careful and detailed assistance with reading and commenting on the manuscript:

Sharon Alter, *William Rainey Harper Community College*
Jeff Ashley, *Eastern Illinois University*
Jenna Bednar, *University of Michigan*
Neil Berch, *West Virginia University*
John Bohte, *University of Wisconsin–Milwaukee*
Shannon Bow O'Brien, *University of Texas–Austin*
William Cassie, *Appalachian State University*
Douglas Clouatre, *Mid Plains Community College*
Gary Crawley, *Ball State University*
Warren Dixon, *Texas A&M University*
Nelson Dometrius, *Texas Tech University*
Jaime Dominguez, *DePaul University*
Nicholas Easton, *Clark University*
David H. Folz, *University of Tennessee*
Michael E. Greenberg, *Shippensburg University*
Donald Haider-Markel, *University of Kansas*
William Hall, *Bradley University*
Susan Hansen, *University of Pittsburgh*
Dana Michael Harsell, *University of North Dakota*
Lisa Langenbach, *Middle Tennessee State University*
William Lester, *Jacksonville State University*
Madhavi McCall, *San Diego State University*
Bryan McQuide, *University of Idaho*
Scott Moore, *Colorado State University*
Lawrence Overlan, *Bentley College*
Kelly Sills, *Washington State University–Vancouver*
Zachary Smith, *Northern Arizona University*
Kendra Stewart, *Eastern Kentucky University*
Charles Turner, *California State University–Chico*

We hope and expect that each of them will be able to find traces of their numerous helpful suggestions throughout this final product. Also, we owe a special thanks to Bruce Stinebrickner at DePauw University for giving the second edition of this text such a thorough edit.

In addition, we express our appreciation to a group of political scientists who pay attention not only to Washington, D.C., but also to what is happening throughout the rest of the country: the dean of governor-watchers, Thad Beyle, formerly of the University of North Carolina; Bruce Cain, University of California, Berkeley; Burdett Loomis, University of Kansas; Alan Rosenthal, Rutgers University; and Larry Sabato, University of Virginia. All generously contributed their expertise when contacted by Alan Greenblatt.

Governing
**States
and Localities**

CHAPTER 1

Introduction

to State and Local Government

They Tax Dogs in West Virginia, Don't They?

Is government going to the dogs? State and local governments raise revenues in many different ways, including varying levels of income, sales, and property tax. They can tax virtually anything, including dogs. In some places a man's best friend is not only a family pet, but also a source of money for government.

What are the advantages and disadvantages of federalism?

What is the comparative method, and why is it a useful way to talk about state and local governments?

What role do state and local politics play in determining how much certain services—like a college education—cost?

1

It doesn't take much to convince Vincent Del Casino Jr., chair of the Geography Department at California State University (Cal State) at Long Beach, of the importance of state politics. It takes even less to convince Phillip Bautista, a student at Fresno State. The state of California, fiscally speaking, all but imploded in 2009, and the political fallout left Del Casino, Bautista, and everyone else in the state struggling to deal with the collateral damage.

A lot went into California's fiscal crisis. There was, of course, what some have labeled the 2008–2009 Great Recession, the biggest economic contraction to hit the United States since the Great Depression of the 1930s. California state government didn't exactly have its finest hour in response to the crisis. Gov. Arnold Schwarzenegger backed a series of ballot initiatives designed to reform the state's budget process. The voters overwhelmingly rejected them. As the state careened toward a financial abyss—a projected $24 billion deficit—the representatives in the ideologically split legislature seemed less interested in grabbing the wheel than in grabbing each other's throats. Looming behind all of this were decades of voter-approved ballot initiatives that limited government's ability to, well, govern.

By the time the political mist had semi-cleared in mid-2009, it became clear that the state's political fix to the financial crisis was going to have an enormous impact across virtually all public-sector services. The Cal State system is one example. The budget finally approved by the legislature and signed by Governor Schwarzenegger cut nearly $100 million of state support from the system, with more cuts anticipated for the future.[1] Overall, the Cal State system was facing a deficit of roughly half-a-billion dollars in 2009–2010. How was that gap closed? With a 20 percent hike in tuition, faculty and staff furloughs, larger classes, and smaller enrollments.[2]

The gap left Del Casino trying to figure out how to "slash our very modest teaching budget" and wondering what is going to happen to one of the largest systems of higher education in the nation when "the state can't manage its affairs and fulfill its own policies and goals."[3] Bautista, on the other hand, wasn't dealing in the billions the state government was juggling, the millions the college system was scrambling for, or even the tens of thousands Del Casino was trying to find. The impact on him was smaller: $306 for an initial tuition hike and another $672 that was added on top of the first. Doesn't sound like much in the greater scheme of things, but it meant that Bautista couldn't pay for maintenance on his car.

California's fiscal woes are perhaps a high-profile example of the impact of state politics on people's lives, but the end result is common enough. If you follow state and local politics far enough, you end up in the day-to-day lives of people you probably are familiar with (yourself, for example). Bautista is just a college student—maybe just like you—trying to figure out how to scrape up a thousand bucks to cover a tuition bill and wondering if his Toyota Corolla will get him to class for another semester.[4] State politics doesn't just affect his educational opportunities, it affects his ability to get an oil change.

Convincing college students that state and local politics is important and worthy of their attention used to be a tough sell. These days . . . not so much. Why should you care about state and local politics? There are lots of ready answers to such a question these days, starting with the tuition bill; and not just if you live in California—virtually every public higher education system has been hammered over the past couple of years by the faltering economy. Yet it's worth considering this question from a broader perspective; it's not just public college and university communities that have their daily lives shaped by state and local politics. The first goal of this book is to make the case that *everyone*—not just college students—has a vested interest in knowing more about state and local government.

The Impact of State and Local Politics on Daily Life

Regardless of who you are and what you do or want to do, if you reside in the United States, state and local governments play a large role in your life. Regardless of what you are interested in—graduating, a career, relationships—state and local governments shape how, whether, and to what extent you are able to pursue these interests. To follow up on the obvious example, consider your college education. The vast majority of college students in the United States—more than three-quarters—attend public institutions of higher education.[5] Public colleges and universities are created and supported by state governments. For many readers of this book, the opportunity to get a college education is possible only because each state government created a system of higher education. For example, Cal State is one of three major higher education systems in California, along with the University of California and the California Community College System. State governments require that taxpayers subsidize the operation of these education systems; in other words, tuition in public colleges and universities picks up only a fraction of the actual costs of education. The rest comes from the taxpayers' pockets via the state government. When the subsidy falls, tuition, as Phillip Bautista found out, goes up. On average, about 36 percent of a public college's revenue comes from money that the state appropriates, or sets aside. Less than 20 percent comes from tuition and fees

Students at public universities in California need little convincing of the importance of state politics. Facing extreme fiscal stress, state government over the past couple of years has slashed its support for higher education, which has hit students directly in the pocketbook. Here, University of California, Los Angeles (UCLA) students Andrea Flores (L) and Kendall Brown (R) and their peers protest a 32 percent tuition increase approved by the UC Board of Regents in November 2009.

paid by students.[6] Public colleges and universities get about $8.3 billion in direct appropriations from state and local governments every year.[7]

Even if you attend a private college, the state government may still play a significant role in covering the costs of your education. A quarter of the students at private, nonprofit schools receive grants or other forms of financial aid directly funded by state governments.[8] In fact, undergraduates at private colleges receive on average more than $2,000 in state grants or other financial aid from state or local government. Not including tuition, that amount of financial aid is several hundred dollars more than the average undergraduate at a public college receives from the state.[9]

State governments do not just determine what opportunities for higher education are available and what they cost. Some states have curriculum mandates. You may be taking a course on state and local politics—and reading this book—because your state government decided that it was a worthy investment of your time and money. In Texas, for example, a state politics course is not just a good idea—it's the law. According to Section 51.301 of the Texas Education Code, to receive a bachelor's degree from any publicly funded college in the state, students must successfully complete a course on state politics.

Think that's a lot of regulation? The government's role in shaping your college education is actually pretty small. Compared to the heavy involvement of state and local governments in shaping K–12 education, colleges have free rein. Roughly 90 percent of students in grades 9–12 attended public high schools.[10] Local units of government operate most of these schools.[11] Private grade schools also are subject to a wide variety of state and local government regulations, ranging from teacher certification and minimum curriculum requirements to basic health and safety standards. Whether you attended public or private school—or were home-schooled—at the end of the day you had no choice in the decision to get a basic grade school education. Although the minimum requirements vary, every state in the union requires at least a grade school education.

State and local governments do not exist simply to regulate large areas of your life, even if it sometimes seems that way. Their primary purpose is to provide services to their respective populations. In providing these services, state and local governments shape the social and economic lives of their citizens. Education is a good example of a public service that extends deep into the daily lives of Americans, but it is far from the only one. The roads you use to get to school are there because state and local authorities built them and maintain them. The electricity that runs your computer comes from a utility grid regulated by state government, local government, or both. State and local governments are responsible for the sewer and water systems that make the bathroom down the hall possible. They make sure that the water you drink is safe and that the burger, sushi, or salad you bought in your student union does not make you sick.[12] State governments determine the violations and punishments that constitute the criminal law. Local governments are responsible primarily for law enforcement and fire protection. The services that state and local governments supply are such a part of our lives that in many cases we only notice their absence—when the water does not run, when the road is closed, or when the educational subsidy either declines or disappears.

The Comparative Method in Practice: Yes, They Really Do Tax Dogs in West Virginia

Recognizing the impact of state and local government may be a reasonable way to spark an interest in the topic, but interest alone does not convey knowledge. A systematic approach to learning about state and local government is necessary to gain a coherent understanding of the many activities, responsibilities, and levels involved. In this book, that systematic approach is the **comparative method**, which uses similarities and differences as the basis for systematic explanation. Any two states or localities that you can think of will differ in a number of ways. For example, they really do tax dogs in West Virginia. The state authorizes each county government to assess a fee for every dog within that county's jurisdiction. This is not the case in, say, New Jersey, where dogs live tax free.[13] Another example: Texas has executed hundreds of criminals since the moratorium, or ban, on the death penalty was lifted in the 1970s; other states have executed none.

In recent elections, Georgians sent a mixture of Republicans and Democrats to the House of Representatives (seven Republicans and six Democrats

COMPARATIVE METHOD

A learning approach based on studying the differences and similarities among similar units of analysis (such as states).

in 2008). The people of Massachusetts sent just Democrats (all ten seats in 2008). Differences between states and localities do not just involve such oddities as the tax status of the family pet or such big political questions as the balance of power in the House of Representatives. Those of you who do something as ordinary as buying a soda after class may pay more than your peers in other states or cities. Some readers of this book are certainly paying more in tuition and fees than those in other colleges. Why?

The comparative method answers such questions by systematically look-ing for **variance**, or differences, between comparable units of analysis. For our purposes, states are one comparable unit of analysis. Local governments—governments below the state level, such as county boards of commissioners and city councils—are another. Governments at each of these levels, state or local, have basic similarities that make meaningful comparisons possi-ble. One way to think of this is that the comparative method is based on the idea that you can learn more about apples by comparing them to other apples rather than to oranges or bananas.

For example, governmentally speaking, all fifty states have a lot in com-mon. Their governmental structures are roughly the same. All have a basic division of power among the executive, legislative, and judicial branches of government. All have to operate within the broad confines of the single set of rules that is the U.S. Constitution. There's a bit more variety below the state level, with many different kinds and levels of local government (coun-ties, municipalities, townships, and so forth), but broadly speaking all these governments share a basic set of responsibilities and all have to operate within the rules set down within their respective state constitutions. These similarities among states and among local governments make mean-ingful comparisons possible. Paradoxically, what makes such comparisons meaningful is not by looking at similarities, but at differences.

The states share similar political structures and follow the same overall set of rules, but they make very different choices. These differences have consequences. Take, for example, college tuition and fees. As noted earlier, there is a direct relationship between the size of a state govern-ment's contribution to higher education and a student's average tuition bill. Underlying this relationship is a set of differences that explains why your tuition bill is high (or low) compared to tuition charged by colleges in other states. Simply put, your tuition bill is comparatively higher (or lower) depending on the size of a state govern-ment's subsidy to higher education; this is a lesson hundreds of thousands of students have become all too painfully aware of in the past year or two. These sorts of meaningful differences extend far beyond how much you're

VARIANCE

The difference between units of analysis on a particular measure.

> Governments at each of these levels, state or local, have basic similarities that make meaningful comparisons possible. One way to think of this is that the comparative method is based on the idea that you can learn more about apples by comparing them to other apples rather than to oranges or bananas.

paying for your college education. A similar difference explains why some of you will pay more for a soda after class than others. The sales tax on a can of soda ranges from 0 to 9 percent, depending on the city and state, hence the different prices in different locales.[14] These examples demonstrate the essence of the comparative method—from your tuition bills to the price of soda, differences between political jurisdictions make a difference in the daily lives of citizens.

Such differences can lend themselves to very sophisticated and very useful statistical analyses. For example, exactly how much is a tuition bill influenced by state support of public higher education? A professional policy analyst can use data on state higher education funding and tuition rates at state universities and colleges to provide a precise estimate of the relationship between the contributions from state government and your tuition bill. On average, for every appropriation of $1,000 per student by state government, tuition and fees at public four-year universities fall by a little more than $200.[15] Of course, the reverse is also true. For every reduction of $1,000 per student in state aid, tuition goes up by an average of $200.

This basic approach of looking for differences that make a difference can be used to answer a broad range of "why" questions. For example, we know that how much a state gives to higher education helps determine how much you pay in tuition. So, why do some states provide more support to higher education than others? This is a question about one difference (variation in how much state governments spend on higher education) that can be answered by looking at other differences. What might these differences be? Well, they could range from partisan politics in a state's legislature to a state's traditions and history to its relative wealth. As a starting point for using the comparative approach to analyze such questions, consider the following basic differences among states and among localities.

Sociodemographics

The populations of states and localities vary enormously in size, age, and ethnicity. The particular mix of these characteristics, or **sociodemographics**, in a specific state or community has a profound impact on its politics. California is the most populous state in the nation, with about 37 million residents. It is a racially and ethnically diverse 37 million, with only 42 percent non-Hispanic whites and with many first-generation or second-generation immigrants. Roughly 12 percent of Californians live in poverty. Compare this with New Hampshire, which has about 1.3 million residents, 93 percent of whom are non-Hispanic whites and only about 7 percent of whom live below the poverty line.[16] These population characteristics present different challenges to the governments in these two states. Differences in populations are likely to promote different attitudes about and policies on welfare, affirmative action, bilingual education programs, even the role and responsibilities of government in general.

SOCIODEMOGRAPHICS

The characteristics of a population, including size, age, and ethnicity.

And it gets better. All these population characteristics are dynamic. That is, they change. Between 2000 and 2005, the population of Flagler County, Florida, grew by more than 50 percent.[17] During roughly the same time period, the population of Arthur County, Nebraska, shrank by more than 10 percent. Such population expansions and contractions create very different problems and policy priorities for local governments—the struggle to accommodate new growth in a fast-developing area versus the challenge of maintaining even basic services in a rural county in which there are ever fewer taxpayers to tax. Or consider the population of the entire state of Florida, which was still growing in 2008, but at the slowest annual rate seen in three decades. That gearing down of population growth is expected to influence everything from housing starts to job creation to state and local tax collections.[18]

How might sociodemographics be related to, say, your tuition bill? Consider the age distribution from young to old of a state's population. There is less demand for college education among those older than sixty-five than there is among those in the traditional undergraduate demographic of eighteen to twenty-four. Given this, states with a higher percentage of their populations in older age groups face a different set of education policy pressures than those with higher concentrations in younger groups. States with large aging populations are likely to face less demand for higher education spending and more demand for public programs, such as healthcare, that address the needs of the elderly. Why do some states provide more support to higher education than others? At least a partial answer to this question is that different sociodemographics create different demands for higher education.

Study Map 1-1 for a moment. Believe it or not, you are actually looking at the United States. The reason the states look so strange is that this is a special kind of map called a cartogram. Instead of using actual geographical space to determine the size of a particular area represented in the map—the number of square miles in each state, for instance—cartograms use other variables to determine how size is represented. This cartogram measures the size of each state's population, another useful way to compare states. Notice that some states that are geographically actually pretty big, like New Mexico at 122,000 square miles, are very small on this map because they have small populations. Other states that are geographically actually really small, like Connecticut (with only 5,000 square miles), look much bigger on this map because they have large populations. Some states, like Virginia, don't look that different in size at all.

Culture and History

States and localities have distinct "personalities" that are apparent in everything from the "bloody bucket" shoulder patch worn by the Pennsylvania National Guard to the drawl that distinguishes the speech of West Texas

Utah is the country's fastest growing state, with a 2.5 percent increase in its population in 2008. The previous population-growth champ, Nevada, was hit hard by a plunge in economic development in cities like Las Vegas and saw its growth rate nearly halved to an annual increase of 1.8 percent.

MAP 1-1 Population by State

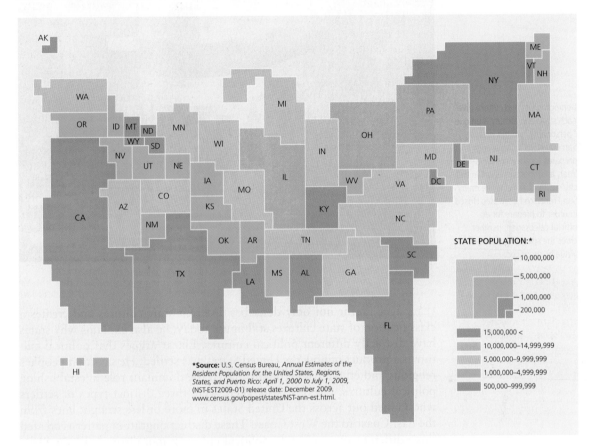

STATE POPULATION:*

— 10,000,000
— 5,000,000
— 1,000,000
— 200,000

15,000,000 <
10,000,000–14,999,999
5,000,000–9,999,999
1,000,000–4,999,999
500,000–999,999

*Source: U.S. Census Bureau, *Annual Estimates of the Resident Population for the United States, Regions, States, and Puerto Rico: April 1, 2000 to July 1, 2009*, (NST-EST2009-01) release date: December 2009. www.census.gov/popest/states/NST-ann-est.html.

natives. Some states have been part of the Union for more than two hundred years and still project an Old World connection to Europe. Hawaii and Alaska became states within living memory and are more associated with the Old West and the exoticism of the Pacific. New York City prides itself on being a cosmopolitan center of Western civilization. The visitor's bureau of Lincoln, Nebraska, touts its small-town ambience and Middle American values. These differences are more than interesting variations in accent and local points of pride. They are visible symbols that represent distinct values and attitudes. Political scientists generally accept that these differences extend to government and that each state has a distinct **political culture**, identifiable general attitudes and beliefs about the role and responsibility of government.

Daniel Elazar's *American Federalism: A View from the States* is the classic study of political culture. In this book, first published more than forty

POLITICAL CULTURE

The attitudes and beliefs broadly shared in a polity about the role and responsibility of government.

Demographics and culture give each state and locality a unique "personality." In this picture, San Francisco's Chinatown prepares for the Chinese New Year, an important event in the city's calendar. Yet while many San Francisco businesses closed in order to prepare for an official celebration, in other cities the special day passed virtually unnoticed.

years ago, Elazar not only describes different state cultures and creates a classification of state cultures still in use today, he also explains why states have distinctly different political cultures. Elazar argues that political culture is a product of how the United States was settled. He says that people's religious and ethnic backgrounds played the dominant role in establishing political cultures. On this basis, there were three distinct types of settlers who fanned out across the United States in more or less straight lines from the East Coast to the West Coast. These distinct migration patterns created three different types of state political cultures: moralistic, individualistic, and traditionalistic.[19]

States with **moralistic cultures** are those in which politics is the means used to achieve a good and just society. Such states tend to be clustered in the country's north (New England, the upper Midwest, and the Pacific Northwest). Elazar argued that the Puritans who originally settled the Northeast came to the New World seeking religious freedom. Their political culture reflected a desire to use politics to construct the best possible society. This notion, that government and politics represent the means to the greater good, creates a society that values involvement in politics and views government as a positive force for addressing social problems. This general orientation toward government and politics spread along the northern and middle parts of the country in successive waves of migration. Wisconsin, for example, is a classic moralistic state. First settled by Yankees, and later by Scandinavians, Germans, and Eastern Europeans, the state has long had a reputation for high levels of participation in politics (for example, high levels of voter turnout), policy innovation, and scandal-free government.

States with **individualistic cultures** have a different view of government and politics. In individualistic cultures, people view government as an extension of the marketplace, something in which people participate for individual reasons and to achieve individual goals. Government should provide the services that people want, but it is not viewed as a vehicle to create a "good society" or to intervene in private activities. Politics in individualistic states is viewed like any other business. Officeholders expect to be paid like professionals, and political parties are, in essence, corporations that compete to provide goods and services to people. Unlike those in moralistic states, as long as the roads are paved and the trains run on time, folks in individualistic states tend to tolerate more corruption in government.

Why? In individualistic states, "Both politicians and citizens look upon political activity as a specialized one," Elazar writes, "and no place for amateurs to play an active role."[20] The roots of this view of government, according to Elazar, comes from the English, Scottish, Irish, and Germans who initially settled in states like Maryland, New Jersey, and Pennsylvania. They came to the United States in search of individual opportunity, not to construct some idealized vision of the good society. This "every man for himself" attitude was reflected in politics, and the individualistic culture was carried by subsequent waves of migration into places like Illinois and Missouri.

New Jersey is a good example of an individualistic state. The state, as political scientist Maureen Moakley puts it, "Has always been more of a polyglot than a melting pot."[21] Originally settled by waves of poor and uneducated immigrants in pursuit of the American Dream, in more recent times it has become home to more than a million foreign-born residents and large racial and ethnic minority populations. The result is a fragmented political culture in which many residents feel more connected to their local communities than to the state. One poll conducted in 2003 found that only one in twenty-five residents could correctly identify which party controlled the state's government.[22] Not surprisingly given all this, New Jersey has strong laws that give the state's more than five hundred local governments more power than localities in other states.

In **traditionalistic cultures**, politics is the province of elites, something that average citizens should not concern themselves with. Traditionalistic states are, as their name suggests, fundamentally conservative, in the sense of preserving a well-established society. Like moralistic states, traditionalistic states believe that government serves a positive role. But there is one big difference—traditionalistic states believe the larger purpose of government is to maintain the existing social order. Those at the top of the social structure are expected to play a dominant role in politics, and power is concentrated in the hands of these elites. Traditionalistic states tend to be rural states (at least historically) in which agriculture, rather than a broader mix of competing commercial activities, is the main economic driver.

Traditionalistic cultures tend to be concentrated in the Deep South, in states such as Georgia, Mississippi, and South Carolina. In these states,

INDIVIDUALISTIC CULTURE

A political culture that views politics and government as just another way to achieve individual goals.

TRADITIONALISTIC CULTURE

A political culture that views politics and government as dominated by elites.

A Difference That Makes a Difference:
Is It Better to Be a Woman in Vermont or a Gal in Mississippi?

According to the Institute for Women's Policy Research (IWPR), it is better to be a woman in Vermont than a gal in Mississippi.

Why? Well, in its 2004 analysis of the status of women in the states, the IWPR had several reasons for ranking Vermont as the best state for women and Mississippi as the worst. For example, in Vermont women had greater economic autonomy and enjoyed greater reproductive rights than women in Mississippi. This is only a partial answer to the question, however. To learn the rest of it, we must ask: *Why* do women have greater economic autonomy and more reproductive rights in Vermont than in Mississippi?

The comparative approach to answering this question involves looking for other differences between Vermont and Mississippi. Differences that might explain the variance in the status of women. Some candidates for those explanatory differences are presented in Table 1-1. This table shows the top five and the bottom five states in the IWPR rankings, the dominant political culture in these states, and the percentage of state legislators who were women in 2009. Notice any patterns?

You may have caught that each of the top five states has either a moralistic or an individualistic culture. All of the bottom five states have traditionalistic cultures. Therefore, political culture might explain some of the difference in women's status. States in which the dominant political values stress the importance of everyone getting involved might offer more opportunities for women. So might states in which such values emphasize hard work as the predominant basis for getting ahead in life. States in which the dominant political values stress leaving the important decisions to established elites might offer fewer opportunities because, traditionally, elites have been male.

Also, take a look at the proportion of women in the state legislatures. On average, about one-third of state legislators in the top five states are women. In the bottom five states, that average is more than halved—only about 15 percent of state legislators are women. This is a difference that can have considerable impact. A number of studies show that women legislators tend to support more progressive policies, are more likely to pay attention to women's issues, and are more likely to push these issues into law.*

Thus, states that have more women in their legislatures are more likely to respond to issues such as reproductive rights, violence against women, child-support policies, and family-leave benefits. All these contribute to IWPR's calculations. Why is Vermont a better state for women than Mississippi? A comparative answer to that question is that Vermont has a political culture that is more likely to encourage and support political participation by women and it also has a greater female presence in its state legislature.

TABLE 1-1

Politics and the Status of Women in the States: Some Variables

Five Best States for Women	Dominant Political Culture	Percentage of State Legislators Who Are Women
1. Vermont	Moralistic	37.2
2. Connecticut	Individualistic	31.6
3. Minnesota	Moralistic	34.8
4. Washington	Moralistic	32.7
5. Oregon	Moralistic	26.7
Five Worst States for Women	**Dominant Political Culture**	**Percentage of State Legislators Who Are Women**
46. Oklahoma	Traditionalistic	11.4
47. Arkansas	Traditionalistic	23.7
48. Kentucky	Traditionalistic	15.2
49. South Carolina	Traditionalistic	10.0
50. Mississippi	Traditionalistic	14.4

Sources: Center for American Women and Politics, "Fact Sheet: Women in State Legislatures 2009," available at www.cawp.rutgers .edu/fast_facts/levels_of_office/documents/stleg.pdf; Institute for Women's Policy Research, *The Status of Women in the States*, 2004, available at www.iwpr.org/States2004/ SWS2004/index.htm; Daniel Elazar, *American Federalism: A View from the States* (New York: Crowell, 1966).

*Michele Swers, "Understanding the Policy Impact of Electing Women: Evidence from Research on Congress and State Legislatures," *PS: Political Science and Politics* 34, no. 2 (2001): 217–220.

politics is significantly shaped by tradition and history (an argument about the official recognition of Confederate flags, for example, can be a major election-year issue in such states). Like the settlers of individualistic states, those who settled the South sought personal opportunity. The preindustrial, agrarian economy of the South, however, led to a culture that was little more than a variation of the feudal order of the European Middle Ages. As far back as the 1830s, French aristocrat and writer Alexis de Tocqueville noted that "as one goes farther south . . . the population does not exercise such a direct influence on affairs. . . . The power of the elected officials is comparatively greater and that of the voter less."[23]

Few states today can be considered "pure" examples of any of these cultures. In other words, most states have elements of two of the cultures or of all three. For example, a number of traditionalistic states, like Florida and Georgia, have seen a huge influx of people from northern states, people who often are not from traditionalistic cultures. The Deep South is also considerably more urban than it used to be. Such changes tend to add elements of the moralistic and individualistic cultures into the traditionalistic mix.

Even with such changes, however, for most states one of Elazar's three political cultures is likely to be dominant, as Map 1-2 shows. Numerous studies have found that the dominant political culture shapes politics and

MAP 1-2 Dominant Political Culture by State

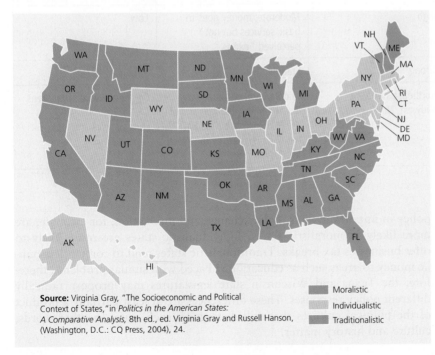

Source: Virginia Gray, "The Socioeconomic and Political Context of States," in *Politics in the American States: A Comparative Analysis*, 8th ed., ed. Virginia Gray and Russell Hanson, (Washington, D.C.: CQ Press, 2004), 24.

Moralistic
Individualistic
Traditionalistic

TABLE 1-2

Political Cultures at a Glance

	Elazar Classification		
	Moralistic	**Individualistic**	**Traditionalistic**
Role of Government	Government should act to promote the public interest and policy innovation.	Government should be utilitarian, a service provider.	Government should help preserve the status quo.
Attitude of Public Representatives	Politicians can effect change; public service is worthwhile and an honor.	Businesslike. Politics is a career like any other, and individual politicians are oriented toward personal power. High levels of corruption are more common.	Politicians can effect change, but politics is the province of the elites.
Role of Citizens	Citizens actively participate in voting and other political activities; individuals seek public office.	The state exists to advance the economic and personal self-interest of citizens; citizens leave politics to the professionals.	Ordinary citizens are not expected to be politically involved.
Degree of Party Competition	Highly competitive	Moderate	Weak
Government Spending on Services	High	Moderate; money goes to basic services but not perceived "extras."	Low
Political Culture	Strong	Fragmented	Strong
Most Common in . . .	Northeast, northern Midwest, Northwest	Middle parts of the country, like the Mid-Atlantic; parts of the Midwest, like Missouri and Illinois; parts of the West, like Nevada	Southern states, rural areas

policy in important ways. Policy change and innovation, for example, are more likely in moralistic states. Individualistic states are more likely to offer businesses tax breaks. Traditionalistic states tend to commit less public money to areas such as education.[24] Faced with similar problems, therefore, the Texas and Wisconsin state legislatures may propose radically different policy responses. These differences are at least partially a product of the political cultures that still distinguish each state. In other words, culture and history matter.

These cultural differences certainly are apparent when it comes to supporting higher education. Moralistic states commit considerably more resources to higher education than governments in individualistic and traditionalistic states. They spend about 13 percent more per capita on colleges and universities than states with the other two cultures. Because moralistic states are those in which attitudes support higher levels of commitment to the public sector, these spending differences make sense in cultural terms. Why do some states provide more support to higher education than others? Apparently, another part of the answer is that some political cultures see higher education in more communal than individual terms.

Economy

The relative size and health of a state's economy have a huge impact on its capacity to govern and provide public services. The per capita gross state product—the state equivalent of the gross national product—varies from about $26,000 in Mississippi to $64,000 in Delaware.[25] (See Map 1-3.) This means government in Delaware has the ability to tap a greater amount of resources than government in Mississippi. The difference in wealth, in effect, means that, if Delaware and Mississippi were to implement identical and equivalent public services, Mississippi would have a considerably higher tax rate. This is because Mississippi would have to take a greater proportion of its smaller amount of resources than Delaware. These sorts of differences also are visible at the local level. Wealthy suburbs can enjoy lower tax rates and still spend more on public services than economically struggling urban or rural communities.

Regional economic differences do not just determine tax burdens and the level of public services. They also determine the relative priorities of particular policy and regulatory issues. Fishing, for example, is a sizable industry in coastal states in the Northeast and Northwest. States like Maine and Washington have numerous laws, regulations, and enforcement responsibilities tied to the catching, processing, and transporting of fish. Regulating the economic exploitation of marine life occupies very little government attention and resources in places such as Kansas and Nevada, although agriculture in the former and gambling in the latter create just as many policy challenges and demands for government action.

Regardless of the basis of a state's economy, greater wealth does not always translate into more support for public programs. States with above average incomes actually tend to spend *less* per capita on higher education. Why would less wealthy states concentrate more of their resources on higher education? There are a number of possible explanations. Education is a critical component of a postindustrial economy, so states that are less well off may direct more of their resources into education in hopes of building a better economic future. Citizens in wealthy states may simply be better able to afford higher tuition costs. Whatever the explanation, this example

MAP 1-3 **Economy by State**

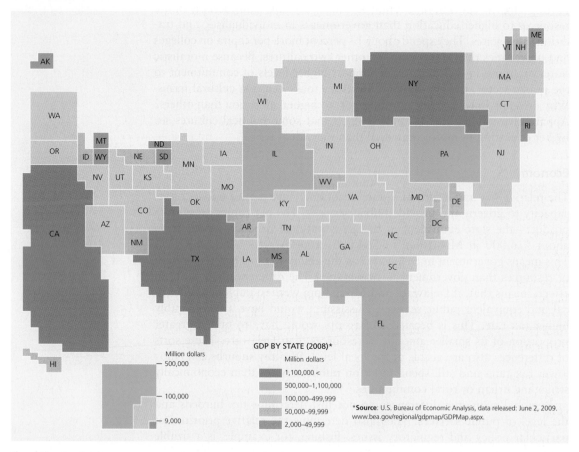

GDP BY STATE (2008)*

Million dollars

■	1,100,000 <
■	500,000–1,100,000
■	100,000–499,999
■	50,000–99,999
■	2,000–49,999

Million dollars
— 500,000
— 100,000
— 9,000

*Source: U.S. Bureau of Economic Analysis, data released: June 2, 2009. www.bea.gov/regional/gdpmap/GDPMap.aspx.

The relative size of state economies is measured in terms of gross state product. Notice how big states with small economies (Montana and Alaska) compare to small states with big economies (New Jersey and Massachusetts).

shows another advantage of employing the comparative method—it shows that sometimes the obvious assumptions are not always the correct ones.

Geography and Topography

There is wild variation in the physical environments in which state and local governments operate. Hawaii is a lush tropical island chain in the middle of the Pacific Ocean, Nevada encompasses a large desert, Michigan is mostly heavily forested, and Colorado is split by the Rocky Mountains. Such geographical and topographical variation presents different challenges to government. State and local authorities in California devote considerable time and resources to preparing for earthquakes. Their counterparts in Texas spend comparatively little time thinking about earthquakes, but they do concern themselves with tornadoes, grass fires, and hurricanes.

Combine geography with population characteristics and the challenges become even more complex. Montana is a large rural state in which the transportation logistics—simply getting students to school—can present something of a conundrum. Is it better to bus students long distances to large, centrally located schools? Or should there be many, smaller schools within easy commuting distance for relatively few students? The first is cheaper. Larger schools can offer academic and extracurricular activities that smaller schools cannot afford. But the busing exacts a considerable cost on students and families. The second alternative eases the transportation burdens, but it requires building more schools and hiring more teachers, which means more taxes. Geographical and population differences often not only shape the answers to such difficult policy issues, they pose the questions.

Consider the variety of seasonal weather patterns that occur within the enormous geographical confines of the United States. In Wisconsin, snow removal is a key service provided by local governments. Road-clearing crews are often at work around the clock during bad weather. The plows, the crews, and the road salt all cost money. They all require a considerable investment in administration and coordination to effectively do the job. In Florida, snow removal is low on local governments' lists of priorities for good reason—it rarely snows in the Sunshine State. On the other hand, state and local authorities in Florida do need to prepare for the occasional hurricane. Less predictable and less common than snow in Wisconsin, it only takes one hurricane to create serious demands on the resources of local authorities.

And, yes, even basic geography affects your tuition bill, especially when combined with some of the other characteristics discussed here. Many large public colleges and universities are located in urban centers because central geographical locations serve more people more efficiently. Delivering higher education in rural areas is a more expensive proposition simply because there are fewer people in the service area. States with below average population densities tend to be larger and more sparsely populated. They also tend to spend more on higher education. Larger government subsidies are necessary to make tuition affordable.

Recognizing the Stakes

The variation across states and localities offers more than a way to help make sense of your tuition bill or to explain why some public school systems are better funded or to understand why taxes are lower in some states. These differences also serve to underline the central role of states and localities in the American political system. Compared to the federal government, state and local governments employ more people and buy more goods and services from the private sector. They have the primary responsibility for many of the issues that people care about the most, including education, crime prevention, transportation, healthcare, and the environment. Public opinion polls often show that citizens place more trust in their state and local governments than in the federal government. These polls frequently express citizens' preference for having the former relieve the latter of a greater range of policy responsibilities.[26] With these responsibilities and expectations, it should be obvious that state and local politics are played for high stakes.

> Compared to the federal government, state and local governments employ more people and buy more goods and services from the private sector. They have the primary responsibility for many of the issues that people care about the most, including education, crime prevention, transportation, healthcare, and the environment.

High stakes, yes, but it is somewhat ironic that state and local governments tend to get less attention in the media, in private conversation, and in curriculums and classrooms than their federal counterpart.[27] Ask most people to think about American government and chances are they will think first about the president, Congress, Social Security, or some other feature of the national government. Yet most American governments are state or local. Five hundred thirty-five elected legislators serve in the U.S. Congress. Thousands of legislators are elected at the state level, and tens of thousands more serve in the legislative branches of local government.

In terms of people, state and local governments dwarf the federal government. The combined civilian workforce of the federal government (about 2.7 million) is less than half the number of people working for a single category of local government—more than 6 million people work for public elementary and secondary schools alone.[28] Roughly 5 million state employees and more than 13 million local government employees punch the time clock every day. (See Map 1-4.) In terms of dollars, state and local governments combined represent about the same spending force as the federal government. In 2006, state and local government expenditures combined totaled approximately $2.5 trillion.[29]

The size of state and local government operations is commensurate with their twenty-first-century role in the political system. After spending much of the twentieth century being drawn closer into the orbit and influence of the federal government, states and localities spent the century's last two decades, and much of the first decade of the twenty-first, aggressively asserting their independence. This maturing of nonfederal, or subnational, government made its leaders and its policies—not to mention its differences—among the most important characteristics of our political system. The Great Recession of 2008–2009 made that importance all too clear. As the economy went south and the budget gaps went north, state and local governments were forced into a painful process of cutting budgets. As pretty much any college student at a publicly supported college or

MAP 1-4 Number of Government Employees by State

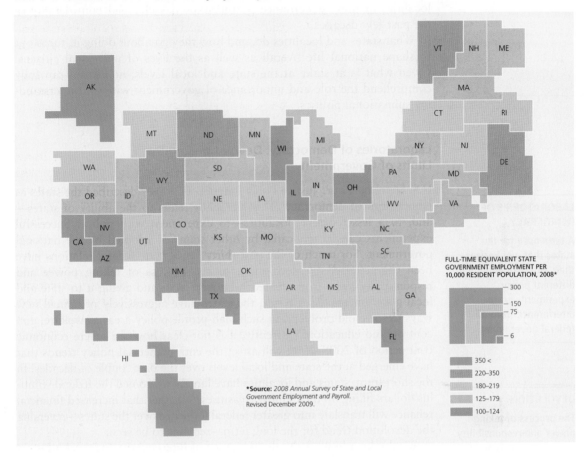

FULL-TIME EQUIVALENT STATE
GOVERNMENT EMPLOYMENT PER
10,000 RESIDENT POPULATION, 2008*

- 300
- 150
- 75
- 6

350 <
220–350
180–219
125–179
100–124

*Source: 2008 Annual Survey of State and Local
Government Employment and Payroll.
Revised December 2009.

university can attest, when state and local governments start hurting the pain is felt by, well, everyone. What is at stake in state and local politics turns out to be not just what *you* are interested in, but just about anything that anyone is interested in. This is one of the reasons why the federal government in 2009 passed a massive economic stimulus package that sent billions of dollars pouring into state and local treasuries. If you want a quick and direct path into the nation's economic, social, and political heart, then state and local governments are the obvious routes.

The context of the federal system of government, and the role of state and local governments within that system, is given more in-depth coverage in chapter 2. Nonetheless, it is important to recognize now that governance in the United States is more of a network than a hierarchy. The policies and politics of any single level of government are connected and intertwined with the policies and politics of the other levels of government in a complex web of interdependent relationships. The role of states and localities in these governance partnerships has changed considerably in the past few decades.

What states and localities do, and how they go about doing it, turns out to shape national life overall as well as the lives of individual citizens. Given what is at stake at the state and local levels, no citizen can fully comprehend the role and importance of government without understanding subnational politics.

Laboratories of Democracy: Devolution and the Limits of Government

U.S. Supreme Court Justice Louis Brandeis famously described the states as **laboratories of democracy**. This metaphor refers to the ability of states—and, to a lesser extent, localities—to experiment with policy. Successful experiments can be replicated by other states or adopted by the national government. For much of the past thirty years, state-federal relations have been characterized by **devolution**, or the process of taking power and responsibility away from the federal government and giving it to state and local governments. As a result, the states have aggressively promoted new ways to solve old problems in such high-profile policy areas as welfare, gun control, and education. Currently, it is not clear how the severe economic contraction of 2008–2009 will affect the entrepreneurial policy trends that have emerged at the state and local levels over the past couple of decades. In the short term, states and localities have largely welcomed the federal stimulus dollars filling up their empty treasuries. Whether that increased financial reliance will translate into greater federal influence over the states—reversing the devolution trend for the long term—remains to be seen.

We'll take a look at the development of intergovernmental relations in the next chapter, but it is important here to recognize that how state and local governments exercise their independent decision-making authority is dependent on a number of factors. Some of these factors are external. The U.S. Constitution, federal laws and regulations, nationwide recessions, and the like constrain what states and localities can and cannot do. Internal factors, such as the characteristics of a particular state, also play a critical role in setting limits on what the state decides to do.

The big three of these internal factors are wealth; the characteristics of the state's political system; and the relative presence of organized interest groups, those individuals who organize to support policy issues that concern them. Public programs cost money. Wealth sets the limits of possible government action. Simply speaking, wealthier states can afford to do more than poorer states. For most states, this is currently the biggest limiting factor on independent policy action at the state and the local levels. Simply put, many subnational governments do not have the money to launch expensive new policy initiatives. Indeed, many of these governments have not had the

---

LABORATORIES OF DEMOCRACY

A term used for the states that emphasizes their ability to engage in different policy experiments without interference from the federal government.

DEVOLUTION

The process of taking power and responsibility away from the federal government and giving it to state and local governments.

Washington, D.C., is an odd hybrid of local, state, and federal governments. Technically, it is a federal city, the only such political jurisdiction in the United States. Although granted varying levels of autonomy throughout its history, D.C. is ultimately ruled by Congress, making it the only local government that draws its power directly from the federal, rather than a state, government.

money to keep funding their existing programs and services at current levels. While a big factor, money is not the only factor that influences policy directions at the subnational level. Political system characteristics are the elements of the political environment that are specific to a state. States in which public opinion is relatively conservative are likely to pursue different policy avenues than states in which public opinion is more liberal. States in which Republicans dominate the government are likely to opt for different policy choices than states in which Democrats dominate. States with professional full-time legislatures are more likely to formulate and pursue sustained policy agendas than are states in which legislators are part-timers who only meet periodically. States in which the government perceives an electoral mandate to reform government are more likely to be innovative than are states in which the government perceives an electoral mandate to retain the status quo.[30] Organized interest group activity helps determine what sort of policy demands government responds to. Governments in states with powerful teachers' unions, for example, experience different education policy pressures than governments in states in which teachers' unions are politically weak. These three factors constitute the basic ingredients for policymaking in the states. Specifics vary enormously from state to state, and the potential combinations in this democratic laboratory are virtually infinite.

Localities face more policymaking constraints than states do because they typically are not sovereign governments. This means that, unlike states, local governments get their power from the level of government above them rather than directly from citizens. The states have much greater control over local governments than the federal government has over the

Local Focus: **The Federal City**

Riddle me this. It is a city. It is sort of a state. It is ruled by Congress. What is it? It is the District of Columbia, otherwise known as Washington, D.C. It is also the nation's capital, and it is surely the most unusual and unique local government in the country.

Technically, Washington, D.C., is a federal city. Article I, Section 8, Paragraph 17 of the U.S. Constitution gives Congress the power to rule over an area not to exceed ten square miles that constitutes the seat of national government. Yet it has never been quite clear what that means in terms of governance. Should Congress rule the city directly? Should the citizens of the city be given the right to elect a representative government? If they do this, should the government be subordinate to Congress or should it be counted as an equivalent to a state and be free to make any laws that do not violate the U.S. Constitution?

Throughout its history, these questions have been answered very differently. In the early 1800s, the district was a strange collection of cities and counties, each governed by different means. Washington City and Georgetown were municipalities run by a chief executive (a mayor) and a legislature (a council). Depending on the time period, however, the mayors were sometimes appointed by the federal government and sometimes elected. In addition to the two cities, there were also two counties. Maryland laws governed Washington County; Virginia laws governed Alexandria County.

In the 1870s, Washington City, Georgetown, and Washington County were combined into a single governmental unit, a federal territory with a governor

appointed by the president and a legislature elected by the territorial residents. This eventually became the District of Columbia, or Washington, D.C. For most of its history, commissioners appointed by the federal government governed the district. It was not until 1974 that the residents of Washington, D.C., gained home rule and the right to elect their own mayor and council.

This mayor-council arrangement, however, is unlike any other municipal government in the United States. The laws passed by the council have to be reviewed and approved by Congress. The laws that govern federal-state relationships treat the district as a state, even though it is not a state and cannot operate like one. The mayor is not considered the head of a federal agency, but he or she is expected to act like one when seeking appropriations from Congress.

This odd hybrid of local, state, and federal governments is reflected in the unique electoral status of Washington, D.C., voters. Voters in the district have a local vote, but only half of a federal vote. They can vote for the president but not for a member of Congress. They can vote for a mayor and council, but they have no voting representative in Congress. Yet Congress has the power to overturn laws passed by the council. The district now has three electoral votes. Prior to 1963, it had none and D.C. voters could not cast a ballot for president.

All this makes Washington, D.C., the nation's most unusual local government. It is the only municipality that is a creature of the United States rather than of a state constitution, and as such, it is the only really national city in the country.

Source: Selected material from Council of the District of Columbia, "History of Self-Government in the District of Columbia," 1997, available at www.dccouncil.washington.dc.us.

states. Yet, even though local governments are much more subordinate to state government than state government is to the federal government, they do not simply take orders from the state capital. Many have independent taxing authority and broad discretion to act within their designated policy jurisdictions.

These policy jurisdictions, nevertheless, are frequently subject to formal limits. The authority of school districts, for example, extends only to funding and operating public schools. State government may place lids on districts' tax rates and set everything from minimal employment qualifications to maximum teacher-to-pupil ratios. Yet, even within this range of tighter restrictions, local governments retain considerable leeway to act independently. School districts often decide to contract out cafeteria and janitorial services, cities and counties actively seek to foster economic development with tax abatements and loan guarantees, and police commissions experiment with community-based law enforcement. During the past two decades, many of the reforms enthusiastically pursued at all levels of government—reforms ranging from innovative new management practices to the outright privatization of public services—have had their origins in local government.[31]

What all this activity shows is that states and localities are not only the laboratories of democracy but also the engines of the American republic. States and localities are not just safe places to engage in limited experimentation, they are the primary mechanisms connecting citizens to the actions of government. It is for exactly this reason that one of the central federal government responses to the economic crises of 2008–2009 was to financially shore up local and state governments.

> States and localities are not just safe places to engage in limited experimentation, they are the primary mechanisms connecting citizens to the actions of government.

Conclusion

There are good reasons for developing a curiosity about state and local governments. State politics determine everything from how much you pay for college to whether your course in state and local governments is required or elective. Above and beyond understanding their impact on your own life and interests, studying state and local governments is important because of their critical role in the governance and life of the nation. Subnational, or nonfederal, governments employ more people than the federal government and spend as much money. Their responsibilities include everything from repairing potholes to regulating pot. It is difficult, if not impossible, to understand government in the United States and the rights, obligations, and benefits of citizenship without first understanding state and local governments.

This book fosters such an understanding through the comparative method. This approach involves looking for patterns in the differences among states and localities. Rather than advocating a particular perspective on state and local politics, the comparative method is predicated, or based, on a systematic way of asking and answering questions. Why is my tuition bill so high? Why does Massachusetts send mostly Democrats to the U.S. House of Representatives? Why are those convicted of capital crimes more likely to be executed in Texas than in Connecticut? Why are sales taxes high in Alabama? Why is there no income tax in South Dakota? Each of these questions can be answered by comparing states and looking for systematic patterns in their differences. The essence of the comparative method is to use one difference to explain another.

The study of state and local politics has been organized into three distinct sections. The first section consists of four chapters designed to set the basic framework, or context, for studying state and local politics. Included here are chapters on federalism, state constitutions, political participation, and political parties and interest groups. The second section covers the institutions of state and local government: legislatures, executives, courts, and bureaucracy. Although elements of local government are discussed in all these, there are also two chapters in this section devoted solely to local politics and government. The final section covers a series of distinct policy areas: budgets and taxes, education, healthcare, crime, and the environment. These chapters not only cover areas of substantive policy interests but also offer concrete examples of how a broad understanding of the context and institutions of state and local governments can be combined with the comparative method to promote a deeper understanding of the politics of states and localities.

Key Concepts

comparative method (p. 7)
devolution (p. 22)
individualistic culture (p. 13)
laboratories of democracy (p. 22)
moralistic culture (p. 12)
political culture (p. 11)
sociodemographics (p. 9)
traditionalistic culture (p. 13)
variance (p. 8)

Suggested Readings

Elazar, Daniel. *American Federalism: A View from the States.* New York: Crowell, 1966. The classic work on political culture in the states.

Gray, Virginia, and Russell Hanson, eds. *Politics in the American States: A Comparative Analysis.* 9th ed. Washington, D.C.: CQ Press, 2007. One of the better-known comparative studies of state politics and policies. Periodically updated.

Morgan, Scott, and Kathleen O'Leary Morgan. *State Fact Finder Series 2010.* Washington, D.C.: CQ Press, 2010. Comprehensive reference on all aspects of the states. Good source for comparative research.

Van Horn, Carl, ed. *The State of the States.* 4th ed. Washington, D.C.: CQ Press, 2005. Thorough overview of the trends in state politics and in political institutions.

Suggested Web Sites

http://quickfacts.census.gov/qfd. U.S. Bureau of the Census Web site that lists state rankings on population, per capita income, employment, poverty, and other social and economic indexes.

http://sppq.press.illinois.edu. Web site of *State Politics & Policy Quarterly,* an academic research journal devoted to studying state-level questions.

www.csg.org/csg/default. Web site of the Council of State Governments (CSG), an organization that represents elected and appointed officials in all three branches of state government. Publishes on a wide variety of topics and issues relevant to state politics and policy.

CHAPTER 2

Federalism

The Power Plan

States and the federal government, like it or not, need each other. The states rely on the federal government to help fund a wide range of programs and policies, and the federal government needs the states to implement those policies and programs. To forge an effective working partnership, key state and federal policymakers need to constantly communicate. Here, President Barack Obama talks to the Democratic Governors Association on Thursday, October 1, 2009, in Washington, D.C.

Why does the federal government seem to be gaining power while the states lose it?

What are the advantages and disadvantages of federalism?

Why would some businesses prefer to be regulated by the federal government rather than state governments?

I n 2007, many states and localities wanted nothing more from the federal government than to be left alone. Gridlocked, unresponsive, and seemingly incapable of meaningful movement on key domestic policy issues like healthcare and immigration, state and local officials increasingly saw the feds as unhelpful or even irrelevant to their own increasingly ambitious policy agendas. As California governor Arnold Schwarzenegger put it, "All the great ideas are coming from state and local governments. . . . We're not going to wait for Big Daddy to take care of us."[1] New York City mayor Michael Bloomberg agreed with him, and together they posed for a *Time* magazine cover headlined, "Who Needs Washington?"[2] It was supposed to be a rhetorical question, but the state of California and the city of New York—in fact, just about all states and localities—were soon to get a harsh and unexpected answer. Who needs Washington? They do.

Many of the policy innovations championed by Schwarzenegger, Bloomberg, and their colleagues were casualties of the Great Recession of 2008–2009. Rather than seeking bold new solutions and pursuing new paths away from the paternalistic feds, cities and states were struggling to achieve old-fashioned solvency and went hat in hand to "Big Daddy." Big Daddy was generous: With the American Recovery and Reinvestment Act (ARRA) of 2009, the federal government injected $787 billion into the U.S. economy, with much of that money funneled directly to state and local governments. That included roughly $85 billion for California and $6 billion for New York City (see for yourself how the Golden State and the Big Apple are spending all that cash at www.recovery.ca.gov and www.nyc.gov/html/ops/nycstim/html/home/home.shtml). Washington sent so much money to the states that in the first quarter of 2009, for the first time in history, federal grants became the single largest source of revenue for state governments. At an annual adjusted rate of $437 billion, states were getting more money coming from Big Daddy than from their own income, property, or sales tax levies.[3]

You'd think states and localities would be grateful for the federal government's money shower, and for the most part, they were. Yet some state and local officials publicly confessed they were more than a little uncomfortable with the federal government's covering their checks. Big Daddy, the thinking went, was more accurately described as a sugar daddy, and like most sugar daddies, the feds wanted something for their money. The fear was that the "something" wanted by the feds was exactly what

Schwarzenegger and Bloomberg had so enthusiastically extolled in *Time* magazine: the policymaking independence of the subnational governments.

You see, the stimulus money was not free in the sense that states and cities got to do as they pleased with it. Accepting federal cash meant accepting the federal policy priorities, which did not always coincide with those of the governments who would actually spend the money. Gov. Mark Sanford of South Carolina pleaded publicly with the federal government to be allowed to spend stimulus dollars as his state saw fit, and he was particularly concerned about taking on long-term, and very expensive, policy responsibilities that his state would be dealing with long after the federal stimulus dollars had dried up.[4] A handful of mostly conservative, Republican governors, echoed this concern, expressing worries that the federal government stimulus plan was, in effect, piling debt upon debt and surrendering state sovereignty to the federal government for a short-term and short-sighted budget fix. Gov. Bobby Jindal of Louisiana pointed out the federal money would be gone in three years, and before accepting any of it, states would be wise to examine all the strings that came attached to it.[5]

Despite some public grumbling about the strings attached, few state and local officials actually turned down any federal stimulus dollars. Financially speaking, the rock of hard cash from Washington was a whole lot better than the hard place of imposing higher taxes on a sinking economy. Yet, although broadly considered a good deal, trading a measure of policymaking independence for much needed cash nonetheless raises a series of critically important questions about the political system and the role of state and local governments within that system.

The United States is somewhat unusual in that by design its subnational governments—especially states—are assigned a central domestic policymaking role and are supposed to enjoy a high degree of independence from the central government. This importance and independence are products of **federalism**. Federalism is a political system in which national and regional governments share powers and are considered independent equals. This system of shared powers is critical to understanding the politics of states and localities, and the central role they play in the U.S. political system. The question at the heart of it all is: Who—the federal government or the state governments—has the power to do what? In the words of University of Chicago law professor Cass Sunstein, the debate over the distribution of powers between the state and federal levels holds "the ultimate fate of measures safeguarding the environment, protecting consumers, upholding civil rights, protecting violence against women, protecting endangered species, and defining criminal conduct in general and banning hate crimes in particular."[6] Diluting the power of subnational governments to

FEDERALISM

Political system in which national and regional governments share powers and are considered independent equals.

> The question at the heart of it all is: Who—the federal government or the state governments—has the power to do what?

make independent decisions on such issues is the key concern accompanying their sudden financial dependence on the federal government. Do we want the federal government using its budgetary power to impose its preferences on these and a wide range of issues? Or do we want these policy conflicts handled at the state and local level?

How these questions are ultimately answered will affect the lives of virtually all citizens in the United States. This chapter provides a basic understanding of federalism, its history and evolution in the United States, and its implications for politics and governance for states and localities.

Systems of Power

We typically think of a nation as being ruled by a single sovereign government, that is, a government that depends on no other government for its political authority or power. This does not mean, however, that every nation has one government. Power and policy responsibility are distributed throughout any given political system in one of three ways and all typically involve multiple levels of government. (See Figure 2-1.) The first option is to concentrate power in a single central government. Nations in which legal authority is held almost exclusively by a central government are known as **unitary systems**. Unitary systems typically do have regional and/or local governments, but these can exercise only the powers and responsibilities granted them by the central government. In other words, these governments are not sovereign; how much or how little power they are allowed to wield is up to the central government, not the citizens of a particular locality. The United Kingdom is a good example of a unitary system. Although the United Kingdom has a strong tradition of local government and has set up regional legislatures in Scotland and Wales and (intermittently) in Northern Ireland, power is concentrated in the nation's Parliament. If it so chooses, Parliament can expand or contract the powers and responsibilities of these lower governments or even shut them down entirely (this has happened periodically in Northern Ireland).

In contrast to unitary systems, confederal systems concentrate power in regional governments. A **confederacy** is defined as a voluntary association of independent, sovereign states or governments. This association stands the power hierarchy of a unitary system on its head. In a confederacy, it is the central government that depends on the regional governments for its legal authority. The United States has experimented with a confederal system twice during its history. The Articles of Confederation was the first constitution of the United States. It organized the U.S. political system as an agreement of union among sovereign states. The national government consisted of a legislature in which all states had equal representation. There was no national executive branch, such as the presidency, and no national judiciary, such as the Supreme Court.

UNITARY SYSTEMS

Political systems in which power is concentrated in a central government.

CONFEDERACY

A political system in which power is concentrated in regional governments.

FIGURE 2-1 How It Works: Systems of Government

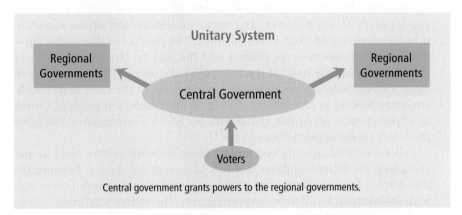

Unitary System

Regional Governments

Central Government

Regional Governments

Voters

Central government grants powers to the regional governments.

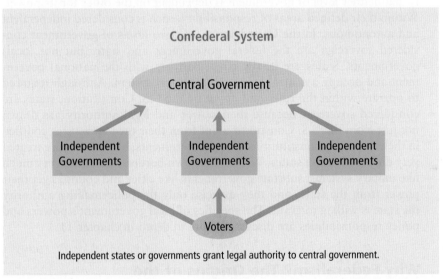

Confederal System

Central Government

Independent Governments

Independent Governments

Independent Governments

Voters

Independent states or governments grant legal authority to central government.

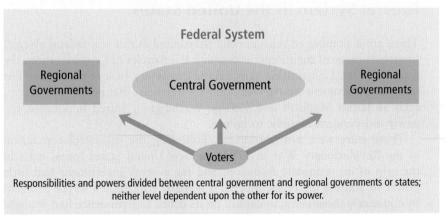

Federal System

Regional Governments

Central Government

Regional Governments

Voters

Responsibilities and powers divided between central government and regional governments or states; neither level dependent upon the other for its power.

This confederal system was adopted during the Revolutionary War and remained in effect for more than a decade. Many of the nation's founders saw its many flaws, however, and wrote its replacement at the Constitutional Convention of 1787 in Philadelphia. The product of that gathering—the U.S. Constitution—was ratified in 1788 and replaced the Articles of Confederation as the basis of the U.S. political system.[7] The second experiment with confederacy began in 1861 at the onset of the Civil War. Southern states seeking to secede from the Union organized their political system as a confederacy. All of this ended with the South's surrender in 1865 and the return of the seceded states to the Union.

Federal systems operate in a middle range between unitary systems and confederacies. Responsibilities in a federal system are divided between the two levels of government, and each is given the appropriate power and legal authority to fulfill those responsibilities. The system's defining feature is that neither level of government is dependent on the other for its power. Within their defined areas of responsibility, each is considered independent and autonomous. In the United States, the two levels of government considered sovereign are the federal government and state (but not local) governments. States are legally equal partners with the national government and occupy a central role in the political system. Although required to operate within the rules laid down by the U.S. Constitution, states are considered sovereign because their power and legal authority are drawn not just from the U.S. Constitution but from their own citizens as codified in their own state constitutions. Local governments, by the way, are treated very differently from states. Within their own borders, states are very much like unitary systems; substate governments like cities and counties get their power from the state, and they exercise only the policymaking authority the state is willing to grant. The specifics of local government's powers and policy responsibilities are discussed more in depth in chapter 11.

Why Federalism? The Origins of the Federal System in the United States

There are a number of reasons why the United States is a federal system. Largely because of their experiences with the Articles of Confederation, the framers of the Constitution rejected the possibility of a confederacy. The national government was so weak under the Articles that prominent figures, such as James Madison and George Washington, feared it doomed the newly independent republic to failure.

These fears were not unfounded. Following the successful conclusion of the Revolutionary War in 1783, the new United States found itself in the grip of an economic recession, and the central government had little power to address the crisis. Indeed, it actually contributed to the problem by constantly threatening to default on its debts. Independence had brought political freedom, but it also meant American-made products now were in head-to-head competition with cheap, high-quality goods from Great Britain. This made consumers happy but threatened to cripple American businesses. The economic difficulties pitted state against state, farmer against manufacturer, and debtor against banker. The weak central government really did not have the power to attempt a coordinated, nationwide response to the problem. It could do little but stand by and hope for the best.

As internal tensions mounted within the United States, European powers still active in the Americas threatened the nation's very sovereignty. Spain shut down shipping on the Mississippi. The British refused to withdraw from some military posts until the U.S. government paid off its debts to British creditors. George Washington believed the United States, having won the war, was in real danger of losing the peace. He said that something had to change in order "to avert the humiliating and contemptible figure we are about to make on the annals of mankind."[8]

For a loose coalition of the professional classes that called themselves Federalists, that "something" was obviously the central government. This group of lawyers, businessmen, and other individuals, drawn mostly from the upper social strata, sought to create a stronger and more powerful national government. Americans, however, were not particularly enthusiastic about handing more power to the central government, an attitude that is not so different from today. Most recognized that the Articles had numerous flaws, but few were ready to copy the example of the British and adopt a unitary system.

Two events in fall 1786 allowed the Federalists to overcome this resistance and achieve their goal of creating a more powerful national government. The first was the Annapolis Convention. This meeting in Maryland's capital convened to try to hammer out an interstate trade agreement. Few states sent delegates. Those who did show up had strong Federalist sympathies. They took advantage of the meeting and petitioned Congress to call for a commission to rewrite the Articles of Confederation.

The second event was Shays's Rebellion, named after its leader, Daniel Shays, a hero of the recently won Revolutionary War. The rebellion was an uprising of Massachusetts farmers who took up arms in protest of state efforts to take their property to pay off taxes and other debts. It was quickly crushed, but with further civil unrest threatening to boil over into civil war and with mounting pressure from powerful elites within the Federalist ranks, the Continental Congress was pushed to call for states to send delegates to Philadelphia in summer 1787. The purpose of the meeting, which came to be known as the Constitutional Convention, was the rewriting of the Articles of Confederation.

Once convened, the group quickly abandoned its mandate to modify the Articles of Confederation and decided to write an entirely new constitution. In doing so, the Federalists who dominated the convention rejected confederacy as an adequate basis for the American political system. Their experience under the Articles had taught them that a central government subordinate to the states was not much of a government at all. What they wanted was a government capable of effectively dealing with national problems, and this meant a strong central government whose power was independent of the states.

Some Federalists, notably Alexander Hamilton, were attracted to the idea of a unitary government, but such a system was never seriously considered at the Constitutional Convention. Popular sentiment did not favor a unitary system, which was understandable given that the Revolutionary War had been fought in no small part because of the perceived arrogance and abuse by a central government toward its regional subordinates (the states were originally colonies of the British crown). Political realities also argued against pushing for a unitary system. To have any legal force the new constitution would have to be ratified by the states, and it was highly unlikely the states were going to voluntarily agree to give up all of their powers to a national government. Federalism was thus the only practical option.

Yet a federal system represented more than the political price that had to be paid to achieve a stronger national government. The founders were attempting to construct a new form of **representative government**, a form of government in which citizens exercise power indirectly, on the basis of a paradox. Convention delegates wanted a more powerful national government, but at the same time they did not want to concentrate power for fear it would lead to tyranny. Their solution to this problem was to create a system of separated powers and checks and balances. They divided their new and stronger national government into three branches—legislative, executive, and judicial—and made each branch partially reliant on the others to carry out its own responsibilities. This made it difficult for any single group to gain the upper hand in all three divisions of government and gave each branch the power to check the excesses of the other branches.

A similar set of goals was achieved by making state and national governments co-equal partners. By letting states remain independent decision makers in a wide range of policy arenas, power was divided between the national and subnational levels of government. The national government was made more powerful by the new constitution, but the independence of the states helped set clear limits on this power.

The Advantages and Disadvantages of Federalism

Federalism solved a political conundrum for the founders and helped achieve their philosophical aims of dispersing and separating power. Yet federalism is not necessarily better than a confederal or a unitary system, just different. In the United States, the pros and cons of federalism have benefited and bedeviled the American political system for more than two centuries.

REPRESENTATIVE GOVERNMENT

A form of government in which citizens exercise power indirectly by choosing representatives to legislate on their behalf.

There are four key advantages to the federal system. (See Table 2-1.) First, it keeps government closer to the people. Rather than the federal government's imposing a "one size fits all" policy, states have the freedom and authority to match government decisions to local preferences. This freedom also results in the local variance in laws, institutions, and traditions that characterizes the U.S. political system and provides the comparative method with its explanatory strength.

Second, federalism allows local differences to be reflected in state and local government policy and thereby reduces conflict. Massachusetts, for example, tends to be more liberal than, say, Alabama. California has a much more ethnically and culturally diverse population than Nebraska. Rather than having the various interests and preferences that spring from state-to-state differences engage in a winner-take-all policy struggle at the federal level, they can be accommodated at the state level. This reduces the friction among interests and lessens conflict.

Third, independent subnational governments allow for flexibility and experimentation. The states, as Supreme Court justice Louis Brandeis famously put it, are "the laboratories of democracy." Successful policy innovations in one state can be adopted by other states and copied by the federal government.

Fourth, independent subnational governments make it easier to achieve at least some national goals. For example, by sending so much stimulus money to state and local governments the federal government was able to achieve its goal of a geographically comprehensive boost to the economy. State and local governments had a vast array of plans and projects—everything from new roads to hiring police officers—that could increase jobs,

TABLE 2-1

Advantages and Disadvantages of Federalism

Advantages	Disadvantages
Allows for flexibility among state laws and institutions.	Increases complexity and confusion.
Reduces conflict because states can accommodate citizens' interests.	Sometimes increases conflict when jurisdictional lines are unclear.
Allows for experimentation at the state level.	Duplicates efforts and reduces accountability.
Enables the achievement of national goals.	Makes coordination difficult.
	Creates inequality in services and policy.

Emergency management provides a classic example of how federalism shapes policy. The Federal Emergency Management Agency (FEMA) is a critical component of any government response to disaster, but its effectiveness is tied to its integration with and support from state and local governments.

stimulate sales, and generally get the economy moving. By funneling money through states and localities, the federal government was deliberately trying to get those economic benefits quickly and efficiently. Rather than having the federal government independently plan the roads or determine personnel needs in specific localities, it simply took advantage of what states and localities already do.

Along with its benefits, however, federalism also confers a set of disadvantages. First, while allowing local differences does keep government closer to the people, it also creates complexity and confusion. For example, if you own a nationwide business, you have to deal with state *and* federal regulations—fifty-one sets of regulations in all. That means, among other things, fifty-one tax codes and fifty-one sets of licensing requirements. And many communities also have their own restrictions and requirements to meet as well.

Second, federalism can increase conflict as easily as reduce it. The Constitution is very vague on the exact division of powers between state and federal governments. This results in a constant struggle—and a lot of litigation—in an effort to resolve which level of government has the responsibility and legal authority to take the lead role in a given policy area. For example, who should challenge drug companies that make false or misleading claims about their products? In January 2007, thirty states settled with the Bayer Corporation for $8 million over safety concerns about a cholesterol-reducing drug that had since been pulled from the market. But just weeks earlier, the makers of four purported weight-loss drugs agreed to pay $25 million to settle allegations by the Federal Trade Commission that they had made unproven claims about the effectiveness of their products. Similar cases, but one was ruled on at the state level and the other at the national level.

Third, although federalism promotes flexibility and experimentation, it also promotes duplication and reduces accountability. For example, local, state, and national governments have all taken on law enforcement responsibilities. In some areas, this means there may be municipal police departments, a county sheriff's department, and the state patrol, plus local offices of the Federal Bureau of Investigation and the U.S. Drug Enforcement Agency. The responsibilities and jurisdictions of these organizations overlap, which means taxpayers end up paying twice for some law enforcement activities. When these agencies are unsuccessful or ineffective, it also is hard to figure out which is responsible and what needs to change.

Fourth, the federal system can make it hard to coordinate policy efforts nationwide. For example, police and fire departments on opposite sides of a state border, or even within adjacent jurisdictions in the same state, may have different communication systems. It is hard to coordinate a response to a large-scale emergency if the relevant organizations cannot talk to each other, but the federal government cannot force state and local governments to standardize radio equipment.

Finally, a federal system creates inequality in services and policies. The quality of public schools and welfare services, for example, depends heavily on the choices state and local governments make. This inevitably means that some states offer better educational opportunities and do more for the needy than others.

The Constitutional Basis of Federalism

The relationship between national and state governments is like a sibling rivalry. It is hard to imagine either level of government getting along without the other, yet because each is independent and focused on its own interests, conflict is common. The ink was barely dry on the newly ratified Constitution before the federal government and the states were squabbling over who had the power and authority in this or that policy area. In writing the Constitution, the founders recognized that the differences between states and the federal government were likely to be a central and lasting feature of the political system. Accordingly, they attempted to head off the worst of the disputes—or at least to provide a basis for resolving them—by making a basic division of powers between the national and state governments.

The Constitution grants the federal government both enumerated and implied powers. **Enumerated powers** are grants of authority explicitly given by the Constitution. Among the most important of these is the **national supremacy clause** contained in Article VI, section 2. This states that the Constitution "shall be the supreme law of the land; and the judges in every state shall be bound thereby." In other words, federal law takes

ENUMERATED POWERS

Grants of authority explicitly given by the Constitution.

NATIONAL SUPREMACY CLAUSE

The constitutional clause stating that federal law takes precedence over all other laws.

Policy in Practice: FEMA and Federalism

By any measure, Hurricane Katrina in 2005 was a disaster. In its wake, the storm left 1,500 people dead, tens of thousands homeless, $80 billion in property damage, and an embarrassing example of how a federal system can fail. Even though the storm is now a half decade in the past, it continues to expose weak links in the relationship between different levels of government.

Those problems were readily apparent in the planning for, and response to, the actual storm. In New Orleans, city government failed to put together any feasible evacuation plan. The federal government came off as simply inept; it had recently adopted a National Response Plan (NRP), a supposed blueprint to guide effective federal government response to national disasters. But nobody really understood what it meant, and the NRP failed its first real test. State government officials got into heated arguments with federal and local officials over who was to blame for what.

Some of this can be forgiven. It's easy to play Monday Morning Quarterback; it's a lot harder to stitch together local, state, and federal operations into a cohesive team in the middle of a Category 3 hurricane and a humanitarian disaster. Yet years after the storm, Katrina continues to provide lessons about the downsides of federalism. Consider the poststorm rebuilding efforts, which included flood protection, economic redevelopment, rebuilding infrastructure, and homeowner assistance. All of these are ongoing efforts in New Orleans—and they are still not being coordinated. For example, federal aid is being used by the state to help people rebuild houses in places where no local flood protection plan is in place—or

may ever be in place—and where the city officials are not guaranteeing they will be able to provide basic services like sewer and water. It's a classic case of one of the most serious downsides of federalism—one government not knowing what the other government is doing.

Katrina is just one example of how emergency management has evolved within the federalist system in a peculiarly American way. Prior to 1950, there really was no federal emergency management system. The federal government involved itself in natural disasters like earthquakes, floods, storms, and fires on an ad hoc basis, or not at all. This changed in 1950 with the passage of the Disaster Relief Act, which authorized the president to declare locations disaster areas, which in turn allowed state and local governments to receive federal aid to deal with the disaster.

An unintended consequence of this was that the federal government's primary role came to be supplying grants to state and local governments. FEMA was created in 1979 to coordinate federal government responses to national disasters. In helping out with disasters, FEMA didn't exactly build a sterling reputation. Judging its performance following Hurricane Hugo in 1989, Sen. Ernest Hollings, D-S.C., declared FEMA to be "the sorriest bunch of bureaucratic jackassess" he'd ever known.

Nevertheless, FEMA became very popular with state and local governments, especially when it began awarding mitigation (disaster preparation) grants in the 1990s. These grants allowed state and local governments to get federal money before any disaster had actually happened. FEMA also became very popular with presidents because it allowed them to distribute

PREEMPTION

The process of the federal government overriding areas regulated by state law.

precedence over all other laws. This allows the federal government to preempt, or override, areas regulated by state law. In recent decades, the federal government has aggressively used this power to extend its authority over states in a wide range of policy issues, so much so that **preemption** has been called "the gorilla that swallows state laws."[9]

money to different constituencies. The definition of *disaster* was stretched wider and wider to get the flow of federal money to states and localities. In 1996, President Bill Clinton declared a record 75 disasters—an average of more than one a week—allowing him to distribute millions in federal aid in what just happened to be an election year.

Although the intergovernmental cooperation centered on FEMA developed into a well-oiled example of cooperative or fiscal federalism, what tended to get left behind was any real progress on effective coordination among the three levels of government in the face of actual disasters. And that coordination is essential. Local governments have a critical role because local police, firefighters and the like are invariably the first responders to any major domestic emergency. But these efforts have to be meshed with federal responses (say, deploying the National Guard, setting up emergency field hospitals, and coordinating the transportation of equipment to clear debris). If they are not, the left hand of government doesn't know what the right hand is doing, which can amplify rather than reduce the misery of a real crisis like Katrina.

There have been numerous attempts to pull off this difficult management act. Following the terrorist attacks of 9/11 the George W. Bush administration effectively gutted FEMA, handing over its prime responsibilities to the Department of Homeland Security (DHS), which in turn produced the NRP as the blueprint for effective domestic emergency management. Unfortunately, it was so dense even the people who managed to read it were not sure what it meant, and its inadequacies were cruelly exposed during Katrina.

Following Katrina, the Bush administration made another serious attempt to come up with a national blueprint for managing emergencies. This relied heavily on centralizing authority in the federal government's hands and shifting much of this authority to the military. This set off constitutional alarm bells in state capitols and city halls, where officials did not want civilian control ceded to the military whenever a hurricane hit or a river burst its banks (one of the strongest critics of the plan was President Bush's brother, Florida governor Jeb Bush). In the end, Congress basically rescued FEMA from its DHS doghouse and sought to restore it to its more high-profile role of the 1990s.

Americans have become accustomed to expecting their government(s) to step in when bad things happen, and if anything, these expectations have increased since Katrina. The scale of those expectations means the federal government and FEMA will likely have expanded roles in any future nonmilitary emergency, whether it's another hurricane or a flu pandemic. Yet it's equally clear that that one of the central challenges for FEMA is not just preparing for the next disaster, but figuring out how to make FEMA work with federalism.

Sources: Richard P. Nathan and Marc Landy, "Who's in Charge? Who Should Be?" Nelson A. Rockefeller Institute of Government, June 2, 2009, available at http://rockinst.org/pdf/disaster_recovery/gulfgov/gulfgov_reports/2009-06-02-Whos_in_Charge.PDF; Martha Derthick, "The Transformation That Fell Short," Nelson A. Rockefeller Institute of Government, August 2009, available at http://rockinst.org/pdf/disaster_recovery/gulfgov/gulfgov_reports/2009-08-Transformation_That_Fell.pdf; Donald F. Kettl, "The Disaster Tripwire," *Governing* magazine, December 1, 2008, 16.

Other enumerated powers are laid out in Article I, section 8. This part of the Constitution details a set of **exclusive powers**—grants of authority that belong solely to the national government. These include the power to regulate commerce, to declare war, and to raise and maintain an army and navy. Article I, section 8 also confers a set of

EXCLUSIVE POWERS

Powers given by the Constitution solely to the federal government.

concurrent powers to the national government. Concurrent powers are those granted to the national government but not denied to the states. Both levels of government are free to exercise these prerogatives. Concurrent powers include the power to tax, borrow, and spend.

Finally, this same section of the Constitution gives the national government **implied powers**. The basic idea behind implied powers is that the authors of the Constitution realized they could not possibly list every specific power that the national government would require to meet the needs of a developing nation. Accordingly, they gave Congress the flexibility to meet unforeseen challenges by granting the federal government a set of broad and largely undefined powers. These include the **general welfare clause**, which gives the federal government the authority to provide for "the general welfare of the United States," and the **necessary and proper clause**, the ability for Congress "to make all laws which shall be necessary and proper" to carry out its responsibilities as defined by the Constitution. (See Table 2-2 for an explanation of these and other provisions.)

TABLE 2-2

U.S. Constitution's Provisions for Federalism

What It Is . . .	What It Says . . .	What It Means . . .
Article I, section 8 (Commerce Clause)	The Congress shall have Power . . . To regulate Commerce with foreign Nations, and among the several States, and with the Indian Tribes. . . .	Gives Congress the right to regulate interstate commerce. This clause has been broadly interpreted to give Congress a number of implied powers.
Article I, section 8 (Necessary and Proper Clause)	The Congress shall have Power . . . To make all Laws which shall be necessary and proper for carrying into Execution the foregoing Powers, and all other Powers vested by this Constitution in the Government of the United States, or in any Department or Officer thereof.	An implied power giving Congress the right to pass all laws considered "necessary and proper" to carry out the federal government's responsibilities as defined by the Constitution.
Article IV, section 3 (Admission of New States)	New States may be admitted by the Congress into this Union; but no new State shall be formed or erected within the Jurisdiction of any other State; nor any State be formed by the Junction of two or more States, or Parts of States, without the Consent of the Legislatures of the States concerned as well as of the Congress.	Allows the U.S. Congress to admit new states to the union and guarantees each state sovereignty and jurisdiction over its territory.
Article IV, section 4 (Enforcement	The United States shall guarantee to every State in this Union a Republican Form of Government, and shall protect each of them	Ensures that a democratic government exists in each state and protects states

TABLE 2-2, continued

What It Is . . .	What It Says . . .	What It Means . . .
of Republican Form of Government)	against Invasion; and on Application of the Legislature, or of the Executive (when the Legislature cannot be convened) against domestic Violence.	against foreign invasion or insurrection.
Article VI (Supremacy Clause)	This Constitution, and the Laws of the United States which shall be made in Pursuance thereof; and all Treaties made, or which shall be made, under the Authority of the United States, shall be the supreme Law of the Land; and the Judges in every State shall be bound thereby, any Thing in the Constitution or Laws of any State to the Contrary notwithstanding.	States that federal law takes precedence over all other laws.
Tenth Amendment	The powers not delegated to the United States by the Constitution, nor prohibited by it to the States, are reserved to the States respectively, or to the people.	Guarantees a broad, but undefined, set of powers be reserved for the states and the people, as opposed to the federal government.
Fourteenth Amendment	All persons born or naturalized in the United States, and subject to the jurisdiction thereof, are citizens of the United States and of the state wherein they reside. No state shall make or enforce any law which shall abridge the privileges or immunities of citizens of the United States; nor shall any state deprive any person of life, liberty, or property, without due process of law; nor deny to any person within its jurisdiction the equal protection of the laws.	Prohibits any state from depriving individuals of the rights and privileges of citizenship and requires states to provide due process and equal protection guarantees to all citizens.
Sixteenth Amendment	The Congress shall have the power to lay and collect taxes on incomes, from whatever source derived, without apportionment among the several States, and without regard to any census or enumeration.	Enables the federal government to levy a national income tax, which helped further national policies and programs in subsequent years.
Seventeenth Amendment	The Senate of the United States shall be com-posed of two Senators from each State, elect-ed by the people thereof, for six years; and each Senator shall have one vote. . . . When vacancies happen in the representation of any State in the Senate, the executive authority of each State shall issue writs of election to fill such vacancies: Provided that the legislature of any State may empower the executive thereof to make temporary appointments until the people fill the vacancies by election as the legislature may direct.	Provides for direct election of Senators, rather than election by each state's legislature.

The Constitution says a good deal about the powers of the federal government but very little about the powers of the states. The original, unamended Constitution spent much more time specifying the obligations of the states than it did defining their power and authority. The obligations list includes Article IV, section 2, better known as the **full faith and credit clause**. The clause requires all states to grant "full faith and credit" to each other's public acts and records. This means that wills, contracts, and marriages that are valid under one state's laws are valid under all. Under the **privileges and immunities clause**, states are prohibited from discriminating against citizens from other states. The idea here was to prevent people traveling across states or temporarily residing in a state because of business or personal reasons from becoming the targets of discriminatory regulation or taxation.

The Constitution also sets out an often criticized system of electing the nation's president and vice president. The presidency goes not to the candidate who wins the most votes but, rather, to the one who wins the most states. Article II, section 1 charges the states with appointing electors—one for each of the state's U.S. senators and representatives—who actually choose the president based on the winner of the state's popular vote. (If the Republican candidate gets the most popular votes, the state's delegation is made up of Republican Party loyalists who vote for the Republican nominee.) A presidential candidate needs a majority in the electoral college, which requires the votes of at least 270 of the 538 state electors, to be named the winner.

Other than these responsibilities and explicitly granting the states the right to enter into compacts, or binding agreements, with each other on matters of regional concern, the Constitution is virtually silent on the powers of the states. This lopsided attention to the powers of the federal government was a contentious issue in the battle to ratify the Constitution. Opponents of the document, collectively known as Anti-Federalists, feared that states would become little more than puppets of the new central government. Supporters of the Constitution sought to calm these fears by arguing that states would remain sovereign and independent and that the powers not specifically granted to the federal government were reserved for the states. As James Madison put it, in writing the Constitution the Federalists were seeking "a middle ground which may at once support due supremacy of the national authority," but would also preserve a strong independent role for the states.[10]

Madison and his fellow Federalists offered to put these assurances in writing. In effect, they promised that if the Constitution were ratified, the first order of business for the new Congress would be to draft a set of amendments that spelled out the limits of central government power and specified the independence of the states. Although Anti-Federalist skepticism remained, the Federalists kept their promise. The First Congress formulated a series of changes that eventually became the first ten amendments to the Constitution and are collectively known as the **Bill of Rights.**

Most of these amendments set specific limits on government power. The aim was to guarantee certain individual rights and freedoms, and at least initially, they were directed at the federal government rather than state governments. The **Tenth Amendment**, however, finally addressed the power of the states. In full, the Tenth Amendment states: "The powers not delegated to the United States by the Constitution, nor prohibited by it to the states, are reserved to the states respectively, or to the people." This provided no enumerated, or specific, powers to the states, but those implied by the language of the amendment are considerable. The so-called reserved powers encompass all of the concurrent powers that allow the states to tax, borrow, and spend; to make laws and enforce them; to regulate trade within their borders; and to practice eminent domain, which is the power to take private property for public use. The reserved powers also have been traditionally understood to mean that states have the primary power to make laws that involve the health, safety, and morals of their citizens. Yet the powers reserved for the states are more implied than explicit, and they all rest in an uneasy tension with the national supremacy clause of Article VI.

After the Tenth Amendment, the **Fourteenth Amendment** is the most important in terms of specifying state powers. Ratified in 1868, the Fourteenth Amendment is one of the so-called Civil War Amendments that came in the immediate wake of the bloody conflict between the North, or the Union, and the South, or the Confederacy. The Fourteenth Amendment prohibits any state from depriving individuals of the rights and privileges of citizenship and requires states to provide due process and equal protection guarantees to all citizens. The Supreme Court has used these guarantees to apply the Bill of Rights to state governments as well as to the federal government and to assert national power over state power in issues ranging from the desegregation of public education to the reapportioning state legislatures.

The implied powers of the federal government, the limitations set on states by the Fourteenth Amendment, and the undefined "leftovers" given to the states by the Tenth Amendment mean that the scope and the authority of both levels of government are, in many cases, dependent upon how the Constitution is interpreted. The Constitution, in other words, provides a basic framework for solving the sibling-rivalry squabbles between the states and the federal government. (See Figure 2-2.) It does not provide, however, an unambiguous guide to which level of government has the primary power, responsibility, and authority on a broad range of policy issues. This, as we will see, means that the U.S. Supreme Court is repeatedly thrust into the role of refereeing power disputes between national and state governments.

BILL OF RIGHTS

The first ten amendments to the Constitution, which set limits on the power of the federal government and set out the rights of individuals and the states.

TENTH AMENDMENT

Constitutional amendment that guarantees a broad, but undefined, set of powers be reserved for the states and the people.

FOURTEENTH AMENDMENT

Constitutional amendment that prohibits states from depriving individuals of the rights and privileges of citizenship and requires states to provide due process and equal protection guarantees.

FIGURE 2-2 Powers of National and State Governments

National Government Powers	Concurrent Powers	State Government Powers
Coin money	Tax	Run elections
Regulate interstate and foreign commerce	Borrow money	Regulate intrastate commerce
Tax imports and exports	Charter banks and corporations	Establish republican forms of state and local government
Make treaties	Take property (eminent domain)	Protect public health, safety, and morals
Make all laws "necessary and proper" to fulfill responsibilities	Make and enforce laws and administer a judiciary	All powers not delegated to the national government or denied to the states by the Constitution
Make war		
Regulate postal system		**Powers Denied**
		Tax imports and exports
Powers Denied		Coin money
Tax state exports		Enter into treaties
Change state boundaries		Impair obligation of contracts
Impose religious tests		Enter compacts with other states without congressional consent
Pass laws in conflict with the Bill of Rights		

Source: Adapted from Samuel Kernell and Gary C. Jacobson, *The Logic of American Politics,* 2d ed. (Washington, D.C.: CQ Press, 2003), 75, Figure 3-2.

The Development of Federalism

Although clearly establishing a federal political system, the provisions of the United States Constitution leave considerable room for disagreement about which level of government—the federal or state—has the power to do what. Disagreements about the scope and authority of the national government happened almost immediately when the First Congress convened in 1789. The issue of a national bank was one of the most controversial of these early conflicts and the one with the most lasting implications. Alexander Hamilton, secretary of the treasury under President George Washington, believed a central bank was critical to stabilizing the national economy, but there was nothing in the Constitution that specifically granted the federal government the authority to create and regulate such an institution.

Lacking a clear enumerated power, Hamilton justified his proposal for a national bank by using an implied power. He argued that the necessary and proper clause implied the power to create a national bank because the bank would help the government manage its finances as it went about its expressly conferred authority to tax and spend. Essentially, Hamilton was interpreting *necessary* as "convenient" or "appropriate." Secretary of State Thomas Jefferson objected, arguing that if the Constitution was going to establish a government of truly limited powers, the federal government needed to stick to its enumerated powers and interpret its implied powers very narrowly. He thus argued that the *necessary* in the necessary and proper clause should be properly interpreted as "essential" or "indispensable." Hamilton eventually won the argument, and Congress approved the national bank. Still, the issue simmered as a controversial—and potentially unconstitutional—expansion of the national government's powers.

The issue was not fully resolved until 1819 when the Supreme Court decided the case of *McCulloch v. Maryland*. This case stemmed from the state of Maryland's attempts to shut down the national bank, which was taking business from state-chartered banks, by taxing its operations. The chief cashier of the national bank's Baltimore branch refused to pay the tax, and the parties went to court. The Supreme Court, in essence, backed Hamilton's interpretation of the Constitution over Jefferson's. This was important above and beyond the issue of a national bank. It suggested that the Constitution gave the national government a broad set of powers relative to the states. Key to this early affirmation of the federal government's power was U.S. Chief Justice John Marshall, whose backing of a broad interpretation of implied powers laid the foundation for later expansions in the scope and authority of the federal government.

The full impact of *McCulloch v. Maryland,* however, would not be felt for some time. For the most part, the federal government began to feel its way into the gray areas of its constitutional powers pretty cautiously. Federalism went on to develop in four distinct stages—dual federalism, cooperative federalism, centralized federalism, and new federalism—and the first of these stages leaned toward the more limited role of the federal government favored by Jefferson.

Dual Federalism (1789–1933)

Dual federalism is the idea that state and federal governments have separate jurisdictions and responsibilities. Within these separate spheres of authority, each level of government is sovereign and free to operate without interference from the other. It represents something of a middle ground in the initial interpretations of how the Constitution divided power. On one side of the debate were Federalists like Hamilton, who championed a nation-centered view of federalism. They wanted to interpret the Constitution as broadly as possible to give the national government supremacy over the states.

On the other side were fierce **states' rights** advocates like John Calhoun of South Carolina, who served as vice president in the administrations of John Quincy Adams and Andrew Jackson. Supporters of states' rights wanted the federal government's power limited to the greatest possible extent and saw any expansion of it as an encroachment on the sovereignty of the states. In the 1820s and 1830s Calhoun formulated what became known as the **compact theory** of federalism. The idea was that the Constitution represented an agreement among sovereign states to form a common government. It interpreted the Constitution as essentially an extension of

DUAL FEDERALISM

The idea that state and federal governments have separate and distinct jurisdictions and responsibilities.

STATES' RIGHTS

The belief that states should be free to make their own decisions with little interference from the federal government.

COMPACT THEORY

The idea that the Constitution represents an agreement among sovereign states to form a common government.

the Articles of Confederation, meaning that the United States was more a confederal system than a federal one.

The compact theory argued that, because sovereignty ultimately rested with the states, the states rather than the Supreme Court had the final say in how the Constitution should be interpreted. The states also had the right to reject federal laws and make them invalid within their own borders. This process was known as **nullification,** and the compact theory took it to an extreme. Calhoun argued that states could reject the entire Constitution and choose to withdraw, or secede, from the Union. In the 1820s, national policies—especially a trade tariff—triggered an economic downturn in the southern states, which created wide support for nullification and **secession** arguments. These extreme states' rights views were not completely resolved until the Union victory in the Civil War ended them for good.

Dual federalism walked the line of moderation between the extremes of **nation-centered federalism** and **state-centered federalism.** Basically, dual federalism looks at the U.S. political system as a layered cake. The state and federal governments represent distinct and separate layers of this cake. To keep them separate, advocates of dual federalism sought to limit the federal government to exercising only a narrow interpretation of its enumerated powers. If the Constitution was to be interpreted broadly, that interpretation should favor the states rather than Congress. This became the central operating philosophy of the U.S. Supreme Court for much of the nineteenth century and is most closely associated with the tenure of Chief Justice Roger B. Taney, who served from 1836 to 1864. Unlike his predecessor John Marshall, Taney was much less sympathetic to arguments that interpreted the federal government's powers broadly.

The dual federalism doctrine gave rise to some infamous court decisions on the powers and limitations of the federal government. Perhaps the best-known is *Scott v. Sandford* (1857). This case that dealt with Dred Scott, a slave taken by his master from Missouri, a slave state, to Illinois, a free state, and on into what was then called the Wisconsin Territory, where slavery had been outlawed by the Missouri Compromise of 1820. This federal law stipulated which new states and territories could and could not make slavery legal. After his master's death, Scott sued for his freedom, arguing that his residence in a free territory had legally ended his bondage. Scott's case was tied to the Missouri Compromise, which the Supreme Court subsequently ruled unconstitutional. The justices' justification was that Congress did not have the enumerated, nor the implied, power to prohibit slavery in the territories. Thus, Scott remained a slave, although his owners voluntarily gave him his freedom shortly after the Supreme Court decision. He died of tuberculosis in 1858, having spent only one of his nearly sixty years as a free man.

Cooperative Federalism (1933–1964)

In theory, dual federalism defines and maintains a clear division between state and national governments and sets a clear standard for doing so. If the

---

NULLIFICATION

The process of a state's rejecting a federal law and making it invalid within state borders.

SECESSION

The process of a government or political jurisdiction withdrawing from a political system or alliance.

NATION-CENTERED FEDERALISM

The belief that the nation is the basis of the federal system and that the federal government should take precedence over the states.

STATE-CENTERED FEDERALISM

The belief that states are the basis of the federal system and that state governments should take precedence over the federal government.

The Sixteenth Amendment gave the federal government the power to levy an income tax. It does not require long lines at the post office every April, although it can seem that way. The last-minute rush to file tax returns ahead of the April 15 filing deadline can mean long lines at post offices like this one in Guilderland, New York.

federal government has the enumerated power to take the disputed action or make the disputed law, it has supremacy over the states in the particular case; if it does not have the enumerated power, then the Tenth Amendment reserves that power for the states and state preferences take precedence.

The problem was that its clarity in theory rarely matched the complex realities of governance in practice. State and national governments have shared interests in a wide range of issues, from education to transportation. To cleanly divide these interests into separate spheres of influence was not only difficult, in many cases it was not even desirable. Even at the height of the dual federalism era, the states and the federal government were collaborating as much as they were fighting. The federal government, for example, owned vast tracts of land in the Midwest and West, and it made extensive grants of these lands to the states to help develop transportation and education systems. Many of the nation's best-known state universities got their start this way, as land-grant colleges.

In the nineteenth century, the federal government also gave out cash grants to support Civil War veterans housed in state institutions, gave money to the states to support agricultural research, and loaned federal man-power—primarily U.S. Army engineers—to help state

> Even at the height of the dual federalism era, the states and the federal government were collaborating as much as they were fighting.

and local development projects.[11] Rather than a layered cake, some experts believe a more appropriate metaphor for federalism is a marble cake with the different levels of government so thoroughly mixed with each other that they are impossible to separate. (See Figure 2-3.)

Certainly as the nation became increasingly industrialized and more urban, state and federal interests became increasingly intertwined. As the nineteenth century drew to a close and the twentieth century began, the federal government undertook a significant expansion of its policy responsibilities. In 1887, it began to regulate the railroads, a policy with enormous significance for the economic development of states and localities. In economic and social terms, this was roughly equivalent to the federal government of today announcing its comprehensive regulation of the Internet and software manufacturers. By fits and starts, dual federalism gradually fell out of favor with the Supreme Court. The Court instead began to interpret the powers of the federal government very broadly and to allow the jurisdictions of state and national governments to gradually merge.

Several events accelerated this trend. In 1913, the Sixteenth Amendment was ratified, giving the federal government the ability to levy a nationwide income tax. The new taxing and spending authority helped further national policies designed during the next decades.[12] The First World War (1914–1918) resulted in a significant centralization of power in the federal government. The Second World War (1939–1945) centralized that power even further. The need to fight global conflicts pushed the federal government to assert the lead role on a wide range of economic and social issues. Even more important to the long-term relationship between state and national governments was the Great Depression of the 1930s, a social and economic catastrophe that swept aside any remaining vestiges of dual federalism.

The central catalyst for a fundamental change in the nature of state-federal relations was the election of Franklin Delano Roosevelt to the presidency in 1932. In an effort to combat economic and social malaise, Roosevelt aggressively pushed the federal government into taking a lead role in areas traditionally left to the states, and in the 1930s the federal government became deeply involved in regulating the labor market, creating and managing welfare programs, and providing significant amounts of direct aid to cities. The general approach of Roosevelt's so-called New Deal agenda defined the central characteristics of **cooperative federalism**—using the federal government to identify the problem, set up the basic outline of a program to address the problem, and make money available to fund that program and then turning over much of the responsibility for implementing and running the program to the states and localities. This arrangement dominated state and federal relations for the next three decades.

COOPERATIVE FEDERALISM

The notion that it is impossible for state and national governments to have separate and distinct jurisdictions and that both levels of government must work together.

Centralized Federalism (1964–1980)

Having all levels of government addressing problems simultaneously and cooperatively paid dividends. It combined the need to attack national

FIGURE 2-3 The Varieties of Federalism

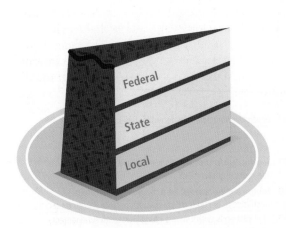

Layer Cake Federalism

Marble Cake Federalism

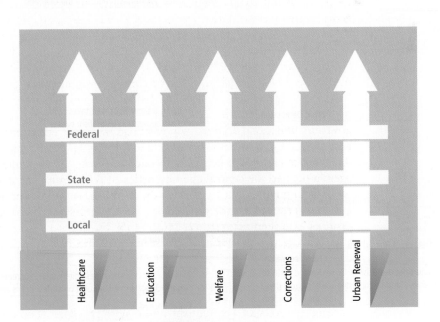

Centralized or "Picket Fence" Federalism

FIGURE 2-4 Key Dates in the History of American Federalism

Revolutionary War starts	1775	1776	Declaration of Independence adopted
Articles of Confederation ratified	1781	1783	Revolutionary War ends
Annapolis Convention	1786	1786	Shays's Rebellion
Constitutional Convention drafts new constitution	1787	1788	U.S. Constitution ratified
First Congress adopts Bill of Rights	1791		
McCulloch v. Maryland establishes that the federal government has a broad set of powers over the states	1819		
Roger Taney sworn in as chief justice; adopts dual federalism as model for federal-state relations	1836	1832	South Carolina attempts to nullify federal law
		1857	*Scott v. Sanford* demonstrates the limits of the federal government
Southern states experiment with confederacy as Civil War starts	1861	1860	South Carolina secedes from the Union in December; hostilities between North and South begin a month later
		1865	Civil War ends with Union victory; Thirteenth Amendment abolishes slavery
Fourteenth Amendment passes	1868		
		1887	Federal government regulates the railroads
Sixteenth Amendment passes	1913		
Great Depression	1930	1933	Franklin Delano Roosevelt takes office; Era of cooperation federalism begins
Era of centralized Federalism begins	1964		
Election of Ronald Reagan and emergence of New Federalism	1980	1972	Richard Nixon begins revenue sharing
Supreme Court decides *Bush v. Gore;* George W. Bush receives Florida's contested electoral votes and becomes president	2000	1986	William Rehnquist becomes chief justice; Supreme Court begins to look more favorably on states' rights arguments
		2008 –2009	Great Recession

problems with the flexibility of the decentralized federal system. Cooperative federalism, however, also signaled a significant shift in power away from the states and toward the federal government. The key to this power shift was money, specifically federal **grants-in-aid**, which are cash appropriations given by the federal government to the states. An ever-increasing proportion of state and local budgets came from federal coffers. At the beginning of the nineteenth century, federal grants constituted less than 1 percent of state and local government revenues. By the middle of the 1930s, federal grants accounted for something like 20 percent of state and local revenues.[13]

For the next thirty years, the federal government continued to rely on grants to administer programs, including the 1950s construction of the federal highway system that Americans drive on today. The 1960s marked a shift, however. **Centralized federalism**, ushered in with Lyndon Baines Johnson's presidency, further increased the federal government's involvement in policy areas previously left to state and local governments. It is commonly associated with Johnson's Great Society program, which used state and local governments to help implement such national initiatives as the Civil Rights Act and the War on Poverty. Sometimes it is referred to as "picket-fence federalism," due to its many crosscutting regulations.

Those initiatives meant more money—and more regulations—for states and localities. The federal government aggressively began attaching strings to this money through **categorical grants**. Federal-state relations evolved into a rough embodiment of the Golden Rule of politics—he who has the gold gets to make the rules.

Richard Nixon's administration took a slightly different tack. It cut some strings but continued to increase the number of grants doled out by the federal government.[14] In the late 1960s, the administration pioneered the idea of **general revenue sharing grants**, federal funds turned over to the states and localities with essentially no strings attached. Although popular with states and localities—from their perspective it was "free" money—this type of grant-in-aid had a short life span; it was killed by the Ronald Reagan administration in the early 1980s.

Federal grants, strings or no strings, do not sound so bad on the surface. Money is money, and a government can never have too much. The problem was that the grants were not distributed equitably to states and localities, and a central feature of cooperative federalism was the often fierce competition to control and access these revenues. The politics became complex. One form of these politics was between the states and the federal government over what type of grant should be used for a particular policy or program. States and localities favored federal grants with fewer strings. Congress and the president often favored putting tight guidelines on federal money because this allowed them to take a greater share of the credit for the benefits of federal spending.

Perhaps the most important dimension of the politics of grants-in-aid, however, was the federal government's increasing desire to use its purse strings to pressure states and localities into adopting particular policies and

GRANTS-IN-AID

Cash appropriations given by the federal government to the states.

CENTRALIZED FEDERALISM

The notion that the federal government should take the leading role in setting national policy, with state and local governments helping to implement the policies.

CATEGORICAL GRANTS

Federal grants-in-aid given for specific programs that leave states and localities with little discretion on how to spend the money.

GENERAL REVENUE SHARING GRANTS

Federal grants-in-aid given with few constraints, leaving states and localities almost complete discretion over how to spend the money.

laws. Beginning in the 1960s and 1970s, cooperative federalism began a new, more coercive era with the rise of ever more stringent grant conditions. These included **crosscutting requirements**, or strings that applied to all federal grants. For example, one condition to receive virtually any federal government grant is an assessment of the environmental impact of the proposed program or policy. Accordingly, most state and local governments began writing—and defending—environmental impact statements for any construction project that involved federal funds.

The federal government also began applying **crossover sanctions**. Crossover sanctions are strings that require grant recipients to pass and enforce certain laws or policies as a condition of receiving funds. One example is the drinking age. The federal government requires states to set twenty-one as the minimum legal drinking age as a condition of receiving federal highway funds.

Increasingly, the strings came even if there were no grants. State and local governments were issued direct orders, essentially were commanded, to adopt certain laws or rules, such as clean water standards and minimum wage laws.[15] These **unfunded mandates** became a particular irritant to state and local governments. Even when there was broad agreement on the substance of the mandate, subnational governments resented the federal government's taking all the credit while leaving the dirty work of finding funds and actually running the programs to the states and localities.

Congress eventually passed a law banning unfunded mandates in the mid-1990s, but it is full of loopholes. For example, the law does not apply to appropriations bills—the laws that actually authorize the government to spend money. In fiscal year 2006, the National Conference of State Legislatures estimated the federal government shifted $22.5 billion in costs to the states. Despite the law, Congress continues to pass laws that subnational governments must obey and to pass on the costs of these to the states.[16]

New Federalism (1980–2002)

Centralized federalism's shift of power toward the national government always faced opposition from states' rights advocates, who viewed the growing influence of the national government with alarm. By the end of the 1970s, centralized federalism also was starting to face a practical crisis—the federal government's revenues could not keep up with the demand for grants. With the election of Ronald Reagan in 1980, the practical and ideological combined to create pressure for a fundamental shift in state and federal relations.

Reagan was not the first president to raise concerns about the centralization of power in the national government. A primary reason for Nixon's support of general revenue sharing, for example, was the attraction of giving states more flexibility by cutting the strings attached to federal grants. It was not until Reagan, however, that a sustained attempt was made to reverse the course of centralized federalism. Reagan believed the federal government had overreached its boundaries, and he wanted to return power and flexibility to the states. At the core of his vision of state-centered **New Federalism** was the desire to reduce federal grants-in-aid. In return, states would be given more policymaking leeway with the money they did get through **block grants**.

Reagan's drive to make this vision a reality had mixed success. The massive budget deficits of the 1980s made cutting grants-in-aid a practical necessity. Reducing the federal government's influence over states and localities turned out to be another matter. Reagan, like many conservatives, was a modern heir to a states' rights perspective that dated back to the Anti-Federalist movement. This means he believed that government should be as close to the voters as possible—in the city hall or the state capitol—rather than far away in Washington, D.C. Yet believing that government should be closer to the people in the abstract is far different from putting that belief into practice. Taking power from the federal government did advance a core philosophical belief of the Reagan administration, but it also created problems for Reagan supporters, who were not shy about voicing their displeasure.

Such core conservative constituencies as business and industry quickly realized that dealing with one government was much less of a headache than dealing with fifty governments. They almost immediately began to put counterpressure on the movement toward expanded state policymaking authority. The result was something of a push-and-pull, with the Reagan administration trying to shove power on to the states with one set of legislative priorities and yank it back to the federal government with another.

Ultimately, Reagan did succeed in cutting grants-in-aid. He consolidated fifty-seven categorical grants into nine new block grants. General revenue sharing and another sixty categorical grants were eliminated entirely. This reduced the amount of money sent to the states while increasing their ability to act independently.[17] Yet Reagan also engaged in a number of fairly aggressive preemption movements and backed a number of unfunded mandates. This reduced the independence of states and forced them to fund programs they did not necessarily support.

The seeds of New Federalism had a hard time taking root at the national level, but its roots sank fast and sank deep at the state and local levels. States were caught between the proverbial rock of a cash-strapped federal government and the hard place of the demand for the programs traditionally supported by federal funds. They slowly and often painfully worked themselves out of this dilemma by becoming less reliant on the federal government. States aggressively began pursuing innovative policy approaches to a wide range of social and economic problems. By the 1990s, as one author puts it, there was, "a developing agreement among state and national political elites that states should have greater authority and flexibility in operating public programs."[18]

The effort to take power away from the federal government and give it to the states was broadly supported by public opinion, which consistently

States under Stress: Is Devolution Dead?

A couple of years ago, nobody could have imagined what the federal government would be up to these days. It is the major stockholder in the world's largest insurance firm, many of the nation's largest banks, and two of the three American auto companies. Federal money—an estimated $223 billion in 2009 and 2010—is now the single largest source of revenue for states and localities. That's more cash than the states get from income, sales, or property taxes.

Shocking as it seems now, back then many of us had convinced ourselves that the nation's states, cities, and counties really weren't all that dependent on the federal government anymore; devolution had progressed to the point where states and locals could make policy and administer programs themselves. What the feds mostly needed to do was stay out of the way. Not any more. Governments all over the country need the federal government's deep pockets. The interesting question is whether this changes the relationships in the federal system for a while—or for good.

Unquestionably, the Barack Obama administration is determined to reassert federal authority across a wide range of areas, particularly in the regulation of insurance, banking, and finance. That is making state regulatory officials very nervous, even though the administration insists it wants to exert authority as a partner with the states, not as an adversary. The president personally has ordered federal agencies to stop preempting state laws and even to rescind past preemptions. "Throughout our history," his recent directive reads, "state and local governments frequently have protected health, safety and the environment more aggressively than has the national government."

The sudden turnaround in federal-state relationships has created its share of ironies. For example, in the middle of 2009 the White House handed California and thirteen other states a significant victory in their long battle with Washington over energy and environmental policy by adopting California's tough standards for greenhouse gas emissions and automobile fuel efficiency. Score one for state independence and policy experimentation, which finally beat federal resistance after a long battle.

Yet at the same time that California was winning this policy battle with the feds, the state was in such fiscal stress it was also asking the federal government to guarantee $13 billion in short-term state debt—a guarantee the federal government declined to provide. It's not just California that is asking for federal government bailouts, lots of municipalities, through their members of Congress, are requesting federal assistance to offset losses suffered when Lehman Brothers went bankrupt. House finance chair Barney Frank is pushing legislation to have the federal government, in effect, insure municipal bonds in an effort to thaw a frozen municipal bond market.

The bottom line is that, if you are a governor or a mayor and you want to put a bright face on what's happening to federal-state relations right now, you can call it "collaborative federalism." But the federal government is not just talking to governors and mayors about what they need. The feds are telling them to start cooperating more with each other, so we may finally be on the road to some version of regionalism. If so, it will very likely be a regionalism crafted and monitored from the top down in the nation's capital, not from the bottom up by mayors and governors.

Devolution may be on hold just until the economic crisis abates, or it may be dead for the long term. Nobody knows. For now, however, make no mistake. Washington is back in charge.

Source: Adapted from Peter Harkness, "Potomac Chronicle: Devolution? What's That?" *Governing* magazine, July 2009.

showed Americans placing more trust in state and local governments compared to the federal government.[19] In the 1990s, the Clinton administration championed the idea of devolution, an extension of New Federalism that sought a systematic transition of power from the federal to the state level in certain policy areas.

Probably the best-known example of devolution is the Personal Responsibility and Work Opportunity Reconciliation Act of 1996, popularly known as the law that "ended welfare as we know it." The law, which Clinton signed under Republican pressure during the 1996 presidential campaign after vetoing it twice, ended Aid to Families with Dependent Children (AFDC) and replaced it with a block grant. In essence, the law embodied the deal between state and federal governments that embodied devolution—the federal government would provide less money, and the states would get more policymaking authority.

Like its parent, New Federalism, the devolution revolution faced strong resistance, often from an old enemy. Conservatives, at least rhetorically, still were the strongest states' rights advocates. Yet when states' rights conflicted with key portions of the conservative political agenda, conservative groups still fought tenaciously for federal supremacy over the states, just as they had during the 1980s. An example of this contradictory behavior is the 1996 Defense of Marriage Act. This federal law was proposed in the wake of movements in Hawaii and Vermont to legalize same-sex unions. Now, remember, the full faith and credit clause means that a contract made under the laws of one state is legally recognized and binding in all states. So, if one state made same-sex unions legal, it raised the possibility that the other forty-nine would have to recognize civil unions as the legal equivalent of marriage. There was a strong push from many traditional states' rights advocates for the federal government to, in essence, grant states exceptions from their full faith and credit obligations. The Defense of Marriage Act did this. It also put the federal government into the business of defining what constitutes a marriage, an area traditionally left to the states.[20]

Michigan was the first state to plow its roads and to use the yellow dividing line on its highways.

Ad Hoc Federalism . . . and a Return to Centralized Federalism? (2002–present)

The mixed commitment to New Federalism is perhaps best exemplified by the presidency of George W. Bush. Bush came to the White House from the Texas governor's mansion and, at least on the surface, was a strong supporter of the principles of New Federalism. He established the Interagency Working Group on Federalism and charged it with finding ways to cut through the regulatory red tape that often accompanies grants-in-aid. Shortly after being inaugurated, he convened a meeting of the nation's governors and told them his administration would aggressively seek to transfer power from Washington, D.C., to the states. He told the National Conference of State Legislatures that he wanted to preserve local control of schools and prevent federal encroachment on this traditional policy. The actual record of the Bush administration was considerably at odds with these New Federalism sentiments. For example, Bush's signature domestic policy was the No Child Left Behind Act, which asserted federal control over important aspects of education. In revamping emergency management policy, the Bush administration not only sought to centralize control in the federal government's hands but alarmed many by seeking to militarize what had traditionally been under civilian authority. Peter Harkness, editor of *Governing* magazine, sums up the Bush administration's record on federalist matters thus: "The administration has mandated more, preempted more and run roughshod over state initiatives that didn't conform to its own ideology."[21]

Part of Bush's departure from the New Federalism philosophy was driven by recession and war. Throughout the history of the United States, power has become centralized in the national government during times of crisis—it simply is better equipped to deal with national economic challenges or international conflict. The Bush administration found itself struggling with a soft economy at the beginning of its term and a disastrous slide into economic recession at the end of its term. In between, much of its focus was devoted to a global war on terrorism in response to the devastating attacks of September 11, 2001.

In the eight years of the Bush administration, the commitment to New Federalism dissolved more or less entirely. Although a number of high-profile policies sought to centralize power in the federal government's hands, the federal government, focused on two wars and other foreign policy matters, either could not or would not act on a broad set of domestic policy issues critical to states and localities. Rather than the administration's relying on any guiding philosophy like Dual, Cooperative, or New Federalism, Bush-era state-federal relations were described as entering a new era of **ad hoc federalism**.[22] Ad hoc federalism is the process of choosing a state-centered or nation-centered view of federalism on the basis of political or partisan convenience. In other words, the issue at hand, not a core philosophical commitment to a particular vision of federalism, determines a policymaker's commitment to state or federal supremacy.

This was not necessarily a bad thing for states or localities. As the opening section of this chapter suggests, in the first decade of the twenty-first century, states and localities aggressively moved into the domestic policy vacuum created by federal government inactivity. For example, the federal government failed to ratify the Kyoto treaty on global warming, but more than seven hundred U.S. cities decided independently to adopt its provisions. The federal government could not pass an immigration law, but Georgia, Colorado, and Oklahoma did.[23] As Gov. Schwarzenegger and Mayor Bloomberg told *Time* magazine, they were doing just fine without Big Daddy and just wanted the federal government off their backs.

This state of affairs was ended by the Great Recession of 2008–2009, which shook up state-federal relations and shifted power decisively toward the federal government. Part of this shift was prompted by the nature of

AD HOC FEDERALISM

The process of choosing a state-centered or nation-centered view of federalism on the basis of political or partisan convenience.

economic shock. For example, the financial industry was widely seen as helping precipitate the economic downturn by making irresponsible loans and underestimating risk. To prop up the financial system, the federal government pumped billions into the system, in the process becoming a major stockholder in many banks (not to mention part-owner of the world's largest insurance company and two of the major domestic car manufacturers). Historically, banks and insurance companies have been regulated by state and federal governments, but with the federal government the only entity with deep enough pockets to have prevented an implosion on Wall Street, few doubt that the regulatory authority over these sectors of the economy will take a significant shift toward Washington, D.C., and away from the states.

Those same deep pockets are also paying for what amounts to a resurrection of centralized federalism, with the federal government setting policy priorities, deciding what to spend on those priorities, and delegating to the states the administration of the approved programs. This is not so much a premeditated attempt by the federal government to usurp the power of the states as it is a recognition that the empty coffers of states and localities need to be filled, that only the federal government has the capacity to provide that much cash, and that the federal government is not going to give away that money without getting its policy priorities attended to. Still, some are already starting to wonder if the federal governments' new position of chief piperpayer will lead to Washington, D.C., calling the policy tunes for the long or the short term. As one observer has put it, the question is not just whether the recession has changed federal-state relations; it has, and more authority is clearly flowing to the feds. The really interesting question "is whether the relationships in the federal system have altered for a while—or for good."[24]

The Supreme Court: The Umpire of Federalism

Article VI, the national supremacy clause of the Constitution, declares that the Constitution, laws passed by Congress, and national treaties are the "supreme law of the land." This does not mean that the states are always subordinate to the national government. Don't forget—the Tenth Amendment also counts as part of that supreme law. However, it does mean that federal courts often have to referee national-state conflicts. Because it has the final say in interpreting the Constitution, the Supreme Court is, in effect, the umpire of federalism. Its rulings ultimately decide the powers and limitations of the different levels of government.

The Rise of Nation-Centered Federalism on the Court

Throughout U.S. history, the Supreme Court has cycled through trends of state-centered and nation-centered philosophies of federalism. As you have already seen, the early Supreme Court under Chief Justice John Marshall pursued a fairly broad interpretation of the federal government's powers in such cases as *McCulloch v. Maryland*. Marshall's successor, Roger Taney, took the Court in a more state-centered direction by establishing dual federalism as the Court's central operating philosophy. The shift from dual federalism to cooperative federalism required a return to a more nation-centered judicial philosophy. Although the Court initially took a more nation-centered track in its rulings following the Civil War, it was not until the Great Depression and Roosevelt's New Deal that a decisive tilt in its rulings cleared the way for the rise of cooperative federalism and the centralization of power in the national government.

A number of New Deal programs—including the Agricultural Adjustment Act, which provided federal subsidies to struggling farmers—at first were struck down by the Court. In a series of 5–4 rulings, the Court declared these programs to be unconstitutional expansions of federal power. In 1937, a frustrated Roosevelt proposed "packing" the Court as a way to prod it into fully accepting cooperative federalism. Under this plan, every time a justice turned seventy and did not retire, the president could appoint an additional judge to the Court. Roosevelt's scheme would have allowed him to alter the balance of power on the Supreme Court by packing it with up to six more members.

Reaction to this plan was largely negative. The proposed law reached Congress pretty much dead in the water—and it is remembered today as one of the Roosevelt presidency's few public relations disasters. Law or not, however, the court-packing plan had the desired effect. As it became apparent that Roosevelt was serious about pursuing a significant shake-up, the Supreme Court switched direction and began to rule in favor of key New Deal proposals. This included upholding the constitutionality of the first Social Security Act.

The shift toward a liberal interpretation of the federal government's powers dominated the Supreme Court's operating philosophy for much of the next sixty years and is exemplified by *United States v. Darby Lumber Co.* (1941). The substantive issue at stake was whether the federal government had the power to regulate wages. The Supreme Court said yes, but the decision is of more lasting interest because of the majority opinion's dismissive comment on the Tenth Amendment. Supposedly the constitutional lockbox of state power, the amendment, according to the Court, did little more than state "a truism that all is retained which has not been surrendered." In other words, the Tenth Amendment was simply a basket for the "leftover" powers the federal government had not sought or did not want.

During and after the New Deal era, the Supreme Court also accelerated a trend of broadly interpreting Congress's powers to regulate interstate commerce. It did this through its interpretation of the **interstate commerce clause**. In *Wickard v. Filburn* (1942), the Court ruled that the clause gave Congress the power to regulate what a farmer can feed his chickens. In *Heart of Atlanta Motel v. United States* (1964) and *Katzenbach v. McClung* (1964), the justices ruled that it gave Congress the power to regulate private acts of racial discrimination.

INTERSTATE COMMERCE CLAUSE

The constitutional clause that gives Congress the right to regulate interstate commerce. This clause has been broadly interpreted to give Congress a number of implied powers.

Governing States and Localities

A series of such decisions over the course of more than fifty years led some judicial scholars to conclude that the Supreme Court had essentially turned the concept of enumerated and reserved powers on its head. In effect, the assumption now seemed to be that the federal government had the power to do anything the Constitution did not specifically prohibit.[25] The states and localities were drawn ever closer into subordinate satellite roles in orbit around the federal government. This situation continued until just before the turn of the twenty-first century. At that point, the Court once again began siding with the states over the federal government.

A Tenth Amendment Renaissance or Ad Hoc Federalism?

By the mid-1990s, the Supreme Court was dominated by justices appointed by new federalists. Reagan, who had campaigned on his intention to nominate federal judges who shared his conservative philosophy, appointed four. He also elevated a fifth, William Rehnquist—originally appointed by Nixon—to the position of chief justice. Reagan's vice president and presidential successor, George Bush, appointed two more justices. The end result was a Supreme Court chosen largely by conservative Republican presidents who wanted limits set on the federal government's powers and responsibilities. The justices obliged.

In a series of narrow—mostly 5–4—decisions in the 1990s, the Court began to back away from the nation-centered interpretation of the Constitution that had dominated its rulings during the era of cooperative federalism (see Table 2-3). *United States v. Lopez* (1995) was a significant victory for states' rights and a clear break from a half century of precedent. This case involved the Drug Free School Zone Act of 1990, which made it a federal crime to possess a firearm within one thousand feet of a school. Following a good deal of precedent, Congress justified its authority to regulate local law enforcement by using a very liberal interpretation of the interstate commerce clause. The Supreme Court disagreed and argued that the commerce clause granted no such authority.

Similar reasoning was used by the justices in *United States v. Morrison* (2000) to strike down the Violence Against Women Act (VAWA). Congress had passed this law in 1994 out of concern that the states, although having primary responsibility for criminal law, were not adequately dealing with the problem of violence against women. The key provision of the VAWA gave assault victims the right to sue their assailants in federal court. Congress argued that it was authorized to pass such a law because fear of violence prevented women from using public transportation or going out unescorted at night. Such fears, the reasoning went, placed limits on economic opportunities for women. This argument made the connection to commerce and Congress's constitutional authority. The Supreme Court again rejected this broad interpretation of the commerce clause.

TABLE 2-3

Key U.S. Supreme Court Rulings Regarding Federalism, 1995–2006

United States v. Lopez (1995)	Court strikes down a federal law prohibiting possession of firearms near public schools. State claim upheld.
Seminole Tribe of Florida v. Florida (1996)	Court rules Congress cannot allow citizens to sue states in a federal court except for civil rights violations. State claim upheld.
Printz v. United States (1997)	Court strikes down federal law requiring mandatory background checks for firearms purchases. State claim upheld.
Alden v. Maine (1999)	Court rules that Congress does not have the power to authorize citizens to sue in state court on the basis of federal claims. State claim upheld.
United States v. Morrison (2000)	Court strikes down federal Violence Against Women Act. State claim upheld.
Reno v. Condon (2000)	Court upheld a federal law preventing states from selling driver's license information. State claim overturned.
Bush v. Gore (2000)	Court overrules Florida Supreme Court action allowing hand recounts of contested election ballots. State claim overturned.
Alabama v. Garrett (2001)	Court rules that state employees cannot sue their employers in federal court to recover monetary damages under the provisions of the Americans with Disabilities Act. State claim upheld.
Lorillard Tobacco Co. v. Reilly (2001)	Court strikes down Massachusetts laws regulating the advertising of tobacco products. State claim overturned.
Kelo v. City of New London (2005)	Court rules that government can seize private property for public purposes, including economic development. State claim upheld.
Gonzales v. Oregon (2006)	Court rules U.S. attorney general overstepped his authority by threatening to eliminate prescription-writing privileges for doctors who follow state law allowing physician-assisted suicide. State claim upheld.

SOVEREIGN IMMUNITY

The right of a government to not be sued without its consent.

At the same time that it was narrowly interpreting the Constitution to limit federal power, the Supreme Court after 1990 began to interpret the Constitution broadly to expand state power. Notably, the Court made a series of rulings that broadly interpreted the Eleventh Amendment's guarantee of **sovereign immunity** to the states. Sovereign immunity is essentially "the right of a government to be free from suits brought without its consent."[26] In cases such as *Seminole Tribe of Florida v. Florida* (1996) and *Alden v. Maine* (1999), the Supreme Court adopted an interpretation of the Eleventh Amendment that limited the right of citizens to sue states for violations of federal law. These rulings not only lessened the power of the federal government over the states, they arguably gave the states more power over their own citizens.

Although these and other rulings resurrected the Tenth Amendment and underlined the independent power of the states, there has been an element of inconsistency to Supreme Court decisions since 1990. In *Bush v. Gore* (2000), the Supreme Court seemed to abandon its commitment to states' rights by overruling the Florida Supreme Court and ordering a halt to the contested recount of presidential ballots. Democratic presidential nominee Al Gore indisputably won the popular vote in 2000, but the outcome of the presidential election was decided by Florida's electoral votes. Gore and Bush ran neck and neck in this state, the decision was so close that a series of controversial and hotly contested recounts were undertaken with the approval of the Florida courts. In effect, the U.S. Supreme Court overturned the state court's interpretation of state law—which allowed the recounts—and decided the presidency in favor of George W. Bush. Another decision that favored federal power over state power came in *Lorillard Tobacco Co. v. Reilly* (2001). Here, the Court overturned a Massachusetts law that regulated the advertising of tobacco products. The Court argued that federal law—specifically, the Federal Cigarette Labeling and Advertising Act—legitimately preempts state law on this issue.

The Court also trumped ten states that have legalized marijuana for medical purposes. In *Gonzales v. Raich* (2005), the Court, led by its more liberal justices, ruled that federal law enforcement officers, prosecutors, and judges can prosecute and punish anyone possessing marijuana. The ruling weakened the states' laws; however, it did not overturn them because state and local officials need not participate in the efforts to seize medical marijuana.[27] Just six months later, however, the Court upheld a state law related to serious illnesses when it ruled in *Gonzales v. Oregon* (2006) against the federal government's challenge of Oregon's law that allows physician-assisted suicide. In recent years, the Court has reviewed a number of preemptions of state law on everything from banking regulation to labor arbitration, and, for the most part, it has sided with federal authority.[28]

> It is ideology—not a firm commitment to a particular vision of state-national relations—that ultimately decides how a justice rules in a particular case.

Some scholars argue that these sorts of inconsistencies have long been characteristic of the Supreme Court's federalism rulings. It is ideology—not a firm commitment to a particular vision of state-national relations—that ultimately decides how a justice rules in a particular case.[29] Therefore, a Court dominated by conservative appointees will occasionally depart from the state-centered notion of federalism if a nation-centered view is more ideologically pleasing, whereas a Court dominated by liberal appointees will do the opposite. The Supreme Court, like the president, also finds it hard to resist the temptations of ad hoc federalism.

Conclusion

The Constitution organizes the United States into a federal political system. This means that the states are powerful independent political actors that dominate important policy areas. Many of these policy areas are those with the most obvious and far-reaching roles in the day-to-day lives of citizens. Education, law enforcement, utility regulation, and road construction are but a handful of examples. The independence they are granted under the federal system allows states a broad leeway to go their own way in these and many other policy areas.

The resulting variation has a number of advantages, such as making it easier to match local preferences with government action and allowing states and localities to experiment with innovative programs or policies. There are also a number of disadvantages. These include the complexity and difficulty in coordinating policy at the national level. The interests of state and national governments overlap in many areas. Because of this and because the Constitution does not clearly resolve the question of who has the power to do what in these arenas of shared interest, conflict is inevitable.

What is the future of federalism? In the past decade, the federal government's commitment to New Federalism has faded, to be replaced by a much more ad hoc approach to state-federal relations. Under the Bush administration, the federal government veered away from the devolutionary trends of the 1990s and made numerous efforts to shift power to the national government. Yet at the same time, the federal government made little progress on many high-profile domestic issues such as the environment and immigration, leaving states and localities to become the primary policy innovators in these areas. The economic shocks of 2008 and 2009 caused a significant retrenchment among subnational governments, which suddenly found themselves heavily reliant on the federal government as a major revenue source. Whether this portends a full reversal of New Federalism, with power concentrating in the hands of the federal government for the long term, remains to be seen. In the short term, however, there is little doubt the federal government will accumulate more authority for the simple reason that propping up big portions of the public and private sectors requires a lot of cash, and, like it or not, only the federal government has the power to print money.

Yet even as circumstances force the federal government to take a more central role, states remain sovereign governments with considerable independence for policy action. The bottom line is that the federal system has evolved into a complex web of intergovernmental relationships that recognizes the practical necessity of cooperation among all levels of government. This creates a situation ripe for continued conflict between state and federal governments, conflicts that in many cases will have to be resolved by the Supreme Court. The Court recently has exhibited some inconsistency in its own commitment to favoring states' rights in resolving state-federal conflicts. Yet, regardless of how these conflicts are ultimately resolved, the future undoubtedly will find states and localities continuing to play a central role in the U.S. political system, both as independent policymakers and as cooperative partners with the federal government.

Key Concepts

ad hoc federalism (p. 58)

Bill of Rights (p. 45)

block grants (p. 55)

categorical grants (p. 53)

centralized federalism (p. 53)

compact theory (p. 47)

concurrent powers (p. 42)

confederacy (p. 32)

cooperative federalism (p. 50)

crosscutting requirements (p. 54)

crossover sanctions (p. 54)

dual federalism (p. 47)

enumerated powers (p. 39)

exclusive powers (p. 41)

federalism (p. 31)

Fourteenth Amendment (p. 45)

full faith and credit clause (p. 44)

general revenue sharing grants (p. 53)

general welfare clause (p. 42)

grants-in-aid (p. 53)

implied powers (p. 42)

interstate commerce clause (p. 60)

national supremacy clause (p. 39)

nation-centered federalism (p. 48)

necessary and proper clause (p. 42)

New Federalism (p. 55)

nullification (p. 48)

preemption (p. 40)

privileges and immunities clause (p. 44)

representative government (p. 36)

secession (p. 48)

sovereign immunity (p. 62)

state-centered federalism (p. 48)

states' rights (p. 47)

Tenth Amendment (p. 45)

unfunded mandates (p. 54)

unitary systems (p. 32)

Suggested Readings

Ellis, Richard E. *The Union at Risk: Jacksonian Democracy, States' Rights, and the Nullification Crisis.* New York: Oxford University Press, 1990. A history of the states' rights movement and the nullification crisis of the 1820s and 1830s.

Kendall, Douglas T. *Redefining Federalism: Listening to the States in Shaping "Our Federalism."* Washington, D.C.: Environmental Law Institute, 2004. An examination of recent federalism cases before the U.S. Supreme Court from the Community Rights Counsel, a nonprofit law firm that assists state and local governments in health and welfare cases.

Peterson, Paul E. *The Price of Federalism.* Washington, D.C.: Brookings Institution, 1995. Overview of how federalism operates in the United States; documents how federal-state relations have evolved.

Storing, Herbert J., and Murray Dry. *What the Anti-Federalists Were For.* Chicago: University of Chicago Press, 1981. Explains why the Anti-Federalists opposed the U.S. Constitution and fought for the Bill of Rights.

Walker, David B. *The Rebirth of Federalism: Slouching toward Washington.* 2nd ed. Washington, D.C.: CQ Press, 1999. Comprehensive history of federalism in the United States and an assessment of current problems and issues.

Suggested Web Sites

www.federalismproject.org. Web site of the Federalism Project, a program sponsored by the American Enterprise Institute that promotes New Federalism ideas.

www.ncsl.org/statefed/statefed.htm. Web site sponsored by the National Conference of State Legislatures that is dedicated to state-federal issues.

www.nga.org. Web site of the National Governors Association that includes a section devoted to state-federal relations.

www.publius.oxfordjournals.org. Web site of *Publius*, a scholarly journal dedicated to the study of federalism.

www.supremecourtus.gov. Web site of the U.S. Supreme Court; includes text of the Court's opinions.

CHAPTER 3

Constitutions
Operating Instructions

Unlike the U.S. Constitution, state constitutions are changed on a regular basis, often to accommodate highly specific laws and policies. Ballot initiatives are one way states alter their constitutions. In 2008, California voters narrowly approved Proposition 8, a ballot initiative defining marriage as a union between a man and a woman and halting that state's same-sex marriages.

3

What impact do state constitutions have on our lives?

Why do state constitutions differ?

How do constitutions determine what state and local governments can and cannot do?

In 2000, Floridians boarded a bullet train to nowhere.

That November they became notorious nationwide for voting in almost even numbers for George W. Bush and Al Gore. But another ballot item stirred up controversy statewide, too. Voters passed a constitutional amendment that mandated the construction of a high-speed rail system that would connect five of the state's largest cities. The measure detailed the type of railroad—"a high-speed monorail, fixed guideway, or magnetic levitation system"—and set a deadline of November 1, 2003, for the start of construction, but left out the project's pesky price tag, estimates of which ranged from $6 billion to $22 billion.

Gov. Jeb Bush vowed to fight the rail program. True to his word, he repeatedly vetoed budget allocations to fund the bullet train, and the November 1, 2003, deadline came and went. In 2004, he and state treasurer Tom Gallagher spearheaded a movement to repeal the high-speed rail amendment. Opponents of the train raised $4 million to spread their message. Their campaign resonated with voters, who were concerned about the train's cost after an especially destructive hurricane season. In 2000, 53 percent of voters passed the bullet train amendment; in 2004, about 64 percent ordered the train back to the station.[1] (Florida's officials may not have wanted the state constitution to force them to spend money on high-speed rail, but they were content to ask the federal government to underwrite the project with funds from the 2009 American Recovery and Reinvestment Act.)

The bullet train back and forth was just one of dozens of fights that have been waged over Florida's constitution in recent years. Since 1976, voters have approved wide-ranging changes to the document, including the "Sunshine Amendment" that widened access to government meetings and documents, a controversial measure limiting school class sizes, and an amendment that made it unconstitutional to use fishing nets that could trap turtles.[2] In many cases, they have battled over measures that in other states might have been proposed statutes, not constitutional amendments. But in Florida, citizens interested in affecting state government through **direct democracy** must petition for changes to the constitution. State law blocks them from proposing statutes, even though it would be easier to undo a statute if opinions changed or the state ran short of cash.[3]

DIRECT DEMOCRACY

A system in which citizens make laws themselves rather than relying on elected representatives.

State constitutions have an enormous impact on state governments and policymaking—and on us. They affect the education we receive, the employment opportunities we enjoy, the political culture of the states in which we live, and the rights we do (or don't) have. State constitutions and the rights and powers they provide also vary widely. This chapter explores how the role that state constitutions allow citizens to play significantly affects governing. California's constitution embraces the idea of direct democracy. The **electorate**, or those individuals who can vote, can make its opinions known at the voting booth. Ballot initiatives and referendums allow voters to override the decisions of the state's elected officials—or even remove the officials entirely—with ease. In contrast, New York's constitution does not. Its politicians are famously insulated from voters' demands, and decisions are made by a handful of senior elected officials.

What explains the tremendous variation among state constitutions? A state's constitution reflects its historical experiences, its political culture, its geography, and its notions of what makes good government. Alabama's constitution, for instance, was drafted in 1901 by a small group of wealthy planters and reflects their fears that rapid industrial development would threaten the "best" form of government—that is, planter government. Although some resisted it at the time, the state's generally traditional political culture made these ideas broadly acceptable.[4] As time passes and a constitution becomes more entrenched, it begins to shape a state's culture and determine the range of political possibilities. Alabama remained a traditional state at least in part because its constitution thwarted industrialization and modernization; although the constitution has been amended more than seven hundred times, the state has resisted changing many of those features. And Alabama is not alone in this regard. Many of the differences in subnational politics can be traced directly to the state constitutions.

In recent years, state constitutions have become more important, not less. Since the 1990s, the U.S. Supreme Court has handed down a number of decisions, some of which have strengthened state governments at the expense of the federal government and others that have trumped state law. The Court's insistence on determining the boundaries of federalism and evaluating state laws and regulations—a form of activism sometimes referred to as **judicial federalism**—even gained former chief justice William Rehnquist the nickname "Governor Rehnquist."[5]

State supreme courts also are becoming more assertive. In 1977, Supreme Court justice William Brennan, a former New Jersey state supreme court justice, wrote a famous article for the *Harvard Law Review* that noted that state constitutions afford their citizens another layer of rights above and beyond the rights protected in the U.S. Constitution. He urged state courts to pay more attention to these rights and to assert themselves more forcefully. They have. In the past decade, for example, state supreme courts in California, Connecticut, Iowa, and Massachusetts have ruled that their constitutions guarantee equal marriage rights to same-sex

ELECTORATE
Individuals who can vote.

JUDICIAL FEDERALISM
The idea that the courts determine the boundaries of state-federal relations.

FIGURE 3-1 **How It Works: Alabama's State Constitution: The More Things Change, the More They Stay the Same**

Since 1819, Alabama has adopted six different constitutions. The most recent was ratified in 1901 and consists of more than 360,000 words. The bulk of this comes from the 798 amendments that make it the world's longest operating constitution. It was the product of a constitutional delegation comprising 155 white males who, like convention president John Knox, were mostly large planters. They wished to hold back the industrialization that had left the state in great debt. Knox, however, described its primary purpose as "secur[ing] white supremacy." African American voters were stripped of voting rights, and interracial marriage was forbidden. Civil rights advocate Booker T. Washington, among others, condemned the document. Many of these provisions are now defunct or have been retracted.

Some still persist, however. For instance, the constitution still contains a statute that calls for racially segregated education. (A call in 2004 to remove the provision was narrowly defeated in the state legislature.) Other provisions allow the continuing disfranchisement of many citizens, delay of economic development, and denial of governing powers to localities. The constitution is accused of encouraging unproductive government action; the state legislature spends more than half of its time debating issues that have only local relevance, and two-thirds of

the constitutional amendments address issues specific to one town or county.

Over time, six different governors have tried to change the existing 1901 document. In each case, they were met with resistance from the legislature, the state supreme court, or powerful planters and industrialists.

Is Alabama's constitution set in stone forever? How can it change? There are two ways to change it: a constitutional convention or article-by-article amendments.

In 2006 and 2007, there seemed to be some headway toward reform. Rep. Demetrius Newton, D, sponsored a bill that would have allowed voters to convene a citizens' convention. Supporters wore shirts proclaiming, "We're unhappy because our constitution is crappy," and rallied outside the state capital during House debates. Newton, however, withdrew the bill in early May 2007, citing a lack of votes from fellow legislators, who had likely been swayed by a group called the Alabama Farmer's Federation. Today, Alabama Citizens for Constitutional Reform continues to advocate for an overhaul of the 1901 document, but the group has yet to realize its goals.

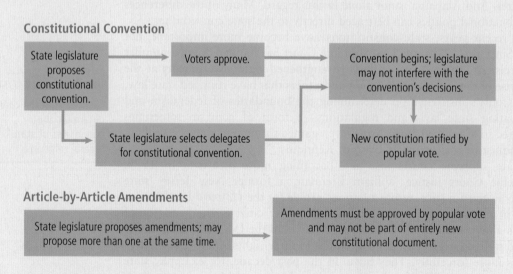

Constitutional Convention

State legislature proposes constitutional convention. → Voters approve. → Convention begins; legislature may not interfere with the convention's decisions.

State legislature selects delegates for constitutional convention.

New constitution ratified by popular vote.

Article-by-Article Amendments

State legislature proposes amendments; may propose more than one at the same time. → Amendments must be approved by popular vote and may not be part of entirely new constitutional document.

Source: Alabama Citizens for Constitutional Reform, www.constitutionalreform.org/whatswrong1.shtml.

couples. (See box on page 87.) State governments have become even more powerful actors in the U.S. political system, and ever more assertive courts have found new rights in the state constitutions. This means that the documents that reflect and determine what state and local governments can and cannot do have become even more important to understanding politics in the United States.

What State Constitutions Do: It's Probably Different than You Think

Mention "the constitution," and chances are good that your listener will think instantly of the U.S. Constitution. The founders have gotten more than 225 years of good press for their work in 1787. Schoolchildren memorize, "We the People of the United States, in order to form a more perfect Union . . ." and venerate the document's wisdom. Yet the U.S. Constitution is only half of the story. As residents of the United States, we live under a system of **dual constitutionalism,** in which the federal government and state governments are co-sovereign powers. Both run in accordance with the rules laid out in their respective constitutions. Despite the important role that state constitutions play in establishing our rights and organizing our local and state governments, most people know very little about them.

The U.S. Constitution and all state constitutions share some common functions. They set forth the roles and responsibilities of governments, describe the basic institutional structure of the government, and establish procedures for these institutions to operate by. Most state constitutions reflect the influence of the U.S. Constitution. They create three primary branches of government (legislative, executive, and judicial) and provide a general governmental framework. Like the U.S. Constitution, they all contain something roughly equivalent to a bill of rights that spells out the rights of citizens and places specific limits on governmental powers. Most state constitutions place these rights firmly in the context of **natural law**, also known as **higher law**, a tradition that holds that these rights are not political creations but divine endowments. Such **constitutional amendments**, or changes, are meant to ensure these rights for citizens.

Yet in many ways it is misleading to compare state constitutions with their better-known federal counterpart. Consider these important differences.

Permanence. The U.S. Constitution is widely seen as the document that created the United States—the embodiment of the founders' wisdom. As such, politicians and the public alike hold it in the highest regard. It has lasted more than two centuries and has been formally changed only twenty-seven times. In contrast, state constitutions are amended and even replaced much more frequently. Most states have replaced their original constitutions at least once. California is currently on its second constitution.

DUAL CONSTITUTIONALISM

A system of government in which people live under two sovereign powers. In the United States, these are the government of their state of residence and the federal government.

NATURAL LAW, OR HIGHER LAW

A set of moral and political rules based on divine law and binding on all people.

CONSTITUTIONAL AMENDMENTS

Proposals to change the constitution, typically enacted by a supermajority of the legislature or through a statewide referendum.

New York is on its fourth. Louisiana is on its eleventh. In fact, one political scientist has estimated that the average state constitution lasts for only about seventy years.[6]

Length. The federal constitution is a relatively short document. At about 7,400 words, it is shorter than most chapters in this book. In contrast, state constitutions tend to be much longer—about twenty-six thousand words on average. Some are much, much longer. New York's constitution and California's ruling document are each roughly fifty thousand words long. The longest state constitution, Alabama's, is more than forty-five times the length of the U.S. Constitution.[7]

Specificity. Why are state constitutions so much longer than the federal constitution and so much more likely to change? Part of the answer has to do with the different functions of the federal constitution versus those of state constitutions. The U.S. Constitution is primarily concerned with setting up the basic structures and procedures of government. State constitutions do these things too. However, state constitutions often set forth procedures and address policies in much greater detail than the federal constitution. Whereas the federal constitution creates a framework for government, state constitutions often get into the policy details. South Dakota, for instance, was one of several states that once sanctioned its state prison to produce twine and cordage. Oklahoma's constitution mandates that home economics be taught in school; Maryland's regulates off-street parking in Baltimore. Political scientist Christopher Hammons has estimated that 39 percent of the total provisions in state constitutions are devoted to specific matters of this sort. In contrast, only 6 percent of the U.S. Constitution deals with such specific issues.[8]

> Whereas the federal constitution creates a framework for government, state constitutions often get into the policy details. South Dakota, for instance, was one of several states that once sanctioned its state prison to produce twine and cordage.

Embrace of Democracy. The U.S. Constitution creates a system of representative democracy; it purposefully rejects direct democracy as a basis for governance. The founders went to great pains to check "the whimsies of the majority" by designing a system of checks and balances that deliberately keeps policymaking at arm's length from the shifting winds of popular opinion. During the Progressive Era in the early 1900s, many states revamped their constitutions to do just the opposite. This was particularly true of the newer western and midwestern states in which old school politics were less entrenched and political cultures tended toward the moralistic or individualistic.

Progressive reformers believed old constitutional arrangements were outmoded and that citizens should have an opportunity to participate

State constitutions contain provisions on everything from free speech to parking fees, from how to organize government to how to build a pipe. Oklahoma's constitution, for example, requires schools to offer courses in the "domestic sciences." Unsurprisingly, state constitutions tend to be considerably longer than the U.S. Constitution.

directly in making laws. Moreover, they worried that state legislatures had been captured by wealthy special interests. In other words, they thought that representative democracy was working for the benefit of a few rather than for the benefit of all. Their solution was to give the people the ability to amend their constitutions and pass laws directly through the use of referendums and ballot initiatives. Thus, in many cases, state constitutions champion direct democracy in a way that the U.S. Constitution purposefully does not.

Finances. Congress and the White House can run up as much national debt as they can persuade bond buyers to swallow. In contrast, thirty-two state constitutions require the legislative and executive branches to balance their budgets. Another seventeen states have statutes that mandate balanced budgets. Only Vermont can choose to run up debt like the feds. Even state constitutions that do not require a balanced budget take a much more proscriptive, or restrictive, view of budget matters than does the U.S. Constitution. California's constitution, for instance, mandates that almost 40 percent of the state budget go toward education, a requirement that has constrained legislators' options when faced with budget shortfalls.

Other state constitutions mandate a specific style and format for the laws that allow the transfer of money to the executive branch. These are known as **appropriations bills.** During the 1990s, some states, including Arizona, Colorado, Nevada, Oklahoma, and South Dakota, amended their constitutions to require supermajorities—two-thirds or three-fifths of the

APPROPRIATIONS BILLS

Laws passed by legislatures authorizing the transfer of money to the executive branch.

electorate—instead of simple majorities of the legislature to increase revenues or taxes.[9] Sometimes the constitutions get more specific still, prohibiting legislators from attaching "riders" to appropriations bills and requiring
a single subject for each bill. (Riders are amendments or additions unre-
lated to the main bill.) Not surprisingly, state legislators sometimes try to
evade these strict requirements. As a result, state judges tend to be much
more involved in monitoring the budget process than their federal counterparts. In 2004, for instance, the Ohio Supreme Court reminded legislators
that it would strike down any laws passed in violation of the state's single-
subject rule.

There's another important and surprising difference between the U.S.
Constitution and state constitutions—the scope of the documents. The U.S.
Constitution's original purpose was to organize a federal government with
sharply limited powers. In contrast, state governments have a wider field of
activities. As the Tenth Amendment of the U.S. Constitution makes clear,
all powers not expressly delegated or forbidden to the federal government
are reserved for the states. In other words, the range of responsibilities
patrolled by state governments is much larger than the federal government's. Given this fact, it is not surprising that state constitutions change
more quickly and tend to be longer, more detailed, and more varied.

The Evolution of State Constitutions

COLONIAL CHARTERS

Legal documents drawn
up by the British crown
that spelled out how the
colonies were to be
governed.

The first state constitutions were not technically constitutions at all. Rather,
they were **colonial charters** awarded by the king of England. These charters
typically were brief documents giving individuals or corporations the right
to establish "plantations" over certain areas and govern the inhabitants
therein. King James I of England granted the first charter in 1606. It created
the Virginia Company of London, which in 1607 established the first English settlement in North America at Jamestown in what is now the state of
Virginia.

As the colonies expanded, many of these charters were amended to give
the colonists "the rights of Englishmen." Just what those rights were, however, was not entirely clear. Britain's constitution was not (and is not) a
written document. It is a tradition based on the Magna Carta of 1215 and
on a shared understanding of what government should and should not do.
From the start, some colonies took an expansive view of their rights and
privileges. The Massachusetts Bay Colony, like other English settlements in
North America, was organized as a corporation and was controlled by a
small group of stockholders. But whereas the charters of the other companies remained in England within easy reach of the British courts, Puritan
leader John Winthrop took his colony's along when he sailed for the New
World in 1630. This made it difficult for the English government to seize
and revoke the charter if the company misbehaved or operated illegally,

which it soon did. The Puritans excluded nonchurchgoers from local governments, punished people who violated their sense of morals, and generally behaved like an independent polity. This misbehavior eventually incurred the displeasure of King Charles II, who revoked the charter in 1691. Massachusetts then received a new royal charter that provided for a royal governor and a general assembly—a form of governance that lasted until the Revolutionary War nearly a century later.[10]

When the colonies won their independence, it was clear that the colonial charters had to be replaced or at least modified. It was less clear what should replace them. Some colonial leaders believed that the Continental Congress should draft a model constitution that every state should adopt. Richard Henry Lee, a Virginia politician, explained the idea in a letter to John Adams in May 1776: "Would not a uniform plan of government, prepared for America by the Congress, and approved by the colonies, be a surer foundation of unceasing harmony to the whole?"[11]

Adams thought not. Although he liked the idea of uniform state constitutions in principle, Adams worried about what would happen in practice. He believed that effective government required a strong executive. The colonists' experience dealing with royal governors, however, had created an aversion to executive power. Adams feared that the Continental Congress would create governments dominated by powerful **unicameral legislatures** or even do away with governors altogether and create a special committee of legislators to handle the everyday business of governing. This would violate what he saw as the wise precautionary principle of the **separation of powers**.

Ultimately, despite being a unicameral body itself, the Continental Congress rejected that particular idea. Instead, it passed a resolution that urged the thirteen colonies to reorganize their authority solely "on the basis of the authority of the people."[12] This set the stage for the states to create their own varied blueprints for government.

After independence was declared and secured, the states convened special assemblies to draft new constitutions. Most adopted lightly modified versions of their old colonial charters. References to the king of England were deleted and bills of rights added. In most of the new states, power was concentrated in the legislative branch to diminish the possibility of tyrannical governors appearing in the political arena.

The First Generation of State Constitutions

This first generation of state constitutions created powerful **bicameral legislatures**—with a few exceptions. Georgia, Pennsylvania, and Vermont opted for unicameral legislatures. Governors and state judiciaries were clearly subordinate in most cases. In fact, legislatures often appointed both the governor and judges. No one envisioned that one day a state supreme

UNICAMERAL LEGISLATURES

Legislatures that possess only one chamber. Nebraska is currently the only state with a unicameral legislature.

SEPARATION OF POWERS

The principle that government should be divided into separate legislative, executive, and judicial branches, each with its own powers and responsibilities.

BICAMERAL LEGISLATURES

Legislatures that possess two chambers, typically a house of representatives, or assembly, and a senate.

court would have the power to overrule the acts of a legislature on the grounds that its laws were unconstitutional. Indeed, the states that did provide for a constitutional review entrusted that function to a special "council of revision" or to "councils of censor."

Nor did the early state constitutions embrace the now commonplace idea of "one person, one vote." Every early state constitution except Vermont's restricted voting access to white males who met certain minimum property requirements. Vermont gave the vote to every adult male. Supporters of a limited **franchise** defended these limitations as essential to the new republic. Without property qualifications, John Adams warned,

> There will be no end to it. New claims will arise; women will demand a vote; lads from 12 to 21 will think their rights are not enough attended to; and every man who has not a farthing will demand an equal voice with any other, in all acts of the state. It tends to confound and destroy all distinctions, and prostrate all ranks to one common level.[13]

Indeed, Adams wanted to restrict the franchise even further by setting still higher property requirements.

In practice, the actual requirements necessary to achieve the right to vote varied widely. Some states, such as New Hampshire, let all white male taxpayers vote. This reflected the fact that New Hampshire was a state of small landowners with a fairly egalitarian political culture. However, even this fair state specified a higher threshold of property ownership that must be met should a man wish to hold office. In Virginia, a state with a more hierarchical political culture dominated by a small group of wealthy landowners and planters, the property qualifications were stiff. Only white males who owned at least twenty-five acres and a twelve-foot by twelve-foot house, or fifty acres unsettled, or a town lot with a twelve-foot by twelve-foot house could vote. It is not entirely clear how many people met these qualifications. Most scholars, however, believe that in the more democratic northern states 60–80 percent of white males could vote. Needless to say, women and minorities could not.

Over the course of the nineteenth century, the franchise was expanded gradually, although in a very uneven and often unjust fashion. A number of southern states, for example, only rewrote their constitutions to allow minorities to vote as part of the price for their readmission to the Union after the Civil War. African American rights also were enshrined in the Fourteenth Amendment of the U.S. Constitution. Yet, despite these protections, gains for African Americans proved short-lived. In the last decade of the 1800s, African Americans' ability to vote and to participate in all aspects of society were harshly limited by the passage of **Jim Crow laws**. These laws provided for the systematic separation of races and sharply restricted access to the franchise, and they permitted the outright intimidation of African Americans.

FRANCHISE

The right to vote.

JIM CROW LAWS

Measures passed in the last decade of the nineteenth century that sought to legally and systematically separate blacks and whites.

A Difference That Makes a Difference:
The Peculiar Constitution of Early Pennsylvania

The original American colonies were established for very different purposes. The Massachusetts Bay Colony, for example, started off as a haven for a persecuted religious sect. The Puritans were determined to create, in the words of Massachusetts's first governor, John Winthrop, "a city upon a hill" to serve as an example of a holy community for all people. Other colonies, such as Virginia, began as business ventures. Still others, including Pennsylvania, were both.

Pennsylvania's first colonial charter reflected the colony's dual purposes as a religious settlement and an investment. It illustrates how state charters were created to serve very particular goals—and how "rights" that Americans now take for granted, such as the right to self-governance, were by no means obvious to this country's founders.

The colony started out as a business venture. In 1681, William Penn received a proprietary interest—the controlling share—in what is now the state of Pennsylvania as repayment for a debt that England's King Charles II owed Penn's father. Penn was already deeply involved in land speculation in North America. He and eleven other investors already owned East Jersey (present-day New Jersey). Soon after buying into Pennsylvania, they acquired a lease on Delaware.

Penn, however, wasn't just a businessman. He was also a devout Quaker, a member of a peace-loving religious group that was often at odds with the official Church of England. Pennsylvania was to Penn "a holy experiment"—a unique chance to found a province dedicated to Quakerism's unique vision of equality and religious freedom.

William Markham, Penn's deputy, was sent in 1681 to establish a seat of government for Penn's new colony. Penn also instructed his representative to construct a

"City of Brotherly Love"—Philadelphia. One year later, Penn himself arrived in his fledgling colony. His first major action was to draw up a constitution, or charter, for his new colony, which he called "the Frame of Government." His second major act was to establish friendly relations with the American Indians in the area—an unusual action that reflected his pacific religious beliefs.

In many ways, the Frame of Government echoed Quakerism's progressive dogmas. Penn's constitution guaranteed religious freedom to everyone who believed in God. It also set forth a humane penal code and encouraged the emancipation of slaves. In contrast, the early settlers of Massachusetts were interested not in individual religious freedom but in establishing a just Puritan society. As a result, the functions of local churches and town governments were intertwined in early Massachusetts. Indeed, the colony was governed as a virtual theocracy for its first two hundred years.

However, the Pennsylvania model was not a uniform triumph of humane liberalism. Penn did use his charter to protect his business interests. The Frame of Government provided for an elected general assembly, but it also concentrated almost all power in the executive branch of government, which was controlled by Penn and the other proprietors.

It was not long before colonists began to chafe at some of the less progressive features of William Penn's early constitution. He was forced to return to Pennsylvania in 1701 and issue a new constitution, the Charter of Privileges, which granted more power to the provincial assembly. However, the conflict between proprietary and antiproprietary forces did not diminish until 1776. That year, noted revolutionary Benjamin Franklin led a convention to assemble and approve a new constitution for the state as it struggled for independence from Great Britain.

Women fared only slightly better. Wyoming began to allow women the vote in 1869. By 1912, only thirteen states had followed suit. It took the Nineteenth Amendment, ratified in 1920, to secure the right to vote, or suffrage, for all women nationwide. This was also the culmination of the Suffrage Movement of the nineteenth century.

The limitations on the franchise imposed by many early state constitutions did little to promote good governance. State legislatures quickly developed an impressive record of corruption and fiscal extravagance because some of the men who had the legal right to vote also had money to influence politicians, an easy task in many states. But the era of unlimited legislative power did not last very long. New territories entering the Union, such as Indiana and Mississippi, opted for elected governors, as did older states that began to revise or replace their constitutions in the 1820s. The intention was to create more balance among the branches of government and allow all voters (not just the rich ones) more of a voice in deciding who would run a state. By 1860, South Carolina was the only state with a governor selected by the legislature.[14] In hindsight, the nineteenth century is seen as a period of tumultuous constitutional change.

Formal Constitutional Changes

Every state constitution provides a method for making changes. Fourteen states actually require citizens to periodically vote on whether or not they want to convene a **constitutional convention**. Voters can decide if they want to amend or replace their state's constitution.[15]

CONSTITUTIONAL CONVENTION

An assembly convened for the express purpose of amending or replacing a constitution.

In the early nineteenth century, suggesting such change could be an exciting—and dangerous—business. In 1841, a patrician attorney and renegade lawmaker by the name of Thomas Wilson Dorr convened an illegal constitutional convention. Its task was to replace Rhode Island's colonial charter with a more modern and progressive constitution. The aged document still limited the franchise to voters owning land valued at $134 or more at a time when other states had long since abandoned such requirements. Dorr's supporters elected him "governor" the following year on a platform that proposed allowing all white males—even Catholic immigrants, a group viewed with great suspicion—to vote, which caused the sitting governor to order him arrested and tried for treason. Thus began the Dorr War, or Dorr's Rebellion. His supporters then attempted to seize the arsenal in Providence but were repelled when their cannons failed to discharge. A month later, Dorr and his followers tried again. This time a force of militiamen and free blacks from Providence repelled them.[16] Still, Rhode Island's establishment got the hint. A new, more liberal constitution was quickly enacted.

The amendment process has since become a bit more routine in most states. Amending or replacing a state constitution is typically a two-step process. First, a constitutional amendment or a new constitution must be proposed and meet a certain threshold of support. Then it must be ratified.

There are four primary ways to propose changes to state constitutions: legislative proposals, ballot initiatives or referendums, constitutional conventions, and constitutional commissions.

MAP 3-1 Number of Constitutions per State

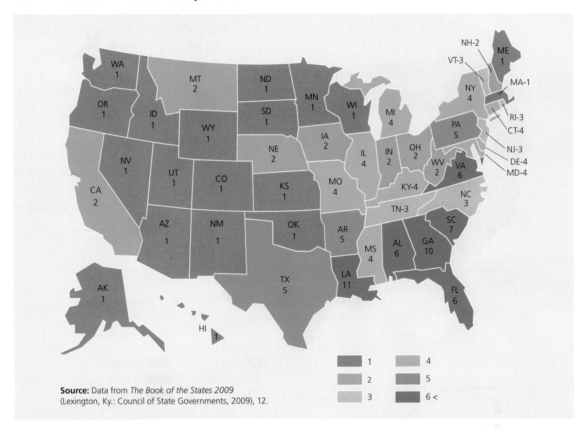

Source: Data from *The Book of the States 2009*
(Lexington, Ky.: Council of State Governments, 2009), 12.

Legislative Proposal

Most attempts to change a state's constitution begin with a legislative proposal. Forty-nine state constitutions allow the state legislature to propose constitutional amendments to the electorate as a whole.[17] In seventeen states, a majority vote in both houses of the legislature suffices to send a constitutional amendment on for **ratification**. However, most states require a supermajority for a constitutional amendment to go into effect. Some states set the bar even higher. The constitutions of eleven states—Delaware, Indiana, Iowa, Massachusetts, Nevada, New York, Pennsylvania, South Carolina, Tennessee, Virginia, and Wisconsin—require their legislatures to vote for a constitutional amendment in two consecutive sessions before it can be ratified.[18] In principle, some state legislatures also can propose completely new constitutions to voters. However, no state legislature has successfully proposed a wholesale constitutional change since Georgia did so in 1982.

RATIFICATION

A vote of the entire electorate to approve a constitutional change, referendum, or ballot initiative.

MAP 3-2 Number of Amendments Adopted per State

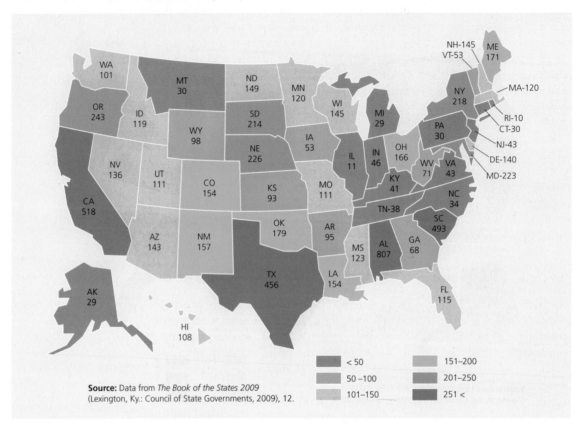

Source: Data from *The Book of the States 2009*
(Lexington, Ky.: Council of State Governments, 2009), 12.

Legend:
< 50
50–100
101–150
151–200
201–250
251 <

Ballot Initiatives and Referendums

BALLOT INITIATIVE

Process through which voters directly convey instructions to the legislature, approve a law, or amend the constitution.

REFERENDUMS

Procedures that allow the electorate to either accept or reject laws passed by the legislature.

Eighteen states give voters another way to propose constitutional amendments—**ballot initiatives** or popular **referendums**. These ballot measures offer citizens a way to amend the constitution or to enact new legislation without working through the legislature. South Dakota was the first state to provide ballot initiatives, in 1898, but it was only after Oregon embraced them in 1902 that the push for direct democracy really got underway. In the sixteen years that followed, nearly two dozen states followed Oregon's lead. The last state to approve ballot initiatives was Mississippi in 1992, some seventy years after its state supreme court tossed out its first ruling, which allowed initiatives.[19] Since then, just two measures have qualified for the ballot. Both failed.

How ballot measures work in practice varies widely from state to state, although there are some common elements to the process. In most states, citizens must first provide the text of their proposal to an oversight body, usually the secretary of state's office or a legislative review committee. Then they need to gather enough signatures to place the proposal on the ballot. This threshold varies widely among states, Wyoming sets the bar high, requiring a number of signatures equal to 15 percent of the votes cast for governor in the last election. It's easier in Colorado, where proponents need only gather signatures equal to 5 percent of the votes tallied for secretary of state in the last election. The signatures are verified, again by the secretary of state or the attorney general. Proposals that pass each test make it on to the ballot at the next election.

Ballot measures typically combine the proposal and ratification stages of the amendment process. Once a proposed amendment is on the ballot, it usually requires a simple majority to pass and become part of the constitution, although some state constitutions do require supermajorities. The practical result is laws without lawmakers; the initiative is commonly employed to seek policy changes that, for whatever reason, are not being considered or undertaken by the legislature.

Constitutional Conventions

The most freewheeling approach to changing or replacing a state constitution is to convene a constitutional convention. Massachusetts, whose constitution was drafted in 1780 and is the nation's oldest, was the first state to adopt a constitution via a convention. Most other states quickly followed. Currently, the only states that make no provisions for changing their constitutions through the use of constitutional conventions are Arkansas, Indiana, Mississippi, New Jersey, North Dakota, Pennsylvania, and Texas.

More than 2,300 initiatives have been included on state ballots since 1904. Oregon leads the nation, with 349 initiatives presented by December 2007.

A constitutional convention typically begins when a state legislature passes a resolution that calls for a statewide referendum on whether a convention should be held. If a majority of the electorate votes in favor of the proposal, then the next step is to hold elections for convention delegates. In most states, a law is passed that provides for the election of convention members from local election districts. Of course, there are exceptions. The legislatures of Georgia, Louisiana, Maine, South Carolina, South Dakota, and Virginia can call a constitutional convention without the approval of the electorate. Iowa holds an automatic constitutional assembly every ten years, and Alaska's lieutenant governor can propose a constitutional convention through a ballot question if one has not occurred within the last decade.

Once delegates are selected, a constitutional convention can convene. Members are free to amend, revise, or even replace their state's constitution; a constitutional convention can change the existing document in any way it sees fit or write an entirely new constitution. Ultimately, its handiwork goes before the electorate as a whole to be voted in or cast out.

Or it can do nothing at all. In 1974, Texas convened a convention to rewrite its creaky 1876 constitution. Members spent several months drafting a new constitution, but when it came time to vote on their handiwork, a majority of the delegates unexpectedly came out against it. The next year, the state legislature voted to put the constitution the convention had drafted to the public anyway as a referendum. The voters turned it down.[20]

State legislators tend to be wary of constitutional conventions and rarely convene them. The reason for this caution is that once convened a constitutional convention theoretically can reexamine any and all aspects of state and local government. Lawmakers who approve a convention might end up initiating a process that leads to more far-reaching changes than they had expected. Increasingly, the average voter seems to share this skepticism. Voters in Alaska, Montana, and New Hampshire have rejected referendums that would have provided for constitutional conventions. In fact, the last constitutional convention was held in 1986 in Rhode Island.[21] More recently, however, calls have been heard for a convention to reform California's constitution, which includes a series of contradictory provisions: some mandate spending, but others restrict taxation. The irony is, voters approved the amendments that made the document so at odds with itself—and now they may have a hand in forcing its overhaul.

> State legislators tend to be wary of constitutional conventions and rarely convene them. The reason for this caution is that once convened a constitutional convention theoretically can reexamine any and all aspects of state and local government.

Constitutional Revision Commissions

CONSTITUTIONAL
REVISION
COMMISSIONS

Expert committees
formed to assess a
constitution and suggest
changes.

If constitutional conventions are for the bold and trusting, then **constitutional revision commissions** are often the cautious technocrat's preferred route to constitutional change. Constitutional revision commissions typically consist of a panel of citizens appointed by the governor, by the state legislature, or by both. The commissions suggest—but cannot mandate—changes to their state constitutions. Between 1990 and 2000, seven states—Alaska, Arkansas, California, Florida, New York, Oklahoma, and Utah—convened constitutional commissions.

Two states go even further in their enthusiasm for constitutional commissions. Florida's constitution requires that a constitutional revision commission convene every twenty years. It also gives this commission a unique power—the right to present proposed changes directly to voters for their approval or rejection. Florida's last constitutional revision commission met in 1998. It recommended thirteen changes to the state constitution, including a proposal to allow local governments to expand the background checks and waiting period requirements on gun sales. That led the head of Florida's chapter of the National Rifle Association (NRA) to decry the proposal as a power grab and to issue a warning that gun owners might vote down all constitutional changes, even changes with universal support, should the proposal pass.[22] The commission refused to back down. Six months later, more than 70 percent of voters supported the measure.

The other state with an unusual constitutional revision commission is Utah, the only state whose commission is permanent. Utah Constitutional Revision Commission members are appointed by the governor, by the leaders of both houses of the legislature, and by sitting commission members. Unlike Florida's commission, Utah's commission can issue its recommendations only in the form of a public report to the governor.

Ratification

Once an amendment has been proposed and found acceptable, it must be ratified before it can go into effect. In most states, this is a straightforward process. First, the proposed constitutional amendment or new constitution is put before the voting public in the next statewide election. Then, the electorate either approves or rejects it. Two states add a twist to this process. In South Carolina, a majority of both houses of the state legislature must vote to approve a constitutional amendment—after the successful popular referendum—before the amendment can go into effect. In Delaware, approval by a two-thirds vote in two successive general assemblies gets a constitutional amendment ratified. As already discussed, the ballot initiative essentially combines the proposal and ratification stages. Once a proposed amendment is qualified for the ballot, it usually requires only a simple majority to become part of the constitution.

Informal Methods for Changing Constitutions

In recent years, voters and legislators nationwide have generally resisted making major changes to their states' constitutions. However, many state constitutions have changed dramatically in informal ways. The most common route of informal constitutional change is via the state supreme courts. For instance, this is the case when a court interprets an existing constitution in a way that creates a new right, such as the right to an adequate or equitable education (discussed in chapter 13, on education).

Sometimes constitutional changes also come about from **judicial review**. In December 1999, the Vermont Supreme Court directed the state legislature to pass a law that provided for civil unions. Its rationale? The court found that because the state constitution was "instituted for the common benefit, protection and security of the people," the state government could not refuse to provide the benefit of marriage to gay people. To those who objected that the state constitution, which was enacted in 1793 and is a model of brevity at 8,200 words, said nothing about gay marriage,

JUDICIAL REVIEW
The power of courts to assess whether a law is in compliance with the constitution.

Procedures for Constitutional Amendment by Legislature

MAP 3-3 Legislative Vote Required for Proposal

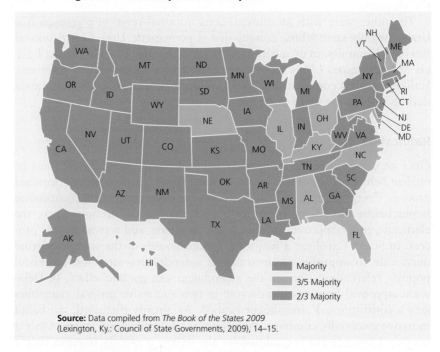

Majority
3/5 Majority
2/3 Majority

Source: Data compiled from *The Book of the States 2009*
(Lexington, Ky.: Council of State Governments, 2009), 14–15.

MAP 3-4 Consideration by Two Sessions Required

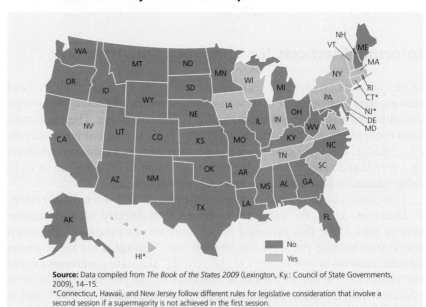

No
Yes

Source: Data compiled from *The Book of the States 2009* (Lexington, Ky.: Council of State Governments, 2009), 14–15.
*Connecticut, Hawaii, and New Jersey follow different rules for legislative consideration that involve a second session if a supermajority is not achieved in the first session.

MAP 3-5 Vote Required for Ratification

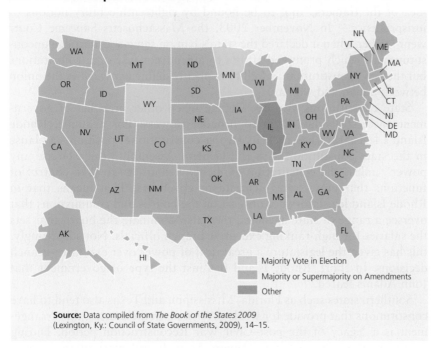

Majority Vote in Election

Majority or Supermajority on Amendments

Other

Source: Data compiled from *The Book of the States 2009*
(Lexington, Ky.: Council of State Governments, 2009), 14–15.

MAP 3-6 Limitation on Number of Amendments Submitted at One Election

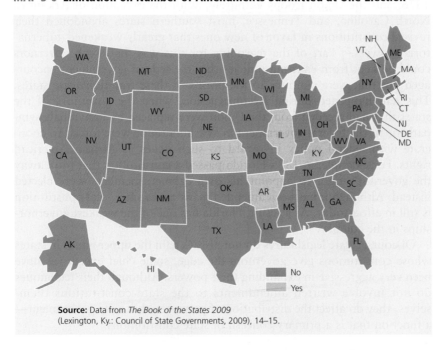

No

Yes

Source: Data from *The Book of the States 2009*
(Lexington, Ky.: Council of State Governments, 2009), 14–15.

the court explained that its job was "to distill the essence, the motivating idea of the framers," not to be bound by eighteenth-century notions of jurisprudence.[23] In November 2003, the Massachusetts Supreme Court went further when it declared the state's ban on same-sex marriage unconstitutional, which prompted efforts to amend not just state constitutions but the U.S. Constitution as well to explicitly define *marriage* as the union between a man and woman.

State constitutions also can change when other branches of government successfully lay claim to broader powers. For example, Rhode Island's legislature has used its strong constitutional position—a clause in the state constitution says the General Assembly "can exercise any power" unless the constitution explicitly forbids it—to take control of functions that most states delegate to governors. That means that in Rhode Island legislators not only sit on the boards and commissions that oversee a range of state agencies; they also dominate the board that sets the salaries for high-ranking executive branch officials. Not surprisingly, this has given the legislature a great deal of power over executive-branch decisions. In short, Rhode Island has just the type of government that John Adams feared.

RECONSTRUCTION

The period following the Civil War when the southern states were governed under the direction of the Union Army.

Southern states such as Florida, Mississippi, and Texas also tend to have constitutions that provide for weak governors. In these cases, this arrangement is a legacy of the post–Civil War **Reconstruction** period. During Reconstruction, the victorious Union Army forced most of the former Confederate states to replace their constitutions. Reconstruction ended in 1876, and the Union troops withdrew. With the exception of Arkansas, North Carolina, and Tennessee, most southern states abandoned their revised constitutions in favor of new ones that greatly weakened gubernatorial powers.[24] Part of the reasoning for this was that weak governors could be kept from enacting policies that the federal government encouraged but that were contrary to the norms of these traditionalistic states. This had happened during Reconstruction, when the governors of the states that had seceded from the Union were replaced by individuals sympathetic to the federal government in Washington or were forced to cooperate with federal policy in regard to such issues as African American rights. For example, in 1885 Florida passed a constitution that took away the governor's right to appoint his own cabinet; members were elected instead. Although it has been amended many times since, that constitution is still in effect today. As a result, Florida has one of the weakest governorships in the country.[25]

Of course, state legislatures do not always gain the upper hand. In states whose constitutions give governors the edge, some chief executives have been very aggressive in expanding their powers. Although their techniques do not involve written amendments to the state constitutions themselves, they do affect the distribution of powers within state government—a function that is a primary concern of state constitutions.

Governing States and Localities

A Difference That Makes a Difference:
State Constitutions and the Right to Marry

"By the power vested in me, by the state of. . . ." These words are repeated by wedding officials every day, in every state. States control who can marry and when. In Nebraska, teens younger than nineteen need their parents' permission to marry, while over the state line in Kansas, people can walk down the aisle at eighteen. A number of states prohibited interracial couples from marrying until 1967, when the U.S. Supreme Court declared Virginia's law unconstitutional in *Loving v. Virginia*. Today, the debate rages around gay marriage. Just five states—Connecticut, Iowa, Massachusetts, New Hampshire, and Vermont—and the District of Columbia have legalized the unions, while thirty states' constitutions have been amended to prohibit them. Several additional states recognize domestic partnerships or civil unions, which grant couples some of the same state-level benefits of marriage.

Legalization of gay marriage has been achieved through judicial review (in Connecticut, Iowa, and Massachusetts) and legislation (New Hampshire and Vermont). Gay marriage has had a less fortunate time at the polls, where voters have rejected it time and time again—most recently in Maine in 2009, after Gov. John Baldacci signed a law to allow the practice. The most high-profile fight was waged in California in 2008 over Proposition 8, a ballot measure that sought to amend the state's constitution to define *marriage* as between one man and one woman—and to put a stop to the same-sex marriages that had begun there in June 2008, after the state supreme court ruled that the state's ban was unconstitutional. After both sides spent more than $55 million on their campaigns, voters narrowly approved Prop 8. Approval of new same-sex marriages was halted, but the state continues to consider the more than 18,000 couples who wed legally as married.

The victory of Proposition 8 prompted further debate among proponents of gay marriage, some of whom wonder whether the continued defeat at the polls means they should wait to wage new legalization campaigns across the states. But the fight over Prop 8 isn't over—and it's not even limited to within the state's borders anymore. In April 2009, Theodore Olson, the former U.S. solicitor general, filed a brief in federal court challenging the amendment.

Sources: Christine Vestal, "Gay Marriage Legal in Six States," Stateline.org, June 4, 2009, available at www.stateline.org/live/details/story?contentId=347390; "Same-Sex Marriage: Breaking the Firewall in California?" Ballotwatch, Initiative and Referendum Institute, October 2008; Jo Becker, "A Conservative's Road to Same-Sex Marriage Advocacy," *New York Times,* August 18, 2009, available at www.nytimes.com/2009/08/19/us/19olson.html.

There is another way to change state constitutions—simple neglect. Sometimes state governments just stop enforcing obscure or repugnant sections of their state constitutions, effectively changing the constitution in the process. No politician today would dare to argue for denying the vote to individuals simply because they are poor or do not own land or belong to a minority group, yet until 1999 Texas's constitution contained a provision that limited the right to vote to citizens who owned land and paid a poll tax. The state government had stopped enforcing these objectionable requirements long before, but had neglected to actually repeal them. Likewise, Alabama's constitution outlawed interracial marriages until an amendment overturned the ban in 2000, a provision that had been informally dropped years earlier.

Why State Constitutions Vary

Without a doubt, state constitutions vary widely from state to state. What explains these differences? Four factors seem particularly important: historical circumstances, political culture, geography, and changing notions of good government.

To better understand how historical circumstances and culture can create a constitution—and then be shaped by that constitution—consider the case of Texas. The Lone Star State's current constitution was written in 1876, soon after federal troops had withdrawn and Reconstruction had ended. During Reconstruction, a strong Unionist governor backed by federal troops had governed the state, centralized police and education functions in state hands in Austin, and generally defied the white Democrats who had been in power before the Civil War. So Texas followed in the footsteps of other southern states and drew up a constitution whose purpose was to ensure that the state would never again have an activist state government. Toward that end, the new constitution allowed the legislature to meet only infrequently, limited the governor's power over the executive branch, and provided for an elected judiciary. The document's sole progressive feature was a provision that for the first time allowed women to continue to own their own property after they were married.[26]

White Democrats' antipathy to Reconstruction explains much of the content of Texas's 1876 constitution; the state's political culture explains why its constitution has endured to the present. Political scientist Daniel Elazar classifies Texas as a traditionalistic-individualistic state that, in his words, "places a premium on limiting community intervention" and "accepts a natural hierarchical society as part of the ordered nature of things."[27] Although Elazar's categories have blurred in recent years, state constitutions continue to bear out his categories. In short, Texas's constitution is well suited to its political culture—a culture that views strong activist government with suspicion.

In contrast, a constitution that allowed the legislature to meet only every other year would suit a moralistic state poorly. Not surprisingly, moralistic states like Michigan, Minnesota, and Wisconsin allow their legislatures to meet far more frequently than does Texas. Because they envision fairly robust styles of governance, the constitutions in these states allow their legislature to meet throughout the year, creating what are, for all intents and purposes, full-time professional legislatures.

New England's propensity for short, framework-oriented constitutions is a variation based noticeably on geography. One political scientist has hypothesized that such a variation may reflect the fact that New England states are small and relatively homogenous and that their citizens are thus less inclined to fight to include policies they support in their states' constitutions.[28]

Of course, history, political culture, and geography aren't the only factors that determine the kind of constitution a state will have. Another important factor is the changing sense of what works best. In the early nineteenth century, many states concluded that a system in which the legislature operates with unbridled power simply did not work well. So they changed their constitutions in ways that strengthened the chief executive. Eighty years ago, groups like the National Municipal League argued that state constitutions should be more like the federal constitution; that is, they should be much shorter documents that provide a framework for governance rather than long documents that get into the details of the policies. That argument gave rise to the **model constitution**, a kind of ideal that states interested in "improving" could adopt. During the 1960s and 1970s, many states did revise their constitutions in ways designed to make their governments more effective, although the last edition of the model constitution was written in 1968.

Since the mid-twentieth century, however, some political scientists have questioned the assumptions behind the model constitution movement. To these revisionists, the fact that most state constitutions outside of New England are long and policy rich is actually a good thing—a healthy sign of an engaged electorate. Revisionists argue that, although Americans have essentially left it to the U.S. Supreme Court to interpret and on occasion to change the federal constitution, citizens have defended their right to participate by shaping their state constitutions.[29]

> **MODEL CONSTITUTION**
> An expert-approved generic or "ideal" constitution that is sometimes used by states as a yardstick against which they can measure their existing constitutions.

> Of course, history, political culture, and geography aren't the only factors that determine the kind of constitution a state will have. Another important factor is the changing sense of what works best.

How State Constitutions Differ

The most obvious ways in which state constitutions differ involve their length and ease of amendment. These are not simply cosmetic differences. Rather, they almost always reflect the different functions that state constitutions serve. Vermont has the shortest state constitution. Like the U.S. Constitution, its goal is primarily to establish a framework for effective government. This is true to a lesser extent of other states in New England as well.

In contrast, constitutions in other regions of the country tend to be longer and more specific in their policy prescriptions. In most states, voters and interest groups that want to accomplish a goal like increased state spending on education will lobby the governor or the legislature. In California, a state with a long policy-specific constitution that provides for a high degree of direct democracy, people often attempt to amend the

Virginia's executive mansion is the oldest continuously occupied governor's residence in the United States. It has been the home of Virginia's governors since 1813.

constitution instead. Although the majority of political scientists wring their hands about this tendency, it undeniably gives Californians a role in shaping their constitution that voters in regions of the country like New England lack.

Operating Rules and Selection for Office

State constitutions create varying organizational structures and operating rules for the constituent elements of state government. They establish different methods and requirements for serving in state politics. Some of these differences reflect the historical differences among states, as well as different political cultures and geography. Other differences reflect different notions of what makes good government. Sometimes these notions can be quite quirky. Consider the following, for example. To serve as the governor of Oklahoma, a state of 3.6 million people, you must be at least thirty-one years old. In contrast, to be the chief executive of California's population of 36 million, you need only be eighteen. You can lead one of the nation's largest states, but don't try to get a beer or a glass of wine at your fund-raisers!

In addition, state constitutions differ widely in how many statewide elected positions they create and how those positions are filled. One of the most important of these differences has to do with the judiciary. At the federal level, judges are selected by the president and approved by the U.S. Senate. Things work very differently in the states. Most give their governors the right to nominate state supreme court justices, often from a list of names chosen by a judicial screening commission. Eighteen states—Arkansas, Georgia, Idaho, Illinois, Kentucky, Louisiana, Michigan, Mississippi, Missouri, Nevada, North Carolina, North Dakota, Ohio, Oregon, Pennsylvania, Texas, Washington, and West Virginia—select their supreme court justices and lower level judges in elections.

Many states use a hybrid of appointment and elections called the Missouri Plan to select and retain judges. Named after the state in which it was first adopted, the plan calls for a governor to appoint a judicial nominating commission. This commission then recommends candidates to fill vacancies on the bench. It presents a list of three carefully vetted, or selected, candidates to the governor, who selects one to fill the vacancy. The nominee assumes the office, but first must be approved by the voters, usually during the next general election. Once approved, the judge faces periodic retention elections. As long as the voters approve, the judge retains office.[30]

Seemingly small institutional differences can have a big impact on how state governments work. A governor with strong veto powers, for example, may have an easier time getting a recalcitrant legislature to consider the executive's point of view on a particular piece of legislation than one who does not. Elected judges are more likely to uphold the death penalty in capital crimes than those more insulated from the ballot box.[31] In short, the different operating rules embedded in state constitutions lead to very different types of governance.

Distribution of Power

State constitutions make very different decisions about where power should reside. Although all state constitutions make at least a bow toward the principle of the separation of powers, in actuality, many have given one branch of government a preponderance of power. Under some state constitutions, the reins of government are clearly in the hands of the legislature or general assembly. Other states have amended their constitutions in ways that give their governors the upper hand.

As previously discussed, some state constitutions clearly give the state legislature an advantage over the governor in the struggle for preeminence. Rhode Island is the classic example. Yet, even though strong state legislatures still may be the norm, in recent decades constitutional changes in many states have bolstered their governors' powers. More than forty state constitutions now give governors the important power of the **line-item veto**, the ability to veto certain portions of appropriations bills while approving the rest. Exactly what counts as an item, and thus what is fair game for a governor's veto pen, is often unclear. As a result, line-item veto court cases have become a common part of the legal landscape.

Some states go even further. In Wisconsin, for example, the state constitution allows a governor the power to strike out an appropriation entirely and write in a lower figure.[32] Former Wisconsin governor Tommy Thompson pushed the power of the partial veto to strike passages and even individual words from bills that came to his desk. In some cases, Thompson would strike individual letters from bills to create entirely new words and meanings and change the entire meaning of the legislation. Critics came to call Thompson's creative writing "the Vanna White veto." In one case, Thompson used the Vanna White veto and his Scrabble skills to transform a piece of legislation from a bill that set the maximum detention period for juvenile offenders at forty-eight hours into one that allowed for a ten-day detention period, a move that enraged the Democratic legislature.[33] Voters later amended the constitution to prohibit that particular veto maneuver. Yet, despite the controversies that surrounded such actions, during his record fourteen-year reign, none of Thompson's more than 1,900 budget vetoes was ever overturned by the legislature.[34]

The power structures set up by the constitutional systems of some states resist easy classification. Take Texas, for example. The fact that the legislature meets for only five or six months every other year might lead you to think that power in Texas resides primarily with the governor. Not

LINE-ITEM VETO

The power to reject a portion of a bill while the rest remains intact.

Illinois governor Pat Quinn vetoed the first budget passed by legislators in 2009 because it failed to include the tax increase he favored. Governors have wide-ranging authority to veto budget bills.

so. In fact, the Texas constitution arguably makes the office of lieutenant governor the most powerful in the state. In Texas, the lieutenant governor presides over the Senate; appoints Senate committees and assigns bills; and chairs the powerful Texas Legislative Council, which is responsible for researching and drafting bills. Indeed, many observers attribute George W. Bush's two successful terms as governor to his close relationship with his lieutenant governor, Bob Bullock, a Democrat.

Rights Granted

State constitutions not only create different mechanisms of governance and give governments different sets of constraints and powers, they also confer different rights to citizens. For example, the U.S. Constitution does not explicitly create a right to privacy, although the U.S. Supreme Court did define a limited right to privacy in *Griswold v. the State of Connecticut* (1965). In contrast, Montana's constitution states that "the right to individual privacy is essential to the well-being of a free society and shall not be infringed without the showing of a compelling state interest."[35] As a result, courts in Montana—and in Kentucky and Tennessee—have interpreted their state constitutions to protect adults' freedom to engage in consensual oral or anal sex that until quite recently was illegal in many other states.[36]

Representative Government versus Direct Democracy

One of the most striking differences among state constitutions is the degree to which they have (or have not) embraced direct democracy. Most Americans celebrate the United States as a democracy, but the founders believed that they were establishing something somewhat different—a representative democracy. This is a form of government in which qualified representatives of the public make the decisions. Direct, or pure, democracy was viewed with suspicion by most of the founders. "[A] pure democracy, by which I mean a society consisting of a small number of citizens, who assemble and administer the government in person, can admit of no cure for the mischiefs of faction," warned James Madison, one of the primary authors of the U.S. Constitution, in his famous argument for the document in *The Federalist,* No. 10:

A common passion or interest will, in almost every case, be felt by a majority of the whole . . . and there is nothing to check the inducements to sacrifice the weaker party or an obnoxious individual. Hence it is that such democracies have ever been spectacles of turbulence and contention; have ever been found incompatible with personal security or the rights of property; and have in general been as short in their lives as they have been violent in their deaths.[37]

In other words, Madison believed that entrusting a simple majority with the power to carry out its will would lead to fickle and tyrannical behavior and to a government that teetered between anarchy and autocracy.

The U.S. Constitution's solution to the problem of pure democracy was to create a representative government or, as Madison saw it, government by a small group of elected officials "whose wisdom may best discern the true interest of their country."[38] In accordance with this belief, the U.S. Constitution created an upper chamber—the Senate—whose members would be selected by state legislatures from among their eminent men. The document also created an electoral college to elect the president. Both of these decisions were made to insulate the federal government from the whims of the majority. The Constitution makes no provision for direct democratic processes. There is not a single federal office *directly* elected by the entire nation. Indeed, as we saw in 2000 with the election of George W. Bush, the electoral college system can result in a candidate's winning the presidency after losing the popular vote.

Whereas the creators of the federal government took great care to ensure it was insulated from direct democratic processes, many states decided to do just the opposite during the Progressive Era. By giving their citizens the chance to make laws and change their constitutions directly, the Progressives sought to circumvent legislatures and executives they viewed as being beholden to wealthy special interests. As Robert M. La Follette, a leader of the Progressive Party in Wisconsin and later a governor and senator from the state, put it:

The forces of the special privileges are deeply entrenched. Their resources are inexhaustible. Their efforts are never lax. Their political methods are insidious. It is impossible for the people to maintain perfect organization in mass. They are often taken unaware and are liable to lose at one stroke the achievements of years of effort. In such a crisis, nothing but the united power of the people expressed directly through the ballot can over-throw the enemy.[39]

For politicians like La Follette, direct democratic mechanisms, such as the ballot initiative and the referendum, represented the general populace's best hope for breaking the power of political bosses and moneyed interests. Between 1902 and 1918, direct democracy enjoyed a great vogue in the states. Sixteen states adopted the ballot initiative in that fourteen-year period. After the First World War, ballot initiatives lost some of their luster as popular enthusiasm for Progressive ideas waned. Only five states—Alaska (1959), Florida (1968), Wyoming (1968), Illinois (1970), and Mississippi (1992) have amended their constitutions to allow for ballot initiatives since the end of the Progressive Era.[40] What's more, note where these states are located. The majority of the states that allow direct democracy lie west of the Mississippi River, where the practice fits with much of the West's populist history.[41]

For much of their existence, initiatives and referendums were used sparingly. Then came Proposition 13 in California. In the 1970s, taxpayer activist Howard Jarvis and retired real estate salesman Paul Gann launched what at first seemed a foolishly impractical campaign to roll back California property taxes and cap the rate at which they could grow. Their campaign struck a chord with many Californians. The state's booming economy had sent property values skyrocketing. Higher property assessments led to higher real estate taxes, which created a huge revenue boom for the state and local governments. Indeed, at the time the state government had a $5 billion annual surplus. Yet, despite the public outcry for relief from rising property costs, Gov. Jerry Brown and the politicians in Sacramento could not agree on a tax reduction plan.

In 1978, California voters passed Proposition 13 and took the decision out of their hands. It directed the state to roll back real estate taxes to 1975 levels and decreed that property assessments could not increase by more than 2 percent a year, regardless of inflation. Most localities previously had reassessed real estate taxes every two years. Proposition 13 decreed that property could be reassessed only when it was sold. The legislation also cut property tax receipts in half and marked the beginning of a nationwide "taxpayer revolt." The revolt culminated in the election of former California governor Ronald Reagan to the presidency two years later.

For California's political establishment, the passage of Proposition 13 was viewed with great trepidation. Politicians worried that it would cripple their ability to pay for the schools and infrastructure that had contributed so much to California's post–Second World War successes. These fears proved well founded. In the wake of Proposition 13, California went from having one of the best-funded public school systems (in the top third in terms of per pupil spending) to having one of the worst (in the bottom third). The proposition put such draconian limits on the ability of local governments to raise revenues that municipalities and counties became increasingly dependent on the state for their funding—so much so that ten years later, in 1988, California teachers' unions pushed through Proposition 98, which mandated that upward of 40 percent of California's general revenue go to education.[42]

In addition to complicating government finances and drastically reducing the flexibility of lawmakers in California, the success of Proposition 13 revived interest in ballots in the twenty-four other states in which they

Qwest Field, home of the Seattle Seahawks, was made possible by a ballot initiative that provided $300 million in public financing for construction of the stadium. The team's owner, billionaire and Microsoft cofounder Paul Allen, financed the successful ballot initiative.

were permitted. In the three decades from 1940 through 1970, there was an average of nineteen ballot initiatives per two-year election cycle in the United States. In the 1980s, that number shot up to fifty initiatives in the average election cycle. In the 1990s, it hit seventy-six ballot initiatives per election cycle.[43] Many of these initiatives were proposed constitutional amendments. Their sheer numbers indicate that states with the initiative are now engaged in an almost continuous cycle of changing their constitutions. These changes are increasingly less about broad questions of good governance and more about pushing narrow agendas.

In the past two decades, ballot initiatives have been used to push through some of the most controversial political issues in the entire country. Oregon voters used a ballot initiative to narrowly (51–49 percent) approve physician-assisted suicide in 1994. In California, voters have used initiatives to impose some of the nation's strictest term limits on elected officials (Proposition 140), to end affirmative action (Propositions 209 and 96), to deny education and health benefits to families of illegal immigrants (Proposition 87), to spend $3 billion on stem-cell research (Proposition 71), and to recall a sitting governor and replace him with an action movie star.

The initiative process has become big business. In 2004, more than $200 million was spent waging battles over California's ballot measures alone.[44] Several companies are devoted to gathering signatures and getting issues placed on the ballot for anyone who can afford their services. To those who have used them successfully, ballot initiatives are a tool to circumvent a hostile legislature and act on the will of the majority. But most political scientists and close observers of state politics have a different viewpoint. To them, ballot initiatives only reinforce the wisdom of the founders in their decision to keep direct democratic processes out of the U.S. Constitution. A number of those who have examined initiatives conclude that they have been hijacked by those with deep pockets and by individuals who use them to further their own self-interests.

Veteran *Washington Post* political reporter David Broder describes ballot initiatives in scathing terms:

> At the start of a new century—and millennium—a new form of government is spreading in the United States. It is alien to the spirit of the Constitution and its careful system of checks and balances. Though derived from a reform favored by Populists and Progressives as a cure for special-interest influence, this method of lawmaking has become the favored tool of millionaires and interest groups that use their wealth to achieve their own policy goals—a lucrative business for a new set of political entrepreneurs.[45]

Exploiting the public's disdain for politics and distrust of politicians, interest groups with deep pockets now have a mechanism to literally rewrite state constitutions to advance their own agendas. For example, in 1997 Microsoft co-founder and Seattle Seahawks owner Paul Allen made an end-run around a balky state legislature and spent $6 million on a ballot initiative that required the state to foot much of the cost for a new stadium for his team. It proved to be a good investment; the initiative passed by 51 percent. Although this was welcome news for many football fans, most political scientists probably see it as an illustration of the very problem that Madison identified in *The Federalist* No. 10. In some ways, the initiative has created a very odd form of governance in which citizens live under laws that are often resisted by their elected governments. With its ability to make sweeping changes in state constitutions, the initiative process could radically change the American system of government in the next few decades.

Constitutions for Local Government?

For the most part, substate governments, such as school districts, counties, and many municipalities, are considered subordinate arms of the state. They may seem like autonomous political units, but they in fact operate under state constitutions and at the discretion of state governments. The courts generally have viewed only the federal government and the states as sovereign entities with the right to determine how their authority should be exercised. The authority and power of local governments is largely confined, if not outright dictated, by the states.

There are some exceptions to this rule. The **municipal charter** is a key example. In a rough sense, these charters are similar to the charters that served as the governing documents for the original colonies. Legally, most municipalities are corporations, and their charters describe the purposes of the municipality and the processes for achieving these objectives. A charter is not a constitution but, rather, a grant of authority derived from a constitution or from state law. Some states have **home rule**, which allows municipalities the right to draft and amend their own charters and to regulate local matters within their jurisdictions without interference from the state. Some states have municipal home rule provisions in their constitutions; others grant municipal home rule through legislation. Municipal home rule means some local governments are operated by charters that "can take on many characteristics of a constitution."[46] Even in the most liberal home-rule states, however, state constitutions and state law generally take precedence over municipal charters.

Conclusion

Even though you rarely read about them in the newspaper—much less hear about them on the evening news—state constitutions play *the* critical role in defining the possibilities of politics in most states. All state constitutions set the basic structure of government, apportion power and responsibilities to particular institutions and political actors, and determine the rights and privileges of citizenship. State constitutions reflect states' distinctive political cultures and, in time, reinforce or alter those traditions.

Yet beyond this common core of shared functions, state constitutions vary greatly. Some protect and extend the rights of the individual beyond the guarantees of the U.S. Constitution; others do not. Perhaps the single biggest difference among state constitutions is the degree to which they serve as a venue for policymaking. In western states, whose constitutions provide for a high degree of direct democracy, advocates and interest groups often attempt to enshrine their policy positions in the state constitution. As a result, these states have long, detailed constitutions. In contrast, the constitutions of the eastern states, particularly in New England, more closely resemble the U.S. Constitution.

State constitutions tend to have a bad reputation with political scientists, for understandable reasons. Although many function well, in more than a few instances, they play an outright disruptive role. In states like

Alabama and Texas, antiquated state constitutions have made it difficult for state governments to promote economic development—a function that most people believe the state government should play. In California and other states, interest groups have used the constitution to ensure that the state's general revenues flow toward the programs they support. In the process, they have reduced the ability of elected officials to make spending decisions on their own.

But as political scientist Christopher Hammons has argued from another perspective, the fact that constitutions continue to be a contentious venue for politics in many states is not necessarily all bad. Although it is still theoretically possible to change the U.S. Constitution, for all practical purposes we as a society have given that right over to the U.S. Supreme Court. It takes an extraordinarily contentious issue, such as reproductive rights, to provoke talk about changing the federal constitution. In contrast, citizens continue to exercise their right to tamper with and tweak their state constitutions. Is that all bad?

Key Concepts

appropriations bills (p. 73)

ballot initiative (p. 80)

bicameral legislatures (p. 75)

colonial charters (p. 74)

constitutional amendments (p. 71)

constitutional convention (p. 78)

constitutional revision commissions (p. 82)

direct democracy (p. 68)

dual constitutionalism (p. 71)

electorate (p. 69)

the franchise (p. 76)

home rule (p. 97)

Jim Crow laws (p. 76)

judicial federalism (p. 69)

Suggested Readings

Book of the States. Lexington, Ky.: Council of State Governments. The single best source of information on state constitutions. Updated yearly, it includes a chapter written by a leading researcher with the latest state constitution news.

Matsusaka, John. *For the Many or the Few: Initiative, Public Policy, and American Democracy.* Chicago: University of Chicago Press, 2004. Examines the effect of special interests on the initiative process.

Tarr, G. Alan. *Understanding State Constitutions.* Princeton, N.J.: Princeton University Press, 1998. Offers the most detailed look at state constitutions and avoids the tendency to view them as inferior versions of the federal constitution.

Tarr, G. Alan, and Robert F. Williams, eds. *State Constitutions for the Twenty-first Century: The Agenda of Constitutional Reform.* Albany, N.Y.: State University of New York Press, 2006.

Suggested Web Sites

www-camlaw.rutgers.edu/statecon/statecon_1.html. Web site for Rutgers University Center for State Constitution Studies.

www.iandrinstitute.org. Web site for the Initiative and Referendum Institute at the University of Southern California, a clearinghouse for information about the initiative and referendum processes of the states.

CHAPTER 4

Finance
Filling the Till and Paying the Bills

Dig a little deeper: the severe recession that hit the United States in 2008 crippled state and local government finances. The federal government stepped in with a $787 billion spending package designed to put people back to work and to help states, cities, and counties balance their budgets. The package included tens of billions in transportation spending for "shovel-ready" projects.

4

What are the differences between progressive and regressive tax systems?

Why are property taxes so important to communities?

How does the federal government support state and local budgets?

Are states' revenue and spending programs sustainable?

Vallejo, California, waved the white flag on May 7, 2008. Faced with bills it could not pay, the city declared bankruptcy, becoming the largest California city ever to file for protection from its creditors. Vallejo was some $17 million in the red, but not because it made bad investments or was the victim of a fraudulent city employee.

Put simply, the economy had brought Vallejo crashing down.

As the housing market crumbled first in California and in other states like Arizona and Nevada, it took with it lots of jobs—and lots of revenue. As the city's income dwindled, Vallejo couldn't keep up with its financial obligations, notably paying for its employees' salaries and benefits.[1]

Meanwhile, Vallejo's parent state was not faring much better. As California's **budget deficit** spiraled toward $50 billion, the state cut services, raised taxes, and even began issuing IOUs to its vendors. Finally, it made a plea to the federal government: we need help.

For the federal government, a budget shortfall is an embarrassment, not a crisis. Congress and the president usually agree to cover the shortfall by borrowing money, that is, by selling U.S. Treasury bonds. The situation at the state level is very different. Like virtually every state, California is required by law to balance its operating budget every year. As a result, its shortfall presented legislators and Gov. Arnold Schwarzenegger with some very difficult choices—and they took almost all of them. Policymakers could slash programs or raise taxes, or do some combination of both; and they did. But still the state faced a $7 billion gap that it could not close, and it turned to the federal government for a handout.

Congress and the White House were not eager to ride to states' rescue, but as 2008 turned to 2009, it became increasingly clear that states might not be able to recover on their own from what was becoming the worst economic downturn since World War II. The **revenues** that keep states functioning—especially income, sales, and property taxes—were dropping precipitously, and not just in the Golden State. National unemployment rates rose above 10 percent, with several states approaching 15 percent, dragging down state income tax receipts 27 percent between June 2008 and June 2009.[2] Consumer demand dried up, taking with it state sales tax revenues, and the housing crisis sent property values—and their resulting taxes—tumbling. That all happened just as demand for state services jumped; the demand for Medicaid, unemployment insurance, public colleges, and even libraries increases during a downturn.

BUDGET DEFICIT, OR SHORTFALL

When the money coming into the government falls below the money being spent.

REVENUES

The money governments bring in, mainly from taxes.

About a month after Barack Obama's inauguration, Congress dipped into the federal coffers to pass the **American Recovery and Reinvestment Act (ARRA)**, a $787 billion package designed to stimulate the economy with targeted tax cuts, job creation, and government investments. Almost $300 billion of the stimulus was intended to help prop up state and local government programs, including $87 billion for state Medicaid programs and a $53.6 billion state fiscal stabilization fund, which most states used in 2009 and 2010 to stave off deep cuts to education and emergency services.[3]

But those billions fell short of closing the more than $300 billion in budget gaps that states accumulated between 2008 and 2010[4]—and the stimulus funds are due to be phased out by 2012. States will once again need to find ways to raise revenues, cut spending, and dig under every cushion to find extra dimes.

In 2008, residents of the United States paid approximately $4,283 in state and local taxes per person.[5] Along with **user fees**, those collections raised about $2.2 trillion.[6] State and local governments use these funds and a substantial influx of funds from the federal government to finance local schools and state universities, provide health insurance to very low-income families and people with disabilities, and build highways and mass transit. The money also helps maintain correctional facilities that house more than 2 million people per year and provides police and fire protection to the remaining approximately 300 million of the population. In short, state and local taxes pay for the programs that Americans care most about and that most directly affect their daily lives.

There is a tendency to think of taxes and budgets as dry, technical, and, yes, boring. That is a pretty good description of much of the literature on this subject, but a very mistaken view of the subject itself. Actually, budgets are the subject of some of the most intense political struggles in state and local politics. It is not simply that people care about money, although they certainly do. Budgets are fundamentally about policy. In many ways, they are the central policy documents of government. They determine and reflect much of the policy orientations of elected leaders. If you want to know what your state or local government's priorities are, its budget will tell you.

This chapter discusses how state and local governments raise money, how they decide to spend it via the budget process, and what they spend it on. It examines why state and local governments make such different taxing and spending choices, and it explores the consequences of these very different choices. The chapter concludes with a discussion of how budgetary constraints and challenges are forcing many state and local governments to rethink how they pay for public services.

AMERICAN RECOVERY AND REINVESTMENT ACT (ARRA)

A $787 billion federal government package intended to stimulate economic growth during the recession of 2008–2009.

USER FEES

Charges levied by governments in exchange for services; a type of hidden tax.

> Budgets are fundamentally about policy. In many ways, they are the central policy documents of government. They determine and reflect much of the policy orientations of elected leaders. If you want to know what your state or local government's priorities are, its budget will tell you.

EXCISE, OR SIN, TAXES

Taxes on alcohol, tobacco, and other similar products that are designed to raise revenues and reduce use.

ESTATE TAXES

Taxes levied on a person's estate or total holdings after that person's death.

GIFT TAXES

Taxes imposed on money transfers made during an individual's lifetime.

SALES TAXES

Taxes levied by state and local governments on purchases.

FOCUSED CONSUMPTION TAXES

Taxes that do not alter spending habits or behavior patterns and therefore do not distort the distribution of resources.

REGRESSIVE TAXES

Taxes levied on all taxpayers, regardless of income or ability to pay; they tend to place proportionately more of a burden on those with lower incomes.

TAX BURDEN

A measurement of taxes paid.

Show Me the Money: Where State Revenues Come From

Roughly half the 2006 revenues of state and local governments (the latest year for which comprehensive figures were available as this is written), or about $1.2 trillion, came from six primary taxes.[7] These were **sales taxes,** including **excise taxes,** often referred to as **sin taxes,** on tobacco and alcohol; property taxes; income taxes; motor vehicle taxes; **estate taxes,** also called death taxes; and **gift taxes.** As states struggled to balance their budgets in the last years of the decade, they increasingly turned to all of these taxes for help; they raised almost $24 billion in tax and fee increases in their 2010 budgets alone.[8]

Sales Taxes

In 2006, state and local governments took in $412 billion from sales taxes—about 34 percent of total state and local government tax revenues. About 81 percent of the money raised by sales taxes goes to state governments. In addition, most states allow at least some counties and cities to levy additional sales taxes. Currently, about 7,500 localities do. Some states, such as California, return a small percentage of the sales taxes to the areas in which the purchases were made. Overall, sales tax revenues account for nearly 16 percent of local government tax revenues nationwide.[9]

State governments, and, to a much lesser extent, local governments, also take in significant sums from gasoline taxes and sin taxes on tobacco and alcohol. Different states interpret this type of tax very differently. Other factors often influence what gets taxed and for how much. North Carolina has a large tobacco-growing industry and a tax of only $0.45 on each pack of cigarettes. New Jersey has no large-scale tobacco industry and levies a tax of $2.70 per pack of cigarettes sold.[10]

Politicians like sales taxes because they tend to be less visible than an income tax. As such, they are less likely to cause voters to retaliate against them at the polls. Economists like sales taxes because they are **focused consumption taxes** that do not distort consumer behavior. That is, sales taxes, even relatively high ones, often do not cause consumers to buy less.

This does not mean that they do not receive their share of criticism. Many liberals and advocates for low-income people complain that sales taxes are **regressive.** If Bill Gates buys a grande latte on his way to work, he pays about $0.28 in sales taxes; freshmen at the University of Washington pay exactly the same. The tax is the same, but the students are paying a much higher percentage of their incomes to the government than Mr. Gates is. Put another way, if Bill Gates's income were even a mere $5 million a year and a typical student's income is $2,500 a year, guess how much Bill Gates would have to pay in sales taxes to face the same **tax burden** as a typical student? Give up? His grande latte would have to cost him a whopping but tax-proportionate $566.20. Of course, as already noted, it doesn't really work that way. If and when Bill Gates goes to a coffee shop, he pays the same price and the same sales tax as anyone else.

States often do attempt to make their sales tax less of a burden on low-income residents by exempting necessities such as food, clothing, and electric and gas utilities from taxation. In general, however, states that rely heavily on a sales tax tend to have more regressive tax systems than other states.

Take, for example, Tennessee, a state that relies heavily on a sales tax rather than assessing personal income taxes. Rich and poor alike paid a 7 percent sales tax at the cash register in 2007. However, Memphis residents earning $25,000 a year or less paid an average of 12 percent of their incomes in state and local taxes. That is about $2,993 for a family of three. In contrast, those residents earning $150,000 or more a year paid only 6.5 percent, or $9,718, of their incomes in taxes.[11] So, whereas it *looks* like the $150,000 wage earners paid more, the low-income residents paid a higher percentage of their incomes in taxes than they might have if they lived in a state that relied more on income taxes. That makes Tennessee's tax system highly regressive.

Sales taxes have another problem—they simply are not bringing in as much revenue as they used to. In the words of James Hine, a finance expert at Clemson University, relying on the sales tax "is like riding a horse that is rapidly dying." What that basically means is that the sales tax base is slowly eroding. Two factors seem to account for this. First, services have become a much more important part of the economy. In 1960, 41 percent of U.S. consumer dollars was spent on services. By 2000, that percentage had risen to 58 percent. Yet most sales taxes are skewed toward the purchase of products rather than the purchase of services. Buy a robotic massage chair at the Mall of America in Bloomington, Minnesota, and you'll pay $58.20 in sales tax on that $800 item.[12] Hire an acupuncturist for an hour from a holistic medical center in Bloomington, and you'll pay no sales tax.

Hawaii, New Mexico, and South Dakota have changed their tax codes so that sales taxes now cover most professional and personal services. However, most states have been reluctant to follow suit. Taxing services could put them at a competitive disadvantage. For instance, if Illinois starts to tax accounting services, there probably would be a sudden boom in business for CPAs in nearby Indiana.[13]

The second factor behind faltering sales tax revenues is the rise of the Internet and online shopping. In 1992, the U.S. Supreme Court ruled that states could not force companies to collect sales taxes for them in places where the companies had no physical presence. As a result, most online purchases are tax-free. A study by Donald Bruce, William F. Fox, and LeAnn Luna of the University of Tennessee, Knoxville, put the overall losses of sales tax revenue from Internet sales at $8.6 billion in 2010 and the predicted losses as high as $11.4 billion per year by 2012.[14]

For states such as Texas and Tennessee that don't have income taxes and that rely heavily on sales tax revenue, this trend is a big problem. To make up

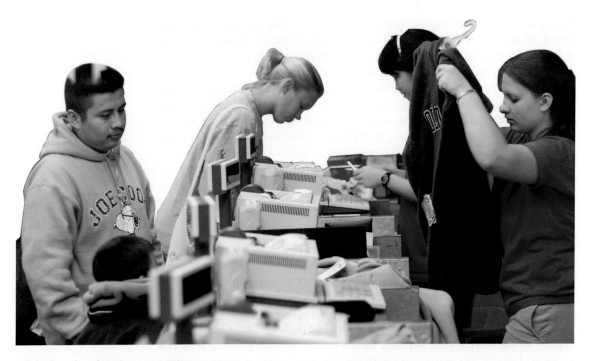

Will that be cash or charge? Either way, these shoppers at the Mall of America in Bloomington, Minnesota, got a break from sales tax on their clothing purchases. Minnesota is one of numerous states that consider clothing an essential item and, therefore, waive any sales taxes. Other states, such as New Hampshire, have no sales tax at all, which makes their malls and shopping outlets very popular with shoppers from neighboring states.

for the kind of revenue loss that Bruce, Fox, and Luna predict, Texas would have to raise its current statewide sales tax rate from 6.25 to 7.86 percent.[15]

The U.S. Congress has rejected states' pleas to stop exempting online retailers from collecting the taxes, citing the difficulty the companies would have complying with very different state sales tax codes. In 2007, Congress extended the moratorium on online taxation until 2014. Absent federal intervention, states have banded together to collect online taxes. Dozens of states joined the Streamlined Sales Tax Project, agreeing to simplify their tax codes in exchange for the chance to convince retailers to voluntarily collect the taxes. The project went live in October 2005, with 150 retailers signing on in eighteen states.[16] By January 1, 2010, more than 1,200 companies participated in twenty-three states.[17] Several states, led by New York, jumped ahead of the project by passing laws mandating that Amazon.com and other similar companies collect sales tax on purchases residents make from affiliates located in state. Amazon challenged the law, but the New York Superior Court upheld the state's law in 2009.[18]

Property Taxes

The second largest source of tax revenue for state and local governments is property taxes. In 2006, property taxes raised approximately 30 percent, or $359 billion, of total state and local government tax revenues. Most sales tax revenues go to state governments, but almost all property taxes go to local governments. As a result, property taxes are by far the most important source of revenue for local government. Approximately 72 percent of local government tax revenues, but only a tiny fraction (2 percent) of state tax revenues, comes from property taxes.[19]

Just about every local government relies on property tax revenues, but property tax rates vary widely from community to community. Most Americans who own homes or condominiums face an effective tax rate of about 1.39 percent.[20] The word *effective* simply acknowledges that some places have exemptions and adjustments that make the effective tax rate lower than the nominal tax rate. You can figure out the nominal tax rate by dividing the amount of tax paid by the amount of taxable income. The effective tax rate is found by dividing the amount of tax paid by the amount of total economic income.

In other words, if you own a condo worth $100,000, you probably pay about $1,390 a year in property taxes. In Manchester, New Hampshire, however, you'd pay $2,840 in property taxes on that same condo. That's because New Hampshire has an effective tax rate of 2.84 percent, which is one of the highest among cities across the country. Why are New Hampshire's property tax rates so high? Largely because the state has no income tax and no sales tax. That limits the state government's ability to raise funds. It also means that the state does not offer its towns the levels of financial support that most state governments do. As a result, whereas most local governments receive 25 percent of their total revenues from property taxes, local governments in New Hampshire are forced to rely on property taxes for 53 percent of their total revenues.[21]

The Education Connection. Property taxes are important for another reason. They pretty much finance elementary and high school education. On average, school districts receive about 43 percent of their funding from local governments.[22] In most states, where you live determines how many education dollars your children receive. Wealthy communities with high housing values raise the most money from property taxes. School districts in these areas tend to have the most educational resources. Conversely, school districts in the poorest areas have the fewest resources. For instance, in New York during the 2003–2004 school year, the most prosperous school districts spent about $2,319 more per student than the least prosperous school districts.[23]

In recent years, this funding gap has begun to narrow. State governments have taken larger roles in financing public education in response to a string of lawsuits that challenged the constitutionality of financing arrangements that provide the poorest children with the fewest resources. Nationwide, school districts with the highest levels of poverty spent $825 less per student during the 2003–2004 school year than did school districts in areas with the lowest levels of poverty.[24]

Hawaii's state government has taken over financing the local schools completely. Many view such a system as more equitable than a traditional, property tax–supported system. However, efforts to equalize school finances also can have unintended consequences, as the state of California discovered. (See box on page 500 of chapter 13 on education.)

The Pros and Cons of Property Taxes. Property taxes generally are paid twice a year as a large lump fee. As such, they tend to be highly visible and extremely unpopular with the public. However, local officials like them because property tax receipts are historically less volatile and more predictable than other types of taxes. Local revenue departments assess the value of houses and businesses and then send their owners a bill, so they know exactly how much revenue a property tax will yield.

In most instances, taxes seem worse when the economy is bad. Property taxes are the exception. They tend to rise most sharply when a town or city is experiencing an economic boom and housing prices are soaring. In these circumstances, an upsurge in property values can lead to a backlash.

The most famous of such backlashes occurred in California in 1978. In response to years of rising property values and related taxes, Californians passed Proposition 13. This piece of legislation capped the property tax rate at 1 percent of a property's purchase price and froze property assessments at their 1978 levels until the property is resold. Newcomers have to pay property taxes based on the actual value of the house.

To this day, Proposition 13 is hotly debated. Conservatives have long praised the movement that gave rise to it. They say that it was the harbinger of the conservative politics that former California governor Ronald Reagan would bring to Washington three years later. Most experts, however, believe that its effects have been devastating. These individuals point to Proposition 13 as the sole reason California transformed from one of the most generous contributors to public education to one of the least generous.

Even the most liberal electorates can be goaded into atypical action by rising property tax rates. In 1980, Massachusetts voters passed Proposition 2 1/2. Property tax increases were capped at, you guessed it, 2 1/2 percent. As a result, towns that want to increase spending by more than that, for such needs as increased funding for education, have to hold special override sessions. Towns also have come to rely on user fees (a phenomenon examined later in this chapter).

Many state and local governments have attempted to ease the burden of property taxes on senior citizens and, in some cases, other low-income individuals. In about fifty Massachusetts towns, senior citizens can reduce their property taxes by performing volunteer work. Cook County, Illinois, limits property tax rate increases by tying them to the national rate of inflation.[25] Despite these efforts, tensions between retirees living on fixed incomes and parents eager to spend more on local schools are commonplace. These pressures can be particularly acute in areas with large numbers of retirees living on fixed incomes. Indeed, some "active-adult retirement communities" ban children altogether.

Another hidden cost of property taxes is worth noting. You might think that commercial and residential property owners are the only ones who pay, right? You're off the hook if you rent, right? Wrong! Most economists believe that landlords pass the cost of property tax increases to renters in the form of rent increases.

> Most economists believe that landlords pass the cost of property tax increases to renters in the form of rent increases.

Income Taxes

Personal **income taxes** account for 22 percent of all state and local tax revenues.[26] That makes income tax revenues the third most significant source of state and local government income. In some ways, however, this figure conceals more than it reveals. Almost all income tax revenues go to state governments.[27] In many states, personal income taxes are assessed on a graduated scale, so higher wage earners pay a greater percentage of their pay in taxes. This structure tends to make state tax systems that rely more heavily on the income tax than on the sales tax more **progressive**.

Of course, this is not true for every state. As previously mentioned, nine states make do without income taxes. Alaska, Florida, Nevada, South Dakota, Texas, Washington, and Wyoming impose no income taxes at all. New Hampshire and Tennessee impose taxes only on certain types of income.

As discussed earlier, states that do not have an income tax usually rely heavily on the sales tax. But Alaska, Delaware, Montana, New Hampshire, and Oregon have no statewide sales tax. Oregon has managed this by—drum roll, please—relying heavily on a state income tax. In fact, in 2006, Oregon's income tax provided 45 percent of its total tax revenues—the most of any state.[28] Voters in Oregon endorsed—and even increased—the state's reliance on its income tax in January 2010 by approving an increase in the tax rate on the highest wage earners—the first time they'd approved such an increase since 1930.

So, Alaska and New Hampshire have neither income taxes nor sales taxes. How can that be? For Alaska, the answer is the Prudhoe Bay oilfields. But New Hampshire just makes do. According to Donald Boyd of the Rockefeller Institute, New Hampshire's state government simply does less than most state governments. The state relies almost exclusively on local governments to finance elementary and secondary education rather than raising state revenue for this purpose. Unlike many other states, it also has managed to avoid court orders to spend dramatically more on secondary school education. It is able to do all this, in part, because the income of the average New Hampshire resident is one of the highest in the country. People are able to pay for a lot of goods and services for themselves.

These states are the exceptions. On average, Americans pay about $866 a year in state income taxes.[29] However, residents of states with high tax rates, such as Maryland, Massachusetts, New York, and Oregon, pay significantly more in income taxes. (See Table 4-1.)

INCOME TAXES
Taxes on income.

PROGRESSIVE TAX SYSTEM
System in which the tax rate paid reflects the ability to pay.

TABLE 4-1

State Individual Income Tax Rates, 2008

State	Tax Rate (%)		Number of Brackets	Income Brackets		Personal Exemption			Federal Tax Deductions
	Low	High		Low	High	Single	Married	Children	
Alabama	2.0	5.0	3	500[b]	3,000[b]	1,500	3,000	300	*
Alaska	No state income tax								
Arizona	2.59	4.54	5	10,000[b]	150,000[b]	2,100	4,200	2,300	
Arkansas[a]	1.0	7.0[e]	6	3,899	32,600[b]	23[c]	46[c]	23[c]	
California[a]	1.25	9.55[w]	6	7,300[b]	47,900[b]	98[c]	196[c]	98[c]	
Colorado	4.63		1	Flat rate		None			
Connecticut	3.0	6.5	3	10,000[b]	500,001[b]	13,000[f]	26,000[f]	0	
Delaware	2.2	6.95	6	5,000	60,001	110[c]	220[c]	110[c]	
Florida	No state income tax								
Georgia	1.0	6.0	6	750[g]	7,000[g]	2,700	5,400	3,000	
Hawaii	1.4	11.00	12	2,400[b]	200,001[b]	1,040	2,080	1,040	
Idaho[a]	1.6	7.8	8	1,320[h]	26,418[h]	3,650[d]	7,300[d]	3,650[d]	
Illinois	3.0		1	Flat rate		2,000	4,000	2,000	
Indiana	3.4		1	Flat rate		1,000	2,000	1,000	
Iowa[a]	0.36	8.98	9	1,407	63,316	40[c]	80[c]	40[c]	*
Kansas	3.5	6.45	3	15,000[b]	30,000[b]	2,250	4,500	2,250	
Kentucky	2.0	6.0	6	3,000	75,000	20[c]	40[c]	20[c]	
Louisiana	2.0	6.0	3	12,500[b]	50,000[b]	4,500[i]	9,000[i]	1,000[i]	*
Maine[a]	2.0	8.5	4	4,949[b]	19,750[b]	2,850	5,700	2,850	
Maryland	2.0	6.25	8	1,000	1,000,001	2,400	4,800	2,400	
Massachusetts[a]	5.3		1	Flat rate		4,400	8,800	1,000	
Michigan[a]	4.35		1	Flat rate		3,300	6,600	3,300	
Minnesota[a]	5.35	7.85	3	22,770[j]	74,781[j]	3,650[d]	7,300[d]	3,650[d]	
Mississippi	3.0	5.0	3	5,000	10,000	6,000	12,000	1,500	
Missouri	1.5	6.0	10	1,000	9,000	2,100	4,200	1,200	*r
Montana[a]	1.0	6.9	7	2,600	15,401	2,110	4,220	2,110	*r
Nebraska[a]	2.56	6.84	4	2,400[k]	27,001[k]	118[c]	236[c]	118[c]	
Nevada	No state income tax								
New Hampshire	State income tax limited to dividends and interest income only								
New Jersey	1.4	10.75	8	20,000[l]	1,000,000[l]	1,000	2,000	1,500	
New Mexico	1.7	4.9	4	5,500[m]	16,000[m]	3,650[d]	7,300[d]	3,650[d]	
New York	4.0	8.97	7	8,000[x]	500,000[x]	0	0	1,000	
North Carolina	6.0	7.75[n]	3	12,750[n]	60,000[n]	3,650[d]	7,300[d]	3,650[d]	
North Dakota[a]	1.84	4.86	5	34,000[o]	373,650[o]	3,650[d]	7,300[d]	3,650[d]	
Ohio[a]	0.618	6.24	9	5,000	200,000	1,550[p]	3,100[p]	1,550[p]	
Oklahoma	0.5	5.5[q]	7	1,000[b]	8,701[b]	1,000	2,000	1,000	*r
Oregon[a]	5.0	11.0	5	2,000[b]	250,000[b]	176[c]	352[c]	176[c]	*r
Pennsylvania	3.07		1	Flat rate		None			
Rhode Island	3.8	9.9[y]	5	33,500[y]	372,950[y]	3,650[d]	7,300[d]	3,650[d]	
South Carolina[a]	0.0	7.0	6	2,740	13,701	3,650[d]	7,300[d]	3,650[d]	

TABLE 4-1, continued

State	Tax Rate (%)		Number of Brackets	Income Brackets		Personal Exemption			Federal Tax Deductions
	Low	High		Low	High	Single	Married	Children	
South Dakota	No state income tax								
Tennessee	State income tax limited to dividends and interest income only								
Texas	No state income tax								
Utah	5.0		1	Flat rate		t	t	t	
Vermonta	3.55	8.95	5	33,950	372,950u	3,650d	7,300d	3,650d	
Virginia	2.0	5.75	4	3,000	17,000	930	1,860	930	
Washington	No state income tax								
West Virginia	3.0	6.5	5	10,000	60,000	2,000	4,000	2,000	
Wisconsina	4.6	7.75	5	10,220v	225,001v	700	1,400	700	
Wyoming	No state income tax								
District of Columbia	4.0	8.5	3	10,000	40,000	1,675	3,350	1,675	

Source: The Federation of Tax Administrators, from various sources, www.taxadmin.org/fta/rate/ind_inc.pdf.
Notes: Asterisk indicates income tax is deductible on federal income tax return.

a Sixteen states have statutory provisions for automatic adjustment of tax brackets, personal exemption, or standard deductions to the rate of inflation. Massachusetts, Michigan, Nebraska, and Ohio index the personal exemption amounts only.

b For joint returns, the taxes are twice the tax imposed on half the income.

c Tax credits.

d These states allow personal exemption or standard deductions as provided in the Internal Revenue Code (IRC).

e A special tax table is available for low-income taxpayers, reducing their tax payments.

f Combined personal exemptions and standard deduction. An additional tax credit is allowed ranging from 75 to 0% based on state adjusted gross income. Exemption amounts are phased out for higher-income taxpayers until they are eliminated for households earning over $61,000.

g The tax brackets reported are for single individuals. For married households, the same rates apply to income brackets ranging from $1,000 to $10,000.

h For joint returns, the tax is twice the tax imposed on half the income. A $10 filing tax is charged for each return, and a $15 credit is allowed for each exemption.

i Combined personal exemption and standard deduction.

j The tax brackets reported are for single individuals. For married couples filing jointly, the same rates apply for income under $33,280 to over $132,221. A 6.4% alternative minimum tax (AMT) rate is also applicable.

k The tax brackets reported are for single individuals. For married couples filing jointly, the same rates apply for income under $4,800 to over $54,000.

l The tax brackets reported are for single individuals. For married couples filing jointly, the tax rates range from 1.4 to 10.75% (with nine income brackets) applying to income brackets from $20,000 to over $1 million.

m The tax brackets reported are for single individuals. For married couples filing jointly, the same rates apply for income under $8,000 to over $24,000. Married households filing separately pay the tax imposed on half the income.

n The tax brackets reported are for single individuals. For married taxpayers, the same rates apply to income brackets ranging from $21,250 to $100,000. Lower exemption amounts allowed for high-income taxpayers. For tax years 2009 and 2010, a surcharge that equals 2% of total liability for taxpayers with income over $60,000 single filer ($100,000 joint) and 3% of total liability for income over $150,000 ($250,000).

o The tax brackets reported are for single individuals. For married taxpayers, the same rates apply to income brackets ranging from $56,850 to $373,650. An additional $300 personal exemption is allowed for joint returns or unmarried head of households.

p Plus an additional $20 per exemption tax credit.

q The rate range reported is for single individuals. For married couples filing jointly, the same rates apply to income brackets ranging from $2,000 to $15,000.

r Deduction is limited to $10,000 for joint returns and $5,000 for individuals in Missouri and Montana, and to $5,600 in Oregon.

s Federal Tax Liability prior to the enactment of Economic Growth and Tax Relief Act of 2001. Or taxpayers have the option of computing tax liability based on a flat 7.0% (6.5% in 2009) of gross income.

t Tax credits are equal to 6% of federal standard/itemized deductions (without state taxes paid) and 75% of federal personal exemption amounts. The credit amount is phased out above $12,000 in income ($24,000 for joint returns).

u The tax brackets reported are for single individuals. For married couples filing jointly, the same rates apply for income from under $56,700 to over $372,950.

v The tax brackets reported are for single individuals. For married taxpayers, the same rates apply to income brackets ranging from $13,620 to $300,000.

w An additional 1% tax is imposed on taxable income over $1 million. Tax rates are scheduled to fall by 0.25% after 2011.

x The tax brackets reported are for single individuals. For married taxpayers, the same rates apply to income brackets ranging from $16,000 to $500,000.

y Or an alternative flat rate of 6.5%. Rates reported are for a single filer calculated based on a tax of 25% of federal liability using IRC in 2001. For married couples filing jointly, the same rates apply to income brackets ranging from $56,700 to $372,950.

Other Tax Revenue Sources: Cars, Oil, and Death

Car registrations, death, and oil and other natural resources also are major sources of state revenues. In 2006, car registration fees brought in more than $20 billion to state and local governments. Estate taxes, sometimes called death taxes, and gift taxes brought in another $4.8 billion.[30]

Thirty-nine states levy **severance taxes** on natural resources that are removed, or severed, from the state. Some states are quite creative about devising severance taxes. Washington, for example, taxes oysters and salmon and other game fish caught in state. But despite some creative taxing, the only states that raise real money from severance taxes are states with significant coal, oil, and natural gas reserves, such as Wyoming and Alaska.

Other Sources of Income: Fees, Charges, and Uncle Sam

The total tax revenues discussed so far add up to about $1.2 trillion. That is a lot of money, but it accounts for less than half of the $2.7 trillion that state and local governments took in in 2006. The rest of the money came from user fees and other charges, insurance trust money, and intergovernmental transfers.

In 2006, state and local governments raised $538 billion from "charges and miscellaneous fees." That is $126 billion more than they raised from sales taxes.[31] Little charges like university tuitions, public hospital charges, airport use fees, school lunch sales, and park permits make a big difference. Recently, states have increased fees to help close budget deficits and avoid more prominent tax increases. The pattern accelerated as tax revenue fell off in recent years; enacted 2010 budgets included $5.3 billion in fee increases.[32] State and local governments earned another $125 million from utility fees and, yes, from liquor sales and licenses.[33] (See Table 4-2.)

TABLE 4-2

The Five States That Rely Most on Revenue from Fees, Charges, and Interest, 2006

State	Percentage of Total Revenue
Alaska	37.4
Indiana	30.1
South Carolina	27.9
Delaware	27.8
Alabama	25.3
U.S. Average	19.7

Source: "State & Local Revenue from Fees, Charges & Interest as % of Total Revenue, 2006," *State and Local Sourcebook*, online supplement to *Governing* magazine, 2010, http://sourcebook.governing.com/subtopicresults.jsp?ind=667.

States under Stress: Balancing the Books on the Backs of Students

On campuses across the country, large gatherings on college quadrangles often mark the start of spring. Except that in March 2010 students weren't playing Frisbee or studying for midterm exams when they took to the grounds at more than one hundred schools nationwide. Instead, they were protesting the widespread tuition increases and staff layoffs that states instituted as part of budget-balancing maneuvers. More than thirty states cut aid to public colleges and universities in 2009 and 2010, although some cuts were backfilled using federal stimulus dollars. But what's happened recently is part of a larger trend: college tuition—both public and private—has increased far faster than the rate of inflation over the last three decades.

The demonstrations gathered steam beginning in fall 2009, when the California regents approved a plan to increase tuition 32 percent during that state's severe budget crisis. "Students are paying more and getting less, and they have every right to be outraged about that," said California State University chancellor Charles Reed.

It's true that states can pass the buck to students in a way that they cannot to prisoners in state prisons. But many are searching for ways to minimize the negative effects of cost cutting. In Louisiana, one of Gov. Bobby Jindal's priorities is to increase the share of Louisiana degrees awarded at community colleges by making four-year schools more selective. Louisiana assigns money to schools based on performance standards, such as graduation rates, and it is one of a growing number of states that intend to fund schools based on the number of degrees they produce—not the number of students they enroll.

Virginia Tech has taken a different approach. Nearly five thousand students take math in a 60,000-square-foot box called the Math Emporium. The former department store houses 537 computers; in front of these, the students sit side by side but taking many different courses: algebra, geometry, or calculus. The students show up when they want and leave when they want. Instructors roam the warehouse-like space looking for those who have placed red cups on their computers—the signal for help. Students can stop working on a lesson whenever they're confident they know it, probably saving the university money.

Maryland has realized more than $120 million in savings from its Efficiency and Effectiveness Initiative, an effort to save money anywhere and everywhere, without hurting the quality of education. Some of the changes the system made were fairly mundane but effective. It launched collaborative purchasing across its campuses to lower prices. It required faculty to spend more time teaching, thereby lowering personnel costs. And, similar to Louisiana, it began directing more of its young people to community colleges, at least to start. The live-in nature of college, after all, is a big part of what makes it expensive. Schools pay for dormitories, sports stadiums, cafeterias, and healthcare facilities. Without those buildings, community colleges come with much lower price tags. Want evidence that the initiative is working? Maryland's in-state tuition did not increase between 2006 and 2010. Part of the reason for that can be traced to politics. In Martin O'Malley's successful campaign for governor in 2006, he spent hundreds of thousands of dollars producing ads promising to control tuition costs, and he sought to keep that promise.

But even that much belt tightening might not be enough to stop the flow of red ink. A recent legislative study projected that Maryland's system will be $700 million short of funds over the next decade.

Sources: Mary Beth Marklein, "Students Rally Today for Quality Education; Walkouts, Rallies vs. Budget Cuts, Layoffs," USA Today, March 4, 2010, D6; The Fiscal Survey of States (Washington, D.C.: National Governors Association and National Association of State Budget Officers, fall 2009); adapted from Josh Goodman, "Can Higher Ed Control Its Costs?" Governing magazine, November 2009, available at www.governing.com/node/4514.

Insurance Trust Funds

Looking at the amount on a pay stub before any deductions are taken out can be pretty impressive. Looking at the actual amount of the paycheck can be a bit disappointing. What people may not realize is that they are not the only ones paying these taxes and fees. Their employers often have to match these payroll taxes and deductions. These **insurance trust funds** go to their state governments and to the federal government. Ultimately, the contributions are invested to support Social Security and retirement programs, workers' compensation and disability programs, and other related insurance programs that benefit employees.

Intergovernmental Transfers

The final portion of state and local government revenues comes from **intergovernmental transfers** of money. In the case of state governments, that means transfers from the federal government. In the case of local governments, that means transfers from state governments. In 2008, the federal government provided some $461 billion to state and local governments, or enough to cover 27 percent of state and local expenditures.[34] When the 2009 and 2010 budget figures are finalized, that $461 billion may be as much as $600 billion per year, accounting for 30 percent or more of expenses, thanks to the federal stimulus package.[35] (See Map 4-1 for a more detailed state breakdown of ARRA funding.)

Approximately 90 percent of federal funds go to specific state programs. Medicaid, the joint state-federal health insurance program for low-income people and people with disabilities, is by far the largest recipient. It receives about 43.6 percent of all federal funds that go to state governments.[36] Education (both K–12 and post–secondary school), transportation projects, and public welfare also receive significant federal funding. Most of these funds cannot be used on just anything. States must spend them on certain programs and often in a certain fashion.

During the 1960s, local governments and some neighborhood organizations also received substantial federal funding. Many of these programs have since ended or have been scaled back drastically. Aside from the stimulus bill, local governments get only about 4 percent of their total revenues from the federal government. Adding to the problem for localities is that states have reduced their support for local governments, too, as one tool to help balance their own budgets. In 2002, intergovernmental revenue transfers from state governments accounted for 33 percent of total local government revenues; by 2006, that share had fallen to 30 percent.[37]

Localities generally have welcomed the money, but the relationship between state governments and county and city governments has not always been an easy one. Over the course of the past decade, many city and county governments have found themselves stuck with unfunded mandates. These requirements have been imposed on them by federal or state legislation that forces them to perform certain tasks but fails to provide them with the

INSURANCE TRUST FUNDS

Money collected from contributions, assessments, insurance premiums, or payroll taxes.

INTERGOVERNMENTAL TRANSFERS

Funds provided by the federal government to state governments and by state governments to local governments.

MAP 4-1 American Recovery and Reinvestment Act Funds Awarded by State, 2009

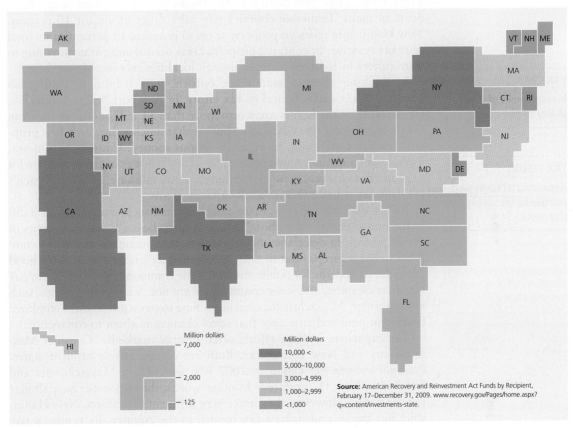

Million dollars
— 7,000

— 2,000

— 125

Million dollars

■	10,000 <
■	5,000–10,000
■	3,000–4,999
■	1,000–2,999
■	<1,000

Source: American Recovery and Reinvestment Act Funds by Recipient, February 17–December 31, 2009. www.recovery.gov/Pages/home.aspx?q=content/investments-state.

money to carry out those tasks. Transfers of money and responsibilities, however, continue to be commonplace during economic downturns.[38]

Taxing Variations among State and Local Governments

Generalizations about state and local finances should not obscure the fact that different states and localities tax themselves in very different ways and at very different rates. The first striking difference concerns the very different tax burdens that states choose to impose on themselves. In 2008, Connecticut residents paid the most per capita in state and local taxes of any state in the country—$7,007. However, New Jersey residents faced the largest tax burden. They returned 11.8 percent of their incomes to state and local governments, the highest percentage of any state in the country. In contrast, residents of Alaska, Florida, Nevada, and Wyoming faced some of the lowest state and local tax burdens in the country. On average, in 2008 residents paid 9.7 percent of their incomes a year in state and local taxes.[39]

State and local governments do not just choose to tax themselves at different rates. They also choose to tax themselves in different ways. Residents of many Tennessee counties pay sales taxes of almost 10 percent. New Hampshire relies on property taxes to generate 18 percent of its total state tax revenue. In contrast, property taxes do not contribute anything to state coffers in fourteen states, although localities rely heavily on them.[40]

TAX CAPACITY

Measurement of the ability to pay taxes.

TAX EFFORT

A measure of taxes paid relative to the ability to pay taxes.

In thinking about a state's tax burden, it is helpful to distinguish between its **tax capacity** and its **tax effort**. In Newport Beach, California, for example, many homes are worth more than $1 million—a far cry from the price tags of a few years ago—but on that much value, even low property tax rates are going to bring in serious money. Conversely, Odessa, Texas, with a median home price of $66,700, is not going to generate a lot of property tax revenue, no matter how high its rates are. Newport Beach's tax capacity is high; Odessa's tax capacity is low.

Rather than tax capacity, many political scientists prefer to look at a different measurement—tax effort, or tax burden. Basically, measurements of tax effort seek to determine the proportion of its income that a given community chooses to pay out in taxes. A community's tax effort is also a good proxy for its appetite for public services. Some communities are willing to pay for street cleaning, and some communities are not. Some communities, such as Cambridge, Massachusetts, even are willing to pay a government employee to drive around and announce that street cleaning is about to commence.

Tax capacities and tax efforts often diverge markedly. Consider Massachusetts and New Hampshire. Both are comparatively affluent states. Personal income per capita in 2007 was $49,142 in Massachusetts and $41,144 in New Hampshire.[41] In other words, the two states have similar tax capacities. However, they make very different tax efforts. New Hampshire has the second lightest tax burden in the country. Its residents pay about $3,642 a year in state and local taxes. In contrast, residents of neighboring Massachusetts pay about $5,377.[42]

Explaining Tax Variations

What accounts for such differences? Primarily, the two states have very different political cultures. New Hampshire prides itself on its rugged individualism. Its motto is "Live Free or Die." Residents tend to want the government to stay out of their way. In contrast, Massachusetts was founded as a commonwealth. The founding document of the Massachusetts Bay Colony describes a single "Body Politic" dedicated to the "general good" of the colony.[43] In this tradition, state and local governments are seen as effective ways of advancing that general good. Thus, higher taxes and larger governments are more acceptable.

Political culture is not the only important variable that explains the very different tax efforts among states. Factors such as geography, geology, demographics, and history also influence the choices that state and local governments make.

Geography. One obvious, but easily overlooked, factor that influences state tax policies is geography. Some states use sales tax policy as a competitive edge. Delaware proudly recruits shoppers from nearby Mid-Atlantic states to its outlet malls with its "no sales tax" advertisements. In contrast, Hawaii charges a 4.5 percent tax on nearly everything sold, including many services. How does it get away with the practice? Well, unless residents are willing to fly to the mainland for their sundries, they don't have much choice but to pay up.

Geology. Geology plays an important role in some state economies too. This is most notably true in oil-rich and natural-gas-rich states like Alaska and Wyoming. Thanks in large part to Prudhoe Bay, state and local governments in Alaska were able to spend $15,924 per person in 2006 while maintaining the lightest tax burden in the country.[44] Indeed, Alaska's Permanent Fund sends each eligible citizen a yearly **dividend** check, typically for around $1,500, as a way of distributing the oil wealth.

DIVIDEND

A payment made to stockholders, or in Alaska's case, residents, from the interest generated from an investment.

Demographics. Demographics play an important role in determining the attitudes of state and local governments toward taxes. This is particularly true at the local level. Consider a city with a strong local economy and rising house prices. Such a city attracts a large number of young workers with children. These are people who might very well want to spend more money on local schools and are willing to deal with rising property tax revenues. However, as mentioned previously, for seniors living on fixed incomes, rising house prices and rising property taxes might spell disaster. During economic booms, conflicts between parents and retirees are a common feature of local politics.

The Economic Cycle. Even when states make similar tax efforts and have similar cultures, state and local finances are distributed very differently from state to state. That is because different states and cities have very different economies.

Different states are situated at different points on the economic cycle. Industrial states, such as Michigan and Indiana, experience economic downturns first. Texas historically has had a counter-cyclical economy. When rising oil prices threaten to push industrial states into recession, Texas tends to do well. The same is true of Wyoming and Alaska.

Yet as important as demographics, geography, history, and political culture are, these variables do not always explain the actual financial choices that state and local governments make. Take Mississippi, for example. One of the most religious and politically conservative states in the country, Mississippi is the buckle of the Bible Belt. In 1990, however, Mississippi passed riverboat gambling legislation. This legislation allowed casino operators to build full-sized casinos on barges moored permanently to the shoreline. The

> Texas historically has had a counter-cyclical economy. When rising oil prices threaten to push industrial states into recession, Texas tends to do well.

goal was to turn the northwestern town of Tunica, which had gained a measure of renown after the television show *60 Minutes* profiled it as the poorest city in America, into Las Vegas East.

Nevada and Mississippi have completely different political cultures. Political scientist Daniel Elazar describes Mississippi as a traditionalistic state and Nevada as an individualistic state. In short, Nevada has the kind of political culture that we might expect to produce, well, Las Vegas. Mississippi does not. Today, however, the hamlet of Tunica has more casino square-footage than the East Coast gambling hotspot Atlantic City, in the individualistic state of New Jersey. Clearly, political culture isn't everything.

Debt

The final source of money for state and local governments comes from debt, generally issued in the form of **bonds.** These are financial instruments with which state and local governments promise to pay back borrowed money at a fixed rate of interest on a specified date. The interest rates paid by the governments depend largely on the government's bond ratings. The ratings are issued by three private companies—Moody's, Standard and Poor's, and Fitch—and are based on the governments' fiscal health; many states' bond ratings have fallen during the current recession. A rating of AAA is the best, whereas anything lower than BBB is considered "junk bond status" and would send a government's interest rates skyrocketing. No state has ever fallen below BBB.[45]

State and local governments, as well as quasi-governmental entities like utility and water authorities, use bonds to finance **capital investments,** typically infrastructure upgrades such as new roads, new schools, and new airports. There are two types of bonds: **general obligation bonds,** which are secured by the taxing power of the jurisdiction that issues them, and **revenue bonds,** which are secured by the revenue from a given project, such as a new toll road. For state governments, capital investments are projects like highways, power plant construction and pollution control, and even land conservation. Because general obligation bonds must be approved by voters, state and local governments turn to revenue bonds more often.

Local governments use bonds to finance programs like school construction, sewage and water lines, airports, and affordable housing. Investors like them too. The earnings from most state bonds are exempt from state income taxes.

In 2006, state and local governments issued $339 billion in bonds.[46] **Municipal bonds,** called munis, are generally safe and attractive investments, particularly for the rich. Municipal bondholders usually are exempted from paying federal or state taxes on income they receive from bonds. Sometimes, however, municipal finances go disastrously awry. In 2009, Jefferson County, Alabama, the largest county in the state, announced it would file for bankruptcy after defaulting on $3 billion in bonds to finance its sewer system. (See box on page 119 for more.)

Local Focus: Bonds and Broken Budgets

The story of how Jefferson County, Alabama, waded into budget and bond muck stretches back to 1993, when the Cahaba River Society, a group dedicated to preserving the river that flows through Birmingham, complained that the county's sewer system was discharging raw sewage into waterways. Federal officials issued a consent decree in which Jefferson County promised to upgrade the system.

The county paid for the upgrade by issuing $3 billion in bonds. As sewer rates rose to meet those costs and Jefferson County struggled under its debt, county officials looked for a way to lessen the loan payments. In 2002 and 2003, they refinanced their bonds with variable-rate and auction-rate securities. (Auction-rate securities are bonds for which the interest rate is reset at auctions every few weeks.)

Auction-rate securities were supposed to be safe, but the auction-rate market collapsed in February 2008. Then the bond insurance companies that were backing the county's debt suffered their own fiscal problems and their credit was downgraded. The result: Jefferson County's interest rates skyrocketed, much like a homeowner's whose subprime mortgage had just reset. The county's revenue from sewer fees could not cover the borrowing costs. On April Fool's Day 2008, Jefferson County failed to make its payment on its debt. Instead, it reached an agreement with its creditors to pay the interest and get an extension on the principal—agreements that left the county of 660,000 teetering on the edge of bankruptcy.

County commissioners and other Alabama political players developed a variety of ideas to solve the sewer mess—to no avail. Without a solution in sight, the county made massive cutbacks: reducing department budgets by one-third, cancelling road maintenance contracts, closing courthouses, and laying off hundreds of county workers. "We're having to downsize this government to the point that it may not be able to operate," County Commissioner Bettye Fine Collins said in 2009.

Variations on the Jefferson County story could play out elsewhere because the recession significantly weakened local governments' financial footing. According to Richard Lehmann, publisher of a newsletter that tracks bond defaults, there were only twenty-nine municipal defaults in 2007, totaling $300 million. In 2008, those numbers skyrocketed to record highs of 150 defaults, totaling $7.8 billion. But muni bonds have historically been a better bet than corporate bonds, and that held true even in 2008, when corporate bond defaults hit $167 billion. Market experts think bond-rating downgrades, common in recessions, are still far more likely than all-out defaults.

But Harrisburg, Pennsylvania's capital city, may combine both scenarios. The city sat on the brink of bankruptcy in early 2010, nearly unable to repay the bondholders who had financed a $300 million incinerator. Moody's, a bond-rating agency, wasn't willing to wait and see; it downgraded the city's rating to junk bond status in February 2010.

Sources: Karen Pierog, "Default, Bankruptcy Fears Overhang U.S. Muni Market," Reuters, February 16, 2010; adapted from Josh Goodman, "Drained," *Governing* magazine, August 2009.

The Budget Process

Once state and local governments have raised money from taxes, user fees, and bonds and have received money from intergovernmental transfers, they must decide how to spend it. These decisions are made during the **budget process.**

Most state and local governments budget for one **fiscal year.** Unfortunately for fans of simplicity in government, the fiscal year is not the same

BUDGET PROCESS

The procedure by which state and local governments assess revenues and set budgets.

as the calendar year. The federal government's fiscal year runs from October 1 to September 30. Most state and local governments generally begin their fiscal year on July 1. Alabama, Michigan, New York, and Texas are the exceptions. As a result, when legislatures debate the budget, they are almost always debating the budget for the coming fiscal year.[47] Twenty-one states pass two-year budgets.[48]

Budget time lines do vary from state to state, but the budget process itself is quite similar. It begins with instructions from the governor's budget office or the mayor's budget office. The executive branch agencies are told to draw up funding requests for the upcoming year. During the fall, the budget office reviews the spending requests and helps the chief executive develop a unified budget for the executive branch.

BALANCED BUDGET

A budget in which current expenditures are equal to or less than income.

Most chief executives unveil their budgets in state-of-the-state addresses in January. In forty-five states, governors and mayors are required by law to submit a **balanced budget** to the legislature or city council. The legislative body reviews the budget, authorizes spending on certain programs, appropriates the necessary money, and presents its budget to the chief executive to sign into law.

Despite some groups' moral objections to gambling, states have turned to casinos like this one floating on the Mississippi River in Dubuque, Iowa, to help raise much-needed revenues.

As a guard against fiscal excess and abuse, forty-nine states have statutory or constitutional requirements that state legislatures must enact a balanced budget. Only Vermont is free to run up debt as it pleases.[49] All but five states also have laws that require lawmakers to save a certain portion of state revenues in so-called rainy day, or budget stabilization, funds. States can draw on these funds during times of recession, when revenues fall. Although rainy day funds rarely offset the revenue drops that occur during a recession, they do provide some cushion for the lawmakers who have to balance state budgets. In 2009 and 2010, for example, rainy day funds helped close more than $35 billion of states' budget gaps—funds that would have otherwise had to come from more severe program cuts or greater tax increases.[50] (See box on page 130.) Many local governments face similar requirements due to state requirements or their own municipal codes.

There are, of course, exceptions. In states such as Arkansas, Mississippi, and South Carolina, legislatures take the lead role in formulating the initial budget plan. Legislative bodies also take the lead in county and city governments with weak chief executives, such as Los Angeles, California. In many western states, citizens and special interests have become players in the budgeting process via ballot initiatives.

Expenditures, or Where the Money Goes

In fiscal year 2006, state and local governments spent approximately $8,393 for every man, woman, and child in the country.[51] (See Table 4-3.) So, where did the money go?

Wages. Salaries are the single largest source of **expenditures** for state and local governments—roughly $611 billion in 2006. State and local governments are the biggest employers in the United States. In 2006, state governments employed 5.3 million people nationwide. Local governments employed another 14.7 million people.[52]

Education. Education has long been the single largest functional spending category for state and local governments. In 2006, state and local governments spent $71 billion on education. Approximately 73 percent of that went to elementary and secondary schools; the remaining 27 percent went to community colleges and state universities.[53]

Primary and secondary education traditionally has been the preserve of local governments. In most states, elected local school boards hire superintendents and principals, select curriculums that align with state standards, and develop school budgets. Local governments typically spend about 38 percent of their funds on schools.[54]

State governments now provide half of all funding for K–12 education. State dollars increasingly are used to train teachers, reduce the number of students in classrooms, promote the use of computers and high-speed

EXPENDITURES
Money spent by government.

North Dakota's spending grew 12.6 percent between 2008 and 2009. Nevada's spending dropped 10.2 percent during the same period.

TABLE 4-3

State and Local Revenues, Expenditures, and Debt, 2006 (in millions of dollars)

State	Total Revenues	Total Expenditures	Total Debt Outstanding at End of Fiscal Year
Alabama	36,029	35,095	22,310
Alaska	13,247	10,788	9,449
Arizona	45,324	42,763	34,655
Arkansas	20,798	18,503	11,815
California	406,020	366,120	299,534
Colorado	41,128	37,064	39,932
Connecticut	33,554	31,502	32,228
Delaware	8,467	8,292	6,087
Florida	151,624	140,638	119,674
Georgia	65,307	63,053	42,086
Hawaii	11,999	11,018	9,504
Idaho	10,850	9,330	4,442
Illinois	108,037	100,995	110,788
Indiana	51,062	44,033	34,347
Iowa	24,840	23,102	13,806
Kansas	21,602	20,295	19,907
Kentucky	31,152	29,514	32,480
Louisiana	39,729	35,314	24,733
Maine	11,700	10,713	7,473
Maryland	48,367	44,280	30,673
Massachusetts	66,603	61,910	86,940
Michigan	87,652	76,757	70,825
Minnesota	48,830	44,820	36,618
Mississippi	24,015	22,109	11,161
Missouri	44,202	39,551	33,957

TABLE 4-3, continued

State	Total Revenues	Total Expenditures	Total Debt Outstanding at End of Fiscal Year
Montana	8,019	6,948	5,787
Nebraska	17,006	15,320	9,336
Nevada	20,363	18,818	20,581
New Hampshire	9,376	9,028	9,952
New Jersey	85,517	82,928	79,281
New Mexico	18,452	16,404	10,707
New York	266,263	240,996	241,407
North Carolina	67,479	64,330	43,938
North Dakota	5,772	4,926	3,486
Ohio	107,494	97,514	63,658
Oklahoma	26,811	23,967	15,244
Oregon	36,149	30,549	26,919
Pennsylvania	109,300	104,228	106,042
Rhode Island	10,272	9,667	8,945
South Carolina	34,676	34,234	32,159
South Dakota	6,062	5,210	4,560
Tennessee	47,256	44,399	27,931
Texas	179,331	160,231	165,572
Utah	20,781	18,527	15,327
Vermont	5,732	5,390	3,854
Virginia	61,647	55,853	46,388
Washington	63,055	56,588	56,655
West Virginia	14,044	12,387	8,937
Wisconsin	47,967	45,316	38,834
Wyoming	7,885	5,972	1,947

Source: *State and Local Sourcebook,* online supplement to *Governing* magazine, 2010, available at http://sourcebook.governing.com.

Internet access, and fund "accountability" and testing regimes. In 2008, 21.6 percent of state expenditures went to K–12 education.[55]

State governments also devote a portion of their expenditures to higher education—10.2 percent of total expenditures in 2008.[56] Spending on higher education is the third largest item on state budgets. Tuition covers about 36 percent of the costs of higher education.[57]

Unlike highways, which receive some of their funding from dedicated gasoline taxes, legislatures typically appropriate funding for higher education from general revenue funds. This is known as **discretionary spending**. When economic times are good, institutions of higher learning and the voters and future voters who enroll in them often benefit from considerable largesse. When the economy slides into recession, however, the fact that institutions of higher education do not have a dedicated source of funding makes them particularly vulnerable to cutbacks. At least thirty-three states cut higher education spending to help balance their budgets in 2009.[58]

Healthcare. Since the late 1990s, healthcare spending has surged dramatically. For state governments, spending on healthcare is now greater than for any other single item.

Medicaid is the largest and most expensive state-run health program. When it was established in 1965, it was viewed as a limited safety net for the very poor and disabled. However, the number of low-income, uninsured Americans has grown, and medical care has become more expensive. The program has grown at an enormous rate as a result. In 1970, state governments spent $2 billion on the program, and the federal government kicked in another $3 billion. By 2008, the states and the federal government spent $311 billion on the program, up from $298 billion just a year earlier.[59] State Medicaid programs now provide health insurance to more than 60 million people and account for 20.7 percent of total state spending.[60] And healthcare costs are growing faster than any other category of government expenditures.

The Medicaid program is also an excellent example of **fiscal federalism**. The federal government picks up most of the program's costs, while states take responsibility for administering the program itself.

Medicaid is also an **entitlement** program. Most programs receive a specific appropriation during the budget process and can spend no more. Entitlements like Medicaid are different. States and the federal government are obligated by law to provide health insurance to low-income individuals who qualify for the program, regardless of the cost. If states have an unexpected surge of applicants and they have not set aside enough money for Medicaid, tough.

States do have some leeway in determining how generous they want their state Medicaid programs to be. They enjoy similar discretion with another joint state-federal program, the State Children's Health Insurance Program (CHIP). In most states, this program provides health insurance for children living in families whose primary wage earner makes up to

---

DISCRETIONARY SPENDING

Spending controlled in annual appropriations acts.

FISCAL FEDERALISM

The system by which federal grants are used to fund programs and services provided by state and local governments.

ENTITLEMENT

A service that government must provide, regardless of the cost.

---

twice the federal poverty level. In 2009, this amount was $44,100 for a family of four. (See Table 4-4.)

During the boom of the late 1990s and the recovery of the mid 2000s, some states made a major effort to extend health insurance via Medicaid and CHIP. Many healthcare advocates saw Medicaid and CHIP expansions as the most promising approach to extending health insurance to some of the roughly 45 million Americans who do without it. Nineteen states continued their efforts even as they faced significant budget shortfalls, but at least fifteen others began cutting coverage in 2009. Two states froze CHIP enrollment, one reduced eligibility for low-income parents, and others increased CHIP waiting periods and premiums.[61]

Medicaid increasingly serves another function as well. It is the only governmental program that pays for long-term care, such as nursing homes and assisted living facilities. Private nursing homes and assisted living facilities can cost as much as $3,500 a month. Few seniors or disabled individuals can afford these costs for very long. As the number of Americans ages eighty-five and older increases from about 5.7 million in 2010 to a projected 8.7 million in 2030,[62] a growing number of elderly citizens will find themselves in need of such services.

TABLE 4-4

Department of Health and Human Services Poverty Guidelines, Maximum Yearly Income, 2009

Size of Family Unit	48 Contiguous States and Washington, D.C.	Alaska	Hawaii
1	$10,830	$13,530	$12,460
2	$14,570	$1 8,210	$16,760
3	$18,310	$22,890	$21,060
4	$22,050	$27,570	$25,360
5	$25,790	$32,250	$29,660
6	$29,530	$36,930	$33,960
7	$33,270	$41,610	$38,260
8	$37,010	$46,290	$42,560
For each additional person, add	$3,740	$4,680	$4,300

Source: *Federal Register* 74, no. 14 (January 23, 2009): 4199–4201.

Local governments spend much less on healthcare than state governments do, or only about 7.5 percent of total expenditures. This is not to say that local governments do not make an important contribution. In 2006, state and local governments spent $110 billion supporting local public hospitals, or $30 billion more than they spent on police protection.[63] All these funds came directly from the local governments. Many of these hospitals serve as healthcare providers of last resort to people without health insurance. In the event of a terrorist attack involving biological weapons, many of these hospitals would serve as society's defense of first resort.

Welfare. The topic of welfare has been one of the most contentious issues in U.S. politics for a long time. Welfare is an entitlement program. While states have some leeway to determine eligibility, they cannot deny or restrict benefits to qualified individuals. From 1965 to 1996, women with young children were eligible to receive monetary assistance through a welfare program known as Aid to Families with Dependent Children (AFDC).

In 1996, Republicans in Congress and President Bill Clinton joined forces to pass the Personal Responsibility and Work Reconciliation Act, which abolished AFDC and replaced it with the Temporary Assistance for Needy Families (TANF) program. TANF disbursed federal money to states in block grants and gave them considerable freedom in determining how they wanted to spend those funds. Many liberals predicted that such welfare "reform" would result in disaster. Instead, the number of people on welfare rolls declined dramatically. Between 1994 and 1999, the welfare caseload declined by nearly 50 percent, from approximately 4 million people to 2 million people.[64]

Welfare continues to be a politically contentious issue. Yet, from a financial viewpoint, it is actually a pretty minor program. In 2008, state governments spent a total of $25 billion on TANF, that is, about 1.7 percent of total state expenditures.[65]

Fire, Police, and Prisons. In 2006, state and local governments spent $113 billion on fire and police protection. They spent an additional $62 billion on prisons and correctional facilities.[66] State and local government spending on police protection and prisons varies widely. New York City, a city of 8 million people, employs a police force of 37,000. That works out to one police officer for every 216 people. In contrast, Los Angeles, a city of 3.8 million, employs only 10,000 police officers. That equals only one police officer for every 380 people.

States also have very different levels of enthusiasm for funding prisons. In fiscal year 2008, Florida devoted 4.8 percent its state spending to prisons. That is a level of spending more than 1 percentage point higher than the national average and reflects Florida's incarceration rate, which is

FIGURE 4-1 How It Works: A Year in the Life of a State Budget: Idaho's Budgetary Process

Most folks first hear about state budget priorities through their governor's state of the state address, the forum in which most state budgetary news is presented. In reality, budget planning begins well in advance of this address and involves all three branches of government to some degree. In Idaho, each year in May (after the last of the potatoes have been planted), that state's Division of Financial Management (DFM) starts sowing its own seeds: overseeing the development of that state's budget for the coming fiscal year. This is the beginning of what is really an eighteen-month process: the planning for fiscal year 2012, for instance, will actually get underway about mid-year in 2010.

This chart shows how the process works in Idaho:

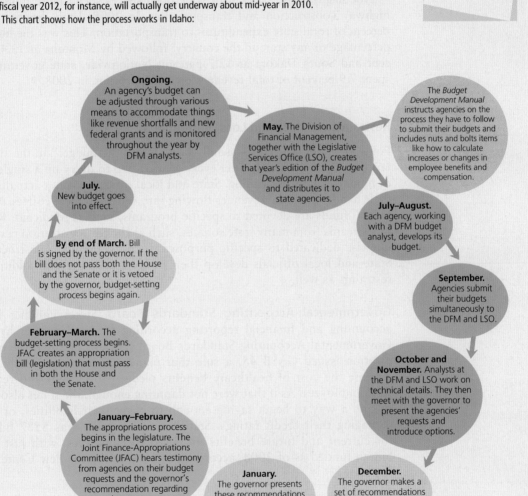

Ongoing. An agency's budget can be adjusted through various means to accommodate things like revenue shortfalls and new federal grants and is monitored throughout the year by DFM analysts.

May. The Division of Financial Management, together with the Legislative Services Office (LSO), creates that year's edition of the *Budget Development Manual* and distributes it to state agencies.

The *Budget Development Manual* instructs agencies on the process they have to follow to submit their budgets and includes nuts and bolts items like how to calculate increases or changes in employee benefits and compensation.

July–August. Each agency, working with a DFM budget analyst, develops its budget.

September. Agencies submit their budgets simultaneously to the DFM and LSO.

October and November. Analysts at the DFM and LSO work on technical details. They then meet with the governor to present the agencies' requests and introduce options.

December. The governor makes a set of recommendations that becomes the executive budget.

January. The governor presents these recommendations to the legislature at the start of the legislative session.

January–February. The appropriations process begins in the legislature. The Joint Finance-Appropriations Committee (JFAC) hears testimony from agencies on their budget requests and the governor's recommendation regarding those requests.

February–March. The budget-setting process begins. JFAC creates an appropriation bill (legislation) that must pass in both the House and the Senate.

By end of March. Bill is signed by the governor. If the bill does not pass both the House and the Senate or it is vetoed by the governor, budget-setting process begins again.

July. New budget goes into effect.

Source: State of Idaho's Division of Financial Management, "Budget Process." http://dfm.idaho.gov/citizensguide/budgetprocess.html.

among the ten highest in the country. In contrast, West Virginia's state government spent only 1.1 percent of its state budget on corrections.[67]

Highways. In 2006, state and local governments spent $135 billion on highways and roads.[68] Most of this money came from dedicated revenue sources, such as the gasoline tax. In addition, the federal government kicked in another $32 billion from the federal highway trust fund and other sources.[69]

Not surprisingly, states with wide open spaces spend more money on highway construction and transportation. In 2008, Utah devoted 22.1 percent of total state expenditures to transportation. This was the highest percentage of any state in the country, followed by Montana at 13.4 percent and South Dakota at 12.7 percent. Nationwide, state governments spent 7.9 percent of total revenues on transportation in 2008.[70]

Restraints on State and Local Budgeteers

Politicians and journalists usually talk about "the budget" in the singular, as if elected officials meet every year or two to divvy up a single pot of money. That's misleading. State and local officials cannot actually lay their hands on all the revenues flowing into state and local coffers. Most federal funds are devoted to specific programs, such as Medicaid. Revenue streams from many state sources, such as the car registration tax, are likewise dedicated to specific purposes, such as highway construction. State and local officials develop their budgets under several additional restraints as well.

Governmental Accounting Standards Board. States conduct their accounting and financial reporting according to standards set by the Governmental Accounting Standards Board (GASB). In 2004, the organization issued GASB 45, a rule that mandated that states tally and disclose the cost of healthcare benefits pledged to current and retired state employees. As if that were not daunting enough, the states also had to find a way to begin saving enough to cover their liabilities, or risk damaging their credit ratings. States' actual liability was $587 billion for current and future benefits promised to employees, with just $32 billion funded as of 2008, according to a report by the Pew Center on the States.[71]

Unfunded Mandates. For years, state officials complained bitterly about the federal government's habit of mandating that states achieve a goal, such as an environmental cleanup, but then failing to provide any money to pay for it. State officials viewed such unfunded mandates as an affront to the notion of federalism itself. In 1995, Congress did something surprising. It passed legislation that curtailed dramatically the practice of imposing unfunded mandates on state governments. This measure alleviated some of the pressures on states, but it did not end the problem. Ironically, in the late 1990s, state governments increasingly imposed unfunded mandates on county and city governments. Evidently, many state governments were no more able to resist the temptation to set goals and make someone else pay for them than the federal government had long been.

As detailed in chapter 2, under federalism the state governments and the federal government are co-equals, at least in theory. If the federal government encroaches too much on state prerogatives, the U.S. Supreme Court can step in and strike federal actions down. But states are not federations; indeed, within their own borders they are more accurately described as unitary systems. Local governments are not equal partners with state governments. In most cases, state governments are free to intervene in local arrangements as they please. Beginning in the late nineteenth century, many states did extend the sovereign powers of government to local governments by passing legislation that provided for home rule. Communities could enact charters and ordinances, change their names, and annex their neighbors without the permission of the legislature. They also controlled their own budgets and property taxes.

At the time, California was one of the strongest home-rule states. In recent years, however, that has changed. California cities now control less than half of their discretionary spending. The state tells them what they must do with the rest. The situation is even worse for California's counties. They have the final say over less than one-third of the money they spend.[72]

Ballot Initiatives and the Budget Process. California's experience illustrates one of the most significant trends in state finances—the growing use of ballot initiatives to shape and restrain state tax systems. According to Bill Piper of the Initiative and Referendum Institute, voters put 130 tax initiatives on ballots nationwide between 1978 and 1999. Roughly two-thirds of them were antitax initiatives that cut, limited, or eliminated taxes in some way. Of these, forty-one passed. In fact, a whopping 67 percent of all antitax initiatives that came up for a vote between 1996 and 1999 passed.[73]

When citizens put their hands directly on the tax levers, it often gets much harder for state and local governments to pay the bills. California is just one name on a list of states that are choking on tax and spending policies put in place by voters. Colorado, Oregon, and Washington are only a few of the other states that have dealt with financial problems caused by ballot initiatives, problems that grew more severe during budget crises.

Policy in Practice: Saving for a Rainy Day

Forty-eight states have some sort of budget stabilization fund that is designed as a savings account of last resort. Many raided these so-called rainy day funds in 2009 and 2010 when they weren't just raining, but *pouring*, red ink. Thanks to the tens of billions they'd socked away years earlier, they were able to draw on at least $35 billion to help close budget gaps and prevent more drastic program cuts and tax and fee increases. Twenty-five states used the monies to help balance their 2009 budgets; another sixteen did the same in 2010. Several states, including Maine and Alabama, drained the funds completely. Ohio left 89 cents in its kitty.

States had built their rainy day funds to an average of 11.5 percent of expenditures before draining them down to 4.8 percent in 2010—or just 2.7 percent, if you don't include Texas and Alaska. Both states continued to sit on their well-stocked funds into 2010. Comparatively, Texas and Alaska fared better, budget-wise, than many of their peers across the country in 2009 and 2010, so it made sense when they didn't tap their reserves. But in other states, policymakers were questioned about why they had chosen to leave their rainy day funds intact. Indiana governor Mitch Daniels refused to dip into his state's $1 billion fund, and the governors of Mississippi, Tennessee, and Wyoming battled with legislators over whether to use the accounts to avert greater budget cuts. Those advocating not to spend down the accounts contended that with forecasts calling for several more years of budget stress, they needed to hold on to them for an even rainier day. "While we all want to be optimistic, and I am optimistic about the long-term future of this state, I am not prepared to bet our financial future and to dip into those reserves," Wyoming governor Dave Freudenthal, a Democrat, told the Republican-controlled legislature. "I think we need to hold onto them."

Soon enough, the conversation will turn to filling the funds back up. The Center on Budget and Policy Priorities and the Government Finance Officers Association have recommended that states dedicate as much as 15 percent of general fund revenues to the accounts, but attaining that goal seems unlikely. "Politically, 5 percent is probably about as high as you can go before people complain that you're sitting on all this cash," says Scott Pattison, executive director of the National Association of State Budget Officers.

Officials in at least one state think they need more of a rainy day cushion than they had this time around. Kansas is one of just two states without a budget stabilization fund. Gov. Mark Parkinson wants to amend the state constitution to allow for an emergency fund, which would require approval from voters. Parkinson sees that as a better strategy than the state's cutting $1 billion from the budget again, as it did in 2010. "It is time that we take steps to make sure that the state never again finds itself facing this kind of fiscal challenge," Parkinson said. "There are many reasons for the budget problems that we have. One is that we came into last year without an emergency fund. This is unacceptable."

Sources: Pamela M. Prah, "Is It 'Raining' Hard Enough?" Stateline.org, February 22, 2010; Rob Silverblatt, "States Draw Down Rainy Day Funds," Stateline.org, August 27, 2009; *The Fiscal Survey of States* (Washington, D.C.: National Governors Association and National Association of State Budget Officers, fall 2009).

These maneuvers have influenced individual tax changes. They also have been known to paralyze state legislatures and local governments. Fifteen states have passed initiatives or referendums that require more than 50 percent of the vote, or supermajorities, on tax decisions made by the state legislatures. In Montana, for example, a supermajority is three-quarters of the legislature. State senator Roy Brown sees changing tax policy as pretty much impossible. "We can't even get a three-fourths majority vote to go to the bathroom," he told the *Billings Gazette* in November 2002.[74]

Conclusion

State and local governments rely on six major types of taxes to fund the operations of government: property taxes; income taxes; sales taxes; sin, or excise, taxes; user fees; and gift taxes. Each of these taxes has distinct pros and cons. Local governments like property taxes because they set the rates and thus control exactly how much revenue is raised. However, when property taxes rise, seniors and people on fixed incomes often suffer. Income taxes tend to be more progressive; sales taxes are more regressive. The exact configuration of taxes in any given state reflects that state's history and political culture. Tax revenues, in turn, support the budget process by which state and local governments set their spending priorities. Increasingly, governments are relying on user fees—collected in relatively small, but frequent, amounts—to supply key revenues.

State and local government finances can be difficult to unravel. However, this is an area that citizens are well advised to watch. Not only do the budget decisions of state and local governments determine the services that individuals enjoy and how much they pay in taxes, but this also is often the arena in which the priorities of public life are sorted out. Is it fair or unfair to ask wealthy citizens to pay a higher percentage of their income in taxes? States such as Texas and Florida, which have no income taxes, have in a sense decided that it is unfair. States like California, which has an income tax, have reached a different conclusion. Should everyone pay more in taxes to extend healthcare to low-income citizens? Massachusetts's tax policies suggest that its answer is yes. Many states in the Deep South have reached different conclusions. In short, the consequences of budget decisions are very real.

There is another reason to pay close attention to state and local finances. Recovery from the most severe recession since World War II may be sluggish, and states' revenue systems are not set up to make the most of today's evolving economy. To get back in the black, states almost certainly will need to change. States like Tennessee that rely heavily on sales tax revenues face particularly serious long-term challenges. As Internet sales and dollars spent on untaxed services continue to grow, sales tax revenues in particular will most likely continue to falter. This will create a need for new revenue-raising measures. Yet states with ballot initiatives may well find new approaches blocked by antitax sentiments at the voting booth.

States have turned to the federal government for help. Congress and the White House responded with the largest stimulus package in history, but even its billions were not enough to solve states' short- or long-term budget problems. As a result, in the coming years states will have to focus as never before on the programs and priorities that drive their taxing and spending decisions. Later in this book, we examine some of the most important state and local government programs in more detail. In many states, they almost certainly will need to change soon.

Key Concepts

American Recovery and Reinvestment Act (ARRA) (p. 103)

balanced budget (p. 120)

bonds (p. 118)

budget deficit, or shortfall (p. 102)

budget process (p. 119)

capital investments (p. 118)

discretionary spending (p. 124)

dividend (p. 117)

entitlement (p. 124)

estate taxes (p. 104)

excise, or sin, taxes (p. 104)

expenditures (p. 121)

fiscal federalism (p. 124)

fiscal year (p. 120)

focused consumption taxes (p. 104)

general obligation bonds (p. 118)

gift taxes (p. 104)

income taxes (p. 109)

insurance trust funds (p. 114)

Suggested Readings

State Expenditure Report. Washington, D.C.: National Association of State Budget Officers. Report printed annually since 1987; details state expenditure data.

The Trillion Dollar Gap. Washington, D.C.: Pew Center on the States. A fifty-state study of state pension and other post-retirement liabilities.

Suggested Web Sites

http://sourcebook.governing.com. Web site of *Governing* magazine's *State and Local Sourcebook*. Annually updated data provide easy access to a wide range of information on state and local government finances.

www.cbpp.org. Web site of the Center on Budget and Policy Priorities. Founded in 1981, the center studies fiscal policy and public programs at the federal and state levels that affect low-income and moderate-income families and individuals. An excellent source of information on state budget issues.

www.census.gov/compendia/statab. The U.S. Census Bureau provides an online version of the *Statistical Abstract of the United States*. Section 8, "State and Local Government Finances and Employment," provides a wealth of information on state and local government revenue and spending.

www.gao.gov. Home page of the Government Accountability Office, which is tracking the use of stimulus funds in sixteen of the largest states.

www.nasbo.org. Web site of the National Association of State Budget Officers.

www.ncsl.org. Web site of the National Conference of State Legislatures. NCSL's fiscal program produces periodic state budget and tax updates, and tracks state actions to close budget gaps.

www.propublica.org/ion/stimulus. "Eye on the Stimulus" page of ProPublica, a nonprofit investigative journalism organization.

www.recovery.gov. The federal government's Web page dedicated to tracking ARRA.

www.recovery.org. Site developed by government contractor Onvia to track ARRA spending at the federal, state, and local levels.

www.rockinst.org. Home page of the Rockefeller Institute of Government, which produces some of the best data and research on state revenues nationwide.

CHAPTER 5

Political Attitudes and Participation

Venting and Voting

Nancy Lucke of Houston attends a Tea Party rally on tax day, April 15, 2009. Thousands around the country participated in antitax protests that day, kicking off a movement that became a major force in American politics early in the Obama presidency.

5

What causes some states or localities to change party preferences?

How do state regulations affect voting?

How do politicians tune into what citizens are thinking?

Was the 2008 election a fluke?

Barack Obama won the presidency by taking a larger share of the popular vote than any Democrat since Lyndon Johnson in 1964. He won states that had favored Republicans for decades by building a coalition that included unusually large shares of the votes cast by African Americans, Hispanics, and those under thirty.

But Democrats running for governor in 2009 in New Jersey and Virginia were not able to hold that coalition together—or, at least, inspire Democratic-leaning voters to turn out in the same numbers they had a year earlier. As Republicans looked to make gains in Congress and the states in 2010, some political analysts began to wonder whether Obama's victory represented a realignment in American politics, or just a personal victory for him and a renunciation of the Bush presidency, but not of the Republican Party (also known as the Grand Old Party, or GOP).

In the run-up to the 2008 election, demographic trends so favored Democrats that Larry J. Sabato, director of the University of Virginia's Center for Politics, worried that America was on the cusp of returning to a "one-and-a-half party system."[1] From the 1930s until 1980, Democrats dominated and were generally favored to control Congress and win the White House, barring a bad economy or disastrous war. Ronald Reagan's big win in 1980 and the ensuing Republican resurgence brought about the first real two-party competition the country had known for decades, Sabato said. But it was possible Democrats would once again hold the upper hand for the foreseeable future.

In 2010, Sabato said that there is still a "growing, underlying Democratic edge in the electorate" and that the nation is still "headed for the party-and-a-half system."[2] And William H. Frey, a demographer at the Brookings Institution, suggested that Obama's candidacy in 2008 may have represented a possible future for American politics. It was both "post-ethnic" in its appeal to upper-income whites as well as racial minorities and "post-boomer" in its appeal to millions of "millennial" voters (those born since 1982). But Frey cautioned that Obama's candidacy may also represent the shape of a political future that hasn't yet fully arrived. The trends that benefited him in 2008—the size of the youth vote and the increasing size of the upscale Democratic electorate—are continuing but may not yet be sufficiently in place to overcome the type of traditional, white, working-class voters who had long dominated American politics and were often skeptical of Obama. "Maybe 20 years down the road there will be more of the Obama group overall, but for now everything is split," Frey said. "It's not 2030 yet."[3]

After the release of the 2000 census figures, some Republican strategists recognized that their party faced a serious, long-term demographic challenge. Rich Bond, a former Republican National Committee chairman, told the *Washington Post,* "We've taken white guys about as far as that group can go. We are in need of diversity, women, Latino, African-American, Asian."[4]

During the 1950s, whites made up more than 90 percent of the electorate (95 percent in 1952).[5] During the decades since, African Americans have secured their place in the voting booth through the passage of civil rights laws, and the Latino share of the population has skyrocketed. In 2008, whites made up 76.3 percent of the electorate, their lowest share ever. African Americans made up 12.1 percent of the electorate while Hispanics constituted 7.4 percent.[6] Voting participation had increased among ethnic minorities from 2004, while white participation had declined.

But Republican candidates in 2009 erased many of the gains Democrats had made among suburban voters, and other groups appeared to be disaffected with Obama's party heading into the 2010 elections. Neither young voters nor African Americans were expected to turn out in the same kind of numbers that had helped propel Obama's victory. And Latinos, who helped Obama carry several states, openly talked about staying home in large numbers due to dissatisfaction with progress on federal immigration legislation.

All this demonstrates two things. First, demographics are not destiny. Although many groups show a propensity for voting for one party or the other—African Americans for Democrats, regular church-goers for the GOP—no group votes entirely as a bloc. Second, even when such groups give overwhelming support to one party's candidates, they do not do so forever.

During the presidency of George W. Bush, pundits routinely characterized states as either "Republican red" or Democratic blue" (based on the colors that broadcast and cable networks used to show how states voted on election nights). But that was never entirely accurate. States may have tended to vote one way for president but the opposite for governor or other important offices.

But, even if it was always something of a myth that states are either red or blue and thus entirely predictable in their partisan voting habits, it does appear to be the case that plenty of counties and other smaller clusters of people increasingly vote for one party over the other. That's why there are so few competitive U.S. House or state legislative seats. Now technology and demographic breakdowns borrowed from commercial marketers, such as guessing voter preferences according to the types of magazines a person subscribes to, are used to micro-target individuals. The goal is to crack open each subdivision and make a good guess about which residents are liberal and which ones are conservative—even when the bulk of their neighbors vote in the opposite way.

The reason for this, of course, is that, if it is not safe to predict how people will vote based on where they live, it is probably a safer bet to predict their preferences based on the issues they care about and the interest groups they belong to. Interest groups, as discussed at greater length in chapter 6, are organizations that attempt to influence policymakers. Although most people will rarely, if ever, call or write to members of Congress or state officials, many of them will belong to some group that makes a case for a particular position on an issue.

Interest groups can bring resources to a campaign in return for attention to their issues by candidates. But all voters do not belong to an interest group—or think of themselves as being part of one—and politicians know that their careers depend on more than financial contributions from these organized interests. Come election time, they need the support of the vast majority of people who do not belong to such groups and who do not pay close attention to politics on a regular basis.

Given all this, how do politicians figure out what the voters back home are thinking, when it seems that the only people they hear from at the capitol or city hall are part of some organized group? How can they pay attention to the needs and desires of the majority of constituents who do not speak out and do not subscribe to *Guns & Ammo*, much less to their local paper?

This chapter answers those questions, and also looks at how voters maintain or change the political cultures and preferences of their states and districts over time. Some of the mechanisms for change discussed include elections and the avenues for direct democracy, such as ballot initiatives and referenda. Public opinion—and how and whether politicians respond—is another factor that influences political outcomes.

Elections

Unquestionably, we have created an odd paradox as a nation. We like elections—we hold more of them than any other country on earth—yet we consistently score one of the lowest voter turnout rates of any democracy in the world.

State political cultures are reflected and sustained through elections, when a majority, or **plurality**, of voters elects officials who more or less reflect that majority's political beliefs. Elections for public office are the fundamental process of representative democracies. More bluntly, they are the main way that the will of the people connects to and influences the actions of government. Each state must determine what constitutes a valid

PLURALITY

The highest number of votes garnered by a candidate for a particular office but short of an outright majority.

vote. Election laws are set and controlled by the states. There is much variation between them as to how easy or how hard it is for citizens to vote. Some of those differences have been smoothed away in recent years by federal laws and court decisions. Differences do remain, however, and they largely reflect the types of political cultures that Elazar describes (and that are outlined in previous chapters).

These differences, in turn, affect national politics. The way that people vote in their own state—the type of access that they have to the ballot—helps determine the success or failure of presidential candidates and the makeup of Congress. For about one hundred years after the Civil War, for example, Republicans were not a true national party. They had next to no presence in the South, which still resented Republican intrusions during the Civil War and Reconstruction in support of abolition, suffrage, and equal opportunity for African Americans. That is one reason Democrats held the region for decades. In fact, the Republican Party of the nineteenth century bore a closer resemblance in some ways to the Democratic Party of today than to its twenty-first-century GOP descendant. Times and political parties change, however. These days, the South is one of the pillars of Republican strength. The region's continuing conservatism now fits well within the GOP.

Southern states and the less populous, rural states in the Mountain West tilt toward Republican interests and form a bloc that helps elect presidents through its disproportionate share of the Electoral College. Each state's Electoral College votes are equal to the size of its congressional delegation. Because each state is guaranteed at least two U.S. senators and one U.S. representative, the Electoral College gives a minimum of three votes to each state, regardless of population. This means that the voting power of smaller states in the Electoral College is disproportionately larger than their population, whereas the voting power of bigger states is disproportionately lower.

For example, in 2008 California had fifty-five electoral votes to represent a population of nearly 37 million. In that presidential election, then, each of California's Electoral College votes represented about 668,000 people. Contrast that with Wyoming, which had the minimum of three Electoral College votes but had a population of only about 532,000. Each of Wyoming's Electoral College votes, in other words, represented about 177,000 people. Political analyst Steven Hill, director of the political reform program at the New America Foundation, calls this "affirmative action for low-population states."[7] This is one reason that George W. Bush could win the presidency in 2000 despite losing the popular vote.

The Mountain West also may be shifting. The region retains its traditional libertarian response to government in that it wants to be left alone by a federal government that owns the vast majority of the land in many western states. However, some libertarian-leaning westerners have been put off by the national Republican Party's intrusion into private matters,

FIGURE 5-1 How It Works: Elections Procedures in Oregon, 2006

Think voting is complicated? Try running an election. In Oregon, as elsewhere, these are complicated affairs, requiring hundreds of pages of rules and regulations—305 pages, to be exact—designed to ensure fairness and preserve democratic processes. Oregon's 2005–2006 "Election Laws" codebook covers everything from voter registration to recall procedures. And that's just the start. There's a good chance that in the run-up to the 2006 elections, every major party candidate for state office in Oregon reluctantly cracked open the 41-page candidate's manual, which detailed the hoops and hurdles facing them and no doubt whetted their appetite for the 184-page campaign finance manual. Anyone interested in sponsoring an initiative or referendum got a 69-page primer. Voters themselves were treated to a 2-volume, nearly 200-page voter's pamphlet. This timeline reveals only a fraction of the process leading up to election day.

Anytime prior to election	**Prospective initiative or referendum petition may be filed.** Petitioners are urged to leave ample time to draft the initiative, gather signatures, face possible appeals, and receive certification. Deadlines for each part of the process depend upon the date upon which the prospective initiative was first filed. Signatures for referendum petitions must be filed for verification no later than the ninetieth day after the legislature adjourns.
September 8, 2005	**Deadline by which prospective candidates for state office must have registered** to vote as a member of the party they plan to represent.
March 7, 2006	**Candidate filing deadline.** Candidates may file to run for office either by declaration or by nomination. Most candidates for state office form a candidate committee by opening a campaign account and filing a Statement of Organization for Candidate Committee (SEL 220) and Campaign Account Information form (SEL 223) with the Elections Division.
	Candidates filing by nomination for statewide office must gather signatures from active registered voters in at least seven counties. Signatures must be from at least 5 percent of the precincts from each of these counties.
March 9	**Voter's pamphlet filing deadline for the primary election.** Candidates submit material for inclusion in the voter's pamphlet. Required documents include: three copies of the Candidate's Statement for State Voters' Pamphlet, a Statement of Endorsement, a list of phone and fax numbers for contacts, the filing fee, and two identical 5 × 7 black and white photos.
March 10	**Deadline for withdrawing a candidacy or nomination.** Second thoughts? The deadline is 5 p.m.
March 20	**Corrections on an insufficient Voter's Pamphlet filing due.**
March 31–May 12	**Campaign contribution and expense reports.** Candidates receiving more than $2,000 in contributions before the primary election must file contribution and expenditure reports. The first report is due no later than March 31, and all subsequent filings, including supplements, must be filed no later than May 12.
April 1	**Ballots mailed to long-term absent voters (overseas and military).**
April 17	**Ballots mailed to out-of-state voters.** Qualified absentee voters include those absent on business, senior citizens, disabled persons, those prevented by employment from registering, out-of-state-and out-of-precinct residents, those absent for religious reasons, students, and those temporarily out of jurisdiction.
April 19–21	**Voters' pamphlets are mailed.**
April 25	**Voter registration deadline for the primary elections.**
April 28–May 2	**Ballots mailed to voters, other than long-term and out-of-state.** Oregon voters are allowed to vote by mail. Ballots are due by 8 p.m. on election day.
May 16	**Primary election held.**

FIGURE 5-1, continued

June 5, 2006	County Elections Officials deliver abstract of votes for the primary election.
June 15	Elections Division must complete primary post-elections procedures and by which candidates must have filed post-elections campaign contributions and expenses reports.
July 7	**Signatures for ballot measures and amendments due.** Statutory measures require 75,630 valid signatures, and constitutional amendments require 100,840.
August 29	Candidate filing deadline for the general election.
August 29	Voters' pamphlet filing deadline for the general election.
September 1	Deadline for withdrawing a candidacy or nomination.
September 7	Elections division certifies the state measures to be voted on to each county elections official for placement on the official ballot by this date.
September 8	Deadline to provide corrections on an insufficient Voter's Pamphlet filing.
September 23	Ballots mailed to long-term absent voters (overseas and military).
October 2–November 3	Campaign contribution and expense reports for the general election must be filed between these dates.
October 9	Ballots mailed to out-of-state voters.
October 17	Voter registration deadline (21 days before election) for the general election.
October 20–24	Ballots mailed to voters other than long-term and out-of-state voters.
November 7	**General election held.** Oregon does its voting by mail. Other states open their doors as early as 6 a.m. and some close as late as 9 p.m.
November 27	Deadline for county elections officials to deliver abstract of votes for the general election.
December 7	Deadline by which the Elections Division must complete post-elections procedures and by which candidates must file post-election campaign contribution and expense reports.
January 5, 2007	Last date to file supplements to the post-election campaign contribution and expense reports.

such as the attempt in 2005 to keep Terri Schiavo, a brain-damaged Florida woman, on life support against her husband's wishes. This resistance to government intervention in private affairs has given Democrats an opportunity to capitalize on social issues that Republicans frequently have championed. There were no Democratic governors in eight Mountain West states in 2002; today there are five. Colorado, which was long dominated by Republicans, now has both a Democratic governor and legislature.

Similar resistance in the suburbs to conservative stances on social issues has helped Democrats in recent elections. In St. Louis County, Missouri, for instance, Democrat Jeanne Kirkton won a state House seat in 2008 that had been Republican as long as anyone could remember and had been represented for the previous thirty-two years by Republican women who were fiscally conservative but who all supported abortion rights and were liberal on other social issues. That year, Republican primary voters rejected a moderate female candidate in favor of a man who took a hard line against abortion and favored school vouchers. Kirkton won on a platform of support for gun control and stem-cell research, while Jay Nixon carried the county in winning back the governorship for the Democrats.

In Missouri, as the Democratic core vote continued to extend outward from the central city of St. Louis, Republicans were left with less room with which to work. They needed to turn out voters en masse in dozens of sparsely populated rural and exurban counties to offset not just the big cities but also their losses in the suburbs. "Running statewide for a Republican is a harder challenge," said Mike Gibbons, a GOP state senator from St. Louis County who lost in his 2008 bid for state attorney general. "You have to gain a substantial margin in the smaller counties. That means you have to travel all over the state, and you also have to compete in suburban areas to hold them close."[8]

A similar dynamic has played out in suburban parts of California, Colorado, New York, and numerous other states in recent years, as suburbs have become more dense and diverse, with more immigrants settling outside the central cities that had long been most attractive to newcomers. "The so-called inner-ring suburbs are now almost as dense and almost as politically Democratic as the central cities," says Lawrence Levy, director of the Center for Suburban Studies, at Long Island's Hofstra University.[9]

This was particularly noteworthy in Virginia, where Democrats ran up big margins in suburbs outside Washington, D.C., that helped propel them to victories in gubernatorial and U.S. Senate elections in recent years. But Republicans certainly noted the phenomenon. In 2009, Republican Robert McDonnell spent more than 75 percent of his direct mail budget targeting suburban voters, especially in Northern Virginia. His mailings were devoted to broad issues such as the economy and education, with targeted mailings sent to groups concerned with particular issues, as well as ethnic groups such as Koreans, Filipinos, Vietnamese, and African Americans. When his opponent, Creigh Deeds, sought to portray him as a right-wing "culture warrior," McDonnell's mailings targeted moderate suburban women, stressing his devotion as a father of three professional women and his record as state attorney general. McDonnell's inroads into what had become a Democratic stronghold helped propel him to a landslide victory.

A Voice for the Public

Elections may be how citizens can speak out for their beliefs, and they may give states a voice in national politics, but you wouldn't know it from the interest they generate among the general public. The franchise appears to be diminishing, with the act of voting on the decline. People do not feel well connected to government. Some hate it. Fewer than half the voting-age population cast ballots in presidential elections. In elections in which congressional or statewide offices are at the top of the ticket, the percentage drops to less than 40 percent. For municipal elections, turnout rates are generally less than 20 percent.

Voting does tend to pick up for competitive races, when voters feel like they have a genuine choice and might make a real difference. The major political parties, however, have reconciled themselves to the reality that millions of people feel their vote does not count. (Sometimes they are even accused of suppressing turnout and using negative ads and other means to sour people who might vote for the other side.)

Upset that an estimated 4 million evangelical Christians did not vote in 2000, Karl Rove, President George W. Bush's lead political adviser, designed a reelection campaign in 2004 to motivate these voters through use of such issues as limitations on stem-cell research and bans on gay marriage. Other issues were used to appeal to other blocs of voters, but Bush's reelection campaign was designed primarily to motivate his base voters rather than to reach across the political spectrum and appeal more broadly. The strategy worked, at least in the short run.

The idea that voters are most easily motivated by appealing to a few core issues also has promoted the growing use of ballot initiatives as a means of promoting turnout. For instance, Ohio's vote in favor of a constitutional ban on gay marriage in 2004 is said to have helped turn out conservatives who in turn helped Bush carry that year's most contested state. Two years later, liberals, looking for weapons of their own, ran initiatives for minimum wage increases on half a dozen state ballots. Some political scientists have found evidence that controversial ballot initiatives do increase turnout, particularly in nonpresidential election years.[10]

But the idea that most voters are motivated by a single issue, or a handful of issues, oversimplifies things in much the same way that the red state–blue state divide flattens our perception of actual electoral behavior. It is true that the majority of voters remain loyal to one party over the other throughout most of their voting lives. They can be convinced to cast votes—or even to change their votes—by any number of factors. The state of the economy, the health of a state's budget, corruption scandals, or the course of a military conflict may change minds and voting habits. "Each election forces one to revisit such topics as to what's effective in voter mobilization or who you aim at," says independent political analyst Rhodes Cook. "White evangelicals and moral values were the story after 2004, while independents and moderates seem to be the story of 2006."[11]

> The idea that voters are most easily motivated by appealing to a few core issues also has promoted the growing use of ballot initiatives as a means of promoting turnout. For instance, Ohio's vote in favor of a constitutional ban on gay marriage in 2004 is said to have helped turn out conservatives who in turn helped Bush carry that year's most contested state.

After 2008, the story seemed to be young voters. Turnout rates have been particularly abysmal for college students and other young people. In an online chat in 2003, political analyst Stuart Rothenberg wrote,

> All non-voters are irrelevant and unimportant, and I am skeptical about efforts by the right, left, or radical center to motivate large numbers of non-voters. It seems that every election we talk about bringing new people into the system, but the 2004 contest is likely to be about which party motivates its base and sways swing voters.[12]

As we look forward, the question is whether young people, who turned out in record numbers to support Obama in 2008, will continue to vote or return to old habits of indifference.

State Supervision of Elections

It seems obvious, but elections are fundamental to democracy. They are the source of authority for governmental decisions and power. On these occasions, a majority of eligible citizens presumably gives its blessing to officeholders who will determine the course of policy. Elections are the main conduit for citizens to express their pleasure or displeasure with governmental decisions. If voters are unhappy with the decisions that their elected officials have made, they can turn them out of office during the next election. For all the system's faults, politicians and parties have to win approval from voters at regularly scheduled intervals if they are to remain in power.

The U.S. Constitution gives states the authority to determine "the times, places and manner of holding elections." In nearly every state, the secretary of state has the practical duty of running elections: setting dates, qualifying candidates, and printing and counting the ballots. In a few states, the lieutenant governor or a state election board may oversee these chores. The states, in turn, rely on the counties or, in some cases, cities to run the polls themselves. The localities draw precinct boundaries and set up and supervise polling places. In many cases, they have the main responsibility for registering voters. Following the election, county officials count up the ballots and report the results to the appropriate individual, such as the secretary of state, who then tabulates and certifies the totals.

The style of ballots varies. California currently uses a random alphabet system to decide the order in which candidate names appear, rotating the starting letter of that alphabet in each state assembly district. The **office group ballot**, also known as the **Massachusetts ballot**, lists candidates' names, followed by their party designation, under the title of the office they are seeking (governor, state representative, and so on). The other major type of ballot is called the **party column ballot**, or the **Indiana ballot**, which "arranges the candidates for each office in columns according to their party designation."[13] Seventeen states make it even easier for citizens

OFFICE GROUP (MASSACHUSETTS) BALLOT

A ballot in which candidates are listed by name under the title of the office they are seeking.

PARTY COLUMN (INDIANA) BALLOT

A ballot in which the names of candidates are divided into columns arranged according to political party.

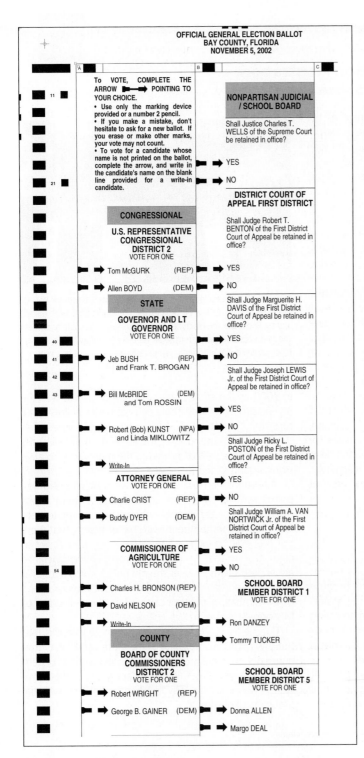

OFFICIAL GENERAL ELECTION BALLOT
BAY COUNTY, FLORIDA
NOVEMBER 5, 2002

OFFICIAL BALLOT, GENERAL ELECTION
BARBOUR COUNTY, WEST VIRGINIA
NOVEMBER 5, 2002

The two main types of ballots are the office group ballot and the party column ballot. These sample ballots from elections in Florida and West Virginia show the differences between the two basic approaches to ballot design. The West Virginia ballot exemplifies the party column ballot, which lists the candidates in columns that indicate their party designation. The Florida ballot, on the other hand, emphasizes office rather than party. This is the key feature of the office group ballot, which lists candidates by name and party under the title of the office they are running for.

Policy in Practice: Automation Frustration: Electronic Voting Still Has Some Bugs

Fifty-five freshman members were sworn in to the U.S. House in 2007. All but thirteen were Democrats. The fact that one particular Republican had won a seat, however, was controversial. Vern Buchanan claimed Florida's 13th District seat with a margin of just 369 votes, while more than 18,000 votes had gone missing, meaning voters had made selections for lower-level ballot races but not for Congress. Most of the missing votes were in the most Democratic county in Buchanan's congressional district. But, rather than being due to fraud or cheating, the botched vote appeared to have been a case of simple mechanical error.

That's how it's gone with electronic voting machines. For all the horror stories about how hackers can break into them and change results, the real problems have been caused by plain old error. In the few years since many states and counties began adopting ATM-style voting machines—prodded by the federal Help America Vote Act (HAVA) of 2002—most of the problems have been caused by ordinary machine error or human error.

There's been plenty of human error. During elections in 2006, voters in major cities such as Denver, Cleveland, Chicago, and Baltimore experienced long delays or other problems simply because poll workers hadn't been instructed properly on how to operate the machinery. "You're dealing with a population of poll workers that is fairly stagnant, that is aging, that is generally not familiar with the latest and greatest in technology," says Dan Seligson, editor of Electionline.org.

Lawrence Norden, a voting expert at New York University's Brennan Center, says that many of the problems have resulted from the fact that governments switched so rapidly to electronic voting systems. Because the kinks are still being worked out, numerous states, and the federal commission that advises them on voting rules, are leaning toward requiring some form of paper printout of votes, so that recounts are more feasible in situations such as the Florida 13th District race.

There was some irony to the fact, after all, that Buchanan had succeeded Katherine Harris, who had presided over Florida's controversial presidential voting

Many states and localities have shifted to high-tech, electronic voting machines in the past few election cycles. The results have been mixed, and some criticize the machines for being overly vulnerable to hackers. The machines also suffer from some very low-tech drawbacks. Here a touch-screen ballot machine is temporarily out of service in a very busy polling place . . . because it ran out of paper.

in 2000 as the state's chief election officer. It was the myriad problems with thousands of paper ballots—in a race that George W. Bush won by just 537 votes after the U.S. Supreme Court put an end to the lengthy recount process—that triggered the mass move to electronic voting in the first place.

Although the new systems have problems, Norden points out that there are some upsides. There is less doubt about voter intent—whom they meant to vote for—than there had been with paper ballots that were not properly "punched." Votes now are also easier to count than in the old days. "Electronic voting machines are an improvement over the old punch cards and lever machines, primarily because they're easier to use," says David Kimball, a political scientist at the University of Missouri–St. Louis.

But, he adds, "One of the unfortunate things is that there was this rush among some states and local governments to quickly switch to a new voting system without maybe carefully considering what that new system was and how it worked and what the potential problems might be."

Source: Original piece reported and written for this book by Alan Greenblatt.

to vote for party nominees—voters can cast a **straight ticket** vote for all of one party's nominees with one computer click or pull of the lever. This is a practice in decline, however, with several states having abolished it, most recently Missouri, in 2006.[14]

Each state's election code determines the specific details about ballots, and perhaps most important, the order in which offices and candidates will appear. This varies considerably among the states. By 1992, about 80 percent of the states had replaced paper ballots with punch cards, machines in which voters pull a lever next to the names of the candidates of their choice, or optical scan voting machines.[15] Voters in many states use electronic systems resembling automated teller machines (ATMs), but many states are pushing for a paper trail to allow the electronic results to be verified. All but a handful of states tabulate votes for write-in candidates, although victories or even significant showings by such candidates are few and far between.

A few cities, including Minneapolis and San Francisco, use instant-runoff voting (IRV) for municipal elections. Rather than picking one candidate, voters rank all the choices. If one candidate receives more than 50 percent of the vote, he or she wins. But if no one receives a majority of the votes, the candidate with the lowest number of votes is disqualified and his or her supporters' second-place choices are redistributed among the remaining candidates. This process continues until someone emerges with a majority. The benefit of such a system, supporters say, is that a candidate who is acceptable to a majority of voters will win, as opposed to a winner-takes-all election in which a candidate with only, say, 30–40 percent of the vote comes out on top of a large split field. The Academy Awards switched to an IRV or preferential voting system for Best Picture in 2010.

Regulating the Parties

A state's authority to print ballots or purchase voting software gives it enormous control over which parties and candidates are presented to the voters. Until the late nineteenth century, parties themselves printed the ballots, which obviously encouraged voters to select a straight ticket of their chosen party's nominees. The advent of the **secret ballot**, also known as the **Australian ballot**, led the states to print their own ballots and, therefore, to determine which parties should appear on ballots. "From there," writes Kay Lawson, a retired San Francisco State University political scientist, "it seemed but a short step to requiring that parties show a minimum level of support to qualify."[16]

The Republican and Democratic parties are themselves regulated at the state level by a bewildering array of varying state laws. Some states provide detailed regulations for party organization, activities, and nominating procedures. Others are silent on many specific matters. According to political

STRAIGHT TICKET

Originally, ballots that allowed voters to pick all of one party's candidates at once; today, voting for all of one party's candidates for various offices—for instance, voting for all Democrats or all Republicans.

SECRET (AUSTRALIAN) BALLOT

A ballot printed by the states that allows voters to pick and choose among different candidates and party preferences in private.

scientist V.O. Key, the traditional Democratic one-party control of the South, although now a thing of the past, led to the introduction of the political primary. Voters had no real choice in the general election, so primaries gave them a real say in who ultimately would hold an office.[17] These days, nearly every state holds primary elections to pick party nominees for state offices, although some states, such as Virginia, still nominate candidates at party conventions. (A fuller discussion of political parties is found in chapter 6.)

Major parties may not like all the state ballot regulations they have to comply with, but the rules in many states seem designed to favor them over new or minor parties and independent candidates. Prior to the 1968 Supreme Court decision in *Williams v. Rhodes,* it was possible for states to have no mechanism in place to qualify new parties for their ballots. Even today, according to Richard Winger, editor of the newsletter *Ballot Access News,* new parties in eleven states cannot qualify for the ballot before they have picked their candidates, who must be listed on their ballot access petition, the collection of voters' signatures.[18]

The Court's decision meant that a state no longer could require that a certain percentage of signatures be collected in each county. But that did not mean states could not erect new roadblocks to keep out aspiring parties or candidates. Nine states changed their laws to require that signatures be collected in each congressional district. This kept ballot access elusive for candidates or parties that had most of their support in a particular city or region. Fifteen states also placed time constraints on when signatures could be collected; for example, California and Ohio require new parties to qualify even before the election year begins. Virginia blocks petitioners from gathering signatures outside their home congressional district. In Texas, voters who participated in major party primaries are not allowed to sign a petition to get a new party on the ballot; the state also requires citizens to know and affix their voter registration numbers next to their signatures on petitions. Similarly, Alabama, Arkansas, New York, and Virginia require signers to supply their precinct numbers. Quick—what's your precinct number?

In its 1971 decision in *Jenness v. Fortson,* the Supreme Court upheld a Georgia law that requires minor parties or independent candidates to collect signatures that represent 5 percent of the total number of votes cast in the last election for the office. Independent or minor party candidates for governor in 2006 had to accrue 101,295 signatures to qualify for the gubernatorial ballot. That is a lot of signatures for a new political player, and it is more than double the amount of votes the one minor party candidate for the office received in 2002. Not surprisingly, no new minor party or independent candidate has qualified for the ballot in Georgia since 1964.[19]

Minor parties and independent candidates continue to file lawsuits challenging such restrictions, but the Supreme Court ruling has emboldened several other states to erect strict barriers against access to the ballot. States such as Alabama, North Carolina, Oklahoma, and West Virginia have the most difficult requirements for parties and candidates to meet. In West Virginia, for instance, the law requires circulators who are trying to collect signatures to tell everyone they approach, "If you sign my petition, you can't vote in the primary." That happens to not be true—but it is the law. Why make a law requiring circulators to fib to voters? Well, the fib benefits the major parties by keeping out the competition, and the major parties write the laws.

For third parties and independent candidates, it can be a real challenge to gain access to the ballots on any of the states discussed here. Given what we know about Elazar's theory about southern, or traditionalistic, states and their hierarchical attitude toward politics, it should not surprise us that these states have the most restrictive ballot access laws. That does not mean that hundreds of minor party and independent candidates have not overcome all these hurdles and more to win spots on statewide ballots. A couple of them have even won election as governor—for instance, in Minnesota in 1998 and Maine in 1994 and 1998. Their place on a ballot one year, however, is no guarantee that members of their parties will qualify the next time around. Alabama requires that a minor party poll at least 20 percent of the vote for governor to win an automatic qualification for the next ballot. Half a dozen other states require at least 10 percent. Given all the restrictions, Lawson concludes, "The laws have been effective in keeping minor parties off the ballot in election after election."[20]

Why all the restrictions? Keeping minor parties off the ballot naturally helps the two major parties. Those who are in power control the rules that keep them in power. In Georgia, bills to loosen the state's restrictions have been introduced at least seven times over the last twenty years. They have always failed.

Restricting Voters

States do not just regulate the access of parties to the ballot. They also regulate the interaction of citizens with that ballot. They determine who can register to vote and how they can register. Changes in federal law over the years have removed many of the initial barriers that states had imposed to restrict voting rights, based on property ownership, literacy, race, sex, and age. But there are still differences among states in how easy they make it for citizens to register—a necessary step toward having the chance to vote in every state except North Dakota, which does not require voter registration.

In the early years of the nation, most eastern states required citizens to own property in order to vote. Those requirements diminished over time, in large part because the western frontier states lacked the type of class structure that reinforced them. The eastern states, however, soon came up with the idea of imposing literacy tests. New immigrants had to demonstrate knowledge of the state constitution or other complex issues to the satisfaction of the local election official.[21] Native whites who were illiterate often were exempted from this requirement. Southern states took up literacy testing as a means of keeping African Americans from voting because they generally received an inadequate education in schools segregated by race. Literacy tests remained a part of the southern legal landscape until the federal Voting Rights Act of 1965 barred them. (See box on page 154.)

Several amendments to the U.S. Constitution expanded voting rights to include minorities and women. The Fifteenth Amendment was passed following the Civil War and was meant to end discrimination against black men seeking to vote. Until the civil rights movement of the 1960s, however, it was effectively bypassed for a century through literacy tests, intimidation, and other means. The Voting Rights Act of 1965 gave the federal government the authority to review state requirements for registration and voting. In 1964, the Twenty-Fourth Amendment banned the use of poll taxes meant to keep blacks and other poor people from voting. Women received the right to vote with the ratification of the Nineteenth Amendment in 1920. The voting age was lowered to eighteen by the Twenty-Sixth Amendment in 1971. In 1993, Congress passed a law known as "motor voter" registration, which requires states to allow citizens to register to vote when they take tests to receive their driver's licenses.

Why all the effort to get people registered to vote? The purpose of registering voters is to prevent fraud. It prevents people from voting more than once or outside of their home jurisdictions. This makes sense, but throughout the nation's history, many states have used registration laws as a means of making voting inaccessible to some.

Voter fraud has become a contentious topic in recent years, with opinion largely split along partisan lines. Republicans say such measures as requiring voters to show a form of photo identification are necessary to guard against fraud, while Democrats argue that the GOP is simply trying to block access by the poor and minority groups least likely to have such identification—and most likely to vote Democratic. In 2008, the Supreme Court upheld a 2005 Indiana law requiring that voters produce a government-used photo ID at the polls, such as a passport or driver's license. "This notion that somehow voter fraud is a dirty word, I don't understand it, because you're talking about people stealing votes, canceling out legitimate votes," Attorney General Alberto Gonzales testified in 2007.[22]

Political scientist Andrew Hacker wrote after the decision that the justices failed to take into account the hardships that requiring a "license to vote" would impose on the 15 percent of Indiana's voting-age population that has no license. Hacker noted that in Milwaukee County, Wisconsin, 53 percent of African Americans lacked a driver's license in 2005, compared with 15 percent of the adult white population statewide. "Requiring

About 18 percent of the total number of registered voters in Minnesota—542,257—registered to vote on election day in 2008. Minnesota is one of just six states to allow same-day registration.

a driver's license to vote has a disparate racial impact, a finding that once commanded judicial notice," Hacker wrote.[23]

Voter Turnout

It has never been easier to register and to vote, yet fewer and fewer people are actually doing either. Motor voter produced an initial spike in registration, but had little or no effect on the number of people voting. According to Curtis Gans of the Committee for the Study of the American Electorate at American University, **voter turnout** rates have declined by about 25 percent over the last forty years.[24] Turnout did spike for the hotly contested 2004 presidential race, but dropped again in 2006. A record 131 million Americans cast votes in 2008. There are countless reasons why voter turnout has generally declined, including a general disaffection with politics and government, a measurable decline in civic education and newspaper reading, a weakening of such civic-minded institutions as student government and unions, and the changing role of political parties away from engaging and educating voters and toward raising money and providing services to candidates.

Turnout rates are in decline, but they are not declining uniformly across the states. There are many reasons why some states have turnout rates 20 percentage points higher than others, but most of these differences can be explained by political culture, demographics, and party competition. The variations in voter registration laws have relatively little effect at this point.

In general, the closer you live to Canada, the more likely you are to vote. The states with turnout rates of more than 70 percent for the 2008 presidential election, including New Hampshire, Iowa, and Wisconsin, were mostly in the northern tier of the country. The states with lower turnout rates, including Arkansas, Hawaii, Tennessee, and Utah, are in the South or far West. (See Table 5-1.) What explains the difference? Culture, for one thing. Elazar's theory about moralistic states appears to hold up, at least as far as voter turnout goes. "You're talking about states with fairly vigorous political parties, communications media that do cover politics and an educational system more geared toward citizen engagement than other parts of the country," says Gans. A big state like California has a mix of cultures—individualistic and moralistic—according to Elazar.

The moralistic states also tend to be homogenous in terms of demographics. People are more likely to vote if they are better educated, if they are elderly, and if they are white. "In states with high percentage of minorities, you're going to have low turnout," says Steven Hill of the New America Foundation. "States with higher voter turnout, such as Minnesota and Maine, tend to be fairly white states."[25] The moralistic states historically also have bred strong two-party competition. This tends to increase turnout. Citizens in states or districts dominated by one party over the other tend not

VOTER TURNOUT
The percentage of eligible citizens who register to vote and do vote.

TABLE 5-1

Percentage of the Voting-Age Population Casting Ballots in the 2008 Presidential Election

Rank	State	Percentage of Total Voting-Age Population	Elazar Classification	Rank	State	Percentage of Total Voting-Age Population	Elazar Classification
1	Minnesota	70.8	Moralistic	26	Alaska	62.4	Individualistic
2	Maine	70.2	Moralistic	27	Maryland	61.9	Individualistic
3	New Hampshire	69.8	Moralistic	28	Kentucky	61.4	Traditionalistic
				29	Massachusetts	61.3	Individualistic
4	Wisconsin	68.5	Moralistic	30	Alabama	60.8	Traditionalistic
5	Mississippi	68.2	Traditionalistic	31	Connecticut	60.8	Individualistic
6	Louisiana	68.0	Traditionalistic	32	Pennsylvania	60.8	Individualistic
7	Iowa	66.9	Moralistic	33	Kansas	59.8	Moralistic
8	North Dakota	66.3	Moralistic	34	Georgia	59.6	Traditionalistic
9	South Dakota	66.1	Moralistic	35	Idaho	58.8	Moralistic
10	District of Columbia	65.3		36	Indiana	58.8	Individualistic
11	Michigan	65.0	Moralistic	37	New Mexico	57.4	Traditionalistic
12	Montana	64.7	Moralistic	38	Illinois	57.1	Individualistic
13	Nebraska	64.5	Individualistic	39	Florida	56.5	Traditionalistic
14	Ohio	64.5	Individualistic	40	Oklahoma	56.5	Traditionalistic
15	Missouri	64.2	Individualistic	41	New Jersey	56.0	Individualistic
16	North Carolina	63.8	Traditionalistic	42	Tennessee	53.6	Traditionalistic
17	Virginia	63.8	Traditionalistic	43	Arizona	53.3	Traditionalistic
18	South Carolina	63.4	Traditionalistic	44	West Virginia	53.1	Traditionalistic
19	Vermont	63.2	Moralistic	45	Nevada	52.8	Individualistic
20	Delaware	63.0	Individualistic	46	Arkansas	51.8	Traditionalistic
21	Rhode Island	63.0	Individualistic	47	New York	51.5	Individualistic
22	Wyoming	62.9	Individualistic	48	California	51.2	Moralistic
23	Oregon	62.6	Moralistic	49	Utah	50.5	Moralistic
24	Washington	62.6	Moralistic	50	Texas	48.8	Traditionalistic
25	Colorado	62.5	Moralistic	51	Hawaii	46.8	Individualistic

Source: U.S. Census Bureau, Table 407, "Persons Reported Registered and Voted, by State: 2008," available at www.census.gov/compendia/statab/2010/tables/10s0407.xls.

to vote as eagerly. Their candidate of choice is certain to win—or to lose if they are "orphaned" voters whose party is weak in their home state.

Voter turnout rates actually have increased in the South, where many of the historical impediments against registration and voting have declined. There also is more competition between the major parties than had been the case for more than one hundred years. But the region has merely stabilized at a slightly lower turnout rate than the rest of the country. Its high proportion of African Americans and its historical legacy of suppressing their votes and the votes of some whites keep its turnout rates sluggish even though African Americans do tend to vote more than other minorities, such as Hispanics.

Hispanics have long been considered the "sleeping giant" of American politics because of their failure to vote in numbers commensurate with their share of the population. They cast just 6 percent of the ballots in the United States in 2004, barely half as many as blacks, even though they constitute a larger share of the national population. Their numbers ticked upward in 2008, but still trailed well behind blacks who turned out in high numbers in support of Obama. The standard explanation is that Hispanics simply lack the well-established political organizations needed to encourage registration and turnout. But other factors are involved as well. Once you subtract the noncitizens, the percentage of voting-age Hispanics who went to the polls in 2004 was just less than 50 percent—less than for blacks and non-Hispanic whites but by a relatively small margin. As Ruy Teixeira, a Democratic polling expert, says, "People who look at the overall size of the Hispanic population and look at the vote think, 'Oh my God, what if these people ever get mobilized?' . . . But so many of these people can't vote anyway."[26]

Then there's age. The median age of Hispanics in the United States is just twenty-seven, compared with thirty-nine for non-Hispanic whites. A much higher percentage of Hispanics do not vote because they are simply too young. That will change. About 750,000 Hispanics will turn eighteen every year for the next twenty years. It could mean that Hispanic voting rolls will swell enormously—or it could mean that young Hispanics, just like young Americans of every race, will fail to exercise their right to vote in great numbers. Hispanics, in other words, already behave pretty much like everybody else. Given a sufficiently dramatic cause, however, they will turn out.[27] That proved to be the case in 2006 when, according to some estimates, the Hispanic share of the total vote approached 9 percent in a year when immigration became a front-burner political issue.

> Hispanics have long been considered the "sleeping giant" of American politics because of their failure to vote in numbers commensurate with their share of the population. They cast just 6 percent of the ballots in the United States in 2004, barely half as many as blacks, even though they constitute a larger share of the national population.

A Difference That Makes a Difference: How Some States Discourage Voters

Thirty years ago, a political scientist named Robert H. Blank came up with a formula for ranking states according to how easy they made it for their citizens to vote. He came up with fifteen different criteria, including whether they allowed people to vote by absentee ballot for any reason (which was true of thirty-six states), whether they kept polls open for a uniform twelve hours across the state (twenty-nine states), whether they allowed people to register to vote within one month of an election (thirty-five states), and whether they required people to establish residency in the state for more than a year before they could register to vote (twelve states).[a]

According to Blank's scale, traditionalistic states, such as Alabama, Arkansas, and Mississippi, made it hardest for people to vote. These states typically tried to maintain a hierarchical political structure in which white, non-elite citizens—and all African Americans—were discouraged from playing an active role. Obviously, attempting to disenfranchise people (keep them

from voting) was the most blatant way possible to limit access to political decision making. Conversely, the states that did the most to make it easier to register and to vote, such as Idaho, Michigan, and Minnesota, were moralistic states that encouraged political participation among the widest number of people possible. Raymond E. Wolfinger and Steven J. Rosenstone found that voting participation was highest in individualistic states in which government is seen as a marketplace for advancing self-interest among people who have direct interest access to government jobs and contracts.[b]

Since Blank's survey, many of the differences in voting and registration laws among the states have been done away with because of federal intervention. A federal court ruled in 1972 that states could not cut off registration any sooner than thirty days before an election. This effectively eliminated longer state residency requirements. In 1995, the federal government adopted a "motor voter" law, based on a law pioneered in Michigan, to allow citizens to fill out a registration form

"BY TH' WAY, WHAT'S THAT BIG WORD?"

Although once a common voting requirement, literacy tests always flunked Democracy 101. States that required literacy standards used them mainly as a way to disenfranchise minorities. Whites, literate or not, were often exempt, and the standards were unevenly applied. The white male test taker in this cartoon has a much higher chance of passing the test than a minority even though he obviously is not qualified. In addition to literacy tests, voters were required to complete lengthy registration forms, like the four-page example seen here from 1950s whenever they applied for a driver's license. Previously, some states had restricted registration so that prospective voters had to show up at a county registrar's office during limited business hours.

There are still differences among the states, however. North Dakota does not require voters to register at all, while some states, including Minnesota, allow voters to register to vote on election day itself. Since 1998, Oregon has conducted all its elections exclusively by mail, which means that citizens do not need to leave their homes to vote and do not have to vote on one specific day. No question, the states that make it easier for their citizens to vote tend to have the highest voter turnout.

Given the many changes in election laws in recent decades, however, the difference in turnout rates has become less pronounced. Voting in southern states still lags behind the rest of the country but by a much smaller amount than in the days of poll taxes and literacy tests. And some of the reforms have not made that much difference. "Motor voting" produced a surge in registration of about 5 percentage points during the first two years of its operation, but it did not lead to higher voter turnout rates in subsequent elections.

States that make registration harder do discourage voters—but then, their entire political cultures are based on limiting participation. The reverse is true of states with high voter turnouts. Differences in registration laws do not explain their higher levels of political participation as well as their generally inclusive cultures. People tend to vote when they are given a choice—when they think their vote matters. This is why more people vote in states that have healthy competition between the major parties rather than being dominated by just one of them. Other factors explain voting turnout rates as well. People who are better educated, have higher incomes, are white, or are older vote more than people who are young, poor, poorly educated, or members of minority groups.

[a]Robert H. Blank, "State Electoral Structure," *Journal of Politics* 35, no. 4 (November 1993): 988–994.

[b]Raymond E. Wolfinger and Steven J. Rosenstone, *Who Votes?* (New Haven, Conn.: Yale University Press, 1980).

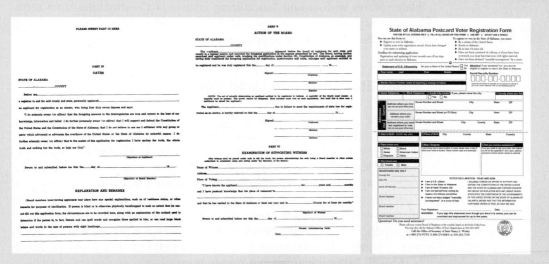

Alabama. These forms asked such questions as, "Give names and addresses of two persons who know you and can verify the statements made above by you relative to your residence in this state, county, and precinct, ward or district." and "Are you a college student? If so, where?" Compare that to the simple one-page Alabama voter registration form of today. The form can be printed out, completed, folded, and mailed like a postcard.

As previously mentioned, there are many other factors that determine rates of voter turnout. Elderly people tend to vote a lot—which is one reason why Social Security and Medicare are always important political issues. Young people, by contrast, rarely vote. People who are wealthy tend to vote more than the poor, and people with higher levels of education vote much more regularly than people with limited education. These are some of the reasons why a high-income state with an educated population, such as Connecticut, has much higher turnout rates than a low-income state where the population is poorly educated on the whole, such as Hawaii.

A competitive election will draw a crowd even in a state that normally has low voter turnout. When people feel like they have a real choice, they are more likely to make the effort to vote. A close three-way race for governor, such as took place in Minnesota in 1998, will produce record turnout, whereas a yawner between a popular incumbent and a no-name opponent will make people sit on their hands. Some states tend to have consistently competitive elections because the two major parties are matched fairly evenly, each getting a roughly equal share of support from the electorate. Other states are one-party states, with Republicans or Democrats dominant. One-party states rarely have competitive elections—but when they do, voter turnout is certain to go up.

In his best-selling 2000 book, *Bowling Alone,* Robert Putnam notes that moralistic states such as Minnesota and the Dakotas have much higher rates of volunteering, attendance at public meetings, and "social trust," as measured by polls, than do traditionalistic states. In other words, voter turnout is just one indication of the overall sense of civic engagement in a place. States with strong "socializing institutions"—anything from membership organizations to news media that still cover politics—are more likely to be places where people are engaged enough to vote.

What Elections Are Used For

Forty-nine states elect a governor and two sets of state legislators: state senators and members of a state house of representatives, delegates, or assemblymen. Nebraska, the only exception, elects a governor and a one-chamber legislature. Beyond that, there is quite a bit of variation among the states in what they allow people to vote for. Some states allow voters to pick a number of statewide officeholders, such as attorney general and secretary of state, whereas in a few places these are appointed positions. Judges are the product of the voting booth in most places but not in about a dozen states. Roughly half the states allow voters to make policy decisions directly through ballot initiatives and referendums.

A look at state elections shows that states have quite different rules about who gets to vote for whom. That, in turn, can affect how a state makes policy. A governor who can appoint his or her entire cabinet is likely to have better success at pushing through his or her own policies than one who has to contend with a group of elected officials, each with his or her own agenda.

All this is putting aside local elections, which also vary considerably. Most large cities, such as Chicago and San Francisco, allow voters to elect a mayor directly. Many smaller cities have what is called a council-mayor format. The city council picks one of its own members to serve as mayor, while the city is administered by a city manager, who is not elected. The same holds true for counties. In some places a county commission picks its own leader, whereas in others voters pick a county executive on their own. Local elections are, for the most part, **nonpartisan**. Candidates do not run under a party label—but, again, there are exceptions, such as the highly partisan elections for mayor of New York City.

Electing the Executive Branch

Until recently in New Jersey, voters elected only their governor of all their statewide officeholders. This has helped create one of the most powerful governorships in the country. It wasn't always so. For centuries, New Jersey governors were much weaker players than the legislature. They were limited to a single term with weak veto and appointment powers. County officials in the state also were quite powerful, at the expense of state officials. That all changed, however, beginning with the new state constitution of 1947. The constitution was pushed through by reformers of the moralistic strain that had always been present, although usually not dominant, in New Jersey politics. The reformers got new powers for the state's governors, including the ability to succeed themselves, authority to appoint not just cabinet officials but also about five hundred board and commission members, and broad authority to reject legislation. New Jersey's governors now can veto all or part of many bills and can issue a conditional veto, meaning a governor can reject portions of a bill while suggesting new language for it.[28]

Compare all that influence with the limited powers of the governor of Texas. In Texas, the governor is only one of twenty-five elected statewide officials—and he or she is not even the most powerful one among them. That distinction belongs to the lieutenant governor. In most states, the lieutenant governor holds a purely symbolic office, with little to do but wait around for something crippling to befall the governor. (New Jersey did not even bother with the office of lieutenant governor, but following a string of gubernatorial vacancies, voters created the position in 2005, which took effect following the 2009 elections.) In Texas, the lieutenant governor is the president of the state Senate and therefore wields tremendous influence over the course of legislation.

In contrast, the governor of Texas can recommend a budget, but he or she has no authority to make the legislature grapple with it seriously.

NONPARTISAN ELECTIONS
Elections in which candidates do not have to declare party affiliation or receive a party's nomination; local offices and elections are often nonpartisan.

Compare that to Maryland, in which legislators can only accept or defeat the governor's spending proposals but can make no fresh additions of their own. The Texas governor appoints the secretary of state and members of many boards or commissions, but many of the latter serve staggered terms. This means that the governor has to work with people who were appointed by his or her predecessor.

As recently as 2003, when a government reorganization bill was debated, efforts have been put forth to provide the governor of Texas with more power. Generally, they have gone nowhere. The state's **plural executive system** illustrates the desires of the framers of the 1876 state constitution to keep too much power out of the hands of any one person or institution. They believed in a separation of powers not just between branches of government but also within the executive branch.[29] The weakened powers of the governor are a reflection of the distrust that Texans had for strong government, in keeping with their constitution's many restrictions on raising taxes.

A couple of other southern and traditionalistic states, such as Alabama and Georgia, also divide power within the executive branch. In 1999, Alabama Democrats in the state Senate sought to strip control of their chamber along with other powers from Lieutenant Governor Steve Windom, a Republican. And they could have done it if only he had left the Senate floor, but Windom refused. To stay present in and to keep control of the chamber for that day, and thus for the rest of his term, he urinated into a plastic jug in the chamber.[30]

Other states chart more of a middle-of-the-road course, electing a handful of statewide officials. In most states, voters elect a lieutenant governor, treasurer, secretary of state, and attorney general. A few states elect other officers as well, such as an insurance commissioner. Some observers believe that appointed officials are removed from political concerns and can make decisions without regard to partisan interests. Others believe that having individual officers answer directly to the public makes them more responsive. Regardless, the fact that many statewide officeholders run for office independently of the governor gives them a power base of their own.

Attorneys general, treasurers, or other statewide officials often have aspirations of becoming governor themselves one day. This leads inevitably to conflict with the sitting governor. During the 1980s in Texas, for example, Democratic attorney general Mark White frequently sparred with Republican governor Bill Clements and eventually unseated him. Today in Texas, every statewide officeholder is Republican, but that has not put an end to squabbling within the executive branch. Caroline Keeton Strayhorn, the state comptroller, has frequently provoked the governor and lieutenant governor, accusing them of using dishonest budget numbers and raising fees excessively. "Sounds like the primary started early this year," Lieutenant Governor David Dewhurst said in 2003.[31]

PLURAL EXECUTIVE SYSTEM

A state government system in which the governor is not the dominant figure in the executive branch but, instead, is more of a first among equals, serving alongside numerous other officials who were elected to their offices rather than being appointed by the governor.

Strayhorn ran unsuccessfully for governor as an independent in 2006.

Legal Offices

Voters pay comparatively little attention to candidates running for some executive branch offices. Races for, say, state treasurer or secretary of state are, for the most part, just not seen as all that exciting. Most often, the party that wins the governorship takes the lion's share of the secondary executive branch offices anyway, so there is not much mystery. These are offices often pursued by legislators or other politicians looking to move up the political ladder. They hope these second-tier positions will firm up their resumés during future bids for prominent offices such as governor.

One office for which the majority-party-takes-all dynamic no longer holds is that of attorney general, the chief law

Minnesota attorney general Mike Hatch applauds Gov. Tim Pawlenty as he arrives at the capitol to deliver his annual State of the State address in 2006. Despite this apparently pleasant moment, the two often feuded, with Hatch challenging and narrowly losing to Pawlenty in that year's election.

enforcement officer in the state. For many years, Democrats completely dominated these positions. That began to change in the late 1990s. (See Map 5-1.) For one thing, the job came to be seen as a more important stepping-stone to the governorship than in the past; in 2007, seven former state attorneys general were serving as governors. McDonnell, the Republican victor in the 2009 Virginia governor's race, had previously served as attorney general, while, in Massachusetts, Attorney General Martha Coakley was the losing Democratic candidate for U.S. Senate against Scott Brown in 2010. Attorneys general in ten other states, including Michigan, South Carolina, Pennsylvania, and California, ran for governor in 2010. Republicans, understandably, became increasingly unwilling to concede this important gateway to the chief executive's office.

Moreover, state attorneys general, who traditionally had concentrated on law enforcement and consumer protection disputes within their states, had joined in a series of multistate settlements that represented an important challenge to corporate interests. They forced a series of settlements in 1998, for instance, that pushed the major tobacco companies to change their marketing strategies and pay states an estimated $246 billion over twenty-five years. Some Republicans believed that these activist attorneys general were engaging in "government lawsuit abuse"—not targeting criminal behavior but, instead, going after companies to achieve changes in policy and regulation that could not be accomplished in the legislative arena. They founded

MAP 5-1 States Attorneys General: Party Affiliation, 2010

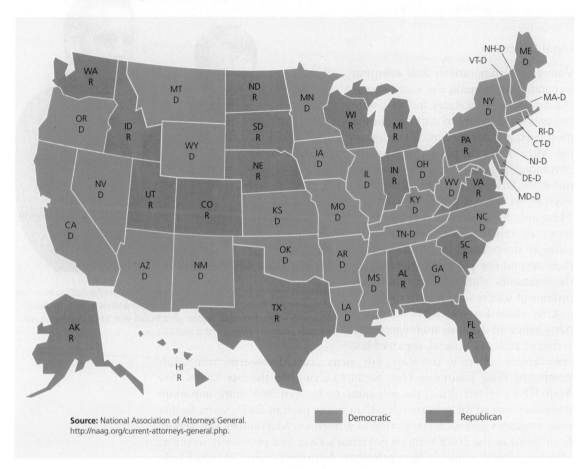

Source: National Association of Attorneys General. http://naag.org/current-attorneys-general.php.

Democratic   Republican

the Republican Attorneys General Association (RAGA) as a campaign wing to elect members of their party to the office and funneled contributions from businesses and conservative interest groups that were threatened by the new activism to their candidates. "Historically . . . attorney general races were off most business people's radar screens," according to Bob LaBrant of the Michigan Chamber of Commerce. In the new environment, he says, "there's greater incentive to get involved in an attorney general race because of the increased involvement of attorneys general across the country in litigation against the business community."[32]

Such interest group money and influence do make a difference. In 2002, the Law Enforcement Alliance of America, an arm of the gun lobby, ran an estimated $1.5 million late-season ad campaign that helped keep the Texas attorney general's office in Republican hands. This was an expanded version of the U.S. Chamber of Commerce's effort in Indiana in 2000, when a $200,000 ad campaign was widely viewed as a leading factor in driving an incumbent Democrat out of office.[33] All told, Republicans have improved their numbers since RAGA's founding from just twelve attorneys general in 1999 to twenty in 2003. (After the GOP lost a couple of seats in 2006, the number of Republican state attorneys general stood at nineteen.) Both parties now believe that campaigns for attorney general will remain more expensive and competitive than they had been historically.

A related phenomenon is affecting judicial elections, which traditionally were sleepy affairs. All but eleven states hold some type of election for judicial posts. These are either direct elections by voters or retention elections used by voters to grant another term to justices appointed by the governor or the state legislature. Until the mid-1990s, judicial campaigns were cheap and fairly ho-hum. What campaign contributions candidates did receive mainly came from trial lawyers, along with unions and other constituencies allied with the Democratic Party. As with the attorney general office, however, all of that began to change during the 1990s. Republicans and their business allies grew weary of seeing their legislative victories in areas such as tort law and workers' compensation overturned by the high courts. In 2000, candidates in supreme court races in twenty states raised a total of $45.5 million dollars, a 61 percent increase over the previous record. The average cost of winning a judicial election jumped 45 percent between 2002 and 2004, while individual races also kept breaking records, with one Illinois contest nearing the $10 million mark in 2004.[34] Elections for individual lower-level court races have broken through the million-dollar barrier also.

The issue of fund-raising by judicial candidates drew attention with the 2008 publication of best-selling mystery writer John Grisham's *The Appeal*. Its plot turns on a rigged Mississippi Supreme Court election. The following year, the U.S. Supreme Court ruled in *Caperton v. Massey* that a case involving a West Virginia Supreme Court justice who had benefited from a $3 million campaign orchestrated by a coal-mining company that had a large case before the court had a conflict of interest. But Chief Justice John Roberts, writing in dissent, noted that the majority had not drawn a clear line in terms of what constitutes the appearance of corruption, which will lead to further confusion.

Direct Democracy

In addition to electing officials to state and local offices, voters can participate in certain forms of **direct democracy**. In about half the states, voters can pass legislation on their own through ballot initiatives or referendums, which also are available in hundreds of municipalities across the country. In twenty-four states, citizens can petition to place a piece of legislation or a constitutional amendment on the ballot for approval or rejection by voters. Also in twenty-four states—mostly the same states—citizens can petition to review a law passed by the legislature and the governor, which they then can accept or reject. (See Table 5-2.)

DIRECT DEMOCRACY
Citizens make laws themselves rather than relying on elected representatives.

TABLE 5-2

Avenues for Direct Democracy

State	Popular Referendum	Ballot Initiative	Constitutional Amendment by Initiative	Recalls of State Officials
Alabama	No	No	No	No
Alaska	Yes	Yes	No	Yes
Arizona	Yes	Yes	Yes	Yes
Arkansas	Yes	Yes	Yes	No
California	Yes	Yes	Yes	Yes
Colorado	Yes	Yes	Yes	Yes
Connecticut	No	No	No	No
Delaware	No	No	No	No
Florida	No	Yes	Yes	No
Georgia	No	No	No	Yes
Hawaii	No	No	No	No
Idaho	Yes	Yes	Yes	Yes
Illinois	Yes	Yes	No	No
Indiana	No	No	No	No
Iowa	No	No	No	No
Kansas	No	No	No	Yes
Kentucky	Yes	No	No	No
Louisiana	No	No	No	Yes
Maine	Yes	Yes	No	No
Maryland	Yes	No	No	No
Massachusetts	Yes	Yes	Yes	No
Michigan	Yes	Yes	Yes	Yes
Minnesota	No	No	No	Yes
Mississippi	No	Yes	Yes	No
Missouri	Yes	Yes	Yes	No
Montana	Yes	Yes	Yes	Yes

TABLE 5-2, continued

State	Popular Referendum	Ballot Initiative	Constitutional Amendment by Initiative	Recalls of State Officials
Nebraska	Yes	Yes	Yes	No
Nevada	Yes	Yes	Yes	Yes
New Hampshire	No	No	No	No
New Jersey	No	No	No	Yes
New Mexico	Yes	No	No	No
New York	No	No	No	No
North Carolina	No	No	No	No
North Dakota	Yes	Yes	Yes	Yes
Ohio	Yes	Yes	Yes	No
Oklahoma	Yes	Yes	Yes	No
Oregon	Yes	Yes	Yes	Yes
Pennsylvania	No	No	No	No
Rhode Island	No	No	No	Yes
South Carolina	No	No	No	No
South Dakota	Yes	Yes	Yes	No
Tennessee	No	No	No	No
Texas	No	No	No	No
Utah	Yes	Yes	No	No
Vermont	No	No	No	No
Virginia	No	No	No	No
Washington	Yes	Yes	No	Yes
West Virginia	No	No	No	No
Wisconsin	No	No	No	Yes
Wyoming	Yes	Yes	No	No
Total # of States with	25	24	18	18

Sources: Data compiled from the Initiative and Referendum Institute at the University of Southern California, www.iandrinstitute.org/statewide_i&r.htm; and the National Conference of State Legislatures, www.ncsl.org/LegislaturesElections/ElectionsCampaigns/RecallofStateOfficials/tabid/16581/Default.aspx.

States under Stress: Tea Party: Powerful Force or Flash in the Pan?

Kari Carender is the child of Democrats and is engaged to someone who voted for Barack Obama for president in 2008. But soon after Obama's presidency set in motion a $787 billion stimulus package, Carender grew upset enough to organize a protest.

Her first rally in Washington state against government spending drew only 120 people. But a week later, her second event attracted 300. Within two months, their ranks had swelled to 1,200 as they joined one of many protests held on April 15—Tax Day—around the country in 2009. Carender, also known as "Liberty Belle," had become one of the first organizers of what became known as the Tea Party movement.

The movement was an expression of anger at the size of government—a backlash against the stimulus, a bank bailout plan that had been passed under President George W. Bush to the tune of $700 billion, and a deficit that in 2009 topped $1.4 trillion. "The Republicans for the last two decades have been a party whose litmus tests have been cultural issues, especially abortion," explained conservative columnist Michael Barone in 2010. "The tea partiers have helped to change their focus to issues of government overreach and spending."[a]

The Tea Party was made up mainly of political newcomers angry about the direction in Washington, D.C. Money and volunteers from their ranks had their effects on a special congressional election in upstate New York in 2009 and the special U.S. Senate election in Massachusetts in 2010. The actual size of their Washington rally on September 12, 2009, was much in dispute, with media outlets such as ABC reporting 60,000 in attendance and organizers claiming more than 1 million.

Regardless of its size—and as yet unknowable staying power—the Tea Party quickly became a real force in American politics. But a force for what? Its opponents accused adherents of incoherence, having no real platform except opposition to President Obama.

But Tea Party adherents resisted being lumped with establishment institutions, including the Republican Party. "This is basically a crowd-sourced party platform, with the smoke-filled rooms and convention logrolling taken out of the picture," blogger and columnist Glenn Reynolds wrote as the Tea Party prepared to hold its first national convention in Nashville in February 2010. "It's a set of ideas developed via an interactive Web site, where voting determines which elements are most important."[b]

Although Tea Party participants mainly concerned themselves with federal issues, they quickly made their presence felt in state-level politics. Candidates who associated themselves with the Tea Party lost Republican gubernatorial primaries early in 2010. But Texas governor Rick Perry was viewed as having successfully beaten back a primary challenge from Kay Bailey Hutchison, a sitting U.S. senator, by embracing many of the Tea Party tenets, notably in the area of states' rights and complaints about federal health and education policies.

Still, some commentators said that the movement not only lacked clear leaders but was too diffuse to have a lasting effect. Populist anger was a major force in American politics early in the Obama era, but it wasn't always clear who most people were mad at. Wall Street was unpopular for exacerbating the worst recession in decades, but attempts in Washington to impose new regulations on financial services were slowed by fears that they would do more to empower the federal government than protect consumers.

Groups such as the U.S. Chamber of Commerce—itself a powerful establishment institution—struck

When citizens or groups other than elected officials put a measure on the ballot to become a law, this is called a popular initiative. When citizens put a measure on the ballot to affirm or reject an action of the legislature or other political actor, this is called a popular referendum. When the legislature places a measure on the ballot to win voter approval (such as a constitutional amendment or bond issue), it is called a legislative responsive chords with its argument that a "big government" approach represented as great a threat as large financial institutions such as banks. "The idea of protecting the little guy seems pretty compelling, but if it can be turned around to say the government is imposing more restrictions, then it's problematic right now," said Vincent R. Reinhart, a former director of monetary affairs at the Federal Reserve.[c]

Liberals grew visibly frustrated that the main vehicle for populist anger in the Obama era directed its concern not at Wall Street but at Washington. Peter Beinart, a Democratic commentator, argued that the Tea Party represented an odd twist on the original vision of populism in America, which saw government as the best means for helping ordinary farmers and workers win power against the privileged few.[d]

Democrats widely circulated the story of a man at a town hall meeting in Simpsonville, South Carolina, who complained to his representative, "Keep your government hands off my Medicare." The member of Congress, a conservative Republican, explained to the man that Medicare is a government-run program.[e]

Democrats felt this served to illustrate the disconnect between people who demand services from government while expressing their disdain for it.

A poll of Tea Party supporters conducted by CBS and the *New York Times* in 2010 showed that they "tend to be Republican, white, male and older than 45." As liberal columnist E. J. Dionne Jr. writes, "This is the populism of the privileged . . . essentially the reappearance of an old anti-government far right that has always been with us and accounts for about one-fifth of the country."[f]

For the Tea Parties, it was clear that government was the enemy. As the Obama administration ran up record deficits and pushed ambitious legislation to regulate not just the financial sector but healthcare and greenhouse gas emissions, the Tea Party message was a powerful one, at least for a highly vocal minority. "A year ago, the Tea Party movement didn't exist," Reynolds wrote early in 2010. "Today, it is arguably the most popular political entity in America. The movement is already more popular than the Republican or Democratic parties, according to a recent *NBC/Wall Street Journal* poll."

Source: Original piece written for this book by Alan Greenblatt.

[a]Michael Barone, "Tea Party Brings Energy, Change and Tumult to GOP," *Washington Examiner,* March 14, 2010, available at www.washingtonexaminer.com/politics/Tea-party-brings-energy_-change-and-tumult-to-GOP-87511912.html.

[b]Glenn Reynolds, "More Impact Is What's Next for the Tea Party," *Washington Examiner,* January 31, 2010, available at www.washingtonexaminer.com/opinion/columns/Sunday_Reflections/More-impact-is-what_s-next-for-the-Tea-Party-movement-83041312.html#ixzz0iC3Z2pcz.

[c]Quoted in Alan Greenblatt, "Populist Push Could Get Lost in the Details," *CQ Weekly,* February 22, 2010, 441.

[d]Peter Beinart, "The Tea Partiers' Phony Populism," *Daily Beast,* February 8, 2010, available at www.thedailybeast.com/blogs-and-stories/2010–02–08/the-tea-partiers-phony-populism.

[e]Philip Rucker, "Sen. DeMint Is a Voice of Reform Opposition," *Washington Post,* July 28, 2009, A1.

[f]E. J. Dionne Jr., "Populism of Privilege," *Washington Post*, April 19, 2010, A15.

referendum. Some referendums are nonbinding—expressing the will of the people but not becoming law—but most are binding and do have the force of law once passed.

In all fifty states, the legislature or other government agencies have the power of legislative referendum. In the decades following independence, citizens in several northeastern states ratified new constitutions; Congress subsequently made legislative referendums for constitutional amendments mandatory for all new states entering the union after 1857.[35]

As discussed in chapter 3, the notion of popular referendums and initiatives really took root after the efforts of reformers from the Populist and Progressive movements. These individuals sought to give citizens more influence over state political systems that they saw as dominated by moneyed interests such as banks, railroads, and mining companies. A majority of the states that have adopted the popular initiative process (under which citizens can collect a certain number of signatures to place issues directly on the ballot) did so in the late 1800s and early 1900s. Most of these states are in the West or Upper Midwest, which had political cultures that welcomed the idea of populist control. Much of the opposition in the eastern and southern states grew out of racist concerns that giving people direct authority to make laws would give too much power to African Americans or new immigrants such as the Irish.

Recent ballot initiatives and referendums have covered a wide range of topics, from legalizing marijuana and allowing physician-assisted suicide to making sure that pregnant pigs are housed in large enough pens (an amendment to the Florida constitution approved by voters in 2002). Many initiatives have to do with tax and spending issues. Sometimes voters send contradictory signals. For instance, in Washington State, voters in recent years have approved limitations on property and other taxes, while at the same time approving such expensive programs as teacher pay increases and class size limitations.

Those who favor the initiative process say that it gives voters a chance to control government directly. Voters know that they are voting for an environmental safety program or a campaign finance law, as opposed to voting for candidates who say that they favor these things but who may act differently once in office. Initiative states do tend to have lower state spending per capita, but that gap generally is bridged by local spending, which tends to run higher in initiative states.[36]

Critics of the initiative process say that it creates more problems than it solves. Because voters are presented with a straight "yes" or "no" choice about spending more on, say, elementary and secondary education, they are not taking into account other competing state priorities, such as transportation or colleges, the way legislators must. Voters can say, as in Washington, that they want both lower taxes and more services but leave legislators and governors few tools for balancing the budget or responding to economic recessions.

Those opposed to initiatives also say that the idea that they express the popular will better than elected representatives sounds good in theory but is flawed in practice. In many states—particularly California—initiatives have become big business. They are not necessarily the expressions of grassroots ideals anymore; instead, they are proposed and paid for by wealthy individuals or interest groups, such as teachers' unions or gambling casinos.

Far and away the most famous and influential modern ballot initiative was Proposition 13, approved by California voters in 1978, which limited property tax rates and made other changes to the state's tax and spending laws (see chapter 3). The initiative was copied successfully in Michigan and Massachusetts, and most states soon placed limitations on their own property tax rates. The success of the proposition fueled the modern initiative movement. There were only eighty-seven statewide initiatives proposed during the entire decade of the 1960s. Since 1978, however, there have been about three hundred initiatives proposed per decade. Ninety-three statewide initiatives were placed on ballots in 1996 alone. That appears to have been the peak year, with supporters of the initiative process complaining since then that state legislatures have placed new restrictions on ballot access and signature collection.

The power of initiatives can be seen in the establishment of legislative term limits, which exist in nearly every state that allows ballot initiatives but in only a couple of states that do not. Term limits, after all, were imposed in virtually every case by voters through ballot measures, not by the legislators themselves. In addition, congressional term limits were a popular idea during the 1990s and were approved in a number of states; however, the U.S. Supreme Court ruled in 1995 that states cannot unilaterally alter the constitutional requirements for holding federal office. State legislators are subject to term limits in fifteen states, but the defeat of a term-limits initiative in Oregon in 2006 has most likely signaled the end of the movement.

Rather than looking to expand term limits, legislators and many others concerned with the effects of term limits on good governance have been seeking to expand the length of time legislators may serve. Term limits are still too popular to repeal, but some people believe allowing legislators ten to twelve years in a chamber, as opposed to six to eight, will make them more expert in grappling with the complex policies they must address. Even these efforts, however, have proven to be tough sells.

Ballots have become regular battlegrounds for a number of other issues. Limitations on reproductive rights, such as parental notification requirements to obtain an abortion, have been debated by voters in many states, as have smoking bans and property rights protections. Although many ballot measures seek to put restraints on government, by limiting state spending, for instance, or by holding judges more accountable for their decisions, voters in recent cycles have rejected these ideas. Public officials were able to make the case that these sometimes rigid restrictions would tie their hands even in emergency situations. Perhaps surprisingly, their arguments were echoed in many states by organized business groups that, although conservative fiscally, were concerned that artificial limits on government would affect their own priorities, such as higher education and transportation projects.

Since 2004, perhaps the most prominent measure on many ballots has been a ban on gay marriage. Many states already had defined marriage as the union of a man and a woman, but following a Massachusetts court decision that found gays had a right to marry, twenty-nine states have changed their constitutions to ban same-sex marriage. Arizona became the first state to oppose a ban in 2006, but voters there approved a more carefully written ban two years later. As noted earlier, some political scientists have suggested that high-profile initiatives do lead more people to vote. Given the attention given to a gay marriage ban in Ohio in 2004, when that state's electoral votes ultimately decided the presidency, there was much coverage in the media that looked at the question of whether the initiative helped President Bush by encouraging social conservatives to vote. "I'd be naïve if I didn't say it helped," Robert T. Bennett, chair of the Ohio Republican Party, told the *New York Times*. "And it helped most in what we refer to as the Bible Belt area of southeastern and southwestern Ohio, where we had the largest percentage increase in support for the president."[37]

Not surprisingly, liberals decided to jump on this particular bandwagon, finding causes, such as minimum wage increases and stem-cell research support, to place on ballots in hopes that more progressive voters would turn out as well. But there is a school of thought that argues that they need not have bothered. Simon Jackman, a statistician at Stanford University, has shown that same-sex marriage initiatives boosted turnout by about 3 percent in the eleven states that had them on the ballot in 2004. On examining data from all of Ohio's counties, however, he concludes that that state's initiative did not boost support for Bush.[38]

Others have noted that it is not an accident that high-profile initiatives tend to appear in closely contested states. "The list of [presidential] battleground states almost exactly matches up with the list of controversial ballot measures this year," said Jennie Drage Bowser, who tracks initiatives for the National Conference of State Legislatures, in 2004.[39]

Beyond initiatives and referendums is perhaps the ultimate expression of popular dissatisfaction—the **recall**. Recalls of local officials are allowed in thirty-six states and 61 percent of U.S. municipalities—more local governments than allow initiatives or referendums. Like ballot initiatives, **recall** laws are mainly the byproducts of the intention of early-twentieth-century reformers to make state governments more responsive to average citizens. Recalls of state officials are allowed in eighteen states. The most famous example of a recall took place in 2003, when California governor Gray Davis was recalled and replaced by Arnold Schwarzenegger.

Before that election, recalls were fairly common at the local level but rare at the state level. Over the past one hundred years, there have been fewer than two dozen recall elections involving state officials, including legislators.[40] The only governor to be recalled before Davis was Lynn Frazier of North Dakota in 1921. Frazier, the state attorney general, and the agricultural commissioner each lost his office after a grassroots movement swelled against scandals in Frazier's government. The only other governor who has ever faced a scheduled recall election was Evan Mecham of Arizona; the legislature saved voters the trouble by removing him from office in 1987.

California makes the recall process pretty easy, requiring fewer signatures as a percentage of the number of people who voted in the last election for the office than in other states. It requires only 12 percent, whereas most states require 25 percent and Kansas requires 40 percent. Gray Davis was unpopular, having won reelection the year before by a small plurality. He also had come to be blamed for the state's $38 billion deficit and electricity crisis.

Public Opinion

Randall Gnant, the former president of the Arizona Senate, says that there is quite a contrast between the politics of today and those of the 1800s. Back then, he says, "It seemed that everybody took part in the political process—there were torchlight parades, party-run newspapers for and against candidates." Today, "We're into sort of a reverse kind of period. Now, almost nobody participates in the electoral process—voter turnout rates are abysmally low." But that does not mean that citizens are not paying any attention to the political process. Given the importance of talk radio, the Internet, and other media that quickly spread public opinion—at least a share of it—the old idea that voters agree to a sort of contract with politicians whom they elect to a two- or four-year term is rapidly becoming dated. Voters are more than willing to express their displeasure about a given policy well before the next scheduled election day. "Try to get somebody interested in electing a candidate and they just don't want to get involved," Gnant points out. "But they are perfectly willing to get involved if somebody does something they don't want them to do."[41]

Citizen opinion usually does not register loudly enough to result in a recall or other formal protest. On most issues that come before policymakers at the state level, citizen opinion hardly seems to exist or be formulated at all. After all, how many citizens are going to take the time to follow—let alone express an opinion about—an obscure regulatory issue concerning overnight transactions between banks and insurance companies?

This lack of interest, or at the very least, this lack of time, begs an important question. If citizens do not or cannot make their feelings known on every issue addressed in the hundreds of bills that wend through the average state legislature each year, how can legislators know that their votes will reflect the will of their constituents? After all, as V.O. Key writes, "Unless mass views have some place in the shaping of policy, all the talk about democracy is nonsense."[42]

Responding to Opinion

Doug Duncan served for a dozen years as county executive of Montgomery County, Maryland, before giving up the job in 2006. Like many veteran officeholders, he found that one of the biggest changes in his job came in the area of communications. "Doing it is half the job," he says, "and the other half is telling people about it so they know how you're spending their money."[43] The old outlets for government officials making announcements or responding to criticism—local daily newspapers and evening TV news broadcasts—have declined in audience or even gone away completely in some cases. Nevertheless, there are more information sources than ever with the growth of the Internet. "The information's there," Duncan says. "It's just a question of how you make it available."

E-mail, listservs, and Web sites devoted to neighborhood concerns or services such as libraries have made it easier for public officials to know what their constituents are thinking—at least, those constituents who are motivated enough to make their opinions known on a given issue. And elected officials have become fairly quick about adopting to new platforms, such as Facebook and Twitter. But let's be realistic—state officials, in particular, cannot know what the majority opinion is in their district about every issue they confront. On most issues, they do not hear from any constituents at all. A few high-profile concerns, such as tax increases or legalizing casino gambling, may lead a newspaper or an interested party to conduct a statewide poll—but even on the rare occasions when there are polls on a state issue, these polls will not break down opinion by legislative district. Given the absence of specific information that each legislator or gubernatorial aide has about how constituents view a particular area, public officials have to rely on a series of clues.

Some political scientists have taken data from various nationwide polls, broken them down by state, and analyzed how well elected officials have reflected the general ideology and desires of the public in their states.[44] What they found is that average state opinion does seem to be reflected in the policy decisions made in individual states. What does *average state opinion* mean? It is the type of things we discussed earlier when talking about Daniel Elazar's classifications of the states. Some states tend to be more liberal overall, whereas others are more conservative. The average citizen's desire—whether in a conservative state like Texas or a more liberal one like Vermont—tends to be pretty well reflected by state laws on issues that range from restrictions on abortion services to welfare spending, the death penalty, environmental protections, and gay rights.[45]

How does this happen? For one thing, elected officials devote an enormous amount of time trying to gauge how opinion is running in their districts. They may not hear from constituents

> For one thing, elected officials devote an enormous amount of time trying to gauge how opinion is running in their districts. They may not hear from constituents on every issue, but they pay close attention to those concerns that are registered through letters and phone calls.

A Difference That Makes a Difference: Town Hall, Version 2.0

Governments can't think of everything. That's why Vivek Kundra, who served as chief technology officer of Washington, D.C., before becoming chief information officer for the Obama White House went to "outsiders," asking for ideas on how to enhance D.C. services through computer applications. He announced the "Apps for Democracy" contest in October 2008. The general public was invited to take data—yes, dry digital data from D.C. files—and turn them into useful and absorbing information for residents, visitors, and government employees.

When the closing bell rang on the thirty-day contest in mid-November, Kundra's office had received forty-seven submissions. The government's cost: $50,000—nearly half of it for prize money. That's cheap for dozens of new and usable applications. If the government had had to develop all of them on its own, it would have taken more than a year and, Kundra estimates, $2.6 million.

Five of the entries were quickly put to use. "That's the power of democratizing data," Kundra says.[a] It fosters the design of quick and nimble applications, allowing citizens to be "co-creators of government." Using the wisdom of crowds is a huge philosophical shift from how government usually runs, he adds.

The whole business of citizens trying to contact governments, and of governments wanting to relay good information to citizens, has always been a creaky process. New tools such as blogs, wikis, and public comment software are smoothing things out a little and allowing governments to enhance some of the traditional ways of communicating with the public.

Carole Brown, who's at the Chicago Transit Agency (CTA), started a blog in 2005 after feeling frustrated by negative newspaper reports on what was happening at the CTA. When Brown read letters to the editor of the newspaper, she realized that readers, angry at the CTA, didn't understand the complexities behind public transportation funding. So Brown blogged away, offering details that riders weren't getting from the press. Today, her blog serves many purposes, from straightening out misconceptions that riders get from other sources to allowing the agency to communicate early and often with transit riders. "My blog is an incredible tool," says Brown. "We're using it to focus on issues most important to our riders, and they have no problem telling us what those are."

At electronic town hall meetings, city officials bring people together in groups of eight or ten at a table with one laptop computer and a trained facilitator. As citizens give their opinions on issues, someone types them up and forwards them to a team of people that gathers and distills the ideas by theme. Concepts that crop up over and over are then flashed on large overhead screens. Eventually those are whittled down to a handful of top priorities by the participants, who vote on them by keypad.

Such a distillation was helpful to San Francisco mayor Gavin Newsom at his first electronic town hall meeting. He already had plenty of information about what lobbyists and professional advocates wanted. What the mayor hoped to find out was what the rest of the city wanted. "The average resident is not typically asked to come or doesn't have time or an entrée to attend a three-hour meeting with the mayor to offer opinions," says Jennifer Petrucione, the mayor's spokeswoman. The virtual town hall was a novel, and helpful, way to find out.

Source: Adapted from Ellen Perlman, "The Missing Link," *Governing* magazine, March 2006.

[a]Ellen Perlman, "The Wisdom of Crowds," *Governing* magazine, February 2009, 46.

on every issue, but they pay close attention to those concerns that are registered through letters and phone calls. They go out and seek opinions by attending religious services and civic events where they can hear the concerns of constituents directly. They use surrogates—such as newspaper articles and interest groups—as ways of determining what is on their

Elected officials do not just have to address the issues they campaigned on, respond to views expressed at the ballot box, deal with the demands of special interest groups, and be attentive to the expectations of political parties. They also have to be prepared to deal with the unexpected. Hurricane Katrina was a dramatic example of this, but other kinds of emergencies, natural or otherwise, happen all the time. Here, Nebraska governor Dave Heineman (right, in blue), and state senator Deb Fischer survey the damage done by a wildfire that destroyed homes in the city of Valentine. State and local emergency agencies were required to control the fire, and other agencies helped deal with the aftermath.

constituents' minds. Susan Herbst, executive vice chancellor and chief academic officer for the University System of Georgia, spent some time earlier in her career hanging out with legislators in Springfield, Illinois. She found that the media were important in shaping public opinion by giving a voice to average people in their stories. The media also shaped the terms of debate. Herbst noted that people in the capital thought that lobbyists often were good indicators of how people felt about an issue: "Staffers seem to think that the nuances and intensity of public opinion are best captured in the communications of interest groups."[46]

This is not to say that using interest groups as surrogates can't be misleading sometimes. The National Rifle Association, for example, may call on its state members to send letters to legislators in numbers that dwarf those mustered by gun control advocates—even in places where a majority favors gun control. "Intense minorities can come off potentially sounding like majorities when in fact they're not," says Illinois Wesleyan University political scientist Greg Shaw.[47] Legislators like to think that they have a pretty good sense of whether a mail-writing campaign has sprung up spontaneously or shows signs of having been organized—everyone signing their name to the same form letter, for example—but sometimes this is easier said than done.

Formal interest groups do not represent every constituent. Some people may favor environmental protection, but not give money to the Sierra Club or the World Wildlife Fund. Some older people actually resist the invitations to join AARP at cheap rates. Still, legislators do gain some sense of how active such groups are in their states and whether they seem to have favorable support at home. A lot of this is inexact, but legislators learn from talking to people whether their constituents are most upset about crime or transportation problems. They are convinced that if they vote for things that voters broadly support, such as mandatory sentencing guidelines for drug offenders or limits on welfare benefits, they will be rewarded politically.

Conversely, a legislator's major fear is of being punished politically. Not getting reelected can be the death knell of a political career. It is important to note, however, that if legislators or governors did not broadly reflect the wishes of the populace that elected them, they would never have won their positions in the first place. In this age of computer-assisted **redistricting**, legislative districts in particular are shaped according to the local political culture, which tends to lean in one ideological direction. A liberal is not going to get elected to a conservative district, ninety times out of a hundred.

Once elected, legislators who want to get reelected are careful not to stray too far from the public opinion in their districts, as best as they can perceive it. They cannot know what the public opinion is about the specifics of every bill, but the fact that not every individual is paying close attention to state politics does not mean that legislators can do whatever they want. Political officials recognize that lobbyists and other interested parties are watching their voting records carefully and can use such information against them, if necessary. "Legislators aren't worried about what their constituents know—they are worried about what an opponent might do with their record in the next election," says Paul Brace, a Rice University political scientist. They act, therefore, as if there is someone or some group out there who has a chance of using a potentially unpopular record against them. "Legislation is written in minutiae, but you know if you vote for it, you'll get an opponent who can dumb it down and use it against you in the next election, and you won't do it."[48]

Some states offer less opportunity for using a politician's record against him or her. In a moralistic state such as Minnesota, there are more daily newspapers paying close attention to state policy matters than in, say, individualistic Wyoming. There are more public interest groups and state-level think tanks closely monitoring St. Paul than there are monitoring Cheyenne. Citizens in states with higher levels of civic engagement are more likely to keep their politicians "honest"—reflecting voters' overall policy desires—than citizens in less-engaged states.

In a state like Idaho or Maryland, one party so completely dominates state politics that only rarely are politicians voted out of office because their records do not reflect public opinion. But even Idaho Republicans or Maryland Democrats can lose—if only in the party primary—if voters sour on their records. All the state capitals have engendered enough of an echo chamber that examines and discusses the work of legislators and other elected officials for an overall sense of their records—conservative or liberal, sellout or crusading—to be known to people who care enough about politics to vote. If those records do not reflect local opinion, the job will go to someone else in the next election.

REDISTRICTING

The drawing of new boundaries for congressional and state legislative districts, usually following a decennial census.

Conclusion

This is a highly partisan era, with little civility or cooperation, it seems, between Republicans and Democrats. But the war between the red and the blue will never be as heated as the war between the blue and the gray—the colors of the North and South during the Civil War. Although voters are divided, they are not as deeply divided as they have been at moments in the country's past, such as the Civil War or Watergate.

That fact is reflected in the recent series of contentious but ultimately narrowly won presidential contests, and on down through other levels of government. As with Congress and the Electoral College, state legislatures have been closely divided, with the two main parties switching leads in total number of seats nationwide throughout the early twenty-first century. The lead among governorships has switched around, too, with Democrats currently up.

The outcomes of recent elections reflect the divided public mood. State and local officials have less ability to control who participates in the political process because of the many changes in voting laws passed at the federal level. They do still maintain a lot of control over whom citizens can vote for through their regulation of political parties and their ability to decide who deserves to get their names on the ballot.

Which state officials citizens get to vote for differs depending on where they live. In most states, citizens vote for several statewide officials such as governor, attorney general, and secretary of state. In others, they might vote only for the governor. Similarly, in some localities, citizens elect the mayor directly whereas in others the mayor is chosen by the city council from among its own membership. Some states allow people to vote directly for judges, while in other states judges are appointed to office. Some localities allow people to vote for school boards; in others, these positions are appointed.

In general, citizens vote for enough officeholders with the authority to control policies that the majority's will generally becomes law. However, because polling is done far more often at the national level than it is at the local or even state level, officeholders sometimes have only an anecdotal sense of what their constituents are thinking. They do pay close attention to what clues they are given and monitor opinion as closely as they can. If they do not create the types of policies that most people want, they are well aware that they are not going to stay in office for long.

Key Concepts

direct democracy (p. 161)

nonpartisan elections (p. 157)

office group (Massachusetts)
    ballot (p. 144)

party column (Indiana)
    ballot (p. 144)

plural executive system
    (p. 158)

plurality (p. 138)

recall (p. 168)

redistricting (p. 173)

secret (Australian) ballot
    (p. 147)

straight ticket (p. 147)

voter turnout (p. 151)

Suggested Readings

Abramowitz, Alan. *Voice of the People: Elections and Voting in the United States.* New York: McGraw-Hill, 2004. A recent look at voting behavior and partisan preferences that suggests some reasons for voter disengagement.

Fisher, Claude S., and Michael Hout. *Century of Difference: How America Changed in the Last Hundred Years.* New York: Russell Sage Foundation, 2006. Draws on census data and polling surveys to present a comprehensive look at demographic, economic, and cultural changes in the United States since 1900.

Patterson, Thomas. *The Vanishing Voter.* New York: Knopf, 2002. A political scientist seeks to explain why voter turnout is falling.

Teixeira, Ruy, ed. *Red, Blue and Purple America: The Future of Election Demographics.* Washington, D.C.: Brookings Institution Press, 2008. A group of political scientists and demographers examine how trends in religion, geography, immigration, income, and class are affecting voting habits.

Wolfinger, Raymond, and Steven Rosenstone. *Who Votes?* New Haven, Conn.: Yale University Press, 1980. A classic study of voter participation in the United States.

Suggested Web Sites

http://fairvote.org. Web site of the Center for Voting and Democracy, which promotes voting and advocates instant runoffs and the abolition of the Electoral College.

http://pewresearch.org. Web site of the Pew Research Center for the People & the Press, which conducts surveys and publishes studies looking at demographic trends that affect politics.

www.lwv.org. Official Web site of the League of Women Voters. Provides a wealth of voter education information.

www.nass.org. Official Web site of the National Association of Secretaries of State. Secretaries of state typically serve as chief election officials, and their offices have primary responsibility for recording official election outcomes.

CHAPTER 6

Parties and Interest Groups

Elephants, Donkeys, and Cash Cows

Interest groups can influence policymakers in a number of different ways. They can make campaign contributions, directly lobby lawmakers, or mount a public pressure campaign. People for the Ethical Treatment of Animals (PETA) uses all three tactics. Its public pressure campaigns often include risqué pictures and appearances to generate attention for the group's cause.

6

Why are political parties weaker than they used to be?

Why are political parties stronger in some states than in others?

How do interest groups influence policymakers?

Col. Aureliano Buendia was a young man when he learned the difference between his country's Liberals and Conservatives in the Gabriel García Márquez novel *One Hundred Years of Solitude*. Liberals, his father explained, fight the authority of the church and the central government and recognize the rights of illegitimate children; conservatives are defenders of public order and morality.

Buendia grew up to lead the Liberal revolutionary forces, without success, in nearly twenty years of civil war. Eventually, his political advisers suggest that he renounce the party's long-standing fight against clerical influence and the rest of the Liberal platform he had been introduced to years before. One adviser, however, speaks against the idea. He points out that they are merely adopting the Conservative platform because it is more popular, even though it represents everything they have fought for so long. Buendia sees things differently. What it means, he says, is "that all we're fighting for is power."[1]

POLITICAL PARTIES

Organizations that nominate and support candidates for elected offices.

This is the classic cynical view of **political parties,** those organized groups that hope to win power by controlling a variety of elective offices, such as mayor or governor. They shift with the winds and pursue whatever policy stances bring them power—even if these stances directly contradict what the parties stood for during the last election. Both major U.S. parties have had moments in recent years when it seemed they had clung to power long after they had run out of guiding ideas. Democrats admitted as much after losing control of Congress in the 1994 elections, and Republicans made similar noises after losing it in 2006. "Every revolution begins with the power of an idea and ends when clinging to power is the only idea left," wrote *Time* magazine reporter Karen Tumulty during the 2006 election season.[2]

Ever since George Washington warned against "the baneful effects of the spirit of party" in his farewell address, many Americans have taken his words to heart. Political disaffection—the feeling that voting really does not make a difference—is why more than half the adult populace of voting age does not do so, whether they are registered or not. "People feel disconnected from parties and think there's no difference between the parties, despite our rhetoric being different," said Royal Masset, a consultant and former political director of the Texas Republican Party.[3]

Real, nonrhetorical differences do exist between the Democratic Party and the Republican Party. Without dwelling too much on specific points, this chapter explains the role of parties in American politics. It looks at how parties, including minor, or third, parties, have evolved; how parties function at the state and local levels; and how their influence differs from state to state. In addition, it takes a look at **interest groups**—individuals, corporations, or associations that seek to influence the actions of elected and appointed public officials on behalf of specific companies or causes.

Political parties are not as dominant in American life as they once were. From roughly the 1820s until the 1940s, parties were a prime organizing force in this country. They not only provided citizens with a political identity but also were a major source of social activity and entertainment—and, in many cases, jobs. Today, parties are not as effective at getting people out to vote or even at organizing them around an issue. However, they do remain important to candidates as a kind of "brand name" identification and as fund-raisers.

Although there are two major national parties, they play larger roles at the state level than they do as national forces. Their respective strength varies widely from state to state and is affected by such factors as the different ways states regulate parties, the differences in the historical roles that parties played within each state, and the amount of competition between the major parties within a given state. In general, the more closely balanced the two main parties are in a state, the more likely that they will have well-funded and well-organized party organizations.

A Primer on Political Parties

Political parties recruit candidates for offices and provide them with support for their campaigns. They give candidates money or help them to raise it and offer logistical and strategic assistance. Just as important, they help coordinate a candidate's message with those of other candidates running for other offices under the party's banner.

Since the 1850s, the vast majority of candidates have run as members of either the Democratic or the Republican Party. Democrats as we know them today evolved from **factional splits** in the earliest days of the American republic. The country started without a two-party system, but factions soon developed. The Federalists, led by Alexander Hamilton, favored a strong central government with power rooted in the industrial North. The Democratic Republicans, led by Thomas Jefferson, emerged as the party opposing the Federalists. They argued for states' rights against a "monarchical" rule by the aristocracy and declared that farmers, craftspeople, and shopkeepers should control their own interests without interference from the capitol.

Jefferson's party, which eventually morphed into the Democratic Party, dominated politics throughout the first half of the nineteenth century. That same time period saw the creation of numerous parties: Whigs, Know-Nothings, Barnburners, Softshells, Hunkers, and Free Soilers. They all had

INTEREST GROUPS

Individuals, corporations, or associations that seek to influence the actions of elected and appointed public officials on behalf of specific companies or causes.

FACTIONAL SPLITS, OR FACTIONS

Groups that struggle to control the message within a party; for example, a party may be split into competing regional factions.

some success, but the Democratic Party of Jefferson and Andrew Jackson dominated so completely that, as the main source of political power, the party split into factions, with northern and southern Democrats arguing over the expansion of slavery. That argument created an opening for a new major party.

The Republican Party was formed in 1854 in opposition to slavery. It soon replaced the Whig Party, which had been formed in 1834 to protest the spoils system politics of Andrew Jackson. The Republican Party, also known as the Grand Old Party (GOP), quickly enjoyed congressional success. Following the election of Abraham Lincoln in 1860, Republicans dominated the presidency for decades to come. Their antislavery stance, however, guaranteed that they were practically nonexistent in the South until the civil rights era of the 1950s and 1960s. Democrats reemerged as the nation's dominant party in the 1930s, when Republicans were forced to take the blame for the Great Depression. The Democrats' New Deal coalition of Southerners, union workers, African Americans, the poor, and the elderly drove American politics well into the 1960s but fragmented after that, resulting in a loss of political control.

Since then, long-standing Democratic majorities at the congressional and state levels have eroded (the party's majorities following the 2008 elections still do not match those of forty years ago), whereas Republicans have held the presidency for most of the past forty years. In 2002, Republicans gained a majority of seats in state legislatures for the first time in fifty years—but their majorities were not overwhelming and were soon lost to the Democrats. Democrat Al Gore won a plurality of the presidential vote in 2000, even as he lost the electoral college vote to Republican George W. Bush. But in 2004 Bush became the first presidential candidate since 1988 to win a majority—51 percent—of the popular vote. Barack Obama repeated this feat in 2008, winning 53 percent of the vote. The narrow margins of presidential victories suggest that, at least at the national level, the two major political parties have spent a decade at roughly equal strength.

It is no secret that contemporary politics is highly competitive. Neither side enjoys a consistent advantage nationally. Candidates from either party are capable of winning statewide offices in nearly every state. Overall support for the parties is, however, split along regional lines. Democrats enjoy more support along the West Coast and in the Northeast, whereas Republicans are dominant in the South and the Plains states. The Upper Midwest and parts of the Mountain West have become the most competitive regions. (Ironically, for a party created to oppose slavery, today the GOP's greatest support is from those areas where slavery once was legal.)

While people are familiar with the Republican and Democratic parties, political parties actually take many different shapes. When people refer to Democrats or Republicans, they are really referring to officials belonging to two umbrella groups that cover a wide variety of parties. Each of the national parties is in reality a consortium of state parties. Party chairs and other representatives from the state parties dominate the national party committees. State parties, in turn, are consortiums of local parties. In some states, local parties are defined by counties. In others, they are defined by congressional districts. Although both the Democratic and Republican parties are active in every state, some state and local parties are more active than others. Parties in densely populated states such as Florida and California are well-funded, professionally run organizations. In less-populated states such as Montana or Idaho, the parties have very small full-time staffs and take on more help just during the few months leading up to an election.

Particular states may have particular dominant political parties, but overall, most other Western-style democracies have much stronger political parties than those in the United States. For example, in the United States, party leaders are not able to nominate candidates of their own choosing. Most candidates are now chosen directly by the voting public through primaries. In fact, even a party's top nominee—its presidential candidate—may not have been the first choice of party leaders. This is much different than is the case in, say, Great Britain. There, political parties are much more centralized. Leadership within the party translates more cleanly into leadership in government. The party, not voters, selects the party's nominee for prime minister.

Here, the national Republican and Democratic parties essentially are made up of state parties. The Republican National Committee, for instance, is made up almost exclusively of state party chairs and one male and one female representative from each state. Representatives from the territories—Puerto Rico, Guam, and the U.S. Virgin Islands, among others—form the rest of the body. U.S. political parties tend to be regulated at the state level. The ways in which they raise and spend money, their organizational structures, and the rules they follow to nominate candidates and place them on ballots all are subject to differing state regulations. How much power the national parties have in relation to the state party shifts over time, as we will see.

That is not to say that parties are not collections of interests. They are conglomerations of people who share some overlapping ideology, or set of political, economic, and social beliefs. These days, Democrats are supported by pro-choice groups and gun control advocates. Environmentalists, trial lawyers, labor union members, and African Americans also tend to be Democrats. Republicans gain support from corporate and small businesses and social conservatives. Party members tend to advocate respect for private property and protection of rights for gun owners. Republicans are also more likely to regularly attend church than are Democrats. These differences, however, are far from absolute. For many people, partisanship represents a

> For many people, partisanship represents a psychological attachment to a political party—a sort of brand loyalty—rather than a rational assessment of personal beliefs and party stance.

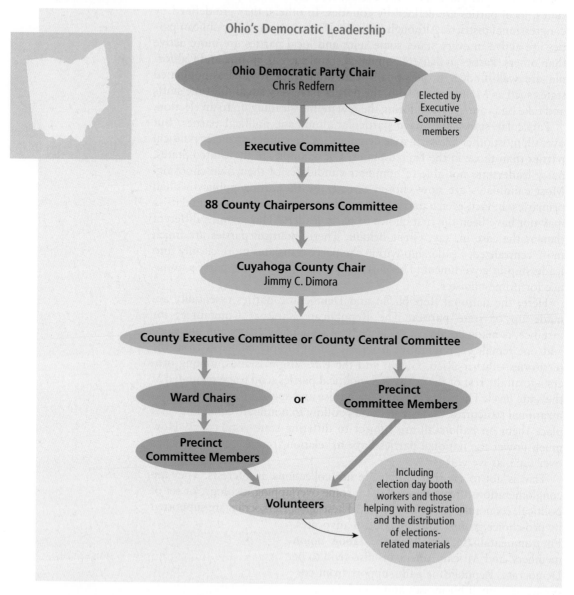

Ohio's Democratic Leadership

Ohio Democratic Party Chair
Chris Redfern

Elected by Executive Committee members

Executive Committee

88 County Chairpersons Committee

Cuyahoga County Chair
Jimmy C. Dimora

County Executive Committee or County Central Committee

Ward Chairs — or — **Precinct Committee Members**

Precinct Committee Members

Volunteers

Including election day booth workers and those helping with registration and the distribution of elections-related materials

psychological attachment to a political party—a sort of brand loyalty—rather than a rational assessment of personal beliefs and party stance.

After Ronald Reagan and other Republicans chipped into Democratic support among certain groups in the New Deal coalition, the Democrats became a famously argumentative group, with various factions within the

FIGURE 6-1, continued

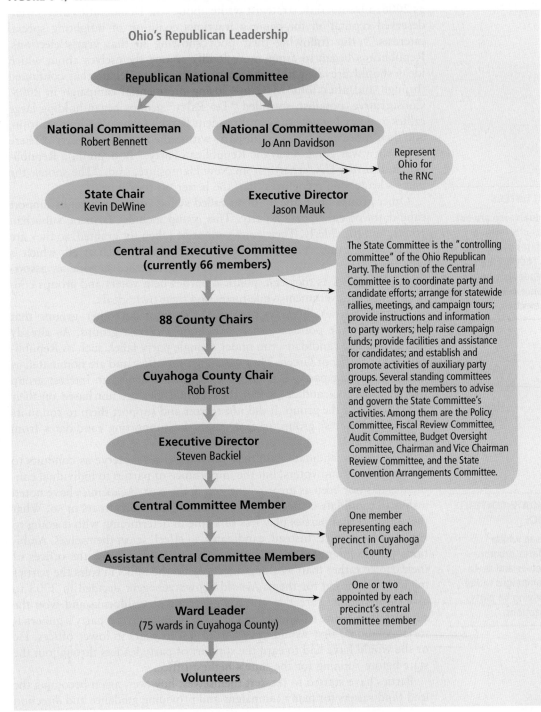

Ohio's Republican Leadership

Republican National Committee

National Committeeman
Robert Bennett

National Committeewoman
Jo Ann Davidson

Represent Ohio for the RNC

State Chair
Kevin DeWine

Executive Director
Jason Mauk

Central and Executive Committee
(currently 66 members)

The State Committee is the "controlling committee" of the Ohio Republican Party. The function of the Central Committee is to coordinate party and candidate efforts; arrange for statewide rallies, meetings, and campaign tours; provide instructions and information to party workers; help raise campaign funds; provide facilities and assistance for candidates; and establish and promote activities of auxiliary party groups. Several standing committees are elected by the members to advise and govern the State Committee's activities. Among them are the Policy Committee, Fiscal Review Committee, Audit Committee, Budget Oversight Committee, Chairman and Vice Chairman Review Committee, and the State Convention Arrangements Committee.

88 County Chairs

Cuyahoga County Chair
Rob Frost

Executive Director
Steven Backiel

Central Committee Member

One member representing each precinct in Cuyahoga County

Assistant Central Committee Members

One or two appointed by each precinct's central committee member

Ward Leader
(75 wards in Cuyahoga County)

Volunteers

party finding it hard to find a common cause with one another. As recently as 2006, a Democratic strategist wrote about "the Democratic Party's well-deserved reputation for being a fractious coalition of infighting special interests."[4] But following their poor showing in that year's elections, Republicans began to argue more loudly among themselves about which ideas should prevail within the party—a fractious debate that continued through and after John McCain's losing presidential campaign in 2008. Conservative, populist, so-called "Tea Party" groups began holding large rallies to decry big government, President Barack Obama's administration, and their more moderate counterparts within the Republican Party. "There is clearly a war going on in the Republican Party," Bob Smith, a Republican and former U.S. senator from New Hampshire, said. "The sooner the party's leadership recognizes that, the better off they'll be."[5]

Other groups are made up of so-called **swing voters** who might support candidates of either major party. This group includes farmers, suburban voters, and the elderly. Their votes cannot be taken for granted, so they are highly sought after. Young people tend not to vote much at all, which is why their concerns often are ignored. Pulling together as wide an assortment of interests as they can, political parties help voters and groups connect with the government while furthering their own ideals.

Political parties, however, remain different from other groups that participate in the political process, including interest groups. As already noted, political candidates run under a single party label, such as Republican, Democratic, or Green. They campaign for office and are nominated as members of that party. In contrast to political parties, an interest group may support the candidates, but their candidacies are not based on their affiliation with the group. It did not recruit and support them to run in its name. The interest group, in fact, might be supporting candidates from several parties.

These same candidates still may rely on parties to serve as conduits to interest groups and voters, but the importance of parties to individual candidates has not been as great recently as in the past. Academics have noted a shift to **candidate-centered politics** over the past thirty years or so. What they mean is that parties play less of a role in determining who is going to run for which office. Instead, candidates, in effect, select themselves. Ambitious people interested in politics and government run for the offices of their choice rather than working their way up the ranks in roles the parties might have chosen for them. Arnold Schwarzenegger decided in 2003 to give up his acting career to run for governor of California and won the support of the state's Republican Party. In the old days, a party's gubernatorial candidate first would have had to put in years in lower offices. He or she would have had to earn the support of party leaders throughout the state before running for the state's highest office.

Parties have started to reassert themselves, however, again becoming the lead fund-raisers for many campaigns and providing guidance and direction

SWING VOTERS

Individuals who are not consistently loyal to candidates of any one party. They are true independents whose allegiance is fought for in every election.

CANDIDATE-CENTERED POLITICS

Politics in which candidates promote themselves and their own campaigns rather than relying on party organizations.

to candidates in the most contested races. During the 2006 campaign, in which Democrats believed they had a shot at taking control of the Michigan state Senate (they failed), their chief strategist sent legislative aides to run campaigns in several close races. Ken Brock, chief of staff to the Michigan Democratic Senate Campaign committee, paid homage to the idea that candidates with a good feel for local issues were crucial. But he was equally interested in "educating our candidates" about the resources, messages, and tactics he believed would work for them. Lansing strategists provided the list of voters that candidates should try to contact. Brock summed up his reasoning: "The way I see it is that they're all highly competent people, but they haven't had the experience of running in an expensive, marginal contest."[6]

Parties are also a primary mechanism for the organization of government. Except for Nebraska, which is nonpartisan, all other state legislatures are organized by party. If the Democrats have a majority of the seats in the Maine House of Representatives, for example, the Speaker and other top leaders will be Democrats and the party will control each committee as well. Not everyone supports this system. George Norris, a U.S. senator from Nebraska who promoted many changes to his home state's political system during the 1930s, argued that state politicians should be nonpartisan. That way, he claimed, they would be judged on their records dealing with issues at home rather than on the question of whether they adhered to positions taken by national parties.

Some things have changed, however. Once the dominant force in U.S. politics—deciding who would run for which office and with how much support—today's political parties are such loose conglomerations of differing interests that they might be better described as marketing organizations. They are brand names that individual candidates choose to apply as a shortcut to identification in the marketplace. For example, to say that you are a Democratic candidate provides voters with a fairly reliable indication that you are for abortion rights legislation. Republicans—those who run for office, if not all rank-and-file party members—nearly always feel the opposite. In other areas, however, such as crime, welfare, and some trade issues, the distinction between party officials is less clear.

Given the overall decline of strong **voter identification** with either major party, today's politics generally centers more around individual candidates than around party politics. Parties have found a new role as support organs. They offer consulting and fund-raising services to self-selected aspirants. They have become "basically what you might call holding companies," says Walter Dean Burnham, a former political science professor at the University of Texas. "They organize cash and spread it around."[7] But now parties are being forced to adapt to legal restrictions on those functions as well. A federal campaign finance law passed by Congress in 2002 and upheld by the Supreme Court in 2003 makes it more complicated for parties to spend money on activities designed to register voters or encourage them to vote. (The Supreme Court reaffirmed the law's

VOTER IDENTIFICATION

When a voter consistently identifies strongly with one of the parties and can be considered, for example, a Democrat or Republican.

constitutionality in 2007.) Although parties still play important roles, often candidates are raising their own money, producing their own TV ads, and creating their own campaign organizations.

This does not mean political parties have become any less important to state and local politics. What they do and how they do it has changed considerably, but democratic politics—and this certainly includes politics in states and localities—is virtually unthinkable without political parties. As a theoretical ideal, or baseline, political scientists use the **responsible party model** as a way to measure and assess political parties. The responsible party model holds that political parties should present clear policy options to voters, that voters will cast ballots based on the options they favor the most, that while in office parties try to create and implement the programs they promise, and that in the next election the parties will be judged by their performance in delivering these programs. In short, this model views political parties as connecting the wishes of citizens to government programs and policies, organizing the government to deliver on those wishes, and acting as the agents used to hold government accountable for delivering on what it promises. These are all highly valuable services to democratic politics, and despite all their changes, political parties have always served these roles, and still do.

Of course, how well parties serve these functions varies from state to state. To have some semblance of a responsible party model, you need at least two competitive political parties offering voters clear choices on policies and programs. You also need parties that actually try to deliver on these policies and programs once they secure a controlling influence in government. Finally, you need voters who pay attention to what the party in power is doing and vote accordingly. States where only one party is competitive at the polls or where there is consistently low voter turnout are less likely to fulfill the promises of the responsible party model.

What Parties Were Like

In their early years, political parties in the United States were a lot more than just brand identifiers and fund-raisers. Many of the social services now provided by local governments, such as food assistance and job placement services, were the province of political parties throughout much of the nineteenth century. For all of the contemporary complaints about the "liberal media," one-sided bloggers, and the domination of talk radio by conservative hosts, today's nonpartisan media are a far cry from the newspapers of the late nineteenth century, which were often openly affiliated with a particular party. The pro-Republican *Chicago Tribune,* on learning that a Democrat had won the 1876 presidential election, ran a headline that read, "Lost. The Country Given Over to Democratic Greed and Plunder."[8] Such an openly partisan statement is unimaginable in the mainstream media of today, although not as unlikely on blogs.

RESPONSIBLE PARTY MODEL

The theory that political parties offer clear policy choices to voters, try to deliver on those policies when they take office, and are held accountable by voters for the success or failure of those policies.

People's party loyalties were so strong because so many of their livelihoods revolved around party interests. Party machines doled out jobs, government contracts, and other benefits to their workers and supporters. The idea was that "offices exist not as a necessary means of administering government but for the support of party leaders at public expense," as one political scientist writes of nineteenth-century party cliques in New York State.[9]

Politics in many cities and some states was totally dominated by these usually indigenous party machines. In Rhode Island, the Democratic Party was dominant through much of the twentieth century, and party leaders accepted little dissent. Only a handful of free-agent candidates were able to pry nominations away from those who had been endorsed by the party. In Providence, the state capital and largest city, only three individuals held the office of mayor from 1941 until 1974. Two of those men were state Democratic Party leaders. Over the same thirty-year period, only two chairs headed the Providence Democratic Party. Both of them doubled as head of the city's Department of Public Works. Party leaders controlled 2,800 jobs, doling them out roughly equally among the various wards, or political districts, within the city.[10]

The close links connecting control of jobs, government spending, and party activity were hardly unique to Rhode Island. Chicago; Nassau County on Long Island, New York; and Pennsylvania were all home to legendary **political machines**, which were also called party machines. A long-standing joke about Chicago politics held that, because they were kept on election rolls, as many dead people voted as living ones. In Oklahoma, the state gave control of most government jobs—the decision-making power over hiring and firing workers—to individual officeholders. These individuals were not afraid to exploit such control for their own benefit. "I have 85 employees—garage men, road workers, janitors, elevator operators—and they work for me when I need them," said a county commissioner. "These people care if I stay in office."[11]

The machine system was self-perpetuating, with control of jobs and power and offices feeding off one another. "Each succeeding election was viewed not as a separate contest involving new issues or new personalities," writes political scientist Joel Sibley, "but as yet another opportunity to vote for, and reaffirm, an individual's support for his or her party and what it represented."[12] Party machines and rival factions ran "slates," or specific lists, of endorsed candidates for offices and lent their backing to the favored candidates. Sometimes this support came at a price. For instance, contenders for the West Virginia General Assembly once had to pay between $250 and $400 for the honor of being listed on one of the various slates in Kanawha County, in which the state capital of Charleston is located.

POLITICAL MACHINES

Political organizations controlled by a small number of people and run for partisan ends; they controlled party nominations for public office and rewarded supporters with government jobs and contracts.

"I have 85 employees—garage men, road workers, janitors, elevator operators—and they work for me when I need them," said a county commissioner. "These people care if I stay in office."

CIVIL SERVICE REFORM.

OFFICE-SEEKER. "St. Jackson, can't you save us? Can't *you* give us something?"

"To the victor belong the spoils." President Andrew Jackson popularized patronage, insisting that public offices should be filled by supporters.

Given party contacts and contracts with private-sector entities, party control of jobs often extended well beyond the borders of government. Sometimes—as was the case in Jersey City, New Jersey—the machines would charge an automatic kickback of, say, 3 percent of public employee salaries. Such trimmings were not always enough to satisfy machine leaders. Clear cases of corruption, such as extorting union funds, running gambling operations, and taking kickbacks on government contracts, often led to the election of reform candidates for mayor and other city and state offices.

There were other backlashes against such obvious corruption. In New Orleans, a Democratic Party political machine called the Old Regulars ruled the city from the 1890s until the mid-1930s. By then, they were the only political force left in Louisiana outside the control of the Populist governor, Huey Long. In 1934 and 1935, Long concentrated all of his powers on changing the machine's management. He limited local control over jobs and triggered a police investigation. He even sent the National Guard into New Orleans. In the end, the machine had no choice but to accept a new city leader and get on board the Long bandwagon.[13]

Breaking up the machines usually took less extreme effort. For one thing, in many states, such as Alabama, Florida, and Michigan, there was little **patronage**—the ability of elected officials or party leaders to hand out jobs to their friends and supporters rather than hiring people based on qualifications. Therefore, there was little motivation to build up a machine. In some places, like Texas, nineteenth-century political parties were weak. They helped administer the election code and tried to remain acceptable to all candidates. In other places, disgust over corruption in politics led to antimachine statutes, such as the imposition of civil service requirements on many government jobs and tougher anticorruption laws. The widespread use of **nonpartisan ballots** for municipal offices is the direct result

PATRONAGE

The ability of elected officials or party leaders to hand out jobs to their friends and supporters rather than hiring people based on merit.

NONPARTISAN BALLOTS

Ballots that do not list candidates by political party; still often used in local elections.

of reforms imposed in reaction to political machines. These ballots, which do not list candidates by political party, are designed to separate city government from party voting.

California may be the best example of a state that had such a progressive reaction against the machines. The state was hostile toward parties, lacked any type of patronage system, and held nonpartisan elections. Precinct and ward organizations were weak, whereas individual candidates were assertive.[14] Party organizations were once banned from endorsing candidates in primary contests. The law also limited state party chairs to two-year terms and required the rotation of chairs on a geographical basis every two years. In 1989, the U.S. Supreme Court threw out the statute and declared it unconstitutional.[15]

But California was the exception to the rule. Throughout the 1800s, most states essentially treated parties as private associations and chose not to regulate them. This remains the position of many other countries today. But, during the twentieth century, that all changed in the United States. States began to regulate parties as though they were public utilities. Such state regulation of political parties is examined later in this chapter.

Parties in the Twentieth Century

At the dawn of the twentieth century, political machines were generally locally based, and local parties were much more important political actors than state parties in states where there were powerful big-city machines. Elsewhere, state parties often were funded and controlled by corporate interests—in many cases by just one interest, such as the DuPont Corporation in Delaware or the Anaconda Copper Company in Montana. Following the Progressive Era reforms in states such as California, state parties became little more than empty shells. As late as the 1970s, many state parties lacked permanent headquarters and were run out of their chairs' homes.[16]

State parties lost much of their influence because of the rise of **primary elections**. Primary elections are used to select candidates who will represent the party in **general elections,** the contest between party nominees to decide which candidate will actually be elected to political office. Rather than through primary elections, which are decided by rank-and-file voters, parties used to pick their nominees through **party conventions,** meetings of a few hundred party officials or supporters. At conventions, party leaders closely controlled most votes and thus had enormous influence over who would or would not become the party's official nominee in the general election. This influence is lost in a primary election; in a primary, the general public has a chance to cast a secret ballot. This gives party officials less direct control over the nominating process. Some states, such as Virginia, still allow for the option of nominating candidates by party conventions, but every state now has a system in place to nominate candidates through primaries. Every party holds a statewide convention, and

PRIMARY ELECTIONS
Elections that determine a party's nominees for offices in general elections against other parties' nominees. Participation in primary elections is sometimes limited to voters registered as members of that particular party.

GENERAL ELECTIONS
The decisive elections in which all registered voters cast ballots for their preferred candidates for a political office.

PARTY CONVENTIONS
Meetings of party delegates called to nominate candidates for office and establish party agendas.

many hold conventions at the local or district level as well. Nowadays, practically anyone who cares to attend a state or local convention can do so. But it still takes some effort or connections to attend a national party convention, especially as a voting delegate.

Direct primaries allow rank-and-file voters to choose nominees for public office through means of a direct ballot. This contrasts with the convention system, in which the role of voters is indirect—voters choose delegates to a convention, and the delegates choose the nominee. At the state level, there are three basic types of direct primaries. **Closed primaries** allow only registered party members to vote in the party's primary, meaning that you must be a registered Democrat to vote for the Democratic nominee for office or a registered Republican to vote for the Republican nominee. This type of primary helps prevent **crossover voting**, in which a member of one party votes in another party's primary (a Democrat voting in a Republican primary, for instance). This practice is not allowed in all states. **Open primaries** allow independents—and in some cases members of both parties—to vote in any primary they choose. Blanket primaries, invalidated in 2000 in the Supreme Court case *California Democratic Party v. Jones*, listed all candidates from all parties on a single ballot and allowed voters in effect to mix and match which primary they participate in. Voters could vote in one party's primary for a particular office, then switch to another party's primary for another office. Louisiana is the only state that retains some elements of a blanket primary. This is essentially a nonpartisan blanket primary—sometimes called a jungle primary—in which all candidates run in the same primary regardless of party. If no candidate wins an outright majority in the primary, the two top vote-getters—regardless of party—go on to a general election face-off. A **runoff primary** sometimes occurs in some states if no candidate receives a majority of the vote. In that case, the top two candidates face off. Map 6-1 shows the state-by-state breakdown of the main types of primaries.

The opposite of the relative openness of primaries is the "smoke-filled room"—an area at a convention that is closed off to the public and in which party barons, some puffing on big cigars, choose a candidate of their liking. It is one of the classic images in American politics. Examples of such cronyism abound. At the 1912 Republican national convention, President William Howard Taft had to stave off a challenge from his predecessor, Theodore Roosevelt. Roosevelt had been able to demonstrate his popularity among the party's rank-and-file by winning every primary that year, save the Massachusetts primary. At the time, however, only a dozen states even held primaries. Taft retained the support of the national party machinery and dominated delegate selection in the nonprimary states. Ultimately, he controlled the convention. Taft was renominated, but he was not reelected. Roosevelt bolted the party, angrily maintaining that Taft's nomination thwarted the will of the "honestly elected majority" of GOP delegates. The split within Republican ranks was enough to allow the

MAP 6-1 Party Affiliation Requirements for Voting in Direct Primaries

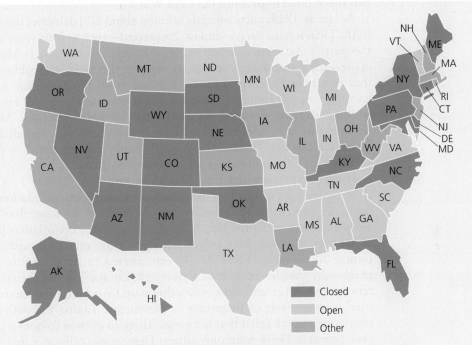

Source: "Primaries: Open and Closed," The Center for Voting and Democracy, February 2008. www.fairvote.org?page=1801.

Notes:

Alaska: Closed caucuses for both parties, but voters may change party affiliation at polls or caucus.

California: Parties may allow voters who decline to state their party affiliation to participate in their primaries. Democrats currently allow registered Democrats and independents to vote in their primary. Republicans currently have a closed primary.

Idaho: Democrats have an open caucus in Idaho, while the Republicans have an open primary.

Illinois: Must vote in primary of same party as last primary the voter participated in. Loosely enforced. Voters may change party affiliation at polls or caucus.

Iowa: Closed caucuses, but voters may change registration at polls.

Kansas: In the Democratic caucus, independent voters can register as Democrat on caucus day. For Republicans it is a closed caucus.

Louisiana: Primaries are closed for presidential elections. For congressional elections, they are effectively open, because Louisiana currently uses a top-two runoff system. They switched to a closed primary used for Congressional races after 2006.

Maryland: Parties can choose to open primaries but both Democrats and Republicans have chosen not to. If a voter does not choose a party, he or she will be recorded as "unaffiliated" and is permitted to vote in any nonpartisan primary in his or her local jurisdiction.

Massachusetts: Registered Democrats and Republicans can only vote for their own party in the primary but independent voters may decide which party they would like to vote for.

Montana: Republicans have a closed caucus, while Democrats have an open primary.

New Hampshire: Registered Democrats and Republicans can only vote for their own party in the primary but independent voters may decide which party they would like to vote for. Unregistered voters can register on election day.

New Jersey: Registered Democrats and Republicans can only vote for their own party in the primary. Any New Jersey voter who has never on a previous occasion voted in a New Jersey primary election may declare a party affiliation at the poll. Independents may also decide which party to vote for.

North Carolina: If registered with a party, you must vote in that party's primary. If unaffiliated, you may choose a party on the day of the primary election.

North Dakota: North Dakota has no voter registration. Voters must only have to prove that they have been a resident for at least 30 days.

Ohio: Must vote in primary of same party as the voter participated in last primary election.

Rhode Island: If voters are registered as "unaffiliated" they may vote in the primary of any party they choose. Once they vote in a primary, however, they are considered a member of that party until and unless they "disaffiliate."

Utah: Currently only Republicans close their primary. Democrats and independents can vote in the Democratic primary. Conventions are held by the political parties prior to the primary.

Virginia: Parties may choose to nominate by convention rather than by primary election.

West Virginia: Republicans have a closed convention while Democrats will hold a primary where unaffiliated voters and independents may participate.

election of Woodrow Wilson, only the second Democrat at that point to win the White House since the Civil War.[17]

As late as 1968, party officials selected about 600 delegates out of 2,600 to the Democratic Party—almost 25 percent—two to four years ahead of the party's national convention. Sen. Eugene McCarthy, D-Minn., had made such a surprisingly strong showing in the New Hampshire primary that he drove President Lyndon Johnson from the race. But Johnson's backing was still enough to help his vice president, Hubert H. Humphrey, win the support of delegates controlled by party officials. McCarthy believed the party rules had cheated him, so he proposed that all delegates be chosen through "procedures open to public participation" in the same year in which the nominating convention took place.[18]

Humphrey recognized that McCarthy and Sen. Robert F. Kennedy, D-N.Y., both of whom had campaigned on anti-Vietnam platforms, had taken 69 percent of the primary vote. Respectful of what that number meant, he wanted to reward their followers with a consolation prize. So Humphrey coupled McCarthy's changes with one proposed by Sen. George McGovern, D-S.D. McGovern wanted to see delegations demographically match—or at least reflect—the composition of the states they represented. More and more states threw up their figurative hands as they tried to meet each of these new requirements. Taking the path of least resistance, they decided that the easiest thing to do was to hold a popular-vote primary. There were only fifteen Democratic primaries in 1968, but by 1980 there were thirty-five. Conventions were reduced to little more than coronation ceremonies.[19]

How State Parties Recovered: Campaign Reform in the Late Twentieth Century

There aren't many smoke-filled rooms at conventions anymore—and not just because of health concerns. Candidates already have been selected by voters through primary elections at that point. Yet conventions are still important networking occasions for officeholders and activists; they also provide occasions for parties to change their internal rules. The action for candidates now is in the primary and general election seasons. This is when they have the chance to woo voters directly, if not personally. Candidates no longer need hierarchical machines to reach voters. The decline of party machines was followed in time by the advent of televised campaign commercials as the dominant mode for trying to persuade citizens to vote.

The increasing reliance on campaign ads, ironically, has led to restored strength for state and national political parties and has spelled the decline of local party strength in federal elections. The move from greeting potential voters in person at party dinners and county fairs to airing TV ads has meant that politicians have had to run more professional campaigns. They hire pollsters to figure out which issues will resonate best in their ads.

Consultants help shape their message on these issues, and media gurus produce the ads and place them during favorable time slots. Once more changing with the times, state parties became important clearinghouses in connecting candidates with consultants. Eventually, they evolved into important consulting organizations themselves.

Every Democratic and Republican state party now has a full-time chair or executive director. Most have other professional staffers as well, who handle fund-raising, communications, field operations, and campaigns.[20] In general, Republican state parties tend to be better funded and, therefore, better run. Democratic state parties, however, often gain equivalent support from their allied groups, such as public-sector unions.

With their massive computer databases, maintained and updated from year to year, political parties help candidates target and reach voters who are sympathetic to their messages. Parties also play an important role in helping interested groups and potential contributors determine which of the party's candidates have a realistic shot at winning. The major parties are not the voter organizers they were in the machine days, when individuals were encouraged to vote "early and often." Parties, however, do still contact up to 25 percent of the electorate in any election cycle. Individuals contacted by parties have a much higher tendency to vote than people who are not contacted, possibly because they feel like the party thinks their votes matter and that's why they were called, or maybe just due to the helpful reminder. While the national parties typically play a greater role in polling and developing issues, "local and state parties [are] particularly important for registering voters and conducting get out the vote campaigns."[21]

One state chair in the 1950s exemplified the move that parties made toward professionalized consulting services. Ray Bliss took over the Ohio Republican Party after it suffered an electoral drubbing in 1948. He immediately began to identify and recruit better candidates. He also looked at ways to encourage citizens to vote, noting that, in 1948, 140,000 rural Republicans did not vote and 150,000 potential Republican voters in urban areas were not even registered. Following Bliss's registration and get-out-the-vote drives, Ohio Republicans in 1950 reelected a U.S. senator, won three statewide offices, and regained control of the state legislature.[22]

For years, Republicans in Ohio were so dominant that they controlled every statewide office and both chambers of the state legislature. The Democratic candidate for state attorney general in 2002 tried to turn this hegemony into a campaign issue, complaining, "What has happened in Ohio is that in many ways we have turned government over to the business community with this one-party rule."[23] That kind of complaint became more salient in 2006, when a series of scandals involving GOP officials and their cronies led to the election of a Democratic governor for the first time in twenty years.

Minority party members enviously keep close tabs on the governing party, and they alert the public and the press to every perceived misstep and abuse. It also is important for minority parties not to get demoralized and to continue to offer voters alternatives, so that candidates from their parties will be in place once the public is ready for a change. For instance, conservative Republicans dominated the Arizona Senate during the late 1990s. It seemed certain that Arizona Speaker of the House Jeff Groscost would join their ranks in 2000 because he was running in a Senate district that heavily favored the GOP. Late in the campaign season, however, Groscost was implicated in a scandal surrounding a massive tax break that aided sports utility vehicle (SUV) owners—including a Groscost friend who sold the vehicles—and cost the state hundreds of millions of dollars. Groscost was beat by his previously unknown Democratic challenger, and the Senate ended up operating under divided control between the parties.

DEALIGNMENT

When no one party can be said to dominate politics in this country.

REALIGNMENT

When popular support switches from one party to another.

Today, the two parties remain so closely competitive nationally that political scientists refer to a period of **dealignment**, meaning that neither party is dominant. In earlier periods of American history, one party or another generally had dominated politics, holding most of the important offices. The two major examples are Republican dominance from the time of the Civil War into the 1920s and the Democratic New Deal coalition, which held power from the presidential election of 1932 into the 1960s. The 1932 election of Franklin D. Roosevelt is the best example of a **realignment**, the switching of popular support from one party to another. Neither party has pulled off a similarly lasting realignment since then in that voters seem about equally supportive of both major parties. Indeed, Republican hopes of creating a "permanent majority" following Bush's 2004 win were dashed quickly when Democrats took control of the U.S. Congress in the 2006 midterm elections, followed by Barack Obama's win in the 2008 presidential election.

State Party Regulation and Finance

It is important to note that the parties, although they are most active during the campaign season, do not dry up and blow away once an election is over. Not only is there planning for the next election—and the one after that and the one after that, in perpetuity—but parties also play an important role in actual government operations. Granted, parties no longer are able to run government strictly to perpetuate their own power, as was true to a certain extent in the machine era. But they still help their most important supporters maintain access to officeholders and other officials.

The Nebraska state legislature is organized on a nonpartisan basis (like most municipal governments). Every other state legislature is organized by party. In other words, if the Democrats hold a majority of the seats in a state's house of representatives, they not only control the leadership, schedule, and agenda of the house, but other Democrats chair the house committees as well. There are exceptions and examples of shared power, particularly when partisan control of a legislature is tied, but these are rare. The more normal state of affairs is for the majority party to rule.

State Party Regulation

Remember that states did not regulate political parties until the beginning of the twentieth century, when the progressive backlash against machine abuse led states to intervene. Political scientists now refer to parties as equivalent to public utilities, such as water and electricity, in which the public has a sufficient interest to justify state regulation.[24] Political parties, after all, are the main conduit for contesting elections and organizing government. The legal justifications that states have used to regulate parties revolve around registration requirements—twenty-eight states and Washington, D.C., register voters by party[25]—because party names are printed alongside those of their candidates on ballots.

Thirty-eight states regulate aspects of the structure of their state and local parties, often in explicit detail, to avoid antidemocratic, machine-boss control.[26] A state sometimes determines, for instance, how the members of a state party's central committee should be selected and how often that committee will meet. It can specify which party organization can name a substitute candidate if a nominee dies or withdraws prior to an election. Such regulation is practiced whether it is in regard to a state party in Minnesota or a local party in Pennsylvania.

A relatively limited number of state parties have challenged the laws in their states in the wake of the 1989 Supreme Court decision, mentioned previously, in which the Court ruled that the state of California did not have the authority to dictate how political parties are organized. The major parties in New Jersey did adopt a number of changes in party structure, but for the most part the parties seem satisfied with the way things are being run under the systems imposed on them by the states.

Nineteen eighty-nine was neither the first time nor the last time the U.S. Supreme Court weighed in on the political party issue. The nation's highest court has issued a number of other decisions in recent years to clarify the legal rights of parties. In a series of cases emanating from Illinois during the 1970s and 1980s, the Court made it clear that "party affiliations and support" are unconstitutional bases for the granting of a majority of government or public jobs, except at the highest levels.[27] In 1986, it ruled that the state of Connecticut could not prevent independents from voting in Republican Party primaries if the GOP welcomed them.[28] This precedent, which allowed the parties rather than the state to determine who could participate in a party's primary, was later followed in several other states. The parties have not always gotten their way, however. In 1999, the Court determined that states have the constitutional right to regulate elections

A total of $6,380,093 was contributed to Hawaii's Democratic and Republican parties in 2008—with $4,505,950 of that going to Democrats.

and prevent manipulation. The ruling blocked a new party in Minnesota from "fusing" with the state's Democratic Party by nominating candidates for election that the Democrats already had nominated.[29]

Campaign Finance

In 1996, the U.S. Supreme Court lifted federal limits on how much parties could spend. Under the new rules, a party could spend as much as it liked to support a candidate, as long as the candidate did not approve the party's strategy or ads or have any say over what the party was doing. The Court decided that no one had the right to restrict **independent expenditures**, those activities that are run without the candidate's knowledge or approval. "We do not see how a Constitution that grants to individuals, candidates, and ordinary political committees the right to make unlimited independent expenditures could deny the same right to political parties," wrote Justice Stephen G. Breyer.[30] A decade later, the Court tossed out a Vermont law that sought to limit fund-raising and the amounts that could be spent by candidates on state campaigns.

In addition to this legal windfall, state parties already had been exempted from a number of federal campaign finance limits. In 1974 and 1976, Congress enacted laws that limited the amount of money candidates could collect from individuals and **political action committees** (PACs). Congress revised the law in 1979 after complaints from party leaders that the new laws almost completely eliminated state and local party organizations from participating in presidential campaigns. The old law, party leaders contended, put too many restrictions on how parties could spend money during a presidential election year. The revised law lifted all limits on what state and local parties could raise or spend for "party building" activities. These included purchasing campaign materials, such as buttons, bumper stickers, and yard signs, and conducting voter registration and get-out-the-vote drives.[31]

It quickly became clear that the more lax restrictions were broad enough to allow for the purchase of TV ads and other campaign-related activities with so-called **soft money** donations, which were nominally meant to support party building. Restrictions on how parties spent soft money, which was raised in increments of $100,000 and more from corporations, unions, and wealthy individuals, were nearly meaningless—as long as the parties did not coordinate directly with candidates. Parties violated the spirit, although not the letter of the law, with state parties acting as virtual soft money–laundering machines for the national parties and for each other. In 2002, Congress revisited the issue and enacted the McCain-Feingold campaign finance law, which blocked the national parties from collecting soft money donations.[32]

Meanwhile, the state parties themselves are no slouches at raising money, as Figure 6-2 shows. Democrats and Republicans at the state level

INDEPENDENT EXPENDITURES

Ad campaigns or other political activities that are run by a party or an outside group without the direct knowledge or approval of a particular candidate for office.

POLITICAL ACTION COMMITTEES

Groups formed for the purpose of raising money to elect or defeat political candidates. They usually represent business, union, or ideological interests.

SOFT MONEY

Money not subject to federal regulation that can be raised and spent by state parties. A 2002 law banned the use of soft money in federal elections.

A Difference That Makes a Difference: That Clean-All-Over Feeling: Maine's Public Financing of Campaigns

Many people believe politics is inherently corrupt. This belief is compounded by the fact that campaign funding comes from individuals, corporations, and unions with a direct interest in the policies and decisions that elected officials make once in office. For this reason, the public financing of campaigns has long held appeal for reformers. "I think it's a very freeing feeling," former Maine state representative Marilyn Canavan, who helped draft a public finance law as head of the state ethics commission, said in 2002. "It means I can make decisions that are right for the people of Maine, and not be concerned in the least whether any campaign contributions are forthcoming."[a]

Through a ballot initiative, Maine set up a voluntary system of public campaign finance for state legislative offices.[b] Anyone who wishes to pursue any state office is granted enough free money to run a credible campaign, as long as a sufficient number of $5 contributions are received upfront to show the candidate's serious intent. In 2008, more than 80 percent of Maine's candidates for the legislature renounced private funding in favor of taking the public money.[c]

But whether Maine has really succeeded in lessening the role of special interests in state politics is a more complicated question. Because there are no restrictions on what the parties can spend—even on behalf of publicly financed candidates—there are those who see the new law as likely to attract more special interest money, not less. Among those skeptics is a former Maine governor, Angus King. The so-called clean elections law, he says, "has a gigantic loophole that really bothers me. You're running as a clean candidate, but the party can spend a million dollars on your behalf. To me, that undermines the whole premise. What you've really done is add a layer of public money to the old system." As if to prove his point, legislative leaders in Maine—even some who initially opposed the clean elections law—have been building up political action committees that raise hundreds of thousands of dollars they can spend supporting candidates of their choice.

A number of other states have enacted partial public finance laws of one sort or another during the past three decades. Some have achieved modest success. Candidates in Minnesota, for instance, tend to abide by spending limits and receive some public financing in return. More commonly, however, public financing has been a failure and largely for one reason. The money available—usually from voluntary tax checkoffs, in which taxpayers designate a few dollars from their tax returns to be spent on campaign finance—is insufficient to pay for the campaigns it is supposed to cover. Wisconsin, for example, became a pioneer when it enacted a public financing law in the late 1970s. But spending limits in Wisconsin have not been raised since 1986, and participation in the voluntary tax checkoff has fallen to less than 10 percent. That means that the amount of public financing grants has dropped to the point where no serious legislative or gubernatorial candidates are willing to choose them instead of taking private contributions. In 2006, Gov. Jim Doyle raised more than $10 million for his winning bid; his challenger, who accepted public financing, was limited to about $1 million in funds.[d]

The more recently adopted laws, including Maine's, allow for inflationary adjustment, and the state has a small population and a low-key political system with a tradition of informal personal campaigning. A clean elections budget of $20,000 comes closer to full funding of a state Senate election in Maine than it would almost anywhere else in the country.

Still, the state's lobbyists and pressure groups are adapting to the law, changing the way they interact with candidates seeking office. Rather than treating candidates like charities, writing out checks and declaring themselves done, interest groups are recruiting candidates themselves and then running issue ads to support them. Such ads do not fall under the clean elections law limits. "People are changing strategies to do the same things they've always done," says Ed McLaughlin, president of the Maine Economic Research Institute. "I expect as time goes by and people get savvy about what they can and cannot do, you're going to see more money come into campaigns. I think part of the intent of the public in passing this law was to take money out of politics. It ain't gonna happen."

[a]Adapted from Alan Greenblatt, "That Clean All-Over Feeling," *Governing* magazine, July 2002, 40.

[b]Arizona has a similar system; five other states have limited programs.

[c]See Maine Commission on Governmental Ethics and Election Practices at www.mainecampaignfinance.com/public/home.asp for complete details of the Maine Clean Elections Act.

[d]Steven M. Levin, "Public Campaign Financing in Wisconsin: Showing Its Age," Center for Governmental Studies, August 2008, available at www.cgs.org/images/publications/cgs_wi_final_081808.pdf.

FIGURE 6-2 State Party Fund-raising over Time

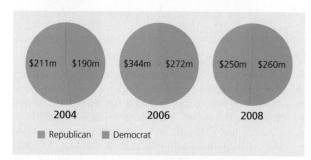

2004	2006	2008
$211m $190m	$344m $272m	$250m $260m

■ Republican ■ Democrat

Source: Data compiled from the National Institute for Money in State Politics, National Overview Maps 2000–2008, www.followthemoney.org/database/nationalview.phtml?l=0&f=P&y=2008&abbr=1.

raised more than $500 million during the 2008 election cycle—a slight dip because of the loss of federal party transfers under McCain-Feingold.[33] But no matter what limitations are placed on campaign finance, money finds its way into the system because the U.S. Supreme Court has held that political expenditures are equivalent to free speech. In January 2010, the Court ruled that political spending by corporations in candidate elections cannot be restricted, a finding that is at odds with the campaign finance laws of at least two dozen states. Says University of Virginia government professor Larry J. Sabato,

There is no way to stop the flow of interested money and there will always be constitutional ways around the restrictions enacted into law. What is so fundamental is that politics and government determine the allocation of goods and values in society. Those goods and values are critical to the success or failure of hundreds of interest groups and millions of individuals. Those groups and individuals are going to spend the money to defend their interests, period.[34]

Party Competition: Why Some States Are More Competitive than Others

The Republican Party came out of the 2002 elections with control over many of the nation's political institutions. Republicans held the White House and the U.S. House of Representatives, and they regained control of the Senate. They defied predictions and held on to a majority of governorships. For the first time since 1952, the party came out ahead in the total number of state legislative seats. Yet their victories did not represent political breakthroughs that they could necessarily bank on. All the Republican majorities were quite narrow, reflecting the level of parity between the two major parties that has kept both of them from firm political dominance for a decade.

Just how narrow were some of the margins? Republicans had only two more governorships than the Democrats. Both congressional chambers were nearly tied; following the 2002 elections, Republicans held 49.6 percent of the nation's 7,400 legislative seats, whereas Democrats trailed just slightly with 49.4 percent of the seats. Republicans held a slight edge in the number of state chambers and legislatures they controlled, but the margins often were slim. In fact, a vacancy in any of a dozen legislative chambers could have resulted in a change of party control.[35] Things got even tighter after the 2004 elections, when the two parties ended up essentially tied in the total number of seats they controlled nationwide.

In 2006, Democrats not only regained control of Congress but made impressive gains at the state level as well. Following that year's elections, Democrats held twenty-eight of the fifty state governorships—their first majority in a dozen years. In addition, Democrats emerged with a 660-seat advantage in state legislative seats. By 2008, Democrats controlled both legislative chambers in twenty-seven states, compared to the Republicans' fourteen. That year, the party didn't win legislative races in only the states where Democrats traditionally dominate; it ran up its margins in states where Republicans only recently had controlled at least one house, such as Minnesota and Oregon.[36]

Historically, most state political cultures have heavily favored one party or the other, as shown in Map 6-2. A well-known example of this is the old Democratic "Solid South." For more than a century, most Southern voters were "yellow dog" Democrats, meaning they would sooner vote

MAP 6-2 Interparty Competition, 2003–2006

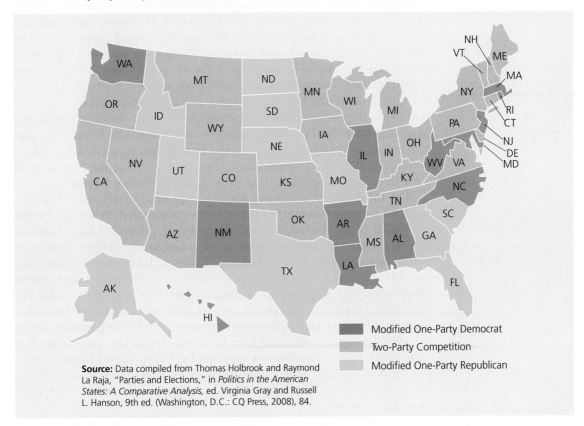

Source: Data compiled from Thomas Holbrook and Raymond La Raja, "Parties and Elections," in *Politics in the American States: A Comparative Analysis,* ed. Virginia Gray and Russell L. Hanson, 9th ed. (Washington, D.C.: CQ Press, 2008), 84.

for a yellow dog than for a Republican. From 1880 to 1944, all eleven states of the old Confederacy voted for Democrats in every presidential election—with a couple of exceptions in 1920 and 1928—elected only Democrats and a few independents governor, and elected only Democrats to the U.S. Senate after popular voting for senators began in 1916.[37] The Democratic hegemony in the South began to break up with the civil rights era that began, roughly, with the elections of 1948.

Today, both parties start out with a fair chance of winning statewide elections in just about every state. That is actually a big change. Republicans are now about even—or dominant—politically in the South, but they have lost their edge in the Northeast, which is now one of the more Democratic sections of the country. Republicans hold the advantage in many states of the Mountain West, but Democrats are stronger along the Pacific Coast. All this was perhaps most noticeable in the 2002 gubernatorial elections, when old party strangleholds finally broke. Georgia elected a Republican governor for the first time since 1868, ending the longest drought for either party in any state before or since. The GOP also took the governor's mansion in other states that had traditionally gone Democratic. These states included Maryland, which elected a Republican for the first time since 1966, and Hawaii, which chose the GOP for the first time since 1959. Democrats, meanwhile, won in Illinois, Maine, Michigan, and Wisconsin for the first time in well over a decade, and they seated governors in Arizona, Kansas, Oklahoma, and Wyoming—states that had been supporting mostly Republicans in recent years.[38] Of the twenty-four new governors elected in 2002, twenty wrested control from a governor of another party. In 2006, most of the Democratic gains at the gubernatorial level came in states that Republicans had left vacant due to term limits or retirement; Maryland governor Bob Ehrlich was the only incumbent Republican who was defeated. Voters elected governors in only two states in 2009, but in both cases, the party in residence at the governor's mansion flipped, with New Jersey and Virginia electing Republicans to replace Democrats.

Why the decline of one-party dominance in nearly every state? One factor is the increased mobility of the American population. In the past people put down roots and perpetuated the political culture of their families, whereas today the country's population is constantly shifting. The many Northeasterners who have moved into the South, for example, do not hold the same cultural memory of the Civil War that kept many conservatives from supporting Republicans. Immigrants to California have made the state more Democratic—Republicans politically misplayed their hand with California Hispanics by pushing an anti-immigrant ballot initiative during the 1990s (a pattern that may have been repeated at the national level in 2006 when House Republicans supported a bill to deport illegal aliens). But the departure of many conservative voters who moved to other Western states such as Nevada and Utah has made the Golden State more Democratic as well.

All of that said, there are still plenty of places that are dominated by a single party. Republicans currently control every statewide office in Texas and seized control of the legislature with the 2002 elections. That means that Democrats have less power in Texas now than they have had for more than a century. This, in turn, means that interest groups are more likely to support Republican candidates because they believe that members of that party will have more say in the function of state government. Once a party loses power, it is at a disadvantage in recovering power. Its traditional allies also will have a harder time pushing their agenda.

Interest groups recognize the fluid nature of political power. Trial lawyers are one of the most important Democratic constituencies, for example, because of their ability to contribute large amounts of campaign cash. In Florida, a state that has become more Republican in recent years, trial lawyers are splitting their donations and support. They are lining up more and more often behind Republicans because they want to get a hearing from the currently dominant party. Some groups, however, are forever on the outs in certain states and communities. Environmentalists have a harder time pushing their legislation in Michigan, because of its historic dependence on the automotive industry, than they do in California. Labor unions have a harder time organizing in traditional right-to-work states in the South than in the Midwest or Northeast.

Also important to remember is that even though the majority of state legislative chambers are politically competitive, most of the seats within them are not. Legislative districts are redrawn following each decennial census. Given computerization and other tools, political leaders are able to predict the likely voting patterns of people on a block-by-block or sometimes house-by-house basis. Following the 2000 census, nearly every district in the country was redrawn in such a way that it became reasonably safe for a candidate of one party over the other. In other words, there are now many safe Democratic districts and safe Republican districts, but there are not a lot of districts that are competitive. That means that most of the competition for a seat will take place in the primary race of the dominant party. If a district looks likely to support a Republican, several qualified candidates might run for the GOP nod; the Democratic nomination probably will not stimulate as much competition.

The Effect of Parties on Political Culture

Democrats are generally more liberal, favoring governmental solutions to social problems. Republicans are generally more conservative, preferring a limited role for government. These are not hard and fast rules, but they are true most of the time and have been true for many decades. As a result, the dominance of one party over the other has had an effect on the political culture of many states. Where there have been successful efforts to mobilize low-income voters through class-based appeals, in places such as Louisiana and Minnesota, government has gotten bigger. If these individuals put someone into office, they expect the support and social programs they were promised.

It is equally unsurprising that politicians who have come to power promising not to raise taxes have kept government growth in check. In New Hampshire, William Loeb, the editor of the Manchester *Union Leader,* came up with the idea of challenging political candidates to sign a no-tax pledge. The pledge became embedded in the state's political culture. Within thirty years, New Hampshire was transformed from a relatively high-revenue state, one that could depend on gaining adequate monies from taxes to fund public programs, to a low-revenue state.[39] The result? Among other things, New Hampshire is the only state in the country that does not offer public kindergarten classes in all school districts.[40]

What may be surprising is the fact that when the parties *really* held real sway—when the machines were more important than any individual officeholder—they were not very interested in expanding government either. Machine politicians wanted to maintain their grip on the government jobs and contracts they already had. This would seem to make sense for a conservative machine, like that run by Sen. Harry Byrd Sr., D-Va., from the 1920s to the 1960s. After all, Byrd and his acolytes shared a respect for balanced budgets and a small public sector. But party machines in general, even progressive ones, usually were not expansionistic. In the machine era, party officials squabbled more over who got control of which government jobs than about changing the number or nature of those jobs. They certainly did not present new government-based solutions to problems. Keeping jobs tied to political loyalties discouraged the creation of a professionalized bureaucracy.

In the meantime, the public did not want corrupt machine politicians to control any more of their money than necessary. Interest groups, such as unions, that might have wanted an expansion of government programs, did not hold enough influence to promote them.[41] As the parties and political machines weakened, however, candidates, party activists, and interest groups became free agents, free to promote all manner of new programs and government expansion.

Party Factions and Activists

Parties are no longer able to reward their followers directly with jobs or other payoffs. Decisions handed down by the U.S. Supreme Court have made it clear that party affiliation is not a constitutional basis on which to decide government hires. Kentucky governor Ernie Fletcher learned that the hard way in 2006 when he and several other top state officials were indicted for hiring supporters. Fletcher had been the first Republican elected to run the state in more than thirty years, and members of his administration were apparently too eager to hire party loyalists for government positions, disregarding the state's merit-hiring law in some instances.

Without party leaders being able to dispense prizes such as jobs, activism and party tasks have become largely volunteer activities. And because people seldom work for free unless they believe in something very strongly, political volunteers have become more ideological. People work for candidates and parties because they believe in specific causes, such as handgun legislation or protections for small business owners.

Just because jobs are no longer the parties' golden eggs does not mean that politicians and parties do not seek to pluck favors from their constituents through policies or promises. Both major parties court the elderly with assurances of healthcare benefits, such as providing prescription drugs through Medicare. The reason is that senior citizens vote and thus are worth courting. Young people, by contrast, tend not to vote. Only 24 percent of Americans thirty years of age and younger voted in 2006, which was the best midterm showing for the young in twenty years.[42] The young voter turnout increased in the 2004 and 2008 presidential elections—51 percent of the population between eighteen and twenty-nine cast ballots in 2008—but the group's participation continues to trail that of older voters by almost 15 percentage points.[43]

Each party has its main constituent groups, but that does not preclude both parties from trying to poach supporters from the other side. Democrats have been at pains in recent years to present a friendly face to business interests, while Republican president George W. Bush courted the Teamsters and building trade unions. Remember, however, that each party is a kaleidoscope of interest groups and can only appeal so much to any one group before it risks alienating support among other groups.

It is obvious that you cannot simultaneously support higher pay for teachers and cutting educational budgets. That is why politicians must perform the neat trick of motivating the true believers within party ranks to support their candidacy during a primary election without pinning themselves down so much that they do not appeal to members of the other party and independents during the general election. Overall, the more contentious the issue, the more a party will try to blur its differences with the other party. Candidates do not want to promise so much to their core supporters—known as the base—that they cannot reach other voters. If you promise a lot of money for public transportation, for instance, that might help you in the city but hurt you in the suburbs.

Both major parties try to appeal to as much of the populace as possible. But their supporters sometimes care more about promoting an issue than they do about winning elections. Interest groups now raise their own funds and use them freely to promote their issues in campaigns. We talk about how interest groups lobby governments a little later in this chapter, but it is worth examining quickly the type of role they can play in contemporary politics.

A 2009 special election for a vacant congressional seat based in Watertown, New York, demonstrates the difficulty that the parties have in maintaining discipline in message and candidate selection. The state GOP nominated Dede Scozzafava, a pro-choice, pro–gay marriage state assemblywoman. Notable figures within the national Republican Party, including former vice presidential nominee Sarah Palin and Minnesota governor Tim Pawlenty, were opposed to Scozzafava's candidacy and publicly backed the Conservative Party candidate instead. Scozzafava dropped out of the race three days before the election and threw her support to Bill Owens, the Democrat candidate and eventual winner.[44]

Numerous interests took an active role in that particular general election campaign that fall, including pro–term limits groups, antiabortion and pro-choice advocates, labor unions, environmental organizations, and antitax groups. In fact, the amount of money the candidates spent on their own campaigns was dwarfed by the amount spent by these and other outside groups. This has become more the rule and less the exception in recent years. In Wisconsin, political races often are dominated by issue ads run by the Wisconsin Manufacturers and Commerce and the Wisconsin Education Association Council (WEAC). Because these two groups care so much about taxes and education, respectively, these issues dominate many races. Politicians and parties have no control over such ads, so they cannot control the agenda. Anything else the candidates might want to emphasize is likely to be drowned out. Nobody disputes that taxes and schools are important, but making them the only subjects in an election detracts from other issues.[45]

By the 1980s, it appeared that candidates were fairly free agents. They were rid of the old party machine apparatus and able to set their own agendas and spread their own messages, largely through broadcast ads. Twenty years later, times changed again. Yes, candidates are now more independent, presenting themselves for party nomination and spending sums they have raised to get into the public eye. The campaigns, however, have become such big business that these funds and this self-motivation often are not enough. Plus, candidates need votes, and to get these votes, they must join ranks with party officials and interest groups that tend to take the candidate's ball and run away with it. Candidates become mere pawns in campaigns that have been overtaken by deep-pocketed interest groups. They stand on the sidelines and watch as the parties or other groups run the greater volume of ads, redefining their campaigns for them.

It is easy to become confused about which is the most powerful—candidates, interest groups, or political parties—and in which situations they hold that power. What is important to remember is that all three are vital parts of the political process and that their relative importance varies depending on the time and place. It is impossible to illustrate every variation, but none of them is ever either nothing or everything. Their roles are entwined.

Pragmatism versus Idealism

Interest groups, just like parties, are most likely to play a prominent role in races that are closely contested or that can tip the partisan balance in a legislature. Redistricting at both the federal and state legislative levels, however, has grown so sophisticated—with so much emphasis placed on making districts safe for incumbents—that relatively few of these races are closely contested. Much of the action takes place in primary contests. But in true swing districts, where either party has a shot at winning, both major parties and all their allies will spend as much money as they can muster to win.

In these cases, party leaders grow frustrated when interest groups trumpet issues that do not appeal to a wider public. The main goal of parties is to win elections, so they are much more interested in fielding candidates who fit the profile of the office in contention than they are in promoting a specific ideology. The Republican National Committee, for example, defeated an attempt in 1998 to pass a party resolution that would have blocked the party from giving any money to candidates opposed to a ban on late-term abortions. Social conservatives were angry that the national committee had spent $760,000 supporting the reelection effort of New Jersey governor Christine Todd Whitman, who had vetoed a state ban on the procedure. "I'm about as pro-life as anybody," said Bob Hiler, Indiana's member of the national committee, "but I just cannot accept a situation in the Republican Party where there is a litmus test if you want to join or be a candidate. I respect the decisions of our national party leaders to place money where it needs to go to ensure that we win that seat."[46]

With just two broad-based national parties, neither can afford to preach an unyielding gospel on any single issue. The people most interested in politics may be motivated by their investment in a particular issue, but if they hang around long enough, they come to realize that no one can win all the time. Perversely, the parties that are best able to keep their troops in line and satisfied with less-than-perfect ideological purity are the parties currently out of power. In other words, the desire to get back into the White House or to hold majority control of a legislature is often strong enough to convince all the quarreling factions to back someone who looks like a winner—even if that candidate is not "perfect" on all of the issues.

But the fact that both parties spend a good deal of time blurring their positions on the most important issues of the day to try to appeal to the most people while alienating the fewest number has made a lot of voters sour on them. As Col. Aureliano Buendia discovered in *One Hundred Years of Solitude,* many Americans believe that politicians do not stand for anything and are more interested in preserving their power than doing the right thing. That is a major reason why voters have become more independent in recent decades and have refused to give lifelong allegiance to one party over the other in the same way that their grandparents did. "It probably would have been better for the parties if the public had become more negative rather than more neutral toward them," writes political scientist

Martin Wattenberg. "Negative attitudes can easily be turned into positive attitudes by better performance or a change in policies. To induce people to care about political parties once again may well be more difficult."[47]

Third Parties and Independents

If millions of people are disenchanted with the Republican and Democratic parties, for a variety of reasons, why isn't there more of a movement toward establishing a viable third, or minor, party as an alternative? After all, in most other democracies, there are numerous parties with strong support. In countries such as Israel and Italy, the leading party typically does not have enough seats in parliament to construct a government on its own and has to enter into a coalition with other parties.

That has never been the case in the United States for a number of reasons. Democrats and Republicans, as we have been exploring, have established wide networks of contacts and supporters—individuals and groups that have long loyalties to one party or the other. They have officeholders at all levels who can help with strategy and fund-raising.

The major parties also have many institutional advantages. For one thing, the United States favors a winner-takes-all system in which the highest vote-getter in a district wins. In some countries, seats are distributed on a percentage basis, so that if a party gets 5 percent of the vote it receives about 5 percent of the total seats available. But if a party took only 5 percent of the vote across the United States, it probably would not win a seat anywhere. In 1992, Texas computer billionaire Ross Perot, the most successful third-party presidential candidate in decades, took 19 percent of the vote but did not carry a single state.

For the 1996 presidential race, Perot established the Reform Party, which he called his gift to the American people. Perot used that gift himself, running for a second time but not doing nearly so well. He had a hard time getting on the ballot in some states—the rules differ in many places and are often complicated. In the state of New York, for instance, a candidate must collect a certain number of signatures from each of the congressional districts to get on the ballot. Many candidates with less financial means than Perot have had difficulty gaining access to ballots. Perot himself was excluded from the presidential debates. The commission running the debates—composed of officials from the Democratic and Republican parties—decided he was not showing enough strength in the polls to warrant being included.

Excluded though he was, Perot nevertheless took 8 percent of the vote in 1996. This was enough to guarantee the Reform nominee in 2000 a spot on all fifty state ballots, as well as $12 million in federal campaign funds. With Perot out of the running, however, the Reform nomination dissolved into chaos. Two separate conventions nominated two separate candidates. The states were left having to decide which candidate deserved the spot on the ballot. "There are no statutes to guide us," said Mike Cooney, Montana's former secretary of state, in 2000 "The Reform Party needed to resolve this issue before it got to this point. It's an internal party problem that has been foisted upon the states and put us all in a bad situation."[48] The eventual Reform nominee proved not to be as much of a factor in the race as did Green Party nominee Ralph Nader. The Reform Party seemed to have self-destructed. Several of the old minor parties that had taken up its banner, such as Minnesota's Independence Party, soon returned to their original names.

Difficulties of Building Support

Many Democrats blamed Nader for the defeat of their candidate, Al Gore. Gore won more popular votes than Republican George W. Bush but was defeated in the electoral college. Some people believe that a third-party candidate will never be anything more than a "spoiler" who deprives major party candidates of needed votes. Others believe that third parties help present a real and needed alternative to the Democrats and Republicans. Unless the major parties are challenged, the thinking goes, they will never change.

The major parties, however, have proven quite adept at co-opting the most popular ideas presented by third-party candidates. Both Democratic and Republican candidates in the 1990s took the idea of a balanced federal budget more seriously because Perot had raised the issue. During the 1930s, Franklin D. Roosevelt lifted many of the ideas of Socialist candidate Norman Thomas. When faced with the rare strong minor-party challenge, a major-party candidate can argue that he offers the best vehicle for presenting any shared ideals—and stands a better chance of beating the other major-party candidate. As noted earlier, Perot's 1992 showing was the best by a third-party candidate since Theodore Roosevelt's in 1912—and neither one of them came close to winning.

> The major parties, however, have proven quite adept at co-opting the most popular ideas presented by third-party candidates. Both Democratic and Republican candidates in the 1990s took the idea of a balanced federal budget more seriously because Perot had raised the issue.

Minor-party candidates have enjoyed more success running for lower offices, but not much. Within a state or a legislative district, there is a better chance that an individual will enjoy enough personal popularity to equalize the playing field against Democrats and Republicans, who typically are better funded and connected. Still, there have been only five governors elected during the last fifty years who were neither Democrats nor Republicans. Two of those five—Walter Hickel of Alaska and Lowell Weicker of Connecticut—had earlier won statewide office as Republicans. Another two were elected in Maine, a state noted for the independent-mindedness of its electorate. The fifth, Jesse Ventura of Minnesota, served only one term, and the would-be successor from his Independence Party finished a distant third in 2002.

At the legislative level, things are just as grim for third-party candidates. Following the 2009 elections, there were only twenty-two third-party or independent state legislators in the United States (not counting nonpartisan Nebraska), out of a total of 7,400. Each of these candidates had dedicated followers. But from a pragmatic perspective—say, as a voter or an interest group interested in seeing your agenda becoming law—it probably makes better sense to support a Democrat or Republican who has a chance of serving in the majority party than it does to pull for a person who will hold just one vote.

A few minor parties have enjoyed a period of success in certain states, such as the Progressive Party during the 1920s in Wisconsin and the Farmer-Labor Party during the 1930s in Minnesota. Over time, however, these parties have been unable to survive the loss of early popular leaders or have been absorbed by one of the major parties. For example, the official name of Minnesota's Democratic Party is still the Democratic Farmer-Labor Party, in reference to its merger with the defunct minor party. The Liberal Party of New York boasted a New York City mayor in the 1960s named John Lindsay. New York is one of the few states that allow candidates to be listed multiple times on a ballot, as the nominee of, for instance, both the Liberal and the Republican parties. In 1980, U.S. senator Jacob Javits was denied the nomination of the state's Republican Party and ran as the Liberal candidate. He succeeded only in splitting the votes of liberals, moderates, and Democrats and helping to elect a more conservative Republican. The Liberal Party disbanded in 2003 after failing to garner enough votes in the previous year's gubernatorial contest to maintain its guaranteed spot on state ballots. "Parties, I suppose, have a life span," said Dan Cantor, executive director of the Working Families Party. "They had their heyday in the [19]50s and [19]60s. It looks like they have come to a full stop."[49]

Ultimately, it is the states that print the ballots and have the authority to decide which parties' nominees are going to be listed on them. It is the states that grant ballot access to parties based on their having won a minimum percentage of the vote in a previous statewide general election. The threshold varies from 1 percent in Wisconsin to as much as 20 percent in Georgia. Such high institutional barriers make minor parties' complaints about two-party dominance of American politics about as fruitless as trying to hold back the tide.

Major Party Support

One other reason minor parties have trouble gaining traction is that people are not, in the main, terribly unhappy with the major parties. The major parties, after all, do devote themselves to appealing to as broad a range of citizens as possible. That said, voter identification with the parties has declined. Some states once allowed voters to vote a straight ticket, meaning they could pull one lever to vote for all the Democratic or Republican candidates on the ballot. Such procedures are now considered quaint. Voters are more and more willing to divide their ballots, a practice called **ticket splitting**. One voter joked, "I vote for the man for president, and give him a Congress he can't work with."

In 1960, the Gallup Organization found that 47 percent of respondents identified themselves as Democrats, 30 percent as Republicans, and just 23 percent as independents or members of other parties. By the 1990s, those numbers had converged. Polling by the Pew Research Center for the People and the Press over a fifty-four-month period in the mid-1990s found an average of 33 percent of the respondents called themselves Democrats, 29 percent Republicans, and 33 percent independents, with a handful naming other specific parties.[50] A poll released by the Pew Research Center in 2009 found that as the proportion of Republicans continued to shrink, Democrats picked up strength, but self-described independents had become the largest of the three groups, with 39 percent of respondents choosing the label—the highest such proportion in seventy years.[51]

Most self-identified independents are not true independents, however. What this means is that their preferences generally do lean toward one of the major parties. "Partisan loyalties in the American populace have rebounded significantly since the mid-1970s, especially among those who actually turn out to vote," concluded political scientist Larry M. Bartels in 2000.[52] Pure independents, those who do not lean toward either party, peaked at 16 percent in 1976. Twenty years later, true independents were just 9 percent of the populace.[53]

The Republicans and Democrats have dominated American politics for 150 years. They have met every challenge—both ideological and structural—and found a way to preserve their near-total control. As political scientist Jeff Fishel puts it,

> If there's any lesson of history about the two major parties in American politics, it is that they're incredible adaptive survivors. They lost the monopoly they had, particularly on candidate recruitment and finance. That certainly does not mean that they're going out of business, just that they have to compete with other groups.[54]

Interest Groups and Lobbies

If many citizens are cynical about political parties, they're even more cynical about interest groups. It's true that lobbyists representing big companies or unions often push for legislation to promote or protect their own narrow interests. But lobbying is how citizens and private companies make their views known to policymakers between election seasons. Sometimes, people even lobby for altruistic reasons rather than self-interest.

TICKET SPLITTING
Voters' or districts' voting for different parties' nominees for different offices—for instance, supporting a Republican for president while supporting a Democrat for Congress.

Consider Daniel Millenson. He was a freshman at Brandeis University who grew alarmed about stories of genocide taking place in the Darfur region of Sudan. Being Jewish and having a "cultural memory" of the Holocaust, he decided he wanted to do something.[55] Millenson established the Sudan Divestment Task Force, which aims to persuade public entities, such as universities and state pension systems, to sell any stock they own in companies that provide revenues or weaponry to the Sudanese government.

Millenson's task force became the leading group coordinating this effort, but other students across the country got involved in similar ways. A handful of students from the UCLA, met in a Westwood living room to talk about the issue starting in 2004 and, because each invited friends, the meetings soon outgrew the living room. Over the next couple of years, hundreds of students got involved. Following a march that included students and film actor Don Cheadle, the University of California's regents agreed to divest from Sudan in 2006. The state of California's public pension systems soon followed. By mid-2008, seventeen other states had similarly divested, with legislation pending in more than a dozen other states.[56]

Millenson and his peers had seen a need to address an issue and created their own interest groups to fill the void. Most interest groups are standing organizations that allow constituencies to petition governments about the decisions that affect them. They are the vehicle for people who are not policymakers, but who are affected by policy, to influence the political process.[57]

As should be apparent by now, interest groups have always been important sources for candidates both of money and of volunteers and other services. They are the organizations that take a direct interest in political activity—both in terms of supporting candidates during an election season and lobbying elected and appointed government officials over policy and spending matters. They differ from parties in that politics and elections are not their whole reason for being. As political scientist Frank J. Sorauf notes, "The American Medical Association devotes only part of its energies to protecting its interests through political action. Not so the political party. It arises and exists solely as a response to the problems of organizing the political process."[58] In other words, the American Medical Association (AMA) may spend millions of dollars annually trying to affect elections and legislation, but it devotes more of its energy to educating its members, promoting good health techniques, and other private activities. This difference in focus leads to a fundamental and obvious trait that separates political parties from special interest groups—political parties run candidates for office under their own label and special interest groups do not.

Interest groups basically come in five flavors. One is a membership group, such as the AMA and Sierra Club, made up of individual members. A second type is the trade association, which represents individuals or organizations in a particular industry or field, such as the National Restaurant Association or the Alliance of Automobile Manufacturers. The third group is the individual institutions themselves, such as Microsoft and General Motors; these larger groups are bound to have lobbyists on staff or devote a significant portion of their executives' time to lobbying. The fourth group is the government lobbyists (sometimes called legislative liaisons), those who represent the interests of one branch of government in front of another. Executive branch officials have aides designated to lobby Congress or a legislature on their behalf, and cities, counties, and states hire lobbyists to make their cases in Washington. The fifth, smaller category is made up of private individuals who lobby on their own behalf for a pet project or against a policy that they find reprehensible.[59]

People and organizations have a constitutional right to petition the government for redress of grievances. That means that they have the right to complain to lawmakers and regulators about their disagreements with laws and how they are enforced. That's what lobbying is. It is worth noting that the government runs some of the most active lobbies. The White House maintains a lobbying shop to try to persuade Congress of the wisdom of its policies. Municipal governments hire lobbyists and associations to protect their interests in their state capitals. There are about 40,000 lobbyists working in state capitals, and the number of associations and related groups has quintupled over the last fifty years. Lobbying in the states is now a $1.3 billion business.[60]

It has become easier to track which interest groups are active in which states. Open up a Web browser and type in the name of a state and "lobbying registration," and you'll be taken to an ethics commission or other state board with which all lobbyists must register. The National Institute on Money in State Politics (followthemoney.org) and the Center for Public Integrity (publicintegrity.org) also offer detailed information about campaign finance and lobbying activity in the states, as well as studies about overall trends.

But looking at raw numbers—who is spending what where—tells only part of the story. It is often difficult to find out which group has influenced the outcome of a specific piece of legislation. Some interest groups play a very public game, like the Sudan Divestment Task Force, but others are more secretive, playing an insider game in which influence is a matter of quiet access to legislators.

That's why many interest groups hire a **contract lobbyist**. This is usually a lawyer or former government staffer or elected official who is valued for possessing valuable insider knowledge and contacts within a particular state capital. Contract lobbyists generally have a number of clients, as a lawyer does. About 20 percent of lobbyists registered to ply their trade in a given capital are contract.[61] They use their relationships and contacts to convince legislators that they should or should not pass a bill. And although lobbyists ignore the executive branch at their peril because spending decisions and regulatory action are carried out there, more lobbying activity happens in the legislative arena. "You don't

CONTRACT LOBBYIST

A person who works for different causes for different clients in the same way that a lawyer represents more than one client.

Policy in Practice: Lobbying for the Environment in the "Old Line" State

Despite growing concerns among scientists, policy-makers, and the public about climate change, consensus on environmental issues has been difficult to reach in recent years in Washington. Consequently, green groups have been pushing their ideas for controlling emissions from cars and power plants at the state level—and doing so with some success.

Maryland is home to several large coal-fired power plants. Environmentalists had tried for years to convince legislators to require these plants to invest in improved filtration of such toxins as mercury, sulfur dioxide, and nitrogen. But they could not overcome the opposition of the power companies and the administration of Gov. Bob Ehrlich, which sent several cabinet members to testify against such legislation in 2005.

"Ain't the beer cold!" boasted Ehrlich's deputy environmental secretary, a former energy company lobbyist, in an e-mail to department colleagues after the bill died in committee.[a]

But circumstances changed as the year wore on. Most significantly, the federal Environmental Protection Agency (EPA) came out with a long-awaited clean air rule that made it clear that Maryland would not meet limitations on health-related pollutants; states not in "attainment" with federal clean air regulations would have significant brakes put on future development. In response, Ehrlich issued new clean air rules addressing the power plants. He didn't go as far as environmentalists had hoped, but the fact that his rules would cost the plants significant amounts of money—which had been the main argument used against previous legislation—made the groups' selling job a lot easier.

The power companies still hoped to stall the "healthy air" bill. They used familiar means, such as campaign contributions to influential legislators and broadcast ads that sought to tie the proposed regulations to hikes in electricity costs in some Maryland jurisdictions.

To combat such messages, several state and national environmental groups decided to work together on the issue, coordinating events and their messages to members and the media. They held an environmental summit at the capitol in Annapolis to highlight the issue while hosting several town hall meetings around the state that were attended by legislators and the general public. They commissioned studies from outside analysts showing that the proposed changes wouldn't cost as much as the power companies claimed and held press events to trumpet such findings.

Like many interest groups, the environmental organizations concentrated their strength by having hundreds of members come to the capitol for a "lobby day," fanning out to meet legislators and their staffs, and making their issue prominent through their presence. Groups that host lobby days can seem to swarm change their minds," said a California lobbyist. "You find ways of making them think they agreed with you all along."[62]

Alan Autry, who was once an actor on the *Dukes of Hazzard* and who later served as mayor of Fresno, came to Washington one day in 2003 to ask for money for his city. He met with members of Congress and a senator who represented his area—who nevertheless needed reminding about Fresno's need for funds for law enforcement and an industrial park. Autry was thrilled when Sen. Barbara Boxer looked him in the eye and pledged her support for a $500,000 study that was the first step toward a major mass transit system in the San Joaquin Valley. "When you sit face to face to get a commitment, that's huge," he said.[63]

all over a capitol, with people wearing buttons or lapel stickers so everyone can see just what concerns them.

The environmentalists also pursued a lobbying strategy that has become common, reaching beyond their own ranks and turning to others for help in promoting their message. In this case, they received significant aid from healthcare professionals, including both doctors' and nurses' groups, as well as from the religious community. "We formed an ad hoc group called the Healthy Air Coalition," said Ed Osann, a consultant to nonprofit groups, including the Natural Resources Defense Council.[b]

Even with all these efforts, compromises had to be made to ensure the bill's passage. One key legislator whose district was home to a power plant—and who had received big campaign donations from energy companies—insisted on softening the penalties for noncompliance. Once both legislative chambers had passed the bill by veto-proof margins, Ehrlich surprised everyone by going ahead and signing it.

Maryland's environmentalists employed similar strategies and realized additional victories in the years following the Healthy Air Act's passage. They returned in 2007 with a "clean cars" bill designed to follow California's strict vehicle emissions standards. Because this bill would affect individual citizens more directly than the power plant regulations, environmentalists took their message not only to the capitol but also to many more citizens to build support for it. One hundred volunteers working with the Chesapeake Climate Action Network (CCAN) placed an estimated 20,000 "tickets" under the windshield wipers of SUVs across the state. These tickets included postcards addressed to Martin O'Malley, who had defeated Ehrlich in November 2006, to urge his support for clean cars legislation.[c] CCAN was among the groups leading the charge in 2009 for passage of legislation mandating a 25 percent reduction in the state's greenhouse gas emissions from 2006 levels by 2020. The environmental lobby celebrated Maryland's becoming just the sixth state required to cut its emissions, but it was joined in supporting the bill by the state's manufacturers and unions—who convinced lawmakers to agree to provisions protecting manufacturing companies from any job cuts as a result of legislation.[d]

[a]Tom Pelton, "Clean Air Law Enacted," *Baltimore Sun,* April 7, 2006, 1A.

[b]Phone interview with Ed Osann, March 1, 2007.

[c]Julie Scharper, "Just the Ticket for a Gas-Guzzler," *Baltimore Sun,* December 10, 2006, 3B.

[d]Pamela Wood, "Global Warming Bill No Longer Out in the Cold," *Capital,* February 11, 2009, A4.

But, although Autry saw the value of coming to "beg" in person, he recognized that most of his time would be spent back in Fresno, running the city day to day. That's why he hired Len Simon, a lobbyist for cities, to keep track of his projects and build support—for a fee of $24,000 a year. Many other city leaders have done the same. For them, Simon walks the corridors of the capitol, reiterating the same points to the same members of Congress, staff members, and executive branch bureaucrats because it is an article of faith in any capital that legislators respond to repetition—if an interest group keeps asking about a project, it must really want it. That kind of pricy persistence pays off. The city of Sandy, Utah, spent almost $200,000 on contract lobbyists in 2007 and claimed more than $1 million

Former actor Alan Autry (right) went on to become the mayor of Fresno, California. As chief executive of a city, Autry understands the importance of lobbying Congress for various municipal projects and programs. That's why he hired Len Simon (left), a contract lobbyist paid a handsome fee to make sure members of Congress know the views of Autry's administration.

in federal earmarks—which a city spokeswoman called a "return on investment."[64]

Legislators often rely on lobbyists to provide them with information, whether it is simply data about an industry's economic outlook or their opinions about whether a bill would cost jobs in legislators' districts. Legislators are always grappling with many issues at once: the state budget, education, the environment, and so on. It is up to lobbyists to keep legislators and their staffs apprised of who favors a particular bill and who would benefit from or be hurt by it. Lobbyists build up relationships with legislators over time, and legislators come to trust some of them for reliable information, even if they hold a differing position on an issue.

Standing in contrast to a contract lobbyist such as Simon is a **cause lobbyist,** who promotes a single-issue agenda, such as medical marijuana or campaign finance reform. A cause lobbyist often plays an outsider's game, using the media to sway public opinion and pressure public officials. Groups who do not have an economic interest in legislative outcomes are able to get away with that tactic because their ideological position is clear for all to see. People like Len Simon engage in **direct lobbying,** dealing directly with legislators in hopes of persuading them. The students trying to get public officials to divest from Sudan were taking an **indirect** approach, building support for their cause through the media, through rallies, and through other ways of influencing public opinion, hoping that legislators would be swayed by the resulting buzz.

Using the media effectively can be trickier for private corporations and other entities directly affected by legislation. The media nearly always portray this third type of lobbyist in a negative light. If a politician sponsors a bill favoring a particular industry and individuals in that industry have made substantial donations to his or her campaign treasury, there are bound to be stories written about that money trail. Numerous states, including Kentucky, Massachusetts, and Minnesota, have passed ethics laws in recent years that preclude lobbyists, who used to wine and dine legislators, from giving them anything of value, even a cup of coffee.[65]

Today, many interest groups try to combine the direct and indirect approaches, hitting up legislators in private meetings for favors while also

CAUSE LOBBYIST

A person who works for an organization that tracks and promotes an issue, for example, environmental issues for the Sierra Club or gun regulation for the National Rifle Association.

DIRECT LOBBYING

A form of lobbying in which lobbyists deal directly with legislators to gain their support.

INDIRECT LOBBYING

A form of lobbying in which lobbyists build support for their cause through the media, rallies, and other ways of influencing public opinion with the ultimate goal of swaying legislators to support their cause.

Governing States and Localities

MAP 6-3 Spending by Lobbyists, 2006

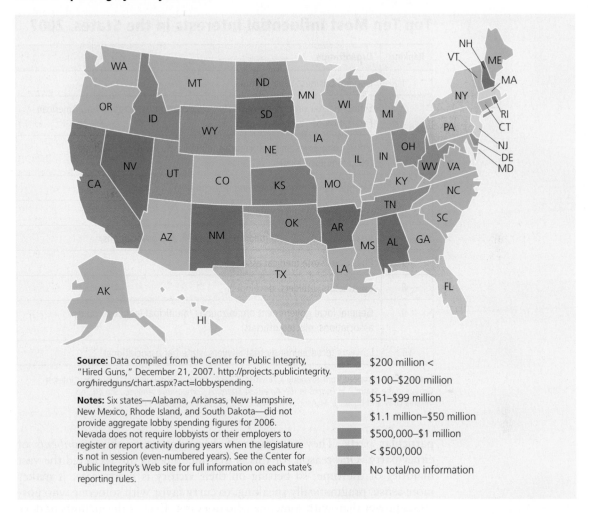

Source: Data compiled from the Center for Public Integrity, "Hired Guns," December 21, 2007. http://projects.publicintegrity.org/hiredguns/chart.aspx?act=lobbyspending.

Notes: Six states—Alabama, Arkansas, New Hampshire, New Mexico, Rhode Island, and South Dakota—did not provide aggregate lobby spending figures for 2006. Nevada does not require lobbyists or their employers to register or report activity during years when the legislature is not in session (even-numbered years). See the Center for Public Integrity's Web site for full information on each state's reporting rules.

Legend:
- $200 million <
- $100–$200 million
- $51–$99 million
- $1.1 million–$50 million
- $500,000–$1 million
- < $500,000
- No total/no information

running public relations campaigns through the media. Groups also are likely to join together in coalitions, hoping that a united front will not only present a more coherent and persuasive message but also prevent any individual group from looking like it is pleading from narrow self-interest. Interest groups often look for surprising allies who will plead their case. For instance, groups wanting to increase funding for afterschool programs will enlist sheriffs to argue that the programs help cut crime by giving young people something constructive to do.

As mentioned earlier, some interest groups tend to be loyal to one party over the other, particularly groups with ideological agendas. But interest groups as a whole do not give most of their support to candidates of a

TABLE 6-1

Top Ten Most Influential Interests in the States, 2007

Ranking	Organization
1	General business organizations
2	Schoolteacher organizations (National Education Association and American Federation of Teachers)
3	Utility companies and associations (electric, gas, water, telephone/telecommunications)
4	Manufacturers (companies and associations)
5	Hospital/nursing home associations
6	Insurance: general and medical (companies and associations)
7	Physicians/state medical associations
8	Contractors, builders, developers
9	General local government organizations (municipal leagues, county associations, elected officials)
10	Lawyers (predominantly trial lawyers, state bar associations)

Source: Data compiled from Anthony J. Nownes, Clive S. Thomas, and Ronald J. Hrebenar, "Interest Groups in the States," in *Politics in the American States: A Comparative Analysis,* 9th ed., ed. Virginia Gray and Russell L. Hanson (Washington D.C.: CQ Press, 2008), 117.

particular party. They give most of their support to the *incumbents* of either party. One reason for this is that incumbents are reelected the vast majority of the time, so betting on their victory is pretty safe. It makes more sense, pragmatically speaking, to curry favor with someone who possesses power than with someone who does not. Even if the incumbent does not subscribe to an interest group's entire program, the group may find it is able to work with the individual on an issue or two.

Another reason that interest groups favor incumbents is because their campaign contributions are based more on rewarding public officials for positions they already have taken than on trying to persuade them to take new positions altogether. In other words, if a legislator already has demonstrated support for gun owners' rights, the NRA will be inclined to support him or her. The group does not give donations to gun control advocates in hopes of changing their minds. The money follows the vote, in most cases, rather than the other way around.

The adoption of bans on gift and other ethical restraints has not stopped the lobbying industry or deterred interest groups. Too much is at stake in too many state capitals for corporations, unions, or cause activists not to play an active role. At the beginning of the twentieth century, one or two powerful home-state companies dominated many state political cultures. State capitals remained old boys' clubs, where just a few powerful interests typically held sway, until about World War II. Since then, states have come to rival Washington in terms of the buzz of activity among competing interests.

About 1,100 different occupations are regulated by states today, and fighting among those industries is never-ending. Art therapists, for instance, want their profession recognized by more state legislatures so that they will be guaranteed reimbursement from insurance companies. Mental health counselors, on the other hand, do not want the added competition and oppose such recognition. Orthopedic surgeons and podiatrists face off over who gets to treat ankle injuries and force legislators to debate whether the ankle is part of the foot. (The Colorado legislature decided it was, opening up the field to podiatrists.) Dog groomers fight veterinarians for the right to brush canine teeth.[66]

Beer is regulated at the state level, which is why Anheuser-Busch InBev, the maker of Budweiser, hires lobbyists in all fifty states. Insurance also is regulated at the state level. Many more industries, in fact, are turning their attention to the states because that is where the federal government and the courts have sent more power. The states have assumed authority over issues such as securities regulation and have taken the lead on issues that have not progressed in Congress. The federal government has failed in recent years to regulate health maintenance organizations, but over the last decade more than forty states have passed bills addressing the topic.

The active role of the state in regulating economic and social activities has induced some industries, such as pharmaceutical companies, to maintain lobbies that are just as powerful in the states as they are in Washington. Others, such as the oil industry, have a major presence at the federal level but are weaker players in most states because state politics largely don't affect them. National companies that are not based in a particular state are likely to hire local contract lobbyists to lend clout to their causes. The consumer products company Johnson & Johnson has its own lobbyists but also maintains memberships in its home state, in the New Jersey Chamber of Commerce, the state's Business and Industry Association, and the New Jersey Health Products Company Group. It also belongs to industry associations in California, Illinois, Massachusetts, and elsewhere. At the national level, Johnson & Johnson belongs to the Pharmaceutical Research and Manufacturers of America, the Health Care Industry Manufacturers' Association, and still other groups.[67]

When an industry has relatively little credibility, it often will turn to allies to represent the public face of its cause. Tobacco companies favor hiring lobbyists who have earned the respect of state legislators as former colleagues or by working for other, less controversial clients. They also seek other groups to take the lead on a lot of their fights. When a state considers

> When an industry has relatively little credibility, it often will turn to allies to represent the public face of its cause. Tobacco companies favor hiring lobbyists who have earned the respect of state legislators as former colleagues or by working for other, less controversial clients. They also seek other groups to take the lead on a lot of their fights.

legislation that will regulate smoking in public places, for example, the most public opponents are more likely to be restaurant groups rather than the tobacco industry. "We're going to participate in a very upfront way," said a Philip Morris spokesman. "But like any other industry, we're going to look to people who share that point of view on any given issue" to take a role as well.[68]

As in the case of tobacco companies fighting smoking bans, lobbyists spend the majority of their time playing defense, trying to kill bills they believe would harm their companies or clients. Still, interest groups and their desires stir up much of the activity in state capitals. "Frankly, the legislature in New Jersey exists for the lobbyist," said one lobbyist there.[69] What he was suggesting is that the governor may want five or six bills passed during a session, while individual legislators may want one or two of their own passed as well. The remaining 99 percent of the thousands of bills introduced in a given year are a wish list of wants and needs by the lobbyists and the interests they represent.

That is why interest groups are an important part of the political landscape in every state. Certain groups play a disproportionate role in particular states, for example, gambling in Nevada or the poultry industry in Arkansas.[70] But the full range of interest groups has crucial influence over the workings of every state. Clive S. Thomas and Ronald J. Hrebenar, two political scientists who have been studying interest group activity in the states for decades, rank the states according to which have policies that are most influenced by interest groups. In no state are interest groups subordinate, that is, consistently outgunned by other policy players, such as governors or political parties.

Those players are stronger in some states than in others. The relative weakness of political parties led Thomas and Hrebenar to argue that interest groups are most powerful in a few states in the South and West, such as Alabama, Nevada, and West Virginia.[71] Certain interest groups may hold greater sway at specific times. The importance of environmental issues, in particular, seems to ebb and flow. But Thomas and Hrebenar note that in the majority of states, the influence of interest groups as a whole remains fairly constant—and fairly strong.

The influence of interest groups is difficult to measure, but it's nonetheless quite apparent, part of the very air that policymakers breathe. Some groups may score a victory here and there: dentists looking for a regulatory change or animal rights' activists looking to ban cockfighting. Other groups have become a permanent part of the landscape, such as business lobbies concerned with taxes, transportation, and education.

There are some interest groups that are powerful everywhere because their members are everywhere. Groups such as teachers' unions, car dealers, restaurant owners, and realtors hold particular sway because they have members in every legislative district, and legislators are more likely to be persuaded by individuals or employers from their home districts. Most realtor lobbying, for example, is handled by volunteer members and state association staff rather than by hired contract lobbyists because realtors tend to be well connected in their communities. They also make it a point to have particular members of their professional community get to know individual legislators from their districts and keep them up to date about their issues of concern. Realtors, like other professions affected at the state policy level, also seek office themselves in part-time legislatures. During the 2005–2006 session, no fewer than twenty-two people who made their living in real estate also served as members of the Utah legislature— including the president of the National Association of Realtors.[72]

Politicians clamor for the support of unions, many of which are strong, outspoken, and well organized. The Service Employees International Union, shown picketing here in 2008, represents 2.2 million members nationwide, including hundreds of thousands of state and local government employees.

Taken together, interest groups are the means through which individual citizens and private companies, as well as governmental bodies, influence the policy decisions that affect their lives or ways of doing business. "I don't believe there are some states where interest groups are stronger and others where they're weaker," said Alan Rosenthal, an expert on state politics at Rutgers University. "In every state, interest groups are important. That's the way interests are represented, through groups."[73]

Conclusion

The essential job of political parties is to nominate candidates for public office. They no longer control many government jobs, but despite changes in campaign finance laws, they have maintained their positions as leading fund-raising organizations. They also perform many other functions in American democracy. They aggregate and articulate political interests and create and maintain majorities within the electorate and within government. They are not the dominant organizing forces they once were, in part because voters and candidates have become more independent than they were a century ago. Parties, however, do still play important roles in recruiting political candidates, supporting them financially and logistically, and helping them market themselves to like-minded voters.

For the past 150 years, two major parties—the Democrats and the Republicans—have dominated politics in the United States. Few candidates not belonging to either of these parties have won office at any level of government, and in most cases, their victories were based on personal appeal rather than support for the third party they represented. The Republican and Democratic parties have been able to adapt to changing times and tastes in ways that have kept them in power, if not always in perfect favor.

With states regulating more industries, interest groups have proliferated so that there are now far more lobbyists than elected officials. Interest groups help push agendas subscribed to by individuals or corporations. Other interest groups push back. Their primary mission is winning as many political offices as possible, so the parties, with varying success, collate and mute the ideological agendas of their interest group allies. Parties cannot afford to have any one group's ideas play such a prominent role that it alienates other groups or voters. It is a difficult balancing act to try to appeal to the majority of voters at any given time while also standing for clear enough principles that most people are willing to support them.

Key Concepts

candidate-centered politics (p. 184)

cause lobbyist (p. 214)

closed primaries (p. 190)

contract lobbyist (p. 211)

crossover voting (p. 190)

dealignment (p. 194)

direct lobbying (p. 214)

factional splits, or factions (p. 179)

Suggested Readings

Black, Earl, and Merle Black. *Divided America: The Ferocious Power Struggle in American Politics.* New York: Simon and Schuster, 2007. Political scientists show that, although one of the two major parties is dominant in most regions, neither can claim a permanent governing majority nationwide.

Gould, Lewis. *Grand Old Party: A History of the Republicans.* New York: Random House, 2003. An excellent recent history of the Republicans from Abraham Lincoln to the present day.

Jewell, Malcolm E., and Sarah M. Morehouse. *Political Parties and Elections in the American States.* 4th ed. Washington, D.C.: CQ Press, 2000. Shows how and why political parties vary at the state level.

Rosenthal, Alan. *The Third House: Lobbyists and Lobbying in the States.* 2nd. ed. Washington, D.C.: CQ Press, 2001. A primer on how interest groups operate in and influence state legislatures.

Witcover, Jules. *Party of the People: A History of the Democrats.* New York: Random House, 2003. Companion to Lewis Gould's *Grand Old Party* that traces the Democratic Party from its Anti-Federalist antecedents to Bill Clinton.

Suggested Web Sites

http://moneyline.cq.com. Congressional Quarterly's MoneyLine Web site providing information on campaign finance, lobbying and lobbyists, and parties and candidates.

www.dnc.org. Web site of the Democratic National Committee.

www.fivethirtyeight.com. Nate Silver's blog covering electoral polling and politics at the national and state levels.

www.followthemoney.org. Web site of the National Institute on Money in State Politics, which tracks political donations and lobbying in all fifty states.

www.gop.com. Web site of the Republican National Committee.

www.irs.gov/charities/political/article/0,,id=109644,00.html. The Internal Revenue Service (IRS) Political Organization Filing and Disclosure site.

www.ncsl.org. Web site of the National Conference of State Legislatures.

www.opensecrets.org. Web site for The Center for Responsive Politics, a nonpartisan organization tracking money in politics.

www.politics1.com/states.htm. Provides links to candidates for most major offices in all the states.

www.publicintegrity.org. Web site for The Center for Public Integrity, which produces among its investigative journalism reports pieces on campaign finance and lobbying activity in the states and Washington, D.C.

CHAPTER 7

Legislatures

The Art of Herding Cats

New Jersey governor Chris Christie, right, and state senator Sandra Cunningham join other volunteers in helping to package Thanksgiving meals at a Jersey City shelter in 2009.

7

Why do so many citizens think that legislatures accomplish so little—or accomplish the wrong things altogether?

What constraints do legislatures face in making effective laws?

Why are some legislators more powerful than others?

State legislatures operate in complex ways, especially when it comes to how members negotiate with their colleagues as they attempt to make laws. Their basic dynamics, however, are fairly similar to how you and your friends decide what pizza to order.

Let's say you're really jonesing for some pizza. The cafeteria is closed and for the sake of argument let's say you've got $5 in cash and your credit cards are maxed out—and the minimum charge for delivery is $10. To get pizza, you need friends. If friends go in on the order, however, you're pretty sure that you won't get your ideal pizza—hamburger with onions and red peppers—because your friends have all made it clear they think that's a disgusting combination. You need to make a deal and that will involve compromise.

You go around your dorm and pretty quickly find four other people willing to go in on a delivery. Of the five people ordering, two of you want some kind of meat, but there are three vegetarians. If all votes are counted as equal, you're going meatless. Similarly, if Democrats hold fifty-three seats in the Indiana House of Representatives and Republicans have only forty-seven, most of the time the Democrats are going to get their way. This is called **majority rule**.

But bills do not always pass according to predictable partisan majorities. Let's change our pizza-ordering scenario. Now it is just you (a young man), your roommate (also a man), and your girlfriend. Your roommate doesn't want hamburger or sausage or pepperoni—and your girlfriend agrees with him! Something similar happens regularly in legislatures, when some members abandon their fellow Democrats or Republicans to vote with the opposing party. For instance, most Democrats might want to pass stricter gun control laws, but some of their rural, more conservative Democratic colleagues might block them by joining with the GOP. This is called **coalition building**.

But your girlfriend actually finds the idea of splurging and enjoying some pepperoni pretty enticing. She also knows that it is not smart policy to favor your roommate's taste over yours. In her heart, she would rather stay vegetarian, but she knows she is better off in the long run if she agrees with you on this. She might even get you to watch that romantic comedy you've been avoiding if she supports your order. In much the same way, legislators often vote for bills that they do not particularly like in order to win support for other priorities. They might want to curry favor with their

MAJORITY RULE

The process in which the decision of a numerical majority is made binding on a group.

COALITION BUILDING

The assembling of an alliance of groups to pursue a common goal or interest.

party leaders, or they might simply want to earn a colleague's help in the future by voting for the colleague's pet bill now. This is called trading votes, or **logrolling.**

Or maybe you have learned that you cannot count on your girlfriend to stick up for you when it's time to call the pizza parlor. So you go around to all your pals in the dorm and plant the idea that what would really be fun tonight would be getting a pizza. You ask only guys you are pretty sure will be good with pepperoni. Just to make sure, you ask Cecilia, whom you know eats more meat than any of the guys. Legislators—and other people concerned with what legislators are up to—do this all time. They try to solicit support from people who are going to vote long before a vote actually takes place so that the result will come out the way they want. This is called lobbying and is similar to the kind of lobbying that interest groups do, as we have seen in chapters 5 and 6.

But let's say that while you are busy polling your friends one of them unexpectedly says that he hates pepperoni worse than poison and that he refuses even to think about sausage. And, surely, you would run into opposition if you dared to ask for anchovies. This sort of thing often happens in legislatures. If there is a bill to increase state spending for abortion clinics, for instance, you can bet that one or more legislators will do everything in their power to block that spending.

There are many ways that an adamant opponent can stop a hated piece of legislation's progress through a chamber, including **filibusters**—endless debates in the Senate. Another way is to attach unwanted amendments, or **riders,** to a bill. The road to a bill's passage into law is twisty and sometimes full of unexpected hurdles. John Dingell, D-Mich., the longest-serving member of the U.S. House of Representatives, perhaps best described the strange relationship between the actual substance of a bill and how it moves through the House when he said in 1984, "If you let me write procedure and I let you write substance, I'll screw you every time."[1]

All these complicated dynamics are why legislative leadership has sometimes been compared to the job of herding cats. "You come into the Senate every day with a wheelbarrow of 33 cats," writes William Bulger, a former president of the Massachusetts Senate. "Your job is to get the wheelbarrow with 17 of those cats to the other side of the chamber."[2]

In all fairness, legislatures were not designed to be simple. The congressional system was designed to be difficult enough to prevent new laws that have not been properly thought through and debated from bothering everybody. "The injury which may possibly be done by defeating a few good laws will be amply compensated by the advantage of preventing a number of bad ones," wrote Alexander Hamilton in *Federalist Paper* No. 73.[3] Most state legislatures share the basic structure of the U.S. Congress, with a house chamber and a senate chamber that each must approve a bill before it can go to the governor to be signed into law. That means that even if a bill makes its way through all the circuitous steps of getting passed by the house, including **committee** fights and winning a majority in the chamber, it can easily die if the senate refuses to sign off on an identical version. "If we passed the Lord's Prayer, we'd send it to the Senate and they'd amend it and send it back," said Bob Bergren, the Speaker of the Montana House.[4] Getting the 150 or so legislators who serve in every state to agree on anything is one of the toughest tricks in politics.

The consequence of this complexity is a grave misperception by the general public about how well legislatures work and how competent individual legislators are. Legislators work hard. They address thousands of bills and constituent complaints every year, but the institutional structures of the legislatures make it difficult for them to respond quickly to the issues of the day. The early part of the twenty-first century also finds the electorate split politically in many states, as well as nationwide, so it is especially difficult to reach an agreement that pleases everyone.

> Legislators work hard. They address thousands of bills and constituent complaints every year, but the institutional structures of the legislatures make it difficult for them to respond quickly to the issues of the day.

The fact is that legislators are mostly working harder to address more complicated problems than in the past. But the public's perception is that they are not getting the job done. Recent studies show that the average person is not in touch with what his or her legislature is up to, considers the legislature to be unnecessarily contentious, and thinks legislators are guilty of talking when they should be acting. Many people believe that legislators are too cozy with the interest groups that provide them with campaign contributions and perhaps other favors. Voters wonder why their representatives do not simply vote the "right" way and go home.

The problem is that there is no one "right" way. Many cross currents blow through every legislature. Some legislators represent liberal **districts**; others represent conservative areas. Some represent cities; others represent farmlands grappling with entirely different, nonurban issues. Legislators acting in good faith will come to different conclusions about what is the right approach to take on any number of issues, from education and transportation to job creation and taxes. All sides get to present their most convincing arguments, but only rarely can a majority of members of a legislature come to an agreement that pleases them all. In their disagreement, they reflect the different opinions of their **constituents**, the citizens back home—which is precisely the way the system is supposed to work.

Let's say that you and your friends are still arguing over pepperoni and the vegetarian combo. Only this time, each choice has an even number of fans. In the end, you decide that you will just go with cheese. Nobody is thrilled about this—none of you gets the toppings you were hoping for—but everyone can live with the choice. This is called **compromise**, and it is the kind of agreement legislators make more than any other. This chapter

Governing States and Localities

gives you a sense of how legislators come to their decisions, who they are, what they do, and how they organize themselves in their institutions. Localities—city and county governments—typically have some form of legislature as well; these are covered in chapter 11.

The Job of Legislatures

During the evening rush hour of August 1, 2007, a bridge that crossed the Mississippi River in Minneapolis, part of Interstate 35W, collapsed. Thirteen people died, and 145 were injured. The bridge collapse triggered a nationwide discussion about the need to update and repair aging infrastructure. Many states that had deferred maintenance and construction of roadways and other infrastructure during tough budget years earlier in the decade stepped up their spending in this area.

Not surprisingly, discussions about infrastructure were especially urgent in St. Paul, Minnesota's capitol just to the east of Minneapolis. In 2008, the legislature approved a $6.6 billion package to pay for transportation needs for ten years, funded by increases in the sales and gas taxes and vehicle registration fees. "We agreed that it was time," said state representative Jim Abeler. "There had been a 20-year bipartisan failure in establishing funding for roads."[5]

But not everyone agreed with the decision. Governor Tim Pawlenty, a Republican, vetoed the package, arguing that its tax increases made it unacceptable. Abeler, along with five other Republicans, joined with Democratic colleagues to override Pawlenty's veto. The Republicans were quickly dubbed the "Override Six" and accused of betraying party principles in enacting a tax hike. Three of the six lost their local party endorsements to party challengers. One was stripped of a top committee vote and decided to retire after a dozen years of service. "If you are going to be a team," the governor said after the vote, "then there are going to be some team rules and team expectations."[6]

The story of the Override Six demonstrates several key points about how legislatures operate today. Everyone understands that it is the job of the legislature to set policy and choose spending priorities for the state, in consultation with the governor—or sometimes despite his wishes, if there's a two-thirds vote to override his veto. Nevertheless, the decisions that legislators make are, by their nature, political. It's difficult to please everybody and often legislators have to balance competing interests. In this case, they had to choose between a demonstrated need for greater investment in infrastructure, on the one hand, and the deep unpopularity of raising taxes, on the other.

State legislatures are not as polarized as Congress, where the members of the two political parties barely speak to one another and seem to castigate the other side as being made up of treacherous enemies as often as they collaborate. But the party caucuses in the state legislatures have grown farther apart in recent years, with less agreement across party lines on matters such as spending priorities. The case of the Override Six was not entirely unusual. Legislative leaders from California to Florida have removed members from leadership posts or desirable committee slots for voting against the party line on important matters—most often on tax or budget votes.

That makes the job of finding the right compromise—getting to an agreed-on set of pizza toppings—that much more difficult. But it also gives voters a clear choice between candidates of the two parties.

What Legislatures Do

All state legislatures share four basic interrelated and often overlapping functions:

- A lawmaking function: They pass laws and create policy for their states.
- A representative function: They provide a means for various groups and individuals to have their interests represented in state policymaking.
- A constituent service function: They offer personalized constituent service to help residents sort out their problems with the state government.
- An oversight function: They oversee the governor and the executive branch and some private businesses through public hearings, budget reviews, and formal investigations.

State legislatures might all address similar issues, including taxes, budgets, and a broad range of other matters such as regulating office safety and requiring sex offenders to register their place of residence with police. Differences in timing, state history, and political culture, however, may cause one state's laws on a topic to differ widely from those of other states. Occasionally, legislatures are pressured to pass uniform laws—as when the federal government insisted that the states raise their legal drinking ages to twenty-one or risk losing highway funding. Louisiana resisted the longest, adopting a minimum drinking age of twenty-one in 1987.

More often than not, laws are adapted to the local scene and are not easily molded to match other states' versions. Large insurance companies are regulated at the state level. They would love to have their agents qualified to sell in every state rather than having to take fifty different qualifying exams. "I'm still not sure what happens if Michigan says you can be an insurance agent if you can sign your name with your eyes shut, and New York says you've got to take a three-year course," said Alexander Grannis, chair of the insurance committee in the New York Assembly. "What happens if someone screws up—if we cancel a Michigan guy's license to practice here for malpractice, does that mean Michigan can retaliate and cancel a New Yorker's right to practice there?"[7]

Within a given state, the media and the public manage to register many failures of a legislature while not giving the institution enough credit for its successes in balancing all the competing interests within the state. Ethics scandals generally receive greater coverage than substantial debates, yet legislators debate and pass laws that cover everything from levels of Medicaid health insurance funding to clean water protections to aid for local governments to workers' compensation payments to the price of milk. In most legislatures, 90 percent of the bills receive almost no media attention and are of interest only to those they directly affect. The media—and with it, the voting public—pay attention only when issues that affect the broadest range of people are considered, such as increases (or cuts) in property tax rates. Legislators do not have the luxury of tuning out when complex and boring but important issues crop up.

One of the arguments against term limits is that legislators have to cope with many complicated issues, getting quickly up to speed on water rights and regional transportation plans. There's the potential that they'll end up reopening fights that had been settled through painful negotiations years earlier, because no one's around who remembers what they'd gone through.

State senators and representatives fight their biggest fights over budgets. Most of their power is derived from the fact that with the approval of the governor they can set fiscal policy, including tax rates. How much the state devotes to each of its programs is a way of revisiting all the problems that never go away. How much is enough to spend on education? How much of that education tab should the state pick up? Although public schools traditionally were funded by local property taxes, most states now pick up one-third of the bill or more. How much money should be spent on healthcare? Should all children be covered,

After serving twenty-six years in the North Carolina House, Joe Hackney took over as Speaker. Signaling a change from his disgraced predecessor, Hackney did something novel when calling for a vote for the first time—he asked fellow legislators if they'd had time to read the bill.

State senators and representatives fight their biggest fights over budgets. Most of their power is derived from the fact that with the approval of the governor they can set fiscal policy, including tax rates.

regardless of their parents' income? How big an investment should the state make in roads or public transportation? How much can be spent overall before the state is taxing individuals and businesses too highly? Practically every state has a constitutional requirement to balance its budget every year, so legislators cannot spend what they do not take in from tax receipts. State legislatures annually address hundreds of such issues, large and small.

Lawmaking

Legislatures tend to be reactive institutions. Early in 2005, Jessica Marie Lunsford, a nine-year-old Florida girl, was raped and buried alive by a convicted sex offender. By the end of 2006, half the states had passed a version of Jessica's Law, which required longer sentences for sex offenders and electronic tracking of their whereabouts following their release from prison. Jessica's Law was just one among hundreds of laws passed by states in recent years in reaction to high-profile sex crimes against children and the attention they received from programs such as Bill O'Reilly's show on Fox News Channel and *To Catch a Predator* on NBC.

Most issues attract far less attention. The New York state legislature grappled with more than 15,000 bills in 2009,[8] which actually represented something of a drop from previous years, while even much mellower Montana takes up about 1,500 a year.[9] Despite this amount of activity—or perhaps because of it—legislators generally do not go looking for issues to address. The typical bill is introduced for one of several reasons: it is a bill that has to be considered, such as the annual state budget; it is a bill dealing with a common problem modeled after another state's legislation; or it is something that an individual or a group outside of the legislature wants considered. These outside influences include constituents, the governor, and lobbyists.

It may not always seem like it, but constituents can have a lot of influence in government. In Massachusetts, for instance, legislators are obliged to consider petitions to introduce bills on any topic that a state resident wants. During the state's debate over same-sex marriages in 2004, for instance, various groups petitioned the legislature with the approaches they favored. In effect, they filed their own amendments.

Governors and the executive branch are also powerful players in the legislative process. They promote ideas they want legislators to work on. These can be bills designed to quickly address relatively small-scale problems, such as the $4 million program to combat wasting disease in deer that the Wisconsin legislature approved in 2002,[10] or larger issues that might be debated for years. For example, the legislature in Washington State has battled for several years over funding for transportation projects in the Puget Sound area and elsewhere. In 2001, legislators failed to agree to Gov. Gary Locke's proposal to spend $9 billion more on roads, despite Locke's calling them into three special sessions. That was in part because

Republicans and Democrats had a hard time coming to an agreement on changes in contracting laws that would require workers to be paid a union wage in rural areas.[11] The legislators and Gov. Christine Gregoire, Locke's successor, finally agreed on a transportation package and a gas-tax increase that voters upheld in 2005. But in 2007 Seattle voters sent them partway back to the drawing board by rejecting two different proposals for the package's centerpiece project. The debate is guaranteed to continue. In 2009, the state agreed to pay $2.4 billion for the Seattle project, but city officials warned that they might not be done enacting the tax hikes needed to pay for their share until 2011.

Finally, lobbyists representing a client such as a beer company or auto manufacturer often will promote draft legislation in hopes that a member of the legislature or general assembly—as legislatures are known in Colorado, Georgia, Pennsylvania, and several other states—will sponsor it as a bill. True.com, an online dating service, convinced legislators in several states in 2006 to introduce legislation requiring such Web sites to conduct background checks of all their users. "I was shocked when I found out that dating services, which market themselves as finding someone's true soulmate, don't provide any kind of even cursory background checks," said Illinois state representative John Bradley, whose bill passed the state House that year. But, even though True.com's founder said he was motivated by an online meeting that ended in murder, his competitors were able to convince legislators that the bill was only a "PR stunt" designed to make True.com's services, which included background checks, look more enticing. They said there was no way of checking on customers, who everyone knew to be fibbers. "There's sort of a joke in the industry that the average person lies by 10 pounds and 10 years," said Eric Straus of Cupid.com.[12]

Although lobbyists may promote bills, they also devote an enormous amount of energy trying to kill other bills. In 2008, the NRA monitored 208 different bills in thirty-eight states, many of which it supported—such as allowing employees to bring guns to the workplace if they kept them in their cars—and many others it opposed. That year, for instance, the Pennsylvania House defeated a proposal to require gun owners to immediately report the loss or theft of firearms to law enforcement officials—the first time in fifteen years that the chamber had considered any significant restriction on gun owners' rights. The state acts as a sort of referee among a lot of competing interests. Any change in state law that someone views as a positive step is likely to adversely affect—or at least frighten—someone else. Whatever gun control advocates want, the gun owners' rights groups will try to stop. "This bill was a defining moment," Kate Harper, a suburban Republican lawmaker who supported the defeated regulation in Pennsylvania, told the *New York Times*. "These are difficult votes for me because it hurts me with my caucus and it also hurts with really strong Republican voters who don't want government interference. On the other hand, I've got soccer moms and people who have never fired a gun and are afraid of them."[13]

Legislators react most strongly to bills in which they have a personal stake or that they know will affect their constituents directly. Let's say that environmentalists are concerned about a river's water quality and want to require new water filters at a paper mill. The mill's owners, concerned that the cost of the filters will be exorbitant, warn that they will have to lay off three hundred employees if the bill goes through. A legislator from that area will have to worry about whether creating a healthier environment is worth being accused of costing people their jobs. Other legislators who live clear across the state from the river and its mill, however, will hold the deciding votes. The people directly affected—the company, the workers, and the downstream residents worried about pollution—will all try to portray themselves as standing for the greater good. If no side is clearly right and favoring one side over the other can do political damage, the bill easily could die. Legislators could then be accused of doing nothing, but they will merely be reflecting the lack of statewide consensus about how to solve the problem.[14]

Representation

The bulk of the work legislators do involves formulating the law and trying to keep an eye on the executive branch, but their primary responsibility is to provide **representation** for their constituents. Basically, they ensure the interests of those they speak for are properly considered as part of decision making at the state level. Sometimes legislators address issues because their constituents are having problems that only a change in the law can address. Medicaid is a shared federal-state program that provides health insurance to the poor. It is an entitlement program, which means that anyone who meets its eligibility requirements is supposed to receive help. But not everyone who is eligible receives that help. In 2001, Garnet Coleman, a Democrat who represented parts of Houston in the Texas House of Representatives, decided to try to change that. The state at that time required as many as fourteen different forms from parents before their children could enroll in Medicaid, and they had to be recertified every few months. Coleman sponsored legislation to reduce all that paperwork to a single four-page form. That change alone was expected to put one-third of the state's 1.4 million uninsured children on the Medicaid rolls.[15] Since then, budget cuts have reduced Medicaid rolls in Texas and many other states. But Coleman simply wanted to change the current rules to make it easier for people who were eligible to be able to apply.

If a problem is real and persistent enough, a state's legislature will address it eventually. Sometimes there is a general recognition that such a long-festering problem just needs to be fixed once and for all. That does not mean the fix is going to be easy. Some states, including Kansas, Ohio, and Pennsylvania, have had to tweak their school-funding formulas continually in response to state supreme court decisions that found their

Local Focus: Taking on the Law in the Land of the Free . . . and the Home of the Silly

Rich Smith, a British journalism student, spent one Christmas Day playing board games. He came across a reference to an obscure law in Florida that made it illegal for divorced women to go parachuting on Sundays. Enchanted by this and a treasure trove of other dumb American laws, he decided to spend the summer after graduation driving all across the United States and breaking every outdated or just plain absurd law he could find. "Tying giraffes to lampposts seemed a funnier way in which to become a felon" than arson or murder, Smith writes in his book about the spree, *You Can Get Arrested for That.**

Smith and a friend attempted to break two dozen laws in all, succeeding in most cases. Many of the laws concerned personal behavior. Traveling east from San Francisco, Smith's first successful crime was to peel an orange in a hotel room, which is illegal throughout California.

He then drove to Globe, Arizona, where it is illegal to play cards on the street against an American Indian, and did just that. He made sure to order plenty of garlic bread along with his pizza in Indianapolis because in that city it is illegal to enter a theater within three hours of eating garlic. He also broke the law by eating watermelon in a cemetery in Spartanburg, South Carolina, and by sleeping on top of a refrigerator in Pennsylvania.

The fashion police have made it illegal to wear a goatee in Massachusetts, so Smith grew one in plenty of time for his visit to that state. He also broke several laws concerning fishing, including his attempt to hunt down marine mammals in a lake in Utah and, of course, his blatant disregard for Chicago's ban on fishing while wearing pajamas. But he lacked sufficient skill to violate Tennessee's stricture against catching a fish with a lasso.

Although Smith managed to break numerous laws, several others defeated him. He failed to find a bathtub to carry illegally across the village green in Longmeadow, Massachusetts, and couldn't persuade a woman in Iowa to kiss him for longer than five minutes (or at all).

Several of his crimes were witnessed by police or private security guards, but perhaps it's in the nature of "dumb" laws that they aren't rigorously enforced. The only time Smith and his buddy got into serious trouble was when they drove ninety-seven miles per hour in a seventy-five-mile-per-hour zone in Wyoming. That time, they got nailed.

*Published by Three Rivers Press, New York, 2006.

---

education systems inadequate. And numerous states, including Mississippi, Pennsylvania, and West Virginia, have changed their tort laws, laws that cover damages to individuals, in the last few years. They have done this to help their doctors and trauma centers afford medical malpractice insurance. Addressing medical malpractice issues is difficult in part because trial lawyers object to any limitations on the punitive damages that people can receive from lawsuits after suffering as a result of medical negligence.

The political reason that this objection by trial lawyers is important is that trial lawyers are influential constituencies in Democratic politics. This is especially true in the Deep South, which has long had a reputation for hefty jury verdicts. States like Alabama and Mississippi traditionally have been hostile to trade unions, having "right to work" laws that have made it difficult for the unions to organize. Elsewhere, in the Midwest and Northeast, where unions are active, they are important donors to Democratic candidates. But where unions are weak, trial lawyers have become the major source of funding for Democrats. The role of such interest groups was discussed in chapter 6.

Legislatures often finish their work on an issue not because of outside pressure but because of internal changes. New leaders in the Arizona Senate in 2001 brought with them solutions to long-standing issues that included understaffing in the state's highway patrol, underfunding of the state's mental health system, and provisioning for water through new contracts. Legislators even managed to repeal antiquated sex laws that made it a crime for unmarried couples to live together.[16] More recently, in 2008, Republicans won control of both legislative chambers in Tennessee for the first time since the Civil War. They quickly began pushing long-sought legislation in areas including the regulation of guns, charter schools, and abortion. "I think every bad bill I've seen in my 10 years got resurrected this year and had a chance of passing," complained Mike Turner, chair of the House Democratic Caucus.[17]

Not surprisingly, states with stagnant leadership or long-term control by one party or the other may have a harder time making breakthroughs. Changes in partisan control bring in new leaders and, with them, new agendas that reflect new priorities and different constituencies. After all, before a bill can even get far enough to be debated, the idea for it must be developed. To get ideas for bills, legislators turn to each other, to staff, to colleagues in other states, and to outside sources such as a company with a cause of its own or a think tank interested in pushing change. As Alan Rosenthal, a leading expert on state legislatures at Rutgers University, points out, "legislation is becoming a national phenomenon." National associations of legislatures, such as the National Conference of State Legislatures and the American Legislative Exchange Council, promulgate ideas that quickly spread from state to state, as do bills pushed by national corporations and interest groups. And states may be addressing new issues that crop up on a similar time frame. In 2007, Rosenthal notes, more than two hundred bills on data privacy were introduced in thirty-nine states, and fifteen states considered legislation to ban or limit trans fats in restaurants. That year, legislatures considered more than 350 bills to address climate change.[18]

Fire-safe cigarettes, as their name suggests, do a lot to prevent accidental fires. They go out when a smoker stops puffing, and they have extra rings of paper that prevent them from burning on their own if a smoker falls asleep or drops a lit cigarette. But tobacco companies always oppose fire-safe cigarettes on the grounds that they cost more to produce. As a Democratic member of Congress from Massachusetts in the 1980s, Jim Shannon fought to require that all cigarettes have these safety features. But his legislation went nowhere because Big Tobacco was able to lobby successfully against this mandate.

But things began to change in 2004 when New York became the first state to mandate fire-safe cigarettes. "Maybe what we need to do is forget about beating our heads against the wall in Congress," Shannon recalls thinking.[19] By that time, Shannon was president of the National Fire Protection Association. This group spends most of its time writing safety codes for equipment like sprinklers and smoke alarms and wasn't the usual sort of public health advocacy group that cigarette manufacturers were used to fighting; it was able to recruit firefighters and marshals to help make its case in more state capitals. Between 2006 and 2009, the group helped persuade forty-four states to enact laws requiring self-extinguishing mechanisms in cigarettes, leaving Wyoming as the only state without such a mandate.

By the end of 2009, the lone holdout hardly mattered. Fire-safe cigarettes had become, de facto, the law of the entire land—especially since the tobacco lobby had given up the fight against them. Instead, tobacco companies worked hard to ensure that no state diverged from the model New York had created. It's one thing to have to meet the specific manufacturing requirements imposed by one state; it would be far more difficult for a national company to have to meet different standards in each state. "If the standards were reasonable and consistent, we could live with them," said Frank Lester, a spokesman for R. J. Reynolds Tobacco Company.[20]

Sometimes, private companies are able, like the firefighters, to go "venue shopping," finding sympathetic legislators in a state who will pass a law that may become a model for other states. But most ideas are still home-grown. Minnesota has an unusually fertile landscape when it comes to ideas for the legislature. More than 750 foundations are active in the state's public life. During the mid-1990s, thirty of them matched funds with the legislature to help nonprofit groups plan for federal budget cuts and changes in welfare law.[21] In addition, the state capital of St. Paul has the now-unusual benefit of being able to mine two major metropolitan daily newspapers—the *Pioneer Press* and the *Star Tribune,* which serves the capital's "twin city" of Minneapolis. Once upon a time, numerous communities were served by two or more competing newspapers. Today, consolidations and foldings have forced most areas to make due with one, if that. Fortunately for Minnesota's legislators, both Twin City papers actively cover public policy. Perhaps as a result, the state was the first to ban smoking in restaurants, the first to allow schoolchildren to choose among public schools, the first to allow charter schools, and the first to enact requirements that people holding comparable jobs receive comparable pay. Such engagement from the media—and, by extension, interest from the public—has become fairly rare. We talk about how the media cover state legislatures a little later on in this chapter.

Texas legislators approved a bill that would allow for random drug testing of thousands of high school athletes in an effort to stamp out steroid use.

Constituent Service

Aside from debating and passing laws, and ensuring that the interests of various groups are represented in decision making, legislators devote a good

FIGURE 7-1 How It Works: A One-Eyed Frog's View of the Legislative Process, or How a Bill *Really* Became a Law in Minnesota

The mechanisms by which a bill becomes a law at the state level are similar to the mechanisms at work at the federal level. And we've all seen the flowcharts that outline the ins and outs: a bill goes in one side, gets debated, marked-up, reported out, and then comes out the other side as a real life law to be implemented, or it gets returned to the legislature for an override, or it gets "killed." You'd be forgiven for thinking that beneath that abstraction lay a more complex and interesting process.

You'd be right. Below is a different flowchart, this one fleshing out what actually happened when a group of Minnesota teens brought to light the fact that the frog population in their area was turning up with extra limbs and missing eyes. About eight months and $151,000 later, the frogs were in much better shape.

In the summer of 1995, Henderson, Minnesota, students discover deformed frogs during a field trip near the Minnesota River. Their findings make headlines in the area.

↓

These headlines prompt the Minnesota Pollution Control Agency to ask for more state funding to research the problem.

Four days later a similar bill is introduced in the Senate by Steven Morse of Dakota.

On January 25, 1996, Rep. Willard Munger of Duluth introduces a bill in the House that would give the Pollution Control Agency $50,000 to fund research into the cause of the deformities.

↓

Students from the Henderson school appear at the state capitol in St. Paul to testify in front of the twenty-four-member House Environment and Natural Resources Committee in support of the proposal. They share photos of the deformed frogs, and tell legislators about what such deformities might indicate about the pollution hazards for the human population.

↓

A similar process takes place in the Senate.

As a result of the testimony, Rep. Virgil Johnson of Caledonia adds an amendment to the House bill requesting an additional $28,000 to fund surveys and public outreach, bringing the requested amount up to $78,000.

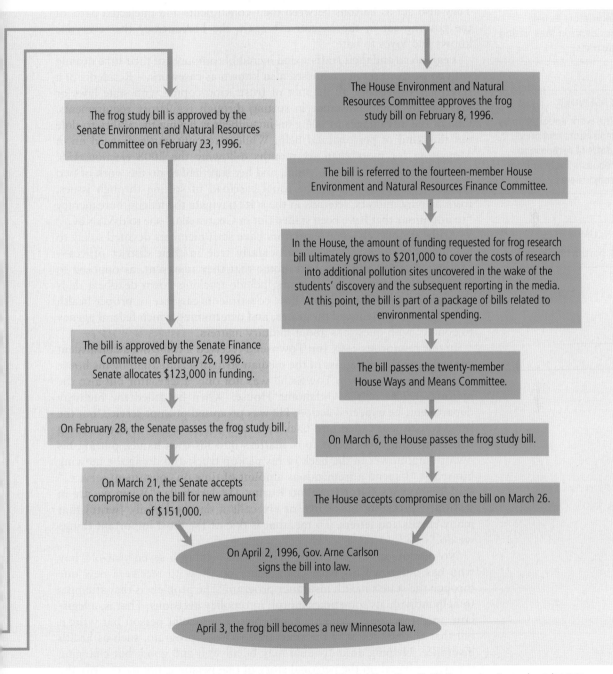

The frog study bill is approved by the Senate Environment and Natural Resources Committee on February 23, 1996.

The House Environment and Natural Resources Committee approves the frog study bill on February 8, 1996.

The bill is referred to the fourteen-member House Environment and Natural Resources Finance Committee.

In the House, the amount of funding requested for frog research bill ultimately grows to $201,000 to cover the costs of research into additional pollution sites uncovered in the wake of the students' discovery and the subsequent reporting in the media. At this point, the bill is part of a package of bills related to environmental spending.

The bill is approved by the Senate Finance Committee on February 26, 1996. Senate allocates $123,000 in funding.

The bill passes the twenty-member House Ways and Means Committee.

On February 28, the Senate passes the frog study bill.

On March 6, the House passes the frog study bill.

On March 21, the Senate accepts compromise on the bill for new amount of $151,000.

The House accepts compromise on the bill on March 26.

On April 2, 1996, Gov. Arne Carlson signs the bill into law.

April 3, the frog bill becomes a new Minnesota law.

Source: Minnesota House of Representatives Public Information Office, "Capitol Steps: How Six Bills Became Law." www.house.leg.state .mn.us/hinfo/How6bil.pdf.

deal of time and energy to **constituent service**. They help clear up problems that citizens are having with public agencies or even private companies. They also act as liaisons between their constituents and unelected parts of the government in the executive branch, the bureaucracy that everyone knows and loves to hate.

Legislators and their staffs spend incredible amounts of their time dealing with constituent service requests, also known as **casework**.[22] Residents of a state may experience all manner of frustration coping with state laws or may merely want assistance in sorting through regulatory requirements. One of the advantages of being an **incumbent** is having the ability to dole out this kind of personalized help. While a recount battle dragged on in Minnesota for more than six months following the 2008 election, U.S. senator Amy Klobuchar, D-Minn., and her staff had to do the work of two senators—handling double the usual caseload of sorting through issues, from helping military veterans in the state navigate the federal bureaucracy "to adoptions that have been stalled out in Guatemala," she told MSNBC.[23]

At the state level, some legislators have staff members devoted solely to helping constituents. This is particularly true in their district offices— offices located in the area back home that they represent, as opposed to their capitol offices. Typical issues include tracking down deadbeat dads for child support, figuring out how constituents can receive proper health coverage under Medicaid programs, and determining which federal agency to contact with questions about military matters.

In one humorous case, Jim Townsend received a call from a constituent complaining that the grass in the median strip of a state road by his house had become overgrown. Townsend was not only a legislator but also the majority leader of the Oklahoma House. When he called the highway department, he expected action. He was promised prompt service, but the same constituent called him back two weeks later to report that nothing had been done. Townsend took matters into his own hands, putting his own riding mower in the back of his pickup truck and doing the mowing himself.[24] "I spend a tremendous amount of time on constituent service," said Tennessee senator Rosalind Kurita, D-Clarksville. "When we are in session, I probably make five or six calls a day and easily [write] that many emails and letters. To me, that is one of the most important things we do."[25]

No one objects to a senator like Kurita helping a seven-year-old boy who has outgrown his wheelchair figure out how to receive a new one through the state's health insurance program. The problem is that attempts to help individuals sometimes morph into policy decisions. That is, a legislator might not only write a letter to help a particular person but write a bill that changes the way the state approaches a program, such as health insurance. Helping an individual may be all well and good, but changing the system based on the personal story of one person is not necessarily the best way to change policies that will affect thousands.

Constituency service, or casework, is an important part of any elected official's job, even if it's not necessarily the most exciting part. Here, Beaufort County (S.C.) councilwoman Margaret Griffin talks to one of her constituents.

Undoubtedly, it is important for legislators to hear about the real-world experiences of their constituents. Because they cannot meet with everybody, however, they need to rely on reports and studies to get a complete picture. They otherwise might be swayed too greatly by personal interactions. The danger of politicians' having to raise significant campaign finance treasuries is not so much that their votes can be bought but that they are much more likely to meet with the people or interest groups that give them the campaign contributions. Campaign donors often give money simply so that they can have access to a legislator when they hand over the check. That means that people who do not or cannot give money may not get heard.

Oversight

Under the U.S. system of checks and balances, legislatures are charged with **oversight**, the task of making sure that the governor and the executive branch agencies are functioning properly. The executive branch is called that because it executes the laws written by the legislature. Legislators are only doing their job when they call governors and executive branch agencies to account through hearings, investigations, and audits for how they are carrying out those laws. Unfortunately, the most ubiquitous form of oversight is a legislator's intervening with administrative agencies on behalf of constituents or constituent groups in ways that are "episodic and punitive."[26]

OVERSIGHT

The role the legislature takes in making sure that the implementation of its laws by the executive branch is being done properly.

Local Focus: Constituent Service: Going the Extra Mile

When John Medinger was a member of the Wisconsin State Assembly, he worked backbreaking hours to do his job—and to make sure that his constituents knew he was doing his job. He needed to let people know how seriously committed he was to representing them and their interests because Medinger is a Democrat who represented a Republican district.

He drove the 137 miles to the capitol in Madison and the 137 miles back home to La Crosse three times a week, even when the legislature was not meeting. When he was in La Crosse, he was in perpetual motion. "If I don't have anything to do at home," he said, "I go sit in a coffee shop and shoot the breeze. I might be home two nights a week to tuck my kids in. I go to every pancake breakfast and every rummage sale. I am always looking for something to do. If there's nothing else, I go to a basketball game and mingle with the crowd."

All that work paid off politically. One year, Medinger got a perfect 100 rating from the American Federation of Labor and Congress of Industrial Organizations (AFL-CIO) but was rated at 29 by the Wisconsin Association of Manufacturers. The La Crosse chamber of commerce endorsed him for reelection anyway. As Medinger once said, "There are some Republicans in my district who could run against me and make my life miserable. . . . But the Republicans can't come up with candidates who will put in 100-hour weeks. So they don't make it."[a] The fact is, no one who interacts with legislators doubts that they work hard. They work long hours meeting with colleagues, constituents, lobbyists seeking a favor for their clients, and business leaders from their districts and across the state.

For all of the clear evidence that politicians work hard, some people still question whether all the meeting and studying and debating those legislators do actually accomplish anything. "A politician's day is long," says satirist P.J. O'Rourke. "He gets into the office early, reads newspaper clippings with his name highlighted, submits to a radio interview with Howard Stern, goes to a prayer breakfast and an ACLU [American Civil Liberties Union] lunch, checks opinion polls, meets with an NRA delegation, makes a friendly call to Al Sharpton, sits in the Inland Waterways Committee hearing room drawing pictures of sailboats and seagulls on a notepad, proposes National Dried Plum Week, votes 'yea' (or is it 'nay'?) on something or other (consult staff), exercises with the president, recovers from a faked charley horse after being lapped on the White House jogging track, watches the signature machine sign letters to constituents, returns a corporate campaign contribution to WorldCom, speaks at a dinner supporting campaign-finance reform, goes home, gets on the phone, and fundraises until all hours."[b]

[a]Quoted in Alan Ehrenhalt, *The United States of Ambition* (New York: Times Books/Random House, 1991), 133.
[b]P.J. O'Rourke, "No Apparent Motive," *Atlantic Monthly,* November 2002, 34.

For example, several years ago, the Arkansas Livestock and Poultry Commission filed suit against a livestock sales barn for failure to meet state regulations concerning an infectious livestock disease called brucellosis. The senator from that district placed language to weaken those regulations in the bill to fund that commission, which prompted the commissioner to resign.[27] The commissioner had taken the funding cut as a signal that his authority was being undermined, so he quit. That kind of scattershot approach—helping a particular constituent at the expense of the public good—is by its nature inequitable. The point of bureaucratic norms is to make sure that regulations and laws are applied fairly and evenly across the board.

Legislators may attack agencies for pursuing policies that hurt their constituents, but it's unfortunately pretty rare for the legislative branch—despite its duty to keep an eye on executive branch functions—to consistently take a hard look at whether ongoing programs are functioning as they should. Aside from unearthing an occasional scandal involving misspent funds, there is little political reward for poking around in the business of the state. Staff aides regularly perform audits and evaluations, but legislatures make only sporadic use of them in making follow-up decisions about funding. Most oversight comes in a less systematic way, through budget reviews and occasional committee hearings. In states that impose limits on the number of terms that legislators can serve, there is even less opportunity to perform oversight. Members have less time to become expert in a particular area and so they often rely more heavily on expert testimony from the very executive branch that they are meant to oversee.

And each program, it seems, has not only agency officials but its beneficiaries and lobbyists who will question the motives of legislators or staffers who seek to audit its work. In other words, there's often not much reward for a legislator in taking the job of oversight seriously. For example, in 2007, the North Carolina legislature created the Program Evaluation Division, which was charged with compiling a scorecard on how state agencies were performing, in much the same way investors might be provided with information about the performance of private companies. John Turcotte, the division's founding director, said his goal was both to "target programs for evaluation that are important to the General Assembly and also look at all state government programs collectively to avoid legislative oversight gaps."[28] Turcotte's first report looked at agricultural research stations. North Carolina had the most of any in the country—twenty-one, compared to only eleven in the much larger state of California—and Turcotte's group concluded that there was no economic or strategic justification for the state to support so many. "That report was like setting off a nuclear weapon in the area of Raleigh," he said. "Any time you question the necessity of an institution or a major component of a program, you will create massive opposition."[29]

Organization and Operation of Legislatures

The U.S. system of representative democracy was designed to be messy. One book has argued that the institutions of democracy should be more popular because they work pretty well, but concedes, "The American political system was not designed for people to understand."[30] Legislatures were created because, even in colonial days, this country was too large and its problems too complex to be addressed by its vast numbers of individual citizens. We elect legislatures in our republican form of government to argue out our problems in a single time and space in sessions at the capitol. The ranks of the legislature have become far more diverse over the last thirty years. Although the average state legislator is still a white male, there are twice as many African Americans and nearly six times as many women serving in legislatures today than there were in 1970. Also over the past thirty years or so, legislatures have become better equipped to do their job by hiring more and better professionally trained staffers. None of these changes, however, have made state legislatures any more popular with the public.

Bicameralism

Legislatures are not, of course, random groups of people hanging around a dorm and picking pizza toppings. Every state has a constitution that describes a body that can pass state laws. In every case but Nebraska, which has a unicameral (or one-house) legislature, legislatures are bicameral (or divided into two houses), pretty much like the U.S. Congress. As mentioned earlier in this chapter, one chamber is normally called either the house of representatives or the assembly and the other is called the senate. The Tenth Amendment of the U.S. Constitution reserves all powers not given to the federal government for the states, and state legislatures can write any state law that does not interfere with federal laws.

The house, or assembly, is considered more of a "people's house," with its members representing fewer people for shorter terms than their colleagues in the senate. The house always has more members, known as state representatives, than the senate. There are 163 representatives in the Missouri General Assembly, for example, but only 34 senators. There are some exceptions, but generally senators serve four-year terms, whereas house members have to be reelected every two years. The two chambers operate independently, with separate leaders, committees, and agendas, although both chambers have to pass the same version of a bill before it can be sent to the governor to be signed into law or vetoed. Nebraska, with its unicameral legislature, is the one exception.

Legislative Leadership

CAUCUS

All the members of a party—Republican or Democrat—within a legislative chamber. Also refers to meetings of members of a political party in a chamber.

Most state legislatures have essentially the same leadership structure, at least for their top positions. At the beginning of a session, each house votes in its speaker. This is generally someone picked beforehand by a **caucus**, or meeting, of members of the majority party. The majority leader and the minority leader rank just below the Speaker of the house. *Majority* and *minority* refer to the respective strengths of the major parties. Either the Democratic or Republican Party may hold the majority of seats in a chamber. (In 2009, fewer than 10 legislators—out of more than 7,000 nationwide—were independents or members of third parties.) In the senate,

TABLE 7-1

Total Number of State Legislators (House and Senate), 2007

State	Senate Members	House Members	Total Members	State	Senate Members	House Members	Total Members
Alabama	35	105	140	Nebraska	49	n/a	49
Alaska	20	40	60	Nevada	21	42	63
Arizona	30	60	90	New Hampshire	24	400	424
Arkansas	35	100	135	New Jersey	40	80	120
California	40	80	120	New Mexico	42	70	112
Colorado	35	65	100	New York	62	150	212
Connecticut	36	151	187	North Carolina	50	120	170
Delaware	21	41	62	North Dakota	47	94	141
Florida	40	120	160	Ohio	33	99	132
Georgia	56	180	236	Oklahoma	48	101	149
Hawaii	25	51	76	Oregon	30	60	90
Idaho	35	70	105	Pennsylvania	50	203	253
Illinois	59	118	177	Rhode Island	38	75	113
Indiana	50	100	150	South Carolina	46	124	170
Iowa	50	100	150	South Dakota	35	70	105
Kansas	40	125	165	Tennessee	33	99	132
Kentucky	38	100	138	Texas	31	150	181
Louisiana	39	105	144	Utah	29	75	104
Maine	35	151	186	Vermont	30	150	180
Maryland	47	141	188	Virginia	40	100	140
Massachusetts	40	160	200	Washington	49	98	147
Michigan	38	110	148	West Virginia	34	100	134
Minnesota	67	134	201	Wisconsin	33	99	132
Mississippi	52	122	174	Wyoming	30	60	90
Missouri	34	163	197	**Total**	**1,971**	**5,411**	**7,382**
Montana	50	100	150				

Source: National Conference of State Legislatures, "Current Number of Legislators, Terms of Office and Next Election Year, January 2007." www.ncsl.org/programs/legismgt/about/numoflegis.htm.

the top leader is known as the president, president pro tem, president pro tempore, or the majority leader.

Certain aspects of the leadership positions remain constant across all the states. For example, a Speaker will typically preside over daily sessions of the house or assembly, refer bills to the appropriate committees, and sign legislation as it makes its way over to the senate or the governor's desk. Leaders appoint committee chairs—in some states, all the members of committees—set or change committee jurisdictions, and offer staff or legislative help to rank-and-file members. They also often help with campaigns, including financial help.

The amount of power invested in the office of Speaker or senate president does vary by state, however. In the Texas Senate, leadership powers are invested in the office of lieutenant governor. Lieutenant governors normally do not possess much formal power, but in Texas, they appoint the members of committees and committee chairs in the thirty-one-member body and decide which bills are considered and when. In some older legislatures, such as those in New Jersey and Massachusetts, the Senate president performs all of those functions, presides over debates, counts votes, and ensures member attendance. In California, those powers rest with the Senate president pro tem. But regardless of how the formal duties are divided up, usually there is one individual who emerges as holding the most power and speaking for the chamber in negotiating with the other chamber and the governor.

With the exception of Nebraska, where parties are actually banned from the nonpartisan unicameral legislature, legislatures are divided along party lines. Not only does the majority party get to pick the top leader, it gets to fill virtually all of the important committee chairs as well. A party majority is worth much more than the comfort of knowing that your fellow Democrats or Republicans will help you outvote the opposition on most bills. To hold the leadership and chair positions means that the majority party gets to set the agenda—deciding which bills will be heard for a vote. Democrats from the 1950s into the early 1990s held a two-to-one edge in the number of legislative seats and controlled many more chambers than the GOP. At the start of this century, however, Republicans pulled into near-ties both in terms of raw numbers of legislators and in how many chambers they controlled. Democrats regained a slight but significant advantage back in the favorable election cycles of 2006 and 2008. At the end of World War II, all but seven of the forty-eight states had united governments, meaning one party controlled the governorship and both legislative chambers. By 1986, only twenty-one of fifty states had united governments.[31] The increasingly competitive nature of legislative politics has meant that every election cycle since 1984 has resulted in at least one tied chamber somewhere.[32]

Some leaders hold their positions for decades, although this is exceptional. Jimmy Naifeh was the Speaker of the Tennessee House from 1991 until his party lost its majority in 2009. Mike Miller started his run as president of the Maryland Senate back in 1987 and was still going strong in 2009. Fred Risser, the nation's longest-serving state legislator and president of the Wisconsin Senate, has held a variety of leadership positions since the 1960s. Climbing the leadership ladder can take no time at all in states with term limits like California and Florida, where House members can serve only six and eight years, respectively, and Speakers are sometimes chosen as a freshman. But Joe Hackney, who became Speaker of the North Carolina House in 2007, had to serve more than a quarter century before attaining that post. "When I came to the legislature, I more or less regarded it as a long-term thing," he says. "It wasn't my plan to be there two or four or six years and quit. It was my plan to make a contribution, and I saw that those who make a contribution built up seniority and experience."[33]

MAP 7-1 Partisan Control of State Government, 1954

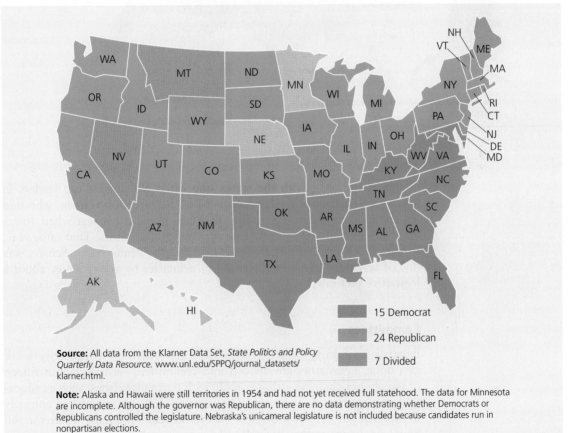

Source: All data from the Klarner Data Set, *State Politics and Policy Quarterly Data Resource.* www.unl.edu/SPPQ/journal_datasets/klarner.html.

	15 Democrat
	24 Republican
	7 Divided

Note: Alaska and Hawaii were still territories in 1954 and had not yet received full statehood. The data for Minnesota are incomplete. Although the governor was Republican, there are no data demonstrating whether Democrats or Republicans controlled the legislature. Nebraska's unicameral legislature is not included because candidates run in nonpartisan elections.

MAP 7-2 **Partisan Control of State Government, 2007**

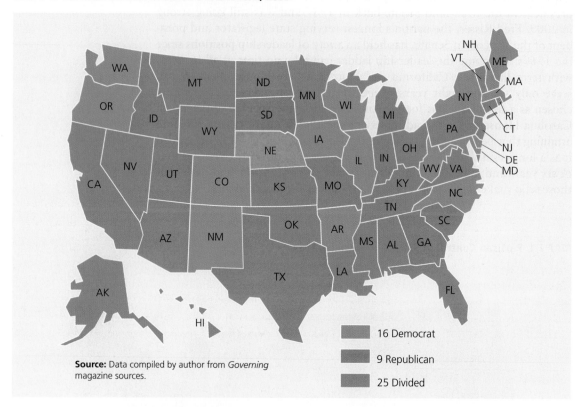

16 Democrat

9 Republican

25 Divided

Source: Data compiled by author from *Governing* magazine sources.

Voters unhappy with the status quo often will unseat top leaders in symbolic decapitations. That happened in 2006 to Bob Garton, who had led the Indiana Senate for twenty-six years but lost his seat when voters grew unhappy about a health insurance perk for senators. That same year, Robert Jubelirer, a twenty-five-year leader in the Pennsylvania Senate, was one of seventeen incumbents ousted in primaries by voters angry about a legislative pay raise.

Committees

Regardless of party control, committees are where most legislative work gets done. Legislators are divided into committees—usually about fifteen or twenty per chamber—that grapple with particular issues, such as education, transportation, and taxes. Thousands of bills are introduced annually in each legislature. Most of these bills never reach the floor where the full house or senate meets. Basically, they never make it past the committee stage to be debated or voted on by the house or senate as a whole. Instead, they are sent to the appropriate committee, where they may be debated and amended but usually die without a hearing. Just as the senate president, house Speaker, or other leader sets the agenda for floor action on bills, so the committee chair decides which bills are going to be heard and receive priority treatment at the committee level.

Members try to serve on the committees where they will have the most influence. The most prestigious committees are the budget committees that set tax and spending levels. Other committees debate policy, but unless funding is provided to pay for those policies, they do not matter very much. Seats on a finance or appropriations committee are highly sought after, but members will also "request appointment to committees, which will give them the most visibility and interest in their districts."[34] Thus, senators from rural districts may want to serve on an agriculture committee. Representatives who previously served on city councils may want seats on the local government committee.

Any member can introduce legislation on any topic, but members of the education committee, for example, are more likely to introduce and influence bills that affect schools. When an education bill is being debated in the full house or senate, other members, who have other specialties, will turn to members of the education committee for guidance about what a bill would do and how they should vote. The same holds true for other issues, such as transportation and healthcare.

Rank-and-File Members

Not every legislator, of course, can be a leader. The majority of legislators—those who provided leaders with their votes—are known as **rank-and-file members** of the legislature. And no legislator—leader or rank-and-file member—can be fully versed on the details of each of the dozens of bills that confront him or her every day during a session. They turn to many sources for information on how to vote. There is a classic notion, posited by political philosopher and statesman Edmund Burke, that divides legislators into **delegates**, who vote according to the wishes of their districts, and **trustees**, who vote according to their own consciences.[35] Given the proliferation of legislation, however, members never hear from a single constituent on probably 90 percent of the bills that they must consider. Instead, they rely for guidance on staffers, other legislators, interest groups and lobbyists, executive branch officials, foundations, think tanks, and other sources.

The fact that legislators cannot rely solely on their own judgment to vote is the source of many people's sense that legislators' votes can be bought—or at least rented. This is ironic, considering that political scientists note that most of the time most legislators are extremely attentive to

RANK-AND-FILE MEMBERS
Legislators who do not hold leadership positions or senior committee posts.

DELEGATES
Legislators who primarily see their role as voting according to their constituents' beliefs as they understand them.

TRUSTEES
Legislators who believe they were elected to exercise their own judgment and to approach issues accordingly.

their districts and vote according to their sense of their desires. Their primary goal, after all, is to win reelection. In addition, most states have made it tougher for lobbyists to get lawmakers' attention. It is difficult under the new ethics rules for a lobbyist to spring for a legislator's cup of coffee, much less treat for lunch. In Kentucky, for example, there are fewer of the nightly receptions that once kept Frankfort well fed, and lobbyists are prohibited from making any personal contributions to candidates for the legislature. "A lot of the principal lobbyists are still here, so folks have had to learn to adapt," says Bobby Sherman, head of the Kentucky legislature's nonpartisan research staff. "It's more work for them. They have to build relationships in a different way, and information delivery is much more important."[36]

All of this is necessary because, as with most things, times have changed. It used to be that rank-and-file members voted pretty much the way they were instructed by their party leaders. In Connecticut, the legislature of the early 1960s was an assemblage of party hacks—members beholden to the party chair for patronage. This meant that most of the legislature's important decisions were made in small meetings to which the public—and even most rank-and-file members—were not invited.

Examples do still exist of members caving in to party or leadership pressure. In his book *Experiencing Politics,* former state representative John McDonough, a Democrat, recounts one afternoon in fall 1995 when he was sitting on the floor of the Massachusetts House of Representatives. The chamber was preparing to vote on a huge tax break for Raytheon, a locally based defense contractor. McDonough thought the tax break was a terrible idea. He considered it a form of corporate blackmail. So he pushed the little red button on his desk and voted against it. Then the majority whip—the party's head vote-counter—came over to see him. "The Speaker wants a green [light] from you on this," the whip said. That did not make any sense to McDonough. The tax break was passing easily. His vote was not needed. The whip did not answer his question as to why the Speaker needed his vote. "He just does," she said. So, McDonough tells us, he caved. A few months down the road, he had his own favorite bill coming up, and he wanted the Speaker's help. He did not want to take any chances. He walked right back to his desk and switched his vote. It was a classic example of trading votes. "Was my switch," he asks, "an example of naked, opportunistic self-interest or of a hard trade-off necessary to achieve a higher good? Anyone can characterize my action either way. The most honest answer is that both perspectives contain some degree of truth."[37]

Such practical decisions are made all the time. Nevertheless, leaders today carry much less weight with members than they did even a generation ago. Leaders these days are no stronger than members want them to be; they often lead by listening. They have to pay attention to customer service and their main customers are rank-and-file legislators. Leaders help other legislators intervene with the governor or the rest of the executive branch and help green-light bills in order to build up political chits. "As long as it wasn't against the law, didn't require that I go to confession, or wouldn't break up my marriage, I did it," recalled Ralph Wright, a one-time Speaker of the Vermont House.[38]

Consider two examples from some years ago. Connecticut House Speaker Irving Stolberg was considered a brilliant legislator, but he was heavy-handed as a leader. When he met with his lieutenants, it was not to consult them on strategy but, rather, to tell them what the strategy would be. Many of the Democrats under him thought he abused his power, so they coupled their votes in 1989 with House Republicans and drove him out.[39] Compare this to a story from across the country the following year. In May 1990, months of work on a workers' compensation reform package threatened to go to waste during a meeting in the office of Oregon House Speaker Vera Katz. Bob Shiprack, chair of the labor committee, grew impatient as the conversation got stuck on the topic of how chiropractors would be treated under the law, so he stormed out. Katz, rather than ordering him to get back to work, ran after him and mothered him, soothed him, and sympathized with his exhaustion. "It disarmed me," Shiprack said. "Vera loves to disarm." Katz's tactic worked, and the workers' compensation package went though.[40]

Leaders cannot bully their way through as they did a generation ago for two reasons. Leadership offices control direct fund-raising efforts designed to build or maintain majorities. The Senate president in Maine, for example, raised more than $450,000 in 2006, in a state where legislative races still can be won with a few thousand dollars. But the leadership efforts are mainly directed at the relatively few competitive races that will make or break a majority. Most rank-and-file members today raise their own money and have greater access to expert advice for hire and separate sources of money, whether from political action committees (PACs) run by industries or labor unions or elsewhere.

We have already touched on the other factor—members do not have to rely on leaders as much as they once did for information about bills or for help writing legislation. The proliferation of lobbyists and the **professionalization** of the legislatures have meant that members have their own resources to draw on.[41]

Apportionment

One more issue that profoundly affects all legislators is **apportionment**. Following the U.S. census, which occurs every ten years, each state draws new lines for its legislative districts. In states with more than one member of Congress, congressional districts are redrawn as well. The **redistricting** process is the most naked exercise of political power in the states. The incumbent party will do everything it can to preserve its hold or, preferably,

PROFESSIONALIZATION
The process of providing legislators with the resources to make politics their main career, such as making their positions full time or providing them with full-time staff.

APPORTIONMENT
The allotting of districts according to population shifts. The number of congressional districts that a state has may be reapportioned every ten years.

REDISTRICTING
The drawing of new boundaries for congressional and state legislative districts, usually following a decennial census.

Compared to earlier generations of legislative leaders who could dictate to the party's rank and file, their contemporary counterparts, like Maine Senate president Beth Edmonds, have to rely more on persuasion and negotiation. For the most part, party leaders in state legislatures no longer have the absolute power to dictate policy and tactics to the legislature's rank and file.

GERRYMANDERS

Districts clearly drawn with the intent of pressing partisan advantage at the expense of other considerations.

MALAPPORTIONMENT

A situation in which the principle of equal representation is violated.

increase its numbers. Each party will seek to draw the maximum number of districts possible that are likely to elect members of its own party. The two major parties will fight each other as best they can to make certain that the other side does not gain the upper hand. "Just like there are no atheists in foxholes, there are no nonpartisans in redistricting," says Paul Green, director of the School of Policy Studies at Roosevelt University in Chicago. "You use whatever leverage you can."[42]

In New York state, slower rates of population growth, relative to other states, has for decades translated into a lost congressional seat or two every ten years. In 2001, the legislature came up with a map that sliced and diced counties and towns in an effort to create new districts that balanced competing political interests in the state. Monroe County, which includes Rochester, was home to 735,000 residents following the 2000 census, more than enough to earn its own congressional seat. Instead, the county was cut into four different congressional districts, including one that stretches one hundred miles in a thin strip along the Niagara River and the Lake Ontario shore to link parts of Buffalo and Rochester and their Democratic precincts.

Political maps that link disparate communities or have odd shapes that resemble earmuffs or moose antlers are known as **gerrymanders,** after Elbridge Gerry, an early nineteenth-century governor of Massachusetts. **Malapportionment** occurs when districts violate the principle of equal representation. In the past, some state legislative districts could have many times the number of constituents as other districts. Votes in the smaller districts, in effect, counted for more. Relatively few people in, say, a sparsely populated rural district would have the same amount of representative clout in the legislature as an urban district with many times the rural area's population.

Legislatures draw the maps in most states, but there are exceptions. Since the 1980s, Iowa's political maps have been created by the nonpartisan Legislative Services Agency. The agency instructs its computers to draw one hundred House districts and fifty Senate districts according to rules that keep population as equal as possible, avoid splitting counties, and keep the districts compact. In contrast to legislature-drawn maps, the agency does not consider party registration, voting patterns, or the political

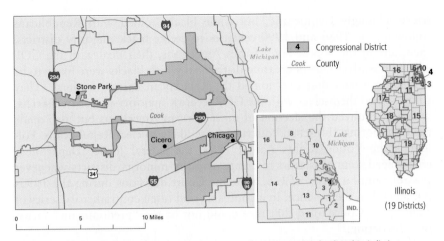

Illinois's Fourth Congressional District is a classic example of a gerrymandered political jurisdiction. It consists of two strips of land running east-west on Chicago's north and south sides. These strips are connected only by a stretch of Interstate 294. The district was drawn this way to capture two majority Hispanic sections of the Chicago area.

territory of incumbents. Largely as a result, partisan control of the Iowa legislature flips just about every ten years. Other states use other commission models. In New Jersey, a bipartisan commission composed of six Democrats and six Republicans is charged with the task of coming up with a plan that can command a majority. If it cannot—which is typical—the chief justice of the state supreme court appoints a thirteenth member to the committee as a tiebreaker. In 2001, the new maps landed the Democrats a majority, and they were able to retake control of the assembly for the first time in a decade and also pulled into a tie in the Senate.

The idea that redistricting needs fixing has become a kind of grail among reformers, but attempts to make redistricting less partisan by taking it out of the hands of legislators have gotten nowhere. Voters in California and Ohio soundly defeated ballot measures in 2005 that would have given redistricting powers to a panel of retired judges or a commission, respectively. But a repeat effort in California in 2008 proved successful. Governor Arnold Schwarzenegger and other sponsors convinced voters to take legislative redistricting out of the hands of the legislators, giving the job to a citizens' commission to be overseen by the state auditor instead. This time around, they left congressional redistricting up to state legislators, guaranteeing that the drawing of those districts would remain political in nature and thus avoiding the opposition of the state's powerful congressional delegation.

Partisanship is the primary concern of redistricting, but it is not the only one. Issues of representation also play a big part. African Americans are overwhelmingly Democratic, but some blacks joined with Republicans following the 1980 and 1990 censuses to create black majority districts, especially in the South. For African Americans, their deal with the GOP offered the advantage of creating districts in which blacks were likely to be elected. It wasn't that they joined the Republican Party, of course. They simply allied themselves with the GOP to draw **majority-minority districts**, which guaranteed the election of more African Americans but also made the neighboring "bleached" districts more likely to elect Republicans. Following the Voting Rights Act of 1982, the federal Justice Department encouraged state legislators to create majority-minority districts whenever possible, until a series of U.S. Supreme Court decisions during the 1990s put an end to the practice. In a confusing and often contradictory series of rulings, the Court ruled that race could not be the "predominant" factor in redistricting.[43]

In most state legislatures, the major goal of redistricting following the 2000 census seemed to be protecting incumbents. Members of the two major parties colluded to draw few competitive districts, preferring to know they would run in "safe" Republican-leaning or Democratic-leaning districts. Drawing districts that were politically safe for current officeholders necessarily meant creating fewer new districts that were likely to elect minorities. That was true even for Hispanics, who were the fastest-growing minority group in the United States during the 1990s, accounting for 60 percent of the population growth in Texas and 80 percent of the growth in California.[44] Nevertheless, the California legislature and the Texas judicial panel that drew that state's maps did not go out of their way to draw new Hispanic-majority districts. Hispanics held only about two hundred state legislative seats in 2001, and their number did not rise appreciably in the 2002 elections. By decade's end, Hispanics had outnumbered African Americans as the nation's largest minority group, but they held less than 3 percent of legislative seats nationwide, compared with more than 8 percent held by African Americans.

State Legislators

If you were to make a composite drawing of the average state legislator, he—and it would be a he—would be white and in his fifties or maybe sixties. He would have had at least some college education, have an income topping $50,000, describe himself as moderate or conservative, and have lived in the community he is representing for at least ten years.[45] There are many, many exceptions to all the aspects of this composite. The type of person who runs for state legislative office has changed a good deal over the past thirty years—there are far more women and African Americans in office and fewer lawyers—but nonetheless, the type of middle- to upper-middle-class American male described here still predominates.

The nation's 7,382 state legislators come from all backgrounds, particularly in the states where the house and senate meet only for part of the year. In states with full-time legislatures, such as California and Pennsylvania, the legislators tend, not surprisingly, to be career politicians who have served in local or other elected offices or perhaps as members of a legislative staff. In states with part-time legislatures, like Arkansas and Indiana, members come from many different walks of life, devoting perhaps one-third of their working hours to politics while earning their living through some other means.

Professional Background

Some employers encourage the political hopes of their employees because they know legislative service can be good for business. This holds true especially for professions most directly affected by state lawmaking, such as big business. Buddy Dyer kept up his law practice while serving in the Florida Senate and in 2002 had to respond to complaints that his bills would have protected his industrial company clients from fines and lawsuits. His defense? "Probably not a bill that goes through the Legislature" did not affect one of his firm's clients.[46]

Other groups enjoy considerable representation within legislative bodies. In 2006, Al Mansell stepped down from his leadership role as president of the Utah Senate to become president of the National Association of Realtors. He stayed in the Senate, however, sponsoring legislation that helped members of his profession. He was one of twenty-two people who worked in real estate who were serving in the Utah legislature at that time. "I've got people who are on county commissions, mayors, state senators," said Chris Kyler, CEO of the Utah Association of Realtors. "Our lieutenant governor was president of our state association about 20 years ago. Our people are involved in the parties, too. We've got precinct chairs and vice chairs and county delegates throughout the state."[47]

Consider public education. Teachers' unions are usually among the most effective lobbying groups in any state, but schools do not necessarily have to rely on outsiders to influence the legislature. Teachers themselves are often members of legislatures, and employees of other institutions of higher learning also may serve. In Maine, state law requires that teachers be granted leave if they want to run for office. Maine's legislature meets for only one-half of the year, every other year. But even that chunk of time is enough to play havoc with a person's work schedule, and there's a good deal of concern in the state that retirees are coming to dominate the legislative chamber.

The reality is that retired people account for only about 12 percent of state legislators nationwide. About 15 percent of legislators are lawyers—a big decline from past decades. In New York, 60 percent of the assembly and 70 percent of the Senate used to be made up of lawyers.[48] Nowadays, the dominant group in legislatures nationwide are people with business backgrounds. They make up about 30 percent of today's legislators. The remaining half or so come from education, healthcare, real estate, insurance, and agriculture.

Demographic Diversity

The number of women legislators has risen dramatically since the "second wave" feminist era of the late 1960s and early 1970s, but their numbers still do not reflect the female share of the overall population. In 1970, women held just 4 percent of all state legislative seats.[49] Their numbers doubled quickly, to 8 percent of all legislators by 1975, and they climbed to 18 percent by 1991. Their ranks held steady at just over 20 percent for about a dozen years before spiking to 23.5 percent after the 2006 elections. Their numbers ticked up to just above 24 percent following the 2008 campaigns. Only six states—Arizona, Colorado, Maryland, Minnesota, New Hampshire, and Vermont—could brag in 2007 that one-third or more of their legislators were women.[50] But, in 2009, the New Hampshire Senate became the first legislative chamber in the nation to have a majority of women members. Women served as its president and majority leader, while another woman served as Speaker of the house.[51]

The number of women entering state legislatures may not be growing exponentially, but the type of women holding house and senate seats has changed. In the old days of the 1970s—about a decade before most readers of this book were born—most women running for office came to politics later in life than men. They had not been tapped to run by party professionals or other "queenmakers." Instead, they jump-started their own careers, drawn into the policy realm out of concerns about their children's schools or their local communities. Men may know from the time they are in school that they want to run for office, says Barbara Lee, who runs a foundation dedicated to helping women run for office, but women often find out later in life that it is important to enter the game because of their specific concerns and experiences.[52] This dynamic has changed to some extent. Women now enter politics at ages comparable to men. Many still tend to care about a set of issues (education, healthcare, and the environment) that are noticeably different from the top priorities of men (taxes and budgets). But sometimes they address such issues because they still find it harder to get on the more powerful finance committees in representative numbers.

Back in the 1970s, when the first relatively large numbers of women legislators entered the capitols, they tended to be less politically ambitious and less likely to enter the ranks of legislative leadership than men. They devoted more attention to constituent service matters and tended to serve on education, health, and welfare committees. They also tended to have less education and come from jobs that were not as good as those held by their male counterparts. During the 1980s, the average socioeconomic status of women legislators improved, and they served on a broader range of committees, but they mostly still focused on issues of women, family, and children. By the 1990s, women legislators held about 15 percent of all legislative leadership positions but were still unlikely to serve on tax committees.[53] Their backgrounds had become more varied, and they had also become more conservative, although they still were more liberal than men—and significantly more likely to initiate legislation than their male colleagues.[54] Women are also more likely than men to successfully get their priority bills through the legislative process.[55]

Women, however, do not alter the fundamental political dynamics in legislatures, perhaps because they remain a fairly small minority in most states. For example, women legislators, by and large, favor reproductive rights, but they do not have an especially powerful impact on a given state's policy regarding this issue. Whether a state devotes much funding toward abortion programs or places a number of restrictions on such programs, including requiring parental notification for minors, depends more on whether the state's overall political culture is liberal or conservative than on whether women make up a large minority of legislative caucuses.[56] Still, women legislators do tend to bring up issues and concerns that would not be raised by an all-male legislature.

This fact is even truer of issues of concern to minorities. African Americans have made gains similar to women in legislatures over the past thirty-five years, growing from a microscopic minority to a larger minority, albeit one that still does not reflect their overall share of the population. Their numbers have doubled to about 625—less than 10 percent of all the legislators nationwide.

Although it is both dangerous and wrong to generalize about any group, the interests of African Americans as a whole have long been fairly stable and predictable. "On questions of public policy, ideology, and candidate choice," writes Kerry L. Haynie in his 2001 book on black state legislators, "African Americans have been the most cohesive and consistent policy subgroup in United States politics."[57] The timing of the increase in numbers of black state legislators was fortunate. Since the 1970s, decisions about issues of importance to African Americans, including Medicaid, student aid, school lunch, community development, welfare, and environmental protection, have devolved from the federal level to the states.[58] In his study of how representatives in Arkansas, Illinois, Mississippi, New Jersey, and North Carolina acted in three different sessions, Haynie found that 55–82 percent of African American legislators introduced bills that addressed issues of particular interest to blacks. White legislators, by contrast, almost never introduced such legislation. In only one of the three years that Haynie studied (1969, 1979, and 1989) did more than one-quarter of nonblack legislators introduce even one bill of interest to blacks.[59] It may sound obvious, but black issues are much more likely to be addressed when African Americans are serving in state legislatures.

More African American legislators does not mean that voting trends change, however. Voting remains polarized along racial lines. Whites will support African American incumbents but are often reluctant to vote for black newcomers. The main reason for the growth in the number of black legislators, therefore, has been the creation of majority-black districts.[60]

Professional versus Citizen Legislators

Legislatures, which were strictly white male playgrounds in the past, have become more inclusive of women and minorities and more attentive to their concerns. But the biggest changes in legislatures over the past thirty-five years have come in the very ways that they do business. Whereas once legislatures were sleepy backwaters in which not much got done—and even less got done ethically—now many chambers are highly professional operations. Most legislatures used to meet for a short time every other year. These days all but a handful meet every year and, in a few cases, nearly year-round. "No single factor has a greater effect on the legislative environment than the constitutional restriction on length of session," two leading legislative scholars wrote long ago.[61]

The most pronounced differences among the states are between "professional" legislatures that meet full-time, pay members a high salary, and employ large staffs and "amateur," or "citizen," legislatures that meet part time, have members who usually hold other jobs, and have smaller staffs. To some extent, all legislatures have become more professional. Even "amateur" legislators devote a third of their time to legislative work. In the early 1940s, only four states—New Jersey, New York, Rhode Island, and South Carolina—met in annual sessions, but that number has climbed continuously.[62] Today, only six states do not meet in regular annual sessions. Expenditures per legislator have increased in nearly every state above the rate of inflation, and today, the most professional legislatures have resources that rival those of the U.S. Congress.[63]

There are many variations among states as to how professional their legislatures are, which profoundly affect their effectiveness, how much institutional strength they have compared to governors, and how popular they are with the public. Some disagreement still exists about whether professional legislators really do a better job than their citizen-legislator cousins. Typically, however, the more professional a legislature, the more effective it is at the essential jobs of drafting and passing laws and overseeing the governor and the executive branch. Most of the more populous states, except Texas, have highly professional legislatures. These professional legislatures are able to provide more resources

TABLE 7-2

State House Demographic Diversity: Total Numbers and Percentages of Legislators Who Are Women, African American, and Hispanic, 2007

State	Total Number of Legislative Seats	Women State Legislators		African American State Legislators		Hispanic State Legislators	
		Total	Percentage of Total Seats	Total	Percentage of Total Seats	Total	Percentage of Total Seats
Alabama	140	18	13	34	24	0	0
Alaska	60	13	22	1	2	0	0
Arizona	90	28	31	2	2	17	19
Arkansas	135	31	23	15	11	0	0
California	120	33	28	9	8	28	23
Colorado	100	37	37	3	3	5	5
Connecticut	187	59	32	19	10	6	3
Delaware	62	6	26	5	8	1	2
Florida	160	37	24	25	16	17	11
Georgia	236	46	20	56	24	3	1
Hawaii	76	25	33	0	0	1	1
Idaho	105	26	25	0	0	1	1
Illinois	177	49	28	29	16	11	6
Indiana	150	22	21	13	9	1	1
Iowa	150	35	23	3	2	0	0
Kansas	165	49	30	6	4	4	2
Kentucky	138	22	16	7	5	0	0
Louisiana	144	22	15	29	20	0	0
Maine	186	54	29	0	0	0	0
Maryland	188	58	31	42	22	4	2
Massachusetts	200	52	26	8	4	5	3
Michigan	148	37	25	19	13	3	2
Minnesota	201	70	35	1	> 1	3	1
Mississippi	174	25	14	42	24	0	0
Missouri	197	44	22	12	6	1	1
Montana	150	39	26	0	0	1	1

continued

TABLE 7-2, continued

State	Total Number of Legislative Seats	Women State Legislators		African American State Legislators		Hispanic State Legislators	
		Total	Percentage of Total Seats	Total	Percentage of Total Seats	Total	Percentage of Total Seats
Nebraska	49	10	20	1	2	1	2
Nevada	63	20	32	7	11	3	5
New Hampshire	424	159	38	1	> 1	2	< 1
New Jersey	120	34	28	10	8	5	4
New Mexico	112	34	30	2	2	44	39
New York	212	52	25	43	20	17	8
North Carolina	170	45	27	26	15	2	1
North Dakota	141	23	16	0	0	0	0
Ohio	132	28	21	16	12	0	0
Oklahoma	149	17	11	6	4	0	0
Oregon	90	24	27	3	3	1	1
Pennsylvania	253	37	15	21	8	1	< 1
Rhode Island	113	25	22	1	1	3	3
South Carolina	170	17	10	28	17	1	1
South Dakota	105	214	20	0	0	0	0
Tennessee	132	24	18	12	9	1	1
Texas	181	43	24	14	8	36	20
Utah	104	23	22	0	0	2	2
Vermont	180	67	37	1	1	0	0
Virginia	140	25	18	17	12	1	1
Washington	147	48	33	3	2	3	2
West Virginia	134	22	16	0	0	0	0
Wisconsin	132	29	22	8	6	1	1
Wyoming	90	15	16.7	0	0	2	2
Total	**7,382**	**1,972**	**24**	**600**	**6**	**238**	**4**

Sources: Center for American Women and Politics (CAWP), "Women in State Legislatures 2010," available at www.cawp.rutgers.edu/fast_facts/levels_of_office/documents/stleg.pdf; National Conference of State Legislatures (NCSL), "Number of African American Legislators 2009," available at www.ncsl.org/default.aspx?tabid=14781; NCSL, "2009 Latino Legislators," available at www.ncsl.org/Default.aspx?TabId=14766.

Note: Percentages are rounded to the nearest whole number.

the influence that interest groups hold, but members of interest groups themselves are often unhappy when things don't break their way. Finally, Rosenthal writes, "people generalize from the worst cases, not the best cases." They do not assume that most legislators are like their own representative or senator, whom they tend to like, but are like "the relative few who are convicted or indicted in a court of law, reprimanded by a state ethics commission or are accused . . . in the media."[69]

By now, however, it should be evident that legislatures, just like books, cannot be judged by the average person's perception of their covers. State legislatures have become more efficient and effective units of government over the past thirty years. At the federal level, Congress has punted on many of the major domestic issues of the last several years, but state legislatures have picked up those balls and run with them. After Democrats took over the U.S. House of Representatives in 2007, they proudly touted a group of priority bills that they were able to pass. Yet many of their signature initiatives, including a minimum wage increase and funding for stem-cell research, already had been approved in numerous states. And the reason that states were pressing hard that year for expanded healthcare coverage programs was that Congress had failed to act in this area and the Bush administration publicly had suggested that states should take the lead on the issue. This dynamic began to change following the election of President Obama in 2008. He quickly took an aggressive approach in areas of policy that states had pretty much had to themselves; nevertheless, states continued to play important roles in helping to shape and implement federal ideas in areas such as climate change, healthcare, and education.

For all of this, legislatures are as unpopular as they have ever been. Following the terrorist attacks of September 11, 2001, polls indicated that the public's faith in government had been restored. Firefighters and cops became popular figures, but elected representatives did not bask in the same sort of glow for very long. If anything, legislators have become more unpopular than they were a generation ago. The increases in staff, in salaries, and in other professional tools that legislators have acquired in recent decades probably have made them better at their jobs. But as they have become more professional, legislatures also have become larger targets of disdain for a public that believes it has little or no use for professional or career politicians. Amateur legislatures hold a stronger appeal to deeply rooted American desires for limited government and limited governmental power.

To a large extent, the general public does not view large staffs and good salaries as ways of ensuring that the legislature does its job in a professional manner. Instead, these increases in legislative resources are seen as yet more proof that politicians want to exploit their offices for personal gain. More than policy issues, the public is quick to anger over such ethical questions as legislative pay raises and other perks for elected officials. "The public does not want the same thing out of a legislature that you think they might want," says John Hibbing, a University of Nebraska political scientist who has written about the unpopularity of legislatures. "The public wants a legislature whose members are not in a position to feather their own nests."[70]

Legislators have done a poor job of selling the idea that what they do is important and necessary in a democracy. "It's our fault" that the legislature is viewed as "dysfunctional," "sheep," and "not independent," says Richard Brodsky, a member of the New York Assembly. "We have never gotten the message out in a coherent way of what we do well and right."[71]

For their part, the media are more concerned with dramatizing conflicts than explaining what are sometimes awfully dry policy matters; therefore, they have not helped legislators to make their case. A primary job of the media in a democracy is to report on what the government is up to, but less and less media attention is devoted to legislatures. Books about such media failings are even more tiresome, if you can believe it, than books about state and local government. But a few points are worth making here.

First, ever since Watergate, the scandal that forced President Richard Nixon to resign in 1974, the press has taken an adversarial position toward the government. People in government, including legislators, are not very good in the first place at getting out the good news about what they are doing or publicizing their successes. And reporters are by their nature skeptics and are good at covering scandals and mistakes. "Skepticism is not just a personality quirk of journalists," says one reporter. "It's a core value, the wellspring of all our best work."[72] The media have made boo-boo coverage practically the mainstay of government reporting. This is not true in 100 percent of the cases, of course, but the press's general attitude toward government was summed up well a few years ago by a reporter in Pennsylvania who told a public official, "Your job is to manage the public business and mine is to report when you do it wrong."[73]

Reporters may be too cynical about what legislators are up to, but a bigger problem might be that there are so few reporters watching them. An *American Journalism Review* survey in 2009 found that there were only 355 full-time newspaper reporters covering the state capitols—a drop of 32 percent since 2003 and only about one-thirteenth the number of journalists who covered the Super Bowl that year. (Although, given the parlous state of journalism, even that number has come down.)[74] That is an average of seven reporters per state, but Georgia, for instance, had only five full-time statehouse reporters. The number of capitol reporters in some other states, such as Michigan, had dropped by nearly half in the previous decade or so. Several states had seen formerly competing papers, such as the *St. Petersburg Times* and the *Miami Herald*, combine forces and share reporters and coverage. The numbers are even weaker for television coverage.[75]

Fewer reporters translate into fewer stories about what legislators are doing to earn their taxpayer-financed livings. The more populous states, such as New York and California, still boast a relatively sizable, if

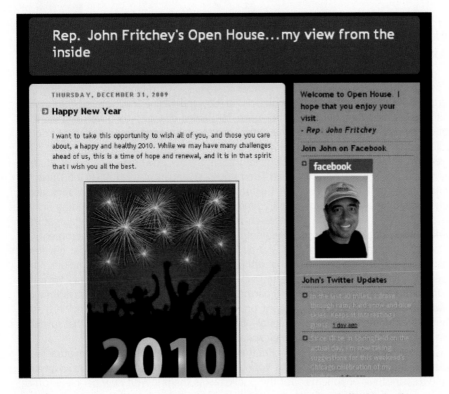

John Fritchey, who has served in the Illinois House since 1996, was the first elected official in the Chicago area to start blogging.

diminished, capitol press corps, but even in these states the legislatures lose out because their stories get lost in the clutter of other news. The South Dakota legislature, when it is in session, is a major source of news in that underpopulated state, but the Illinois General Assembly loses out to coverage of other activities in Chicago and the surrounding area.[76] As a result of diminished coverage, says Gary Moncrief, a political scientist at Boise State University, "I'm not sure the American public is very attuned to the inner workings of legislatures and the fact that they probably do work better today than thirty or forty years ago."[77]

Some of the slack has been taken up by bloggers—nearly every capital is covered by at least a handful. The Texas blogging corps has included political junkies, college students, the producers of a talk-radio show, mainstream journalists, and a couple of state representatives who blog directly from the House floor. Of course, nothing is perfect, and a common complaint about statehouse bloggers, like all bloggers, is that their coverage tends toward the snarky. "We live in a pretty cynical age and the blogs are pretty cynical," said a press aide to the Texas lieutenant governor.

Policy in Practice: Outwit, Outlast, Outplay: Who Really Got the Best Deal with Term Limits?

The biggest change to hit states over the last quarter century has been the advent of term limits. In the fifteen states with term limit laws—which were almost all approved via ballot initiatives by voters sick of career politicians—legislators are limited to serving no more than six, eight, or twelve years in either the house or senate. Although that may sound like a long time, it turns out not to be enough for most legislators to master all the complexities of understanding and formulating a wide range of policy.

Term limits have failed the public's goal of bringing in more "citizen legislators." Instead, legislators are constantly seeking their next political job rather than carving out a career in one chamber for decades. Term limits also have failed to bring in the anticipated and hoped-for substantial numbers of women and minorities to the legislative ranks. The total number of women legislators is up nationwide, but their ranks have actually been slower to grow in states that impose term limits.[a]

But if they haven't fulfilled all their promises, term limits have not been quite the disaster their opponents predicted either. One of the most common predictions—that with members serving so briefly, lobbyists hoarding institutional and policy knowledge would accrue all the power—appears to have missed the mark. Term limits pretty much have been a mixed bag for lobbyists, who must introduce themselves to a new, skeptical set of legislators every couple of years rather than relying on cozy relations with a few key committee chairs. "I don't know one lobbyist who thinks it's a good thing," said Rick Farmer, who wrote about term limits as an academic before going to work for the Oklahoma House. "If term limits are such a good thing for lobbyists, why do so many lobbyists hate them?"

It does seem clear, however, that legislators in term-limited states have lost power to the executive branch—the governors and their staff who actually know how to operate the machinery of government. "Agency heads can outwit and outlast anyone and everyone on the playing field and they have consolidated their power," said one southern legislator-turned-lobbyist.

Academic studies in term-limit states, including California, Colorado, and Maine, have found that legislators make far fewer changes to governors' budgets than they used to, representing many billions of dollars in legislative discretion that is no longer exercised. "The crumbling of legislative power is clear across states," said Thad Kousser, a political scientist at the University of California, San Diego, and author of a book about term limits. "There's no more clear finding in the research than a shift in power where the legislature is becoming a less than equal branch of government."

For all that, it's become common to hear governors and other executive branch officials complain about term limits because the laws mean they lack negotiating partners whose knowledge and expertise they can count on. It seems that no one who works in a state capital—or in the law and lobbying shops that surround any capital—likes term limits.

But there is one group that still finds them attractive—the voting public. Polls suggest that about 75 percent of the public favors them. "With new people in office, you have people with real world experience," says Stacie Rumenap, president of U.S. Term Limits, a group that advocates limits. "Under term limits, you might have a schoolteacher sitting on the education committee."[b]

That sort of suggestion often is made about term limits—you get rid of the professional politicians and get people who know what the real problems are because they themselves are real. And while Idaho and Utah have repealed their limits, efforts to extend or weaken term limits have been rejected several times since 2002 by voters in Arkansas, California, Florida, and Montana.

The main effects of term limits, after all, are procedural. It's difficult to make a convincing case that they have made any one particular policy worse, let alone imperiled the quality of life in any state that observes them. The underlying complaint of term-limits opponents, that they make legislators less powerful, is one reason why many people supported them to begin with.

Source: Adapted from Alan Greenblatt, "The Truth about Term Limits," *Governing* magazine, January 2006, 24.

[a] Peter Slevin, "After Adopting Term Limits, States Lose Female Legislators," *Washington Post*, April 22, 2007, A4.

[b] Interview with Stacie Rumenap, October 4, 2002.

National Conference on State Legislatures's Term Limits Poll: Survey Results, 2003.

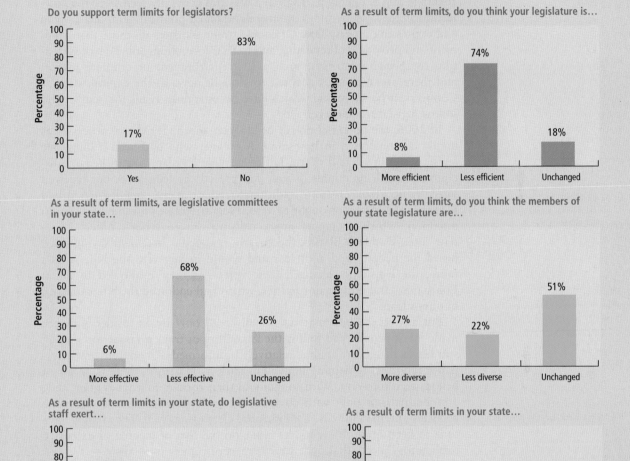

Source: www.ncsl.org/programs/legismgt/about/survrslt.htm.

Note: In 2003, the National Conference on State Legislatures surveyed 134 state legislators, legislative staff members, lobbyists, and others in states with term limits for legislators. The results of a few of the survey questions are shown here.

"The more critical they are, the more readers they get. There are no lines any more between what's fair game and what's not."[78]

Not only are they snarky, but the rise of political blogs such as Minnesota Democrats Exposed and Michigan Liberal represent a return to media coverage that is openly partisan in a way not generally seen since the nineteenth century. Many blogs are merely updated political pamphlets, aping and expressing a party line. Of course, some bloggers do more than comment and provide real reporting and fresh information. Some devote attention to specialized topics, such as the environment or criminal justice, and there are Web sites devoted to straight news at the capitol, such as Connecticut News Junkie, which have become must-reads for people who follow legislatures closely.

In 2006, the potential power of bloggers on the legislative process was amply demonstrated in Louisiana. A blogger who had been a long-time legislative counsel said that a bill to provide legislators with heavily discounted health premiums, which had passed the legislature but received virtually no attention from traditional media outlets, sounded like a bad idea that the governor ought to veto. Blog attention prompted talk radio attention, which prompted angry calls to the governor's office. Three days later, Kathleen Blanco, the governor, issued a statement saying she'd heard the people loud and clear and would in fact veto the bill. What's more, the legislators changed their votes—as they're allowed to do in Louisiana—and both major parties, which had endorsed the bill, came out in opposition.[79]

But having the best material usually read only by an insider audience made up of people who follow the legislature or track an issue for a living still leaves the general public relatively uninformed. Among the few newspaper reporters remaining in capitals such as Hartford, there is an air of beleaguered intensity. With so many of their former colleagues gone, they are charged not only with covering the governor, legislature, and state agencies but, in many cases, politics and elections as well. They barely have time to keep up with events, let alone do the sort of digging or extensive explanatory pieces that once were staples of capitol journalism.[80]

The decline of general coverage and the rise of often partisan commentary and news sites on the Web are among the reasons that amateur legislatures are much more popular with their constituents than are more professional chambers. The urge to return legislatures to their more humble but lovable position as citizen institutions has been the main driver behind the term limits movement. Limits on the number of terms an individual may serve in the house or senate have been approved in most of the states that allow ballot initiatives. As of 2009, there were fifteen states with term limits. The limits range from a low of six years of service per legislative chamber in states such as Arkansas and Maine to twelve years service in Nevada, Oklahoma, and Utah.

Still, governors are the prime political actors in virtually every state. Some are notably more successful than others, but all are seen as leaders. In most states, the governor sets the agenda, largely determining which policy issues will be pursued and how the state budget will look. They are unique among state-level politicians in terms of the media attention they can attract. This helps them promote their causes, but they must rely on other institutional players if they are going to accomplish more than making speeches.

Recently, governors have become a lot better equipped to control the rest of the executive branch—running states in fact as well as in theory. For more than one hundred years after the founding of the American republic, governors were strong in title only, with little real power. In fact, they were hardly more than figureheads. Throughout the last decades of the twentieth century, however, governors were given more and more formal control over the machinery of government at the same time that the federal government shifted greater control of many programs, including welfare, to the states. They have longer terms than they once did and enjoy greater authority to appoint the top officials in virtually every government agency. (Only New Hampshire and Vermont still have two-year gubernatorial terms. The rest of the states have four-year terms. Only Virginia limits its chief executive to a single consecutive term—although two-term limits are common among the states.) These changes were the result of changes in laws in many states that were specifically designed to strengthen the office of governor in hopes of creating greater accountability and coherence in government. They are now, with few exceptions, not just the most famous politicians in their states but also the most powerful.

Governors are expected to be the leading cheerleaders for their states. They are expected to attract business and jobs, to set the political tone, and to manage state affairs. They serve as the primary face and voice of government during natural disasters or other crises. With this much power, of course, comes a great deal of expectation. If a state is not doing well—if it is losing more jobs than its neighbors during a recession, for example, or is running a budget deficit—voters and the media will hold the governor responsible. That is why voters ushered in governors who were not from the incumbent party in nineteen states during the bad budget year of 2002—a feat that may well be replicated amid deeper budget woes in 2010.

Governors are like mini-presidents in each state. Like the president, the governor commands the lion's share of political attention in a

Governors are like mini-presidents in each state. Like the president, the governor commands the lion's share of political attention in a state, is generally seen as setting the agenda for the legislative branch, and is basically the lead political actor—the figure most likely to appear on television on a regular basis. As with the president, governors tend to receive the blame or enjoy the credit for the performance of the economy.

state, is generally seen as setting the agenda for the legislative branch, and is basically the lead political actor—the figure most likely to appear on television on a regular basis. As with the president, governors tend to receive the blame or enjoy the credit for the performance of the economy.

And, like the president, a governor shares responsibility for running the government—implementing laws; issuing regulations; and doing the work of building the roads, maintaining the parks, and performing other public functions—with the help of a cabinet. Presidents appoint their cabinet officials to run the Departments of Defense and Agriculture and the like. Governors have no foreign policy responsibilities, of course, but they do have help in running state-level departments of agriculture, finance, environmental protection, and so on. In most cases, in most states, the governor appoints officials to head these departments. But some other statewide officials, such as attorneys general, often are elected on their own and may even represent another party. We explore the roles of these other executive branch officials in this chapter.

And this chapter also answers these questions: How did governors get to be such powerful players, when for much of U.S. history their offices were weak? Why is this so? Why do some states still give their governors more pomp than power? We look at how the office of governor has changed over the years. We examine the types of power governors can command by virtue of the office and which powers they must create out of the force of personality. We also look at what sorts of people get elected governor and how they get elected. Finally, we survey some of the other important statewide offices, such as lieutenant governor and attorney general.

The Job of Governor

Following the American Revolution, governors had very little power for one simple reason—distrust. Colonial governors, appointed by the British, had imposed unpopular taxes and exploited their positions to make themselves rich. Americans did not want to invest too much power in individuals who might turn into mini-dictators. There was no national president, after all, under the original Articles of Confederation. In the states, most of the power was disbursed by giving it to many individuals holding office in legislatures and on state boards and commissions. Governors in all but three of the original states were limited to one-year terms. While in office, they were not given control over state departments and agencies. Separately elected individuals, boards, or commissions ran these instead. After his state's constitutional convention, one North Carolina delegate said that the governor had been given just enough power "to sign the receipt for his salary."[3]

The number of agencies grew as government became more complex toward the end of the nineteenth century. Lack of central control over these agencies, however, meant that states had difficulty functioning coherently. The U.S. Constitution had done much to improve the political structure in the United States—but not for governors. Governors still lacked the authority to perform in a way that the public expected given their position at the top of the political pyramid. This problem persisted well into the twentieth century.

Lynn Muchmore, a political scientist, sums up the sort of frustrations governors had as late as the 1980s in terms of getting various parts of government to act as they wished. Muchmore lays out a theoretical case of a governor elected on a platform of promoting growth in the state's rural areas and documented the difficulties he had in making good on those promises. In this scenario, the new governor found that the highway department, which was run by a separate commission, had decided a decade ago to complete urban segments of the state's road system. This decision siphoned money away from plans to develop better roads in rural areas. The board that oversaw the public colleges and universities had a policy of phasing out satellite campuses in favor of investing in three urban campuses. The state's department of commerce would not work in any county that did not have a local economic development corporation. Many rural counties lacked such corporations because they did not have the population or tax base to support them. And the state legislature had passed restrictions that denied new businesses breaks on rural utility rates.[4] Despite his promises, the governor's battle to help rural areas was an uphill one.

Not every scenario is so extreme, but it is often the case that state agencies not headed by people appointed by the governor—and therefore not answering to him or her—will have their own constituencies and concerns. They will not have in mind the big picture of how the different parts of state government can best work together to promote the general good. Only the governor sees the whole field in that way.

In recent decades, governors have been granted greater powers in hopes that states will function more efficiently. They now have much more power over appointments than they once did. This means that they are able to put their own teams in place to carry out their policies. They have become important symbols of the state not only at home but also in other states and abroad as ambassadors who promote their states to businesses that they hope to attract.

Terry Sanford, a former governor of North Carolina, sums up the job of the contemporary governor well:

> The governor by his very office embodies his state. He must . . . energize his administration, search out the experts, formulate the programs, mobilize the support, and carry new ideas into action. . . . Few major undertakings ever get off the ground without his support and leadership. The governor sets the agenda for public debate; frames the issues; decides on the timing; and can blanket the state with good ideas by using his access to the mass media. . . . The governor is the most potent political power in the state.[5]

Governors must be multitaskers. They propose legislation, which has to win approval from the legislature. They can implement regulations that help clear up how those laws actually are applied to individuals, businesses, and other groups. Increasingly in recent years, governors have become the strongest advocates and public relations people for their states, traveling to promote tourism and help close deals with out-of-state trading partners that might locate offices or operations in their states. Let us explore all these roles in some detail.

Chief Legislator

Just as the president does not serve in Congress, governors do not sit as members of state legislatures. Like the president, however, they have enormous influence over the work legislatures do. Governors outline their broad proposals in inaugural and annual state of the state addresses. They and their staffs then work with individual legislators and committees to translate these proposals into bills.

Some governors are better at getting what they want from legislatures than others. Why? Part of it is personal charm, but a lot of it has to do with the powers granted to a governor in a given state. In Texas, for instance, most of the influence that the executive branch holds over legislation is given to the lieutenant governor, not the governor. Governors all vary in terms of how much authority they have in blocking bills they do not like through use of the **veto**, or rejection, of the bill. Those variations in authority help to determine how much clout a governor has in the legislature.

Governors never get everything they want from state legislatures, but governors do have a great deal of impact on which bills become laws. There are a number of reasons for this. In every state, bills almost never become law without the governor's signature. Governors can veto them. Legislators can get around a veto, but that often means that they have to pass the bill again by a **supermajority vote**. Supermajority votes are usually votes of two-thirds or more. That means a governor needs the support of only one-third plus one vote in either chamber to sustain his veto. Because it is hard enough to get both legislative houses to agree on a bill in the first place, such a large vote against most governors rarely happens. If you can't pass a law without the governor's approval, it stands to reason that you will want to work with him or her to create a version of the bill that will win such approval.

Another factor that makes governors enormously influential in the legislative process is their command of state budgets. In nearly every state, the main responsibility for creating a state budget rests in the office of the governor. The governor proposes budgets that detail the amount of money that will go to every state agency, welfare program, highway department, and school district. There are often restrictions on how a state must spend much

VETO

The power to reject a proposed law.

SUPERMAJORITY VOTE

A legislative vote of much more than a simple majority, for instance, two-thirds of a legislative chamber's voting to override a governor's veto.

of its money from year to year, whether because of old laws or federal requirements. But a governor gets the first crack at deciding how most of the state's money is going to be spent.

Maryland's governor is the nation's most powerful in terms of setting a state budget, the result of changes prompted by a serious deficit in 1916 for which the legislature took the blame.[6] There, once the chief executive lays out the budget, the legislature cannot add any more money to fund individual departments or programs or shift money among those programs. Legislators *can* reduce the size of appropriations but cannot create programs of their own. In the other states, legislators have more power to tinker. In New York state in 2003, the legislature

Maryland governor Martin O'Malley uses a farm tour to tout his new budget, which includes funds to help farmers promote environmentally friendly practices. While most governors exercise considerable influence over budgets, the Maryland governor has more power than most. A number of legal restrictions make it difficult for the Maryland legislature to make major changes to the budget proposed by the governor.

passed its own budget by overriding the governor's veto. Usually, however, the governor's blueprint gets passed, with legislators making changes only here and there. "As far as legislators are concerned," one political scientist writes, "the ability to create the budget is so powerful that it becomes *the* major tool for a governor in achieving his legislative programs."[7]

While legislatures might set the overall dollar amount that goes to the transportation department, governors might get to decide, for instance, whether bridges are going to be built in particular districts. To get those bridges—or any other goodies they might want—legislators often have to give the governor what he or she wants in terms of passing major initiatives. "Any legislator who says he needs nothing from the governor's office is either lying or stupid," according to one observer of the Alabama political scene.[8] Legislators who belong to the governor's party are inclined to help out anyway because they will be perceived as part of the same team when facing voters in the next election.

Some governors choose to focus only on a few big issues and leave many small matters to the prerogative of the legislature. Others tackle a wide range of problems. How much success a governor enjoys varies greatly according to his or her individual abilities and skills. Yet there is no question that a governor is the most likely person to set the main agenda for the legislature and the state.

Head of State Agencies

Governors at one time had very little control over who ran their states' departments. This meant that people with other agendas could set policy over taxes or healthcare or other issues. Even today, for instance, Texas voters elect twenty-five different statewide officials. Texas governors cannot hire their own choices for such positions as comptroller (the state's chief financial officer), agriculture commissioner, or state supreme court justices.

In most states, that has changed in recent times. Only about half of the governors chose their own cabinet officials in 1969, but nearly all of them do today.[9] (From 1965 to 1979, twenty-one states embarked on comprehensive reorganizations of their executive branches.)[10] In fact, the current trend is to try to merge even large departments so that they do not work at cross-purposes or duplicate work. In 1998, Florida voters decided to shrink the state's cabinet and put more power directly in the governor's office. In Massachusetts, Gov. Mitt Romney created a "supercabinet" position in 2003 that oversaw the state's economic, consumer affairs, and labor departments in hopes of coordinating their budgets and activities. His other attempts to consolidate more power in the governor's office through a major reorganization of the government structure were rejected by the legislature, however. Such mergers do not always make happy marriages. In 2007, Beebe, the Arkansas governor, undid the merger of the state health and human services departments that had been put in place by his predecessor, Mike Huckabee, two years earlier.

The power to appoint people to run state departments offers obvious benefits for governors. They can pick their own people who they know will pursue their policy preferences. If they fail, they can be fired. How much influence a governor has over state education policy, say, or environmental protection still depends on the amount of energy and time the governor can afford to devote to these issues, as opposed to everything else that must be done. One Arkansas governor said that a governor "will spend almost as much time keeping his staff and his cabinet and the people around him happy as he does keeping his constituency happy."[11]

In other words, governors who can appoint their own people to run the government cannot count on accomplishing the administration's major goals. Just like any other boss, governors may be disappointed in the performance of the people working for them. The ability to hire and fire people, however, as well as the ability to determine how much money their departments are going to get, means that governors are truly the leaders of the executive branch of government.

Chief Spokesperson for the State

Mississippi governor Haley Barbour is the first to credit the countless government workers who helped southern Mississippi cope with Hurricane

Katrina, which devastated the Gulf Coast in 2005. But a major crisis such as Katrina also demands a strong leader who can communicate calm to the public and provide "a central decision-making point for when things get balled up or go sideways, which they do," as Barbour says. He excelled at both. Barbour was straight with the facts about the utter devastation in the area, but his own demeanor in public appearances suggested that the state would summon the will to rebuild.[12]

A governor acts as the chief spokesperson and public face of a state's government in good times as well as bad. Governors didn't always think it was part of their job description to attract jobs and industry to their states, but they do now. The template was set for them by Luther Hodges, who served as governor of North Carolina from 1954 to 1961, before becoming U.S. secretary of commerce. Hodges created a business development corporation in his state to supply capital to businesses; changed the state's corporate income tax rates; and employed the expertise of nearby University of North Carolina, North Carolina State University, and Duke University in the creation of the 5,000-acre Research Triangle industrial park, which in turn led to the development of the state's high-tech infrastructure. "My administration was considered by many to be 'industry hungry,'" Hodges once said. "It was!"[13]

New Mexico governor Bill Richardson worked hard to send signals that the state government wants to be as friendly as possible to business growth. New Mexico had the forty-seventh lowest per capita income in the country, so Richardson didn't even wait until his inauguration in January 2003 to begin his sales pitch for his programs and for the state. The day after his election, he got on a plane to talk to executives in California's Silicon Valley in hopes of persuading them to set up operations in New Mexico. Once in office, Richardson proudly boasted that he calls CEOs on a daily basis and "sucks up to them big time."[14]

Other governors perform similar chores. Former Wisconsin governor Tommy Thompson used to host business executives from Minnesota at the opening of fishing season to show off the state's outdoor activities and to try to convince them to locate new facilities there. To combat a significant decrease in travel and tourism in the months following the terrorist attacks of September 11, 2001, Florida governor Jeb Bush wrote letters of thanks to every group that agreed to hold its convention in the state. Governors regularly send out press releases about their role in helping to land new jobs and companies through tax incentives, the creation of cooperative biotechnology ventures, and other economic development activities.

Basically, their main role as chief face of the state is now in sales. They promote their states' benefits to economic interests. They pitch the virtues of low tax rates, good roads and transportation systems, livable communities, well-educated workforces, and anything else they can think of that might seem attractive to individuals scouting potential business sites. Their desire to have good packages to sell has had an effect on their policies, with most governors being afraid to make any moves that might be perceived as unfriendly to business.

That proved to be the case for Colorado governor Bill Ritter. In early 2007, the state legislature swiftly passed a bill that would have made it easier for organized labor to unionize workplaces. Ritter had campaigned with union support and had pledged to union members that he would support such a move. But he surprised everyone by vetoing the bill, deciding that he could not afford to alienate business interests so early in his term when he would need their help on other issues, such as higher education and transportation. "I recognize how deeply disappointed my friends in organized labor will be with this decision," Ritter wrote in his veto message. But he was more worried "about the impact this change would have on our ability to attract new business to Colorado, to create new economic opportunity for all."[15]

Governors do speak out in other roles as well; for example, they appear in tourism brochures. Sometimes they get criticized for this because some see it as promoting their own images at state expense. During the 2006 campaign season, the Maryland legislature called a halt to ads featuring Gov. Bob Ehrlich, who was running for reelection. "If he's really the state's best attraction for tourists, pity Ocean City," commented the *Washington Post* in an editorial.[16]

When their teams are in major bowl games or the World Series, governors are sure to let the media know that they have bet some celebrated state product against those of other governors. More substantively, governors have become important lobbyists in Washington, seeking more federal money for their states. They are the only people that lobby in the nation's capital who can be sure that members of Congress and cabinet officials will meet with them directly rather than having them meet with staff.

Party Chief

Governors are also the leading figures in their party within their states. U.S. senators arguably might be more influential figures, but governors are more important politically at home. Governors command more foot soldiers. They may be able to call on thousands of state workers, whereas a senator's staff numbers in the dozens at most. Not all of a governor's workers are loyal members of the same party—in fact, changes in patronage laws and the creation of a civil service system mean that governors appoint far fewer state employees than they did some decades ago. Governors, however, have more people whose jobs depend on them than do any other elected official.

Governors often pick state party chairs of their liking. They help to recruit and raise money for candidates for other statewide offices and the legislature. They use the media attention they attract to campaign for those they support. For all this, state parties are not as important as they were forty years ago, so governors now devote less energy to political activities than to the nuts and bolts of their own jobs. This does not mean they do not have to pound the political pavement. They are still the titular heads of the party in their states, and no modern politician (who isn't already rich) can avoid the duties of raising campaign contributions.

In their role as head of state, governors often are seen as the building blocks for putting together a winning electoral map in presidential races. Unquestionably, having a popular governor on your side won't hurt you politically. It is taken as an article of faith among pundits and other political experts that governors can help swing their states toward the presidential nominee of their choice through their media presence and ability to sway some percentage of their states' votes. This doesn't always turn out to be the case, however. George W. Bush, then the governor of Texas, did receive a major boost toward capturing the Republican presidential nomination in 2000 when every other Republican governor endorsed him. To the surprise of some, however, they did not help him much in the general election. Republicans then held eight of the ten largest states, but Bush only carried three of them.[17] Bush did a little better in 2004, carrying four out of the five largest states that had Republican governors by then. In 2008, U.S. Senator Barack Obama, D-Ill., broke the pattern of four of the last five presidents' having previously served as governor. Still, seventeen of the forty-four presidents in our history had been governors.

Commander in Chief of the National Guard

Even in this country's earliest days, when governors had few powers, each governor's military position was strong, "with all states designating him as commander-in-chief."[18] Southern governors perhaps most famously used their power to control the National Guard in resisting desegregation during the 1950s and 1960s. The National Guard in each state is a state agency, but the president has the power to federalize it, calling up units to perform federal service. That happened in the civil rights era, when the Guard was ordered to work for the feds against governors who were resisting integration. Today's National Guard is more likely to fight alongside federal soldiers in such places as Iraq.

Governors do not use the Guard as their private armies, however. Instead, they can call out units to respond to natural disasters or riots. Milton Sharp, governor of Pennsylvania during the 1970s, remembered his years in office in terms of emergency responses to floods, a pair of hurricanes, droughts, ice storms, fires, and a gypsy moth infestation rather than in terms of lawmaking and policy agenda setting.[19]

Still, the question of who controls the National Guard has become a politically potent one in recent years. The federal government pays for troop training and many of its operations, and the Supreme Court has found that the feds—not governors—have the final say over where units are deployed.[20]

In 2007, the Department of Defense called up Oklahoma City, Oklahoma's 45th Infantry Brigade, National Guard, for a tour of duty in Iraq, a force of nearly 13,000 troops.

Governors complain that because of this they have been caught short during times of disaster, such as Hurricane Katrina. Fortunately, they have generally been able to make up for these shortfalls in home-state personnel through agreements with other states that send spare troops. Then in 2006 Congress passed a law that made it easier for the White House, rather than the statehouse, to take command of the Guard during times of disaster. All fifty governors signed a letter protesting an earlier version of the law. "We see this as an expansion of the president's authority, a change to allow the possibility that the National Guard would be federalized," said David Quam, a lobbyist with the National Governors Association (NGA).[21] The debate about control over Guard troops has continued into the Obama administration.

Most governors naturally hope to avoid having their tenure defined by the natural disasters and other factors beyond their control that Milton Sharp felt shaped his tenure. Governors have to attend to many political tasks during their time in office. How much success they have in setting their own courses depends on the amount of power they command. That power, in turn, varies a good deal by state and depends not just on the **formal powers** of the office but also on the amount of power individuals in that office can create for themselves.

The Powers of Governors

Anyone who follows sports understands that natural ability does not necessarily translate into success. Some players look great on paper—they're strong, they can run fast, they have whatever skills should help them dominate their sport. But, for whatever reason, these players sometimes squander their talents and are shown up by athletes who are weaker but who nevertheless have a greater understanding of the game, work harder, or simply find a way to win.

It is the same with governors. Some of them look incredibly strong on paper, and their states' constitutions give them powers that their neighbors can only envy. Nevertheless, states that have set up the governor's office to be strong sometimes end up with weak governors. Conversely, states in which the governor's official powers are weak sometimes can have individuals in that office who completely dominate their states' politics. They are able to exploit the **informal powers** of their office—they have managed to create personal powers, as opposed to relying on relatively weak institutional powers.

When we talk about the powers of governors, we obviously do not refer to an ability to cast spells or turn back armies with their wands. If you want to understand why some governors are considered successful or powerful and why others are quickly forgotten even by their supporters, there is an obvious place to start. You need to look at what sorts of power governors are given by right of taking that office. If they do not have the tools to influence policy, they will have a much harder time winning political victories. Yet every governor, even those whom state law does not grant much authority, has enough stature to expect success.

Let us outline the different types of powers that governors actually do have, both the formal—the roles that come as part of the necessary equipment of the office—and the informal powers that these individuals create for themselves by using their office as a platform.

Formal Powers

Most governors have a wide variety of formal powers granted to them by state constitutions or other laws. Among the most important of these are the power to appoint officials to run state agencies, the power to veto legislation, the power to craft budgets, the power to grant pardons, and the power to call legislatures into session. Each of these aspects of a governor's job description is examined in this section.

The Power to Appoint. As mentioned earlier, the first governors in this country lacked **appointment powers**. They could not pick their own people to run state agencies, which made those agencies more independent. Nowadays, governors can pick their own teams, which gives them greater authority to set policy. When John Engler served as governor of Michigan during the 1990s, for example, he put in place a series of appointees with a strong ideological commitment to limited government. These appointees helped him carry out his desire to shrink the state's government. His contemporary, Ann Richards of Texas, set out to change the face of state government by changing the faces of the people within it—appointing women, blacks, and Hispanics to replace the white men who had always run things in Austin.

APPOINTMENT POWERS
A governor's ability to pick individuals to run state government, such as appointing cabinet secretaries.

Because governors cannot run their states alone, they must rely on the work of people they appoint to help carry out broad policy desires. If a governor wants to offer people living in public housing more opportunities to buy their homes, he or she will have a better chance of succeeding if he or she can appoint a housing director who shares those views, as opposed to governors with the same philosophy who have to work with housing directors who answer to independent commissions that oppose privatizing public housing.

Having loyal foot soldiers on your team rather than free agents is important for governors who want things done their way. This is not the only benefit the power of appointment carries with it, however. Governors get to appoint dozens and sometimes thousands of people to full-time government jobs and to commissions and boards. For instance, if you are attending a public college, chances are that the governor appointed the board of governors of your school or university system. These are considered plum jobs and giving them out is a way for a governor not only to influence policy but also to reward campaign contributors or other political allies.

Texas governor Rick Perry (left) is introduced by Texas lieutenant governor David Dewhurst. Although technically the second-ranking executive in the Texas state government, Dewhurst actually may wield more power. Texas governors have very few formal powers. The lieutenant governor, however, presides over the state Senate, sets the agenda, and appoints senators to the committees. This makes Dewhurst the executive with the most direct influence over the legislature.

Of course, there is a downside to the power of appointment, which is the risk of picking the wrong people. Earlier, we talked about former Pennsylvania governor Milton Sharp, who remembered his administration mainly as a time of dealing with natural disasters. It is little wonder he prefers to remember his time in office that way because many of his appointments turned into disasters of his own making. His secretary of property and supplies was sent to prison for contracting irregularities. The same fate befell a member of his turnpike authority. Other members of his administration came under ethical shadows as well. Even though Sharp himself was never touched by scandal, subsequent candidates—including the man who succeeded him as governor—ran campaigns against corruption. They won office by pledging to clean up Harrisburg.[22]

Still, the ability to appoint the heads of departments that run such areas as correctional facilities, educational institutions, highways, and utilities helps define a governor's overall power and influence. In some states, governors can pick their own top people without needing the approval of the legislature. In other states, they do need such approval, although the strength of the legislature's hold over this area varies. Rhode Island voters in 2004 strengthened the governor's appointment powers and weakened the legislature's reach into the executive branch through a ballot referendum that banned legislators from serving on boards and commissions. Conversely, in Texas, a legislative attempt to strengthen the governor's weak appointment powers was defeated in 2003. The primary reason for this was that legislatures and governors often have adversarial relationships—each can be the enemy of the other. Within the political system, all players are reluctant to surrender power to those in another branch or institutional position.

Power to Prepare State Budgets. The most powerful tools governors have may be their ability to shape a state's budget. It gives them enormous influence in their dealings with the legislature. The same is true of their ability to maintain control over state agencies. In most states, agencies and departments submit their budget proposals to a central budget office that works as part of the governor's team. The governor's ability to deny them funds or shift money among departments helps make sure that agencies remain focused, at least to some extent, on the governor's priorities.

Policy in Practice: Governors with Gumption: Policy Innovation and Interstate Influence

Governors are the masters of their political domains—their own states. Sometimes, however, they have an effect that reaches far beyond their own state boundaries. Their ideas can spread to be emulated by their colleagues and can even affect federal policy.

In a political era that considers governors in general to be great lobbyists in Washington, there are some who stand out. Few have had an impact equal to that of Tommy Thompson. Thompson served as Wisconsin's governor from 1987 until President George W. Bush put him in charge of the Department of Health and Human Services (HHS) in 2001. While governor, Thompson had petitioned the HHS for waivers from federal welfare law requirements. One of his first acts on taking office had been to bring together a group of welfare mothers to tell him their stories. He wanted to learn about the obstacles that made it difficult for them to get and keep jobs.

Using these personal stories as motivation, he created a program called Wisconsin Works. The program requires virtually all welfare recipients to work, either at regular jobs that the government has subsidized or in community service. The state increased its spending on child care, healthcare, transportation, and other support services. The combination of Wisconsin's welfare reforms and a healthy economy helped the state cut its welfare caseload by about 65 percent during Thompson's first decade in office, saving more than $1 billion.*

One of Thompson's main pulpits for spreading his gospel of reform and renewal was the NGA. The association is designed as a clearinghouse for governors throughout the country to exchange information, as well as to lobby on behalf of the states in Washington. Thompson's experiments were imitated elsewhere. The innovations that he and other governors came up with formed the backbone of the 1996 federal welfare law. The restructured law put time limits on how long a person could stay on welfare and imposed new work requirements.

In 2001, Maryland governor Parris Glendening—one of Thompson's successors as NGA chair—used the position to push a very different agenda. Glendening was tired of seeing farmland and open fields in his state torn up in favor of development. He thought that new houses and businesses should be built near existing houses and businesses rather than sprawling across the countryside. The excessive development led only to long commutes and environmental degradation.

His Smart Growth Act, which became Maryland law in 1998, is designed to steer the state's money toward the expansion of roads and other infrastructure in such a way as to discourage sprawl and encourage development and redevelopment in settled communities. It does not prevent builders or local governments from creating new projects on virgin land. It merely says that the state no longer subsidizes such projects.

The idea took root, at least for a while. Other governors initially followed Glendening's example. Within a few years, however, sprawl had become a high-profile issue in at least thirty states. Nearly a dozen of these previously had passed sprawl-control measures more or less similar to Maryland's.

Thompson's changes in welfare law are an example of moving the national debate by influencing Congress. Glendening's story is about having an impact by providing a model for—and offering guidance to—other states. In both cases, governors of relatively uninfluential states were able to promote big ideas that changed people's lives across the country.

*Ellen Perlman, "The Welfare Risk-Taker," *Governing* magazine, December 1997, 32.

TABLE 8-1

The Governors: Powers

State or other jurisdiction	Budget making power		Item veto power			Item veto-2/3 legislators present or 3/5 elected to override	Item veto-majority legislators elected to override	Authorization for reorganization through executive order (a)
	Full responsibility	Shares responsibility	Governor has item veto power on all bills	Governor has item veto power on appropriations only	Governor has no item veto power			
Alabama	*(b)	...	*	...	...	...	*	...
Alaska	*	...	...	*	...	*	...	*
Arizona	*(b)	...	...	*	...	*	(c)	...
Arkansas	...	*	...	*	...	...	*	*
California	*(b)	...	...	*	...	*	...	*(d)
Colorado	...	*	...	*	...	*	...	*
Connecticut	...	*	...	*	...	*	...	...
Delaware	*(b)	...	*	...	...	*	...	*
Florida	...	*	...	*	...	*	...	*
Georgia	*	...	...	*	...	(c)	...	*
Hawaii	...	*	*	...	...	*	...	*
Idaho	(e)	(e)	...	*	...	*	...	*
Illinois	...	*	*	...	...	*	...	*
Indiana	*	...	...	...	*	...	...	*
Iowa	...	*	...	*	...	*	...	*
Kansas	*	...	...	*	...	*	...	*
Kentucky	*(b)	...	...	*(f)	...	*	*	*
Louisiana	...	*	...	*	...	...	*(g)	*(h)
Maine	...	*	...	*	...	...	*	...
Maryland	*	...	*	...	...	*	...	*
Massachusetts	*	...	*	...	...	...	*(g)	*(d)
Michigan	*(i)	...	...	*(f)	...	...	*(g)	*
Minnesota	...	*	...	*	...	...	*(g)	*(j)
Mississippi	...	*(k)	*	...	...	*	...	*
Missouri	*(b)	...	...	*	...	*	...	*
Montana	*	...	...	*	...	*(l)	...	*(m)
Nebraska	...	*	...	*	...	*(n)	...	...
Nevada	*	...	...	...	*	...	...	...
New Hampshire	*(b)	...	...	...	*	...	...	...
New Jersey	*(b)	...	...	*	...	...	*(g)	*(o)
New Mexico	*	...	...	*	...	*	...	...
New York	...	*	*	...	...	*	...	...
North Carolina	...	*	...	...	*	...	...	*(p)
North Dakota	*	...	...	*	...	*	...	*
Ohio	*	...	...	*	...	*	...	...

TABLE 8-1, continued

| State or other jurisdiction | Budget making power | | Item veto power | | | | | Authorization for reorganization through executive order (a) |
	Full responsibility	Shares responsibility	Governor has item veto power on all bills	Governor has item veto power on appropriations only	Governor has no item veto power	Item veto-2/3 legislators present or 3/5 elected to override	Item veto-majority legislators elected to override	
Oklahoma	...	*	...	*	...	...	*(g)	...
Oregon	...	*	...	*	...	*	...	*
Pennsylvania	*	...	...	*	...	*	...	...
Rhode Island	...	*	...	...	*	...	...	...
South Carolina	...	*	...	*	...	*	...	...
South Dakota	*	...	...	*	...	*(q)	...	*
Tennessee	...	*	...	*	...	...	*	*
Texas	...	*	...	*	...	*	...	*
Utah	...	*	...	*	...	*	...	*
Vermont	*	...	...	...	*	...	...	*
Virginia	*	...	...	*	...	*(q)	...	*
Washington	*	...	*(r)	...	...	*	...	...
West Virginia	*	...	...	*	...	*	...	...
Wisconsin	*(b)	...	...	*(s)	...	*	...	...
Wyoming	...	*	*	...	...	*	...	...
American Samoa	...	*	...	...	...	...	...	*
Guam	*	...	*	...	...	*	...	*
No. Mariana Islands	...	*	...	*	...	*	...	*
Puerto Rico	...	*	...	*	...	*	...	*(t)
U.S. Virgin Islands	*	...	...	*	...	*	...	*

Source: The Council of State Governments' survey of governor's offices, December 2009.

Key:

* — Yes; provision for.

. . . — No; not applicable.

(a) For additional information on executive orders, see Table 4.5.

(b) Full responsibility to propose; legislature adopts or revises and governor signs or vetoes.

(c) 2/3 of members to which each house is entitled required to override veto.

(d) Authorization for reorganization provided for in state constitution.

(e) The Legislature has full responsibility with regard to setting the state's budget.

(f) Governor may veto any distinct item or items appropriating money in any appropriations bill.

(g) 2/3 of elected legislators of each house to override.

(h) Only for agencies and offices within the governor's office.

(i) Governor has sole authority to propose annual budget. No money may be paid out of state treasury except in pursuance of appropriations made by law.

(j) Statute provides for reorganization by the commissioner of administration with the approval of the governor.

(k) Governor has the responsibility of presenting a balanced budget. The budget is based on revenue estimated by the governor's office and the Legislative Budget Committee.

(l) If the Legislature is not in session when the governor vetoes a bill, the secretary of state must poll the Legislature as to the question of an override but only if the bill had passed by a vote of 2/3 of the members present.

(m) The office of the governor shall continuously study and evaluate the organizational structure, management practices, and functions of the executive branch and each agency.

The governor shall, by executive order or other means within his authority, take action to improve the manageability of the executive branch. The governor may not, however, create an agency of state government by administrative action, except that the governor may establish advisory councils and must approve the internal organizational structures of departments.

(n) 3/5 majority required to override line-item veto.

(o) Executive reorganization plans can be disapproved by majority vote in both houses of the legislature.

(p) Executive order must be approved by the legislature if changes affect existing law.

(q) Requires 2/3 of legislators present to override.

(r) Governor has veto power of selections for nonappropriations and item veto in appropriations.

(s) In Wisconsin, governor has "partial" veto over appropriation bills. The partial veto is broader than item veto.

(t) Only if it is not prohibited by law.

TABLE 8-2

Gubernatorial Executive Orders: Authorization, Provisions, Procedures

State or other jurisdiction	Authorization for executive orders	Civil defense disasters, public emergencies	Energy emergencies and conservation	Other emergencies	Executive branch reorganization plans and agency creation	Create advisory, coordinating, study or investigative committees/commissions	Respond to federal programs and requirements	State personnel administration	Other administration	Filing and publication procedures	Subject to administrative procedure act	Subject to legislative review
		Provisions								**Procedures**		
Alabama	S, I, Case Law	✱	✱	✱	...	✱	...	...	...	✱	...	...
Alaska	C	...	...	...	✱	...	...	...	...	✱	...	✱
Arizona	I	✱(a)	✱(a)	✱(a)	...	✱	...	...	...	✱(b)	...	...
Arkansas	S, I, Common Law	✱	✱	✱	✱	✱	...	...	...	...	...	...
California	I	✱	✱	✱	✱	✱	✱	✱	✱	...	...	...
Colorado	C	✱	✱	...	✱	✱	✱	✱	...	✱	✱	...
Connecticut	C, S	✱	✱	✱	...	✱	...	...	...	✱	✱	...
Delaware	C	✱	✱	✱	✱	✱	✱	✱	...	✱	...	...
Florida	C, S	✱	✱	✱	✱	✱	✱	✱	...	...	✱(c)	...
Georgia	S, I (d)	✱	✱	✱	✱	✱	✱	✱	...	✱	...	...
Hawaii	C	✱	✱	✱	✱	✱	✱	✱	...	✱	✱	✱
Idaho	S	...	I	I	...	I	I	...	...	(b)(e)	...	...
Illinois	C, S	✱	✱	✱	✱	✱	✱	✱	✱	✱	✱	✱
Indiana	C, S, Case Law	✱	✱	...	✱(limited)	✱	✱	✱	...	...	...	...
Iowa	(f)	✱	✱	✱	✱	✱	✱	✱	(g)	✱	✱	✱
Kansas	C, S	✱	✱	✱	✱	✱	...	✱	✱	...	...	(h)
Kentucky	C, S	✱	✱	✱(i)	✱	✱	✱	✱	✱(j)(k)(l)	✱(b)	✱	✱
Louisiana	C, S (m)	✱	✱	✱	✱	✱	✱	✱	...	✱	...	...
Maine	I	✱	✱	✱	...	✱	✱	✱	...	...	...	...
Maryland	C, S	✱	✱	✱	✱	✱	✱	✱	✱(n)	✱	✱	✱(o)
Massachusetts	C, S	✱	✱	✱	✱	✱	...	✱	✱	✱	...	...
Michigan	C, S, I	✱	✱	✱	✱(p)	✱	✱	✱	✱	✱(p)	...	...
Minnesota	S	✱	✱(q)	✱	✱	✱	✱	...	(r)	✱(b)	✱	✱(o)
Mississippi	C, S	✱	✱	✱	✱	✱	✱	✱	...	(s)	(s)	...

TABLE 8-2, continued

State or other jurisdiction	Authorization for executive orders	Civil defense disasters, public emergencies	Energy emergencies and conservation	Other emergencies	Executive branch reorganization plans and agency creation	Create advisory, coordinating, study or investigative committees/commissions	Respond to federal programs and requirements	State personnel administration	Other administration	Filing and publication procedures	Subject to administrative procedure act	Subject to legislative review
		|<-- Provisions -->|								|<-- Procedures -->|		
Missouri	C, S, Common Law	★	I	★	★	★	★	★	★	★(o)	. . .	★(o)(t)
Montana	S, I, Common Law	★	★	★	★	★	★	★	★	★	. . .	. . .
Nebraska	C, S	★	★	★	. . .	★	. . .	. . .	. . .	★	. . .	. . .
Nevada	S, I	★	. . .	I	. . .	★	. . .	. . .	I	. . .	. . .	. . .
New Hampshire	S	★	★(a)	★	. . .	★	★	. . .	★(k)	★	. . .	. . .
New Jersey	C, S, I	★	★	★	. . .	★	★	★	★(u)	★	. . .	. . .
New Mexico	C, S	★	★	★	★	★	. . .	★	. . .	★	. . .	. . .
New York	C, S	★	★	★	. . .	★	. . .	. . .	. . .	★	. . .	. . .
North Carolina	C, S	★	★	★	★	★	★	★	★	★	. . .	★(v)
North Dakota	S, I	★	★	★	. . .	. . .	. . .	. . .	(l)(r)(u) (w)(x)(y)	. . .	. . .	. . .
Ohio	S, I (z)	★	★	★	★	★	★	. . .	. . .	★	. . .	. . .
Oklahoma	C, S	★	★	★	(aa)	★	★	★	. . .	★	. . .	. . .
Oregon	I	★	★	★	. . .	★	★	★	. . .	. . .	. . .	. . .
Pennsylvania	C, S	★	. . .	★(n)(bb) (cc)(dd)	. . .	★	★	. . .	★(dd)	★(b) (bb)	. . .	. . .
Rhode Island	I, Case Law	★	★	★	★	★	★	★	. . .	★	. . .	. . .
South Carolina	S	★	★	★	. . .	★	★	. . .	★	★	. . .	. . .
South Dakota	C	★	★	★	★	★	★	★	★	★	. . .	. . .
Tennessee	S	★	★	★	★	★	★	★	★	★(b)	. . .	. . .
Texas	I	★	★	★	★	★	★	★	. . .	. . .	. . .	. . .
Utah	S, I	★	★	★	★	★	★	★	. . .	. . .	. . .	. . .
Vermont	S, I	★	★	. . .	★(ee)	★	★	. . .	. . .	. . .	. . .	★(ff)
Virginia	S	★	★	★	★	★	★	★	. . .	. . .	★	. . .
Washington	S	★	. . .	. . .	. . .	. . .	. . .	. . .	. . .	. . .	. . .	. . .
West Virginia	C, S	★	★	. . .	. . .	★	★	. . .	. . .	. . .	. . .	. . .

continued

TABLE 8-2, continued

State or other jurisdiction	Authorization for executive orders	Provisions — Civil defense disasters, public emergencies	Energy emergencies and conservation	Other emergencies	Executive branch reorganization plans and agency creation	Create advisory, coordinating, study or investigative committees/commissions	Respond to federal programs and requirements	State personnel administration	Other administration	Procedures — Filing and publication procedures	Subject to administrative procedure act	Subject to legislative review
Wisconsin	S	✳	✳	✳	. . .	✳	✳	. . .	. . .	✳	✳	✳
Wyoming	(gg)	. . .	. . .	. . .	. . .	. . .	. . .	. . .	. . .	. . .	. . .	. . .
American Samoa	C, S	✳	✳	✳	✳	✳	✳	✳	✳	✳(hh)	✳(hh)	. . .
Guam	C	✳	✳	. . .	(ii)	✳	✳	✳	✳	✳	. . .	. . .
No. Mariana Islands	C	✳	I	✳	C	S, I	S	. . .	✳	S	I	. . .
Puerto Rico	C, S, I, Case Law	✳	✳	✳	✳	✳	✳	✳	✳	(jj)	. . .	. . .
U.S. Virgin Islands	C	✳	✳	✳	✳	✳	✳	✳	✳	✳	. . .	. . .

Source: The Council of State Governments' survey, December 2009.

Key:

C — Constitutional
S — Statutory
I — Implied
✳ — Formal provision.
. . . — No formal provision.

(a) Broad interpretation of gubernatorial authority.
(b) Executive orders must be filed with secretary of state or other designated officer. In Idaho, must also be published in state general circulation newspaper.
(c) Under some circumstances the Cabinet must approve before an order becomes law. The Joint Administrative Procedure Committee must make sure agency rules have legislative authority to do so.
(d) Implied from Constitution.
(e) Some implied.
(f) Constitution, statute, implied, case law, common law.
(g) Executive clemency.
(h) Only for EROs. When an ERO is submitted the legislature has 30 days to veto the ERO or it becomes law.
(i) To give immediate effect to state regulation in emergencies.
(j) To control administration of state contracts and procedures.
(k) To impound or freeze certain state matching funds.
(l) To reduce state expenditures in revenue shortfall.
(m) Inherent.
(n) To control procedures for dealing with public.
(o) Reorganization plans and agency creation.
(p) Executive reorganizations not effective if rejected by both houses of legislature within 60 calendar days. Executive orders reducing appropriations not effective unless approved by appropriations committees of both houses of legislature.
(q) If an energy emergency is declared by the state's Executive Council or legislature.
(r) To assign duties to lieutenant governor, issue writ of special election.
(s) Governor is exempt from the Administrative Procedures Act and filing and administrative procedures Miss. Code Ann. § 25-43-102 (1972).
(t) Reorganization plans and agency creation and for meeting federal program requirements.
(u) To administer and govern the armed forces of the state.
(v) Must submit to the secretary of state who must compile, index and publish executive orders. Copies must also be sent to president of the Senate, Speaker of the House, and principal clerk of each chamber
(w) To suspend certain officials and/or other civil actions.
(x) To designate game and wildlife areas or other public areas.
(y) Appointive powers.
(z) Executive authority implied except for emergencies which are established by statute.
(aa) Limited authority in executive branch reorganization/agency creation.
(bb) Filing.
(cc) For fire emergencies.
(dd) To transfer funds in an emergency.
(ee) Subject to legislative approval.
(ff) Only if reorganization order filed with the legislature.
(gg) No specific authorization granted, general authority only.
(hh) If executive order fits definition of rule.
(ii) Can reorganize, but not create.
(jj) Executive orders are filed in the Department of State.

A governor can use the budget process to override old agency decisions, for example, to make sure that the transportation department fully funds bike trails that previously had been ignored. Even when an agency has some independence about how it spends its money, a governor can persuade its officials to fund other priorities—a new law school at a state university, for example—by threatening to withhold some percentage of its overall budget.

Power to Veto. In talking about the governor as chief legislator, we touched on the governor's ability to veto legislation in every state. (North Carolina's governor was the last to win this power, in 1997.) Legislators can override vetoes, but that rarely happens because of supermajority vote requirements. Members of the governor's own party usually are reluctant to vote to override a veto. That means that if the governor's party holds just one-third of the seats in a legislative chamber, plus one, a veto is likely to be sustained—meaning the governor wins.

Legislators, therefore, try to work with governors or their staffs to craft a version of a bill that the governor will sign. There is little point in passing a bill if you know it is going to be rejected. Of course, legislatures sometimes pass a bill just to get it vetoed, making the governor's opposition official and public. That happened often when Gary Johnson was governor of New Mexico during the 1990s. Johnson did not support any bill that increased the size of government, and so he ended up vetoing more than seven hundred bills. Legislators sent him bills that would increase funding for popular programs, such as education, in hopes that his vetoes would make him look bad. Whether that happened or not, Johnson almost always won the procedural battle. Not only was the legislature unable to override his vetoes except in one instance, but he also was reelected to a second term. Conversely, South Carolina governor Mark Sanford—who attracted national attention in 2009 when he disappeared from the state for several days to visit his mistress in Argentina—was already an enfeebled governor. The legislature, which was controlled by his own party that year, overrode Sanford's vetoes on matters ranging from budget priorities and the question of whether to accept federal stimulus funds to payday lending and sex offender policies.

All but seven governors—those in Indiana, Maryland, Nevada, New Hampshire, North Carolina, Rhode Island, and Vermont—have a power known as the line-item veto; that is, they can reject just a portion of a bill. If there is a bill funding education, for example, the governor can accept all of it except for an increase in funding for a school in the district of a legislator who is a political enemy. Governors can use the line-item veto to try to cut spending, as when New York governor George Pataki eliminated spending for more than one thousand items from the state budget in 1998. The governor's ability to cut legislators' pet projects out of the budget forces most of them to support that governor's major initiatives. Congress

States under Stress: Arizona Governor Pays Price for Revenue Fall

Jan Brewer was Arizona's popular secretary of state when her political career took a turn for the worse—she became governor.

With Democrat Janet Napolitano departing the state in 2009 to serve in President Obama's cabinet, Brewer, who is a Republican, stepped in as her replacement. The timing was awful. Between 2007 and 2010, Arizona's revenues dropped by one-third, brought down by the housing bust. When Brewer took office, she faced a $3.4 billion shortfall for fiscal year 2010, out of an overall budget of less than $10 billion.

It wasn't that Brewer was unwilling to cut spending. In 2010, she signed a budget package that made Arizona the first state to eliminate funding for its Children's Health Insurance Program and included cuts in Medicaid deep enough to threaten coverage for 300,000 adults.

But, throughout 2009, Brewer surprised many in Arizona by advocating for a penny increase in the sales tax. Brewer had a long-standing reputation as an opponent of higher taxes, but soon after taking office she proposed a public referendum on a sales tax increase to help balance the budget. Her fellow Republicans, who controlled both houses of the legislature, recoiled. Brewer tried to strike a deal by coupling the sales tax vote with future tax cuts, including a move to a flat income tax beginning in 2012. Democrats rejected that bargain—and Brewer still didn't get the Republican support she needed.

The inability to reach an agreement led to a stalemate lasting many months. In September 2009, Brewer signed some budget bills that, without the sales tax increase, still left the state's finances $1.5 billion out of balance, a shortfall that continued to grow into 2010.

Finally, legislators decided that she was right, that voters deserved the chance to decide for themselves whether they were willing to pay more in taxes. A referendum was put on the ballot in May 2010, which voters approved. But that is hardly likely to be the end of the political battling. Opponents of the plan termed it, correctly, the largest tax increase in Arizona history.

And the issue made Brewer's path to winning a full term of her own much steeper. She drew three opponents in the GOP primary. Even if she could survive that, she faced a tough general election contest against Democratic state attorney general Terry Goddard.

It was an ironic turn of events for Brewer. When she ran for reelection as secretary of state in 2006, the *Arizona Republic* endorsed her as "a partisan worth keeping." She was known as an able administrator, but as a state legislator and Maricopa County official, she had been seen as an aggressive Republican activist. Few people would have predicted that she'd lead a charge against the wishes of her own party in favor of a tax hike.

Source: Adapted from Josh Goodman, "Lonely at the Top," *Governing* magazine, November 2009, 17.

tried to give the president line-item veto authority, but the U.S. Supreme Court ruled the practice unconstitutional in 1998.

When Tommy Thompson was governor of Wisconsin during the 1990s, he used the line-item veto to an unusual degree. Some governors can strike not only projects from bills, but individual words and letters as well. Thompson became notorious for vetoing just enough letters to completely alter the meaning of a bill (see chapter 3). The courts upheld his right to do so, but that power was soon curbed. Nevertheless, in 2005, Jim Doyle, the state's Democratic governor, was able to strike out 752 words from a budget bill in order to cobble together a new, twenty-word sentence that shifted $427 million from transportation to education.[23] Prompted by

Doyle's move—and by near-daily editorials in the *Wisconsin State Journal* newspaper and Web site—the legislature in 2008 further restricted the governor's veto authority. He no longer can stitch together words from different parts of a bill, but he still can delete words from individual sentences, and he can change numbers—quickly converting $100 million into $10 million, for instance. "It seems like each governor gets more creative in their use of the partial veto, and this was clearly an abuse," said state senator Sheila Harsdorf, a sponsor of the successful anti-Frankenstein referendum. "When people saw that veto, it was pretty hard to justify."[24]

Power to Grant Pardons. One clichéd motif of old movies and television was to depict a prisoner about to be put to death, only to be spared by a last-minute pardon from the governor. Governors, like the president, can forgive crimes or commute (change) sentences if they feel a person has been convicted unfairly. They sometimes act on the recommendations of pardon boards, but the decision to pardon is theirs alone and not reversible.

A famous example of the use of pardon power happened in Illinois in 2003. During his last week in office, Gov. George Ryan pardoned 4 prisoners condemned to death and commuted the sentences of the other 167 death-row prisoners to life in prison. Ryan had grown concerned that the number of death-row cases that were being overturned because new evidence, such as DNA lab work, indicated that the death penalty was being unfairly and inequitably assigned. He appointed a commission to study the application of the death sentence and became convinced that the state could not impose the death penalty with such absolute certainty that innocent people would not be put to death. The move gained Ryan international celebrity among death penalty opponents but was criticized by prosecutors and others at home.

Not all governors use their pardon powers in such a high-minded way. In Tennessee in 1979, Lamar Alexander was sworn in as governor three days early to prevent outgoing governor Ray Blanton from commuting the sentences of any more prisoners. Blanton already had granted fifty-two last-minute pardons, and the Federal Bureau of Investigation (FBI) already had arrested members of his staff for extorting money to sell pardons, paroles, and commutations.

The Power to Call Special Sessions. Most legislatures meet only part time and generally have fixed session schedules. When necessary or desired, however, every governor has the power to call legislatures into special session. Nearly half the nation's governors have the ability to set the agenda of a special session. This means that legislators can deal only with those issues that the governor wants addressed.

Special sessions can be useful for governors who want to deal with an issue right away. In recent years, many governors have called special sessions when the state's revenues have fallen short so that the legislatures can

As powerful as they are, there are some things governors may not be able to control. The weather is one. The insurance industry may be another. Florida's Republican governor Charlie Crist tackled both in his first term as he worked behind the scenes and in front of the cameras to pass legislation to stem rising insurance costs in the state.

THE PROBLEM. The disastrous 2004 and 2005 hurricane seasons left many of Florida's homeowners with more than just flattened roofs: it landed them with crushing insurance bills. The cost of insuring a home more than doubled in 2006, and many residents considered leaving the state altogether. Joining a chorus of voices advocating for a host of insurance reforms, Governor Crist urged Floridians to stay put and promised to work with lawmakers to help bring down insurance rates.

That's no small feat. Insuring property in a state that saw nearly $36 billion in storm damages in one year alone is an expensive business—and regulating that industry is the state's responsibility. Even the industry's harshest critics understand that the premiums homeowners pay on a regular basis to insure their homes must keep pace with the amounts that agencies anticipate will be paid out in future claims. That's basic math. But, critics say, insurers' profits have soared in recent years. Some agencies have adopted such misleading or unfair practices as creating differently named subsidiary companies that offer different rates than their parent agencies. Others offer restricted insurance plans to Floridians (for example, they offer auto but not homeowners insurance). Still others refused to offer policies in that state, leaving many without coverage.

In their wake stands Citizens Property Insurance, a state-run agency created in 2002 by the Florida legislature as an insurance "safety net." Under its original rules, homeowners were allowed to switch to Citizens only if they had been denied coverage by a national company or if their premiums were quoted at more than 25 percent higher than Citizens's rates. By 2006, however, Citizens was set to become the insurer for more than half of all of Florida's homeowners—about 1.3 million policyholders—making it the state's largest insurance company rather than the agency of last resort.

With so many homeowners forced to pay exorbitant rates or cut loose from national policies altogether and Citizens stepping in to fill the gap, Governor Crist and Florida's lawmakers were made to reconsider the role that Citizens should (or could) play in wholesale insurance reform.

THE PROCESS. In January 2007 Crist called a week-long special legislative session to try to hammer out a plan. Crist himself brought several aggressive measures to the table, including recommendations to lower threshold requirements for homeowners to get coverage through Citizens, to cap the agency's ability to raise rates, and to crackdown on subsidiaries. He also asked for the power to appoint the company's director. But the hallmark of his plan was to make Citizens more competitive with private insurers. After the special session, the legislature continued the reform debate during its regular session.

Early predictions of Crist's likelihood of success were not good. The insurance lobby came on strong, as did a handful of legislators from his own party, who warned the public that increasing the role of the state-sponsored Citizens was tantamount to socialism and potentially could bankrupt the state. But having once been a state legislator himself, Crist knew how to work the ropes. His main advantage was his stratospheric popularity: he had plenty of political capital, and he wasn't shy about spending it.

To promote his plan, Crist put in rare appearances before several House and Senate committees and stumped to persuade homeowners that the promised rate relief wasn't an illusion. He also traveled to Washington, D.C., to help Florida lawmakers appeal for a national disaster relief fund to help defray costs to that state's homeowners.

Crist and his staff continued to work behind the scenes, too, with the governor's staff "buttonholing" legislators. State senator J. D. Alexander reported that "there had been some political arm-twisting," adding, "You don't go against a governor with a 77-percent approval rating." [a]

Both the House and Senate took up bills that included a number of Crist's original proposals; by the end of their regular session, they'd reached resolutions.

THE OUTCOMES. Crist got a lot of what he wanted. Legislators agreed to freeze Citizens's rates at 2006 levels through 2009. Policyholders will be allowed to choose coverage through Citizens if they receive quotes from national insurers that are more than 15 percent higher than Citizens's annual premiums. Other provisions also are in place to allow the agency to be more competitive with private insurers.

"You put the nail in the coffin this afternoon on the industry that was hurting our people. That's right and just fair and important, and you did it, and God bless you for fighting for the people of Florida," Crist told legislators. "I hear some groans from insurance lobbyists? Tough. That's right. We work for the people, not them." [b]

But Crist didn't get everything he asked for. Legislators killed an amendment giving him the power to appoint Citizens's director. Also rejected was a proposal that would have allowed the agency to write policies for auto, theft, and fire insurance that would have made it better able to amass greater financial reserves and offer lower premiums.

[a] Paige St. John, "Crist Still Pushing for Property-insurance Legislation," *Tallahassee Democrat*. www.tallahassee.com/apps/pbcs.dll/article?AID=2007705030346.

[b] S. V. Date, "Sessions End More Like Recess Than Finale," Palm Beach Post.com. www.palmbeachpost.com/state/content/state/epaper/2007/05/05/m1a_XGR_session_0505.html.

help them cut spending. Sometimes, special sessions allow legislators to focus on a complex issue, such as changing medical malpractice liability laws. Such issues might get lost in the shuffle of a regular session, when most attention is devoted to passing a budget.

Although governors can call special sessions, they typically will not enjoy success unless they can work out deals on their pet bills in advance. "If a governor calls a special session without knowing what the outcome's going to be," said former Mississippi House Speaker Tim Ford, "it's chaos for everybody."[25] Working without a deal already in place, legislators will sit around reading newspapers and eating snacks while their leaders try to hammer out an agreement with the governor. They resent having to give up time from their regular jobs to sit idly in the capital.

And governors may be able to call legislators into special session, but they cannot necessarily make them do anything. In Iowa in 2002, Gov. Tom Vilsack called the legislature back in hopes they would increase funding for education and health, but the legislature adjourned after a single day without debating any bill. "We just came in and went home," said House majority leader Christopher Rants. Vilsack then signed a package of budget cuts he had accepted in meetings with legislators and went on to call a second special session later in the month.[26]

Sometimes the fact that governors have to resort to the use of such powers as calling special sessions or issuing vetoes is a sign of weakness. What it may show is that they could not get what they wanted from their legislatures during the regular course of business.

Informal Powers

The powers just outlined are spelled out in state constitutions and statutes. Governors either have line-item veto authority or they do not. Much of the outcome of a governor's program, however, depends on a governor's individual ability to wield informal powers—the ability to leverage the power and prestige of the office into real influence in a way that may not be replicated by successors. Governors may be personally popular, have a special gift for working with legislators, or have some other skills that help them do their jobs well but that are not based on any authority that the state granted.

Popular Support. One thing that will always help a governor is popular support. A governor who wins with 51 percent of the vote has all of the same formal powers as a governor who wins with 73 percent, but the more popular governor is clearly going to have an edge. Legislators and other officials will accept more readily the need to go along with a popular governor's program because they believe that program is what most voters in the state want. This is especially true if the governor ran strong in their districts. In a case like this, "[l]egislators cannot fail to be impressed," according to political scientist Alan Rosenthal, "for if there is one thing they are sensitive to it is the number of votes candidates receive."[27]

It is a long time between gubernatorial elections—four years in most cases—so to maintain and build on their popularity governors do all sorts of public relations work. They never fail to alert the press to all their good deeds, they appear in other forums—TV shows, groundbreakings, dedications, state fairs, and church socials—where they can impress the public, and they propose legislation that they believe will be popular. The fortunes of governors rise and fall with the health of the economy of their states, but individual governors can make themselves more or less popular depending on how well they appear to address the problems of the day.

Party Support in the Legislature. Having members of their own party dominate the legislature certainly helps governors get their agendas passed. Governors can be successful if the other party controls the legislature, but it is a lot tougher. The reasons are fairly obvious. Republican legislators want to see a Republican governor succeed, and the same holds true, obviously, for Democratic legislators serving under Democratic governors. Voters perceive politicians belonging to the same party as being part of the same team. Therefore, the political fortunes of these politicians will be tied together during the next election. Members of the same party are likely to hold similar positions on such issues as taxes, levels of social service spending, and the environment. "Governors are far more likely to influence legislators from their own party," a pair of political scientists concluded in 2002.[28] Each party naturally is going to try to strengthen the power of the institution it controls and weaken the one it does not, but a party that controls both the executive and legislative branches is going to be able to push through legislation in a cooperative fashion.

Governors are more likely to grant favors to legislators of their own party or raise money for them. This, in turn, makes those legislators more likely to support their programs. Some governors curry favor with legislators because they used to be legislators themselves and still have friends in the house or senate. One-time Tennessee governor Ned McWherter, for example, was a long-time legislator before taking the top office. He concentrated his attention on a few pet initiatives, such as a major overhaul of the state Medicaid system, and went along with whatever his pals in the legislature were thinking on most other matters.

Unified control of government is no guarantee of success for the governor, however. Just as some governors, such as Mark Sanford, have become unpopular with members of their own party in the state legislature, there certainly have been plenty of others who were able to work well with legislatures controlled by the other party. But having to do so only made their jobs tougher. Governors need at least a large enough minority of their own party to sustain their vetoes. This is the only definite way to ensure real influence over the legislative process.

TABLE 8-3

Ranking of the Institutional Powers of Governors, 2007

State	Separately Elected Executive Branch Officials	Tenure Potential	Appointment Powers	Budgetary Powers	Veto Powers	Party Control	Total Score	Rank
Massachusetts	4	5	3.5	3	5	5	4.3	1
Alaska	5	4	3.5	3	5	4	4.1	2
Maryland	4	4	2.5	5	5	4	4.1	2
New Jersey	5	4	3.5	3	5	4	4.1	2
New York	4	5	3.5	4	5	3	4.1	2
West Virginia	2.5	4	4	5	5	4	4.1	2
Utah	4	5	3	3	5	4	4.0	7
Colorado	4	4	3.5	3	5	4	3.9	8
North Dakota	3	5	3.5	3	5	4	3.9	8
Illinois	3	5	3	3	5	4	3.8	10
Iowa	3	5	3	3	5	4	3.8	10
Nebraska	4	4	3	4	5	3	3.8	10
Pennsylvania	4	4	4	3	5	3	3.8	10
Tennessee	4.5	4	4	3	4	3	3.8	10
New Mexico	3	4	3	3	5	4	3.7	15
Arkansas	2.5	4	3	3	4	5	3.6	16
Connecticut	4	5	2.5	3	5	2	3.6	16
Florida	3	4	2.5	3	5	4	3.6	16
Maine	5	4	3.5	3	2	4	3.6	16
Michigan	4	4	3.5	3	5	2	3.6	16
Minnesota	4	5	2.5	3	5	2	3.6	16
Missouri	2.5	4	3	3	5	4	3.6	16
Ohio	4	4	3.5	3	5	2	3.6	16
Washington	1	5	3.5	3	5	4	3.6	16
Delaware	2.5	4	3.5	3	5	3	3.5	25
Montana	3	4	3	3	5	3	3.5	25
Oregon	2	4	3	3	5	4	3.5	25
Wisconsin	3	5	2	3	5	3	3.5	25
Arizona	2.5	4	4	3	5	2	3.4	29
Hawaii	5	4	2.5	3	5	1	3.4	29
Louisiana	1	4	3.5	3	5	4	3.4	29
California	1	4	4	3	5	2	3.2	32
Georgia	1	4	2	3	5	4	3.2	32
Idaho	2	4	2	3	5	4	3.3	32

TABLE 8-3, continued

State	Separately Elected Executive Branch Officials	Tenure Potential	Appointment Powers	Budgetary Powers	Veto Powers	Party Control	Total Score	Rank
Kansas	3	4	3	3	5	2	3.3	32
Kentucky	3	4	4	3	4	2	3.3	32
New Hampshire	5	2	3	3	2	4	3.2	32
Texas	2	5	1	2	5	4	3.2	32
Virginia	2.5	3	3.5	3	5	2	3.2	32
Wyoming	2	4	3.5	3	5	1	3.1	40
Nevada	2.5	4	3.5	3	2	3	3.0	41
South Carolina	1	4	2	2	5	4	3.0	41
South Dakota	1	4	2	2	5	4	3.0	41
Indiana	3	4	2.5	3	2	3	2.9	44
Mississippi	1.5	4	2	3	5	2	2.9	44
North Carolina	1	4	3.5	3	2	4	2.9	44
Alabama	1	4	3	3	4	2	2.8	47
Oklahoma	1	4	1	3	5	3	2.8	47
Rhode Island	2.5	4	3	3	2	1	2.6	49
Vermont	2.5	2	3.5	3	2	2	2.5	50

Source: Thad Beyle and Margaret Ferguson, "Governors and the Executive Branch," in *Politics in the American States,* 9th edition, Virginia Gray and Russell L. Hanson, eds. (Washington, D.C.: CQ Press, 2008).

Separately Elected Executive Branch Officials: 5 = only governor or governor/lieutenant governor team elected; 4.5 = governor or governor/lieutenant governor team, with one other elected official; 4 = governor/lieutenant governor team with some process officials (attorney general, secretary of state, treasurer, auditor) elected; 3 = governor/lieutenant governor team with process officials, and some major and minor policy officials elected; 2.5 = governor (no team) with six or fewer officials elected, but none are major policy officials; 2 = governor (no team) with six or fewer officials elected, including one major policy official; 1.5 = governor (no team) with six or fewer officials elected, but two are major policy officials; 1 = governor (no team) with seven or more process and several major policy officials elected. [Source: CSG, *The Book of the States, 2007* (2007)].

Tenure Potential: 5 = 4-year term, no restraint on reelection; 4.5 = 4-year term, only three terms permitted; 4 = 4-year term, only two terms permitted; 3 = 4-year term, no consecutive election permitted; 2 = 2-year term, no restraint on reelection; 1 = 2-year term, only two terms permitted. [Source: CSG, *The Book of the States, 2007* (2007)].

Appointment Powers: in six major functional areas, including corrections, K-12 education, health, highways/transportation, public utilities regulation, and welfare. The six individual office scores are totaled and then averaged and rounded to the nearest .5 for the state score. 5 = governor appoints, no other approval needed; 4 = governor appoints, a board, council or legislature approves; 3 = someone else appoints, governor approves or shares appointment; 2 = someone else appoints, governor and others

approve; 1 = someone else appoints, no approval or confirmation needed. [Source: CSG, *The Book of the States,* 2007 (2007)].

Budgetary Power: 5 = governor has full responsibility, legislature may not increase executive budget; 4 = governor has full responsibility, legislature can increase by special majority vote or subject to item veto; 3 = governor has full responsibility, legislature has unlimited power to change executive budget; 2 = governor shares responsibility, legislature has unlimited power to change executive budget; 1 = governor shares responsibility with other elected official, legislature has unlimited power to change executive budget. [Sources: CSG, *The Book of the States, 2007* (2007): and NCSL, "Limits on Authority of Legislature to Change Budget" (1998).]

Veto Power: 5 = governor has item veto and a special majority vote of the legislature is needed to override a veto (3/5's of legislators elected or 2/3's of legislators present); 4 = has item veto with a majority of the legislators elected needed to override; 3 = has item veto with only a majority of the legislators present needed to override; 2 = no item veto, with a special legislative majority needed to override a regular veto; 1 = no item veto, only a simple legislative majority needed to override a regular veto. [Source: CSG, *The Book of the States, 2007* (2007)].

Party Control: The governor's party - 5 = has a substantial majority (75% or more) in both houses of the legislature; 4 = has a simple majority in both houses (under 75%), or a substantial majority in one house and a simple majority in the other; 3 = split control in the legislature or a non-partisan legislature; 2 = has a simple minority (25% or more) in both houses, or a simple minority in one and a substantial minority (under 25%) in the other; 1 = has a substantial minority in both houses. [Source: NCSL Web page].

Score: total divided by six to keep 5-point scale.

Unfortunately for governors, divided control of state governments has become common. Voters are more likely to split their tickets and vote for nominees of different parties for different offices. Divided government is likely to make the governorship more difficult because governors must try to convince political competitors to get with their programs. Cooperation becomes consorting with the enemy.

Political scientists have built on the work David R. Mayhew has done in studying divided power between Congress and the White House to examine divided power in the states. It was once commonly thought that divided power necessarily meant that less work got done. That does not appear to be the case. What it may mean is that different types of bills become law. In other words, a Democratic governor might work with a Republican-controlled legislature to create lots of laws, but the nature of these laws might be very different from what it would have been if the governor had worked with a Democratic legislative majority. A Democratic governor working with a Democratic-controlled legislature should be able to pursue legislation more in keeping with party's principles and desires than a Democratic governor who has to compromise with a GOP-controlled legislature.

"[E]ach party attempts to strengthen the institution it commands and to weaken the institution controlled by the opposition," notes one political scientist.[29] In other words, if Republicans hold the governorship, they will try to make that office more powerful at the expense of a Democratic legislature and vice versa. But because power is so often shared these days under divided government, the two parties cannot just attack each other's programs. If they share power, they also share responsibility in the eyes of the voters, and so they have to work together to forge compromises on central issues such as the budget.

Conflict is more likely when the party in opposition to the governor's holds both legislative chambers, which should not be all that surprising. If each party controls one chamber, the governor is much more likely to claim victory.[30] It is all a matter of leverage and pressing the advantages your party has.

Ability to Communicate. We have already touched on the advantage governors have over legislators in regard to media exposure. There is no law that says newspapers and TV stations have to pay more attention to pronouncements from the governor—but that is what happens anyway. Pretty much anything legislators say and do takes a back seat. The governor is a single, well-known individual who is important to every voter in the state. A legislator, by contrast, even a powerful one, is just an individual legislator among 120 or 150 legislators and represents a district that makes up only a fraction of the state.

Smart governors are aware of the power of the mass media in helping to spread their messages. Contemporary governors have large public relations staffs that deal exclusively with the media and make sure that their governors' faces appear on television regularly. A governor's fame adds to the grandeur of the office, making the officeholder appear more potent to legislators, to aides, and to other people who deal with the governor. Power builds on power, in the sense that a governor who becomes famous for pushing through a landmark change in law becomes a more formidable presence in the state in the next policy battle.

Governors have to play both an inside game and an outside game. They have to appeal both to capital insiders and to the public at large. A governor who makes every move based on the ability to turn it into a press release or who appeals to the public by bashing the "corruption" in the capital may score points with the media and the public but soon will have few friends in the legislature. In Illinois, Rod Blagojevich was elected governor by railing against the corruption of state government and did not change his theme song once he took office. He refused even to establish a permanent residence in the state capital of Springfield, commuting from his home in Chicago. "We're going to keep fighting to reform and change the system and give the people a government that stops spending their money like a bunch of drunken sailors," he said toward the end of his first year in office.[31] Needless to say, the legislators whom Blagojevich had likened to drunken sailors were not eager to cooperate with him any more than they had to—even though his own party had a majority in both chambers. They continued to feud with him throughout his tenure—one publicly called the governor "insane" in 2007[32]—and did not hesitate to impeach him in 2009 after federal investigators revealed tapes of phone conversations in which Blagojevich was caught trying to sell Obama's U.S. Senate seat, which the governor had the power to fill following Obama's ascension to the White House.

Blagojevich may be an extreme case, but he is not alone in his criticisms. Many governors have bashed their state legislature. What they have found is that, although it made them popular with the public, it did not help them get their agendas passed. That was the lesson Arnold Schwarzenegger learned. When he was first elected governor of California in 2003, Schwarzenegger continually threatened to take his agenda directly to the people through ballot initiatives and referenda if the legislature refused to go along for his ride. Yet even the Man Who Was the Terminator could not convince voters about items he could not get passed in the legislature.

Schwarzenegger was elected in an unusual recall election at the end of 2003. During his first year in office, Schwarzenegger, a Republican, showed himself to be a savvy negotiator. He outmaneuvered the Democrats who dominated the legislature, making unusual alliances with various groups to get his way on such major issues as an overhaul of the state workers' compensation insurance law and a series of budget packages. He knew how to use his celebrity to focus attention on a problem, win a victory, and then carry that momentum forward into the next fight.

That was his first year. But he lost his way during his second year. He took to calling Democrats "girlie men" for not supporting his priorities and vowed to take his proposals directly to the public in the form of ballot initiatives. Schwarzenegger ended up doing just that. He called a special election in 2005 to determine the fate of his proposals to limit state spending and weaken his opponents through changes in redistricting and campaign spending. How did his gamble pay off? Every one of his proposals went down to defeat, and his own approval ratings slipped to 38 percent. Early polling in 2006 suggested Schwarzenegger would lose his bid for reelection.

Instead, Schwarzenegger staged an amazing comeback. He began cooperating with legislators rather than calling them names. Together, they passed some $40 billion worth of infrastructure projects and a landmark bill to address global warming. Schwarzenegger won a decisive reelection victory. What the actor-turned-politician had learned is that, although the governor calls the tune, he needs other players to join his band to accomplish anything. "Where he has gotten so much of his recent star power is in his ability to work compromises with the legislature," Mark Baldassare, director of research for the Public Policy Institute of California, said early in 2007. "His popularity is derived from working both sides of the aisle to come to a compromise. That's what he's going to have to do, or he will see his star power diminish."[33]

Merging Formal and Informal Powers

Roy Barnes, who served one term as governor of Georgia from 1999 until 2003, had said during his days in the state legislature, "When you are called down to the governor's office, it is a very impressive office, you're talking to the governor, and you know that he controls things that could be good or ill for your district. He controls grants, he controls roads, and other things."[34] In other words, the formal powers of the governor (the ability to control projects) merge with the informal powers (the mystique of the office) to influence legislators and other suppliants.

> In other words, the formal powers of the governor (the ability to control projects) merge with the informal powers (the mystique of the office) to influence legislators and other suppliants.

When Carroll Campbell became governor of South Carolina in 1987, that state's governor's office was among the weakest in the nation. The state's government consisted of seventy-nine separate administrative agencies, and the governor had sole appointment power for only ten of them. Campbell spent three years arguing that the modern executive needs more power to run a state well. He devoted nearly all his attention to the office, using all his informal powers—including the ability to persuade and the ability to keep an issue in front of

TABLE 8-4

Ranking of the Personal Power of Governors, 2007

State	Governor	Electoral Mandate	Position on Ambition Ladder	Personal Future	Job Performance Rating in Public Opinion Polls	Personal Powers Index Score	Rank
Arkansas	Mike Beebe	5	5	5	na	5.0	1
Colorado	Bill Ritter	5	5	5	na	5.0	1
Connecticut	M. Jodi Rell	5	5	5	5	5.0	1
Nebraska	Dave Heineman	5	5	5	5	5.0	1
Vermont	Jim Douglas	5	5	5	5	5.0	1
Ohio	Ted Strickland	5	5	5	4	4.8	6
Arizona	Janet Napolitano	5	5	3	5	4.5	7
Indiana	Mitch Daniels	5	5	5	3	4.5	7
Kansas	Kathleen Sebelius	5	5	3	5	4.5	7
Alaska	Sarah Palin	4	3	5	5	4.3	10
California	Arnold Schwarzenegger	5	5	3	4	4.3	10
Iowa	Chet Culver	4	5	5	3	4.3	10
Mississippi	Haley Barbour	4	5	4	4	4.3	10
Montana	Brian Schweitzer	3	5	4	5	4.3	10
New York	Eliot Spitzer	5	3	5	4	4.3	10
West Virginia	Joe Manchin III	5	3	4	5	4.3	10
Wisconsin	Jim Doyle	4	5	5	3	4.3	10
Alabama	Bob Riley	5	3	3	5	4.0	18
Florida	Charlie Crist	4	2	5	5	4.0	18
Idaho	C.L. "Butch" Otter	4	3	5	na	4.0	18
Kentucky	Ernie Fletcher	4	5	4	3	4.0	18
Michigan	Jennifer M. Granholm	5	5	3	3	4.0	18
New Hampshire	John Lynch	5	1	5	5	4.0	18
New Mexico	Bill Richardson	5	3	3	5	4.0	18
Oklahoma	Brad Henry	5	3	3	5	4.0	18
Oregon	Ted Kulongoski	4	5	3	4	4.0	18
South Dakota	Mike Rounds	5	3	3	5	4.0	18
Delaware	Ruth Ann Minner	5	5	1	4	3.8	28
Georgia	Sonny Perdue	5	3	3	4	3.8	28

continued

TABLE 8-4, continued

State	Governor	Electoral Mandate	Position on Ambition Ladder	Personal Future	Job Performance Rating in Public Opinion Polls	Personal Powers Index Score	Rank
Hawaii	Linda Lingle	5	2	3	5	3.8	28
Illinois	Rod Blagojevich	4	3	5	3	3.8	28
Maryland	Martin O'Malley	4	2	5	4	3.8	28
New Jersey	Jon Corzine	4	2	5	4	3.8	28
Tennessee	Phil Bredesen	5	2	3	5	3.8	28
Texas	Rick Perry	2	5	5	3	3.8	28
Utah	Jon Huntsman	5	1	4	5	3.8	28
Massachusetts	Deval Patrick	5	1	5	3	3.5	37
Minnesota	Tim Pawlenty	2	3	5	4	3.5	37
Missouri	Matt Blunt	2	5	4	3	3.5	37
North Dakota	John Hoeven	4	1	4	5	3.5	37
Pennsylvania	Edward Rendell	5	2	3	4	3.5	37
South Carolina	Mark Sanford	4	3	3	4	3.5	37
Wyoming	Dave Freudenthal	5	1	3	5	3.5	37
North Carolina	Michael Easley	3	5	1	4	3.3	44
Louisiana	Kathleen Blanco	3	3	4	2	3.0	45
Virginia	Tim Kaine	3	1	3	5	3.0	45
Washington	Chris Gregoire	2	2	4	4	3.0	45
Maine	John Baldacci	2	3	3	3	2.8	48
Nevada	Jim Gibbons	3	1	5	1	2.5	49
Rhode Island	Don Carcieri	2	1	3	4	2.5	49

Source: Thad Beyle and Margaret Ferguson, "Governors and the Executive Branch," in *Politics in the American States,* 9th edition, Virginia Gray and Russell L. Hanson, eds. (Washington, D.C.: CQ Press, 2008).

Notes:

Governor's electoral mandate: 5 = landslide win of 11 or more points; 4 = comfortable majority of 6 to 10 points; 3 = narrow majority of 3 to 5 points; 2 = tight win of 0 to 2 points or a plurality win of under 50%; 1 = succeeded to office. [Source: Author's data - www.unc.edu./~beyle]

Governor's position on the state's political ambition ladder: 5 = steady progression; 4 =former governors; 3 = legislative leaders or members of Congress; 2 = substate position to governor; 1 = governorship is first elective office. [Source: Individual governors' Web sites in each state and author's data]

The personal future of the governor: 5 = early in term, can run again; 4 = late in term, can run again; 3 = early in term, term limited; 2 = succeeded to office, can run for election; 1 = late in final term. [Source: CSG, *The Book of the States, 2007* (2007): and author's data.]

Gubernatorial job performance rating in public opinion polls: 5 = over 60% positive job approval rating; 4 = 50 to 59% positive job approval rating; 3 = 40 to 49% positive job approval rating; 2 = 30 to 39% positive job approval rating; 1 = less than 30% positive job approval rating; na = no polling data available. [Source: Author's data]

Governor's personal powers' index score: the sum of the scores for EM, AL, PF, GP divided by 4 and rounded to the nearest tenth, except for those states without a governor's job performance rating where the sum is divided by 3 and rounded to the nearest tenth.

Governing States and Localities

voters and legislators through use of the media—to increase his formal powers. In the end, he won. In 1993, the legislature restructured the government. It consolidated the administration into seventeen departments and gave the governor the power to appoint the directors of twelve of them.

The importance of being dealt such a fine political hand of cards cannot be stressed enough. Governors with constitutional authority to set the budget, to appoint their own people to spend that budget and implement their plans, and to line-item veto to keep legislators intimidated are going to have a lot easier time than their neighbors who lack some or all of those tools. One of those neighbors may be a more skilled politician and ultimately may have more success. People today expect the governor to be a powerful figure in the state and, in most cases, the governors have the tools to be just that. If only because of the power and prestige of the office and the ability to command media attention, a governor holds enormous influence in determining which issues are brought to the forefront and how they are handled.

Becoming Governor and Staying Governor

This chapter has described governors as the most powerful and important political actors in their states. It should come as little surprise then, given the history of politics in this country, that middle-age white males have dominated the job. Women are being elected governor with greater frequency—there were only three elected governor during the nation's first two centuries—but there are still plenty of states that have yet to elect a woman for the top job.[35] In 2007, nine women served as governor, the highest number to ever serve at one time. (Their ranks had been slightly depleted by the time thirty-seven states held gubernatorial elections in 2010, due to retirements and presidential appointments.) In 1873, P. B. S. Pinchback, the black lieutenant governor of Louisiana, was elevated to the post of acting governor for forty-three days, but only two African Americans have ever been elected as governor of any state.[36] Douglas Wilder of Virginia held the job during the first half of the 1990s; Deval Patrick was elected to the office in Massachusetts in 2006. David A. Paterson, who is African American and legally blind, became governor of New York following Eliot Spitzer's 2008 resignation due to a sex scandal. There have been a handful of Hispanic and Asian governors, including Bill Richardson of New Mexico and Gary Locke of Washington state, respectively. In 2007, Bobby Jindal of Louisiana became the first Indian American to be elected governor.

Many nonpoliticians have been elected governor, including Arnold Schwarzenegger, former wrestler Jesse Ventura of Minnesota, and business executives Mark Warner of Virginia and John Lynch of New Hampshire. Most governors, however, have had a good deal of previous government experience. They have served in the U.S. Congress, the state legislature, or other statewide positions such as lieutenant governor and attorney general or even state supreme court justice. Only a handful of independent or third-party candidates have been elected governor in recent years—and none since Ventura in 1998 and Angus King of Maine in 1994 and 1998.

One qualification for modern governors is quite clear—they must have the ability to raise money. Gubernatorial campaigns have become multi-million dollar affairs, particularly in heavily populated states in which television ads are expensive to run because the media markets are competitive and costly. The total campaign costs for the thirty-six governors races in 2002 was $840 million—a jump of 63 percent over the campaigns conducted only four years earlier. Those numbers were a bit skewed by two wealthy candidates in Texas and New York, who spent a combined $140 million on their own races. But, overall, gubernatorial campaign spending was up to about $800 million in 2006, even without such free-spending, self-funding contenders.

Factors Driving Gubernatorial Elections

Like the Winter Olympics, gubernatorial elections in most states have been moved to the second year of the presidential term in what are called "off-year" elections. Thirty-four states now hold their gubernatorial elections in the off-year. Another five states—Virginia, New Jersey, Kentucky, Mississippi, and Louisiana—hold their elections in odd-numbered years. Nine states—Delaware, Indiana, Missouri, Montana, New Hampshire, North Carolina, North Dakota, Utah, and Vermont—hold their elections at the same time as the presidential contest. In addition, New Hampshire and Vermont, the only states that have clung to the old tradition of two-year terms, hold elections for governor every even-numbered year.

The majority of governors are elected in an even-numbered off-year because states want to insulate the contests from getting mixed up in national issues. They want voters to concentrate on matters of importance just to the state instead of diverting their attention to federal issues brought up in presidential campaigns. This was the desire and the intent. But the plan has not been a 100 percent success. Elections for governors are often the biggest thing on the ballot, so voters use the races as a way of expressing their opinions about who is *not* on the ballot. In 1994, when antipathy was running high against Democratic president Bill Clinton, Republicans not only took control of both houses of Congress but also won a majority of the governorships for the first time in more than a decade. In 2002 and 2003, when Republican president George W. Bush was generally popular, Republicans did better than had been expected in gubernatorial contests. But as Bush's popularity sank, so did the ranks of Republican governors. Democrats in 2006 regained the majority of governorships for the first time since 1994, holding twenty-eight states,

TABLE 8-5

Who's Who among U.S. Governors, 2010

State	Governor	Party	Education (highest degree obtained)	First Elected in	Previous Political Life
Alabama	Bob Riley	Republican	University of Alabama	2002	Member, U.S. House of Representatives
Alaska	Sean Parnell	Republican	Seattle University (JD)	—	Lieutenant governor
Arizona	Jan Brewer	Republican	Radiology technician	—	Elected Arizona secretary of state
Arkansas	Mike Beebe	Democrat	University of Arkansas (JD)	2006	Arkansas state attorney general
California	Arnold Schwarzenegger	Republican	University of Wisconsin	2003	Started at the top as governor; previously major movie star
Colorado	Bill Ritter	Democrat	University of Colorado (JD)	2006	Elected district attorney for Denver
Connecticut	M. Jodi Rell	Republican	Attended Old Dominion University and Western Connecticut State University	2006	Lieutenant governor
Delaware	Jack Markell	Democrat	University of Chicago (MBA)	2008	State treasurer
Florida	Charlie Crist	Republican	Cumberland School of Law (JD)	2006	Elected Florida attorney general
Georgia	Sonny Perdue	Republican	University of Georgia (DVM)	2002	Houston County Planning and Zoning Board
Hawaii	Linda Lingle	Republican	California State University, Northridge	2002	Maui County councilmember
Idaho	C.L. "Butch" Otter	Republican	College of Idaho	2006	Member, U.S. House of Representatives
Illinois	Pat Quinn	Democrat	Northwestern (JD)	—	Lieutenant governor
Indiana	Mitch Daniels	Republican	Georgetown (JD)	2004	Chief of staff, Richard Lugar
Iowa	Chet Culver	Democrat	Virginia Tech	2006	Elected secretary of state
Kansas	Mark Parkinson	Democrat	University of Kansas (JD)	—	Elected Kansas lieutenant governor
Kentucky	Steve Beshear	Democrat	University of Kentucky (JD)	2007	Lieutenant governor
Louisiana	Bobby Jindal	Republican	Brown University (note: also Rhodes scholar at Oxford)	2007	Member, U.S. House of Representatives

continued

TABLE 8-5, continued

State	Governor	Party	Education (highest degree obtained)	First Elected in	Previous Political Life
Maine	John Baldacci	Democrat	University of Maine, Orono	2002	Member, Bangor City Council
Maryland	Martin O'Malley	Democrat	University of Maryland (JD)	2006	State field director for Barbara Mikulski's 1986 campaign
Massachusetts	Deval Patrick	Democrat	Harvard University (JD)	2006	Appointed assistant attorney general for civil rights by Bill Clinton
Michigan	Jennifer M. Granholm	Democrat	Harvard University (JD)	2002	Elected Michigan attorney general
Minnesota	Tim Pawlenty	Republican	University of Minnesota (JD)	2002	Eagan City Councilmember
Mississippi	Haley Barbour	Republican	University of Mississippi (JD)	2003	Director, White House Office of Political Affairs
Missouri	Jay Nixon	Democrat	University of Missouri (JD)	2008	Missouri attorney general
Montana	Brian Schweitzer	Democrat	Montana State University (MS)	2004	Appointed to the USDA Farm Service Agency Committee
Nebraska	Dave Heineman	Republican	U.S. Military Academy	2005	Lieutenant governor
Nevada	Jim Gibbons	Republican	Southwestern University (JD)	2006	Member, U.S. House of Representatives
New Hampshire	John Lynch	Democrat	Georgetown University (JD); Harvard University (MBA)	2004	Appointed to the New Hampshire University System Board of Trustees, then chair
New Jersey	Chris Christie	Republican	Seton Hall (JD)	2009	U.S. attorney
New Mexico	Bill Richardson	Democrat	Tufts University	2002	U.S. energy secretary
New York	David Paterson	Democrat	Hofstra University (JD)	—	Lieutenant governor
North Carolina	Bev Perdue	Democrat	University of Florida (EdD)	2008	Lieutenant governor
North Dakota	John Hoeven	Republican	Northwestern University (MBA)	2000	Started at the top as governor; previously president and CEO of the Bank of North Dakota
Ohio	Ted Strickland	Democrat	University of Kentucky (PhD)	2006	Member, U.S. Congress
Oklahoma	Brad Henry	Democrat	University of Oklahoma (JD)	2002	State senator
Oregon	Ted Kulongoski	Democrat	University of Missouri (JD)	2002	Member, Oregon House of Representatives

TABLE 8-5, continued

State	Governor	Party	Education (highest degree obtained)	First Elected in	Previous Political Life
Pennsylvania	Edward Rendell	Democrat	Villanova University (JD)	2002	Elected district attorney, Philadelphia
Rhode Island	Don Carcieri	Republican	Brown University	2002	Started at the top as governor; previously CEO Cookson America
South Carolina	Mark Sanford	Republican	University of Virginia (MBA)	2002	Member, U.S. Congress
South Dakota	Mike Rounds	Republican	South Dakota State University	2002	State senator
Tennessee	Phil Bredesen	Democrat	Harvard University	2002	Mayor, Nashville, Tennessee
Texas	Rick Perry	Republican	Texas A&M University	2000	Member, Texas House of Representatives
Utah	Gary Herbert	Republican	Brigham Young University (no degree)	—	Lieutenant governor
Vermont	Jim Douglas	Republican	Middlebury College	2002	State treasurer
Virginia	Bob McDonnell	Republican	Regent University (JD)	2009	State attorney general
Washington	Chris Gregoire	Democrat	Gonzaga University (JD)	2004	Elected state attorney general
West Virginia	Joe Manchin III	Democrat	West Virginia University	2004	Member, state legislature
Wisconsin	Jim Doyle	Democrat	Harvard University (JD)	2002	District attorney, Dane County
Wyoming	Dave Freudenthal	Democrat	University of Wyoming (JD)	2002	Appointed U.S. attorney, Wyoming

Source: National Governors Association, "Governors of the United States, Commonwealths and Territories, 2010," available at www.nga.org/Files/pdf/BIOBOOK.pdf.

Note: Those individuals not elected to office (—) were elevated to the position following after the elected governor left office for some reason.

compared with the GOP's twenty-two. By contrast, Democrats lost the governorships of both Virginia and New Jersey in 2009—the only two contests held that year—amid voter concern about the economy toward the end of Obama's first year in office.

Overall, however, governors races are still less prone to follow national trends than, say, elections for the U.S. Senate. The reason? Voters understand that the governor's position is important in and of itself. They consider state-level issues carefully when choosing a governor. The dominant concern in most gubernatorial contests is the state economy. Even the most powerful politicians have only limited control over the economy at best, but voters tend to reward or punish the incumbent party based on the economic performance. If a state is faring poorly or doing considerably worse than its neighbors, the incumbent party is likely to struggle.

Economic matters certainly play a role in elections if the state budget is in trouble. Voters consider budget crises a sign of bad management and take their anger out on the governor in many instances. In 2002, most state budgets were suffering shortfalls as revenues dipped due to a recession. Only a dozen governors were reelected that year, whereas a record two dozen freshman governors took office. Of those new governors, fully nineteen succeeded a governor of another party or an independent. In other words, voters in many states were ready for a change and blamed the incumbent party for the state's money problems. The dynamics were a little different in 2006. Although Democrats gained a net six governorships that year, most of their wins came in states where Republican governors were retiring or forced out by term limits. They defeated only one incumbent that year, Bob Ehrlich of Maryland. As mentioned earlier, Republicans took both available prizes—Virginia and New Jersey—in the recession year of 2009.

For most of the twentieth century, Democrats dominated gubernatorial contests, but they lost their edge to Republicans starting in 1994. Yet, in general, momentum over the last several years has swung back and forth between the parties. In 2002, the two parties showed that they were each competitive in nearly every state. Republicans were elected governor for the first time in decades in states such as Georgia, Hawaii, and Maryland. Democrats, on the other hand, were elected in places where their party had struggled for years to win a statewide office, including Kansas, Oklahoma, and Wyoming. The Democrats' 28–22 margin following the 2006 elections was the exact opposite of what the proportion had been before election day, when it had been the GOP that controlled twenty-eight states.

Because gubernatorial elections attract a great deal of media attention, voters are more likely to vote for the person rather than the party. Indeed, voters more often use party as a guide in lower-profile contests such as state legislative races. Voters are better informed about individual gubernatorial candidates. One reason is greater news coverage of the races. Another important factor is the amount of money that candidates for governor spend to publicize themselves. Candidates create extensive organizations that promote their campaigns and use all the modern techniques of political consultants, polling, and media buys. Voters are far more likely, even in less-populous states, to get to know the candidates through TV ads and brochures than through speeches or other personal appearances. In 2002, New York governor George Pataki spent $44 million to win a second term. Even so, he still was outspent by a third-party candidate who spent more than $75 million of his own money. The Democratic candidate in Texas, Tony Sanchez, spent $76.3 million in his losing effort. California governor Gray Davis spent $64 million winning reelection that year.[37] In the 2006 gubernatorial election in Michigan, Dick DeVos, heir to the Amway fortune, spent $35 million of his own money. That helped to make it the most expensive governor's race in Michigan history, but it didn't help DeVos any; he lost by a 14-point margin, his votes having cost him, on average, $22 apiece.

Keeping and Leaving Office

For all of the potential upsets, the office of governor is a pretty stable one these days. States used to change governors just about every chance they got, but that is no longer the case. According to political scientist Thad Beyle, states changed governors on average more than two times each during the 1950s. By the 1980s, however, turnover occurred on average just over once a decade. During the 1990s, the rate climbed back up a bit, so that the average state changed governors 1.4 times.

It is not unusual to see governors get reelected by vote margins that top 70 percent. Not only are they in charge of setting policy, but they also actually get things done. They educate children, build roads, and respond with help when miners get trapped. Translation? They generally are viewed more favorably than legislators. From a constituent's standpoint, what do legislators do, after all, except vote?—and their votes tend to be highly partisan. Governors, on the other hand, have to compromise because of the number of people they must deal with. Of course, there are governors who are polarizing figures, but in the main they are less contentious figures than legislators or members of Congress.

Governors are rarely booted out of office prematurely. In June 2004, Connecticut governor John Rowland resigned after being investigated by the legislature for accepting gifts from a contractor with business before the state. Faced with possible **impeachment** and a federal criminal investigation, Rowland, one of the nation's longest-serving governors at the time, chose to step down. Blagojevich, the disgraced Illinois governor, continued to insist on his innocence even after being impeached in 2009, but awaits trial on criminal charges stemming from his conduct in office. In 2003, Gray Davis was the first governor forced to leave office by a **recall election** since Lynn Frazier of North Dakota was booted out more than eighty years earlier on charges of corruption. Voters felt that Davis had dug California into such a deep hole financially that the state would take years to recover. His liberal views on such issues as gay marriage also had stirred up controversy. Arnold Schwarzenegger won the special election held on the same day as Davis's recall.

Arizona governor Evan Mecham was impeached and convicted in 1987 for impeding an investigation and lending state money to a car dealership that he owned. The previous conviction dates back to 1929, when Henry Johnston of Oklahoma was removed for general incompetency by a legislature with possible political motives. A few governors, including Fife Symington of Arizona (1997), Jim Guy Tucker of Arkansas (1996), and Guy Hunt of Alabama (1993), have resigned following criminal convictions.

IMPEACHMENT

A process by which the legislature can remove executive branch officials, such as the governor, or judges from offices for corruption or other reasons.

RECALL ELECTION

A special election allowing voters to remove an elected official from office before the end of his or her term.

TABLE 8-6

Recall Rules

State	Grounds for Recall	Specific Signature Requirement	Petition Circulation Time	Election for Successor
Alaska	Yes	25%	Not specified	Successor appointed
Arizona	No	25%	120 days	Simultaneous (5)
California	No	12%	160 days	Simultaneous (6)
Colorado	No	25%	60 days	Simultaneous (6)
Georgia	Yes	15% (1)	90 days	Separate special
Idaho	No	20% (1)	60 days	Successor appointed
Kansas	Yes	40%	90 days	Successor appointed
Louisiana	No	33.3% (1)	180 days	Separate special
Michigan	No	25%	90 days	Separate special
Minnesota	Yes	25%	90 days	Separate special
Montana	Yes	10% (1)	3 months	Separate special
Nevada	No	25%	60 days	Simultaneous (5)
New Jersey	No	25% (2)	320 days (4)	Separate special
North Dakota	No	25%	Not specified	Simultaneous (5)
Oregon	No	15% (3)	90 days	Separate special
Rhode Island	Yes	15%	90 days	Separate special
Washington	Yes	25%	270 days	Successor appointed
Wisconsin	No	25%	60 days	Simultaneous (5)

Source: Adapted from the National Conference of State Legislatures and Alan Greenblatt's, "Recall Rules," in "Total Recall," *Governing* magazine, September 2003, 26.

Note: Signature requirement is % of votes cast in last election for official being recalled. Exceptions: (1) % of eligible voters at time of last election; (2) % of registered voters in electoral district of official sought to be recalled; (3) % of total votes cast in officer's district for all candidates for governor in last election; (4) applies to governor or U.S. senator; all others 160 days; (5) recall ballot consists of a list of candidates for the office held by the person against whom the recall petition was filed. The name of the officer against whom the recall was filed may appear on the list; and (6) recall ballot consists of two parts: The first asks whether the officer against whom the recall petition was filed should be recalled. The second part lists candidates who have qualified for the election. The name of the officer against whom the recall was filed may not appear on this list.

More recently, two governors have resigned amid sex scandals: Eliot Spitzer of New York (2008) and Jim McGreevey of New Jersey (2004).

A more common threat to gubernatorial staying power is term limits. Governors in thirty-six states are limited to two terms or two consecutive terms in office. The governor of Utah can spend no more than three terms in office. The only two states that have two-year terms instead of four-year terms—Vermont and New Hampshire—place no limits on the number of terms a governor may serve. Howard Dean served five full terms as governor of Vermont before running for president in 2004.

So what do governors do once they leave office? Several of them, like Dean, run for higher offices like the presidency or Senate. Four out of the last five presidents prior to Barack Obama, in fact, were governors before winning the White House (see box on page 317). Not surprisingly, once in office, these former governors appoint other governors to positions in their administrations. They realize that these individuals know and understand what it means to lead and how to delegate and get things done, so former governors become cabinet members and ambassadors. Former Texas governor George W. Bush appointed five former governors to cabinet positions and an ambassadorship after moving into the Oval Office in 2001; Obama appointed two sitting governors and two former governors to his cabinet in 2009 and, in one of his bipartisan picks, named Republican Utah governor Jon Huntsman his ambassador to China. Governors also regularly run for the U.S. Senate. A dozen senators and one representative serving in 2010 previously had been governors.

Entering the Senate or serving as a cabinet official generally is considered a step up the professional ladder from being a governor. Many politicians, however, find that being governor—able to make and implement decisions, with a large staff and all the machinery of state government at their disposal—is the best job they'll ever have. Dirk Kempthorne, who gave up a Senate seat to run for governor of Idaho in 1998, said that many of his colleagues regretted having to give up the governorship to come to Washington and be just one more legislative voice among many. "They all said that being governor is the best job in the world," Kempthorne said on taking office. "I'm ready to find out."[38]

Many former governors in other positions complain that they never had it so good as back when they were running their states. "My worst day as governor was better than my best day as a United States senator," Thomas Carper, D-Del., said in 2009.[39] Wisconsin's Tommy Thompson openly lamented the second-guessing to which he was subjected as President George W. Bush's HHS secretary during a 2006 appearance before the National Governors Association, an organization he had once chaired. "When you're a governor, you can wake up in the morning and you can have an idea and you can have somebody working on it by 11 o'clock in the morning," Thompson said. "When you go to Washington . . . I get up, get the same idea, go in. Then you have to vet it with 67,000 people who all believe sincerely they're smarter than you."[40]

> A more common threat to gubernatorial staying power is term limits. Governors in thirty-six states are limited to two terms or two consecutive terms in office.

Other Executive Offices

Only the president is elected to the executive branch of the federal government. The vice president is the president's running mate and is elected as part of a package deal. The heads of all the cabinet departments—Defense, Transportation, Energy, Agriculture, and so on—are appointed by the president, subject to Senate approval. Voters do not get to say who gets in and who stays out.

Things work differently at the state level. The governor is the only statewide official elected in every state. Most states, however, also have several other statewide officials elected in their own right. This is a holdover from earlier times when the governor was not invested with much power and authority was distributed among a number of officeholders. Texas still has two dozen officials who are elected statewide, whereas New Jersey elects only the governor. (That changed in 2009, when Garden State voters elected a lieutenant governor for the first time.) Most states have a handful of officials elected statewide; we outline the responsibilities of a few of them here.

Lieutenant Governor

The office of lieutenant governor traditionally has been seen as something of a joke. Lieutenant governors, it's been said, have nothing to do but wait for their governors to resign or die so that they can accrue some real power. That situation has changed in just the last few years. Some states, such as Georgia and Virginia, responded to budget shortfalls of recent years by slashing the budgets and limiting the powers of their lieutenant governors' offices. More states, however, have expanded the purview of the office, recognizing that the security demands created by the terrorist attacks of 2001 mean that there is plenty of work to go around and the skills of the second-in-command should be used more fully.

In Nebraska, for example, Gov. Mike Johanns appointed Lieutenant Governor Dave Heineman to head all of the state's homeland security efforts immediately after the September 11, 2001, terrorist attacks. Minnesota lieutenant governor Carol Molnau was given charge of the state's department of transportation after her election in 2002 and saved the state the $108,000-a-year expense of hiring a separate transportation secretary. Similarly, right after the 2003 election, Kentucky's new lieutenant governor, Stephen Pence, was named secretary of the department of justice, which put him in charge of public safety, corrections and law enforcement, the state police, and vehicle enforcement. "It's rare that the lieutenant governor doesn't have some specific duties," says Julia Hurst, director of the National Lieutenant Governors Association.[41]

In the cases cited here, power was granted to the lieutenant governor because of the desire of the governor. The next person to hold the office

A Difference That Makes a Difference: From State House to White House: Translating a Governorship into a Presidency

How big of an advantage is it to run for the presidency as a sitting governor as opposed to some other position? For more than a quarter century prior to Barack Obama's election in 2008, it looked like it was about as big as they come.

Four of the previous five presidents had been governors: Jimmy Carter, Ronald Reagan, Bill Clinton, and George W. Bush. The one exception was George W. Bush's father, George Bush, who came to the Oval Office after serving as Reagan's vice president. Seventeen presidents in all had served earlier as governor.

The 2008 campaign ended up being dominated by senators, including Obama, John McCain, and Hillary Rodham Clinton. They outpolled a large number of gubernatorial contenders that included Mitt Romney of Massachusetts, Bill Richardson of New Mexico, Mike Huckabee of Arkansas, and Mark Warner of Virginia. And, of course, Sarah Palin was serving as governor of Alaska when McCain picked her as his running mate, an office from which she resigned in 2009.

No wonder so many governors were eager to make a run at the presidency. Compare the record of governors to holders of other offices. No sitting U.S. senator had been elected president since John F. Kennedy in 1960. No member of the U.S. House has been elected since James Garfield, all the way back in 1880.

What makes governors such attractive candidates for the nation's most powerful office? And what makes legislators usually so *un*attractive?

For one thing, governors are the only other politicians who have run governments that are anywhere near as complicated as the federal government. Given the complex nature of some state governments, it may even be a toss-up sometimes as to which is the more difficult—ruling one state or ruling all fifty. True, governors do not formulate foreign policy, but they do have to become experts in running departments that cover everything from taxes and education to public health and public safety. Governors have to run things. Members of Congress just vote. "Because the presidency is no place to begin to develop executive talents, the executive careerist clearly is preferable to the legislator," writes political scientist Larry J. Sabato.[a]

Furthermore, legislators have to vote "yes" or "no" on thousands of issues, so they leave a long paper trail. This trail is a clear record bound to contain more controversial elements than any governor's list of bridges built and budgets balanced. Legislators' records often are distorted in smear campaigns that make use of attack ads and mudslinging. Their vote for a $300 billion bill can become defined by one tiny provision it contained.

Congress is a major part of "official" Washington, and legislators hardly can say they have no connection with what occurs there. Conversely, governors running for the White House can always claim they are Washington "outsiders" who are going to sweep in and clean up the town. Former governor-turned-president Bill Clinton reportedly advised Sen. Joseph Biden, D-Del., that senators had to overcome big handicaps to run for president. Not only did they have their records to explain, but they also had forgotten how to speak the language of the average person. "When you get to Washington, the only people you talk to are the elites: elites in the press, elites among the lobbyists, elites that you hire on your own staff," Clinton told Biden. "You're not regularly talking to ordinary, everyday people."[b] Biden didn't listen to Clinton, launching his second bid for the presidency in 2008 and ultimately being elected at Obama's side that year as vice president. But, then, neither did Clinton's wife, who is currently serving as secretary of state.

Senator Clinton did understand what her husband was saying, however, and began her presidential campaign with a "listening tour." Her initial campaign slogan, "Let the Conversation Begin," was roundly ridiculed on *The Daily Show* and by bloggers.[c]

Governors are able to advertise the fact that they have to talk to "real people" every day. By contrast, the out-of-touch image of Congress and Washington in the public mind hampers members of Congress seeking national office. "It could probably be shown by facts and figures that there is no distinctly native American criminal class except Congress," Mark Twain wrote in his 1897 book *Following the Equator*. Governors running for national office invariably present themselves as fresh alternatives to the tired habits of Washington, promising to change the culture and tone of the nation's capital.

That they fail to do so is almost a given. That opens up the field for the next fresh face from the state of California or Arkansas or Texas. Do not forget that all of the recent governors turned presidents came from the South or West, reflecting the growing populations and political power of these regions.

a Larry J. Sabato, *Goodbye to Good-Time Charlie,* 2nd ed. (Washington, D.C.: CQ Press, 1983), 33.
b E. J. Dionne Jr., "Govs 4, Senators 0. Tough Odds," *Washington Post,* January 4, 2004, E4.
c Linda Feldmann, "Hillary Clinton Targets Women's Vote," *Christian Science Monitor,* February 1, 2007, 1.

may have very different responsibilities or nothing to do at all. In many states, however, the lieutenant governor's responsibilities are laid out by law. In Indiana, for example, the lieutenant governor's portfolio includes the departments of commerce and agriculture. In half the states, the lieutenant governor presides over the state senate and has varying degrees of authority in each of these chambers. In Texas and Mississippi, lieutenant governors play much more than a ceremonial role. Not only do they preside over the Senate, but they also set the agenda and appoint senators to committees. In both states, the lieutenant governor often is referred to as the most powerful figure in the state, with authority in both the executive and legislative branches.

Twenty-five states elect their governors and lieutenant governors as part of the same ticket. (New Jersey opted for this model after two recent governors left office prematurely, electing its first lieutenant governor in 2009.) In eighteen other states, the two are elected separately. The other six states—Arizona, Maine, New Hampshire, Oregon, Tennessee, and Wyoming—don't elect lieutenant governors, although in Tennessee the speaker of the Senate is given the title. Electing the governor and lieutenant governor separately can be a source of mischief, especially if the people elected are not from the same party. Lieutenant governors often assume the powers of the governors when their bosses are out of the state. During the 1970s, Republican Mike Curb of California had a lot of fun appointing judges and issuing **executive orders** while Democratic governor Jerry Brown was busy out of the state doing, among other things, his own presidential campaigning.

Attorney General

Perhaps the statewide office that has undergone the greatest transformation in recent years is that of attorney general. Always referred to as the top law enforcement officer in the state, the attorney general sometimes has duties that have been quite minimal because most criminal prosecutions are taken care of at the county level. But attorneys general have become major political players, finding new power by banding together in multistate consumer protection cases against Microsoft, financial firms, toymakers, drug companies, and the shoemakers Reebok and Keds, among many other examples.

The granddaddy of all such cases was the series of lawsuits filed against the tobacco companies during the mid-1990s. The attorneys general argued that the cigarette makers had engaged in fraud and caused a great deal of sickness and health conditions that the states had ended up paying to treat through Medicaid and other programs. An initial agreement with the industry was not ratified by Congress. Instead, in 1998 the attorneys general settled their lawsuits with the companies on their own. The tobacco companies agreed to pay the states an estimated $246 billion over twenty-five years. More recently, state attorneys general have pursued prominent cases against brokerage firms and pension fund managers. Beginning in

2007, New York State attorney general Andrew Cuomo received at least $13 million in settlements from lenders and universities that had violated state laws with their student loan policies.

Not surprisingly, there has been a backlash against these newly powerful officials. In part, this has been based on the fact that for many attorneys general the job has been a successful launching pad toward the governorship. In 2010, nine former attorneys general were serving as governor, with about as many seeking the office in elections that year. "It seems to be considered the second most prominent and important position to governor," said veteran Arkansas newspaper columnist John Brummett. "The other statewide offices are mostly clerical and pointless."[42]

But the fight over control of the office has largely been ideological. One of the

Andrew Cuomo hopes to follow both Eliot Spitzer, his predecessor as state attorney general, and his father Mario into the New York governor's mansion. He was favored to win the 2010 election.

great philosophical divides in U.S. politics lies between those with opposing views of how business should be regulated. There are those who believe that businesses have a right to conduct their affairs with a minimum of interference from state governments, which only can hinder their productivity and profits. Others believe just as strongly that conducting business in a state is a privilege that confers with it a number of responsibilities that the state has the duty to enforce. The majority of state attorneys general over the past few years have acted as if they were members of the "privilege" camp, and that has fueled the rise of groups designed to combat what the business sector sees as excessive regulatory activism.

Attorneys general have traditionally been Democrats, their campaigns funded by trial lawyers. In recent years, the U.S. Chamber of Commerce and many business groups have spent millions trying to defeat "activist" attorney general candidates. "Historically . . . attorney general races were off most business people's radar screens," says Bob LaBrant of the Michigan Chamber of Commerce. Today, "there's greater incentive to get involved in an attorney general race because of the increased involvement of attorneys general across the country in litigation against the business community."[43] The Republican Attorneys General Association was founded in 1999 to elect candidates who believe that their colleagues have gone too far in pursuit of business regulations and the revenues such cases can generate. Their strategy appeared to work—the number of GOP attorneys general climbed from twelve in 1999 to twenty by 2003, but it has slipped a bit in the years since then.

TABLE 8-7

The Powers of the Offices

In many states, Lieutenant Governors . . .	Secretaries of State . . .	Attorneys General . . .
Preside over the senate	File and/or archive state records and regulations; other corporate documents	Institute civil suits
Appoint committees	Administer uniform commercial code provisions	Represent state agencies and defend and/or challenge the constitutionality of legislative or administrative actions
Break roll-call ties	Publish state manual or directory, session laws, state constitution, statues, and/or administrative rules and regulations	Enforce open meetings and records laws
Assign bills	Open legislative sessions	Revoke corporate charters
May be assigned special duties by governor	Enroll and/or retain copies of bills	Enforce antitrust prohibitions against monopolistic enterprises
Serve as cabinet member or a member of an advisory body	Register lobbyists	Enforce air, water pollution, and hazardous waste laws in a majority of states
Serve as acting governor when the governor is out of state		Handle criminal appeals and serious statewide criminal prosecutions • Intervene in public utility rate cases • Enforce the provisions of charitable trusts • Enforce open meetings and records laws

Sources: Compiled from the National Lieutenant Governors Association, www.nlga.us/Members.htm; *The Book of the States 2003* (Lexington, Ky.: Council of State Governments, 2003), 215, 221, and 224; and the National Association of Attorneys General, www.naag.org/ag/duties.php.

When any institution of government extends its power, there is the likelihood of a counterreaction by some other part of government or by the media or other private-sector forces against it. And the main battleground is always the ballot box. Voters elect those candidates they feel will get the most done for them and for the state.

Other Offices

Every state elects its governor, and most states elect a lieutenant governor and attorney general. In terms of which other offices are held by elected

At the apex of most state court systems is a supreme court. State supreme court justices, such as Mississippi supreme court justices Jess Dickinson (left) and Michael Randolph (right), typically have the final say on appeals from lower courts.

federal case about it." In the real world of crime and legal conflict, there are actually relatively few federal cases because those must involve violations of federal law, federal constitutional rights, or lawsuits that cross state borders. With the exception of celebrity trials like the O. J. Simpson murder case, state courts operate largely below the public's radar.

Yet they are enormously important institutions. The federal U.S. district courts hear several hundred thousand cases a year. By comparison, close to 100 million cases are filed in the lowest state courts every year. These courts have the awesome responsibility of resolving the vast majority of the nation's disputes. If you crash your car or your landlord evicts you, if you get divorced and fight for child custody, if your neighbor's tree lands in your yard, or if your employer won't pay you, then you'll find yourself in a state court. State courts are also where virtually all criminal cases are tried, from drunk driving to murder, from misdemeanors to capital offenses. If you get a serious enough traffic ticket, you will find yourself in a state court.

There are two basic kinds of court cases: **criminal cases** and **civil cases**. Criminal cases involve violations of the law, with the government prosecuting the alleged perpetrator, or criminal. Those found guilty usually go to jail. By contrast, civil cases involve disputes between two private parties, such as a dry cleaner and a customer with badly stained pants. In civil cases, individuals sue each other, usually for financial judgments. Both types of cases start out in **trial court**. If the parties in a case cannot reach agreement through a **settlement** or a **plea bargain**, they go to trial.

Every trial has a winner and a loser. Those unhappy with the trial's outcome can file an **appeal**. Most states have two levels of courts that hear appeals from trial court judgments. The appeal first goes to an **intermediate**

CRIMINAL CASES

Cases that involve violations of the law.

CIVIL CASES

Cases that involve disputes between private parties.

TRIAL COURT

The first level of the court system.

SETTLEMENT

A mutual agreement between parties to end a case before going to trial.

PLEA BARGAIN

An agreement in which the accused admits guilt, usually in exchange for a promise that a particular sentence will be imposed.

appellate court, which reviews the original trial's record to see if any errors were made. After the appellate court has ruled, parties who still are not satisfied can attempt to appeal to the highest state court of appeals, usually called the **state supreme court**. In most states, this court does not automatically have to take an appeal but can pick and choose among cases, typically choosing those whose resolutions will require a clarification of the law. Such resolutions could set a **precedent** that has consequences well beyond the specifics of the case being appealed.

A state supreme court is the highest legal body in the state court system. This gives it the ultimate power to interpret the state constitution. Its decisions are almost always final. Only the U.S. Supreme Court outranks the highest state courts. Even the nine justices in Washington, D.C., however, cannot review—that is, come up with a new decision for—a state supreme court judgment unless it violates the U.S. Constitution or federal law.

When such federal issues are involved, there is no question that state courts must follow the rulings of the federal courts. The chief justice of the Alabama Supreme Court, Roy S. Moore, learned this lesson in 2003 after placing a two-and-a-half-ton monument to the Ten Commandments in the rotunda of the state supreme court building. Federal judges ordered him to move it, ruling that such a display violated the First Amendment's separation of church and state. He refused and ultimately was removed from office for having tried to place himself above the law. In 2006, his former colleague on the court, Justice Tom Parker, expressed anger at other justices for following the U.S. Supreme Court precedent that prohibits the use of the death penalty for crimes committed by minors. Justice Parker unsuccessfully urged his colleagues not to follow Supreme Court opinions "simply because they are precedents."[7]

Trial Courts

More than 100 million cases were filed in state courts in 2007, about one case for every three citizens. These numbers have stayed relatively constant over the last ten years, although they have edged up recently. More than half the cases involved traffic offenses. The number of civil and criminal cases was roughly equal—18.1 and 21.4 million cases, respectively—and there were 7.9 million domestic and juvenile cases.[8] The vast majority of these millions of cases were resolved through plea bargains or settlements. Only a small minority ever went to trial.

When parties do go to trial, they appear before a state court judge in what is often referred to as a **court of first instance**. In this court, nothing has been determined and nothing is a "given." The trial is a blank canvas on which the parties can introduce documentary and physical evidence, such as fingerprints or DNA. Witnesses can testify as to what they saw or heard, and experts can try to help explain complex evidence.

The judge presides over the introduction of evidence; rules on objections, which occur when either of the parties thinks that the other party

A Difference That Makes a Difference:
The New Judicial Federalism

A century ago, state supreme courts were described as being so quiet that "you could hear the justices' arteries clog."[a] No one says this today, and the New Judicial Federalism is one big reason why.

This doctrine describes a new-found reliance on state constitutions to protect those rights not covered by the U.S. Constitution. Under the principles of federalism, each state has its own justice system—distinct from those of its neighbors and from the federal system—and its own constitution. The U.S. Constitution is the supreme law of the land, and no state court can interpret its own state's constitution in a way that limits rights secured by the federal charter. States are free, however, to interpret their own constitutions any way they like, except for that single proviso.

For most of the country's history, state constitutions were overlooked. Rarely were they relied on to overturn state laws, especially on the basis of civil rights. But, starting in the early 1970s, state supreme courts increasingly began to use state constitutions as independent sources of rights. By 1986, Justice William J. Brennan characterized the "[r]ediscovery by state supreme courts of the broader protections afforded their own citizens by their state constitutions [as] . . . probably the most important development in constitutional jurisprudence in our time."[b]

In many legal areas, the actual impact of judicial federalism on civil liberties has not been all that sweeping. It is still true that most state court judges continue to interpret state constitutions in lockstep with interpretations of the U.S. Constitution. One commentator found, however, that in approximately one out of every three constitutional decisions, state courts extended rights beyond federal levels.[c] In some areas, such as the interpretation of rights to exercise religion freely and in search-and-seizure rulings, state courts, relying on their own constitutions, have continued to grant rights after the U.S. Supreme Court's interpretation of the Constitution took a more conservative and restrictive turn.

In other cases, state courts rely on unique constitutional provisions. For instance, state constitutions, unlike the federal document, often commit state governments to the achievement of particular policy ends. The New Jersey constitution requires a "thorough and efficient system of free public schools," the Illinois constitution requires the state to "provide and maintain a healthful environment for the benefit of this and future generations," and the New Mexico constitution requires bilingual education. Relying on explicit provisions like these, state supreme courts have ordered legislatures to restructure the way they finance public education when inequalities are so extreme they rise to the level of constitutional violation.

Today, the new judicial federalism is well established, with more and more cases raising state constitutional issues, sparking a renewed interest in these once-overlooked documents. State supreme court justices are more likely now to take a fresh look at their own constitutions than to slavishly follow the interpretations of the U.S. Supreme Court. Activists also have focused more attention on state constitutions, mounting campaigns to amend them to either extend or curtail rights.

[a] G. Alan Tarr, "The New Judicial Federalism in Perspective," *Notre Dame Law Review* 72 (1997): 1097.

[b] William J. Brennan, "State Constitutional Law," special section of *National Law Journal* 9 (September 29, 1986): S–1.

[c] James N. G. Cauthen, "Expanding Rights under State Constitutions: A Quantitative Appraisal," *Albany Law Review* 63 (2000): 1183, 1202.

---

has said or done something wrong, and issues of admissibility, that is, whether or not it is all right for specific evidence or facts to be included in the trial; and instructs the jury as to the relevant laws. The judge further instructs the jury members that they must apply the laws as stated to the facts as they find them. It is the jury, however, that must decide what the facts are. (In **bench trials**, this is done by the judge.) The jury or the judge

BENCH TRIALS
Trials in which no jury is present and a judge decides the facts.

FIGURE 9-1 How It Works: State Court Structure in Illinois and New York

At a glance, it's easy to see why New York state's court system has been called Byzantine—just compare it to Illinois's (left). Although it encompasses 22 circuits with more than 850 justices, Illinois's single trial court system (its general jurisdiction courts) looks like a model of clarity and simplicity compared to New York's 10 different trial courts (the courts of general and limited jurisdiction). But the differences run deeper than what a simple organizational chart can reveal. New York's three-hundred-year-old town and village justice court system, in particular, has been subject to loud and persistent criticism for cronyism, corruption, fiscal mismanagement, and plain old inefficiency. According to *New York Times* reporter William Glaberson, "the [town and village justice] courts have survived in part because the justices—most of them not even lawyers—have longstanding and deep ties to the upstate political system, and because of the substantial cost of replacing them with more professional courts."[a] With 2,300 justices involved at that level, this would indeed be a tall order.

What can be done? In 2006, New York's former chief judge Judith S. Kaye, the state's top advocate for court reform, recommended changes "across four broad areas: court operations and administration; auditing and financial control; education and training; and facility security and public protection."[b] A few of these proposed changes could be implemented right away, including requiring word-for-word records of court proceedings—a bona fide court transcript—to ensure fairness and the purchasing of recording equipment to make that possible. Other changes would require more

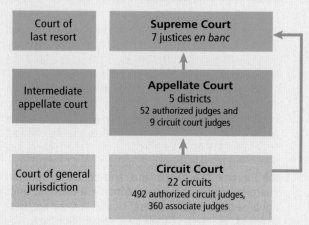

Illinois's State Court Structure

sweeping institutional modifications. Judge Kaye called for state funds to help support the town and village justice courts, which are currently funded and operated locally. This change would require legislative approval. Her most aggressive recommendation—to simplify the trial court structure itself into a more common two-tiered organization—would require an amendment to the state's constitution. Legislators received the proposals coolly. A commission on state court reform backed some of Kaye's ideas in 2008 with its suggestion that the state eliminate as many as five hundred of the justice courts, but New York had not instituted the changes by early 2010.[c]

GENERAL JURISDICTION TRIAL COURTS

Courts that hear any civil or criminal cases that have not been assigned to a special court.

must decide who and what to believe and what happened. Unless this decision is based on a legal mistake, such as improper evidence, hearsay testimony (testimony based on rumor), or a misleading statement of the relevant law, the result typically will be upheld on appeal. The business of the trial court is to examine the facts to resolve the dispute. Subsequent appellate courts review the trial court's application of the law to those facts.

A key distinction among state courts is between **general jurisdiction trial courts** and **limited**, or **special jurisdiction, trial courts**. A general jurisdiction trial court hears any case not sent to a special court, whether it is civil or criminal. The kinds of cases that can be tried in special jurisdiction courts are statutorily limited. Some are limited to cases of less seriousness,

New York State's Court Structure

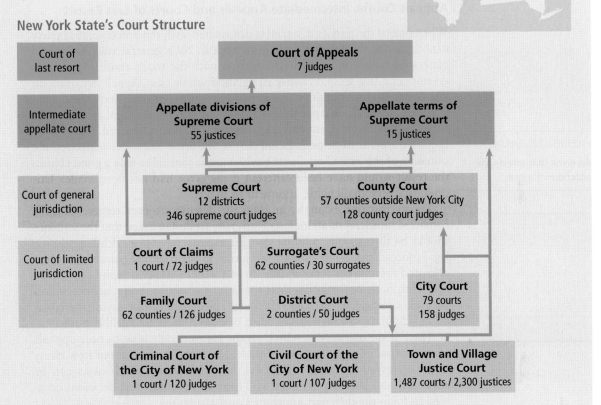

Court of last resort		**Court of Appeals** 7 judges	
Intermediate appellate court	**Appellate divisions of Supreme Court** 55 justices		**Appellate terms of Supreme Court** 15 justices
Court of general jurisdiction	**Supreme Court** 12 districts 346 supreme court judges	**County Court** 57 counties outside New York City 128 county court judges	
Court of limited jurisdiction	**Court of Claims** 1 court / 72 judges	**Surrogate's Court** 62 counties / 30 surrogates	**City Court** 79 courts 158 judges
	Family Court 62 counties / 126 judges	**District Court** 2 counties / 50 judges	
	Criminal Court of the City of New York 1 court / 120 judges	**Civil Court of the City of New York** 1 court / 107 judges	**Town and Village Justice Court** 1,487 courts / 2,300 justices

[a] William Glaberson, "Justice in Small Towns to Be Upgraded," *New York Times,* November 22, 2006, A1.

[b] Judith S. Kaye and Jonathan Lippman, "Action Plan for the Justice," November 2006, available at www.state.ny.us/publications/pdfs/ActionPlan-Justice.pdf.

[c] Joel Stashenko, "Study Supports Elimination of Hundreds of Justice Courts," *New York Law Journal* 240, no. 56 (2008): 2.

such as misdemeanors or civil cases that involve small amounts of money. Others are limited to the types of parties involved, such as juvenile offenders or drug abusers.

Not all states make this distinction between trial courts. Illinois has no limited jurisdiction courts. In contrast, New York, the state with the largest number of judges, is also the state that relies most heavily on limited jurisdiction courts. More than 3,000 of the state's 3,645 judges sit on limited jurisdiction courts.[9] (See Figure 9-1.) The majority of these limited jurisdiction courts over which most of these judges preside are "town and village courts" or "justice courts." In states that do not rely on limited jurisdiction courts, appeals go directly to appellate courts. In states that

LIMITED, OR SPECIAL JURISDICTION, TRIAL COURTS

Courts that hear cases that are statutorily limited by either the degree of seriousness or the types of parties involved.

make the distinction, some issues can be appealed from limited jurisdiction courts to general jurisdiction courts.

Appeals Courts: Intermediate Appeals and Courts of Last Resort

When one of the parties in a trial is dissatisfied with the outcome, that party can challenge the result by filing an appeal. As a general rule, an appeal cannot be based on mere dissatisfaction with the trial's result. Appellants do not get a free second chance to try their whole case. Appellate courts do not decide issues of guilt or innocence or ensure that trials were conducted perfectly. Instead, an appeal must state that there were legal errors in the original trial. But it is not enough to say that an error occurred. Courts also require the error to be **prejudicial**; that is, the error had to have affected the outcome of the case. Appellants have to argue that there was a good chance the result would have been different if the error had not been made. This often is a very challenging argument to make.

PREJUDICIAL ERROR

An error that affects the outcome of a case.

To cite just one example, in 2006 the defense attorney representing the convicted murderer of an Indiana University freshman asked that the sentence should be thrown out, arguing that jurors may have been drinking during legal proceedings. Some of the male jurors in the trial had painted their toenails and raced down a hotel hallway in a bailiff's backless high heels. "Two men with heels on, painting their toenails, it is not a normal activity unless they are intoxicated," he said. The judge ruled against him, saying there was no indication of drunkenness in court or during the actual deliberations.[10]

There is no one way in which all the states decide how to hear appeals from the trial courts. States have made different decisions about how many levels of review to grant an appeal, how to choose which cases can be appealed, and how many judges will hear an appeal. These decisions combine to form the different appellate court structures.

For example, not all states have both an intermediate appellate court and a supreme court. Back in 1957, only thirteen states had intermediate appellate courts. Today, eleven states and the District of Columbia still resolve all their appeals with only one level of review. These states, which include Delaware, Montana, North Dakota, Rhode Island, South Dakota, Vermont, and Wyoming, are less populous—seven have populations of less than 1 million—and thus tend to have fewer cases to resolve. Smaller populations give rise to relatively more manageable caseloads.

The sheer volume of appeals makes it impossible in the majority of states for one appellate court to hear and resolve every appeal. To deal with burgeoning caseloads, most states have created another tier of review. In these states, appeals go first to an intermediate appellate court. Only after they have been reviewed at this level can they move on to the court of last resort, usually the state supreme court. The intermediate court makes it possible for the state judicial system to hear many more appeals and creates the possibility of a second level of appeal.

Intermediate appellate courts range in size from 3 judges (in Alaska, Hawaii, and Idaho) to 102 judges (in California). States with the most judges at the intermediate appellate level usually divide their jurisdictions into specific regions. California, for example, divides these judges into nine appellate divisions. By contrast, New Jersey, with thirty-two appellate judges, has the largest appellate court that is not divided into judicial regions.[11] Regional divisions make the courts more convenient, but they also create a danger. All these different courts may come up with different rulings on the same or similar issues. This has the potential to set different, possibly conflicting precedents for future litigation.

State appellate courts also vary in whether they have **discretionary** or **mandatory jurisdiction**. In other words, in some states the courts have a right to pick and choose which cases they hear. In other states, judges must consider each case, in the belief that everyone has the right to an appeal. It is widely accepted that losers in a single-judge court ought to have the right to at least one appeal to a court with multiple judges.[12] This one appeal, however, is generally considered sufficient to correct any prejudicial errors made in the trial courts. Even in states in which the court of last resort has discretionary jurisdiction, capital punishment appeals may be mandatory.

Two tiers of appellate courts allow petitioners the right to one appeal to the intermediate appellate court, followed by the possibility of a further appeal to the court of last resort. Such a structure allows the supreme court or other courts of last resort to choose whether to hear cases that might have relevance beyond the parties in the case, allowing them to make the law clear to others.

One more variable in the state court system structure involves the number of judges at each level who hear a particular appeal. At either the appellate court level or at the court of last resort level, judges may hear an appeal *en banc*, or all together, or they may sit in smaller **panels**, typically of three judges. Sitting in panels may be more convenient because courts sit simultaneously in different locations. This allows more appeals to be heard and makes the courts more convenient to the parties. However, like regional divisions, this may also lead to problems of unifying doctrine created by various courts at the same level.

States that use panels have a variety of techniques to limit the divergence among panels. These include conferencing drafts of opinions *en banc*. This means that the panel's draft opinions are circulated among all the judges, even those not on the panel. Two states, Texas and Oklahoma, have created a system of two supreme courts with different subject matter jurisdictions rather than having one supreme court sit in panels. In each state, one supreme court has largely civil jurisdiction and one supreme court hears only criminal appeals; each of these courts sits *en banc*. In Texas, the intermediate appellate court has both civil and criminal jurisdiction. In Oklahoma, the intermediate appellate court has only civil

DISCRETIONARY JURISDICTION

The court has the power to decide whether or not to grant review of a case.

MANDATORY JURISDICTION

The court is required to hear every case presented before it.

EN BANC

Appeals court sessions in which all the judges hear a case together.

PANELS

Groups of (usually) three judges who sit to hear cases in state courts of appeals.

jurisdiction—all criminal appeals go directly to the court of last resort for criminal cases. A few states have created a system of intermediate appellate courts with differing subject-matter jurisdictions and then a single court of last resort.

States have mixed and matched all these variables to come up with different ways to organize the appellate court review process. The most common pattern, adhered to by half the states, involves an intermediate appellate court, sitting in panels, that must consider all appeals. The decisions of these panels are then subject to review by a court of last resort, such as a supreme court, sitting *en banc*. Usually, this highest court can hear just the cases it sees fit to hear. In states without an intermediate court of appeals, often the courts of last resort must hear all the cases that are sent to them. However, in two such states, New Hampshire and West Virginia, all appeals are made to a supreme court with discretionary review; the supreme courts in these two states get to pick and choose their cases. In the District of Columbia, all appeals are heard by a court of appeals with nine justices who often sit in panels of three.

In other words, if you lose your case, you will have at least one chance—and usually more than one chance—to get your appeal heard. But you will face a legal labyrinth that involves variations of courts and judges and panels and rules. All of these variations add up to one more reason to hire a good lawyer.

Selecting Judges

How judges are selected is a significant political decision. Historically, such decisions have generated tremendous controversy, and the controversy continues today. Why is there no clear consensus on such an important issue? Controversy is perhaps inevitable. The judiciary is one of the pillars of the U.S. political system, but at the same time, we want to believe that judges are above politics. We like to think that they are independent and will rule only as justice requires, based on the specific facts presented and the applicable law. Of course, judges are only human. That's why we want them held accountable for their decisions. These competing values—independence and accountability—tug judicial selection procedures in different directions. If independence is seen as more important than accountability, it makes sense to appoint judges for lifetime tenures. This is done in the federal system. If accountability is seen as more important than independence, it makes sense to elect judges. Elections are a key element of judicial selection at the state level. Yet they are not the only component; states have formulated a variety of selection systems in an effort to balance the competing values of independence and accountability. These specifics matter. How a state structures its courts and chooses its judiciary may impact the types of decisions made by individual judges.

Almost no two states select judges in the exact same way, although they can be roughly divided into two camps of almost equal size. The first group includes states that choose judges through popular elections, either partisan or nonpartisan. In partisan elections, judicial candidates first run in party primaries and then are listed on the ballot with a designation of their political party. Candidates in nonpartisan elections run on the ballot without any party label. The second group consists of states that have appointed, rather than elected, judges. Under the appointment model, the governor or the legislature may appoint judges. In some states, the choice of whom to appoint is limited to choosing from names advanced by a nominating committee.

To make matters even more confusing, many states use different methods to choose judges at different levels of their judiciaries. States might, for example, choose trial judges by popular election but appoint supreme court justices. What's more, many states employ different methods by region. In Arizona, for example, trial courts in counties with a population greater than 250,000 choose judges through merit selection; less populous districts rely on nonpartisan elections. Indiana holds partisan elections in a portion of its judicial districts and nonpartisan elections in others. Finally, some states that generally elect their judges fill midterm judicial vacancies by appointment.

How states choose their judges has been historically volatile. Movements to change the methods for judicial selection rise up, gain popularity, and then, eventually, are supplanted by the next big reform movement. How a state originally chose its judges had much to do with which reform was in vogue at the time the state entered the Union and ratified its constitution. No single judicial reform ever succeeded in completely replacing earlier methods, however, and so there is tremendous variation among the states in the way they select judges.

Under the U.S. Constitution, the president, with the advice and consent of the Senate, appoints all federal judges. Similarly, the original thirteen states chose to appoint judges, giving the appointment power to one or both houses of the legislature, or less commonly to the governor, either alone or with the consent of the legislature.[13]

Then, in the mid-1800s, during the presidency of Andrew Jackson—a period marked by distrust of government and a movement toward increased popular sovereignty—the appointive system came under attack. Every state that entered the Union between 1846 and 1912 provided for some form of judicial elections.[14] At the dawn of the twentieth century, concern that judges were being selected and controlled by political machines led to a movement for nonpartisan elections. By 1927, twelve states employed this practice.[15]

During the second half of the twentieth century, judicial reformers focused on persuading states to adopt a new method of choosing judges, referred to as merit selection. The variations of merit selection systems

The merit selection of judges, widely adopted by states across the country to fill some or all judicial vacancies, originated in Missouri from a power struggle between Gov. Lloyd Stark, pictured here, and powerful political boss Tom Pendergast.

are discussed in detail in the following section on appointment. Basically, a merit system is a hybrid of appointment and election. It typically is based on a bipartisan judicial nominating commission whose job is to create a list of highly qualified candidates for the bench. The governor appoints judges from this list, who must then face a retention election. The retention election for a newly appointed judge is usually set to coincide with the next general election, and it provides voters with a simple choice: to keep or not to keep the judge on the bench. If the vote is for retention, the judge stays on the bench. If the vote is against retention (this is rare), the commission goes back to work to come up with another list of candidates for the post.

Under some merit systems, all judges (not just newly appointed ones) must face periodic retention elections, although the length of term and other specifics vary from state to state. Missouri became the first state to adopt such a judicial selection method in 1940, which is why judicial merit selection is sometimes referred to as "the Missouri Plan." The movement enjoyed considerable success from the 1960s to the 1980s. The number of states that embraced merit selection for choosing supreme court justices grew from three in 1960 (Alaska, Kansas, and Missouri) to eighteen by 1980.[16]

Recently, however, this movement appears to have lost momentum. Approximately half the states still rely on merit selection to choose some or all of their judges, and no merit selection state has returned to selection through elections. However, since 1990, most states that have considered adopting merit selection, whether for trial courts or appellate level courts, have rejected it. In Florida, for example, a 2000 initiative for the merit selection of trial court judges appeared on the ballot and was soundly defeated in every county.[17] A poll taken in early 2007 showed that an overwhelming majority of Pennsylvanians opposed changing the method of selecting judges from election to appointment.[18] In recent years, several states were debating doing away with merit selection altogether, including Missouri, its home state. Each method for selecting judges and the issues they raise will be addressed at length in the sections that follow. (See Map 9-1 for the systems of selection for each state.)

MAP 9-1 Initial Judicial Selection, by Type of Court

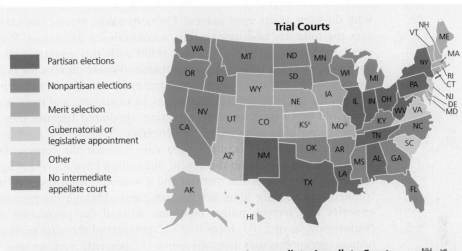

Trial Courts

Partisan elections
Nonpartisan elections
Merit selection
Gubernatorial or legislative appointment
Other
No intermediate appellate court

Source: American Judicature Society, "Methods of Judicial Selection." www.judicialselection.us/judicial_selection/methods/selection_of_judges.cfm?state=.

Notes:

ᶦThe Arizona Constitution provides for merit selection and retention of judges in counties with populations of 250,000 or greater. Counties whose populations are less than 250,000 may adopt merit selection through ballot initiative.

ᶦᶦJudges are selected by merit selection in 17 districts and by partisan election in 14 districts.

ᶦᶦᶦJudges in Kansas City, Springfield, and St. Louis are selected by merit selection; all others are elected by partisan election.

ᶦᵛThe chief justice of the supreme court assigns superior court judges to the appellate court division.

ᵛChosen from among active and retired district judges, retired supreme court justices, and attorneys

ᵛᶦCandidates who want to challenge incumbent justices must be nominated at party conventions. Candidates appear without party affiliation on the general election ballot.

Intermediate Appellate Courts

Courts of Last Resort

Courts

Popular Elections

Why do some states elect judges? Elections allow greater popular control over the judiciary and more public accountability for judges. Proponents argue that such elections are compatible with this country's democratic traditions and that voters can be entrusted to make choices for judges that are as good as those that legislators or mayors would make. To these supporters, the appointment of judges smacks of elitism, and there is a worry about old-boy networks—judges getting appointed because they are the cronies or political allies of elected officials.

Some argue that electing judges can increase the representation of women and minorities on the bench. But studies have found negligible differences between selection method and diversity.[19] Both systems have contributed to a slightly more diverse judiciary, although the percentages of minority and women judges continues to trail the population at large. Nationwide, as of 2005, forty-four (12 percent) of the state supreme court justices were minorities and ninety-five (27 percent) were women.[20] In the judicial elections of November 2006, diversity was a big winner. In twelve states, male and female candidates faced each other for state supreme court seats, and in two-thirds of these elections the women won.[21]

Those on the other side of the argument are critical of judicial elections in general, whether partisan or nonpartisan. They focus on what they see as a threat to the independence of the judiciary posed by the introduction of politics into the selection process. The tone of judicial elections has deteriorated substantially and in a manner that some fear could damage the image of the judiciary. Qualified candidates for office could choose to opt out.

It is a debate about more than academic ideas, however. How a state chooses its judges has a very real political impact, with consequences for judicial impartiality, campaign fund-raising, the role of interest groups, and the character of judicial campaigning. Some point to these problems as reasons to move away from selecting judges through judicial elections and toward a merit selection system. Others argue that the problems can be addressed without abandoning elections altogether but, rather, by tinkering with them. Die-hard supporters of elections see the increased politicization of judicial elections as positive because greater competitiveness translates into more meaningful choices for voters.

Before jumping into the consequences of elections, it is important to remember that elections for state court judges, when they are held, can be either partisan or nonpartisan. Most or all of the judges in eight states—Alabama, Illinois, Louisiana, Michigan, Ohio, Pennsylvania, Texas, and West Virginia—are selected through partisan elections. Another five states (Indiana, Kansas, Missouri, New York, and Tennessee) select some of their judges this way.[22] Nonpartisan elections are held to select most or all judges in thirteen states—Arkansas, Georgia, Idaho, Kentucky, Minnesota,

Mississippi, Montana, Nevada, North Carolina, North Dakota, Oregon, Washington, and Wisconsin—and some judges in another seven states—Arizona, California, Florida, Indiana, Michigan, Oklahoma, and South Dakota.[23] In some cases, labeling a popular election partisan or nonpartisan may be a distinction without a difference. All Ohio judges and Michigan Supreme Court justices run without party labels on the ballots, but the candidates are chosen through party primaries or conventions, and the parties are heavily involved in judicial campaigns.[24]

The legislative and executive branches are clearly political. Representatives of the people are chosen and held accountable through elections. Why shouldn't judges be elected like other powerful players in the political system? Because the judge's role is designed to be different. Judges decide specific cases and controversies based on hearing the evidence. They are supposed to rely only on statutes, case precedent, constitutional law, and the unique facts presented by each case. They are not supposed to rule based on the wishes of those who elect them or with the next election in mind.

A lot rides on the public's belief that a judge will be neutral and impartial. That belief underpins the willingness to bring disputes to the courts and to abide by the results—the keys to both economic and political stability. Judges cannot, as political candidates do, make campaign promises about future decisions without undermining respect for the impartiality and independence of the judiciary. For the same reasons, judges cannot represent specific interest groups or constituents or even the will of the majority. There are times when all judges, when doing their jobs properly, are compelled by the law to make unpopular judgments or to protect the rights of those without political power.

In 1999, U.S. Supreme Court justice Anthony Kennedy pointed out in an interview that there are times for every judge when the law requires the release of a criminal whether the judge likes it or not. To characterize a judge in that case as "soft on crime" betrays a misunderstanding of the judicial process and the constitution.[25] In the same television interview, Justice Stephen Breyer also expressed concerns about the way judicial elections require judges to court public opinion. He asked, "Suppose I were on trial. Suppose somebody accused me. Would I want to be judged by whether I was popular? Wouldn't I want to be judged on what was true as opposed to what was popular? . . We have a different system. And our system is based upon . . . neutrality and independence."[26]

Is this how it really works? Or only how it is *supposed* to work? The highly charged issue of capital punishment makes a useful test case. Why are some courts more likely to impose the death penalty than others? Some research indicates that state supreme court justices facing reelection

> Why are some courts more likely to impose the death penalty than others? Some research indicates that state supreme court justices facing reelection in states in which capital punishment is particularly popular are reluctant to cast dissenting votes.

in states in which capital punishment is particularly popular are reluctant to cast dissenting votes. Researchers Paul Brace and Melinda Gann Hall found that—among politically comparable states—rulings to uphold death sentences are more likely in states with elected judges.[27] Not only that, but the closer supreme court justices are to reelection, the more likely they are to support capital punishment.[28]

Texas and Florida share at least one thing in common—hundreds of inmates on death row with a high volume of death penalty appeals. But the similarity stops there. Texas justices are elected in partisan elections, and they almost never reverse a death sentence. In Florida, however, supreme court justices are merit selected, and the court has one of the nation's highest reversal rates.[29] It is not misguided for a judge facing reelection to fear reversing a death sentence. There are numerous examples of state supreme court justices who were labeled as soft after opposing the imposition of capital punishment in a particular case and were voted off the bench. This occurs even when the unpopular opinions are later held to be correct by the U.S. Supreme Court.[30]

The effects of judicial selection ripple out beyond those cases that tackle politically volatile issues like capital punishment and raise issues of improper influence on the judiciary. Professor Steven Ware reviewed all arbitration decisions made by the Alabama Supreme Court from 1995 to 1999. Justices there are selected through partisan elections, and this period encompassed a shift in the court majority from Democrats to Republicans. In virtually every case—even those that involved bland issues of law that appeared ideologically neutral—Ware found a direct correlation between voting and campaign contributions.[31] The Democrats, funded mostly by lawyers who worked for the plaintiffs, opposed arbitration. The Republicans, financed primarily by business interests, favored it. In 2006, the *New York Times* published the results of an examination of campaign financing over twelve years in regard to the Ohio Supreme Court, finding that justices routinely sat on cases after receiving campaign contributions from the parties involved or from groups that filed supporting briefs. The article found that justices, on average, voted in favor of contributors 70 percent of the time, with one particular justice voting for his contributor 91 percent of the time.[32]

OK, so this all sounds shady, but candidates running for judicial office must raise money. Frequently, this money comes from the very people who have a vested interest in the outcome of cases that are or will be before a judge. Describing judicial fund-raising, Justice Paul E. Pfeifer, a Republican member of the Ohio Supreme Court, said, "I never felt so much like a hooker down by the bus station in any race I've ever been in as I did in a judicial race."[33] But the need to find dollars to run for a seat cannot supersede good judgment. In *Caperton v. Massey* (2009), the U.S. Supreme Court ruled that West Virginia Supreme Court of Appeals Justice Brent Benjamin should have recused himself from a case in which the CEO of the lead defendant had raised $3 million for Benjamin's election. Benjamin was the deciding vote in favor of the defendants.

In Benjamin's case, the $3 million from the CEO of A.T. Massey Coal Co. represented about 60 percent of his electoral war chest[34]—another piece of evidence that the funds required to run a campaign have been skyrocketing, particularly in state supreme court races. Between 2000 and 2009, candidates for state supreme court seats raised more than $200 million, more than double the $83 million they raised in the previous decade.[35] Much of this money comes from lawyers, litigants, and other groups with an interest in the outcome of litigation.

Why do these groups contribute so much money to judicial elections? As with any other political donation, there is at least some truth to the cynic's sense that campaign contributions are a good investment. The president of the Ohio state bar concluded, "The people with money to spend who are affected by court decisions have reached the conclusion that it's a lot cheaper to buy a judge than a governor or an entire legislature, and he can probably do a lot more for you."[36] When the judicial reform organization Justice at Stake surveyed 2,428 state court judges, one-quarter said that campaign contributions influenced their decisions. Even if justices do not allow campaign contributions to affect their decisions, the appearance of a conflict already has been created. A 2002 survey found that 75 percent of voters believe campaign contributions to judges influence decisions.[37]

Single-issue interest groups may target a judge for a specific ruling on a topic such as capital punishment, abortion, or same-sex marriage. Groups may criticize or praise the judge, taking the case completely out of its legal context. Such groups have joined together in the type of coalitions formed in other partisan political contests. Given the power of interest groups, Santa Clara University law professor Gerald Uelmen has observed that judicial independence is most endangered in states with growing death-row populations without any executions, states with laws requiring parental consent for abortions by minors, and states that allow statutory enactments or constitutional amendments by initiative.[38] In two states, Ohio and Kentucky, these three judicial landmines have come together. Both states elect supreme court justices in highly partisan and expensive races on a recurring basis.

Prior to 2002, judges' campaigns generally were subject to codes of judicial conduct that placed tight restrictions on campaigning to prevent judges from discussing topics that might later come before them on the bench. In *Republican Party of Minnesota v. White* (2002), however, the U.S. Supreme Court struck down such restrictions as violations of judges' free speech rights. Since then, interest groups such as the Christian Coalition of Georgia have asked judicial candidates to complete questionnaires, pressuring them to reveal their views on hot-button issues. The groups then target specific "bad" judges for removal. Some candidates themselves have run outspoken campaigns stating opinions on such issues as school funding that will clearly appear before the court.

Campaigns increasingly rely on 30-second TV spots, which can do little more than offer simplistic sound bites about complicated issues. According to Justice at Stake, in 2002 only one in ten of these TV spots was negative; that number had risen to more than one in five by 2004. In the 2000 elections for the Michigan Court of Appeals, the word *pedophile* ran in huge type near the name of the judge that the GOP was accusing of upholding a light sentence for a pedophile. In that same race, the Democratic Party ran ads that declared that the incumbents had ruled "against families and for corporations 82 percent of the time"—a claim the *Detroit Free Press* found "border[ed] on the bogus."[39] These ads do seem to make a difference. In 2004, thirty-four judicial elections featured some form of television advertising, and in twenty-nine of them, the candidate with the most ad expenditures won.[40]

Added to this mix of expensive campaigns and 30-second TV spots is the fact that ordinary citizens have very little information with which to make informed choices about judicial races. Voters commonly vote only for candidates at the top of the ticket, like governors or senators, and leave the ballots for judicial candidates incomplete.[41] Lack of voter participation undermines the public's ability to keep the judiciary accountable. It makes judges more vulnerable to single-issue groups.

In partisan elections, the additional danger is that the political parties may expect favors from the candidates they put forward. In 1976, the Michigan Supreme Court decided a redistricting case in a way that favored Republicans. In the next election, the Democratic Party refused to renominate the court's Democratic chief justice.[42] Thomas Phillips, a one-time chief justice of the Texas Supreme Court, has asked,

> When judges are labeled as Democrats or Republicans, how can you convince the public that the law is a judge's only constituency? And when a winning litigant has contributed thousands of dollars to the judge's campaign, how do you ever persuade the losing party that only the facts of the case were considered?[43]

Appointment

States in which judges are appointed rather than elected can be divided into two general categories: **pure appointive systems** and merit selection systems that rely on a nominating committee.

Federal judges have always been selected through a pure appointive system. The president appoints judges who, if they are confirmed by the Senate, "shall hold their Offices during good Behavior." No state, however, employs precisely this method of judicial selection.

In four states—California, Maine, New Hampshire, and New Jersey—the governor appoints state court judges without a nominating commission.

That is, these governors are not limited in their selections to a list of names provided by someone else.[44] Judges' nominations still require some kind of second opinion, however. In Maine, the governor appoints judges subject to confirmation by a legislative committee whose decision may be reviewed by the Senate. In New Jersey, the state Senate must confirm the governor's appointees, who then serve an initial seven-year term, after which the governor may reappoint them. A special five-member elected council confirms a judicial appointee in New Hampshire. California's governor appoints judges after submitting names to the state bar for evaluation.[45] In **retention elections**, judges run unopposed. The voter may indicate only either a simple "yes" or a "no" on the question of whether the judge should be retained.

Virginia is the only state in which the legislature appoints all state judges without a nominating committee. A majority vote of both houses of the Virginia General Assembly is required to appoint any judge.

Merit selection, initially endorsed by the American Bar Association in 1937, was conceived as a way to limit the intrusion of politics into judge selection.[46] Most states that currently appoint judges rely on a method of merit selection through nominating committees. Twenty-four states and the District of Columbia rely on a merit selection plan for the initial selection of some or all judges. Another ten states use such plans to fill midterm vacancies at some or all levels of court.[47]

What puts the *merit* into merit selection? It is misleading to describe merit selection as if it were a single method for selecting judges because the details vary considerably from state to state. At its core, it requires that the state assemble a nonpartisan nominating committee. This committee forwards a list of names from which either the governor or the legislature chooses a judge. How a partisan, distrustful legislature solves the problem of creating a nonpartisan committee differs in almost every state. Some require parity of political party affiliation for the commission members. Others have adopted extremely complex methods to assure the impartiality of nominating commissions.

Even after the composition of the nominating commission has been determined, states have different ways of choosing its chair, the most influential position. In some states, including Maryland, New Hampshire, and Utah, the governor can exert considerable control over the commission through the ability to appoint its chair.[48] Other states, such as Alaska, Arizona, Colorado, and Utah, designate the chief justice of the state supreme court as chair. Some states allow the commission to choose its own chair, and, finally, New Mexico's constitution designates the dean of the University of New Mexico Law School as the chair of the state's judicial nominating commission.[49]

Usually, the governor chooses the judge from the list forwarded by the commission. In South Carolina and Connecticut, the nominating committee forwards a list of names to the legislature, which then meets in joint session, appointing judges by a majority vote.[50]

RETENTION ELECTIONS

Elections in which judges run uncontested and voters are asked to vote "yes" if they wish to retain a judge in office for another term or "no" if they do not.

The ways in which judges are retained after being appointed also vary. In most states, judges appointed through merit selection serve shorter initial terms, usually one or two years. After that, they participate in retention elections. These special elections were conceived as a means to provide some public participation in the selection of judges while avoiding the intrusion of politics. In some states, notably California and Tennessee, this has backfired. Retention elections have become as fiercely partisan as popular elections.

Some merit selection states have dispensed with elections altogether. For instance, in Connecticut, Delaware, and Hawaii, judges are reevaluated and reappointed by the judicial selection commission. In Vermont, after an initial appointment through merit selection, a judge receives an additional term as long as the General Assembly does not vote against it.[51]

Terms of Office

The length of a judge's tenure is another element in the balance between judicial independence and judicial accountability. In the federal court system, judges serve life terms, limited only by "good behavior." Judges can be removed only through an impeachment process for cause. This life tenure is considered an important element, perhaps the most important element, in ensuring the independence of the federal judiciary.[52] There has never been a conviction of an impeached federal judge based solely on an unpopular judicial decision in the federal system.[53]

With only a few exceptions, state court judges serve fixed terms of office and must therefore seek reappointment or reelection. The rare exceptions include judges in Rhode Island, who serve life terms, and judges in Massachusetts and New Hampshire, who hold their positions until the age of seventy. Judges in states with fixed terms typically serve for less than ten years. New York appellate court judges serve the longest terms in the states—fourteen years—before mandatory retirement kicks in at age seventy.[54] (See Tables 9-1, 9-2, and 9-3.)

Shorter tenures bring with them the increased danger that political interests and pressures will intrude on judicial decision making. Giving judges longer terms allows them to be judged on a more complete record. A judge can more easily put some distance between a particular controversial decision and the election. To look at this another way, research indicates that judges with longer terms of office are more willing to manifest partisanship than judges with shorter terms. For example, researchers Paul Brace and Melinda Gann Hall find that, out of all the judges studied, Democrats with long terms are least likely to support capital punishment, whereas Republicans with long terms are the most likely to support it. This leads them to conclude "term length influences the willingness of individual justices to express their partisanship."[55]

Governing States and Localities

TABLE 9-1

Courts of Last Resort: Terms and Methods of Reappointment by State, 2010

State	Name of Court of Last Resort	Initial Term (years)	Subsequent Terms	Method of Reappointment	Geographical Basis for Selection
Alabama	Supreme	6	6	Reelection	Statewide
Alaska	Supreme	At least 3	10	Retention election	Statewide
Arizona	Supreme	At least 2	6	Retention election	Statewide
Arkansas	Supreme	8	8	Reelection	Statewide
California	Supreme	12	12	Retention election	Statewide
Colorado	Supreme	At least 2	10	Retention election	Statewide
Connecticut	Supreme	8	8	Governor renominates; legislature reappoints	Statewide
Delaware	Supreme	12	12	Gubernatorial reappointment from judicial nominating commission; senate consents	Statewide
Florida	Supreme	At least 1	6	Retention election	Statewide
Georgia	Supreme	6	6	Reelection	Statewide
Hawaii	Supreme	10	10	Nominating commission retains	Statewide
Idaho	Supreme	6	6	Reelection	Statewide
Illinois	Supreme	10	10	Retention election	District
Indiana	Supreme	At least 2	10	Retention election	Statewide
Iowa	Supreme	At least 1	8	Retention election	Statewide
Kansas	Supreme	1	6	Retention election	Statewide
Kentucky	Supreme	8	8	Reelection	District
Louisiana	Supreme	10	10	Reelection	District
Maine	Supreme Judicial	7	7	Gubernatorial reappointment; senate confirms	Statewide
Maryland	Court of Appeals	At least 1	10	Retention election	Circuit
Massachusetts	Supreme Judicial	To age 70	NA	NA	Statewide

continued

TABLE 9-1, **continued**

State	Name of Court of Last Resort	Initial Term (years)	Subsequent Terms	Method of Reappointment	Geographical Basis for Selection
Michigan	Supreme	8	8	Reelection	Statewide
Minnesota	Supreme	6	6	Reelection	Statewide
Mississippi	Supreme	8	8	Reelection	District
Missouri	Supreme	1–3	12	Retention election	Statewide
Montana	Supreme	8	8	Reelection	Statewide
Nebraska	Supreme	At least 3	6	Retention election	Statewide (chief justice); district (associate justices)
Nevada	Supreme	6	6	Reelection	Statewide
New Hampshire	Supreme	To age 70	NA	NA	Statewide
New Jersey	Supreme	7	To age 70	Gubernatorial reappointment; senate confirms	Statewide
New Mexico	Supreme	Remainder of unexpired term	8	Retention election	Statewide
New York	Court of Appeals	14	14	Gubernatorial appointment from nominating commission; senate consent	Statewide
North Carolina	Supreme	8	8	Reelection	Statewide
North Dakota	Supreme	10	10	Reelection	Statewide
Ohio	Supreme	6	6	Reelection	Statewide
Oklahoma	Supreme	At least 1	6	Retention election	District
Oregon	Supreme	6	6	Reelection	Statewide
Pennsylvania	Supreme	10	10	Retention election	Statewide
Rhode Island	Supreme	Life	NA	NA	Statewide
South Carolina	Supreme	10	10	Legislative reelection	Statewide
South Dakota	Supreme	At least 3	8	Retention election	District appointment; Statewide retention
Tennessee	Supreme	Until next general election	8	Retention election	Statewide

TABLE 9-1, continued

State	Name of Court of Last Resort	Initial Term (years)	Subsequent Terms	Method of Reappointment	Geographical Basis for Selection
Texas	Supreme and Criminal Appeals	6	6	Reelection	Statewide
Utah	Supreme	At least 3	10	Retention election	Statewide
Vermont	Supreme	6	6	Vote of general assembly	Statewide
Virginia	Supreme	12	12	Legislative election	Statewide
Washington	Supreme	6	6	Reelection	Statewide
West Virginia	Supreme Court of Appeals	12	NA	Reelection	Statewide
Wisconsin	Supreme	10	10	Reelection	Statewide
Wyoming	Supreme	At least 1	8	Retention election	Statewide

Source: Data compiled from the American Judicature Society, "Methods of Judicial Selection," 2010, available at www.judicialselection.us/judicial_selection/methods/selection_of_judges.cfm?state.

Note: NA = not applicable.

TABLE 9-2

Intermediate Courts: Terms and Methods of Reappointment by State, 2010

State	Name of Intermediate Court	Initial Term (years)	Subsequent Terms	Method of Reappointment	Geographical Basis for Selection
Alabama	Civil Appeals; Criminal Appeals	6	6	Reelection	Statewide
Alaska	Appeals	At least 3	8	Retention election	Statewide
Arizona	Appeals	At least 2	6	Retention election	Division
Arkansas	Appeals	6	6	Reelection	District
California	Appeals	12	12	Retention election	District
Colorado	Appeals	At least 2	8	Retention election	Statewide

continued

TABLE 9-2, **continued**

State	Name of Intermediate Court	Initial Term (years)	Subsequent Terms	Method of Reappointment	Geographical Basis for Selection
Connecticut	Appeals	8	8	Governor renominates; legislature reappoints	Statewide
Delaware	No intermediate appellate court				
Florida	District Courts of Appeal	At least 1	6	Retention election	District
Georgia	Appeals	6	6	Reelection	Statewide
Hawaii	Intermediate Court of Appeals	10	10	Nominating commission	Statewide
Idaho	Appeals	6	6	Reelection	Statewide
Illinois	Appeals	10	10	Retention election	District
Indiana	Appeals	At least 2	10	Retention election	District
Iowa	Appeals	At least 1	6	Retention election	Statewide
Kansas	Appeals	1	4	Retention election	Statewide
Kentucky	Appeals	8	8	Reelection	District
Louisiana	Appeals	10	10	Reelection	Circuit/District
Maine	No intermediate appellate court				
Maryland	Special Appeals	At least 1	10	Retention election	Circuit
Massachusetts	Appeals	To age 70	NA	NA	Statewide
Michigan	Appeals	6	6	Reelection	District
Minnesota	Appeals	6	6	Reelection	Statewide
Mississippi	Appeals	8	8	Reelection	District
Missouri	Appeals	1–3	12	Retention election	District
Montana	No intermediate appellate court				
Nebraska	Appeals	At least 3	6	Retention election	District
Nevada	No intermediate appellate court				
New Hampshire	No intermediate appellate court				
New Jersey	Appellate Division of Superior Court	Appointed by chief justice of supreme court for fixed term			

TABLE 9-2, continued

State	Name of Intermediate Court	Initial Term (years)	Subsequent Terms	Method of Reappointment	Geographical Basis for Selection
New Mexico	Appeals	Remainder of unexpired term	8	Retention election	Statewide
New York	Appellate Divisions of Supreme Court	5 years or through end of supreme court term, whichever is shorter	5	Governor reappoints from nominating commission	Statewide
North Carolina	Appeals	8	8	Reelection	Statewide
North Dakota	No intermediate appellate court; cases assigned to the court of appeals by the supreme court are heard by three-judge panels				
Ohio	Appeals	6	6	Reelection	Appellate district
Oklahoma	Civil Appeals	At least 1	6	Retention election	District
Oregon	Appeals	6	6	Reelection	Statewide
Pennsylvania	Commonwealth and Superior	10	10	Retention election	Statewide
Rhode Island	No intermediate appellate court				
South Carolina	Appeals	6	6	Legislative reelection	Statewide
South Dakota	No intermediate appellate court				
Tennessee	Appeals; Criminal appeals	Until next general election	8	Retention election	Statewide
Texas	Appeals	6	6	Reelection	District
Utah	Appeals	At least 3	6	Retention election	Statewide
Vermont	No intermediate appellate court				
Virginia	Appeals	8	8	Legislative reelection	Statewide
Washington	Appeals	6	6	Reelection	District
West Virginia	No intermediate appellate court				
Wisconsin	Appeals	6	6	Reelection	District
Wyoming	No intermediate appellate court				

Source: Data compiled from the American Judicature Society, "Methods of Judicial Selection," 2010, available at www.judicialselection.us/judicial_selection/methods/selection_of_judges.cfm?state.

Note: NA = not applicable.

TABLE 9-3

Trial-Level Courts: Terms and Methods of Reappointment by State, 2010

State	Name of Trial-Level Court	Initial Term (in years)	Subsequent Terms	Method of Reappointment	Geographical Basis for Selection
Alabama	Circuit	6	6	Reelection	Circuit
Alaska	Superior	At least 3	6	Retention election	District
Arizona	Superior	2 or 4, depending on population of county	4	Nonpartisan election; Retention election	County
Arkansas	Circuit	6	6	Reelection	Circuit
California	Superior	6	6	Reelection	County
Colorado	District	At least 2	6	Retention election	County
Connecticut	Superior	8	8	Governor renominates; legislature reappoints	Statewide
Delaware	Superior	12	12	Governor reappoints from judicial nominating commission; senate consents	Statewide
Florida	Circuit	6	6	Reelection	Circuit
Georgia	Superior	4	4	Reelection	Circuit
Hawaii	Circuit	10	10	Nominating commission	Island
Idaho	District	4	4	Reelection	District
Illinois	Circuit	6	6	Retention election	Circuit/County
Indiana	Superior and circuit	6	6	Reelection	County
Iowa	District	At least 1	6	Retention election	District
Kansas	District	1 or 4 depending upon district	4	Retention election; Reelection	District
Kentucky	Circuit	8	8	Reelection	Circuit
Louisiana	District	6	6	Reelection	District
Maine	Superior	7	7	Governor reappoints; senate confirms	Statewide
Maryland	Circuit	At least 1	15	Nonpartisan election	County/City
Massachusetts	Superior	To age 70	NA	NA	Statewide

TABLE 9-3, continued

State	Name of Trial-Level Court	Initial Term (in years)	Subsequent Terms	Method of Reappointment	Geographical Basis for Selection
Michigan	Circuit	6	6	Reelection	Circuit
Minnesota	District	6	6	Reelection	District
Mississippi	Circuit	4	4	Reelection	District
Missouri	Circuit	6	6	Reelection or Retention election depending on circuit	Circuit
Montana	District	6	6	Reelection	District
Nebraska	District	At least 3	6	Retention election	District
Nevada	District	6	6	Reelection	District
New Hampshire	Superior	To age 70	NA	NA	Statewide
New Jersey	Superior	7	To age 70	Governor reappoints; senate confirms	County
New Mexico	District	Remainder of unexpired term	6	Retention election	District
New York	Supreme and county courts	14/10	14/10	Reelection/reelection	District/county
North Carolina	Superior	8	8	Reelection	District
North Dakota	District	6	6	Reelection	District
Ohio	Common Pleas	6	6	Reelection	County
Oklahoma	District	4	4	Reelection	District
Oregon	Circuit	6	6	Reelection	District
Pennsylvania	Common pleas	10	10	Retention election	District
Rhode Island	Superior	Life	NA	NA	Statewide
South Carolina	Circuit	6	6	Legislative reelection	Circuit and at-large
South Dakota	Circuit	8	8	Reelection	Circuit
Tennessee	District courts	8	8	Reelection	District

continued

TABLE 9-3, continued

State	Name of Trial-Level Court	Initial Term (in years)	Subsequent Terms	Method of Reappointment	Geographical Basis for Selection
Texas	District	4	4	Reelection	District
Utah	District	At least 3	6	Retention election	District
Vermont	Superior; district	6	6	Vote of general assembly	Statewide
Virginia	Circuit	8	8	Legislative reelection	Circuit
Washington	Superior	4	4	Reelection	County
West Virginia	Circuit	8	NA	Reelection	Circuit
Wisconsin	Circuit	6	6	Reelection	Circuit
Wyoming	District	At least 1	6	Retention election	District

Source: Data compiled from the American Judicature Society, "Methods of Judicial Selection," 2010, available at www.judicialselection.us/judicial_selection/methods/selection_of_judges.cfm?.

Notes: Information on trial-level courts refers to highest court at trial-level, for example, those with general, rather than limited, jurisdiction. NA = not applicable.

Judicial Compensation

In addition to selection and tenure, compensation is one of the bellwethers for assessing independence of the judiciary. How a state determines the salaries of its judges and whether those salaries can be reduced makes a difference. The U.S. Constitution forbids reducing federal judicial salaries as a protection for judges who make unpopular decisions. Not all state constitutions include this proscription. In Florida, for instance, the constitution does not prevent the legislature from amending state laws to reduce salaries to discipline judges for unpopular decisions.[56]

According to the National Center for State Courts, at least twenty states have created independent judicial compensation commissions to advise their legislatures on judicial salary levels. The goal of these commissions is to determine the amount necessary to retain and recruit qualified judges and to eliminate the need for judges to lobby for their own salaries. States without such commissions rely on a variety of methods to eliminate partisan bickering over judicial salaries. The District of Columbia links salary increases to those of federal judges. Judges' salaries in South Dakota are linked to annual increases of the salaries of other state employees. In Pennsylvania, salary increases are tied to increases in the Consumer Price Index.[57] (See Table 9-4.)

Not only did the mandate come with no funding, but it also lacked any specifications as to how indigent services must be provided. States and localities, as a consequence, have devised differing systems, with the quality of service provided varying tremendously. Three primary models have emerged throughout the nation, with most states employing public defender programs, **assigned counsel**, or **contract attorneys**, or some combination of these. The method chosen may vary from county to county within a state, or a state may rely primarily on one type and use either of the other types for casework overload or the inevitable cases involving a conflict of interest. Among the nation's one hundred most populous counties in 1999 (the latest figures available), public defender programs were operating in ninety counties, assigned counsel programs in eighty-nine counties, and contract programs in forty-two counties.[76] Public defenders usually serve metropolitan areas and assigned counsel programs or contract programs serve less populous regions.

Public defenders' offices draw on a salaried staff of attorneys. They provide criminal legal defense services either as employees paid directly by the government or through a public or private nonprofit organization. Large public defenders' offices generally employ attorneys who are trained and supervised and who are supported by a staff of investigators, paralegals, and clerical staffers.[77] The American Bar Association has observed, "When adequately funded and staffed, defender organizations employing full-time personnel are capable of providing excellent defense services."[78] The challenge is to adequately fund and staff the offices. In 2009, the Michigan Court of Appeals ruled in favor of criminal defendants who charged that three counties' public defense systems were so underfunded that they failed to provide adequate representation. Put simply, they contended that the system was unconstitutional due to lack of funding—and the courts agreed, sparking debate statewide about potential reforms.[79]

Another system is called assigned counsel; here private attorneys are chosen and appointed either on a systematic or an ad hoc basis and are paid from public funds. Depending on the state, individual judges, assigned counsel program offices, or the court clerk's office may make the appointments. In the oldest type of assigned counsel program, judges make ad hoc assignments of counsel. Sometimes the only basis for these decisions is whoever is in the courtroom at the time. These arrangements frequently are criticized for fostering patronage (the granting of jobs to political allies), particularly in less populated counties.

Most states appoint lawyers from a roster of attorneys available for assigned cases. These rosters are compiled in various ways. Generally, assigned counsel need do no more than put their names on a list to be appointed to cases. There is no review of their experience, qualifications, or competence. Some states, particularly those with organized plans administered by an independent manager, may require specific training before attorneys can be included on the roster. In Maine, all attorneys in

ASSIGNED COUNSEL

Private lawyers selected by the courts to handle particular cases and paid from public funds.

CONTRACT ATTORNEYS

Private attorneys who enter into agreements with a state, a county, or a judicial district to work on a fixed-fee basis per case or for a specific length of time.

A 2005 survey of 2,485 Anchorage residents found that only 6.4 percent of respondents felt defense attorneys were excellent at treating people fairly. Prosecutors and judges fared little better, at 8 and 13.3 percent, respectively.

the local bar are included on the roster unless they choose to be removed.[80] Assigned counsel generally are paid either a flat fee or an hourly rate, in some cases subject to an overall fee cap. Many are paid at very low rates, such that only recent law school graduates or those who were previously unsuccessful in the business of law will agree to take assignments.[81]

Contract attorney programs are another way to provide defense services. A state, a county, or a judicial district will enter into a contract for the provision of indigent representation. These contracts can be awarded to a solo attorney, a law firm that handles both indigent and private cases, a nonprofit organization, or a group of lawyers who joined together to provide services under the contract. The parties may agree to accept cases on a fixed-fee per case basis or to provide representation for a particular period of time for a fixed fee.

Fixed-fee contracts specify the total amount of compensation the lawyer will receive for work on all cases taken during a specified period of time. The contractor must accept all cases that come up during the duration of the contract. For this reason, they are viewed by some as quick fixes that allow the funding body to limit costs and accurately project expenses for the coming year. However, such contracts have been criticized severely by the courts and national organizations like the American Bar Association because to make a profit, the contracting attorney has to spend as little time as possible on each case. Few states rely on them to provide representation for all or even a majority of their indigent defense cases. Instead, they are more commonly used to handle public defender overload or conflicts. Sometimes, a public defenders' office also will contract out a specific category of cases, such as juvenile or traffic offenses. Of the total amount spent on indigent criminal defense in the nation's one hundred largest counties, only 6 percent was spent on contract programs.[82]

Regardless of the model used by a county or state, all depend on adequate funding to successfully provide "effective assistance of counsel." Inadequate funding leads to lawyers' carrying impossible caseloads. Overburdened lawyers make crucial decisions based on too little investigation of the facts and inevitably pressure clients to plead guilty.[83] Many indigent defense systems are plagued by lack of funding and resources, high attorney workloads, and little or no oversight over the quality of services—problems that could result in the conviction of innocent people.[84] "Providing genuinely adequate counsel for poor defendants would require a substantial infusion of money and indigent defense is the last thing the populace will voluntarily direct its tax dollars to fund," writes attorney David Cole. "Achieving solutions to this problem through the political process is a pipe dream."[85]

Yet how secure would you feel if you were wrongly accused of a felony in Virginia, where your appointed lawyer could be paid a maximum of $1,000 to defend you?[86] If you don't plead guilty quickly, your lawyer will lose money on your case. Recently, a wave of successful lawsuits by groups like the American Civil Liberties Union against underfunded and

Local Focus: Maricopa County's Flat Fees and the Death Penalty

You know you're in trouble when you're facing the death penalty and your lawyer would rather go to jail himself than work on your case. In the late 1990s, Phoenix attorney Mike Terribile represented convicted murderer Richard Rivas, but as the case entered the sentencing phase, he refused to do any more work. The reason? Terribile said the flat fee he had received from Maricopa County to handle the case as a contract attorney was not enough to cover his costs. He appealed the payment contract to a judge, saying he would refuse to prepare Rivas's defense if he was turned down, even if that meant being held in contempt and jailed.

As in many jurisdictions, the Maricopa County Public Defenders' Office simply can't handle all the indigent cases it receives—more than 50,000 each year. To alleviate the problem, the county contracts with private attorneys to handle the overflow. The county generally pays about $64,000 for a set of eight cases. Maricopa County administrator David Smith says that's plenty. "If a case settles with just a few hours' work, they [still] get the $8,000," Smith says. He says that there is a

provision in the contract that allows for extra compensation if a case gets complicated, but notes that 97 percent of the cases in the county are plea-bargained out. "We expect that it will all even out." Contract attorneys handling capital cases were paid more— $10,000 at the start and an additional $10,000 if the case went to trial—but those cases demand many more than just a few hours' work.

After years of battle, the county stepped up payments for capital cases to at least $50,000, with the possibility for more based on the number of hours spent on each case. Contract attorneys welcomed the additional money but soon recognized another problem—there were too few of them to staff the county's death penalty cases. Inadequate defense is a major reason why the American Bar Association has called for a death penalty moratorium. "You go to any death penalty state and start asking questions about counsel in those cases and, with very few exceptions, there are substantial problems," says Tye Hunter, former executive director of North Carolina's Indigent Defense Services Commission.

Sources: Adapted from Alan Greenblatt, "Flat Fees and Death Penalties," *Governing* magazine, March 2001, available at www.governing.com/archive/archive/2001/mar/glimpses.txt; Michael Terribile, "And So It Goes" and "We Won, and No One Told Us," Arizona Attorneys for Criminal Justice, July 28, 2007, and January 25, 2006, available at www.aacj.org/news-indigent-defense.php.

overburdened public defenders, assigned counsel programs, and contract attorneys have led legislators to enact reforms that "even the most skeptical observers admit have the potential to bring important changes to the process of criminal justice."[87] Some of these have led to successful injunctions or settlements, increased funding for indigent defense, and improved administration of such programs.[88] Furthermore, the defense community and organizations like the American Bar Association have been focusing on the need for standards for indigent criminal representation. The goal is to educate those policymakers who design the systems by which these legal services are delivered.

Juries

If you vote, pay a utility bill, or drive, you may be called to jury duty at some point in your life. You may be asked to decide whether a defendant in a capital case lives or dies; whether someone spends the rest of his or her life in prison; whether a civil plaintiff, injured and unable to work, should be able to collect damages; or whether a civil defendant must be bankrupted by the large amount of damages ordered to be paid. Service on a jury may require spending days or weeks listening to intricate scientific evidence and expert testimony, listening to conflicting testimony, and deciding who is credible and who is not to be believed. Or you may spend one day in a large room with other potential jurors, break for lunch, and go home at the end of that day without ever hearing a single case.

The right to a jury trial in state criminal proceedings is granted by the Sixth Amendment. Not all criminal prosecutions trigger the right to a jury trial—minor offenses involving a potential sentence of less than six months do not require juries. Neither do juvenile proceedings, probation revocation proceedings, or military trials.

The jury's role in a trial is that of fact-finder. The judge has to ensure a fair and orderly trial, but it is the jurors who must determine the facts of the case. In some instances, parties may agree to forgo a jury trial and, instead, choose a bench trial in which the judge serves as both judge and jury. In a criminal bench trial, the judge alone decides guilt or innocence.

Differences and similarities in how judges and juries rule have been the subject of much research and review. Standard stereotypes might lead you to think that juries are less able to separate emotion from reason than judges or that they decide cases more generously for injured plaintiffs and that grisly evidence in criminal cases may motivate them to decide based on passion or prejudice. Not so. For instance, research shows that civil plaintiffs in product **liability** and medical malpractice cases have more success before judges in bench trials.[89]

> Standard stereotypes might lead you to think that juries are less able to separate emotion from reason than judges or that they decide cases more generously for injured plaintiffs and that grisly evidence in criminal cases may motivate them to decide based on passion or prejudice. Not so.

LIABILITY
A legal obligation or responsibility.

Historically, juries have been composed of twelve people who must come to a unanimous verdict. Since 1970, however, a series of U.S. Supreme Court decisions has allowed states to move away from this standard.[90] In state jury trials, whether unanimity is required depends on the size of the jury. A conviction by a twelve-member jury may be less than unanimous, whereas a six-member jury must have unanimity. A majority of states continue to require twelve-member juries to make unanimous rulings in felony criminal cases, but seven states use six-member or eight-member juries for noncapital felonies. Two states, Louisiana and Oregon, do not require a unanimous verdict in such cases.[91] Most states provide for civil juries of six members or eight members. Those that still require twelve members typically allow parties to agree to smaller juries. Unanimity is not required in most civil trials; instead, most states provide for verdicts based on a supermajority of either five-sixths or two-thirds.

States develop and maintain master lists from which they identify potential jurors. Their sources include driver's licenses, motor vehicle registrations, telephone directories, tax rolls, utility customer lists, voter registrations, and lists of actual voters. It is very hard to avoid ever being called in for jury duty. Jurors must be residents of the county in which the court sits and must generally be eighteen years old, although in Alabama and Nebraska the minimum age is nineteen and in Mississippi and Missouri it is twenty-one. States also usually have some sort of requirement regarding literacy and the ability to understand or communicate in English, or both. South Carolina requires at least a sixth-grade education, and Tennessee explicitly excludes those of "unsound mind" and "habitual drunkards." Most states also require that jurors not be convicted felons.

The provisions for selecting a juror typically are the same for all the trial courts within a state, although some make distinctions between limited and general jurisdiction courts. The formal process of jury selection begins with a *voir dire* examination. This is the process by which prospective jurors are interviewed and examined. Some may be excused following a challenge by one of the attorneys in the case. The primary purpose of this is to impanel, or select, an impartial jury. If it appears during the questioning that a particular juror is biased or has a particular view of the case, that juror may be stricken **for cause**. There is no limit on the number of challenges a party can make for cause. In addition, each party receives a certain number of **peremptory challenges**, meaning the lawyers can kick off jurors for any reason other than race or gender.

VOIR DIRE

The interviewing and examination of potential jurors.

FOR CAUSE CHALLENGE

A lawyer's asking the judge to excuse a potential juror because the individual appears to be biased or unable to be fair.

PEREMPTORY CHALLENGES

Lawyers' dismissing potential jurors for any reason except race or gender.

Defendants' Rights versus Victims' Rights

Crime typically involves at least two actors: a perpetrator and a victim. Traditionally, the criminal justice system in the United States interposes the ideal of public prosecution between the two. That is, all crimes are crimes against the state. The prosecutor, representing the public and not any particular individual, sees that justice is done objectively and fairly. The public's interest, under this system, is distinct from the victim's interest in retribution.

Numerous provisions in the Bill of Rights balance the rights of criminal defendants against the powers of the state. These defendants' rights include:

- The right to be presumed innocent until proven guilty
- The right to be safe from arrest or searches and seizures unless the government has made a showing of probable cause
- The right to a lawyer
- The right to a jury trial
- The right to confront witnesses
- The rights to due process and the equal protection of laws
- If proven guilty, the right to punishment that is not cruel and unusual

The framers' concerns in creating these rights were about overreaching government power. They worried that innocent people otherwise might be railroaded into jail on charges they never had a chance to adequately defend themselves against. There is no mention of the rights of crime victims.

In the last three decades, this balance has undergone a radical transformation. Defendants still have all of the rights listed, but now state courts are increasingly balancing them against a new class of victims' rights. The movement advocating an increasing role for the victims of crime has become a formidable force and has achieved tremendous success in enacting legislation in all the states. The momentum started in 1982, when a president's task force on victims of crime described the United States justice system as "appallingly out of balance." That is not to say that victims were helpless—the number of state laws addressing victims' rights was already in the hundreds. By 1998, however, the number of crime victim–related statutes had soared to more than 27,000. Twenty-nine states had passed victims' rights constitutional amendments.[92]

Today, every state has either a constitutional amendment or a statutory scheme that protects victims' rights. Some predict that the next amendment to the U.S. Constitution will be a victims' rights amendment. Supporters frequently argue that the justice system favors defendants over victims and that, without modification, the system itself constitutes a second victimization. On the other hand, civil rights organizations fear that some victims' rights laws upset the system of checks and balances in the nation's criminal justice system and undercut the basic due process protections designed to keep innocent people out of prison.

The specifics of victims' rights laws vary among the states. A variety of statutes or amendments guarantee that crime victims receive monetary compensation, notice of procedural developments in the case, protection from offender harm, and more attentive treatment from the justice system. The more controversial of such laws are directed toward providing victims with a significantly greater involvement in the actual prosecutions. This includes providing victims the right to confer with the prosecutor at all stages, including plea bargains; the right to attend all stages of the case, even if the victim will be called as a witness; and the right to introduce victim-impact statements at the sentencing phase of the trial.

Perhaps the most controversial and interesting of the victims' rights laws concern victim-impact evidence. This may be particularly true in capital cases in which impact statements have been described as

> highly emotional, frequently tearful testimony coming directly from the hearts and mouths of the survivors left behind by killings. And it arrives at the precise time when the balance is at its most delicate and the stakes are highest—when jurors are poised to make the visceral decision of whether the offender lives or dies.[93]

In 1991, the U.S. Supreme Court reversed itself and ruled that impact statements that detailed the particular qualities of the victim and the harm caused to the victim's family could be admissible in capital sentencing hearings.[94] Today, all states allow victim-impact evidence at the sentencing phase of the trial. Most of the states with the death penalty allow it in capital trials.

Sentencing

The state prison population has ballooned in the last twenty years, from less than 320,000 in 1980 to 2.3 million today.[95] Corrections has been one of the fastest growing items in state budgets and averaged 7 percent of state general fund budgets in 2008.[96] In most states, the judge holds a separate sentencing hearing after the jury finds the defendant guilty. In capital cases, the Supreme Court has held that only a unanimous jury, and not the judge, can sentence a defendant to death.[97] Thirteen states have provisions for a sentence of life without parole if the jury is unable to reach agreement.[98] In noncapital cases, by contrast, it is almost always the judge who sets sentence. Only in Arkansas, Missouri, Texas, and Virginia does the jury choose the sentence. In all states but Texas, the judge is free to disregard the jury's decision.

Sentencing policy involves the balancing of value judgments, such as the perceived severity of the crimes and the perceived severity of different punishments, with the relevance of mitigating circumstances. It must include considerations of the costs to the taxpayers and to society of incarceration. Surveys indicate that attitudes on sentencing follow regional patterns, "with residents of New England demonstrating the greatest tendency to be lenient and residents of central southern states displaying the least leniency."[99] It is not surprising, then, that state sentencing laws vary and that the punishment a convict faces depends not just on what that person did but also on where the crime was committed. Voters in California and Oklahoma, for instance, view drug offenses differently. In California state courts, a cocaine dealer is subject to a two- to four-year prison term. The same offense in Oklahoma brings a minimum of five years and a maximum of life imprisonment.[100]

The amount of discretion given to judges also varies from state to state. Depending on the type of crime or where the defendant is charged, the sentence can be a matter of "do the crime, do the time" or whatever the judge or parole board thinks is best.

A few decades ago, it was possible to talk of a predominant American approach to criminal sentencing. At all levels of the nation's criminal justice system, a concern for rehabilitation and deterrence led states to embrace **indeterminate sentencing**. Legislatures set very wide statutory sentencing margins within which judges had the discretion to impose sentence for imprisonment with little fear of appellate review. The sentence

INDETERMINATE SENTENCING

The judge sentences an offender to a minimum and a maximum time in prison, and a parole board decides how long the offender actually will remain in prison.

was indeterminate because the parole board, not the judge, had ultimate control over the actual release date. Under this system, the discretion of judges and parole boards was necessary to tailor the punishment to the specific rehabilitative needs of the individual defendant. This practice led to wide discrepancies in the sentences imposed for those convicted of the same crime.

Indeterminate sentencing came under attack from several angles during the 1970s. The lack of guidance for judges led to the potential for discrimination in sentencing based on such factors as race, ethnic group, social status, and gender. There was also criticism of the ability of parole boards to successfully determine whether inmates had or had not been rehabilitated. Finally, rehabilitation lost favor as the country entered an era of tough-on-crime rhetoric and a "just desserts" theory of criminal sentencing.[101] Sentencing reform sought to replace indeterminate sentencing with **determinate sentencing**. This led to the adoption of federal sentencing guidelines, a structured system of binding sentencing rules that greatly limited judicial discretion in sentencing in the federal courts.

In contrast to the federal court system, there has been no single sweeping sentencing reform across all fifty states. Some states have made wholesale changes to determinate sentencing laws, but most continue to use indeterminate sentencing.[102]

Yet indeterminate sentencing does not necessarily mean more lenient sentencing. It just means that the actual amount of time served may vary depending on the judge or the findings of a parole board. For instance, before the charges were dropped, Los Angeles Lakers star Kobe Bryant was charged with felony sexual assault in Colorado. The sex offense statutes there are considered among the harshest in the country. Any sentence on a sex assault charge can mean the possibility of life imprisonment. In part, the severity of the sentence depends on the results of a battery of tests. These results are used by judges in sentencing and by parole boards to determine if the prisoner is a continued threat. They include plethysmograph tests, which involve placing an electric band around the penis in an attempt to measure deviant thoughts as the person is shown images of abusive behaviors. Described as "very Clockwork Orangish" by Don Recht, former head of the Colorado Defense Bar, the results are studied carefully nonetheless. Under Colorado's indeterminate sentencing, a convicted sex offender is released only when deemed safe to reenter society.

Most states still rely on indeterminate sentencing, but all states have adopted at least some features of determinate sentencing, although in greatly differing degrees. When it comes to sentencing reform, "the states have served as hothouses of experimentation during the last thirty years, with so much activity that the diversity of provisions among the states has become exceedingly complex."[103] Some of the major reforms adopted include sentencing guidelines, **mandatory minimum sentences** that are imposed for conviction of specified crimes, **habitual offender laws**, and

DETERMINATE SENTENCING

The judge sentences an offender to serve a specific amount of time in prison depending on the crime.

MANDATORY MINIMUM SENTENCES

The shortest sentences that offenders may receive upon conviction for certain offenses. The court has no authority to impose a shorter sentence.

HABITUAL OFFENDER LAWS

Statutes imposing harsher sentences on offenders who previously have been sentenced for crimes.

truth-in-sentencing laws. With the implementation of these reforms, the time served in prison by those convicted has been increasing as a percentage of the sentence imposed. In 1993, the percentage of a sentence that an offender spent in prison was 31.8 percent; that percentage had increased to 44.4 percent by 2005.[104]

All fifty states and the District of Columbia have enacted some form of mandatory minimum prison sentencing.[105] These laws limit judicial discretion by requiring that individuals guilty of specific crimes must go to jail no less than a specified length of time. Such crimes include drug possession or trafficking, drunk driving, and sexual offenses. The mandatory sentencing laws also may take effect if certain acts enhanced the severity of the underlying crime, for instance, if weapons were involved. If a crime involved the use of a deadly weapon, New Mexico requires an additional year for the first offense or three additional years for a second offense. The use of a firearm to commit a crime in Nevada requires a doubling of the sentence for the underlying crime. In Ohio, the use of a deadly weapon requires an additional term of three to six years.[106]

Habitual offender laws also are common among the states. These statutes impose more severe sentences for offenders who previously have been sentenced for crimes. California's "three-strikes" law was a prototype of this kind of legislation. The law states that if a defendant convicted of a felony has one prior conviction for a "serious" or "violent" felony, the sentence is doubled. Defendants convicted for a felony with two prior convictions for "serious" or "violent" felonies receive a life sentence without possibility of parole. The law has been severely criticized for its "unbending harshness," but it has withstood constitutional challenges.[107] Five states have enacted some form of "two or three strikes" legislation.[108] One such state is Michigan, where the sentence is one-and-a-half times the maximum sentence for the second conviction and twice the maximum sentence for a third conviction.[109]

Another sentencing reform movement began in the 1990s. Known as truth-in-sentencing, these laws reduce the amount of discretion parole boards have to shorten sentences for good behavior. They do this by specifying the proportion of a sentence that offenders must serve before they may be considered for parole. Forty-one states have adopted some form of truth-in-sentencing laws.[110] Most, however, still have a parole board with some discretionary release authority and a system in which the incarcerated felons can accumulate "good time" under a specified formula. Arkansas, Louisiana, Vermont, and Wyoming are among the many states that provide for a day of "good time" for each day—or less—served. North Dakota grants five days of "good time" for every month served.

These formulas also can be complicated by the accumulation of work or education credits. Some states, like Illinois, have cut through the confusion by eliminating the "good time" credit for certain serious offenses. Others have eliminated it altogether. Michigan eliminated the concept of "good

TRUTH-IN-SENTENCING LAWS

Laws that give parole boards less authority to shorten sentences for good behavior by specifying the proportion of a sentence an offender must serve before becoming eligible for parole.

time" for all felony offenses committed after December 2000, and the District of Columbia has not offered it since 1994.[111]

As states reduce judges' discretion and increase time that offenders spend in prison, a considerable burden has been placed on the facilities and personnel of the prison system. In response to this, most states are exploring sentencing options for their less serious offenders that are less severe than imprisonment but more serious than ordinary probation.[112] One such option is house arrest. This requires the offenders to remain in their residences for the duration of their sentences. They often are required to wear electronic bracelets around the wrist or ankle that send a continuous radio signal to verify their location.

Many states rely on "intensive probation." This form of probation involves much closer supervision by parole officers with smaller caseloads than the norm. Parolees in these programs typically are required to hold a job, submit to urinalysis, pay restitution to victims, and perform community service. To alleviate prison overcrowding, some states release prisoners to "halfway" houses that assist with their reintegration into the community. Young first-time offenders may be sentenced to "boot camps" for shorter periods and subjected to strict military discipline. Nonviolent offenders may be offered work release; weekend sentencing; alcohol, drug, or mental health treatment; or release subject to appearance at daily reporting centers.

Problems from the Lack of Sentencing Uniformity

Since the 1970s, sentencing reform movements have concerned themselves more and more with the sentencing disparities that occur when judges and parole boards have broad discretion in the sentencing of criminal offenders. Many states felt pressure to reform sentencing, but how they responded varies substantially. State sentencing guidelines, adopted by a minority of states, are not as rigid as the new federal guidelines. State judges also tend to have more discretion than federal judges.

A parallel trend in criminal law involves the increased federalization of crimes that were once the sole domain of the states. Many street crimes, such as low-level gun and drug offenses, are now federal offenses. Law enforcement officials have the choice of sending such cases to federal or state prosecutors and courts, and the cases are subject to the differing sets of sentencing guidelines. The trend away from discretion in sentencing has led to some uniformity nationwide in sentencing in federal courts. Ironically, however, the federal sentencing guidelines and the increased federalization of local crimes have increased the sense of randomness in sentencing within communities. Whether offenders are charged in a state court or a federal court can lead to huge disparities in the sentence for the same offense.

Nationwide, drug and weapons violations result in sentences that are, on average, three times longer in federal courts than in state courts.[113] In some cases, the essentially random chance of being charged in federal court can lead to a death penalty, even where local voters have twice rejected capital punishment, as in the District of Columbia. In some areas, prosecutors have been suspected of "shopping" for either a state or federal trial, depending on the race of the offender. In a region of Massachusetts in the late 1990s, white crack dealers were tried exclusively in state courts, whereas many black dealers were tried in federal courts.[114] When two members of the same community, who do the exact same thing, are subjected to drastically different treatment, it undermines public confidence that justice is being done. This was one of the concerns that led to the passage of sentencing reforms in the first place.

The Case for Court Reform

How state courts are organized is not static or carved in stone. States constantly evaluate their practices and modify procedures to adapt to demographic, economic, and political conditions. This section discusses some reforms being adopted or at least being discussed in most states. Specialized courts to handle drug offenses or family matters are currently in vogue to accommodate increasing caseloads, as are attempts to streamline and speed up court dockets. Given the controversy surrounding judicial elections, many states aren't waiting for major reforms to merit selection but, instead, are focusing on modifying elections to minimize the problems posed by the need for campaign contributions. Finally, this section addresses some of the pressures to reform that stem from the lack of uniformity across the country and within individual states.

The Problem of Increasing Caseloads

Nationwide, violent crime rates are down. State courts, nonetheless, have found themselves on the front lines dealing with the results of societal problems such as substance abuse and family violence since the 1980s. From 1984 to 1999, the U.S. population grew by only 12 percent. During this period, the number of juvenile cases grew by 68 percent, and the number of domestic relations cases grew by 74 percent. Criminal cases, mostly misdemeanors, grew by 47 percent.[115]

In reaction to such growth, many states have created "problem-solving courts." These include community courts, domestic violence courts, mental health courts, and drug treatment courts. Their purpose is to deal decisively with low-level nonviolent crimes. The solutions often involve closely monitored treatment plans meant to stop the revolving door of **recidivism**, or relapses into criminal behavior. Drug courts, with their focus on treatment for nonviolent drug-addicted offenders, contribute to the decline in violent crimes and save local and state governments millions of dollars annually from reduced incarceration rates.

RECIDIVISM

A return to, or relapse into, criminal behavior.

States also have been experimenting with integrated family courts. These courts adopt a holistic approach to all the issues that affect a single family in a single court system. Such integrated courts can address issues more efficiently, especially in cases in which delays can leave children in foster care limbo. Many individuals who appear in such family courts traditionally have been forced, instead, to face multiple proceedings in multiple courts: assault charges in county courts, custody disputes in family courts, and divorce issues in yet another court. The current trend is to put all of a family's problems before a single, informed judge to eliminate conflicting orders and multiple appearances. New York has estimated that its Integrated Domestic Violence Court slashed the number of family court cases from more than three thousand to less than nine hundred in its first two years, reducing delay and duplication and increasing cost-effective case management.[116]

This increased focus on court administration and case management has not been confined to the criminal side of the court calendar. Until just a few years ago, crowded civil dockets and multiyear waiting periods were relatively common in many states. "Back in the 1980s, there was no incentive for an insurance company to settle a case for the first year," said Bill Sieben, who was then president of the Minnesota Trial Lawyers Association. "They knew the case wasn't even going to be nearing a trial for several years."[117] This is becoming less true as states focus on clearing their overcrowded and overly cumbersome civil dockets. Tom Phillips, former chief justice of the Texas Supreme Court, attributed faster-clearing caseloads primarily to the rise of the managerial judge.[118] Most trial judges may insist on a strong case-management system, but a generation ago, when caseloads were smaller and more manageable, not many of them did.

In recent years, not content with merely handing down verdicts, forceful judges have seized control of their courts and made it clear that things will run according to their schedules, not at the convenience of lawyers who never seem quite ready to go to trial. "A very strong component of civil cases is, just set a trial date and the case will go away," said Kevin Burke, formerly the chief judge of the Hennepin County Court in Minnesota. "Left to their own devices, lawyers aren't necessarily going to manage it to a speedy resolution."[119]

State initiatives to speed up dockets, or court case schedules, have included an increased reliance on **alternative dispute resolution**. In certain types of cases, such resolutions now are mandated, and lawyers are required to inform their clients about alternatives to standard court fights. These alternatives usually involve hashing things out in front of an expert mediator. Some courts have been creative in finding appropriately authoritative experts. Hennepin County courts, for instance, refer dry cleaning disputes—stained pants, torn dresses, and busted buttons—to a retired owner of a dry cleaning business for speedy resolution. An accountant may resolve a financial dispute. These innovations increase the efficiency of the court system and free up trial judges for more complex cases.

Several states are experimenting with a **rocket docket** patterned after an innovation in a Virginia federal court. In essence, these fast-tracked dockets impose tight, unbending deadlines on lawyers for the handling of pretrial motions and briefs. In the Vermont Supreme Court, the rocket docket applies to cases that present no novel issue likely to add to the body of case law. Rather than all five justices sitting *en banc* to hear these cases, each month they split and rotate through a smaller and less cumbersome panel of three that is able to reach consensus more quickly. The panel releases its decisions within twenty-four hours in 99 percent of the cases.

Rocket dockets are not always a panacea, however. Florida implemented the approach as thousands of home foreclosures began clogging the courts in late 2006. The foreclosure courts could clear 250 cases a day, each in a matter of minutes. But, although it represented a success for the state, attorneys found fault with the system. The few homeowners who attended the hearings had little time to be heard, and one review of 180 cases in Sarasota found that only one in four had complete paperwork. By late 2009, one judge found a way to slow the rapid-fire process, at least a bit—he gave any homeowners who showed at the courthouse an additional three months to work to save their home or to move.[120]

In Colorado, rapid population growth has led to mounting lawsuits, and courts increasingly have turned to **magistrates** to resolve less important cases. Often a local official or attorney hired on contract, these magistrates have helped the state to stay on top of an 85 percent increase in case filings despite only a 12 percent increase in the number of judges. The magistrates issue preliminary decisions that must then be upheld by a judge, but this is a formality in most cases. This modification is credited with enabling more routine cases to be handled efficiently and allowing more time for more complex cases, but some have complained to the Colorado bar that this reliance on contract attorneys to serve as magistrates decreases the accountability of the judges and does not yield sufficiently clear precedents to provide guidance to the attorneys who must practice before them.[121] Given these concerns, a task force on civil justice reform convened by then governor Bill Ritter recommended that the state create additional district and county court judgeships to alleviate the caseload strain on the system.[122] A 2007 act created forty-three new positions for judges across Colorado.

The Reform of Judicial Selection

Nationally, 87 percent of all state judges face partisan, nonpartisan, or retention elections or some mix of these.[123] As discussed earlier, the trend in recent years has been for these elections to become more and more like the elections for legislative and gubernatorial offices: loud, nasty, and expensive. Some fear that this will lead to a blurring of the distinction between the judicial and political branches of government and throw into question the independent decision making of the judiciary.

ROCKET DOCKET

Fast-tracked cases that often have limited, specific deadlines for specific court procedures.

MAGISTRATES

Local officials or attorneys granted limited judicial powers.

States under Stress: This Court Will Not Come to Order

In Birmingham, Alabama, domestic-relations judge Suzanne Childers keeps a .38-caliber Smith & Wesson revolver under her bench. That, and a can of pepper spray, have served as protection for her courtroom since budget cuts eliminated two deputies' positions. Childers's story is extreme, but hers is not the only courtroom that has been left less safe as a result of the state and local fiscal crisis. In Massachusetts, open court officer positions were not filled between the end of 2008 and early 2010, and in Maine, metal detectors in courthouses go unstaffed. "It's a question of do you want to close courthouses and run (fewer) courthouses with full security? Or do you want to keep all your courthouses open and compromise on security?" said Mary Ann Lynch, a spokeswoman for Maine's court system.[a]

Many states are shutting the doors to the court for several days per month. Hawaii's courts began closing two Fridays per month in November 2009. California does not hold sessions on the third Wednesday of every month; this move is estimated to save the Golden State some $85 million—a fraction of the $414 million deficit in the state courts' 2010 budget.[b] Almost every state is trying to get by with less. A survey conducted by the National Center for State Courts (NCSC) in early 2009 estimated that at least thirty state court systems were facing cutbacks in their 2010 budgets,[c] and budget conditions worsened after the survey responses were collected. Florida laid off 10 percent of its court employees in 2010, and Oregon cut its court employee salaries by 20 percent.[d]

When budget cuts eliminated courtroom security guards, Jefferson County, Alabama, Domestic Court judge Suzanne Childers resorted to keeping a .38-caliber pistol under her desk during session for protection.

Court administrators predicted the cutbacks would be felt across state systems. NCSC reported that the cuts would lead to increased backlogs in civil, criminal, and family court cases. Making matters worse, states expected that the very programs they had implemented to help alleviate backlogs—alternative dispute resolution and problem-solving courts—would themselves end up on the chopping block.

[a] Quoted in Denise Lavoie, "Budget Cuts Force Tough Choices on Court Security," *Seattle Times,* January 10, 2010, available at http://seattletimes.nwsource.com/html/businesstechnology/2010758141_apuscourthousesecuritycuts.html.

[b] Paul Elias, "Calif. Courts to Close 1 Day a Month to Save Money," Associated Press, July 29, 2009.

[c] Daniel J. Hall, "How State Courts Are Weathering the Economic Storm," in *Future Trends in State Courts 2009* (Williamsburg, Va.: National Center for State Courts, 2009).

[d] "Actions and Proposals to Balance the FY 2010 Budget: Criminal Justice," National Conference of State Legislatures, available at www.ncsl.org/?tabid=17240.

Indeed, the U.S. Supreme Court's decision in *Republican Party of Minnesota v. White* (2002) may have brought politics closer than ever to the judicial elections process. A 5–4 majority ruled that the First Amendment does not allow the government "to prohibit candidates from communicating relevant information to voters during an election." This includes judicial candidates who wish to speak publicly about disputed legal matters. At the same time, the Court acknowledged the core responsibility of judges to "be willing to consider views that oppose [their] preconceptions, and remain open to persuasion when the issues arise in a pending case." Today, states that hold elections for judicial offices, such as Ohio, Pennsylvania, and Wisconsin, feature public debates among judicial candidates similar to those held for candidates for legislative office.

The major reform movement of the latter half of the twentieth century was the merit selection of judges, described previously. This movement initially was very successful, but after being adopted by roughly half the states, it has stalled in recent years. Since 1990, all the legislatures that have considered merit selection have rejected it. States seeking to adopt merit selection face both cultural and political obstacles. They face an ingrained cultural belief that elections are a critical part of our democracy that are not to be sacrificed without a fight. Combined with this is the political reality that in most states a change to merit selection would require the legislative super-majority and public approval necessary for a constitutional change.

Recognizing these barriers to adopting merit selection, reformers are focusing on improving popular elections to minimize the threat they pose to judicial independence and impartiality. For example, the unprecedented level of interest group activity in judicial elections has led to recommendations to require the disclosure of campaign contributions. This is an area with First Amendment implications that forces states to tread very carefully. Some states focus their reforms on the dangers inherent in campaign financing and are experimenting with public financing of judicial campaigns. They hope that this will reduce the potential of campaign contributions' influencing or creating the appearance of influencing outcomes. In Wisconsin, revenue to publicly fund the campaigns of state supreme court candidates comes from a $1 state tax return check-off. In 2002, North Carolina became the first state to provide full public financing of elections for appeals court and supreme court candidates who accept spending limits, a program that was encouraged when the U.S. Supreme Court declined to hear arguments in a case contesting its constitutionality.[124]

Conclusion

State and local courts play a profound role in their state governments. They resolve civil disputes and hand out justice in criminal cases. They also protect the citizens of their states from unconstitutional behavior by the political branches of government. Despite the importance of this role, or perhaps because of it, judicial systems differ tremendously from state to state. There are organizational differences from initial trial to final appeal. Judges in some states are elected by voters and in others are appointed by the governor. Such differences reflect each state's unique orientation toward the values of politics, law, judicial independence, and accountability.

The focus in this chapter has been on the players involved as a case works its way through the judicial system. In a criminal case, the elected prosecutor has tremendous freedom to decide which charges to bring against an accused criminal. Anyone charged with a crime has the right to an attorney, and the state must provide attorneys to those unable to afford their own. Usually a public defender takes the case. If a plea bargain is not reached, the case goes to trial, and the fate of the accused rests in the hands of a panel of ordinary citizens who have been called to jury duty. Potential jurors are selected from a pool of individuals who may have done something as simple as pay a utility bill. This does not mean, however, that there is anything simple about a jury's task. Often, this group holds the future of another individual in its hands.

If an accused person is found guilty and sentenced to incarceration, the length of time the offender actually spends in jail depends a lot on how the values of rehabilitation, deterrence, and retribution have played out in a particular state's political system. Differences here can have an enormous impact. One state may try a nonviolent drug offender in a special drug court that focuses on treatment. But another may try the same offense in a general trial court in which the judge has no choice under the rigid minimum sentencing guidelines except lengthy incarceration.

None of the choices that states make in structuring their courts is fixed and unchanging. States are always responding to altered societal or political realities, experimenting with what works, and adapting to political movements. Some of the areas of reform and change examined in this chapter were triggered by the political rise of victims' rights movements, by the realities of changing caseloads, or by a perception that the selection of judges has become increasingly political.

Key Concepts

activist judge (p. 326)

alternative dispute resolution (p. 372)

appeal (p. 330)

assigned counsel (p. 361)

bench trials (p. 331)

civil cases (p. 329)

contract attorneys (p. 361)

Suggested Readings

Brace, Paul, and Melinda Gann Hall. "Studying Comparatively: The View from the American States." *Political Research Quarterly* 48 (March 1995): 5–29. This study examines how politics and methods of judicial selection effect capital punishment decisions in state supreme courts. The authors conclude that party affiliation and whether judges are elected have an impact on how death penalty cases are decided.

Carp, Robert A., Ronald Stidham, and Kenneth Manning. *Judicial Process in America,* 7th ed. Washington D.C.: CQ Press, 2007. A comprehensive look at the state and federal court systems in the United States; covers the foundations, history, organization, and processes, as well as other issues like policy implementation and judicial decision making.

Rottman, David, and Shauna Strickland. *State Court Organization 2004.* Washington, D.C.: Bureau of Justice Statistics, 2006. A basic overview of how the fifty states organize their state court systems. Includes everything from qualification requirements to selection methods to the number of courts and full-time judges serving in a state.

Ware, Steven. "Money, Politics and Judicial Decisions: A Case Study of Arbitration Law in Alabama." *Journal of Law and Politics* 15 (1999): 645. This article presents the results of a study of 106 decisions by the Alabama Supreme Court from January 18, 1995, through July 9, 1999. The study shows the correlation between campaign funding and judicial rulings.

Suggested Web Sites

www.abanet.org. Web site of the American Bar Association, the largest voluntary professional association in the world, with a membership of more than 400,000.

www.ajs.org. Web site of the American Judicature Society, a nonpartisan organization with a national membership that works to maintain the independence and integrity of the courts and increase public understanding of the justice system.

www.brennancenter.org. Web site of the Brennan Center for Justice, a nonpartisan center at New York University that conducts research and advocates on a range of judicial topics, including state court reform and campaign financing.

www.JusticeatStake.org. Web site of the Justice at Stake Campaign, a nonpartisan effort working to keep courts fair and impartial.

www.ncsconline.org. Web site of the National Center for State Courts, an independent nonprofit organization that assists court officials to better serve the public.

www.ojp.usdoj.gov/bjs. Web site for the Bureau of Justice Statistics that includes information and statistics on a variety of areas, including courts, sentencing, crimes, and victims.

CHAPTER 10

Bureaucracy

What Nobody Wants but Everybody Needs

A swimming pool is not what usually springs to mind when you mention bureaucracy. Public agencies, however, come in many shapes and forms, including parks and recreation departments that are responsible for maintaining swimming pools. Publicly run pools, believe it or not, fit right into the formal definition of a bureaucracy.

10

Why do we have so much bureaucracy?

How good—or bad—a job does it really do?

How does technology enable more efficient and effective bureaucracy?

For Avigayil Wardein, setting up a lemonade stand was a way to earn a little pocket money and maybe learn a few business basics. She earned a little pocket money all right, but ended up learning more about bureaucracy than business.

In summer 2003, the six-year-old set up shop at the end of her mom's driveway in Naples, Florida. She quickly began attracting business from thirsty passersby. Within days, however, the police arrived to shut Avigayil down. In Naples, city regulations require a permit for all temporary businesses. Avigayil had not gone to the appropriate agency, filled out the necessary forms, and paid the required $35 permit fee. Because this temporary business permit expires as soon as a vendor shuts down for the day, complying with the rules meant Avigayil was faced with paying $35 per day to satisfy city hall bureaucracy. That was $5 more than her record daily take.

A public agency's ensnaring a six-year-old's lemonade stand in red tape and demanding a daily thirty-five bucks as the price of staying open? One more example, as if we needed it, of everything that is wrong with government bureaucracy, right? Bureaucracy is overbearing, interfering, and a needless complication in citizens' lives, right?

Wrong. In this story, bureaucracy turns out to be more the understanding hero than the heartless villain. Avigayil's lemonade stand was temporarily shut down as the result of a citizen complaint. A neighbor had called city hall and protested the illegal operation of a business. Technically, the complaint was accurate, and the city was legally obligated to respond. An officer was duly dispatched to shut down Avigayil, although he bought a glass of lemonade and was mostly apologetic about the whole process. The city then gave Avigayil a fistful of daily permits—more than enough to keep her business legal for the summer—and waived the fees. She was back in business.[1]

The permits are actually a reasonable rule. They are not designed to shut down lemonade stands run by entrepreneurial elementary school students but, rather, to control temporary vendors like hot dog stands. Left unregulated, the latter could operate anywhere at any time, creating the potential for traffic problems, neighborhood nuisances, and unscrupulous business practices. Avigayil's story highlights bureaucracy's paradoxical nature. On the one hand, it does mean rules and red tape that are inconvenient at best and defy common sense at worst. Yet bureaucracy does not produce or enforce these rules just for kicks. Like it or not, there are good reasons for the rules, and someone wants the bureaucracy to enforce them.

Bureaucracy represents what is perhaps the political system's greatest contradiction. We do not particularly like it, yet we seem unable to live without it. Like a trip to the dentist, bureaucracy often is inconvenient, involves too much paperwork, and can result in a certain amount of pain. Ultimately, however, it turns out to be good for us.

This chapter explores this workhorse of the U.S. political system—the state and local bureaucracies that implement and manage most public programs and services. We discuss what bureaucracy is and why it plays such an important role. Most important, we use the comparative method to arrive at some explanation of why the American political system has so much bureaucracy when many citizens seem to value it so little.

What Is Bureaucracy?

For our purposes, **bureaucracy** is the public agencies and the public programs and services that these agencies implement and manage. Thus, **bureaucrats** are simply the employees of the public agencies. These agencies—generically known as government bureaucracies—usually are located in the executive branches of state and local governments. Although these agencies are very different in terms of the programs and services they manage and deliver, the vast majority of them are organizationally very similar. There is a specific set of organizational characteristics associated with bureaucracy:

Division of labor. Labor is divided according to task and function. Most large bureaucracies, for example, have separate technical, personnel, and financial specialists.

Hierarchy. There is a clear vertical chain of command. Authority is concentrated at the top and flows down from superiors to subordinates.

Formal rules. Bureaucracies are impartial rather than impulsive. They operate on the basis of rationally formulated guidelines and standardized operating procedures.

Maintenance of files and records. Bureaucracies record their actions.

Professionalization. Employees of bureaucratic organizations get their jobs on the basis of qualification and merit.[2]

Virtually all large, complex organizations have these characteristics, not just government agencies. Wal-Mart and IBM have these characteristics and can thus be considered bureaucratic organizations, even though they are private companies. What separates a public bureaucracy like the Department of Motor Vehicles or the local school district from a private bureaucracy like IBM is a difference in goals. In the end, what separates public bureaucracies from private bureaucracies is not what they are, but what they do.

BUREAUCRACY
Public agencies and the programs and services that they implement and manage.

BUREAUCRATS
Employees of public agencies.

PROFESSIONALIZATION
Bureaucratic employees earn their jobs based on qualifications and merit.

What Does Bureaucracy Do?

Public bureaucracies play two fundamental roles in state and local political systems. First, they are the key administrators in the democratic process. They are charged with carrying out the decisions and instructions of elected public officials. This is the central focus of the academic discipline of public administration. Their second role is more controversial. Bureaucracies not only carry out the decisions of the democratic process; as it turns out, they have a fairly important say in what those decisions are.

Bureaucracy as Policy Implementer

The first job of bureaucracy is to be the active manifestation of the will of the state. This is just a fancy way of saying that bureaucracy does what the government wants or needs done.[3] The whole process is known as **policy implementation**. Agencies implement policy by issuing grants and contracts, enforcing laws and regulations, or undertaking and managing programs directly. For example, when elected officials decide to build a new road, they do not adjourn the legislature to go survey land, drive bulldozers, and lay asphalt. It is a public agency that negotiates to buy and survey the land. It is the agency that either issues the contracts to build the road or takes on the job of construction using its own employees and equipment. This is what makes private and public bureaucracy different: IBM and Wal-Mart exist to make money, whereas public agencies exist to serve the public interest by turning the decisions of elected officials into concrete reality.

It is a job staggering in its scope and complexity. Citizens ask government for a lot: roads, education, health benefits, safe drinking water, parks, reliable power grids—the list is virtually endless. Governments respond by passing laws that create programs or policies, which then must be put into action and then managed or enforced. Governments respond, in other words, with bureaucracy. State and local bureaucracies manage not only state and local programs but federal programs as well. The federal government relies on state and local agencies to implement the vast majority of its welfare, education, and highway programs.[4]

In their roles as implementers, managers, and enforcers, state and local government bureaucracies shape the day-to-day lives of citizens more than any other part of government.[5] The single largest form of bureaucracy in the United States is a fundamental part of virtually every community: public schools. Employing more than 3 million teachers, public schools serve almost 50 million students and have a combined budget of $477 billion.[6]

POLICY IMPLEMENTATION

The process of taking the expressed wishes of government and translating them into action.

> Citizens ask government for a lot: roads, education, health benefits, safe drinking water, parks, reliable power grids—the list is virtually endless. Governments respond by passing laws that create programs or policies, which then must be put into action and then managed or enforced.

Other public agencies regulate and set the licensing requirements for professions ranging from lawyers to bartenders. Think of the need to ensure that professionals are qualified to deliver the services they sell. Look around at all the public libraries, swimming pools, and parks that offer recreational and educational opportunities at little or no cost. Think of programs for garbage removal, law enforcement, and fire protection. From the barber who is licensed to cut our hair to the street sweeper who is hired to clean the paths we walk, bureaucracy literally covers us from our heads to our toes.

Inside Erie County, New York, there are three cities; twenty-five towns; fifteen villages; and almost one thousand special fire, sewer, and lighting districts.

Bureaucracy as Policymaker

The second fundamental role of the bureaucracy is more controversial than its job as the government's agent of implementation. Public bureaucracies not only help translate the will of a government into action, in many instances they actually determine the will of the government. Put bluntly, bureaucracies do not just do policy; they also make it.[7] They do this in at least three ways.

The first way is through what has been called the power of the street-level bureaucrat. **Street-level bureaucrats** are the lower-level public employees who actually take the actions that represent government law or policy. In many cases, street-level bureaucrats have the discretion, or ability, to make choices about what actions they do or do not take. In making these choices, they are essentially making policy. For example, the street-level bureaucrat associated with speed limits is the traffic cop. This public employee is actually on the highway with a radar gun making certain that motorists abide by the speed limits specified by state or local law. The legislature may have passed a law setting a maximum highway speed of 65 miles per hour, but if the traffic cop decides to go after only those motorists doing 75 miles per hour or faster, what really is the speed limit that motorists must obey? And who has set that limit? Arguably, it is not the legislature but, rather, the street-level bureaucrat.[8]

This is not to suggest that street-level bureaucrats are power-hungry tyrants. In many cases, they have no choice but to make choices. On a road on which speeding is common, it may be impossible to stop every leadfoot. Doesn't it make more sense to concentrate on the most flagrant offenders who pose the most risks? Street-level bureaucrats have to balance the goals, laws, and regulations relevant to their agencies with the practical demands of the day-to-day situations they deal with. That often means making, not just implementing, policy.

The second way in which bureaucracies make policy is through rulemaking. **Rulemaking** is the process by which laws or mandates approved by legislatures are turned into detailed written instructions on what public agencies will or will not do.[9] Rules are necessary because most laws passed by legislatures express intention, but they do not specify the details of how

STREET-LEVEL BUREAUCRATS

Lower-level public agency employees who actually take the actions that represent law or policy.

RULEMAKING

The process of translating laws into written instructions on what public agencies will or will not do.

to make that intention a reality. For example, the Nebraska state legislature created the Nebraska Games and Parks Commission to enforce a number of laws relating to hunting, fishing, wildlife preservation, and boating. The details of enforcing those laws—such as setting permit fees, determining bag limits for particular types of fish, and designating no-wake zones on lakes—are rules established by the commission rather than laws passed by the legislature. This makes sense. The legislature would quickly become bogged down if it had to delve into the myriad details that must be addressed to put a public program into action. These details are left to individual agencies.

Once a rule is approved, it typically becomes part of a state's administrative code, which is the bureaucratic equivalent of state statutes. These rules have the force of law—violate them and you could face fines. Just ask anyone who has ever been caught fishing without a license. Given this, rules are not left to the discretion of the street-level bureaucrat. Most state agencies have to follow a well-defined process for making rules. This process includes seeking input from agency experts, holding public hearings, and, perhaps, listening to special interests. The Nebraska Games and Parks Commission is required to give public notice of any intention to create a rule and must hold a public hearing to allow interested parties to have their say. If this sounds a lot like the process of making laws in a legislature, it is. Rulemaking is probably the most important political activity of bureaucracy. In effect, it is a large lawmaking operation that most citizens do not even know exists.

Cutting Red Tape? Most people do not associate barbers or beauticians with bureaucracy. Yet most barbers must be licensed and regulated by state and/or local government.

Finally, bureaucracies also contribute to policymaking directly by pursuing political agendas. Street-level discretion and rulemaking are *passive* policymaking in the sense that they involve bureaucrats' responding or not responding to something such as a speeding car or a newly signed bill. Yet bureaucracies and bureaucrats also take *active* roles in politics. This is done in a number of ways. At the state and local levels, the heads of many public agencies are elected. Such positions include everything from county sheriff to state attorney general. As elected officials, these agency heads often make campaign promises, and once in office, they try to get their agencies to deliver on them.

The visibility and importance of these elected state and local agency heads have increased with the rise of New Federalism. They now are widely recognized as critical players in the process of policy formulation, not just policy implementation.[10]

Therefore, some agencies will be the tools used to deliver on a political agenda. It is also true that other bureaucrats, not just elected agency heads, try to influence policy. As we will see later in this chapter, unions are powerful political actors in many states, lobbying for better pay and benefits and getting actively involved in election campaigns.

The implementation and political roles of bureaucracy make it a particular target for citizen concern and, at times, scorn. It is easy to see that we need some bureaucracy. Somebody has to manage all those programs and services we want from government. Yet government bureaucracy has a terrible reputation for inefficiency, incompetence, and mismanagement.[11] Many question whether we have too much bureaucracy, and still others are concerned about the powerful political role of what are mostly unelected officials. Why do we have so much bureaucracy? How good of a job does it really do? Could we get by with less of it? Is there a better way to run public programs and services? Is there too much bureaucracy and too little democracy in state and local government? These are reasonable questions that the comparative method can help answer.

What Is "Enough" Bureaucracy?

Most people believe that, whatever its merits, there is too much bureaucracy in government and in our lives. Undeniably, state and local governments have a lot of bureaucracy. How much? Some insight into the size and scope of state and local agencies can be gleaned from Table 10-1, which lists the number of employees on state and local government payrolls by function. Combined, state and local governments have more than 19 million full-time and part-time employees. Most of these—approximately 14 million versus 5 million—are employees of local rather than state government.[12] Whether at the local or state level, the vast majority of these individuals work in what we would recognize as a bureaucracy.

The numbers contained in Table 10-1 confirm that there are a lot of state and local bureaucrats, but numbers alone give little insight into whether there is too much or too little bureaucracy. In reality, the size of the bureaucracy and the extent of its role in the day-to-day life of any given individual vary from state to state and locality to locality for two main reasons. First, in each locality, citizens make different kinds of demands on each state and local government agency. Some localities need more of one particular resource, whereas others need less. In Eden Prairie, Minnesota, the public demands more cross-country ski trails, and in Yuma, Arizona, it needs more public swimming pools. As a result, the size and role of the public sector can vary significantly from place to place—more demand equals more bureaucracy.

Second, there is no universally agreed on yardstick for measuring what constitutes a "reasonably" sized bureaucracy. Where one person sees a

TABLE 10-1

State and Local Government Employment by Function

Function	Total Individuals (in thousands)	State Government (in thousands)	Local Government (in thousands)
Elementary and secondary education	7,823	59	7,764
Higher education	2,896	2,335	561
Hospitals	1,006	421	585
Police protection	993	106	887
Corrections	730	472	258
Streets and highways	567	242	325
Public welfare	537	237	300
Other government administration	448	175	274
Electric power and gas supply	92	4	88
Judicial and legal	489	60	429
Financial administration	437	174	264
Fire protection	463	0	463
Natural resources	210	161	49
Social insurance	85	85	0
State liquor stores	9	9	0
Other	2,542	588	1,952
All functions	19,327	5,128	14,199

Source: U.S. Census Bureau, *Statistical Abstract of the United States: 2009.*

bloated public sector overregulating citizens' lives, a second sees the same set of agencies providing important public goods and services. At the very least, to compare the size of bureaucracy across states and localities we need to explore not just the total number of public employees but also the size of a specific public sector relative to the size of the public it serves. Table 10-2 shows one way to do this. It lists the states with the five largest and the five smallest bureaucracies as measured by the number of government employees per every 10,000 citizens.

By this measure, the mostly large, urban, and populous states have the *smallest* bureaucracies. More rural, less populous states, conversely, have

TABLE 10-2

States with the Most and the Least Bureaucracy by Number of Employees

State	State Employees (per 10,000 citizens)
Top Five	
Hawaii	602
North Dakota	374
Alaska	372
Delaware	362
New Mexico	314
Bottom Five	
Florida	119
Illinois	122
Pennsylvania	131
California	138
New York	139

Source: U.S. Bureau of Labor Statistics for 2008, as reprinted in *State and Local Sourcebook,* online supplement to *Governing* magazine, 2009.

the *largest* bureaucracies. How can this be? Why would North Dakota have more bureaucracy than California? The answer is actually pretty simple. Fewer people do not necessarily mean less demand on the government. Even the most rural state still needs an educational system, roads, and law enforcement. These are all labor-intensive propositions. Indeed, they may be even more labor intensive in rural states. For example, to serve a widely dispersed population, an educational system either has to build lots of small schools or figure out a way to transport lots of students over considerable distances to a smaller number of large schools. More urban, densely populated states can take advantage of the economies of scale that come with centralized locations. Basically, less bureaucracy is needed where the citizens being served are close by. But whether this will hold true for much longer is uncertain. As this chapter discusses later, governments have spent much of the last decade crunched for cash, and they have saved money by relying on technology to bridge the distances between their offices and those they serve—resulting in a need to pay fewer employees.

The same tale is told when we use expenditures—in this case, the amount of money states spent for services—to measure the size of bureaucracy. Alaska is among the five states with the largest bureaucracies as measured by both number of employees and per capita expenditure. (See Table 10-3.) Not coincidentally, it is also one of only two noncontiguous states—Alaska neighbors Canada rather than the United States, and Hawaii is an island chain in the Pacific. Geographical isolation requires that these states do more for themselves, which means more bureaucracy.

Expenditures and employees tell us something about the size of the bureaucracy, but they do not tell us much about its influence or power over the daily lives of citizens. An undermanned bureaucracy with a small budget still can have considerable impact on the interests of an individual. If you have ever spent time in a university financial aid office, you probably already understand the point here—when people complain about bureaucracy being too big, they often mean the red tape and rules that come with it, not its budget or payroll. For the number of forms you fill out at the financial aid office, you may feel that the bureaucracy owes you a free

TABLE 10-3

States with the Most and the Least Bureaucracy by Expenditures

State	State and Local Expenditures (dollars per capita)
Top Five	
Alaska	15,924
New York	12,499
Wyoming	11,647
California	10,100
Massachusetts	9,622
Bottom Five	
Idaho	6,373
Arkansas	6,587
South Dakota	6,608
Oklahoma	6,699
Missouri	6,775

Source: U.S. Census Bureau, as reprinted in *State and Local Sourcebook,* online supplement to *Governing* magazine, 2009.

meal, but there is only so much money in the pot. It is very easy to recognize this sort of thing as a central part of bureaucracy. It is very hard to measure it objectively. Lacking good measures of "red tape" or "rules" makes it hard to make comparisons. If there are no comparative measures, it is harder to use the comparative method to help show why some bureaucracies have more influence than others.

Despite this, there is little doubt that public bureaucracies in large urban areas probably do have a more powerful role in the day-to-day lives of citizens than those in less populous rural areas. Why? It is not because bureaucracy is more power hungry in cities but, rather, because more concentrated populations require more rules. Building codes are more critical in urban areas because of the associated fire-safety and health risks—a problem with one building can pose risks for those working or living in the surrounding buildings. Building regulations thus tend to be more detailed, and the enforcement of these rules tends to be a higher priority, in urban than in rural areas. In this sense, urban areas do have more bureaucracy than rural areas.

Measuring Bureaucratic Effectiveness: It Does a Better Job than You Think

So far, our application of the comparative method has given us a sense of how big bureaucracy is and why it is so big—because characteristics such as urbanization and geography result in different demands being placed on government. These different demands translate into public agencies of different sizes and with varying levels of involvement in our day-to-day lives. What the comparative method has not told us is how good (or bad) a job public agencies do. The widespread belief is that they are, at best, mediocre managers of public programs and services.[13] Although this negative stereotype is held by many, for the most part it is wrong. Public agencies, as it turns out, are very good at what they do.

How good? Well, in many cases, at least as good as, if not better than, their private sector counterparts. The assumption is that the private sector is more efficient and more effective than the public sector, but numerous studies find this is based more on stereotypes than facts.[14] For example, in the early 1990s, officials in Fort Lauderdale, Florida, decided to shut down the city's pipe-laying operation and instead have the private sector bid on municipal pipe-laying jobs. The idea was to save the city money by getting competitive private-sector bids and eliminating an entire public bureaucracy. A study undertaken by city engineers found that in-house costs for laying pipe were between $68 and $73 per linear foot. Much to everyone's surprise, the initial private-sector bids were up to $130 per linear foot. The city undertook an extensive reorganization of its pipe-laying operations and managed to drop its costs to $43 per linear foot. The private sector responded by cutting its bids in half, into the $50–60 range. Even after these dramatic reductions, however, the private sector still could not do the job as cheaply as the "inefficient" public bureaucracy.

This not only shows that the public sector can be as cost-effective and efficient as the private sector, but it also provides a cautionary tale about the downside of the profit motive. It turns out that the private sector is quite willing to feed at the public trough to fatten its bottom line.[15] There is not much glamour associated with laying utilities, filling potholes, and running public transportation systems, but these are highly valued public services that consume a lot of tax dollars. And contrary to popular perception, public bureaucracies provide these services efficiently and spend these dollars effectively.

It is not just about overall performance. Public agencies come out equal to or better than the private sector on a wide range of employee characteristics used to identify an effective organization. Public- and private-sector employees are roughly equal in terms of their job motivation, their work habits, and their overall competence. Compared to the private sector, however, public-sector employees tend to have higher levels of education, express a greater commitment toward civic duty and public service, abide by more stringent codes of ethical behavior, and be more committed to helping other people.[16] Various studies show that over the past thirty years state and local agencies have become more productive and more professional, and they have done so during an era when they have shouldered an increasing share of the burden for delivering programs and services from the federal government.[17]

There *is* wide variation between and within the states on how well public bureaucracies are managed. Good management has an enormous impact on the capacities and effectiveness of programs and agencies. States that engage in prudent, long-range fiscal planning are better positioned to deal with economic downturns, and they generally can deliver programs more efficiently. States that do a better job of attracting qualified employees with a strong commitment to public service almost certainly are going to be rewarded with more effective public agencies. States that make training their employees a priority are likely to enjoy similar benefits. The bottom line is that well-managed public agencies lower costs and improve results, whereas the reverse is true for badly managed agencies.[18]

Bureaucracies Put to the Test: Who Passes and Who Fails and Why

Which states and localities have the best-run public agencies? The Government Performance Project (GPP) has devoted considerable resources to this question. A project of the Pew Center on the States, the GPP holds state governments publicly accountable for the quality of management within their jurisdictions.[19] It does this by researching management practices and performances in four areas: money, people, infrastructure (roads, bridges, and construction), and information (how states gather, analyze, disseminate, and use information). The GPP then issues grades for performance in

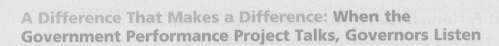

A Difference That Makes a Difference: When the Government Performance Project Talks, Governors Listen

In 2003, Nevada was awarded the dubious distinction of having the worst state tax system in the country, according to a Government Performance Project report, published in *Governing* magazine. The silver state (nicknamed for its silver mines) did few things well when it came to taxes, the vast majority of which were levied on sales and gaming. The system didn't generate enough revenue, was deemed regressive and unfair, and couldn't be adequately administered with the state's existing policies and technology. Nevada earned just one lousy star out of four possible stars for each of these three basic functions. Contrast that evaluation with the magazine's judgment of Hawaii, which received the highest rating for fairness and three of four possible stars in adequacy of revenue.

For Nevada, the report bolstered then governor Kenny Guinn's push for an overhaul of the state's tax system. Although the legislature didn't enact Guinn's exact vision—he called for $1.1 billion in tax increases—later that year, the state House and Senate did approve an $836 million package that instituted state payroll taxes and real estate sales and raised alcohol and cigarette taxes.

For Alabama, also a one-star state, the road to reform was bumpier—and longer. Its rigid tax code, written into the state constitution (which made it next to impossible to change the structure of the system),

provided nowhere near enough revenue to keep the state operating smoothly. What's more, the system was highly regressive, levying income taxes for a family of four beginning at just $4,600, nearly $15,000 below the federal poverty line.

Republican governor Bob Riley was new to his office when the report was issued, but he quickly began advocating a massive $1.2 billion tax reform package. His plan would have reduced taxes for many of the state's poorest residents; however, it was overwhelmingly rejected by a two-to-one margin. The failure didn't deter Riley, who continued to tell whoever would listen about the "immorality" of the state's tax system. In 2006, he returned with a new, smaller tax reform package. This time, the state legislature agreed with the proposal and raised the state income threshold for a family of four to $12,600, the first time it had been raised since 1935. The cut will save Alabamians $60 million a year, with workers earning $20,000 or less annually receiving the bulk of the benefit. No one earning more than $100,000 will be eligible for the tax break.

As Riley was signing the bill into law, he was already gearing up for the next round in his tax fight. But the 2006 tax victory was the governor's only one; a 2008 effort to raise the threshold even further fell short by a single vote in the state Senate.

Sources: Adapted from Katherine Barrett, Richard Greene, Michele Mariani, and Anya Sostek, "The Way We Tax: A 50-State Report," *Governing* magazine, February 2003, available at www.governing.com/gpp/2003/gp3intro.htm; Sean Whaley and Jane Ann Morri, "Guinn Signs Record Tax Increase," *Las Vegas Review-Journal,* July 23, 2003; David White, "Riley Signs Low-Income Tax Cut into Law," *Birmingham News,* April 13, 2006; Philip Rawls, "National Study: Ala. Levies More Income Tax than Any State on Families Living at Poverty Line," Associated Press, November 2, 2008.

each area (see box above). The result is an administrative report card for state governments that is essentially an index of the relative performance of bureaucracy.

Table 10-4 shows the most recent grades issued to the states. The grades show that most state governments are doing at least an acceptable job but that some are clearly doing better than others. These are differences that make a real difference. The quality of public schools and roads, and even the quality of the air we breathe, is dependent in no small measure on the

TABLE 10-4

Government Performance Project, Grades at a Glance, 2008

State	Money	People	Infrastructure	Information	Average Grade
Alabama	C–	B–	C+	C	C+
Alaska	C–	C–	C–	B–	C
Arizona	C+	B–	B–	B–	B–
Arkansas	B–	C–	C+	C–	C
California	D+	C–	B–	C+	C
Colorado	C+	C	C+	C	C+
Connecticut	B–	B–	C+	B–	B–
Delaware	A–	B	B+	B–	B+
Florida	B–	C–	A–	B–	B–
Georgia	B+	A–	B	B+	B+
Hawaii	C+	B–	C	C–	C+
Idaho	B+	C+	B–	C+	B–
Illinois	C–	C–	C	C+	C
Indiana	B+	B	B+	B–	B
Iowa	B+	B+	C+	B+	B
Kansas	B–	C+	C+	B	B–
Kentucky	C+	C+	A–	B	B–
Louisiana	B	B	C+	B+	B
Maine	C	C–	C+	C	C
Maryland	B+	C+	B+	B–	B
Massachusetts	C+	C	D+	C	C
Michigan	C+	B+	A–	A	B+
Minnesota	B+	B–	C+	B	B–
Mississippi	C+	C	C+	C	C+
Missouri	B+	B–	B+	A	B+
Montana	C+	B–	C+	C+	C+
Nebraska	A–	B–	B+	B–	B
Nevada	C+	C–	B–	B–	C+

TABLE 10-4, **continued**

State	Money	People	Infrastructure	Information	Average Grade
New Hampshire	C−	D	D+	D+	D+
New Jersey	C−	B−	C+	C−	C
New Mexico	B−	C	C+	B	B−
New York	C+	B−	B−	C+	B−
North Carolina	B−	B	B−	B−	B−
North Dakota	B	C	B−	C+	B−
Ohio	B	C+	B−	B−	B−
Oklahoma	B−	C+	C−	C	C+
Oregon	C+	C+	C+	B−	C+
Pennsylvania	B	C+	B−	B	B−
Rhode Island	D+	D	C+	C	C−
South Carolina	B−	A−	C−	B−	B−
South Dakota	B+	C+	B	D+	C+
Tennessee	B−	C	B	B	B−
Texas	B	B	B	A−	B+
Utah	A	B+	A	A	A−
Vermont	B−	C+	B+	C−	B−
Virginia	A−	A	B+	A	A−
Washington	A−	A−	B+	A	A−
West Virginia	B	C	C−	C	C+
Wisconsin	C+	B−	B−	C+	B−
Wyoming	B	C+	B	C+	B−

Source: "The Government Performance Project," Pew Center on the States, March 2008.

effectiveness of public bureaucracies.[20] States with better-run bureaucracies provide the best and most effective services and make the most efficient use of taxpayer dollars.

Why are some state and local bureaucracies run better than others? Why does California rate a C, whereas Virginia rates an A-minus? The answers to these questions are found not in the bureaucracy but, rather, in the broader political environment of the states. Ultimately, legislatures and governors are responsible for bureaucratic performance. This is not only because they set the laws that control personnel, management, and training practices; their decisions on a wide range of policy issues have tremendous consequences even for a smoothly running agency. The most obvious example is budgets. States have gone through boom and bust cycles during the past ten years, with economic good times of the 1990s followed by a fiscal crisis shortly after the turn of the century; a few years of prosperity returned before the nation plunged into the worst recession since World War II. Through it all, some states practiced good fiscal management, with legislatures that resisted the temptation to spend excessively and enact large tax cuts. As the economy soured, these states also acted quickly to stabilize revenues.

Other states—like California—did the opposite. These states increased spending during the 1990s and then tried to put off the day of reckoning with creative accounting practices and by dipping into one-time revenue sources. The end result for California was near insolvency—fiscal crises that rocked the public sector, leaving it underfunded, understaffed, and a little shell-shocked, not exactly the ingredients for smoothly running public programs. The comparative method shows us that it is the states that avoided big tax cuts in the 1990s, the states with divided governments in which the governor is from one party and the legislature is controlled by another, and the states with powerful governors that spent less, had better financial management, and had public agencies with higher grades.[21]

Many of the faults attributed to public bureaucracies actually can be traced to legislatures, which give agencies conflicting and confusing missions and often do not provide adequate resources to fulfill these missions. It is the legislatures that demand what is politically expedient, not what is effective or efficient, and then roundly and repeatedly criticize bureaucracy for not performing well. The real surprise is not that some bureaucracies are ineffective or poorly run but that the vast majority of them, most of the time, manage to more or less serve the public interest. And they do so in spite of democratic institutions rather than because of them. At least one professional student of bureaucracy has suggested than any objective view of the joint performance of bureaucracy and representative democracy would lead to the conclusion that what we need is more bureaucracy and less democracy![22]

> The real surprise is not that some bureaucracies are ineffective or poorly run but that the vast majority of them, most of the time, manage to more or less serve the public interest. And they do so in spite of democratic institutions rather than because of them.

That sentiment has taken real shape in some states in the form of increased performance auditing designed to improve the efficiency and effectiveness of government programs. "That's where you find out if money is being spent the way it is supposed to, or whether you're getting the most bang for the buck," says former Colorado state representative Brad Young.[23]

Past perceptions of auditors pegged them as glorified bean counters, but in some states, their independent reports carry significant weight. California's nonpartisan Legislative Analyst's Office has served as a model for other states,[24] and strong legislative support kept Florida's Office of Program Policy Analysis and Government Accountability operating despite multiple efforts by Gov. Jeb Bush to downsize the office.[25] In Washington state, even the citizens see the benefits of performance audits; voters there approved a 2005 ballot initiative that increased the state auditor's authority to study state and local agency performance.

Is There a Better Way to Run Public Programs and Services?

Looking at bureaucracy comparatively, we learn how big it really is, why it is so big, and how well it performs. But is a traditional bureaucracy really the best way to run public programs and services? Do we really need less democracy and more bureaucracy? Do we really need 19 million people on the state and local government payrolls? The short answer is no. Public services and programs could be delivered through competitive bidding by the private sector. Public agencies could be staffed and run by political party loyalists or special interest supporters. Things could be done differently. Before abandoning the traditional public bureaucracy, however, it is worth considering why public agencies are so, well, bureaucratic.

Remember the key characteristics of bureaucratic organizations listed earlier? These turn out to be important advantages when it comes to running public programs and services. For one thing, bureaucracies tend to be impartial because they operate using formal rules, not partisan preference, bribes, or arbitrary judgment. If you need some form of license or permit, if your shop is subject to some form of environmental or business regulation, or if you are trying to receive benefits from a public program, it does not matter to the bureaucracy if you are rich or poor, liberal or conservative, an influential high-roller or an average citizen. What matters to the bureaucracy are the rules that define the application process, eligibility, and delivery of the necessary service or program. Following bureaucratic rules can be maddening, but these rules do help ensure that public agencies are more or less impartial.

The bureaucratic characteristics of hierarchy and record keeping help hold public agencies accountable. Public agencies are expected to be answerable for their actions. They have to justify why they did what they did to legislatures, executives, the courts, and citizens.[26] An action at a lower level of bureaucracy almost always can be appealed to a higher level. Students at most colleges and universities, for example, can appeal their grades. In such appeals, the bureaucrat responsible for issuing the grade—the instructor—is expected to justify to the appeals board and the dean why the grade represents a fair and reasonable application of the rules of the class and the grading policies of the university. Setting rules, requiring records, and setting up a clear chain of authority help ensure that bureaucrats and bureaucracies do

The Commonwealth of Virginia receives gold stars for its bureaucracy—it was one of the three top-ranked states (Utah and Washington were the others) in the most recent ratings conducted by the Government Performance Project. Part of what puts Virginia at the top of the class is the state's practice of holding the more than one hundred cabinet members and agency heads accountable to formal "executive agreements." These are reviewed by the governor and outline clear measurable goals for each agency against which its performance is appraised. Yearly public assessments of each agency are available online.

These scorecards evaluate performance in human resource management, government procurement, financial management, technology, and emergency preparedness. In effect, this is an assessment of those agencies' leaders and their subordinates. The table here shows only a portion of the scorecard for Virginia's executive agencies for 2009 and includes ratings for agencies in the Offices of Administration, Commerce and Trade, Education, Finance, Health and Human Services, and Public Safety. Overall, ten of the fifty-three rated agencies met expectations in every category. The remaining forty-three were rated as needing to make progress in at least one area, including five that were rated as below expectations in at least one area.

Virginia's Executive Branch Agencies 2009 Scorecard

Legend:

M = Meets Expectations   P = Progress toward Expectations   B = Below Expectations   U = Results Unavailable

Agency	Secretariat	Emergency Preparedness	Financial Management	Government Procurement	Human Resources	Information Technology
Compensation Board	Administration	M	M	M	M	P
Department of General Services	Administration	M	M	M	M	P
Department of Human Resource Management	Administration	P	M	M	M	M
Department of Minority Business Enterprise	Administration	M	P	P	M	B
State Board of Elections	Administration	U	P	M	U	U
Department of Business Assistance	Commerce and Trade	B	P	M	M	M
Department of Housing & Community Development	Commerce and Trade	M	M	M	P	P
Department of Labor & Industry	Commerce and Trade	M	M	M	M	M
Department of Mines, Minerals & Energy	Commerce and Trade	M	M	M	M	M
Department of Professional & Occupational Regulation	Commerce and Trade	P	M	M	M	P

E-Government

The history of reform shows the difficulty in coming up with a viable alternative to traditional bureaucracy. This does not mean, however, that bureaucracy is not changing. Indeed, it is changing in fundamental ways. Perhaps the best example of this is how public agencies use information technology. The changes in technology are creating **e-government**, "the delivery of information and services online via the Internet or other digital means."[40] All fifty states and most local governments now have e-government operations that allow citizens to do everything from applying for hunting licenses to submitting small business applications to filing their taxes.[41] Some states, responding to an increasingly virtual society, have taken electronic interaction with citizens a step further by using RSS feeds, webcasts, and podcasts to disseminate information, and they send urgent information, such as Amber Alerts, through e-mail or text messages.[42]

There are a number of key advantages to e-government. It is convenient for citizens (no more waiting in lines) and for governments (shorter lines to deal with). It may promote political participation by facilitating communication between the public and elected officials. A good example of this is the attempt by numerous states, especially in the Southwest, to make all of their Web sites available in Spanish as well as English to make it easier for nonnative speakers to get the information they need. In Texas, all state government Web sites can be accessed in Spanish simply by clicking "En Español."[43] Governments also hope that e-government will allow them to deliver information, public programs, and public services cheaper and faster, and as their budgets deteriorated in 2008 and 2009, a number of state and local agencies began charging higher fees for conducting some services like renewing a driver's license in person rather than online.

States and localities, however, differ widely in their use of technology. A key indicator of the commitment to e-government is the extent to which the Web sites allow transactions. In 2008, 89 percent of government sites offered online services, up from 21 percent eight years earlier; 33 percent of sites accepted credit cards to complete transactions. But just 13 percent were set up for digital signatures.[44] Why are some state and local governments more techno-savvy than others? The most important factor explaining the differences in e-government reform seems to be the professionalism of the state government. Wealthier, more urban states also are more likely to be e-government innovators.[45] Several organizations, including Brown University, the Brookings Institution, and the Center for Digital Government, conduct periodic studies of governments' use of—and skill using—e-government. The groups assess different aspects of state and local governments' use of the Internet, but they all note a tremendous growth in e-government in the early years of the twenty-first century.[46]

Unlike many other reform movements, the rise of e-government does seem to be bringing about important and permanent changes in the administrative arm of government. It is changing how people interact with government, changing their expectations of government, and changing how public agencies are run. For example, in the virtual world there are no boundaries between agencies—they are just a mouse click away. This is forcing those agencies to rethink how they work together. When you make it easier to do business with government online, one of the typical results is an increase in the workload of agency personnel. This can force a rethinking of who does what and why in a public agency. Management reform fads have had a very mixed impact on bureaucracy, but the shift toward e-government has brought broad changes that are here to stay.

Conclusion

Although bureaucracy is often despised and disparaged, it is also clear that government bureaucracy is underestimated and does not get the credit it actually deserves. A wide range of state and local agencies support and deliver the programs and services that make up our social and economic life as we know it. The comparative method shows us that bureaucracy is big— but only as big as we want it to be. If we want less bureaucracy, we can choose to make fewer demands on government. The comparative method also shows that, for the most part, these bureaucracies do their jobs remarkably well. In contrast to the popular stereotype, most public agencies tackle difficult jobs that are unlikely to be done better by any other alternative. Perhaps the most astonishing thing about bureaucracy is how much we take it for granted. Public schools, safe drinking water, working utility grids, and roads are simply there. We rarely contemplate what an astounding administrative and logistical feat is required to make these aspects of everyday life appear so mundane.

Yet, although bureaucracy almost certainly deserves more praise than criticism, there is cause for concern. Its growing role and responsibilities have raised worries about the power that administrative agencies wield in a democratic society. Changes such as the rise of new information technology are forcing bureaucracy to change with the times. The high cost of public services and an ongoing debate about what government should do is shifting more of what was traditionally considered public administration toward the private sector.

Bureaucratic reform movements, at least in some ways, should be viewed with skepticism. Criticizing the bureaucracy is a traditional sport in American politics, and a lot of reforms turn out to be little more than fads that quickly fade when the pleasing rhetoric meets the real-life challenge of delivering the goods. Some reforms, like the rise of the merit system and of e-government, can radically reshape what bureaucracy is and what it does. One thing, however, will almost certainly remain constant. Whatever the government is, and whatever it does, it will rely on bureaucracy to get it done.

Key Concepts

affirmative action (p. 403)

bureaucracy (p. 381)

bureaucrats (p. 381)

collective bargaining (p. 402)

e-government (p. 409)

merit systems (p. 400)

neutral competence (p. 400)

patronage (p. 399)

policy implementation (p. 382)

professionalization (p. 381)

representative bureaucracy
   (p. 404)

rulemaking (p. 383)

seniority (p. 403)

spoils system (p. 399)

street-level bureaucrats (p. 383)

Suggested Readings

Goodsell, Charles. *The Case for Bureaucracy: A Public Administration Polemic.* 4th ed. Washington, D.C.: CQ Press, 2004. A classic argument for why bureaucracy works and why it does not deserve its negative reputation.

Kerwin, Cornelius M. *Rulemaking: How Government Agencies Write Law and Make Policy.* 3rd ed. Washington, D.C.: CQ Press, 2003. A comprehensive look at rulemaking and bureaucracy.

Lipsky, Michael. *Street-Level Bureaucracy.* New York: Russell Sage Foundation, 1980. A classic work examining the policymaking role of the street-level bureaucrat.

Walters, Jonathan. *Measuring Up 2.0: Governing's New, Improved Guide to Performance Measurement for Geniuses (and Other Public Managers).* Washington, D.C.: Governing Books, 2007. A look at real-world performance measurement and management efforts in states and cities.

Suggested Web Sites

www.aspanet.org. Official Web site of the American Society for Public Administration, the largest professional association for those who work for or study public agencies.

www.governing.com. Web version of *Governing* magazine, which is dedicated to covering state and local issues. Includes numerous stories and other resources on agency leaders and performance, e-government, and more.

www.pewcenteronthestates.org. Home to the Government Performance Project, including online results and additional information about government effectiveness and efficiency.

CHAPTER 11

Local Government

Function Follows Form

Ancient Greeks pledged allegiance to their city, not to any nation-state. There are plenty of people who still make a formal commitment to serve local government, including police officers and firefighters. Pictured here is the graduation ceremony of the 36th Alaska Law Enforcement Training class; these individuals will go on to work as municipal police officers and fire marshals and in other law enforcement posts in towns and cities across Alaska.

Why do local governments vary so much within and between states?

How and why have local governments changed over the years?

What are the positive and negative aspects of Dillon's Rule?

How has the Great Recession affected local governments?

11

Ancient Greeks did not pledge allegiance to ancient Greece. At that time and place, the nation-state as we know it didn't really exist. Instead of the nation-state, the patriotic loyalty and civic duty of the Greeks was oriented toward city-states, such as Athens and Sparta. And, boy, did the Greeks take their civic duty seriously.

The Athenian Oath was recited by the citizens of Athens more than two thousand years ago and is still cited as a model code for civic responsibility. Citizens who took this oath pledged, "We will never bring disgrace on this our City by an act of dishonesty or cowardice. . . . We will revere and obey the City's laws, and will do our best to incite a like reverence and respect in those above us who are prone to annul them or set them at naught."[1]

Americans don't quite reach that level of civic commitment to their cities, but attitudes toward local government in the twenty-first century are not as far off from the Greek ideal as you might imagine. The United States has a long tradition of strong local government, which is unsurprising given the political system's founding principles of division and decentralization of power. Woven tightly into the country's political fabric is a mistrust of centralized power, and Americans generally prefer to keep government as close as possible to citizens, where they can keep an eye on it.

Government does not get any closer than local government—the cities, counties, and other political jurisdictions that exist at the substate level. It is this level of government that Americans tend to trust the most, and it is this level of government that citizens generally want to have more rather than less power. One survey, for example, found that roughly a third of citizens believe local government gives them the most for their money. In these sort of bang-for-buck assessments, local governments trump state and federal governments, which suggests that Americans, as a general rule, prefer, value, and trust government down at the grassroots level.[2] Given those beliefs, it is thus somewhat paradoxical that local government is, technically speaking, the weakest level of government of all. The federal government and state governments are sovereign powers, equal partners in the federal system that draw their powers from their citizens. Pull a state out of the federal system and view it independently, however, and what you find is not a federal system but a unitary system. (See Figure 11-1.) Hierarchically speaking, as discussed in some depth in this chapter, states are superior to local governments. Local governments are not sovereign; they can exercise only the powers granted to them from the central authority of the states.

Governing States and Localities

FIGURE 11-1 Substate "Unitary" System

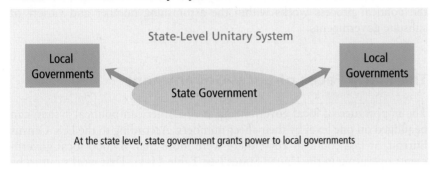

State-Level Unitary System

Local Governments ← State Government → Local Governments

At the state level, state government grants power to local governments

An individual state, however, is a strange sort of unitary system. Whereas a state government is clearly the seat of power, below the state is an astonishing number and variety of political jurisdictions, many of them piled on top of one another and related to one another in no clear organizational fashion. Many of them operate independently of each other even when they occupy the same geographical space and provide services to the same citizens. For example, a city and a school district may overlap each other entirely, but have different governance structures, different leaders, and different purposes. One of these governments is not the boss of the other; the city cannot tell the school district what its tax rate should be any more than the school district can tell the city to build another library.

It is down here in the crazy quilt of local governments that much of the grunt work of the political system takes place. Local governments provide law enforcement, roads, health services, parks, libraries, and schools; they are mostly responsible for regulating (or even providing) utilities, such as sewer and water; they run airports, public transportation systems, mosquito control programs, and community recreation centers. The list goes on. And on. Collectively they represent the public services we encounter most in our daily lives, generally take for granted, and almost certainly could not get along without. No wonder citizens tend to think that local governments give them good value for the money (well, at least compared to what they get from state and federal governments).

Local governments, however, go well beyond just providing services. They must make political and philosophical decisions that affect their residents' quality of life and reinforce values. Many citizens believe local governments have an obligation to provide a safety net for the poor, strike a balance between the need for sufficient revenues and public resistance to high taxation, and referee disputes over land-use planning that pit, say, developers against environmentalists or middle-income homeowners against low-income renters.

In short, local governments are worth getting to know. This chapter examines the powers, responsibilities, and specific forms of local government; how and why these forms evolved; how they differ by state and region; and how the political process works within the astonishing number and variety of substate governments.

The Many Faces of Local Government

The importance of local governments to the American political system can be judged on one level by their sheer numbers. According to the U.S. Census Bureau, at last count in 2007 there were more than 89,000 local governments operating in the United States (see Table 11-1). That works out to be roughly one local government for every 3,450 people.[3]

What form these local governments take, what responsibilities and powers they exercise, and how many of a particular kind exist in a given geographical or demographic area vary wildly from state to state. The number of local governments within a state's boundaries, for example, depends on a state's history, culture, and administrative approach to service delivery. New England states have a tradition of active civic participation and social spending that accommodates a large number of local governing units. By contrast, the South has much less of a tradition of civic engagement in local government, and even today a relatively small number of powerful county leaders dominate such services as school governance.

In terms of differences, local governments make state governments look like they were all stamped from the same cookie cutter. Take the average of 3,450 people for each local government. That number can be misleading because local governments are not evenly spread out demographically. Hawaii has relatively few local governments. It has no incorporated municipalities, just four counties, and the consolidated city-county government of Honolulu. Georgia, on the other hand, has 154 counties, and all of them are vested with municipal-like powers. The city of New York is the largest city in the United States, with a resident population of more than 8 million. The city of Hove Mobile Park, North Dakota, has a population of two. No that's not a typo. As of the last census, Hove Mobile was an incorporated municipality whose population consisted of an elderly married couple living in a trailer park.[4]

Local governments are not evenly spread out geographically, either. They range from villages covering less than a square mile to counties that cover nearly 125,000 square miles. Within or adjacent to their borders may be mountains, deserts, beaches, urban centers, or vast stretches of nothingness. These differences help explain why some local governments are interested in maintaining subways and others worry about maintaining clean beaches.

Political and cultural traditions also vary at the local level. For instance, the degree of loyalty that citizens display toward a local governing entity often depends on whether they personally identify with the area or whether

TABLE 11-1

Number of Government Units, Ranked by State and Type

State	All Government	County	Municipal	Township	School Districts	All Special Districts
Illinois	6,994	102	1,299	1,432	912	3,249
Pennsylvania	4,871	66	1,016	1,546	515	1,728
Texas	4,835	254	1,463	—	1,082	2,291
California	4,344	57	478	—	1,102	2.765
Kansas	3,931	104	627	1,353	316	1,531
Missouri	3,723	114	952	312	536	1,809
Ohio	3,702	88	938	1,308	668	700
Minnesota	3,526	87	854	1,788	341	456
New York	3,403	57	618	929	680	1,119
Indiana	3,231	91	567	1,008	293	1,272
Wisconsin	3,058	72	592	1,197	441	756
Michigan	2,983	83	533	1,242	579	456
Nebraska	2,659	93	530	454	288	1,294
North Dakota	2,699	53	357	1,320	198	771
Colorado	2,416	62	270	—	180	1,904
South Dakota	1,983	66	309	916	166	1664
Iowa	1,954	99	947	—	380	528
Oklahoma	1,880	77	594	—	567	642
Washington	1,845	39	281	—	296	1,525
Florida	1,623	66	411	—	95	1,051
Arkansas	1,548	75	502	—	247	724
Oregon	1,546	36	242	—	234	1,034
Georgia	1,439	154	535	—	180	570
Kentucky	1,346	118	419	—	175	634
New Jersey	1,383	21	324	242	549	247

continued

TABLE 11-1, continued

State	All Government	County	Municipal	Township	School Districts	All Special Districts
Alabama	1,185	67	458	—	131	529
Idaho	1,240	44	200	—	116	880
Montana	1,273	54	129	—	332	758
Mississippi	1,000	82	296	—	164	458
North Carolina	963	100	548	—	—	315
Tennessee	928	92	347	—	14	475
New Mexico	863	33	101	—	96	633
Massachusetts	861	5	45	306	82	423
Maine	850	16	22	466	98	248
Vermont	733	14	45	237	293	144
Wyoming	726	23	99	—	55	549
South Carolina	698	46	268	—	85	299
West Virginia	663	55	232	—	55	321
Arizona	645	15	90	—	301	239
Utah	599	29	242	—	40	288
Connecticut	649	—	30	149	17	453
New Hampshire	545	10	13	221	164	137
Virginia	511	95	229	—	1	187
Louisiana	526	60	303	—	68	95
Delaware	338	3	57	—	19	259
Maryland	256	23	157	—	—	76
Nevada	198	16	19	—	17	146
Alaska	177	14	148	—	—	15
Rhode Island	134	—	8	31	4	91
Hawaii	19	4	1	—	—	15

Source: U.S. Census Bureau, *Census of Governments,* available at www.census.gov/govs/cog/GovOrgTab03ss.html.

Strong attachments to localities are not unusual. New Yorkers love New York, of course, but the sentiment is familiar to any long (or even not-so-long) resident of virtually any city in the United States. These attachments are reflected in public attitudes toward government; local government tends to be more trusted than higher levels of government.

they ignore their membership and regard the area as an artificial construct. Put another way, a Manhattanite probably feels more community pride than, say, a user of the Buncombe County, North Carolina, Metropolitan Sewer District.

All these differences provide multiple opportunities to put the comparative method into practice, but they also can be confusing. Local authority, for example, overlaps—school districts sprawl across municipalities, which, in turn, are covered by counties. A couple may plan on getting married in the city of Chapel Hill, North Carolina, but their marriage certificate will carry the insignia of Orange County, North Carolina. That is because in most states the power to grant marriage licenses is vested in counties, not in cities. Adding to the confusion, the units of government at the substate level vary in their duties and obligations from state to state. Depending on where you live, you may rely on a different set of authorities to get a pothole filled on your street, arrange for a stop sign to be installed at a dangerous intersection, or register your opinion on a bond issue for a new high school.

Despite all these differences, however, there are only three general forms of local government in the United States: **counties, municipalities,** and **special districts.** Counties traditionally are viewed as geographical and administrative subdivisions of states. The exact definition of a municipality varies from state to state, although municipalities generally are political units that are distinguished geographically from counties by being more compact and distinguished legally by being independent corporations rather than "branch offices" of the state government. Special districts cover a huge

COUNTIES

Geographical subdivisions of state government.

MUNICIPALITIES

Political jurisdictions, such as cities, villages, or towns, incorporated under state law to provide governance to a defined geographical area; more compact and more densely populated than counties.

SPECIAL DISTRICTS

Local governmental units created for a single purpose, such as water distribution.

range of local governments. Typically, special districts are single-purpose governments. Unlike counties and cities, which are general purpose governments, special districts usually are created to provide a specific public service rather than a range of services. School districts are a good example. These are geographically defined local units of government created to provide educational services. Other special districts include water management and sewage treatment districts.

The Organization and Responsibilities of Local Governments

Even within each of the three basic categories of local government, there is considerable variation in organizational structure, autonomy, and responsibilities. These categories are distinct enough, however, to wrangle those more than 89,000 local governments in the United States into a general understanding of what local governments are and why they take on the forms they do.

Between the County Lines

To find out what county government is all about, it would be instructive to take a trip to your local county courthouse. There you are likely to find signs pointing you toward a variety of self-explanatory government offices: district attorney, coroner, sheriff, treasurer, and the like. You also may find signs for offices whose purposes are not quite so self evident. President Harry Truman once walked into the courthouse in Allegheny, Pennsylvania, and was taken aback by one of the signs he saw. "What the hell is a prothonotary?" he famously asked. Well, a prothonotary, Mr. President, is the chief record keeper of a civil court. Truman's bewilderment over this obscure county office encapsulates some of the confusion over what county government is and what it does. People might be asked to vote on a prothonotary come election time, but chances are only a small minority knows what the heck a prothonotary is or why the position is necessary.[5]

In your particular courthouse the prothonotary might travel under a less mysterious title, such as clerk of the civil court. Regardless, however, the office of prothonotary points out what county government is often about: the unglamorous, but undoubtedly necessary, administration of central (that is, state) government functions. Civil courts and criminal courts for the most part function under the framework of state rather than county authority. Yet at the county courthouse the court's record keeper, prosecutor, and judge are typically county-level elective offices. It is the county government that represents the local face of the central government.

The unglamorous utilitarian governing unit known as the county grew out of a thousand-year-old tradition brought over from England, where it was known as the shire. (Many English counties still carry this suffix; one of the authors of this book was born in the county of Oxfordshire.) In the United States, counties "are nothing more than certain portions of the territory into which the state is divided for the more convenient exercise of the powers of government," wrote U.S. Supreme Court chief justice Roger B. Taney, in *Maryland ex. rel. Washington County v. Baltimore & Ohio Railroad Co.* (1845).[6] Centralizing day-to-day governance for an entire state in the state capital simply was, and largely still is, impractical. Thus, states divided themselves into smaller geographical units—counties—and created a governance structure within each to provide a local "branch office" of the state government.

Called parishes in Louisiana and boroughs in Alaska, more than three thousand counties are drawn on the maps of the remaining forty-eight states. How many county governments reside within a state varies wildly. Rhode Island and Connecticut are the only states that have no county governments (as more geographically compact states, they have less need for such administrative subunits of state governments). Some states have just a handful. Delaware, for example, has only three counties. Supporting the claim that everything is bigger in Texas, the state has 254 counties, the most in the nation.

Geographically speaking, counties are typically the largest local governments, although, like their numbers, their sizes can vary enormously. Arlington County, Virginia, covers 42 square miles, which is on the smallish side. North Slope Borough, Alaska, encompasses 142,224 (mostly uninhabited) square miles. Measured by population, counties range from 9.8 million in Los Angeles County, California, to forty-two people in Loving County, Texas.[7] (See Tables 11-2 and 11-3.)

Because they generally cover the largest geographical territory, counties bear much of the burden of providing services widely, if not lavishly. The majority of the million citizens in California's Sacramento County, for example, live in unincorporated territory. This means that their property is not part of any city, town, or township that can provide municipal services. Hence, the burden falls on the county to provide these residents with such services as law enforcement, parks and recreation, and storm water management.

The autonomy and authority of county governments also varies considerably from state to state. There are some regional patterns to such differences. For example, in the Northeast, local government traditionally is centered in towns and villages. These are the units of government that attract the most participation, make the most high-profile decisions, and are the focus of most attention. County governments in this region are historically viewed as just the local offices of state government, representing a form of government and governance more remote than the village board.

In the South, counties are also technically creatures of state government in that they were formed and granted their authority by state legislatures.

TABLE 11-2

Twenty-Five Largest U.S. Counties by Population, 2008

Rank	Geographic Area	Population Estimates
1	Los Angeles County, Calif.	9,878,554
2	Cook County, Ill.	5,285,107
3	Harris County, Tex.	3,935,855
4	Maricopa County, Ariz.	3,880,181
5	Orange County, Calif.	2,997,033
6	San Diego County, Calif.	2,974,859
7	Kings County, N.Y.	2,528,050
8	Miami-Dade County, Fla.	2,387,170
9	Dallas County, Tex.	2,366,511
10	Queens County, N.Y.	2,270,338
11	Riverside County, Calif.	2,073,571
12	San Bernardino County, Calif.	2,007,800
13	Wayne County, Mich.	1,985,101
14	King County, Wash.	1,859,284
15	Clark County, Nev.	1,836,333
16	Broward County, Fla.	1,759,591
17	Santa Clara County, Calif.	1,748,976
18	Tarrant County, Tex.	1,717,435
19	New York County, N.Y.	1,620,867
20	Bexar County, Tex.	1,594,493
21	Middlesex County, Mass.	1,473,416
22	Alameda County, Calif.	1,464,202
23	Suffolk County, N.Y.	1,453,229
24	Philadelphia County, Pa.	1,449,634
25	Sacramento County, Calif.	1,386,667

Source: U.S. Census Bureau, "Resident Population Estimates for the 100 Largest U.S. Counties Based on July 1, 2008, Population Estimates: April 1, 2000, to July 1, 2008," available at www.census.gov/popest/counties/CO-EST2008–07.html.

TABLE 11-3

Twenty-Five Smallest U.S. Counties by Population, 2008

County, State	Population	Rank
Loving, Tex.	42	1
Kalawao, Hawaii	117	2
Blaine, Neb.	248	3
King, Tex.	281	4
Arthur, Neb.	338	5
Kenedy, Tex.	388	6
Petroleum, Mont.	436	7
McPherson, Neb.	514	8
San Juan, Colo.	552	9
Thomas, Neb.	583	10
Borden, Tex.	593	11
Grant, Neb.	604	12
Loup, Neb.	619	13
Treasure, Mont.	637	14
Slope, N.D.	675	15
Harding, N.M.	684	16
Kent, Tex.	708	17
Banner, Neb.	735	18
Logan, Neb.	735	19
Hooker, Neb.	736	20
Wheeler, Neb.	807	21
Roberts, Tex.	833	22
Hinsdale, Colo.	840	23
McMullen, Tex.	851	24
Mineral, Colo.	962	25

Source: U.S. Census Bureau, *State and County Quick Facts,* available at http://quickfacts.census.gov/qfd/states/30/30103.html.

Yet, in the South, the county governments are much more likely to be a central focus of local government. County government here tends to be the form of local government that wields the most political power and policy influence and tends to be the focus of local political elites. The reason for these differences primarily has to do with the more urban nature of the Northeast compared to the historically more rural South. Rural areas by definition lack substantial urban centers, which means they lack large and powerful city or village governments. County governments thus occupy the center of local government, and the county seat—the place where county government is physically located—becomes the locus of local politics.

Counties are distinct from municipalities (which are discussed in-depth later), although these distinctions have blurred. County governments are historically rural governments that help conduct state government business. The quintessential county government is a keeper of public records, such as property deeds, birth and death certificates, and mortgages, and an administrator of property taxes, local road maintenance, election results certification, criminal courts, and jails run by county sheriffs. The typical U.S. municipality, on the other hand, performs such day-to-day functions as police and fire protection; sewage disposal; sanitation; and the maintenance of public parks and other infrastructure facilities, including stadiums, airports, and convention centers.

In the messy real world, however, such clear distinctions often disappear. Many modern county governments—particularly urban ones—have their official fingers in these classic city functions as well. In many regions, there is substantial overlap between county and city functions, and county and city governments operate cheek by jowl. For example, in Phoenix, Arizona, the city hall is directly across the street from the Maricopa County administration building.

As a general rule, however, counties tend to be kept on a tighter leash by state governments than are municipalities (especially the large urban cities). In New Hampshire, for example, legislators still approve county budgets. In Texas, each county is required by the state to appoint a county judge-at-large and four commissioners, regardless of whether the county's population numbers in the hundreds or the millions. Counties, in other words, are still in theory and often in practice the administrative subunits of state government.

Perhaps because they often are seen as extensions of state government, counties historically have been treated less generously when state and federal governments make appropriations to local governments. Some of this may be changing, however. Counties were the recipients of billions in federal grants through the American Recovery and Reinvestment Act (ARRA, better known as the 2009 federal stimulus package), and the White House made a point of reaching out to county officials to coordinate effective expenditures of those dollars. For example, Vice President Joe Biden and representatives from a broad range of federal agencies charged with distributing ARRA grants were a prominent presence at the annual meeting of the National Association of Counties in 2009. Biden warned that the stimulus is not "free" money, or as he put it, "No swimming pools. No tennis courts. No golf courses." But he also made it clear that counties were being viewed as an important means of implementing the ARRA. This is because they had a ready made set of policy programs ranging from social welfare to transportation that fit the ARRA's goal of having an impact quickly.[8]

Although county governments, like all other subnational governments, became more dependent on federal grants after the economic woes of 2008 and 2009, they have independent sources of revenue. The primary funding source controlled by county governments is the property tax, which historically accounts for about 30 percent of county government income. Like everything else about local government, however, there is considerable variation in where county governments get their money and what they spend it on. Fairfax County, Virginia, gets about 40 percent of its revenues from property taxes, whereas Orange County, California, gets less than 10 percent of its revenues from property taxes. Other sources of revenue include sales taxes (although not all counties have the legal authority to levy a sales tax), state appropriations, and taxes on everything from cars to hotel rooms.[9]

Just as there are huge variations among counties in terms of revenue, there are similar variations in spending priorities. Where county governments focus their spending depends on geography, politics, and relations with neighboring jurisdictions. A significant chunk of county spending goes to basic social services; public welfare, hospitals, and other healthcare programs account for about 60 percent of county government expenditures. Other categories of expenditure range from roads to sewers to schools to general administration.[10]

The Structure of County Government. There are three basic forms of county government: commission, council-executive, and commission-administrator. What differentiates the three forms is the degree of separation between legislative and executive powers and who is responsible for the day-to-day administration of the executive side of government.

The most common form of county government is the **commission**, which concentrates legislative and executive functions and powers into an elected board of commissioners. For example, it exercises legislative powers by passing county ordinances and approving the budget. And it wields executive powers by being responsible for a broad range of hiring and firing decisions and by exercising considerable control over many administrative offices.

Depending on the state and the county, members of these county-level legislatures may be called county commissioners, supervisors, selectmen, county board members, or judges. In Louisiana, these locally elected

COUNTY COMMISSION SYSTEM

A form of county governance in which executive, legislative, and administrative powers are vested in elected commissioners.

legislators are called parish jurors. In New Jersey, they are boards of chosen freeholders. Whatever their official titles, commissioners are typically a small group elected to serve staggered two- or four-year terms.

The most significant reform of county government since its inception has been to separate the executive and legislative powers by creating an independent county-level executive office. **Council-executive** county governments typically have an independently elected officer who serves as the county-level equivalent of a governor. County executives frequently have powers to veto ordinances passed by the board of commissioners, and they have the authority to appoint key department heads. Thus the main difference between the commission and council-executive forms of government is the approach to separation of powers. (See Figure 11-2.)

Commission-administrator county governments stand somewhere between the commission and council-executive forms. In this form of government, an elected commission retains most legislative and executive powers, but appoints a professional administrator to actually run the government. County administrators usually serve at the pleasure of the commissioners—they can be hired and fired as the county commission sees fit. In practice, commissioners typically delegate considerable powers to administrators, including the power to hire and fire department heads and to prepare a budget for the commission's approval.

Commission-administrator and, to an even greater extent, council-executive structures have been popular reforms to the traditional commission form of county government. Diffuse and ineffective decision making and outright corruption were the primary reasons for the shift away from commissions in the twentieth century. Reformers were concerned that, under the commission approach, power was so diffuse that county governments tended to drift in the absence of clear leadership; also, commissioners too often appointed their friends to important positions. As a result, an increasing number of counties, as many as 15 percent, now are run by elected county executives who exert firm leadership on policy and hiring. This reduces the role of the commissioners to something closer to an advisory level. Another 12 percent of counties are led by appointed administrators. State policymakers have contributed to this trend—Arkansas, Kentucky, and Tennessee now mandate that their counties be headed by elected executives.

Although such reforms have reduced entrenched corruption, even today there are examples of county governments going very badly astray. When this happens, states have still been known to step in and, in effect, put the county government out of business. For example, in 1997, the Massachusetts House of Representatives voted to abolish the government of Middlesex County, which it believed had become a corrupt, debt-ridden, and expensive administrative burden. A handful of county-based positions (for example, the sheriff, district attorney, and register of deeds) were retained as independently elected offices, but much of the guts of the

FIGURE 11-2 How It Works: The Structure of County Government

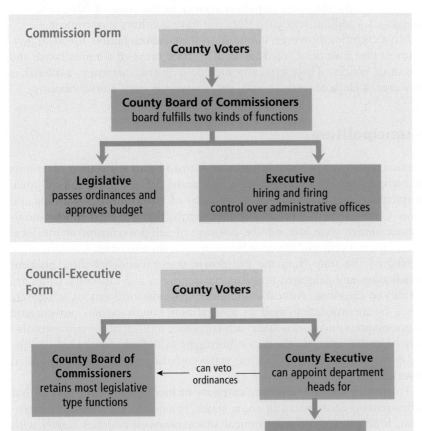

The three basic forms of county government differ on division of powers and in who is responsible for day-to-day administration of county government. In the commission form, voters elect county commissioners who exercise legislative and executive powers and exercise considerable authority over day-to-day administration. In the council-executive form, voters elect commissioners who exercise legislative powers and independently elect a county executive who wields executive powers and serves as the chief administrator. In the commission-administrator form, voters elect commissioners who retain most legislative and executive powers. However, they hire a professional manager to provide day-to-day administration of county government.

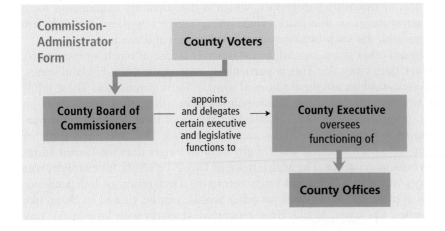

county government was absorbed by the state. That is still the case today; in other words, the most populous county in the state of Massachusetts (roughly 1.4 million residents) does not have a county government.

Most counties, however, continue to have representative forms of government that includes elected heads of a broad range of administrative and executive offices. These typically include a district attorney, a sheriff, a treasurer, a clerk of records, and, yes, sometimes even a prothonotary.

Municipalities

A municipality is a political jurisdiction formed by an association of citizens to provide self-governance within a clearly defined geographical area. Municipalities encompass two basic forms of government: townships and cities. **Cities** are corporations. In other words, they are legal entities incorporated under state law for the purpose of self-government at the local level. This is a central difference between counties and cities. Counties were created by the state from the top down; states mandated these political jurisdictions and delegated to them certain powers and functions. Cities are bottom-up creations. A local community seeks the authority of self-governance by incorporating itself as a legal entity with certain powers and responsibilities under state law. Such corporate municipal governments also may be called villages, towns, or boroughs (although, somewhat confusingly, *towns* and *boroughs* in some states can also refer to nonincorporated governments).

Townships are an interesting category of local government that all but defies general description. In some states, townships are shells of government, little more than geographical subdivisions of counties vested with little in the way of responsibility or power. In other states, townships are vested with a considerable range of responsibilities and essentially function as mini-county governments. They typically are run by a board of commissioners or township supervisors, which is just a county commission form of government in miniature. These more active townships typically are responsible for such functions as snowplowing rural roads.

In still other states, townships (or towns) exercise as much, or even more, power than cities do. This is particularly true in the New England states, where townships are the traditional form of local governance. These kinds of townships function as municipalities. Like cities, they are bottom-up institutions, political entities formed by groups of local citizens for the purpose of self-governance. Many are incorporated, like cities, and some of them have been working units of government longer than the United States has been in existence. The Maine town of Dover-Foxcroft, for example, was incorporated in 1769, eight years before the Declaration of Independence was approved.[11] Townships, in other words, can be viewed as being like counties, like cities, or like large geographical spaces with little in the way

CITIES

Incorporated political jurisdictions formed to provide self-governance to a locality.

TOWNSHIPS

Local governments whose powers, governance structure, and legal status vary considerably from state to state. In some states, townships function as general purpose municipalities; in others, they are geographical subdivisions of counties with few responsibilities and little power.

of a governance structure within them. Which of these descriptions is accurate depends on state law and the traditions of local governance.

What distinguishes cities and the city-like townships from counties and county-like townships is that they are formed by associations of citizens rather than being brought to life as designated subunits of states. Municipalities are general purpose governments that provide a range of public services and address a variety of political issues at the local level. They are brought into existence because groups of citizens, usually those concentrated in compact urban areas, wanted to exercise a degree of political self-determination over their community. Accordingly, they incorporated, bringing to life a legal entity—a municipality—that grants them the right to a broad degree of self-governance.

Governance arrangements at the municipal level vary even more than at the county level. In municipalities, there is variation in the powers of the executive, or **mayor**, and the legislature, typically a **city council**. A strong role often is played by an appointed administrator, or **city manager**, who is given the day-to-day responsibility for running municipal operations. There are four municipal governance systems: the mayor-council system, the city manager system, the commission system, and the town meeting system.

Mayor-Council Systems

One of the most common forms of municipal governance is the **mayor-council system**. It is distinguished by a separation of executive and legislative powers. According to the International City/County Management Association (ICMA), approximately 43 percent of U.S. cities use this system. Executive power is vested in a separately elected mayor, although the powers that a mayor actually is allowed to exercise vary considerably.

The mayor-council system can be broken down into **strong mayor** and **weak mayor systems**. In discussions of city governance, these terms have less to do with a politician's personality than with the powers that a given mayor enjoys when stacked up against the powers of the city council and the bureaucracy. Under the strong mayor system, the executive is roughly the municipal-level equivalent of a governor. Strong mayors exercise a great deal of power, and typically they have the authority to make appointments to key city offices, to veto council decisions, to prepare budgets, and to run the day-to-day operations of municipal government in general.

The strong mayor system is most common in the Northeast and the Midwest. One example of a strong mayor in action is Carleton S. Finkbeiner, who was elected mayor of Toledo, Ohio, in 1994. Early in his tenure, he overrode resistance from school authorities and placed uniformed police officers in every junior high school and high school as a way to reduce violence. The policy has taken some cops off the street, but it also has created trust with students and is a preventive approach that has

MAYOR
The elected chief executive of a municipality.

CITY COUNCIL
A municipality's legislature.

CITY MANAGER
An official appointed to be the chief administrator of a municipality.

MAYOR-COUNCIL SYSTEM
A form of municipal governance in which there is an elected executive and an elected legislature.

STRONG MAYOR SYSTEM
A municipal government in which the mayor has the power to perform the executive functions of government.

WEAK MAYOR SYSTEM
A municipal government in which the mayor lacks true executive powers, such as the ability to veto council decisions or appoint department heads.

reduced drug and gang problems by providing mentors and role models for students. The U.S. Conference of Mayors cited the program as an example of best practice in 2000.[12] What Finkbeiner demonstrated was the ability of a strong mayor to independently make important policy decisions. Making such decisions can often be controversial, although it doesn't seem to have hurt Finkbeiner. With one term-limit-enforced break to host a TV show on public affairs, he served three full terms as mayor between 1994 and 2009.

A weak mayor system retains the elected executive, but this is more of a ceremonial than a real policymaking office. In weak mayor systems, the executive, as well as legislative, power is wielded by the council. Executives in weak mayor systems still can exercise considerable influence, but they have to do this by using their powers of persuasion rather than the authority vested in their office. In many cities where mayors have limited powers, individuals with strong personalities have nevertheless been able to exert huge influence. They do this by fostering cooperative relationships with their powerful city managers. Examples are Pete Wilson, the mayor of San Diego in the 1970s, and Henry Cisneros, the mayor of San Antonio in the 1980s.

In both strong and weak mayor systems, the council serves as the municipal-level legislature and can wield extensive policymaking power. No major policy or program can get far in a city without massaging from the city council. Councils average six members, but in many large jurisdictions twelve to fourteen members are elected. Los Angeles, for example, has fifteen. Chicago has a whopping fifty council members, and New York City has fifty-one.

City councils exert a major influence over a city's livability. They steer policies on such vital issues as zoning and urban renewal, as have the councils in Los Angeles and Philadelphia, for example. In recent years, they have been pivotal in the pursuit of public-private partnerships. In Indianapolis, for instance, the city council has worked with the city's mayor and administrators to save taxpayers $100 million by opening up service contracts to competitive bidding. The money saved by contracting out such services as wastewater treatment, asbestos abatement, recycling, street sweeping, and server billing goes toward public safety and airport improvements.[13]

In cities where councils lack discipline, however, quirky personalities can impede progress. In St. Louis, the board of aldermen has twenty-nine members. Back in the 1950s, these aldermen enjoyed a major say in decisions that affected zoning, development, and highway location. But, by the start of the twenty-first century, critics complained that the board micromanaged and encouraged parochialism (a limitation of views or interests) and balkanization (the division of an area into small, often hostile units).

Elected with as few as eight hundred votes, some of these personally ambitious individuals have embarrassed their communities by spending more time squabbling among themselves than teaming up to make principled decisions. For many aldermen, however, the personal stakes are

FIGURE 11-3 Strong Mayor–Council Form of Government

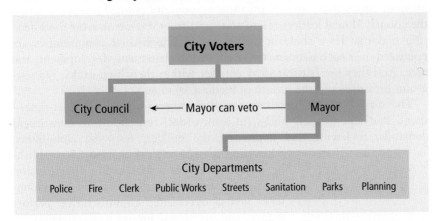

Source: John P. Pelissero, "The Political Environment & Cities in the 21st Century," in *Cities, Politics & Public Policy: A Comparative Analysis,* ed. John P. Pelissero (Washington, D.C.: CQ Press, 2003), 15.

FIGURE 11-4 Weak Mayor–Council Form of Government

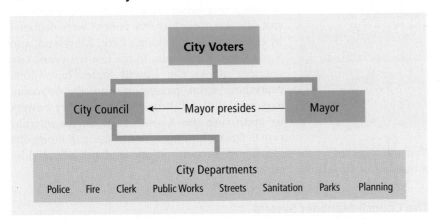

Source: John P. Pelissero, "The Political Environment & Cities in the 21st Century," in *Cities, Politics & Public Policy: A Comparative Analysis,* ed. John P. Pelissero (Washington, D.C.: CQ Press, 2003), 15.

higher than is commensurate with their actual power. Neighborhood **wards** have little influence, for example, on developers and corporations whose view of the city includes many wards. Ward aldermen can't implement a broad vision because the real executive power is in the mayor's office. In addition, they do not always know about deals being cut in other wards. Yet, sometimes, just one or two individuals can hold up a hand and make the entire city come to a halt.[14]

WARDS

Divisions of municipalities, usually representing electoral districts of the city council.

A survey taken in 2001 by the National League of Cities showed an array of issues that cause frustration among city council members across the country. Local leaders resent state and federal controls over their decision making. They chafe at the degree to which their communities are polarized over such issues as taxation, traffic abatement, development, and race. And they are frustrated by conflict within their own ranks, interest-group pressure, and the nature of media coverage.

The survey also found that council members—who work part-time—spend the bulk of their hours (in rank order) responding to constituent demands, reviewing and approving the budget, resolving complaints, addressing the city's "real problems," establishing objectives and priorities, establishing a vision for the community's future, establishing long-term goals, overseeing administrative performance, and overseeing program effectiveness.[15]

City councils have also been known to weigh in on national, and even international, issues with or without the approval of the mayor or city manager. In the 1980s, for example, when proposals for a joint U.S.-Soviet freeze on nuclear weapons was being discussed by U.S. arms control officials, "nuclear-free zones" were declared by city councils in Takoma Park, Maryland, and Santa Cruz, California. In the last ten years, city councils across the United States have done everything from passing resolutions opposing expanded FBI antiterrorism investigatory powers to approving the Kyoto Protocol, an international treaty limiting greenhouse gas emissions that was rejected by the federal government but independently adopted by a number of subnational governments.

> City councils have also been known to weigh in on national, and even international, issues with or without the approval of the mayor or city manager. In the 1980s, for example, when proposals for a joint U.S.-Soviet freeze on nuclear weapons was being discussed by U.S. arms control officials, "nuclear-free zones" were declared by city councils in Takoma Park, Maryland, and Santa Cruz, California.

The Council-Manager System

COUNCIL-MANAGER SYSTEM

A form of municipal governance in which the day-to-day administration of government is carried out by a professional administrator.

Rather than separating executive and legislative functions, the **council-manager system** is based on the principle of separating the political and administrative functions of government. This separation is achieved by having a council make policy decisions but placing their implementation in the hands of a professional administrator, usually called a city manager, hired by the council. (See Figure 11-5.)

The origins of this system are in the Progressive reform movement that swept through government at all levels at the turn of the nineteenth century. As discussed elsewhere in the context of state-level party politics, a century ago political machines ran the typical large city in the United States. Places like Boston, Chicago, and New York were governed

FIGURE 11-5 Council-Manager Form of Government

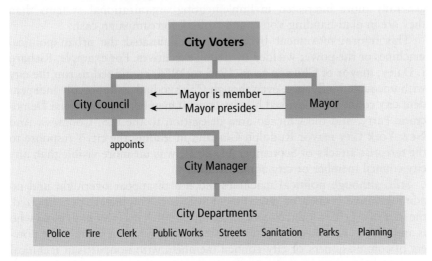

City Voters

City Council ← Mayor is member — Mayor
← Mayor presides —

appoints

City Manager

City Departments

Police   Fire   Clerk   Public Works   Streets   Sanitation   Parks   Planning

Source: John P. Pelissero, "The Political Environment & Cities in the 21st Century," in *Cities, Politics & Public Policy: A Comparative Analysis,* ed. John P. Pelissero (Washington, D.C.: CQ Press, 2003), 16.

by charismatic politicians who took advantage of their ties to ethnic minorities, such as the Irish or the Italians. Patronage jobs were given out to their personal friends, whose chief qualification was that they were campaign supporters. Elections were fraught with partisanship, which produced high incumbent reelection rates. Many machine insiders got themselves elected as city commissioners and were given authority to run individual departments, including police, fire, or sanitation services. This resulted in politically powerful, but often corrupt and incompetent, municipal governments.

During the first half of the twentieth century, reform groups began pressuring city governments to become more professionalized and less politicized. The National Municipal League (now the National League of Cities), which focuses on small to medium-size cities, was one such group. The U.S. Conference of Mayors, whose members head larger cities, and the ICMA were two others. In the belief that the top vote-getters in a given city may not be the best managers, the National Municipal League drafted a model charter that laid out the powers of mayors, city councils, and administrators.

In 1913 Dayton, Ohio, became the first major U.S. city to create a position for a strong manager, largely in response to suburbanization (the establishment of residential communities on the outskirts of a city) and the rise of an educated middle class. The idea was that a government run by a professional city manager would be less prone to corruption and partisan favoritism than those led by the classic big-city mayor. Such managers are generally more interested in implementing organizational systems than they are in glad-handing voters and trolling for campaign cash.

This reform movement by no means eliminated the urban political machines or the power wielded by strong executives. For example, Richard J. Daley, mayor of Chicago from 1955 to 1976, continued to run the city with unequaled influence, even though Chicago had a supposedly independent city council. He swayed his city council members, the national Democratic Party, and the Chicago-area delegation to the U.S. Congress. And New York City mayor Rudolph Giuliani, in leading the city's response to the terrorist attacks of September 11, 2001, was far more visible than any city council member or city administrator.

Still, although political machines did not disappear overnight and no administrative branch of government was ever completely depoliticized, the idea of a professional city manager took root. This is an individual who is appointed, not elected, and who, at least in theory, can counter the powers of commissioners or city council members with nonpartisan technical administrative expertise. In some cities, this manager is paired with a mayor. The mayor acts as more of a ceremonial figurehead and seldom blocks anything wanted by the manager or the council members. Supported by a legislative body that is elected by popular vote and that meets about every two weeks to deal with policy issues, the manager is empowered to hire and fire all city employees, set pay scales, prepare an annual budget that is approved by elected officials and implemented by staff, and make policy recommendations.

Today, the council-manager system of city government is seen in more than 3,000 cities, or 49 percent of communities with populations of more than 2,500. (See Table 11-4.) It is most popular in medium-size cities,

TABLE 11-4

Most Common Forms of City Government in the United States, 2007*

Council-Manager	3,511 (49 percent)
Mayor-Council	3,116 (43.5 percent)
Commission	143 (2.0 percent)
Town Meeting	339 (4.7 percent)
Representative Town Meeting	62 (0.9 percent)

Source: International City/County Management Association. www.icma.org/upload/library/2007-04/ {F55E2557-92E4-4791-9DFC-FB9D282E3DF1}.doc.

*Represents only those cities with populations of 2,500 or greater.

primarily in the South and the West. The reason council-manager cities are concentrated in these population areas is that smaller cities cannot afford a full-time manager's salary and big cities tend to want a more partisan mayor. However, there are exceptions to this rule. Large cities that use a manager-council system include Dallas, Texas, and San Diego and San Jose, California.[16]

And the trend toward professionalization continues. A survey conducted by the ICMA showed that the percentage of city managers with advanced degrees rose from 27 percent in 1971 to 73 percent in 1995. Managers are also less likely to use volunteer committees to farm out work and more likely to use a professional staff. They supervise the systems that provide detailed financial controls and report transparency. For example, in Phoenix, Arizona, the city manager issues a monthly report that details the percentage of ambulance calls answered in fewer than ten minutes, the total number of nights individuals spent in homeless shelters, how many rounds of golf were played on public courses, and how many square miles of streets were swept.

Commission Systems

Similar to their county-level counterparts, municipal **commission systems** concentrate executive and legislative powers into a single elected body. These bodies make key policy decisions in the same way a legislature does. Yet each commissioner is also the head of an executive department. Commissioners run for office not as representatives in a legislative body but as the head of a particular city department: commissioner for public safety, commissioner for public works, and so on. Most commission systems also have a mayor, but this is not an independent executive office. The position usually is held by a commissioner chosen to preside over commission meetings; it is not an independent executive office but more of ceremonial position.

As a form of municipal (as opposed to county) governance, the commission system originated in Galveston, Texas, in the early 1900s. Galveston had suffered a devastating hurricane that killed thousands and left the city in ruins. The existing city government proved ineffective in dealing with the aftermath of this disaster. In response, the Texas legislature approved a completely new form of municipal government—the commission system—to try to deal with the huge task of rebuilding the city. It proved successful; Galveston was rebuilt and put back on the civic track.

This success led other municipalities to follow Galveston's lead and adopt the commission form of governance. The commission system's success, however, has been limited, and only a relative handful of cities currently operate under it. Its main drawbacks are two. First, the merging of elected and administrative positions leads to commissioners' becoming the entrenched advocates of their departments. Second, winning an election and administering a large bureaucracy turn out to be

CITY COMMISSION SYSTEM

A form of municipal governance in which executive, legislative, and administrative powers are vested in elected city commissioners.

very different skills. Good politicians, in other words, do not always make good department heads.

Only about 2 percent of municipalities with populations greater than 2,500 use the commission form of government.[17] The drawbacks of commission governments are much the same as the drawbacks of commission systems at the county level—executive authority is so diffuse it tends to produce a government with no real direction. Because commissioners serve as the head of their own departments, with no real central authority above that position, commission systems at the municipal level function as a legislature consisting of elected executives. This can make coordinating departments difficult and providing a strong sense of direction for the government overall even harder.

Town Meetings

The **town meeting form of government** is largely unique to the United States and is mostly found in towns in New England states (in New England, towns are basically municipalities, although they may also have some of the functions traditionally associated with county government in other states). Although not a particularly widespread form of local governance, it is probably the oldest, and it is certainly the most democratic. Its origins are rooted in the religious communities that made up early colonial settlements in New England. A high premium was put on consensus in these communities, and the town meeting evolved as a means to reach such widespread agreement. Such meetings allowed citizens to have a direct role in deciding which laws they would pass and who would be responsible for implementing and enforcing these laws. In many cases, the politics were worked out before the actual town meeting, with neighbor talking to neighbor across their fences and in taverns. The grassroots agreements hashed out in these informal discussions then were expressed as community consensus in the town meeting.[18]

What all this boils down to is that the legislative functions are concentrated in the citizens themselves. A town meeting is convened through a warrant, or an announcement of the date, time, and place of the meeting and the items to be discussed. It is open to all community citizens, and all have an equal vote in matters of town policy. Such legislative power often is exercised directly; for example, budgets are approved by town meetings. Some authority, however, may be delegated to a representative board, whose members are called selectmen. The board of selectmen exercises whatever authority is granted to it and is responsible for seeing that policies enacted in the town meeting are carried out.

Towns also have incorporated some elements of the council-manager system by voting to hire professional managers to handle the administrative side of government. The manager system seems to work well with this type of government; for example, roughly 30 percent of the

The town meeting form of government is largely unique to the United States, and even in the United States is mostly confined to the Northeast. In this form of local governance, legislative powers are vested in citizens who exercise those powers during a town meeting of local residents. Here, residents in Strafford, Vermont, are meeting to discuss local issues and elect town clerks.

towns in Maine—most of them small communities with fewer than 2,500 residents—have managers but hold town meetings as well.[19]

The town meeting is probably the most idealized form of government that has ever existed in the United States. Thomas Jefferson, for example, saw this grassroots democratic approach to self-governance as, "the wisest invention ever devised by man."[20] Alexis de Tocqueville, the nineteenth-century French aristocrat who wrote one of the most celebrated analyses of the American political system, referred to towns as the "fertile germ" of democracy.[21] For even modestly large communities, however, this approach simply isn't practical. A gathering of citizens that runs into the thousands would be too unwieldy, and the likelihood of getting broad agreement from such a large group on any number of policy issues is pretty low. This goes a long way toward explaining why this approach is thus largely confined to smaller communities in New England.

Special Districts

Special districts, for the most part, are fundamentally different from the other forms of local government already discussed. Counties and municipalities are general purpose governments that provide a broad range of public services within their given jurisdictions. Special districts, on the other hand, are mostly single-purpose governments. They are created to provide a specific service that is not being provided by a general purpose government.

With few exceptions, special districts exist outside the consciousness of the average citizen. More than 30,000 special districts have been created across the country—and often across borders of other units of government—to administer single programs or services. One of the exceptions to this, and the most common form of special district, is the school districts. Next in line, and much lower in profile, are sewer and water system districts, which account for about one-third of special districts nationwide. These are followed by districts for fire protection and housing.

Still other districts administer transportation, soil conservation, mosquito control, and even libraries. Commuters may not know it, but hundreds of thousands of them use some pretty well-known special districts every day. The Port Authority of New York and New Jersey, Boston's Massachusetts Bay Transportation Authority, and the Washington Metropolitan Area Transportation Authority of the District of Columbia collectively cover hundreds of square miles and cross dozens of government borders.

Why use special districts to provide single programs or services? Why not just have the county or municipality add that service to its governing portfolio? Well, in certain situations, single-purpose governments can seem attractive solutions to political and practical problems. For example, special districts sometimes are implemented as a way of heading off threats of political annexation of one local government by another. They also are used as a tool for community and business improvement. Freed of local tax authority, administrators of special districts often can get infrastructure items built and services provided without dipping into any one locality's funds. For example, farmers in special water districts, particularly in the West, are eligible for discounted federal loans to help them with irrigation. In addition, special districts can use private-sector business techniques in management, such as paying market rates instead of government rates to contractors.

Working within Limits: The Powers and Constraints of Local Government

Local governments, regardless of their particular form, differ from the state and federal government in a fundamentally important way—they are not sovereign. This means that local governments draw their power not from the citizens they serve but from the government immediately above them—the state government (this is why states considered

Oklahoma was one of five territories to gain statehood in the twentieth century. At one point, American Indians initiated efforts to create a state from land in the Indian and Oklahoma territories. Today, the state is home to the most members of recognized tribes in the country, and like other native groups in the United States, many of these have their own government and judicial systems.

Policy in Practice: Eminent Domain and Local Power

Although local governments are not sovereign, this does not mean they are powerless. Many local governments, for example, have the power of eminent domain, or the right to take private property without the owner's consent.

The Fifth Amendment to the U.S. Constitution compels any government exercising such powers to offer the owner just compensation for the property taken. That, however, often does little to mollify people who have their lives or communities uprooted to make way for a new road or a new development.

Eminent domain became a hot topic recently because of a U.S. Supreme Court decision. In *Kelo v. New London* (2005), the court ruled that homeowners could be forced to sell not just to a city but to private developers who would add to the city's tax base. In effect, the court said that local governments have a central role in planning and that economic development cannot be halted simply because some property owner objects.

At first blush, this seems to be a significant boost to the power and reach of local governments. The political fallout from the *Kelo* ruling, however, also has provided an instructive lesson in Dillon's Rule. In the wake of the Court's decision, a number of states immediately moved to curb local powers of eminent domain. There undoubtedly would have been more immediate action

by state legislatures except for the fact that many of them were not in session when the ruling was announced. A few states, including Nevada and Utah, anticipated the ruling and passed new restrictions on eminent domain before the Supreme Court made its decision.

Eminent domain, in other words, may be a power exercised by local governments, but it is one of the most unpopular exercises of power taken by any level of government. Any time a local government uses eminent domain it often finds its power challenged not by a court or another level of government but by its own citizens. For example, when Cypress, California, decided to force a church to sell to make way for a Costco store, the political fallout was so negative that local officials backed off and sought a less confrontational (and more expensive) settlement.

"Elected officials rightly know that they cannot go around taking property at will," says Indianapolis mayor Bart Peterson, who has taken the lead on this issue for the National League of Cities. Eminent domain is an important and sweeping power given many local governments, and it remains an important tool to aid economic development. Like most powers exercised by local government, however, the power of eminent domain is far from absolute.

Source: Alan Greenblatt, "Land Law," *Governing* magazine, August 2005.

---

in isolation are referred to as unitary governments in the introduction to this chapter).

This is not to say that local governments are powerless. Far from it. Local governments are charged with the primary responsibility for delivering a broad range of public services (such as education, law enforcement, roads, and utilities), and they have broad authority to levy taxes and pass regulations and ordinances (an ordinance is a law passed by a nonsovereign government). Local governments can also exercise the power of eminent domain (see the Policy in Practice feature "Eminent Domain and Local Power" on this page). Yet, despite all their responsibilities and powers (not to mention their sheer numbers), not all forms of local governments are, at least technically, equal partners in government. They are subordinate to the state governments from which they are granted their power.

Why is this the case? The short answer is the Tenth Amendment to the U.S. Constitution. Local governments are not mentioned anywhere in the U.S. Constitution, which divides power between the federal and state governments. Despite the long-standing cultural practice of having strong local governments, legally they fall under the purview of the Tenth Amendment's guarantee of state sovereignty. This means the power to determine the scope of authority of local governments is among those "reserved to the States respectively, or to the people." In other words, states get to say what localities can and cannot do. They set the limits and define the terms.

Dillon's Rule

DILLON'S RULE

The legal principle that says local governments can exercise only the powers granted to them by state government.

The legal doctrine that defines the division of power between state and local governments is known as **Dillon's Rule**, named after Iowa Supreme Court justice John F. Dillon. In addition to having a fine legal mind, Dillon was a highly respected and well-read scholar of local government. An argument he formulated in 1868 has served ever since as the basis for understanding and justifying the power—or, more accurately, the lack of power—of local government. Dillon's Rule is built around the legal principle of *ultra vires,* which means "outside one's powers." In a nutshell, it states that local governments are limited to the powers expressly granted to them by their state and to those powers indispensable to the stated objectives and purposes of each local government.

> Dillon's Rule is built around the legal principle of *ultra vires,* which means "outside one's powers." In a nutshell, it states that local governments are limited to the powers expressly granted to them by their state and to those powers indispensable to the stated objectives and purposes of each local government.

What Dillon essentially did was build a legal argument that the Tenth Amendment secured power for the states but not for local governments. As Dillon himself put it in his famous 1868 ruling in *City of Clinton v. the Cedar Rapids and Missouri Railroad*, local governments are "mere tenants at the will of their respective state legislatures." The rule has structured legal thinking on the power of local governments ever since, although it has always had its critics and opponents. It was challenged as early as the 1870s, when Missouri legislators rewrote the state constitution specifically to allow municipalities a degree of independence from the constraints of state government.[22]

responsible for the building and maintenance of extensive road systems, as well as for enforcing traffic and safety laws on those roads. That's an expensive proposition, and counties generally welcome state and federal money to support these critical public services. Yet the golden rule—he who gives the gold makes the rules—means those funds inevitably come with strings. The obligations that come with the money, in the form of state or federal mandates, are not nearly as popular as the cash. This sets up a love-hate relationship between local authorities and the state and federal governments above them. In addition, state and federal governments are frustrating because they restrict the decision-making freedom of local authorities. The restrictions and conditions, however, are often the price of the intergovernmental grants that underwrite important local government functions.

Participation in Local Government

Local governments are distinguished from state and federal governments not only by their power (or lack thereof) but also by their politics. Comparatively speaking, state and federal politics are dominated by political parties, which contest elections, mobilize voters, and organize government. Things are different down at the local level where more than two-thirds of local governments are nonpartisan. Since the decline of the big-city political machines of the early twentieth century, candidates for county boards and city councils run on their personal competence for the most part rather than on ideology or past affiliation. Only 17 percent of city councils hold partisan elections, according to the ICMA. Yet in some cities, partisan labels that have been abolished officially continue to play a role unofficially. This has occurred in Chicago. Even though they have been officially abolished since the 1930s, partisan labels have remained in play as Democrats continue to dominate the heavily African American city.

Council members usually run in **ward,** or **district, elections.** The advantage of organizing such elections on the basis of defined geographical areas is that they assure each neighborhood of having a local on the city council who knows their streets and residents by name. This is especially important for minorities who may be grouped together by housing patterns. Very large cities, however, have to balance the desire to have districts small enough so that council members really know the neighborhood concerns with the practical concerns of having a municipal legislature that has a reasonable number of members. In some places, the population of council districts are themselves the equivalent of a mid-size city. Los Angeles, for examples, is split into fifteen city council districts. Because Los Angeles has a population of roughly 3.8 million, that means each district has something like a quarter million constituents.

WARD, OR DISTRICT, ELECTIONS
Elections in which voters in a municipal ward vote for a candidate to represent them on a council or commission.

Although their ranks in high office are far below the roughly 50 percent of the population they represent, women hold some of the most important leadership positions in local government. Here, U.S. district judge Vanessa Gilmore swears in Annise Parker (center) as mayor of Houston, the nation's fourth largest city. In addition to being only the second female mayor of Houston, Parker is the first openly gay mayor of a city with more than 1 million residents. Accompanying Parker is her partner Kathy Hubbard (right).

AT-LARGE ELECTIONS

Elections in which city or county voters vote for council or commission members.

Other jurisdictions permit candidates to run in **at-large elections**. This means that they can hail from any part of the jurisdiction. The advantage of having candidates run at-large, and the reason most cities opt for it, is that it makes room for a greater pool of highly qualified and talented people who, presumably, look at the interests of the city as a whole rather than just the parochial interests of a ward or neighborhood. Some city charters require a combination of ward representatives and at-large members. But it can get controversial. In 1991 in Dallas, court-ordered redistricting required a switch from an at-large system to one in which fourteen members were chosen by districts. The result was that more Hispanics and blacks won seats.

There is perhaps no better example of the unique nature of local politics than the town meetings that define local governance in New England. Usually held twice a year when the elected council or clerk issues a warrant, or agenda, these gatherings epitomize direct democracy in action. Citizens can do everything from passing a budget to opposing a developer's plan for a new golf course. There simply is no equivalent to this comprehensive citizen legislature at the state or federal level, nor, as a practical matter, could there be.

One of the paradoxes of local government is that, although it is the level of government that citizens support the most, it is the level of government they participate in the least. The turnout in local elections is often half the national average of 55 percent voter turnout in a presidential election. This reflects a general indifference among many citizens toward the prosaic affairs of local government. Neighborhood volunteer and community development organizations, although often run by articulate and dedicated activists, often involve as little as 3–12 percent of the local population.[26]

Yet the absence of popular fervor in local issues does not mean that local offices are not important. Indeed, politics at this level can have implications for state and even national politics. For example, local government offices often serve as proving grounds for up-and-coming politicians who go on to higher office at the state or national level. New immigrants, particularly Asians and Latinos, increasingly are working their way into public office on this level. By the end of the twentieth century, one-third of all cities with more than 200,000 residents had elected either a Hispanic or black mayor.[27] In 2007, there were over 5,000 elected Hispanic or Latino officials, with the majority holding local offices and with many of those in state and federal offices coming from a local government background. Representative Nydia Velázquez, D-N.Y., for example, was the first Puerto Rican American woman elected to Congress and serves as the chair of the influential Congressional Hispanic Caucus. She began her career as a member of the New York City Council.

The increase in black local officials during the final third of the twentieth century was dramatic. According to the Washington-based Joint Center for Political and Economic Studies, from 1970 to 2001 the number of black mayors rose from 48 to 454, the number of black city council members rose from 552 to 3,538, and the number of black county commissioners rose from 64 to 820.

Women also have made great gains, although far from reaching their proportion as half the total population. According to the Center for American Women and Politics in Washington, D.C., in July 2009 204 mayors of cities with populations of more than 30,000 were women. These included the mayors of Baltimore, Maryland; Fresno, California; and Atlanta, Georgia. Added to their number in December 2009 was Annise Parker, who won a runoff race to become mayor of Houston, Texas, the fourth largest city in the United States.

Where partisan affiliations are allowed at the local level, there have been some historically important divisions among voters. For example,

Democratic candidates have tended to draw votes from minority groups, Catholics, and the liberal intelligentsia. Republicans have tended to draw votes from WASPs (white Anglo-Saxon Protestants), big business, and law-and-order enthusiasts. This is changing, however. In New York City in 2001, billionaire Michael Bloomberg, who had switched from the Democratic Party to the Republican Party, spent millions of dollars of his own money to win an upset victory over Democratic public advocate Mark Green. Part of his success was that he was able to attract Hispanic voters.[28]

The payoff for winning local office is more likely to come in the form of visibility and personal satisfaction than in cold hard cash. Mayors, many of whom work part time, earn an average of less than $10,000 per year. New York mayor Michael Bloomberg shelled out more than $100 million to win a third term in 2009, but declines to take a salary; he works for a token $1 per year. Typically, mayors of big cities get considerably more than that. Los Angeles mayor Antonio Villaraigosa's salary was $223,000 per year, although in 2009 he proposed reducing his compensation by 12 percent as part of a package to deal with the city's financial woes. Council members generally earn less than mayors. In most small and medium-size cities, being a member of the city council is more of a public service than a part-time job. Even in large mayor-council cities—where being a member of the city council is a full-time job—the average compensation is less than $40,000 per year.[29]

On the other hand, the job of professional city or county manger tends to be a fairly well-compensated, white-collar position. According to the ICMA, city managers made about $92,000 per year in 2003 and county managers a little more. According to payscale.com (a Web site devoted to compensation analysis), city managers across a number of states averaged about $100,000 per year in 2010 (check out the compensation numbers yourself at www.payscale.com/research/US/Job=City_Manager/Salary/by_State). The weekly average workload for council members in small, medium, and large cities is twenty, twenty-five, and forty-two hours, respectively. The typical number of hours they spend doing services for constituents has risen to 35 percent of their time. In larger cities with mayor-council systems, more than 90 percent of elected officials have staffs at their disposal, compared to only 50 percent in smaller cities, according to the National League of Cities.[30]

Not surprisingly, 66 percent of city council members in a National League of Cities survey said they wanted a raise. Many citizens oppose large salaries for their local officials, particularly at the school board level, because they feel the

> Many citizens oppose large salaries for their local officials, particularly at the school board level, because they feel the nominal fees they receive are not an hourly wage but, rather, a stipend that honors public spiritedness.

nominal fees they receive are not an hourly wage but, rather, a stipend that honors public spiritedness.

The Road Ahead

The forms and functions of local governments have evolved through myriad permutations, nearly all of them designed to produce leaders and practices that maximize both efficiency and responsiveness to voters. Yet few local governments can go it alone. In the first five years of the twenty-first century, local governments suffered considerably as recession squeezed their budgets. By 2006, most local governments had significantly improved their fiscal outlooks, helped by a hot real estate market that improved property tax revenues. The real estate market, however, began to cool in 2006, signaling that market forces were about to put downward pressure on the growth of property tax revenues. That pressure became an overwhelming force in 2008 and 2009 as the national housing bubble burst, the country slid into the deepest economic recession since the Great Depression, and local governments faced a fiscal crisis.

In response to plunging sales and property taxes, local governments were forced to take some drastic actions. A 2010 survey by the Center for State & Local Government Excellence reported that nearly 70 percent of state and local governments had enacted hiring freezes, more than 40 percent had made lay-offs, and roughly one-third had instituted furloughs (nonvoluntary unpaid leaves) and reformed employee benefit packages to reduce costs.[31] A similar survey by the ICMA highlighted the sweeping changes that the Great Recession brought specifically to local government. More than 80 percent of respondents to the ICMA survey said the financial crisis had affected local government operations and that in response city and county managers were making hard choices about deferring capital projects and maintenance, increasing fees, and cutting some services altogether. Tellingly, the overwhelming majority of respondents in the ICMA survey (67 percent) reported that the changes forced by the Great Recession were not temporary; local government management professionals saw the wrenching contractions as a new "business norm" for the foreseeable future. As Jason Gage, city manager of Salina, Kansas, put it, "Some of the changes we've implemented will continue once the recession ends. We will continue to emphasize performance, explore ways to restrict staffing, and this has been a wake up call to pay close attention to our daily expenditures."[32]

IMCA director Robert O'Neill Jr. says that there is a silver lining to the Great Recession's brutal impact on local governments—the possibility of creative destruction. O'Neill argues that the fiscal crisis has forced local governments to become more efficient, more adaptable, and more focused on seeking out new and creative ways to address long-standing problems. Although local governments may be smaller in a postrecession era, they are

States under Stress: Unionized Labor Faces Tougher Times with Local Governments

Negotiating labor contracts in the middle of the Great Recession is not exactly a union's dream scenario. Workers at GM and Ford can tell you that. But so can city employees in St. Petersburg, Florida, and employees of San Francisco's Bay Area Rapid Transit Authority (BART). Like the private sector, the public sector is increasingly telling its unions it doesn't have the money to fund current salary obligations, let alone wage increases. Public-sector unions are increasingly recognizing that this claim is not a negotiating tactic by public managers; it's simply a fact of life.

In summer 2009, for example, then St. Petersburg mayor Rick Baker declared a fiscal emergency and sought to reopen a union contract that called for pay raises for city employees in 2010. Alarmed about giving up a contractually guaranteed benefit, the unions persuaded Baker to back off. But 2010 is the last year of the contract, and the unions can read a balance sheet as well as a mayor. Rick Smith, head of the Florida Public Services Union (FPSU) in St. Petersburg, said that the union recognizes that negotiations are going to be more about how to help weather the crisis than about how much more will end up in the paychecks of union members.

Unions are facing what's been termed the toughest collective bargaining landscape in generations, with much of the focus on how much to give up rather than how much to get. BART went through a nasty fight with its unions in 2009 over a contract renewal. When the dust settled, the unions agreed to a four-year deal that has no pay increases, reduces overtime, and calls for employees to contribute more toward their health insurance premiums. In some circles, that counts as a union success.

This clash between the unbalanced bottom lines of local governments and the collective bargaining agents that represent public employees can make for heated conflicts. Ask Philadelphia mayor Michael Nutter, a one-time "friend of labor" who sought to save money with a budget that called for trimming labor costs by $25 million over five years. The AFSCME, whose affiliates represent blue- and white-collar city workers in Philadelphia, responded to his proposed budget trimming with large anti-Nutter rallies and calls for strikes.

The problem for unions is that the Great Recession is having a long-lasting impact on local government finances. Labor contracts up for renewal in the past two years and in the foreseeable future are running head-on into a new reality where local governments simply do not have the revenue streams they had four or five years earlier. Yet, at the same time that money to pay public employees is getting scarcer, the demand for government services—and therefore the demands on public-sector employees—is increasing at the local level. Steve Kriesberg, an AFSCME official, points out the cross-pressures that this creates for local governments: "When you take away 20 percent of revenues from a jurisdiction, there's just no way to fill that kind of hole. At the same time, you're seeing a greater demand for government services. You start thinking about the big picture, and you can give yourself a headache."

What to do? Some localities are getting creative. In Springfield, Oregon, unions cut a deal with the city to make raises contingent on prevailing financial conditions. The FPSU in St. Petersburg has talked to the city about setting aside some of its affordable housing stock for city employees (with the real estate market in the tank, affordable housing is something some cities have in far too great abundance). Other suggestions range from shifting to 38-hour workweeks to providing incentives for public employees to use public transportation.

The bottom line is that the business of local government has undergone a real shift, and that extends to the labor market. Unions, at least the realistic ones, are seeking to find solutions with their management counterparts.

Source: Adapted from Jonathan Walters, "For Unions, Tough Bargaining Times," *Governing* magazine, October 2009.

likely to be tougher and better equipped to address bigger problems with fewer people, less cash, and more creativity. Experiencing a fiscal crisis of historic proportions is forcing localities to question everything about their way of doing business and, O'Neill argues, that's not necessarily a bad thing for the long term.[33]

Despite the rough ride over the past few years, the long-term durability of governments at the town, city, county, and special-district levels continues to be seen in the variety of ways each responds to its own unique circumstances, not just economic trends but the full array of particular traits and challenges unique to every locality. There is no shortage of candidates willing to pay the price in time, sweat, and sacrificed income that it takes to make a go of it in the modern world of local elected offices. These small-scale leaders continue to debate and organize to provide valued services using a process consistent with a loftier vision of democracy. De Tocqueville noted nearly two hundred years ago that democracy in America was practiced unusually effectively at the local level, where "inhabitants with the same interests" manage to provide "all the elements of a good administration."[34] At least in this way, recession or not, local government hasn't changed much at all.

Conclusion

De Tocqueville viewed local governments in the United States as sort of mini-republics. He saw them as civic entities in which citizens were closest to government and in which government reflected accurately what citizens desired. In many ways, that perspective is still valid. Local governments wield actual power, and they are responsible for important programs and services. They come in a bewildering variety of types, many of which reflect state or regional history, culture, and preferences. Taken as a whole, all these differences can seem confusing. Yet in any single place—your hometown or local county—the government and what it does or does not do probably seem perfectly reasonable and natural.

Local government certainly remains the most common form of government in the United States, and it is still the form of government the average citizen is most likely to come into contact with on a day-to-day basis. Counties, municipalities, and special districts build and maintain roads, police those roads, run schools, manage libraries, and provide other programs and services too numerous to list. And they do all of this while employing very different approaches to government. Some are run by powerful executives, others are run by more egalitarian councils or commissions, and still others are mostly run by professional managers.

Yet local government is far from ideal. These mini-republics are constrained by Dillon's Rule. They tend to have relatively low voter turnout for elections. The idiosyncrasies of local government structure can mean electing someone with no real administrative experience to run a complicated bureaucracy with a multimillion-dollar budget. Local governments today face significant challenges, most notably dealing with the fallout of the Great Recession, which has increased demand for their services even as it has decimated their revenues. Just because the politics is local does not mean it is less difficult.

Key Concepts

at-large elections (p. 446)

charter (p. 443)

cities (p. 428)

city commission
   system (p. 435)

city council (p. 429)

city manager (p. 429)

commission-administrator
   system (p. 426)

council-executive
   system (p. 426)

council-manager
   system (p. 432)

counties (p. 419)

county commission
   system (p. 425)

Dillon's Rule (p. 440)

general act charters (p. 444)

home rule (p. 443)

mayor (p. 429)

mayor-council system (p. 429)

municipalities (p. 419)

special act charters (p. 444)

Suggested Readings

Garvin, Alexander. *The American City: What Works, What Doesn't,* 2nd ed. New York: McGraw-Hill, 2002. A comprehensive reference to urban planning and design in the United States that analyzes key projects initiated in 250 urban areas.

Kemp, Roger L., ed. *Forms of Local Government: A Handbook on City, County, and Regional Options.* Jefferson, N.C.: McFarland, 2007. Each chapter covers a different level of government, and the sample charters provided describe the laws that form the basis of government.

Orfield, Myron. *Metropolitics: A Regional Agenda for Community and Stability.* Washington, D.C.: Brookings Institution, 1997. Using the example of the twin cities of Minneapolis and St. Paul, Minnesota, the author presents a system of regional government meant to improve schools, create affordable housing, and protect the environment and quality of life.

Pelissero, John P., ed. *Cities, Politics, and Policy: A Comparative Analysis.* Washington, D.C.: CQ Press, 2003. Through case studies and cross-sectional analyses of a variety of urban areas, this book shows how scholars find patterns and draw conclusions that offer insights beneficial to all communities.

Suggested Web Sites

www.brookings.edu. Web site of the Brookings Institution, one of Washington, D.C.'s oldest think tanks, which pursues independent, nonpartisan research in such areas as metropolitan policy and governance.

www.census.gov. Web site of the U.S. Census Bureau, which is responsible for collecting and tabulating data on the population and demographics of the United States.

www2.icma.org/main/sc.asp. Web site of the International City/County Management Association, whose mission is to create excellence in local government by developing and fostering professional local government management worldwide.

www.naco.org. Created in 1935, the National Association of Counties is the only national organization that represents county governments in the United States.

www.natat.org. The National Association of Towns and Townships seeks to strengthen the effectiveness of town and township governments by exploring flexible and alternative approaches to federal policies to ensure that smaller communities can meet federal requirements.

www.nlc.org. Web site of the National League of Cities, the oldest and largest national organization representing municipal governments in the United States.

www.usmayors.org. Web site of the U.S. Conference of Mayors, which is the official nonpartisan organization of the 1,183 U.S. cities with populations of 30,000 or more.

CHAPTER 12

Metropolitics

The Hole Problem of Government

Critics of urban governance argue that there is a hole in local government. Not a hole quite as literal as this one, but rather the general absence of meaningful regional government. While many issues—such as transportation and highway maintenance—are essentially regional in nature, there is a notable lack of regional political jurisdictions.

12

What is the "hole" in government?

Why do the decisions of one local government affect the decisions of other local governments?

Why do patterns of growth create pressure for new forms of local government?

Allegheny County, Pennsylvania, has a lot of governments. There is the county government, of course. You've probably also heard of the county seat, Pittsburgh, a city famed for football (the Steelers are six-time Super Bowl champs), ketchup (the headquarters of the H.J. Heinz Company), and steel (in the early twentieth century, Pittsburgh accounted for half of the nation's steel manufacturing). Pittsburgh is a major metropolitan city, with a general purpose government organized under a mayor-council system.

Chances are, however, that you can't name even a tiny fraction of all the governments in Allegheny County, even if you live there. If you can, you have a remarkably good memory. For example, there are more than one hundred municipalities in the county. Pittsburgh is the biggest, but there are eighty-five other cities or boroughs within the county limits. (In Pennsylvania, a *borough* is a general purpose municipal government.) Add to that forty-two townships and forty-four school districts. Then, there is a mix of other special districts—everything from the West Mifflin Sanitary Sewer Municipal Authority to the Allegheny County Hospital Development Authority. If anyone bothered to count (and as it happens, someone has), that person would find a grand total of 273 local governments in Allegheny County.[1]

That works out to be 1 government for every 2.56 square miles, or 1 government for every 4,526 residents.[2] Like we said, Allegheny County has a lot of governments. All those political jurisdictions add up to a lot of differences and, you guessed it, those differences make a difference. There are more than a hundred police departments and more than two hundred volunteer fire companies.[3] There are different public works departments, dispatch centers, library systems, purchasing operations—you get the point. There are a lot of differences. And how do they make a difference? Well, in taxes for one thing.

Consider that someone owning property valued at $100,000 in Pine Township on the county's northern edge will pay about $589 in municipal taxes annually. A similarly valued property in the city of Pittsburgh will cost its owner $1,549 in taxes.[4] In other words, the property tax burden can vary by a factor of three, depending on where the property is located within a county's borders. Of course, not everybody pays taxes for the same public services. What public services are available, and the quality of those services, also will vary from place to place.

Governing States and Localities

Keeping up with all this variation can cause a headache. So can trying to make rational sense of it. The problem with large urban areas like Pittsburgh and its immediate surrounding areas is that the fragmented political system is not really designed to deal with the realities of governing. In Allegheny County, there are a lot of governments engaged in providing the same services, and each has its own political leaders, governance structure, and bureaucracy. Some say this is a bad thing. Splitting the responsibilities of local government into literally hundreds of small slices adds up to a lot of redundant inefficiency.

It also makes it incredibly difficult to coordinate an effective response to a wide range of problems that have multijurisdictional causes and consequences. Consider traffic. Authorizing, say, the construction of a new industrial park means there will be a lot of new commuters. Chances are that many of these commuters will live in other communities, which they will drive through on their way to work. Those communities face increased pressure on their transportation infrastructures and have to deal with the expensive consequences of a more heavily used transportation system. In other words, a decision by one local government can have important implications for other local governments. This not only makes coordination difficult, but it can lead to a lot of hard feelings and conflict.

Other individuals, however, say "*vive la difference*." Pittsburgh and Allegheny County are like most other major metropolitan areas in that for a lot of people they are pretty terrific places to work, live, go to school, and raise a family. So what if there are a lot of local governments? The positive side to having a lot of different municipalities, townships, and counties with their different tax rates and levels of public services is choice, and lots of it. All those differences mean people can choose to live in a place that has the right mix of taxes and public services to suit their individual preferences. Of course, this assumes they actually have the resources and the knowledge to make such choices, an assumption that more than one political scientist has questioned.

This chapter explores the consequences of all these differences and what they mean for everything from effective environmental policies to dealing with racial segregation, poverty, crime, political inequality, and traffic congestion. Addressing such problems in places like Allegheny County is hard because it demands that not just one or two governments do something but that dozens—or even hundreds—of governments do something. And whatever that something is, it needs to be effectively coordinated if it is going to provide a reasonable solution to the problem. And there's the rub. According to some, the organization and structure of government at the local level not only makes it hard to forge solutions to certain problems, it makes finding those solutions harder.

The previous chapter discussed the different forms of local government and different ways of organizing local government. This chapter focuses more on the importance and difficulty of coordinating all those different localities. Most Americans live in urban areas like Allegheny County, areas where local governments are cheek to jowl and piled on top of one another. The central economic and social problems that governments must address in these areas are regional rather than local in nature. Yet the United States has no tradition, and few examples, of regional government. It has a lot of local governments with limited abilities and limited incentives to act regionally. How to fashion coherent responses to regional problems is the central challenge of local governance in urban areas. This problem has become particularly acute in the wake of the Great Recession. The federal government is increasingly recognizing that local economies are defined by metro regions rather than by the sometimes arbitrary geographical lines of states or localities. Boosting the economy means targeting these metro areas for grants and other programs, which can be difficult when there is little or no governance infrastructure specifically designed to tie the polyglot mix of local governments into a coherent policy agenda. It raises questions about how governments below the state level are organized, as well as fundamental questions of political power, especially questions that deal with who has the authority to make policy and who has to pay for it.

As it turns out, rural areas are facing the same governance challenges, although for different reasons. Rural areas are being forced to grapple with regional-level coordination issues because shrinking populations cannot provide the tax base to support general purpose governments in small communities. Thus, local governments in rural areas, like local governments in urban areas, are feeling their way toward more cooperative arrangements, sharing the burden of providing public services, and even considering mergers. So, urban or rural, the biggest challenge for all is dealing with a world in which the problems are regional but the governments are local.

The Missing Level of Government

You might not have noticed, but according to some scholars there is a hole in the organizational structure of the federal system. The basic organization of the federal government, and the powers and responsibilities of state and federal governments, is covered by the U.S. Constitution. The organization of the state governments and the powers and responsibilities of state and local governments are covered by individual state constitutions. The hole is at the regional level. There is nothing in the Constitution, and virtually nothing in state constitutions, that addresses even the notion of regional government, let alone its organization or powers and responsibilities.

In some ways this is understandable. The federal arrangement set up by the Constitution is the bedrock of the U.S. political system and is deeply woven into the fabric of society. No one seriously proposes to fundamentally alter this arrangement. Even though it stands on less legal authority—local governments, remember, are not sovereign—there is a strong tradition of local government. People tend to be oriented toward their local communities and tend to place more faith in city hall than in the state or national capital. In contrast, there are no strong legal foundations for regional governments and no strong tradition of regional government either. It is the poor relation of the U.S. political system: little thought of and, outside the community of urban scholars and a handful of officials, not much loved.

Yet the majority of local governments in the United States are, like the 273 governments of Allegheny County, embedded in a larger metropolitan region. These regions have similar policy challenges and problems that have common sources and call for common solutions. This absence of some sort of regional umbrella government has been called a "fundamental flaw in America's governance structure." Why? Because "[m]etropolitan regions have become the most important functional units of economic and social life in almost all modern societies."[5] Labor and jobs, for example, rarely are concentrated in a single local political jurisdiction. The bottom line is that localities are intertwined economically and socially but are governed as if such matters can be isolated within the preexisting geographical boundaries of political jurisdictions.

Consider Shelby County, Tennessee, which a pretty urban place (Memphis sits within its borders) and is located just outside Arkansas and Mississippi. One of the major economic players in this region is the Memphis Regional Medical Center (colloquially known as "The Med"), which is the only Level 1 trauma center in a 150-mile radius. Residents across the border in Arkansas certainly rely on it to provide key emergency medical services. Yet because it is in a different state The Med cannot recover all the costs incurred for providing those services to Arkansas residents. Federal law, for example, prevents states from sending Medicaid dollars to pay for services outside state borders. The Med delivers roughly $12 million worth of services to Arkansas residents per year and gets about $24,000 back in reimbursements. Everyone recognizes the importance of The Med, but getting it adequately funded is a struggle. A. C. Wharton Jr., the mayor of Shelby County, argues that keeping The Med open is obviously a regional issue and should be addressed at a regional level. The problem is the relative lack of any systematic mechanism to coordinate a regional response to the problem. This is a big reason why Wharton has pushed for the Memphis and Shelby County governments to consolidate. That would surely help, but counties and municipalities in different states—even if they are economically and socially intertwined—are likely to stay separate entities. Federal and state constitutions recognize states, counties, and municipalities. Regions, not so much.[6]

The underlying problem is that political geography no longer lines up with economic and social geography. At the center of much of economic and social life in the United States is not a city or a county but a metropolitan area. According to the U.S. Census Bureau, a **metropolitan area** is

METROPOLITAN AREA

A populous region typically comprising a city and surrounding communities that have a high degree of social and economic integration.

a region with "a large population nucleus, together with adjacent communities having a high degree of social and economic integration with that core." It is important to note that this definition sees a metropolitan area as comprising "one or more entire counties."[7]

For data gathering and reporting purposes, the federal government formally defines metropolitan areas using the concept of a **metropolitan statistical area (MSA)**, an area with a city of 50,000 or more people, together with adjacent urban communities that have strong ties to the central city. As of 2008, there were 366 metropolitan statistical areas in the United States (there were 8 more in Puerto Rico). More than 80 percent of U.S. residents live in such metropolitan areas, with 30 percent living in central cities.[8] These metros are where some of the most important policy challenges of the twenty-first century are not just concentrated but irretrievably interconnected. Consider traffic congestion. According to metro scholar Bruce Katz, roughly 60 percent of all the vehicular miles logged in the United States occur in the top one hundred metros. This reflects not just the population concentration of those areas, or just the challenges of traffic congestion and the transportation infrastructure, but global warming (that concentration of traffic produces a lot of greenhouse gases) and the effects of global trade, shipping, and freight.[9]

Local governments in these metros, like it or not, simply cannot confine their problems or their ambitions to within their own borders, any more than they can independently control global trade or air pollution.

MAP 12-1 Pittsburgh Metropolitan Statistical Area and Surrounding MSAs

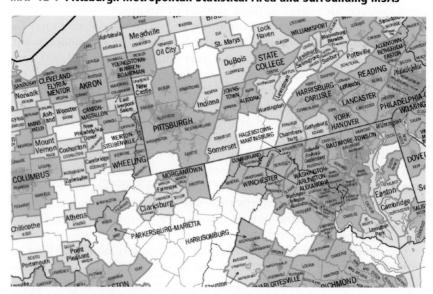

Source: U.S. Census Bureau, Population Division.

In metros, the cities, their suburbs, and the counties in which they are geographically located all blend together into a dense urban concentration. According to the U.S. Conference of Mayors, nearly half of the fifty most populated cities in the United States were packed into just 100 square miles. These population centers account for an astonishing 85 percent of U.S. employment.[10]

But there are even bigger units to consider. These dense metropolitan areas often bump into each other, forming an even larger urban geographical area referred to as a **megalopolis**. A *megalopolis* is an urban area made up of several large cities and their surrounding urban areas—in effect, a string of MSAs (see Map 12-2). Megalopolises are not confined by county borders, and they are not necessarily confined by state borders either. For example, one of the largest megalopolises in the country starts at Philadelphia, Pennsylvania, and runs through the state of New Jersey. They may not even be confined by national borders, as in the case of Detroit, Michigan, and Windsor, Ontario, in Canada. Another example of a cross-national megalopolis is El Paso, Texas, and Juárez, Mexico.

MEGALOPOLIS

An urban area made up of several large cities and their surrounding urban areas.

MAP 12-2 **Metropolitan and Micropolitan Statistical Areas of the Continental United States**

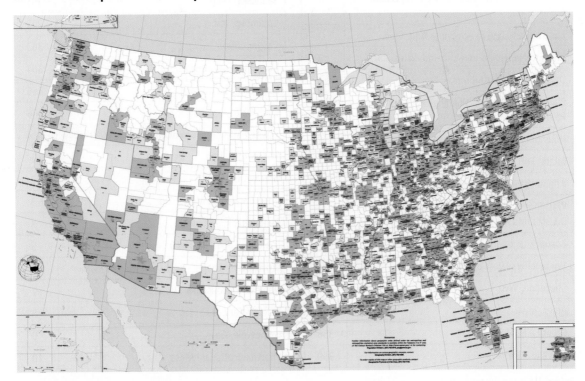

Source: U.S. Census Bureau, Population Division.

Because these metropolitan areas span not just county but also state and even national borders, it is incredibly difficult to exercise any form of centralized planning over their growth and operation. Like Allegheny County, there are literally hundreds of governments making thousands of decisions, and these often are made with little coordination or thought to their regional effects. This fragmentation of political authority not only makes it hard to address regional problems, it is arguably the cause of some of them.

Take, for example, the rise of so-called **edgeless cities**. These are sprawling unplanned office and retail complexes that are not pedestrian friendly and often become ghost towns at night. They do have obvious economic attractions—they mean jobs, sales taxes (people who work in them buy stuff, even if it is just gas and incidentals at a convenience store), and also property taxes (office complexes are valuable properties).

EDGELESS CITIES

Office and retail complexes without clear boundaries.

TABLE 12-1

Metropolitan Statistical Areas at a Glance

Ten Largest MSAs by Population, 2008	Rank
New York-Northern New Jersey-Long Island, N.Y.-N.J.-Pa.	1
Los Angeles-Long Beach-Santa Ana, Calif.	2
Chicago-Naperville-Joliet, Ill.-Ind.-Wisc.	3
Dallas-Fort Worth-Arlington, Tex.	4
Philadelphia-Camden-Wilmington, Pa.-N.J.-Del.-Md.	5
Houston-Sugar Land-Baytown, Tex.	6
Miami-Fort Lauderdale-Miami Beach, Fla.	7
Atlanta-Sandy Springs-Marietta, Ga.	8
Washington-Arlington-Alexandria, D.C.-Va.-Md.-W.V.	9
Boston-Cambridge-Quincy, Mass.-N.H.	10

Ten Smallest MSAs by Population, 2008	Rank
Cheyenne, Wyo	356
Ames, Iowa	357
Great Falls, Mont.	358
Corvallis, Ore.	359

Danville, Ill.	360
Sandusky, Ohio	361
Columbus, Ind.	362
Casper, Wyo.	363
Hinesville-Fort Stewart, Ga.	364
Lewiston, Idaho-Wash.	365
Enid, Okla.	366

Top Ten MSAs by Percentage Change, 2000–2006	Rank
St. George, Utah	1
Greeley, Colo.	2
Cape Coral–Fort Myers, Fla.	3
Bend, Ore.	4
Las Vegas–Paradise, Nev.	5
Provo-Orem, Utah	6
Naples–Marco Island, Fla.	7
Raleigh-Cary, N.C.	8
Gainesville, Ga.	9
Phoenix-Scottsdale-Mesa, Ariz.	10

Source: U.S. Census Bureau, Population Division, 2008.

Yet, whatever local benefits they produce, they also export a set of costs to the larger region. Most of the people who work in edgeless cities commute home to greener residential areas. This means such developments segregate and put considerable geographical distance between where people live and where people work. The end result—traffic congestion and smog—affects all communities in the region, but individually there is not much any local government can do about such problems.

Sprawl: How Metropolitan Regions Grow

The fragmented nature of governance in metropolitan areas creates an interconnected set of problems that are difficult to address in a systematic and coordinated fashion. To understand the causes and consequences of these problems, as well as the challenges involved in effectively addressing them, it helps to have a little historical background on the roots of metropolitan growth.

Metropolitan areas are a relatively new concept. As recently as the 1920s, scholars recognized that the growth of suburbs, rapid and easily accessible transportation, and new forms of communication were transforming urban areas into a new social and economic phenomenon. They also recognized that existing forms of local government were ill-equipped to deal with this new urban reality, and some even went so far as to call for a new form of metropolitan government to address the gap between state and local political jurisdictions.[11]

It was not until after World War II, however, that the country really saw the explosive growth of metropolitan areas and the broad-scale governance problems that accompanied this growth. In some ways, this growth was inevitable. A population boom created enormous pressure for new development, and that development typically took place on the periphery of large cities or urban areas in the form of low-density suburban housing and commercial developments. This created an interrelated set of problems that can be traced to the catch-all phenomenon of **sprawl**. Often used as a generic term for the rapid growth of any metropolitan area, sprawl is considered by most urban scholars to be a particular type of growth. There is no universal definition, but this type of growth does have set of specific characteristics:

Single-use zoning. One of the central political powers of local government is control over land use. This power is typically exercised through **zoning laws**. These laws can allow land to be used for a mix of commercial, recreational, and residential developments, or for single uses, when land is used for single-purpose developments. Local governments in metropolitan areas have tended to favor the latter approach. The end result is geographical separation between the places where people work, live, and play.

SPRAWL
The rapid growth of a metropolitan area, typically as a result of specific types of zoning and development.

ZONING LAWS
Regulations that control how land can be used.

LOW-DENSITY DEVELOPMENT

Development practices that spread (rather than concentrate) populations across the land.

Low-density development. The growth of metropolitan areas has not only been defined by single-use developments but also by low-density developments. In effect, local governments have exercised their powers over land use to dictate that the growth in metropolitan areas will be out rather than up. Rather than multifamily developments like high-rise condominiums and apartments, suburbs and other urban municipalities have favored single-family developments. These developments make for lower population densities, but obviously they also require more land. For example, the population of the Milwaukee, Wisconsin, metropolitan area increased roughly 3 percent between 1970 and 1990; but geographically the metro area increased by 38 percent. Los Angeles is a classic case of how low-density development can consume vast stretches of land. Population-wise, Los Angeles grew about 45 percent between 1970 and 1990; land-wise, it grew by 300 percent.[12]

LEAPFROG DEVELOPMENT

Developments that jump—or leapfrog—over established developments, leaving undeveloped or underdeveloped land between developments.

Leapfrog development. Leapfrog developments jump—or leapfrog—over established developments, leaving undeveloped or underdeveloped land between developments. This puts a particular strain on infrastructure, not just on roads but also on water and sewer facilities. Having developments that bypass undeveloped land means that utilities have to be stretched out further to serve these developments.

Leapfrog development is partially driven by the economic incentives of developers. Most established municipalities like to create uniform requirements for developments within their own jurisdictions, for example, by enforcing specific building codes. They may even impose what are sometimes called **impact fees**. Municipalities charge builders of new housing or commercial developments impact fees to help offset the costs of extending services such as parks, schools, law enforcement, and fire protection services to these developments. A new housing development, for instance, may require the building of a new fire station, and impact fees can help offset that cost. It is not hard to see then why developers often favor building in unincorporated areas, typically on land with a geographical separation from municipal borders that is still close enough to make for an easy commute. The land in unincorporated areas tends to be cheaper, and there are fewer regulations to deal with.

IMPACT FEES

Fees that municipalities charge builders of new housing or commercial developments to help offset the costs of extending services.

CAR-DEPENDENT LIVING

Owning a car for transportation becoming a necessity; an outcome of low-density development.

Car-dependent living. Developing metropolitan areas through single-use, low-density developments means citizens have to be highly mobile. Getting from a suburban home to a job in a commercial office development and from home to the kids' soccer game on the weekend pretty much requires an automobile. In low-density housing developments, it is often impossible—or at least impractical—to do something like "run to the corner store." Getting a six-pack to watch the game or a bag of sugar to bake cookies, or even arranging a play date for the kids, requires transportation. Because public transportation systems are, for the most part, not set up for convenient and efficient transportation across large, multijurisdictional geographical areas, having a car becomes a necessity for living in metropolitan areas.

Between 1950 and 1990 the population of the United States increased by about 40 percent, but the number of miles traveled in cars increased 140 percent. The imbalance between population growth and the growth in automobile use is a direct consequence of how land has been developed in metropolitan areas. The rise of car-dependent living exacts an environmental toll. Governments have done a reasonably good job of controlling "point" sources of pollution (concentrated sources of pollutants that tend to be limited in number, like factories or power plants) over the past three decades or so. However, nonpoint sources of pollution are harder to identify and control because they consist of many sources, each putting out a relatively small amount of pollutants but collectively having a large-scale impact on the environment. Cars are a classic example of a nonpoint source of pollution and are a major cause of air quality problems in metropolitan areas.[13]

One of the consequences of development patterns in urban metropolitan regions is traffic congestion. Because people tend to live in one place and work in another, commuting by car is part of the daily routine for millions of Americans. Traffic back-up along Lake Shore Drive in Chicago is common for area drivers.

Fragmentation of land use powers. A key characteristic of sprawl is the division of powers among local political jurisdictions, in particular the power over land use. Local governments frequently have strong incentives to use these powers in a way that provides local benefits for those within the particular local jurisdiction but creates costs for neighboring communities.

These basic characteristics have defined the growth and development of many major metropolitan areas in the United States during the past half century or so. The result is largely unplanned growth (no systematic coordination to balance local benefits with regional costs) that spreads out across ever-larger geographical regions, gobbling up previously rural areas and replacing them with low-density, single-use developments.

The Cons of Metropolitan Growth

By now it should be fairly obvious that metropolitan growth characterized by sprawl results in problems like traffic congestion and smog. Yet many academics who study urban politics and growth also believe that these development patterns produce a wide range of other problems. These problems include the concentration of poverty and crime into certain neighborhoods; segregation by race and class; and inequality in public services, fiscal resources, and political power.

As new low-density housing developments began popping up around core cities after World War II, the middle and upper classes began moving from the cities to the suburbs. There were "push" and "pull" reasons for the migration of the better-off classes to the suburbs. One reason was the lure of the lifestyle—the home with the white picket fence on a leafy suburban lane—that "pulled" people out of the city. Another was the racial desegregation of public schools in the 1960s and 1970s; increasing numbers of less well-off nonwhites began to make up an ever greater proportion of urban schools, acting as an incentive for whites to move, "pushing" them out to the suburbs.

The racial—and perhaps racist—undertones of this demographic shift have been repeatedly noted by academics.[14] Because the middle and upper classes were largely white, this demographic phenomenon became known as **white flight**. As whites left the dense, multiuse neighborhoods of cities for the lure of single-family homes on large lots in suburbia, minorities became concentrated in the core urban areas. Because racial minorities also were much more likely to be less socioeconomically well-off than whites, this also meant that inner-city neighborhoods became poorer.

As neighborhoods became poorer, the remaining middle class felt more pressure to decamp to the suburbs and a self-reinforcing trend set in; the poor and ethnic minorities became increasingly concentrated in core city neighborhoods. In the past couple of decades, this trend has started to occur in the suburbs themselves. Minorities who managed to get far enough up the socioeconomic ladder to move to an inner-ring suburb have triggered another round of white flight; as these comparatively less white, less well-off people move into the inner-ring suburbs, the better-off move farther out. The end result is the increasingly racial and socioeconomic homogeneity of particular political jurisdictions.

Some local political jurisdictions are well-off and tend to have property values that support high-quality public services. Middle- and upper-class suburbs, for example, tend to have high-quality public schools. So do **exurbs**, or municipalities in more rural settings that serve as bedroom communities, with residents commuting in to jobs in the cities or suburbs during the day and returning to their homes after work. This tends to be in stark contrast with some inner-city neighborhoods and inner-ring suburbs in which poverty is concentrated. Property values are low in such neighborhoods, which means that they cannot support high-quality public services.

It is important to note that the end result is economic *and* racial segregation based on housing patterns. This trend is made apparent by school districts. In some urban areas, for example, African Americans make up less

WHITE FLIGHT

A demographic trend in which the middle and upper classes leave central cities for predominantly white suburbs.

EXURBS

Municipalities in rural areas that ring suburbs. They typically serve as bedroom communities for the prosperous, providing rural homes with easy access to urban areas.

Governing States and Localities

than 3 percent of the total population but constitute 70 percent of the enrollment in school districts.[15] These are invariably schools that serve poor communities where crime and other social problems place enormous strains not just on public education but also on social and economic opportunities in general. While people can, and do, experience challenge and struggle out in the suburbs, such communities are much more likely to have the fiscal capacity to support such public services as good school systems. And because good schools play an important role in determining where the middle class wants to live, again this becomes a self-reinforcing trend.

In other words, here is a difference that makes a big difference to the quality of life of millions of people. Place matters because wealth is segregated by community across metropolitan regions, communities that are themselves concentrated in different political jurisdictions. As one well-known study of metropolitan politics and policy concludes, where you live in a given metropolitan area both affects your quality of life and shapes your social and economic opportunities. Place affects access to jobs, public services, levels of personal security (crime tends to be higher in some socioeconomically stressed neighborhoods), availability of medical services, and even the quality of the air you breathe (the people commuting in from the exurbs contribute to urban smog, but escape to the cleaner rural air after the work day is done).[16]

Take the issue of jobs. Two-thirds of all new jobs are created in suburbs (think of big-box stores like Wal-Mart and Home Depot that dot suburban landscapes—they represent a lot of jobs). The people who most desperately need some of those jobs, and the social and economic opportunities they represent, are concentrated in poorer inner-city neighborhoods. Three-quarters of all welfare recipients live either in the central cities or in poorer rural areas.[17] These people cannot move to the suburbs where the jobs are because they cannot afford the expensive homes that typify low-density, single-use housing developments. Buying and operating a car also are expensive propositions that can levy a harsh financial toll on those less well-off. That leaves public transportation, which, because of the huge geographical spaces that have to be covered, is often inefficient.

Critics of the consequences of sprawl argue that the end result will be metropolitan areas that continue to promote and reinforce economic and racial segregation and create disparities in the tax base that lead to huge differences in the quality of public services among local political jurisdictions. On top of that, from a regional perspective, the patterns of metropolitan growth are economically inefficient (jobs and the labor market are

> Place matters because wealth is segregated by community across metropolitan regions, communities that are themselves concentrated in different political jurisdictions. As one well-known study of metropolitan politics and policy concludes, where you live in a given metropolitan area both affects your quality of life and shapes your social and economic opportunities.

disconnected) and environmentally dangerous (all those cars pump out a lot of toxic emissions).[18]

Government Reform in Metropolitan Areas

Racial and economic segregation, inequities in the tax bases and public services, and, above all, political fragmentation that creates difficulty in coordinating rational and effective responses to regional challenges—the problems of governance in metropolitan areas are well known. But what can be done about them?

There are a number of strategies for rationalizing government in metropolitan areas, all of which either have been implemented or considered to various degrees in virtually all major urban areas. The **reform perspective** pushes for such rationalization and begins with the assumption that the key problems and challenges of governance in metropolitan areas are regional in nature and, as such, should be addressed regionally. Proponents also tend to argue that many of the problems have been created by political fragmentation in the first place in that there are lots of smaller governments making decisions that may produce local benefits but export the costs to other jurisdictions. If the root cause of these problems is political fragmentation, government consolidation is the obvious solution. In other words, new regional governing structures should be created to fill the hole in the federal system, governments that are better positioned to effectively respond to the interconnected problems of large metropolitan areas.[19]

There is no universal response to filling that hole, however. Instead, there are a number of different strategies that range from creating new pan-regional governments to eliminating long-standing local jurisdictions.

Regional Governments

Adherents of the reform perspective are strong advocates of creating regional authorities to address regional problems. This can be done in a couple of ways.

First, new government structures can be created to sit above existing political jurisdictions and be given the authority to oversee regional land-use planning. This sort of approach has been popular with a number of civic activists from the reform tradition. Former Albuquerque mayor David Rusk, Minnesota state representative Myron Orfield, and syndicated columnist Neal Pierce have all been popular champions of pan-regional planning authorities. There are a couple of well-known examples of such regional planning authorities that are frequently cited by such advocates as examples of the benefits of taking a top-down approach to land-use regulation.

REFORM PERSPECTIVE

An approach to filling gaps in service and reducing redundancies in local governments that calls for regional-level solutions.

One of the best known of these is the Metropolitan Service District in Portland, Oregon, called "Metro." Metro is a true regional government that covers Clackamas, Multnomah, and Washington counties and the twenty-five municipalities in the Portland metropolitan area. It is governed by an elected legislature (a six-member council) and an elected executive (the council president).[20] Metro exercises real regulatory authority in areas such as land-use planning, regional transportation, recycling and garbage disposal, and a host of other areas that are regional rather than local in nature.

A number of academic observers have concluded that the Portland top-down approach to regional planning has reaped considerable benefits compared to metropolitan areas that have no comparable regional governance. For example, white flight in Portland has been markedly less than in other cities. Compared to many other major cities, the middle class—especially young, highly educated individuals—tend to settle in the central city rather than in the suburbs or nonmetropolitan areas.[21]

One of the notable characteristics of the Portland Metro is the presence of an **urban growth boundary (UGB)**. A UGB controls the density and type of development by establishing a boundary around a given urban area. Land inside the UGB is slated for high-density development; land outside the UGB is slated for lower-density, rural sorts of development. In effect, this is a planning regulation that forces cities to grow vertically rather than horizontally and, thus, sets limits on sprawl and the problems it generates.

Critics of UGBs argue they have a significant downside. By limiting the land available for development, UGBs drive up prices for land in particular and real estate in general. The end results are high property values and limited supplies of affordable housing. This does not seem to have happened in Portland, however, at least to any extreme. In fact, property values there are considered reasonable compared with the rest of the West Coast. The success of the UGB in Portland has been used by reformers to promote the adoption of similar policies in other urban areas. Three states—Oregon, Tennessee, and Washington—now mandate cities to establish UGBs.

Regional Councils

Most metropolitan areas lack any form of regional government with the authority and standing of Portland's Metro. There are, however, a large number of regional planning authorities that provide at least a rudimentary form of coordination among the local governments packed into metropolitan areas.

Probably the most common attempt to rationalize local policymaking across multijurisdictional metropolitan areas is the formation of regional councils. A **regional council** is "a multi-service entity with state and locally-defined

URBAN GROWTH BOUNDARY (UGB)
The border established around urban areas that is intended to control the density and type of development.

REGIONAL COUNCIL
A planning and advisory organization whose members include multiple local governments. Regional councils often are used to administer state and federal programs that target regions.

boundaries that delivers a variety of federal, state and local programs while continuing its function as a planning organization, technical assistance provider and 'visionary' to its member local governments."[22]

Regional councils are made up of member governments, such as municipalities and school districts, although other nonprofit, civic, private, or academic organizations also may be included. They originated in the 1960s and 1970s as a vehicle for delivering state and federal programs to regional areas. Since then, they have grown to become an important means of making and coordinating regionwide policy and planning in such areas as land use, transportation, economic development, housing, and social services. In effect, regional councils are a way to recognize that decisions made in one community can have knock-on effects in neighboring communities and that it therefore makes sense to address some problems regionally rather than locally. There are 516 such bodies in the United States, and of the roughly 39,000 general purpose local governments in the country (which include counties, cities, municipalities, villages, boroughs, towns, and townships) about 35,000 are served by a regional council.[23]

A related form of regional authority is the **metropolitan planning organization (MPO)**. MPOs are regional organizations that decide how federal transportation funds are allocated within a regional area. MPOs are interesting because they represent a specific recognition by federal law that regions—as opposed to localities—are central functional policy units. The Intermodal Surface Transportation Efficiency Act of 1991 (ISTEA) mandated that every metropolitan region had to identify an institution (an MPO) to serve as the central coordinating authority for federal transportation funds in that area. These MPOs have the responsibility of developing transportation plans and programs for their metropolitan regions. All transportation projects involving federal money—which is to say virtually all major transportation projects—have to be approved by an MPO. Some MPOs administer billions of dollars in federal transportation grants, and control over such large amounts of money, coupled with the MPOs' authority over critical transportation programs, translates into major political clout.[24]

Regional councils and MPOs, however, should not be confused or equated with Portland's Metro. They are different in the sense that they are more a vehicle for intergovernmental cooperation than an actual form of government with executive and legislative authority independent of local government interests. Formal organizations of local governments in metropolitan areas have existed in some form or another for decades; regional councils and MPOs are just the more common and better-known examples. Hashing out roles and responsibilities, not to mention making decisions, involves a complicated—and often contentious—give-and-take among the local governments that constitute the membership of these regional bodies.

For example, most formal organizations of local governments, in metropolitan areas at least, began by allowing every member to have an equal voice in the organization. What this meant was that a small rural township

MAP 12-3 California's Metropolitan Planning Organizations' Boundaries

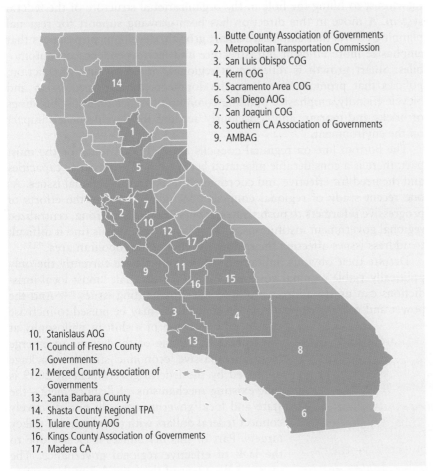

1. Butte County Association of Governments
2. Metropolitan Transportation Commission
3. San Luis Obispo COG
4. Kern COG
5. Sacramento Area COG
6. San Diego AOG
7. San Joaquin COG
8. Southern CA Association of Governments
9. AMBAG

10. Stanislaus AOG
11. Council of Fresno County Governments
12. Merced County Association of Governments
13. Santa Barbara County
14. Shasta County Regional TPA
15. Tulare County AOG
16. Kings County Association of Governments
17. Madera CA

Source: Association of Metropolitan Planning Organizations. http://terrains.com/gallery/ampo/ampo_map.php.

had exactly the same influence on regional issues as a core city, even though it had a fraction of the population. Figuring out more representational, equitable, and democratic decision making in these regional bodies has been, to put it mildly, a challenge. Smaller jurisdictions are, understandably, loathe to give up their influence to bigger neighbors for fear of having their interests take a back seat. The bigger neighbors, in turn, resent having their interests yoked to the interests of much smaller communities.

Intergovernmental institutions such as regional councils are, at best, confederal sorts of regional governments that are creatures of the often conflicting interests of their members. This complicates decision making and makes it harder for these bodies to exert firm regulatory authority over critical areas such as land use. Still, in most parts of the country they come the closest to filling the hole in the organizational structure of the federal system. A move in this direction has been growing support for regional planning efforts that emphasize **smart growth**, development practices that emphasize more efficient infrastructure and less dependence on automobiles. Smart growth is reflected in regional, or even single-jurisdiction, policies that promote mixed-use developments that are pedestrian and bicycle friendly, emphasize building community rather than just buildings of bricks and mortar, and consciously account for development's impact on the environment.

The bottom line on regional councils and MPOs is that, for the most part, there is a considerable mismatch between their governance capacities and the need for effective and coordinated responses to regional issues. As one recent study of regional councils concludes, "Despite the efforts of progressive reformers to push strategies encouraging . . . strong, centralized regional government institutions, most regional institutions find it difficult to address issues affecting the quality of life in a metropolitan area."[25]

Despite their obvious limitations, these councils are currently the only politically viable regional governance mechanisms that, "most local jurisdictions can use to address multiple and cross-cutting issues."[26] And the power and role of regional councils and MPOs may be poised to increase considerably because of a shift in philosophy at the federal level. One of the lessons to emerge from the massive economic stimulus package approved by the federal government in 2009 is that existing mechanisms of disbursement—the state and local governments—do not effectively connect federal dollars with their intended policy targets. Part of this disconnect is clearly due to the lack of effective regional governance. The overarching intent of the federal stimulus money was to stimulate the economy, and that means targeting metro areas where much of the nation's economic activity takes place. Stimulus dollars, however, for the most part went to states and localities that were scrambling to get their individual shares of the federal pie. Powerful metro-level governments with the ability to effectively address key issues across political jurisdictions got less stimulus money because for the most part they simply don't exist. The Obama White House has signaled that in the future it prefers to see federal aid tied to increased regional cooperation, and that puts regional councils and MPOs in a good position to see their governance capacities increase (see the States under Stress feature "Tying Federal Funding to Regional Cooperation," page 473).

SMART GROWTH

Environmentally friendly development practices, particularly those that emphasize more efficient infrastructure and less dependence on automobiles.

> One of the lessons to emerge from the massive economic stimulus package approved by the federal government in 2009 is that existing mechanisms of disbursement—the state and local governments—do not effectively connect federal dollars with their intended policy targets. Part of this disconnect is clearly due to the lack of effective regional governance.

States under Stress: Tying Federal Funding to Regional Cooperation

If the Obama administration gets its way, how the federal government interacts with states and localities across a wide range of policy areas is about to be redefined, and that change will reshape the entire structure and process of dispensing federal funds and steering federal policy.

The White House has embraced a concept, advanced largely by the Brookings Institution's Metropolitan Policy Program, that stresses the primacy of the nation's metro regions—cities or clusters of cities, plus their inner and outer suburbs and some rural areas that are linked to them economically. The Brookings mantra is that these regions are the economic drivers of the country; they do, after all, contain three-quarters of the American population and generate most of the nation's economic activity. So, the idea is for Washington to start approaching the governments below its own level not as separate states, cities, and counties but as metros.

Soon after it took office, the administration started pushing its domestic agencies to find a more regional approach to dealing with all subgovernments. Federal departments in charge of housing, transportation, energy, the environment, labor, and small businesses are trying to coordinate hundreds of programs addressing a wide range of activities. And the expectation is that the efforts they will be funding—clusters of governments acting collaboratively—must be similarly integrated. If they are, great. If not, no dough.

The 2009 federal stimulus money was mostly subject to the old rules because Washington wanted to pump it out as fast as possible and didn't have time to write new rules. A New York Times analysis of more than 5,000 transportation projects in the first few months under Obama showed that "the 100 largest metropolitan areas are getting less than half the money from the biggest pot of transportation stimulus money. In many cases, they have lost a tug of war with state lawmakers that urban advocates say could hurt the nation's economic engines."

This could be the last time federal funds are distributed that way. Top managers in all the relevant agencies seem serious about forcing metropolitan collaboration, particularly when it involves more than one area of domestic policy. At HUD, Secretary Shaun Donovan (former commissioner of housing in New York City) and Deputy Secretary Ron Sims (former executive of King County, Washington) already have budgeted $150 million to implement the collaborative effort.

Bruce Katz of the Brookings Institution predicts optimistically that the growing recognition of the importance of metro areas "will stimulate a new generation of political and policy organizing at the metro scale." He believes this will include reinvigorating and funding long-dormant MPOs that were resuscitated sixteen years ago when Congress passed a landmark transportation bill, only to be largely ignored in more recent years.

Of course, there are problems with this strategy, both practical and political. As columnist Mary Newsom of the Charlotte Observer points out, far too many MPOs still seem to believe that " 'transportation' means only highways" and that regional organizations are little more than instruments for the protection of local turf. The Charlotte metropolitan region, Newsom notes, "is home to four separate MPOs, or five, depending on how you count. So transportation planning here is completely fragmented—and Charlotte gets shorted when dollars are divvied."

That's true in a lot of places because governors and legislatures like to spread the funds around their states rather than concentrating them in metros. And they may not be too interested in changing the process or the rules. But that is exactly what the Obama administration is pressuring them to do.

Federalism scholar Paul Posner of George Mason University has some doubts about how successful the new administration's metro initiative will be, not only because states and locals have the political clout to avoid ceding too much authority but also because "the feds have a track record of good intentions over the past 50 years" that have ultimately amounted to very little.

But Posner concedes that some incremental progress is taking place. "The lesson learned," he says, "might be that the only way the federal government will succeed in institutionalizing regionalism is if it follows and supports demand from the bottom of our system, rather than seeking to create and impose demand from the top. Where the demand exists and the regional institutions are strong, there is promise. But where they are not, then progress will be much slower."

Source: Peter Harkness, "Tying Federal Funding to Regional Cooperation," Governing magazine, September 2009.

Many local governments also engage in looser, informal cooperative arrangements rather than creating formal institutions such as regional councils or MPOs. This sort of cooperation is known as an **interjurisdictional agreement (IJA)**, an increasingly common form of intergovernmental cooperation. IJAs may take the form of a binding agreement. For example, a town may contract with the county for law enforcement services or for dispatch services. Other IJAs may be much more informal and rest on nothing more than a good faith agreement between two or more local governments to jointly provide a service or work together on planning or management issues. No one really knows how many IJAs there are or how effective they are in promoting an effective integrated response to regional problems. Given the shortcomings of more formal institutions like regional councils and MPOs, however, they often represent one of the few viable alternatives for multijurisdictional governance.[27]

Government Consolidation

One way to regularize or rationalize governance in a metropolitan region is to create a pan-regional institution. As already discussed, this can be done either through the creation of a new form of government (such as Portland's Metro) or through a formal institution of intergovernmental cooperation, such as a regional council. A second approach is to reduce the number of governments through merger or consolidation. This is typically done by merging a city with a county.

On the face of it, this makes a good deal of sense. Cities and urban counties share the same geographical space and provide similar services. A classic example is law enforcement services. Think of an urban county sitting on top of a large city. The county will have a sheriff's office; the city will have a police department. Each can have its own jails, dispatch centers, training facilities, and purchasing departments. It strikes many that there is a lot redundancy and inefficiency in duplicating these services in such close quarters. Why not consolidate at least some of these functions? That is exactly what Des Moines, Iowa, and Polk County did with their city and county jails. The county and city jails sat on opposite sides of the Des Moines River—directly across from each other—and consolidating facilities and operations just seemed to make sense.

If consolidating operations can reduce redundancy and improve efficiency, why not go whole hog and merge municipal and county governments into a single government? Cities and counties often duplicate bureaucracies and paperwork, so there seems to be an obvious logic to **city-county consolidation**. With as many as 75 percent of all major urban areas in the United States contained within single counties, it would seem to make sense that such mergers would be common and easy. But they aren't, and it doesn't.

According to the National Association of Counties, of the nation's more than three thousand counties only thirty-three (roughly 1 percent) have consolidated with cities. Since 1990, there have been only about six successful mergers, although many more have been considered.[28] Unsuccessful efforts include Gainesville, Florida, with Alachua County and Spokane, Washington, with Spokane County.

Despite the glacial pace of city-county consolidation, it is an idea that has been around for a long time. The earliest consolidation dates back to 1805, when the city of New Orleans was consolidated with New Orleans Parish (remember, in Louisiana counties are called parishes). The practice even enjoyed an era of popularity in the 1960s and 1970s.

Proposals for consolidation often come in response to a state initiative or a regional challenge. For example, the citizens of Jacksonville, Florida, in Duval County, were experiencing industrial waste in their river, underachieving high schools, and clashes between city and county officials during the 1960s. Local business leaders lobbied the state legislature for help. The legislature created a commission that proposed a consolidation plan. The plan was approved in 1967 by the legislature and, subsequently, was approved by the voters in a referendum.

For the most part, this merger has worked for the two governments involved. But even after the merger, there were municipalities in Duval County (Atlantic Beach, Baldwin, Jacksonville Beach, and Neptune Beach) but outside Jacksonville city limits that continued as independent local governments. These communities periodically have considered splitting off from Jacksonville/Duval and forming a new county (Ocean County) as a means to recover a county government less tied to the city of Jacksonville. Thus far, however, these efforts have not progressed beyond the discussion stage, and all these municipalities remain a part of Duval County.

Still, only a few dozen mergers in two hundred years leaves a lot of cities and counties sitting right on top of each other duplicating services. Why haven't city-county consolidations happened more often? The answer in part has to do with who supports and who opposes the mergers when they are proposed.

Consolidation typically is favored by business groups and others who favor efficiency in government spending and regulation over local control of government. These individuals seek a reorganization of government to reduce bureaucratic redundancy and to allow communities to speak "with one voice." The politics of consolidations, however, are tricky. Middle-class suburbanites may be concerned that mergers will benefit mostly downtown residents while raising taxes in the suburbs; inner-city minorities may fear their voting power will be diluted. Elected officials reflect these concerns and perhaps add some of their own. Consolidated governments mean fewer elected politicians and, most likely, fewer public employees. This creates internal pressure to resist merger movements.

TABLE 12-2

Consolidated City-County Governments

City-counties operating primarily as cities		Metropolitan governments operating primarily as cities		Areas with county-like office in other governments (city, township, special district, state)	
Alaska	City and borough of Anchorage	Tennessee	Hartsville and Trousdale County	Florida	County of Duval (City of Jacksonville)
	City and borough of Juneau		Lynchburg and Moore County	Georgia	County of Clarke (City of Athens)
	City and borough of Sitka		Nashville and Davidson County		County of Muscogee (City of Columbus)
	City and borough of Yakutat				County of Richmond (City of Augusta)
California	City and county of San Francisco			Hawaii	County of Kalawao (State of Hawaii)
Colorado	City and county of Broomfield			Indiana	County of Marion (City of Indianapolis)
	City and county of Denver			Kentucky	Lexington-Fayette Urban County
Hawaii	City and county of Honolulu			Louisiana	Parish of East Baton Rouge (City of Baton Rouge)
Kansas	Unified Government of Wyandotte County and City of Kansas City				Parish of Lafayette (City of Lafayette)
Montana	Anaconda-Deer Lodge County				Parish of Orleans (City of New Orleans)
	Butte-Silver Bow County				Terrebonne Parish Consolidated Government
				Massachusetts	County of Nantucket (Town of Nantucket)
					County of Suffolk (City of Boston)
				New York	Counties of Bronx, Kings, New York, Queens, and Richmond (all part of the City of New York)
				Pennsylvania	County of Philadelphia (City of Philadelphia)

Source: *2002 Census of Governments,* vol. 1, no. 1, Government Organization, GC02(1)-1 (Washington, D.C.: United States Department of Commerce, Bureau of Census), Appendix B.

A Difference That Makes a Difference: Marrying a City with a County

January 2003 saw the birth of the Louisville-Jefferson Metro government. The new government was the result of a long-disputed merger of Kentucky's most developed and populous entities: the city of Louisville and Jefferson County. Advocates of what would become the largest such consolidation in the United States since 1970 had finally driven home their case after three failed attempts to persuade voters, going back to the 1950s.

The idea is that consolidation will allow struggling downtown Louisville to share the benefits of the job growth previously concentrated in the suburbs. Rivalry between competing bureaucracies should ease, paperwork for businesses in such areas as building codes should shrink, and regional planning to relieve traffic congestion should be streamlined.

No longer will the county, run by a judge-executive with authority over more than eighty municipalities, have veto power over tax and annexation proposals. Under the new rules, if both the county and the city have a law on the books for a certain issue, the county law prevails. If the city has a given law and the county doesn't, then the existing city law now covers both areas.

The idea seemed so promising that representatives from cities such as Fresno, California; Buffalo, New York; Milwaukee, Wisconsin; and Cedar Rapids, Iowa came to study its implementation.[a]

For cities with expansion potential that is "inelastic," the term used by author and former Albuquerque mayor David Rusk, consolidation becomes a tempting alternative to annexation or boundary change. Rusk said in his 1995 book *Cities without Suburbs* that consolidation is a way to amplify economic power and project it over a greater area.

Resistance most commonly comes from suburbanites who are not attracted by the idea of forming a common identity with a city that in many cases is impoverished and suffering from crime and poor public schools. Perhaps suburban taxpayers are reluctant to pay for infrastructure improvements in other jurisdictions—urban sewer and water lines, for example—when many residents of rural areas and newly suburbanized neighborhoods paid for their own septic tanks and wells.

Politically, many urban minorities feel that their autonomy and influence will be diluted in a greater metropolitan entity. Those living in surrounding unincorporated areas may feel left out of the political mix altogether.[b] Indeed, with the Louisville merger, the percentage of African Americans in the total population shrank from 34 to 19 percent.

But there are grounds for optimism. With change from city to metro region, resulting in the land area rising from 60 to 386 square miles, and the population tripling, rising from 256,231 to 693,784, the average education level, median income, home price, homeownership rate, and employment rate also all rose. The number of high school graduates rose from 76 to 82 percent, the median household income rose from $28,843 to $39,457, and home ownership rates rose from 52.5 to 64.9 percent.

[a]Alan Greenblatt, "Louisville: Anatomy of a Merger," *Governing* magazine, December 2002.

[b]Ann O. Bowman, "Urban Government," in *Handbook of Research on Urban Politics and Policy in the United States*, ed. Ronald K. Vogel (Westport, Conn.: Greenwood Press, 1997), 139.

There is also plain old-fashioned community loyalty. The point has been made before about the strong tradition of local government in the United States. People identify with their local governments and tend to trust them (at least compared to state and federal governments). There is no tradition of regional government, and citizens and public officials treat these new and unknown entities with a degree of mistrust.

All this combines to make city-county consolidations a tough political undertaking, even when most objective observers agree they make a good deal of sense. Allegheny County and the city of Pittsburgh, for example, have been flirting with the issue of consolidation for more than a decade. A series of blue-ribbon panels, committees, and commissions have studied the pros and cons of an Allegheny-Pittsburgh consolidation, and they have mostly come to the same conclusion. "There's no question you could save money and provide much better service," states David O'Laughlin, who served on one such panel.[29]

There has been some progress. The city and county have managed to consolidate some operations, for example, 911 call centers, fingerprinting duties, and some court functions. But a full-scale merger, despite its apparent advantages, still seems a long way off. In 2006, yet another panel was formed to study city-county consolidation, and in 2008, it recommended that a merger take place. As of 2010, there was still no merger. Allegheny County and the hundreds of governments within its borders sometimes cooperate and sometimes feud, but they retain their local political independence. The bottom line is that local governments as a general rule do not want to share customers and definitely do not want to put themselves out of business.[30]

Like a good marriage, the consolidation of a city and a county depends critically on partners that trust each other and can make equal contributions to the merger. For example, Phoenix, Arizona, has won awards for its state-of-the-art management innovations. On the other hand, surrounding Maricopa County has a reputation for management inefficiency. Good luck in getting those two governments down the aisle.[31]

Annexation

ANNEXATION

The legal incorporation of one jurisdiction or territory into another.

Rather than forming new governments like Portland's Metro or merging old ones, another option for dealing with the problems of sprawl, traffic congestion, and uneven economic development is to make the existing political jurisdictions bigger. **Annexation** is the legal incorporation of one jurisdiction or territory into another. Usually, the jurisdiction that does the annexing is the more politically powerful, whereas the "annexee" is weaker and may not be enthusiastic about becoming the latest addition to a larger municipal neighbor. This approach is relatively common in the South and West, regions where there are large tracts of unincorporated land adjacent to major cities. Cities such as El Paso, Houston, and Phoenix have annexed hundreds of square miles and, in doing so, have turned themselves into regional governments by sheer geographical size. Oklahoma City, for example, has more than 600 square miles within its city limits, with much of that added over the years through annexations.[32]

Annexation is principally a tool used by municipalities that want to control development along their peripheries and engage in planned expansions of their tax bases. Remember that cities like to create uniform requirements on area developers, whereas developers tend to favor unincorporated areas where land is cheaper and there are fewer regulations. One option for cities to put a stop to this and impose a more coherent and orderly plan on metropolitan growth is to simply annex that unincorporated land.

A city government that wishes to annex a tract of land must organize the citizens of an unincorporated area to sign a petition. Some communities seek to expand by annexing prospectively, working to incorporate a still-undeveloped parcel of land farther out from a suburban parcel already being transformed from woods or farmland into subdivisions. This, in turn, may alienate rural landowners, including farmers, who value their traditional identity separate from that of the city.[33] Annexing, in short, can create a lot of conflict, with some residents of unincorporated areas seeing it as a land grab that threatens to develop their rural communities out of existence.

Given this sort of conflict, it should not be too surprising to find that states make it tough for cities to annex new land. For example, in 1963 the California legislature created fifty-eight local agency formation commissions (LAFCOs) as boundary watchdogs to discourage annexation. Among other things, LAFCOs are supposed to discourage urban sprawl. However, because urban sprawl pretty much describes metropolitan growth in the past four decades in large parts of the state, many Californians believe that these commissions are too weak to deal with rapid suburbanization.

Annexation can make sense from a big-picture perspective in that it can help impose the orderly expansion of urban municipalities, but there is no getting around the fact that it creates losers as well as winners. And the losers often are not interested in losing at all. For example, in Ohio, townships and counties are pushing for more say over annexations, deliberately trying to limit the ability of municipalities to gobble up unincorporated land in the name of development.[34]

Annexation also has natural limits—there has to be land available to annex. Although municipalities tend to have the upper hand over sparsely populated, unincorporated territories, if they bump up against another city, it's a different story. Unlike cities in the South and West, cities in the North and East are more likely to be ringed by incorporated suburbs; in effect, core cities are fenced in by other cities, with no real option to expand. Pittsburgh, for example, covers about 58 square miles—a fraction of Oklahoma City's 600-plus square miles. Outside of a merger with Allegheny County, it is unlikely that Pittsburgh is going to grow to anywhere near the geographical size of Oklahoma City.

The Case against Reform: Public Choice and the Tiebout Model

Although metropolitan areas undoubtedly have problems, not everyone agrees that these problems require stronger regional governments. Indeed,

In June 2006, Anaheim, California, became the first major U.S. city to go wireless. Residents can subscribe to the service on a monthly basis, and visitors can purchase temporary usage capabilities.

some argue that some of the underlying problems have been exaggerated, or at least not balanced adequately against the benefits of metropolitan growth.

Backing this argument is the fact that cities are, for the most part, pretty decent places to live. Core cities have not been swirling down into a uniform death spiral of relentless flight to the suburbs, leaving poverty, racial segregation, and crime. In many MSAs, the core cities remain the economic and social hubs of the region. Scholars and musicians, business leaders and actors—people in a wide range of fields are still more likely to be attracted to the city to pursue their opportunities and dreams than to an exurb or single-use housing tract. Core cities remain exciting places, centers of innovation and culture, shopping and business activity.

So, despite the undeniable downsides to growth patterns in metropolitan areas, there are also some positives, at least for some people. First and foremost are the quality of life benefits. That house in the suburbs can be a pretty darn nice house, in a pretty darn nice neighborhood. Good-quality schools are not hard to find in the suburbs, and neither are relatively crime-free developments with nice parks and maybe even a golf course nearby. This looks pretty attractive to those who have the means to take advantage of such opportunities. The same developments that often are castigated by academic critics of urban planning (or the lack thereof) can be job-generating machines.

For example, many consider Levittown in Nassau County, New York, to be the original "cookie cutter" modern suburban housing development. Eventually totaling more than 17,000 homes, Levittown was built in an unincorporated area in the late 1940s and early 1950s. It was, literally, a community built from the ground up. First came the housing development; then public services (schools and parks) followed. Levittown served as a model for suburban growth across the United States, and what is notable about it for present purposes is that it was designed as an affordable housing development. The houses were nothing fancy—brand-new they cost under $8,000, which even by the standards of the early 1950s was a good price for a single-family home. What they offered was not economic segregation for the moneyed class but, instead, the American dream of home ownership for a generation of World War II veterans.[35]

And the middle and upper classes have not abandoned every neighborhood in every city. Indeed, some decaying urban areas have undergone a renaissance, with old warehouses being turned into upscale condos and downtown neighborhoods becoming the focus of thriving cultural scenes. This process of physical rehabilitation of urban areas, which attracts investment from developers and drives up property values, is known as **gentrification**. Gentrified neighborhoods do present something of a double-edged sword, however. Although gentrification clearly can resuscitate decaying areas, the rise in property values means that poorer people (the original residents) can no longer afford to live there. In essence, gentrification creates pockets of middle-class wealth within cities.

GENTRIFICATION

The physical rehabilitation of urban areas, which attracts investment from developers and drives up property values.

In short, there is a glass half-full perspective that sees innovation and vitality, high standards of living, and social and economic opportunities; this contrasts with a glass half-empty perspective that focuses on segregation, smog, and economic inequality. There are also strong theoretical reasons that argue against any large-scale movement to replace multiple local jurisdictions with larger regional governance structures.

Public choice is a model of politics that views governments and public services in market terms. In public choice models, governments are seen as producers of public services and citizens are seen as consumers. As in most markets, competition among producers is seen as a good thing. With lots of local jurisdictions, citizens can choose their favored "producer" by moving to the city or town that has the mix of taxes and public services that suits them best. If that local government fails to satisfy the individual citizen consumer—in other words, its taxes go too high or its public services drop too low—they can vote with their feet and move to another jurisdiction with a more attractive tax–public service package.

Multiple jurisdictions mean multiple producers, a set of competing "products" in the form of different mixes of taxes and public services. That competition keeps governments responsive to their constituents and puts pressure on these governments to be efficient and to keep the quality of public services as high as possible and taxes as low as possible. If local governments are inefficient, that is, their taxes are high and their public services are poor, they risk having their constituents move to another jurisdiction that offers a better deal.

From a public choice perspective, concentrating local governments into regional governments, either through formal or informal mechanisms, risks a considerable downside. Government consolidation basically represents the creation of monopoly service providers and brings with it all the problems of monopolies that are well understood from private markets: lack of response to consumers, high costs, and indifferent quality.

This perspective on local government was most famously articulated by Charles Tiebout in the 1950s. The **Tiebout model** of local government calls for a metro area made up of a series of micropolitical jurisdictions. If each jurisdiction can control its tax-service package, fully mobile citizens will respond to the available packages by gravitating to the one that suits them best. Or, as Tiebout put it, the mobility of citizens will provide "the local public goods counterpart to the private market's shopping trip."[36]

In addition to highly mobile citizens, the Tiebout model also requires informed citizens. If people do not know what different governments are offering in the way of alternative tax-service packages they are not going

In short, there is a glass half-full perspective that sees innovation and vitality, high standards of living, and social and economic opportunities; this contrasts with a glass half-empty perspective that focuses on segregation, smog, and economic inequality.

PUBLIC CHOICE MODEL
A model of politics that views governments and public services in market terms; governments are seen as producers of public services and citizens are seen as consumers.

TIEBOUT MODEL
A model of local government based on market principles wherein a metro area is made up of a series of micropolitical jurisdictions that, on the basis of their services and costs, attract or repel certain citizens.

to be very good local government "shoppers," and local governments may be able to take advantage of that ignorance by becoming lazy and inefficient producers of public goods and services.

If the mobility and information requirements are met, the Tiebout model makes a strong theoretical case for political fragmentation in metropolitan areas, obviously arguing against the reform perspective of pushing for government consolidation. From the Tiebout model perspective, a regional government or a merged city and county government represents a big monopoly, which is likely to produce a large inefficient bureaucracy that is unresponsive to citizens and that has little incentive to keep quality high and costs low.

The "if" on the mobility and information requirements, however, is a big one. A number of scholars have argued that citizens are neither fully mobile nor fully informed. The constraints on mobility are fairly obvious; where you can live is determined by how much money you can earn. This means the well-off, if they so choose, can be fairly mobile. The less well-off, on the other hand, are more likely to find their mobility limited by their pocketbooks. They simply cannot afford to move to better neighborhoods, even if they want to, because property prices are too high. There are some important implications here. The Tiebout model, remember, makes a good case that local governments will be responsive to people who have a real exit option, in other words, people who can pack up and move if they do not like what the local government is doing. If those people are defined by wealth, it means governments in metropolitan areas are likely to be more responsive to the concerns of the well-off than to those of the poor.

The requirement that citizens be informed also turns out to be a fairly restrictive burden on using the Tiebout model as a practical template for metropolitan governance. As it turns out, most people have only a vague notion of the details of the tax-service packages offered by their own local government, let alone what the tax-service packages of neighboring local governments offer. Three political scientists, William Lyons, David Lowery, and Ruth Hoogland DeHoog, undertook one of the more comprehensive field tests of the Tiebout model in the early 1990s. They surveyed citizens who lived in what they termed "monocentric" metropolitan areas (areas where there was a consolidated city-county government) and "polycentric" metropolitan areas (places defined by a range of smaller political jurisdictions). They found there was no difference in citizens' reported satisfaction with public services in the two types of metropolitan settings, that mobility was extremely low in both settings (the probability of moving was 2.66 percent in polycentric areas and 1.32 percent in monocentric settings), and that citizens were better informed in monocentric than polycentric settings.[37] These findings raise considerable questions about whether the Tiebout model can serve as a practical guide to governance in metropolitan areas.

In the 1990s, the Tiebout model was reworked by a group of political scientists who argued that the central idea did not require that *all* citizens be mobile and highly informed. It just required that *enough* citizens have these characteristics to force government to be responsive to their interests. The question, of course, became what sort of citizens would be motivated enough to inform themselves about local government and be willing to use that knowledge to form the basis of buying property.

The logical test case for this argument seemed to be school districts. Schools are an important consideration in buying real estate, and if anyone was going to have the motivation to bone up on local government, it would be parents moving into a new school district. A survey of people who recently had bought homes in Suffolk County, New York, revealed that these recent movers were more informed than long-time residents. If wealthy movers tend to be highly informed, it suggests there might be a subgroup of citizens who resemble those in the Tiebout model.[38] Whether this small subgroup is enough to create market-like pressures for efficiency on local governments, however, remains a point of contention.[39]

Regardless, the Tiebout model demonstrates that there is a theoretical case to be made for political fragmentation in metropolitan areas. Coupled with high suburban standards of living and gentrification in the core cities, there is a reasonable counterargument to the calls for more centralized government in metropolitan areas.

Rural Metropolitics

Rural governments frequently face a different set of challenges than the urban areas discussed thus far. For example, some rural counties are dealing with shrinking and aging populations, as younger people shift from rural agricultural areas to more metropolitan areas in search of educational, social, and economic opportunities.

Consider that in Kansas roughly three-quarters of the state's 105 counties lost population between 2000 and 2004.[40] This reflects a population exodus that tracks a massive consolidation in agriculture as family farms give way to massive corporate operations. Fewer farms means fewer agricultural jobs, which means that younger people move to the cities where the jobs are, leaving smaller rural communities with fewer shoppers, fewer schools, and fewer businesses. That is a recipe for decline that can be hard to reverse.

Rather than white flight, rural states such as Iowa, Kansas, and Nebraska face **rural flight**, the movement of the young and the middle class to more urban areas. Although the underlying cause is different, the end result can be pressure for a solution that sounds familiar to any veteran of the political battles over urban growth—regional government. Iowa, for example, is a mostly rural state. It has a population of roughly 3 million and roughly a

RURAL FLIGHT

The movement of rural youth and the middle class to more urban areas.

MAP 12-4 Population Changes by County, Iowa, 2000–2008

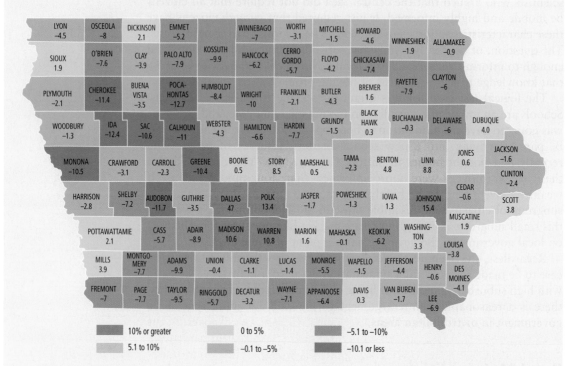

LYON −4.5	OSCEOLA −8	DICKINSON 2.1	EMMET −5.2		WINNEBAGO −7	WORTH −3.1	MITCHELL −1.5	HOWARD −4.6	WINNESHIEK −1.9	ALLAMAKEE −0.9
SIOUX 1.9	O'BRIEN −7.6	CLAY −3.9	PALO ALTO −7.9	KOSSUTH −9.9	HANCOCK −6.2	CERRO GORDO −5.7	FLOYD −4.2	CHICKASAW −7.4		
PLYMOUTH −2.1	CHEROKEE −11.4	BUENA VISTA −3.5	POCA-HONTAS −12.7	HUMBOLDT −8.4	WRIGHT −10	FRANKLIN −2.1	BUTLER −4.3	BREMER 1.6	FAYETTE −7.9	CLAYTON −6
WOODBURY −1.3	IDA −12.4	SAC −10.6	CALHOUN −11	WEBSTER −4.3	HAMILTON −6.6	HARDIN −7.7	GRUNDY −1.5	BLACK HAWK 0.3	BUCHANAN −0.3	DELAWARE −6
										DUBUQUE 4.0
MONONA −10.5	CRAWFORD −3.1	CARROLL −2.3	GREENE −10.4	BOONE 0.5	STORY 8.5	MARSHALL 0.5	TAMA −2.3	BENTON 4.8	LINN 8.8	JONES 0.6
										JACKSON −1.6
HARRISON −2.8	SHELBY −7.2	AUDOBON −11.7	GUTHRIE −3.5	DALLAS 47	POLK 13.4	JASPER −1.7	POWESHIEK −1.3	IOWA 1.3	JOHNSON 15.4	CEDAR −0.6
										CLINTON −2.4
									MUSCATINE 1.9	SCOTT 3.8
POTTAWATTAMIE 2.1	CASS −5.7	ADAIR −8.9	MADISON 10.6	WARREN 10.8	MARION 1.6	MAHASKA −0.1	KEOKUK −6.2	WASHINGTON 3.3		
									LOUISA −3.8	
MILLS 3.9	MONTGO-MERY −7.7	ADAMS −9.9	UNION −0.4	CLARKE −1.1	LUCAS −1.4	MONROE −5.5	WAPELLO −1.5	JEFFERSON −4.4	HENRY −0.6	DES MOINES −4.1
FREMONT −7	PAGE −7.7	TAYLOR −9.5	RINGGOLD −5.7	DECATUR −3.2	WAYNE −7.1	APPANOOSE −6.4	DAVIS 0.3	VAN BUREN −1.7	LEE −6.9	

Legend:
- 10% or greater
- 5.1 to 10%
- 0 to 5%
- −0.1 to −5%
- −5.1 to −10%
- −10.1 or less

Source: Population Division, U.S. Census Bureau, Table 1: Annual Estimates of the Resident Population for Counties of Iowa: April 1, 2000 to July 1, 2008 (CO-EST2008-01-19). Release Date: March 19, 2009.
Note: The April 1, 2000, estimates base reflects changes to the Census 2000 population resulting from legal boundary updates, other geographic program changes, and Count Question Resolution actions. All geographic boundaries for the 2008 population estimates series are defined as of January 1, 2008.

thousand general purpose governments. That works out to be thirty-six general units of government for every 100,000 residents.[41] Most counties in Iowa do not have a lot of people; what they have is a lot of government. (See Map 12-4 for county-by-county population changes in Iowa.)

That makes government tremendously inefficient; in rural areas, there are redundant layers of government sitting on stagnant tax bases. That puts upward pressure on property taxes, and it also creates incentives to make government more efficient. Consolidating governments is one way to do this, and this is an option that increasingly is being considered in rural states. Schools are typically among the first sets of merger candidates. As student populations decrease in a rural community, it is harder to fund a comprehensive K–12 school system. If there is another community within busing distance, it can make a good deal of financial sense to split

Governing States and Localities

The law was due for reauthorization in 2007, but debate stalled in Congress, and policymakers punted until well into President Barack Obama's administration. Obama called for a rewrite of NCLB but not a wholesale change, to the disappointment of some, including teachers' unions. His plan—just released and under consideration in early 2010—would eliminate "adequate yearly progress," but would set up other accountability mechanisms and encourage continued competition, as introduced with Race to the Top, in exchange for additional federal funding.

NCLB is a classic example of the push and pull of federalism. Since the days of Horace Mann, nineteenth-century Massachusetts education chief and the father of the American **common school**, education has been a function of state and local governments. As president, Ronald Reagan even proposed eliminating the federal Department of Education. The advent of NCLB, however, dramatically boosted the federal role in education, intensified accountability pressures, and did much to place all state and local school entities on a similar path toward change.

At a time when schooling was reserved mostly for families able to afford tutors or boarding schools, Mann's endeavor was school reform for radicals. The one-room schoolhouses he inspected as the first secretary of Massachusetts's **state board of education** were crude and ill equipped. Many of the teachers were poorly paid and trained, and regular attendance by students was not even required by law. Through personal advocacy and his widely circulated writings, Mann did much to build up the state as the primary actor in the fledgling experiment of public education in the United States.

A century and a half of impassioned debate has passed since Mann's time. The years have yielded few certainties in American education. What is undisputed, however, is the way the quest for good schools is intertwined with democratic civic ideals. The everyday rough-and-tumble over curriculum and budgets pays constant heed to this country's founding ideals of individual dignity, the promise of social mobility, and government by consent of the governed.

It was not just for public relations that President Lyndon B. Johnson viewed education as "the answer to all our national problems."[4] A former teacher himself, Johnson launched what he called the Great Society initiative. This was a series of new federal programs designed to curb poverty and expand opportunities for the nation's disadvantaged. It rested, as he said in one speech, on "abundance and liberty for all"[5] and led the federal government to make its first major forays into education policy.

Given the variety of policy approaches permitted under the U.S. system of federalism, education has always been governed, to the extent possible, by states and localities. In 2008, elementary and secondary education accounted for the largest share of state government spending—34.5 percent of general funds—according to the National Association of State Budget Officers.[6] Members of all parties and followers of various philosophical

COMMON SCHOOL

In a democratic society, a school in which children of all income levels attend at taxpayer expense.

STATE BOARD OF EDUCATION

Top policymaking body in each of the fifty states, usually consisting of appointees selected by governors.

leanings agree that education has the most impact on economic growth and civic engagement.

The nation's universal compulsory education laws mean that all taxpayers, not just families with school-age children, are required to support society's bid for an educated citizenry. Education is a field that brings out panic in some parents who feel their child's whole future is at stake with every report card. It is a field that allows ambitious politicians to make names for themselves by vowing to make schools more accountable. Candidates promise to get better results in the classroom from taxpayer dollars. They do this despite occasional resistance by professional educators, who value autonomy and resent burdensome regulation.

The stakes have always been high. But it was in the final decades of the twentieth century that political leaders and many in the general public shifted to a mindset that public education was in dire and ongoing need of fixing. The 1983 report *A Nation at Risk* was commissioned by the Reagan administration; it declared that the United States was just that because a rising tide of mediocrity in schools invited defeat by a foreign power.

That report set in motion a continual movement with such themes as **back to basics**, new curriculum **standards**, and **high-stakes standardized testing**. The movement involved not just teachers and parents but also federal and state legislators, local **school boards**, courts, advocacy groups, and even the national political parties. And this wave of reform continues well into the twenty-first century.

Organization and Leadership: Schools Have Many Bosses

The United States is one of the few industrialized countries with no national ministry of education. The U.S. Department of Education was created in 1978, but the primary authority for running schools rests with the fifty states. This is in accordance with the Tenth Amendment edict that the powers not delegated by the Constitution to the federal government are reserved to the states. An exception is the District of Columbia; its board of education derives its funds from the city's appropriation from Congress.

As far back as the 1780s, state legislatures have been given the task of schooling the citizenry. For example, in 1857, Minnesota's constitution proclaimed that the "stability of a Republican form of government depend[ed] upon the intelligence of the people, it is the duty of the legislature to establish a general and uniform system of public schools."[7] In other words,

> Legend has it that a national education chief in Europe can look at a clock on any given weekday and know precisely which lesson is being taught in classrooms across a country.

the consensus was that creating a well-educated population not only helped individual citizens prosper but also helped entrench the democratic process.

Fifty varying traditions make for a lot of bosses in a democratic approach to education. A system that permits local innovations and variations is a far cry from the systems in Europe. Legend has it that a national education chief there can look at a clock on any given weekday and know precisely which lesson is being taught in classrooms across a country.

Modern state legislatures, working with state **departments of education**, are the players that deal with major state policy questions and large-scale resource issues. A state legislature can raise teacher salaries statewide, equalize funding among districts, and set up health benefits and retirement plans for the state's pool of teachers. It can borrow money by floating state bonds to provide schools with construction funds, which commits taxpayers to long-term debts.

The states are also the main players in determining **teacher licensure procedures**. For example, they determine whether or not teacher candidates must take a standardized test and how schools are awarded **accreditation**.

The more complex state decisions are proposed and implemented by an experienced educator who is the chief state school officer. The governor can appoint these officials, as in Iowa, Maine, and New Jersey. Or they can be appointed by a state board of education, as in Louisiana, Utah, and Vermont. Sometimes, they are elected on a partisan ballot, as in North Carolina and Oklahoma, or on a nonpartisan ballot, as in North Dakota and Oregon. They work closely with state boards of education. These boards also can be appointed or elected, depending on the state, and their members usually represent each region of a state.

Further down the chain are the **local education agencies (LEAs)**, which have been formed in nearly 15,000 **school districts** scattered over cities, counties, and townships. School districts are staffed with full-time professionals, but they carry out policies set by school boards or other locally elected officials.

The extent of policymaking authority enjoyed by each LEA or district is determined by a state's legislature. In Horace Mann's region of New England, local control is strong. The population of states in the Deep South traditionally has been poor and rural. Many citizens are suspicious and untutored in the workings of government. As a result, the legislatures of these states have retained a more centralized role.

Even within states, there are huge differences in economies, traditions, and demographics. Think of rural, mountainous northern California versus densely populated, arid southern California. Also, northern Virginia, an affluent suburban area of Washington, D.C., that tends to favor active government, is very different from Virginia's rural areas, in which folks tend to favor limited government.

DEPARTMENTS OF EDUCATION
State-level agencies responsible for overseeing public education.

TEACHER LICENSURE PROCEDURES
The academic degrees, work experience, and performance on adult standardized tests that a state requires before a teacher candidate can be certified to work in a school district.

ACCREDITATION
Certification process in which outside experts visit and evaluate a school or college to vouch for minimum quality standards.

LOCAL EDUCATION AGENCIES (LEAs)
School districts, some of which may be cities, counties, or subsets thereof.

SCHOOL DISTRICTS
Local administrative jurisdictions that hire staff and report to school boards on the management of area public schools.

The degree of flexibility in education that states can give to localities depends greatly on scale. It also depends on the degree to which local citizens feel passionate about participating in school governance. The nation's school districts are a patchwork quilt that evolved as individually as the states themselves. Texas, for example, contains more than one thousand school districts. These vary widely, from the liberal college town of Austin to the conservative business center of Dallas. By contrast, rural, and still largely undeveloped, Hawaii is administered as one district.

In large cities such as Los Angeles, schools are administered under a centralized authority. This is why the district is called Los Angeles Unified. New York City, the nation's largest school district with more than 1 million students, has tried both centralized and decentralized approaches. In 2002, Mayor Michael Bloomberg won approval from the state legislature to eliminate the city's thirty-two separate school boards and centralize control. The intent was to reduce what some viewed as administrative bloat so that the new chancellor, Joel Klein, could experiment with such reforms as charter schools and be held accountable for results. Mayors and school boards across the country watched New York closely as Klein and Bloomberg began implementing changes, including new admissions policies for the city's most desirable programs, the creation of more than three hundred small and charter schools, and even cash incentives for students displaying academic progress.[8] The program's many detractors did not prevent the state legislature from renewing mayoral control in 2009.

Five years into New York's experiment, in April 2007, the mayor of Washington, D.C., Adrian Fenty, won the approval of the city council to take over the city's troubled school system from the city school board. Fenty appointed Michelle Rhee, a Teach for America alumna, the district's new chancellor. Like Klein, Rhee vowed to transform a troubled school system, and she proved her willingness to turn long-ingrained practices upside down by shutting more than twenty schools, firing underperforming principals—including the head of her own daughters' school[9]—and proposing teacher salaries of up to $130,000. Three years into her appointment, Rhee made headlines once again when she struck a deal with the teachers' union that would weaken tenure provisions for teachers but pave the way for double-digit merit-based pay increases.[10]

School boards are quintessentially U.S. democratic institutions that got their start in the Progressive Era at the end of the nineteenth century. These citizen boards were envisioned as a way to end the spoils system. Individuals would no longer be able to show partisan and political favor by awarding jobs to their followers. This would make way for the shared pursuit of effective public education.

Looking back now, that promise seems quaint, given that political interest groups continue to target school board elections. In Virginia, for example, school board elections were abolished in the early 1950s because southern white traditionalists feared that too many candidates were sympathetic to the then-growing school desegregation movement. It was not until 1992 that elected members once again replaced appointed members. In addition, during the 1990s, conservative Christian political activists zeroed in on school board elections as battlegrounds for their agenda of promoting school prayer and eliminating sex education.

Some critics say school boards actually produce fewer school improvements than they do campaign bumper stickers. (See box on page 496.) That is one reason they were curbed by city governments during the 1990s in Boston, Chicago, Cleveland, and Detroit.[11] Faced with stagnating test scores and an exodus of families to private or parochial schools, urban leaders argued that emergency action to arrest the decline of the schools was more important than the democracy of a thousand voices.

Large urban school districts, including New York and Washington, D.C., have been experimenting with centralizing control over public schools. Washington, D.C., mayor Adrian Fenty chose Michelle Rhee, an alumna of Teach for America, to run the district's schools. Rhee made headlines with sweeping changes, including pushing for more accountability and layoffs of hundreds of teachers.

The idea is that a centralized authority figure, such as a mayor or school chief, is accountable in the mystifying field of school reform. Appointees from an elected mayor are more likely to take decisive action and worry less about glad-handing, returning campaign favors, and seeking reelection. The jury is still out on such propositions, and proposals to abolish elected school boards tend to appear only in districts that are in dire straits.

The challenges facing school boards are formidable. Keep in mind that by law a public school must accept all students who live within its jurisdiction. This makes planning tricky. Many school boards do not have taxing authority, but most prepare budgets for approval by the county board or city council, which must balance education spending against spending on police and fire protection and transportation. It is the board that hires the superintendent, who hires the principals, who, in turn, hire the teachers who taught you to read.

Money Matters

The greatest share of school funding comes from the states. On average, states paid for 47.6 percent of a school's costs in 2007. Compare this to the 43.9 percent that came from local jurisdictions and the just 8.5 percent that came from the federal government. (These figures are the most recent available and predate the infusion of stimulus money, which greatly boosted the federal government's share of education spending in 2009 and 2010.)[12]

Policy in Practice: Do School Board Races Improve Education or Simply Create More Bumper Stickers?

At the bottom of the ballot, far below the household names seeking the presidency or a seat in Congress, appear the names of candidates for your local school board. Most, rest assured, are fine people. But with voter turnout often as low as 20 percent in off-year elections, school board races are sometimes derided as wasteful exercises dominated, in the worst cases, by personally ambitious, underqualified, single-issue ideologues. Yet school districts, governed mostly by boards, make up one-sixth of the nation's local governments.[a]

According to the National School Boards Association (NSBA), 93 percent of the members of the nation's 14,890 school boards are elected and 2.8 percent are appointed. The remainder serve on boards with both elected and appointed members. Today, only 10 percent of the country's 95,000 school board members declare a party affiliation. Most run and pay for their bumper stickers using their own funding, without the typical baggage of campaign donations from business groups or trade unions (other than teachers' associations). In large cities, such as San Diego, Milwaukee, and Los Angeles, candidates can spend tens of thousands of dollars.

Although some complain that school board incumbents are firmly entrenched, school board races actually seem competitive, at least compared to congressional races. An NSBA survey showed that from 1998 to 2001, 47.4 percent of the races produced no defeats for incumbents. In the U.S. Congress, the incumbency retention rate is well over 90 percent.

Among the most vocal critics of elected school boards are superintendents, whose function as chief executive officers of school districts sometimes can be thwarted by the boards, which have power to hire and fire them. They argue that school board members, who are paid little or nothing, often take office with little understanding of nuts-and-bolts management issues and that many need training. Princeton University molecular biology professor Lee Silver, after a frustrating term as an elected school board member in his college town, proposed that boards be abolished and replaced by a committee of professional educators. "There isn't a single thing school boards do well," he writes. "On the contrary, what they do more often than not is to get in the way of school district administrators who are perfectly able to run the schools by themselves."[b]

But abolishing elected school boards is unlikely. Instead, some are trying to reform them from the inside out. Don McAdams, a former Houston school

Many states and localities raise school funds from income tax and sales taxes. Twenty-four states dedicate funds raised through the morally controversial practice of running a state lottery. Those gambling dollars add up. In California, the lottery generates 2 percent of the state's education funding, and in 2005, the Florida lottery transferred more than $1 billion to the schools.[13] The bulk of school funds, however, come from the local property tax. This tax is based on the assessed value of a taxpayer's home, usually a percentage of each $100 in assessed value.

There is a logic to this. All taxpayers in a given community are believed to benefit from a quality school system—it helps maintain attractive real estate values and helps create an educated workforce. And the tax system is progressive, meaning that homeowners whose property is worth more pay more in nominal amounts, although all pay the same percentage. Most board member, now directs the Center for Reform of School Systems, whose aim is improving boards' performance. He argues that, instead of being irrelevant or impediments to reforming public education, boards are vital government organizations. "School districts are essential units of change," he says. "They're the ones that have to build civic capacity and sustain it over time."[c]

Gail Littlejohn, a retired executive in Dayton, Ohio, applied McAdams's theories when she spearheaded an effort to reinvent that city's school board. Littlejohn found three like-minded candidates and raised more than $120,000—an unheard-of amount for a Dayton school board election. Her group took office in November 2001. The newly composed board replaced the superintendent and remade the district's finance office, directing more money to classroom instruction, creating a new reading program, putting math and reading coaches in classrooms, and reconstituting low-performing schools. And with the University of Dayton, it set up an academically rigorous high school that has begun attracting students who most likely would otherwise have gone to private or charter schools.

The result: Test scores in the district began to rise. After a 2002 report saying that Dayton schools were in "crisis," the Council of the Great City Schools began reporting on their turnaround. The challenge for Dayton, and for any school district with an elected board, is to be able to sustain reform efforts beyond the first blush of enthusiasm. Dayton learned this first when one of Littlejohn's allies was unseated by a union-backed candidate who was unhappy with the new board's priorities. Littlejohn herself left the board in 2007—to take a position with McAdams's organization—and by the time she departed, just one of her original running mates remained on the board. Still, McAdams counsels that reform will take time. "This takes patience," he says. "The voters don't always send us ideal candidates, but democracy's a messy business."

[a]This statistic and information about the Center for Reform of School Systems and Dayton, Ohio, adapted from Rob Gurwitt, "Battered School Boards," *Governing* magazine, May 2006, available at www.governing.com/archive/archive/2006/may/school.txt.

[b]Lee M. Silver, "Why I'm Giving Up on School Boards," *School Administrator*, Web edition, February 1998, available at www.thefreelibrary.com/Why+I%27m+Giving+Up+on+School+Boards.-a077288672.

[c]Gurwitt, "Battered School Boards."

mortgage companies inconspicuously collect most of these tax funds for homeowners. The money is then kept in a homeowner's personal escrow account until the tax is due.

The downside of property taxes is that, as property values gain in value, the assessment and corresponding property taxes also rise—irrespective of whether a homeowner's income is rising along with it. This vicious circle is what fueled passage of California's famous Proposition 13 in 1978. This statewide ballot measure capped property taxes and ignited a tax revolt in other states. (See box on page 500.)

An even deeper problem with funding schools via the property tax is the fact that wealthier districts are able to keep theirs at an attractively low percentage rate and still produce enough revenue dollars to support good schools. For example, in affluent Beverly Hills, California, property was—and still is—very expensive. Yet the tax rate cited in *Serrano v. Priest* (1971), a famous school funding equity case, was only $2.38 per $100 in assessed value. Place this up against the $5.48 per $100 in the low-income Baldwin Park area. There the schools were demonstrably inferior, and the community was able to spend only half the amount that was spent in Beverly Hills. The California Supreme Court agreed that families in Baldwin Park were being denied a "fundamental right" to quality schools.[14] The court ordered the legislature to find a way to make school funding more equitable.

A slightly different principle was spelled out by the U.S. Supreme Court in the 1973 ruling in *San Antonio Independent School District v. Rodriguez.* In this case, attorneys for a largely Mexican American population found that their clients were paying a tax rate 25 percent higher than people in nearby affluent school districts. These less affluent districts, however, were able or willing to fund schools with only 60 percent of the amount enjoyed by wealthy San Antonio neighborhoods. Here the Supreme Court acknowledged the disparities but ruled that equal school funding is not a federal constitutional right: "The Equal Protection Clause does not require absolute equality or precisely equal advantages," the justices wrote. Despite this ruling, the precedent was set. State courts began to see themselves as protectors of poor and rural students, and the school funding equity movement at the state level gathered more steam.

These two cases launched a decades-long movement of constitutional litigation on school funding that has spread to nearly every state. It pits the principle of local control against pressures to close the gap between wealthy and poor districts. Jurists, educators, parents, and tax activists continue to fight about the key to school equity.

In the 1970s, most courts, like California's, ruled in favor of greater equalization among districts. After some judicial setbacks, the momentum slowed in the 1980s before gaining ground again in the courts of the 1990s. Nowhere was this drama played out more visibly than in Vermont, where a 1997 state supreme court ruling prompted the legislature to enact the controversial Act 60. The act forces wealthier districts that want to upgrade their schools to share their added funds with schools in poor districts.

Understandably, citizens in affluent districts like to see their tax dollars spent in their own communities, and they will lobby and push to keep their schools the best. Many middle-class and upper-class taxpayers say they paid extra for their homes so that their children could attend schools that do not lack for essentials. Citizens in poor districts, by contrast, argue that dilapidated school buildings, meager resources, and teachers at the low end of the profession's already low pay scale are the chief reasons for the achievement gap between their children and those in wealthier districts. (See Map 13-1.) They assert that resources should be distributed among all districts so that all students receive an essentially equitable level of education. Should individuals from less affluent areas be denied access to a good

MAP 13-1 Spending per Student 2005–2006

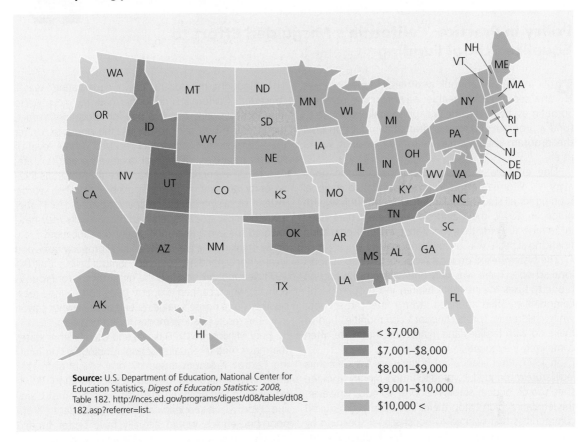

Source: U.S. Department of Education, National Center for Education Statistics, *Digest of Education Statistics: 2008,* Table 182. http://nces.ed.gov/programs/digest/d08/tables/dt08_182.asp?referrer=list.

Legend:
- < $7,000
- $7,001–$8,000
- $8,001–$9,000
- $9,001–$10,000
- $10,000 <

education? Must funneling more resources into disadvantaged communities require "penalizing" affluent communities?

Responses among state legislatures to court orders on school funding have varied. The issue has not always broken down easily along conservative-liberal lines. Indeed, the percentage of per-pupil expenditures has risen most steeply during periods of conservative ascendancy, such as the 1920s and 1950s.[15] This demonstrates the degree to which creating quality schools is a near-universal value.

Researchers examining the role that money plays in learning have created models that attempt to factor in such variables as a school's percentage of student dropouts, graduation rates, teacher salaries, and enrollment. (See Map 13-2.) These models also look at the percentage of children living in poverty and those in female-headed households, how many students have disabilities and how many of these have severe disabilities, and how many students possess limited English proficiency.[16] Few believe that

Policy in Practice: California's Misguided Effort to Equalize School Funding

Policymakers often look at different types of taxes and see interchangeable ways to raise revenue. Sometimes, however, the way policymakers decide to fund a program can have a dramatic impact on how the program itself works—or on whether it works at all.

One example of a well-intentioned reform gone awry is California's effort to provide equal educational funding for all students in kindergarten through twelfth grade. In 1971, the California Supreme Court ruled in *Serrano v. Priest* that the state's existing education financing scheme was unconstitutional.

The system relied on local property taxes to support local schools. There was only one problem. Relying on property taxes meant that children in "property rich" communities often attended lavishly financed schools, while children in "property poor" communities had to make do with facilities and instruction that were often completely inadequate.

In 1977, after years of such litigation, the California legislature responded. It voted to funnel money from the state's large budget surplus to local schools. However, the legislation didn't stop there. The state also required communities that wanted to boost school spending by raising local property taxes to share the additional funds they brought in with other school districts.

In hindsight, this "district power equalization" was ill conceived. Californians no longer had any incentive to raise local property taxes to pay for education. In fact, the incentive was now to do just the opposite. Under the new system, each district received a base level of support regardless of its local tax revenue and tax rate. As a result, every district had an incentive to set its local property tax rate as low as possible. In other words, instead of raising education spending to a new higher level for most students, equalization actually may have lowered the average amount spent on education.

By breaking the link between local property taxes and local school spending, some economists believe that the 1971 *Serrano* decision laid the groundwork for Proposition 13, which capped property taxes and banned reassessment of a house's value as long as the owner stayed in it. The result was less money for everyone.[a]

New Mexico, South Dakota, and Utah—other states that have tried to equalize school funding by confiscating "extra" revenues raised by local school districts—also have ended up driving school funding down rather than up. According to Harvard economist Caroline Hoxby, "It appears that some students from poor households would actually have better funded schools if their states had not attempted such complete equalization."[b]

[a]William Fischel, "How Judges Are Making Public Schools Worse," *City Journal,* summer 1998.

[b]Caroline Hoxby, "All School Finance Equalizations Are Not Created Equal," *Quarterly Journal of Economics* 116, no. 4 (2001): 1228.

pouring money into a school district automatically produces improvements. As a result, they also attempt to consider such human factors as the degree of cooperation among teachers, rates of absenteeism, and the extent of disruptive behavior in classrooms.

Most important, researchers try to isolate precisely how monies are best spent inside schools to derive the most benefit. Areas in which increased funding translates into student learning gains, according to one study, included spending on instruction, central office administration, and teacher-student ratios. Areas that demonstrated less of a payoff included funds for school-level administration, overall **capital outlays**, and salaries for teachers with advanced degrees.[17]

CAPITAL OUTLAYS

A category of school funding that focuses on long-term improvements to physical assets.

MAP 13-2 **Student Enrollment in Public Schools by State, Fall 2005**

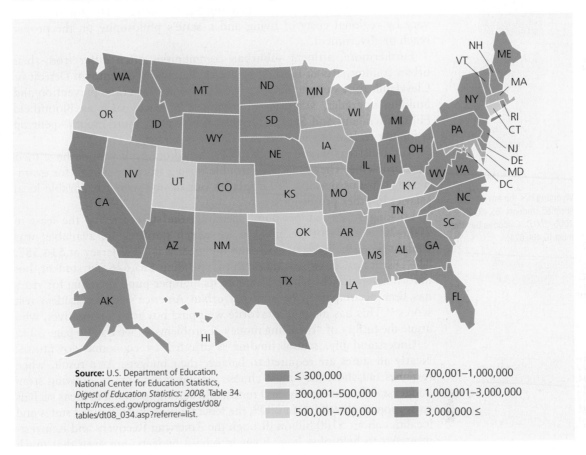

Source: U.S. Department of Education, National Center for Education Statistics, *Digest of Education Statistics: 2008,* Table 34. http://nces.ed.gov/programs/digest/d08/tables/dt08_034.asp?referrer=list.

≤ 300,000
300,001–500,000
500,001–700,000
700,001–1,000,000
1,000,001–3,000,000
3,000,000 ≤

Since the movement for new standards and accountability gained ground in the 1990s, school funding battles have shifted from an emphasis on equalization toward an effort to achieve adequacy, or what is required to get students to meet high standards.[18] To determine how much per-pupil spending is adequate for a school district, some states convene a panel of experts who use their professional judgment to pick the resources needed by schools, determine the costs of acquiring these resources, and then adjust their recommendations in favor of the needier districts. Examples of such states are Maine, Oregon, and Wyoming. Other states use the **successful schools model**, wherein groups of schools whose students have done well according to state standards are examined for their average per-pupil costs, which are then applied across the state. Examples of these states are Illinois, Mississippi, and Ohio.[19]

The funding appropriated by state legislatures depends on the input expected of localities. New York state, for example, reports the nation's

SUCCESSFUL SCHOOLS MODEL

Education model that uses observed spending levels in the highest-performing schools as the model from which to calculate necessary spending in other, lower-performing schools.

Wyoming has the fewest enrolled students (85,193 in 2006–2007). California has the most (6,406,821).

largest disparity in per-pupil spending between affluent and less-affluent districts, with the richer areas spending $2,319 more.[20] The amounts also vary by regional costs of living and a state's philosophy on the proper reach of government.

Furthermore, affluent suburban communities often differ from their urban counterparts in funding priorities. Parents in downtown Detroit or Cleveland, for example, may want extra monies for crime prevention and building upgrades, whereas suburbanites in places such as Bloomfield Hills, Michigan, and Shaker Heights, Ohio, want more money spent on computer technology and extracurricular programs.

Rural districts in states such as South Dakota or Wyoming have their own problems. They may have trouble raising teacher salaries, for example, if it means pushing those salaries out of line with comparable local salaries in other professions.

Looking strictly at per-pupil spending, the state offering the least in 2005–2006 (the most recent year for which statistics are available) was Utah at $6,629. The state spending the most was New Jersey at $16,587. The District ofColumbia ranked third, spending $15,626 per student, but unfortunately for the nation's capital, its high per-pupil spending for years has been accompanied by some of urban America's lowest student test scores.[21] This has made it a favorite whipping boy for conservatives, who argue the futility of "throwing money at problems." (See box on page 503.)

Understandably, school funding is affected by economic downturns. Nearly all states are required to balance their budgets. As a result, when revenues fall short they must choose among raising taxes, drawing from budget stabilization (rainy day) funds, and cutting spending in areas such as corrections and welfare. In 2009, the federal government handed states and localities about $100 billion through the American Recovery and Reinvestment Act to help plug huge holes in school budgets, but even that much wasn't enough. By spring 2010, local, state, and federal officials were warning the public of massive cuts to classroom learning and more teacher layoffs as revenues continued to skid. "We are doing things and considering options I never thought I'd have to consider," Peter C. Gorman, superintendent of North Carolina's Charlotte-Mecklenburg school district, said in April 2010.[22] (See box on page 522.)

To school reformers, these state funding cuts were embarrassing. They came at a most inopportune time, too—just as the states needed to invest more resources to show progress under the NCLB.

New Pressure to Perform

Except in the minds of some nostalgists, it is doubtful there ever was a halcyon era of consensus among education's disparate stakeholders. There are far too many views about the nation's public schools to have all parties agree that they at some point achieved a satisfactory level of quality.

502

Local Focus: Got an Alternative to Throwing Money at Schools? Tell It to Kansas City

In August 2003, a judge in Kansas City, Missouri, issued a ruling that ended a labyrinthine, high-profile lawsuit over school desegregation and unequal funding between the city's urban and suburban schools. The postmortems offered by attorneys and educators were eye-popping: In twenty-six years, $2 billion had been spent; multiple court rulings had gone back and forth that had required tax increases and redrawing of boundaries; and fifty-five dilapidated schools were renovated while seventeen new ones were built, including a new $32 million magnet high school designed to attract suburban students by featuring, among other assets, an Olympic-size pool and indoor track. Magnet schools place a strong emphasis in a particular subject area, for example, music, science, drama, or math. Students are selected through an application process instead of being assigned based on residence, as in traditional public schools.

The main goals of the litigation, however—the recruitment of more white students to the mostly black inner-city schools and improved academic achievement by minorities—went largely unfulfilled. One of the series of judges who handled the epic case was reported to have confessed, "Maybe I created too expensive a school system."[a]

The degree to which money should factor as an ingredient in any recipe for school improvement is among the least settled disputes in education research. Conservatives have long argued the futility of "throwing money at problem schools." Indeed, school districts plagued by "bureaucratic bloat," embezzlement scandals, and rigid regulation and paperwork do not inspire school reformers to push additional funds as a panacea. If a funding shortage is the cause of underperformance, critics ask, how do you explain the fact that students often perform better at private and Catholic schools, some with tuitions of less than $3,000? And how can you explain the fact that students in the other countries of the Organization for Economic Cooperation and Development outperform American children on reading and math tests, even though the per-pupil spending rates in these mostly European countries are nearly half the U.S. average?[b]

Such critics argue that competently run schools provide "added value." This, they say, has as much to do with academic rigor as with simple dollars. They offer case studies in which infusions of cash failed to prompt a noticeable rise in test scores.[c] Washington, D.C., is commonly cited in such debates; its per-pupil spending is the second-highest nationwide, yet its students regularly score among the lowest on standardized tests.

Backers of increased school spending argue that, in most cases, higher test scores are linked to affluent districts. They dramatize the "savage inequalities" in resources between districts, using a phrase coined from Jonathan Kozol's 1991 book of the same name. Who wants to teach or learn inside a run-down and filthy building? Liberals emphasize that greater spending is needed in districts with a preponderance of children from low-income homes and uneducated parents. They note that some children also are more expensive to educate; the National Center for Education Statistics (NCES) calculates that special education students need 2.3 times the student average and that poor students need 1.2 times the student average.

The lack of consensus on this question is one reason the fifty states and the District of Columbia vary so widely in how much they spend. (See Map 13-1.) The jury is still out on measuring the role of funding. As the Kansas City drama confirmed, money may not be a guaranteed solution to troubled schools. But most communities feel obliged to spend goodly amounts in the course of finding one.

[a]Quoted in Donna McGuire, "Judge Ends Desegregation Case after 26 Years and $2 Billion," *Kansas City Star*, August 14, 2003.

[b]Center for Education Reform, "Spending More but Educating Less," available at www.edreform.com. See also Herbert J. Walberg, "Spending More while Learning Less: U.S. School Productivity in International Perspective," Thomas B. Fordham Foundation report, 1998, available at www.edexcellence.net.

[c]Eric A. Hanushek, "Assessing the Effects of School Resources on Student Performance: An Update," *Educational Evaluation and Policy Analysis* 19 (1997): 141–164.

> Traditionalists who hearken back to the classic education taught in the early twentieth century sometimes forget that in 1900, only 6 percent of children in the United States finished high school. Back then, the best that most could count on was a solid job in, say, manufacturing. For many, college wasn't an option.

Today's charge that schools are going to the proverbial hell in a hand basket also was heard throughout the 1940s and 1950s.

This charge intensified in 1957 after the Soviet Union launched its *Sputnik* satellite. Americans feared that U.S. students had fallen behind the country's cold war rivals in science and math. Traditionalists who hearken back to the classic education taught in the early twentieth century sometimes forget that in 1900, only 6 percent of children in the United States finished high school. Back then, the best that most could count on was a solid job in, say, manufacturing. For many, college wasn't an option.[23]

The current crisis over performance was set in motion during the early 1980s by the Reagan administration. Education secretary Dr. Terrell Bell lit a fire under sometimes resentful educators in 1983 by publishing *A Nation at Risk*. This report ranked states by school achievement data. Today, there are continuing laments that test scores are plummeting, kids don't know U.S. history, and graduates arrive in college or in the workplace unable to write a declarative sentence.

It is true that school test scores have been stagnant for many years. It is hard to argue that a yawning achievement gap has not persisted between the preponderance of black and Hispanic students at the lower end of the achievement scale and the frequently more affluent whites and Asians near the top. Yet test scores are not locked into a downward spiral. Those who choose to see the school performance glass as half full point to the nation's ever-replenishing supply of successful entrepreneurs. Look at the country's proliferation of Nobel Prize winners, they say. Step back and admire how its corporations continue to dominate the world economy. If public education plays a foundational role in supporting the economy and promoting new knowledge, clearly America's schools are doing something right.

Yes, a disturbing 82 percent of respondents to the annual Gallup Poll for *Phi Delta Kappan* magazine gave the nation's overall school system a grade of less than A or B. But far more—more than 50 percent in 2009—assigned those same grades to the performance of their own local schools.[24] Is it fair to blame a school for its students' performance, defenders ask, without considering each child's opportunity to learn? What about the income disparities that subject poorer kids to inferior schools—schools that, however well-intentioned their staff, present a less rigorous curriculum, under-qualified teachers, low expectations, resource disparities, and a disruptive climate? These students also tend to suffer from performance anxiety, negative peer influences, racial discrimination, sketchy preschool attendance, and homes in which the value of learning is not emphasized. Back and forth—the debate roars on.

Teaching to the Test

Meanwhile, on the front lines of education, the main performance indicator for schools remains not grades, not satisfaction surveys, not oral exams—but, rather, the standardized test, an indicator that has taken on new significance in the era of NCLB. Critics bemoan the trend of "teaching to the test," which skews classroom time toward the subjects covered on the tests, often at the expense of classes such as art and music. In 2007, nearly three-fourths of school districts reported reducing elementary school instructional time in at least one subject to make more time for reading and math, the subjects tracked by NCLB.[25]

A thriving commercial testing industry has grown up to supply schools with inexpensive, mass-produced tests for quick computerized scoring of large numbers of students from kindergarten to twelfth grade. Familiar giants in this multibillion-dollar industry include the Comprehensive Test of Basic Skills; the Iowa Test of Basic Skills; and the Stanford Achievement Test (SAT; note that this is not the SAT, Scholastic Assessment Test, many of you took when applying to colleges).

Each publisher has developed procedures to continually rotate questions, keep the tests statistically valid and as free as possible from cultural bias, and minimize scorekeeping errors. And all for good reason. When things go awry, the result can be lawsuits. Some of these tests are **criterion referenced** and are intended to measure mastery of a given subject as defined by state standards. Most, however, are **norm referenced**, meaning that students are graded on how well they approach the mean student score on that same test administered across the country.[26]

A large number of states have their own tests. Resistance among the advocates of local control to proposals made in the 1990s for a national student test caused such tests to continue to be permitted under the NCLB. Florida has its Florida Comprehensive Assessment Test (FCAT), Virginia has its Standards of Learning, and New York has its Regents Exam. Critics still question whether these tests are properly aligned with a given district's or state's curriculum and whether such tests are comparable to those used in other states.

In an effort to provide some uniformity and continuity in testing, the federal government has administered its own test since 1969—the **National Assessment of Educational Progress (NAEP)**. Nicknamed "the nation's report card," it is administered in volunteer sample districts to students in grades four and eight. Over the years, NAEP scores have remained essentially flat, with subgroups' scores rising and falling. Since the early 1990s, fourth and eighth graders have shown improvement in math but little change in reading ability. The federal government used to track twelfth graders' scores as well, but it has not released the information in recent years because fewer high schools have agreed to participate in the testing.[27]

CRITERION REFERENCED TESTS
Standardized tests designed to gauge a student's level of mastery of a given set of materials.

NORM REFERENCED TESTS
Standardized tests designed to determine how a student's mastery of a set of materials compares with that of a specially designed sampling of students determined to be the national "norm" for their age group.

NATIONAL ASSESSMENT OF EDUCATIONAL PROGRESS (NAEP)
The only regularly conducted, independent survey of what a nationally representative sample of students in grades four, eight, and twelve know and can do in various subjects; known as the "nation's report card."

TRENDS IN INTERNATIONAL MATHEMATICS AND SCIENCE STUDY (TIMSS)

A regularly updated study launched by the United States in 1995 that compares the performance in science and mathematics of students in forty-six countries.

Another key performance indicator coordinated by the U.S. Department of Education is the **Trends in International Mathematics and Science Study (TIMSS)**. Designed to compare the academic achievement of students in forty-eight countries, the 2007 TIMSS study found, for example, that the scores for U.S. fourth and eighth graders exceeded the TIMSS averages for both math and science. Students in the United States beat out those in Italy and Australia in math, but trailed Japan and Singapore in science. And although U.S. school reform advocates frequently point out the superior academic performance of students in many other countries as a sign of the urgent need to introduce more resources and more accountability measures, the 2007 TIMSS results showed that American students had made progress in math between 1995 and 2007. (Science scores held about constant in the same time frame.)[28]

Many of the countries that participate in TIMSS run schools that have established rigid tracks, one for college-bound elite students and one for the remainder who normally attend vocational schools. In the United States, all students have an equal opportunity to advance, at least in theory. Most students applying to college endure the stomach-churning tests known as the SAT and the less widely used ACT (which is used primarily in the Midwest). Designed by the private nonprofit Educational Testing Service and run by the private nonprofit College Board, the SAT is designed to be a predictor of college achievement. The test has been renamed and recalibrated on several occasions. What began as the Scholastic Aptitude Test became the Scholastic Assessment Test. Thirty years of annual scores from this test have prompted much anguish.

In the early 1980s, a study found that the average scores had fallen by 81 points from 1963 to 1977—from 478 down to 429 on the verbal test and from 502 to 470 on the math test. During the 1990s and early part of the twenty-first century, however, the College Board had reason to be upbeat; in an August 2003 report, the board reported the highest level of math scores in thirty-five years. Then the College Board revised the test once again, adding a writing section and including higher-level math. By 2009, students had shown a slight improvement in their math scores over the previous decade, while critical reading skills had slipped slightly.[29]

Beyond standardized testing—and both before and after passage of the NCLB—one performance indicator that is gaining ground is the measurement of high school graduation rates. But historically, the states have applied a patchwork of methods for figuring these rates. Experts point out that it is tempting for districts to arrive at a school's rate simply by subtracting the number of dropouts from the number collecting a diploma. The problem with that is that some dropouts transfer to other schools in a **General Equivalency Degree (GED) program**, get their GEDs on their own, or are incarcerated.

These missing students are hard to track down. Only ten states have spent the money required to perform a longitudinal study of the fate of such

GENERAL EQUIVALENCY DEGREE (GED) PROGRAM

A series of tests that can be taken to qualify for a high school equivalency certificate or diploma.

students. Some schools are embarrassed by such "failures" and choose to sweep them under the rug. Indeed, in 2003 the school district for Houston, Texas, previously run by former education secretary Roderick Paige, suffered under the glare of the national spotlight when it was revealed that the city's high schools had been underreporting dropout rates to appear to be performing better under the state's accountability plan. The underreporting—a citywide dropout rate of 1.5 percent, when the actual figures were between 25 and 50 percent—was uncovered by a principal. His school reportedly had had no dropouts; unfortunately, he personally knew of some. Fallout from the scandal caused several high officials to be fired.[30]

For these reasons and others, graduation rates are not fully reliable. In 2005, the governors of all fifty states signed on to a formula proposed by the National Governors Association: divide the number of students receiving a diploma in a given year by the number of students entering ninth grade for the first time that same year. However, few states implemented the change, leading U.S. Secretary of Education Margaret Spellings to issue a regulation mandating in October 2008 a single dropout rate formula to be used across the country.[31]

Many Brands on the School Reform Shelf

It is one thing to theorize about how to improve schools and quite another to implement real-world programs that get results. Decades of promising techniques—and sometimes utopian promises—have rotated through solutions that span everything from **site-based management** to early-reading programs to smaller class sizes, to name just a few. No consensus has materialized, only more debate. Still, the main schools of thought on school reform can be boiled down to the following.

Standards and Accountability

The **standards movement** first drew attention at a 1989 education summit in Charlottesville, Virginia. Attended by President George Bush and state governors, including future president Bill Clinton, the summit created a national panel to set and monitor education targets that would become **Goals 2000**, or the Educate America Act. That same year, the Kentucky Supreme Court struck down the entire state education system, which prompted the enactment of the **Kentucky Education Reform Act** the following year. This paved the way for the standards movement nationwide.

The premise was simple. Standards require laying out in advance what students should be able to do at each grade in each subject, aligning tests to that content, and then evaluating who reaches the standard. Without question, determining what students should know in each subject area was a task for professional associations. The National Council

SITE-BASED MANAGEMENT

A movement to increase freedom for building administrators such as school principals to determine how district funds are spent at a given school.

STANDARDS MOVEMENT

Effort to create benchmarks of adequate learning in each subject for each grade level so that students and teachers can be evaluated on the mastery of this predetermined material.

GOALS 2000

The Educate America Act, signed into law in March 1994, which provided resources to states and communities to ensure that all students reached their full potential.

KENTUCKY EDUCATION REFORM ACT

The 1990 law passed in response to court findings of unacceptable disparities among schools in Kentucky and considered the most comprehensive state school reform act to date.

of Teachers of Mathematics produced the earliest standards. As momentum built in the early 1990s, the Clinton administration worked to give the movement a national framework in its reauthorization of the **Elementary and Secondary Education Act**, originally passed in 1965.

Prodding from governors and the business community produced considerable progress on the integration of a standards-based approach. Fully forty-nine states laid out standards. Iowa—the lone holdout—proudly leaves standards to local school districts. By summer 2002, forty-seven states were issuing "report cards" on student achievement. Not quite half were breaking the data down by racial subgroups, level of income, or limited English proficiency. Among teachers, according to an *Education Week* survey, eight in ten reported that their curricula were now more demanding. Six out of ten said their students were writing more.

Not that this wasn't all to the good, but the problem with standards, teachers say, is that there are too many to cover in one school year.[32] There is no consensus that standardized tests truly measure learning, given that some children who perform well in written and oral and problem-solving situations do not test well, perhaps due to pressure. Plus, many who test well forget what they memorized soon after.[33] More recently, forty-eight states banded together—Alaska and Texas were the holdouts—to propose common standards, but each still needs to decide whether to adopt the guidelines.[34]

Part of what stands in the way is the issue of textbooks and curriculum development. Twenty-nine states are open territory states that allow individual districts to purchase their own textbooks and develop their own curriculums. This means that children are using different learning materials in different grades at different schools, even if the state has subject standards. The actual learning levels may not be represented accurately on standardized tests, state-authored or otherwise.

The other twenty-one states are adoption states. This means that not only are there state standards but there is also a standard statewide curriculum. Often, the state legislature or a specially appointed panel determines which books will be used in every grade at every public school in the state. Even among adoption states, however, curriculums and standards vary widely. This also can cause students' education levels to be misrepresented. For example, a student moving from Texas to California (both adoption states) will not have learned the same material in the same grade. If forced to take a standardized test, especially a state-sponsored one, the child may fail.

Whether in an open territory state or an adoption state, at the high school level standardized tests are truly high stakes. By 2009, twenty-six states had policies in place to deny high school diplomas to students who fail end-of-course exams.[35] That means students can fail to graduate even if they have passing grades. This not only breaks the hearts of families, it can cost a student a college acceptance. It also opens schools up to embarrassment from lowered graduation rates. Such fears are the reason that Alaska, Arizona, and Maryland delayed the implementation of high-stakes tests.[36] But most of the states using high-stakes graduation tests do allow for an alternate pathway to graduation for students who cannot pass the exams but can demonstrate mastery of the material, and between 2006 and 2008, about 95 percent of high school seniors in Alabama, California, and Massachusetts had passed the compulsory reading and math tests.[37]

The achievement aims expressed in the standards movement were undeniably noble. Goals 2000 included such aspirations as all children beginning school ready to learn and then graduating with demonstrated competencies. It vowed that there should be more professional development for teachers and greater parental involvement. Graduation rates were to be increased to 90 percent. All schools would be drug-free and violence-free, and U.S. students would rocket to first place in the world in math and science.

The question the standards movement never fully answered, however, dealt with accountability. What happens if students fail? Should students, teachers, principals, schools, or all of the above be penalized? As the turn of the millennium came and went, no one could argue that whoever was accountable had done their jobs. Nor could anyone claim that the lofty goals had been achieved. All of this became a somewhat moot point, however, when the George W. Bush administration abolished the Goals 2000 infrastructure to make way for the NCLB.

Recruiting Good Teachers

Recent research has demonstrated that the single most important factor in student learning, more important than curriculum, family income, student health, or parental involvement, is good teaching.[38] Economists have even quantified the effect, estimating that the best teachers give their students an extra year's worth of learning and perhaps 50 points on standardized tests.[39] This is particularly true for minorities, so many of whom enter school socially or economically disadvantaged.

Problem is, demographic projections point to a shortage of teachers that could exceed 2 million during the first decade of the twenty-first century. The absence of qualified teachers also is worse in high-poverty schools. These schools suffer from a heavy turnover in teaching staff, and the number of teachers with less than three years experience is 20 percent, versus 15 percent for other school districts.

The shortage is acute in certain subject areas: special education, mathematics, science, bilingual education, and technology. This is in part due to the fact that teacher salaries often are too low to attract candidates who can earn more at high-tech firms and corporations. School districts must make do, then, with whomever they have to teach the necessary courses. The use of teachers by school districts, however reluctantly, to instruct in

TABLE 13-1

Percentage of Schools Failing to Make Adequate Yearly Progress (AYP)

State	2006–2007	2007–2008	State	2006–2007	2007–2008
Alabama	16	17	Montana	10	28
Alaska	34	41	Nebraska	n/a	n/a
Arizona	28	26	Nevada	31	38
Arkansas	39	28	New Hampshire	41	59
California	33	48	New Jersey	28	n/a
Colorado	25	40	New Mexico	55	68
Connecticut	32	40	New York	n/a	n/a
Delaware	30	30	North Carolina	n/a	n/a
Florida	67	76	North Dakota	9	36
Georgia	18	31	Ohio	38	36
Hawaii	35	60	Oklahoma	n/a	n/a
Idaho	73	44	Oregon	21	35
Illinois	24	31	Pennsylvania	23	28
Indiana	46	n/a	Rhode Island	20	26
Iowa	9	9	South Carolina	61	82
Kansas	11	10	South Dakota	17	n/a
Kentucky	21	29	Tennessee	16	15
Louisiana	n/a	n/a	Texas	10	14
Maine	26	38	Utah	25	20
Maryland	23	16	Vermont	12	38
Massachusetts	37	50	Virginia	26	26
Michigan	17	20	Washington	35	n/a
Minnesota	38	49	West Virginia	19	20
Mississippi	17	14	Wisconsin	4	7
Missouri	30	60	Wyoming	6	25

Source: *An Analysis of State AYP Results for 2007–08* (Alexandria, Va.: National School Boards Association, 2008).

Note: n/a = not applicable.

areas in which they do not hold degrees affects between 4 and 16 percent of high school students in the liberal arts, according to the Department of Education.[40]

One piece of the NCLB aims at improving this record. It originally called for all teachers of core subjects to be "fully qualified," defined broadly as holding a teaching license and showing command of the subjects they teach, by the 2005–2006 school year. When the U.S. Department of Education realized that most states were unlikely to meet this deadline, it declared them compliant if they could demonstrate "good faith and effort" toward meeting the goal. All but seven passed the test.[41] A survey of states and school districts revealed, however, that few believe the NCLB requirement has significantly improved teacher quality.[42]

Colleges and universities that have schools of education are working to improve the quality of their graduates and to provide aspiring educators with more substantive knowledge and less jargon and abstract pedagogy. Many current researchers believe that teachers with the most content knowledge in their field are most effective in raising student achievement. This suggests that the techniques of working with young people and diagnosing student impediments are best acquired on the job.[43]

Alternative licensure programs that provide appropriate training, mentoring, and testing to interested individuals now are permitted in twenty-four states and the District of Columbia. Examples of such programs include Troops to Teachers, which opens up classroom jobs to former military personnel, and Teach for America, which involves recent college graduates who want to fight poverty. Thousands of teachers enter the profession through these programs each year.

Many Schools, Few Resources

Teach for America places its newly minted teachers in urban and rural schools, a boon to districts that have difficulty recruiting and retaining quality instructors. On average, teachers in rural school districts earn 88 percent of the salaries of their nonrural counterparts. While rural schools do have lower crime and dropout rates than urban schools, teachers in rural districts—home to 19 percent of public school students—must also contend with the perpetual challenges of few opportunities for professional development, limited curriculums, and threats of school and district consolidation.[44]

The consolidation of small rural schools has been controversial since it began back in the days of Horace Mann and his one-room schoolhouse. The practice, often pursued by states and districts in search of cost savings, picked up steam throughout the twentieth century. According to the National Center for Education Statistics (NCES; part of the U.S. Department of Education), the nation's 117,108 school districts in the 1937–1938 school year had been cut back to 13,924 by 2007–2008. During that same

School reform efforts have brought a new focus on test scores as proof of student improvement and achievement. Standardized tests have become common nationwide, and students in at least twenty-six states must pass exams prior to graduation.

time period, enrollment grew from 25.5 million students to 49.2 million.[45] States continue to propose consolidation plans, despite conflicting evidence of the strategy's success.[46] West Virginia closed more than three hundred schools between 1990 and 2005, and Iowa consolidated 14 percent of its districts during the same period.[47] And proposals picked up steam later in the decade as municipal and state budgets plunged steeply downward. Through its consolidation law, Maine has cut seventy-five school districts, resulting in hundreds of thousands in savings. Other states are eyeing yet more drastic measures. Mississippi governor Haley Barbour asked a blue-ribbon committee to develop a plan for cutting districts by one-third, and in 2009, Pennsylvania governor Edward G. Rendell recommended reducing the state's school districts from five hundred to one hundred, although his plan failed to gain traction among legislators.[48]

Backlash against further consolidation—but the continuing realization that cost savings need to be made—has some districts and states rethinking their strategies and turning, yet again, to technology. Distance learning is more than just correspondence courses; it encompasses videoconferencing and online learning modules and can vastly expand learning opportunities for both students and teachers.[49] This is not to say that computers are a panacea for all of the ills plaguing rural school districts—after all, they still have to come up with the money to invest in the technology—but proponents argue that it is a strong alternative to closing schoolhouse doors.

Choosing Wisely: Alternatives to Public Schools

School choice, always guaranteed to stir up emotions, has been brought to the forefront of the education debate by NCLB. Schools that fail to make adequate yearly progress for two consecutive years are deemed "in need of improvement," giving parents the right to transfer their children to another public school. NCLB has not led to a high volume of student transfers; polls show the public would rather reform the public school system from within. Alternatives such as charter schools and voucher programs excite varying levels of support.[50] Nevertheless, reformers continue to promote school choice, and parents are taking advantage of the options available. The percentage of students attending their assigned public school fell from 80 percent in 1993 to 73 percent in 2007.[51]

Charter Schools

Entrepreneurs who want to launch their own schools with public money have been applying to run **charter schools** since the early 1990s. These schools are less an educational philosophy than a variation on school governance. Charter schools range in theme from Montessori to the fact-based niche curriculum called Core Knowledge to ranching to online (distance) learning. Sponsors have included former public and private school principals, parent groups, universities, social service agencies, and nonprofits such as the YMCA. By 2007, more than four thousand charter schools had sprung up in the thirty-nine states that have enacted charter laws, with more than 1.2 million students enrolled.[52] The approach is poised for greater adoption because President Obama has made public school alternatives a cornerstone of his education reform proposals, including Race to the Top.

CHARTER SCHOOLS
Public schools, often with unique themes, managed by teachers, principals, social workers, or nonprofit groups. The movement was launched in the early 1990s.

In principle, students who attend charter schools are given the same per-pupil expenditure as students in mainstream schools, although the founders often must scrounge to find facilities. The willingness of a state to encourage the establishment of charter schools depends on the condition of its public schools and the energies of would-be charter school founders. Some states set up special chartering boards. Others allow local school boards to approve the applications.

Overall, state charter laws vary. Arizona's loose regulations provide start-up funds, a fifteen-year authorization, and the freedom for existing private schools to convert to charter status. States with strict charter laws, such as Kansas, provide no start-up funds, allow only a three-year term before a charter school must seek a renewal, and cap the number of schools permitted.[53]

Backers see charter schools as laboratories of innovation that bypass staid bureaucracies and satisfy the parental desire for choice. Evidence of the academic achievement of charter schools is modestly favorable but not spectacular. Some have been forced to close due to corruption, such as embezzlement by administrators, or a failure to attract enough families or maintain a physical facility. In one high-profile case, California's largest charter school operator announced in August 2004 that it would be closing at least sixty campuses amid an investigation into its academic and financial practices, leaving 10,000 students stranded just weeks before the start of the school year.[54] In addition, critics worry that charter schools will balkanize public education and that they may be exploited as a way to avoid dealing with unionized teachers. They also fear that these schools may present an administrative headache to those school superintendents charged with monitoring against abuses of funds.

To determine whether charter schools should be scaled up and duplicated throughout the country, researchers do not just want to know whether a charter's own students' test scores improve. They also want to know if the schools these children's families chose to leave are using the departures as an incentive to do better.[55] To that end, studies have been carried out. Advocates of charter schools, including the George W. Bush administration, suffered a blow in August 2006 when a long-awaited study of test scores by the U.S. Department of Education revealed that fourth graders in charter schools scored significantly lower than their peers in traditional public schools.[56] (See Table 13-2.)

But there are also plenty of individual charter school success stories. Charter schools have been embraced by the chancellor of the nation's largest school system, that of New York City, and Los Angeles mayor Antonio Villaraigosa has even started his own charter school organization. More than 26,000 D.C. public school students—one in three—attend the city's 60 charter schools, and they have scored higher than their traditional school counterparts on standardized tests.[57]

Some studies suggest that tracking students over time might provide additional favorable findings. Tom Loveless, director of the Brown Center on Education Policy at the Brookings Institution, conducted a two-year study of 569 charter schools in 10 states. He found that, although charter school students do score lower on state tests, over time they progress faster than students in traditional public schools. Other proponents believe that students in charter schools also score lower, in part, because they were farther behind to begin with in their previous, traditional schools.[58] A comparison study by Stanford University researchers of charter and traditional public schools in fifteen states and Washington, D.C., found that

TABLE 13-2

Charter School Scores

	Percentage of Fourth Graders at or above Basic Level in . . .			
	Math		Reading	
	Charter Schools	Other Public Schools	Charter Schools	Other Public Schools
Gender				
Male	69	77	55	58
Female	68	75	60	65
Race				
White	84	87	73	74
Black	51	54	37	39
Hispanic	58	62	45	43
Income				
Eligible for Public Lunch	53	62	39	45
Not Eligible	81	88	72	76
Location				
Central city	58	67	50	51
Non-central City	79	80	66	66

Source: U.S. Department of Education, Institute of Education Sciences, National Center for Education Statistics, National Assessment of Educational Progress (NAEP), 2003 Reading Charter School Pilot Study, December 2004.

charter school students in poverty and English-language learners earned higher scores than their traditional school counterparts. Across all students, however, 37 percent of charter schools fared worse than the traditional schools.[59]

Vouchers

Considered a more radical reform than charter schools, **school vouchers** have been proposed in some form since the 1950s. The idea is to mimic government grants used in higher education by giving interested families a set amount of public money that can be used at any accredited school: public, private, or parochial (religious). Voucher enthusiasts want to provide parents with more choice, to break up the "monopoly" of the public education bureaucracy to boost competition, and, more recently, to advance the rescue of low-income black families from failing schools in low-income neighborhoods as a civil right.

SCHOOL VOUCHERS

Movement dating to the 1950s to allow taxpayer dollars to be given to families to use at whatever public, private, or parochial schools they choose.

Charter schools have grown across the country as alternatives to traditional public schools. President Barack Obama has made school competition, including the encouragement of charter schools, a hallmark of his proposals to reform the No Child Left Behind Act and the nation's education system.

Opponents worry that vouchers spell the beginning of the end of society-wide efforts to maintain and improve universal public education. They note that private schools can be selective about which students they accept. In addition, the proposed amounts for vouchers are often less than half of actual tuition. In some communities, the number of available slots at area private schools is insufficient for the number of interested applicants. Voucher proponents aren't without counterarguments, however. They assert that the programs create competition that forces public schools to improve and that they give lower-income students opportunities they might not otherwise have.[60]

Critics also object to the potential for religious indoctrination at parochial schools. Despite these concerns, in June 2002, the U.S. Supreme Court ruled that vouchers can go to a religious school as long as the school's chief purpose is education—in other words, a school that offers a comprehensive secular curriculum, albeit with religious rituals and instructors, as opposed to a Sunday school or bible study.

For each of these reasons, vouchers generally have failed when put to the voters on state ballot initiatives, including in Michigan and California in 2000 and Utah in 2007.[61] In 2006, the Florida Supreme Court struck down the state's voucher program, a key part of then governor Jeb Bush's education plan, as unconstitutional. Efforts to reinstate part of the program at the ballot box in 2008 failed when the court rejected the questions due to technicalities.[62]

Since the early 1990s, however, voucher experiments have been underway at long-troubled and racially isolated schools in Cleveland, Ohio, and Milwaukee, Wisconsin. Cleveland's voucher program, which served 5,800 students during the 2005–2006 school year, was folded into Ohio EdChoice. This statewide voucher program offers 14,000 renewable scholarships to students attending schools considered in "academic emergency" or on "academic watch," the state's two lowest rankings for school performance.[63]

Milwaukee's program offers vouchers worth up to $6,500 to low-income families who may send their children to 1 of 125 participating private schools. The program included only secular schools when it started, but in 1995 it expanded to include parochial schools, a measure protected by the 2002 Supreme Court ruling. By 2006, religiously affiliated schools constituted about 70 percent of the participating schools. In 2006, Wisconsin governor Jim Doyle signed a bill to raise the number of vouchers issued annually from 15,000 to 22,500 in exchange for increased accountability, including standardized testing and accreditation.[64] A report conducted by School Choice Wisconsin, a school voucher advocacy group, found higher graduation rates among students enrolled in the voucher program between 2003 and 2008.[65]

A number of other studies have documented achievement gains among students who use vouchers.[66] Certainly any program that is selected by parents eager for change has an improved chance for students to gain ground. But studies by the U.S. Department of Education and by University of Illinois researchers found public and private school students perform similarly when test scores are adjusted for race and other factors, and a congressionally requested study by the U.S. Government Accounting Office (GAO; later called the Government Accountability Office) of the Milwaukee and Cleveland experiments "found little or no difference in voucher and public school students' performance" in the schools of those two cities.[67]

Home Schooling

A major school reform movement gaining popularity is **home schooling**. According to a 1999 survey by the U.S. Department of Education, an estimated 850,000 students were being taught at home. By 2007, that number had jumped by 29 percent to more than 1.5 million, according to the NCES.[68]

Home schooling champions have organized a legal defense network and a lobbying effort. As the movement has grown, it has organized sports leagues, field trips, proms, and graduation ceremonies. And there are plenty of home school success stories, including Harvard acceptances and solid scores on standardized tests.

Home schooling advocates are a diverse group, but the two main strands are fundamentalist Christians and "free-school" advocates who favor more student choice of subject matter. Parents who can make the time to home-school like the security and personal imprint they can leave on their youngsters. An NCES study found that 30 percent of those surveyed wanted the flexibility to teach moral or religious lessons. Another 31 percent cited concerns about the environment of traditional schools.[69]

Of course, throughout the history of this country, there always have been those who have chosen to teach their children at home. The modern

HOME SCHOOLING

The education of children in the home; a movement to grant waivers from state truancy laws to permit parents to teach their own children.

movement, however, really started taking off in the 1980s. State governments have accommodated home schoolers to varying degrees. Some require parents to have a bachelor's degree to home-school. Others require a curriculum to be submitted for approval, and still others give parents a choice of giving their children a standardized test selected by the school district or hiring their own qualified evaluator.

Michael Farris, leader of the Home School Legal Defense Association, based in Purcellville, Virginia, has been at the forefront of the national movement. His organization ranks states based on how tightly or loosely they regulate home schooling. States with no requirements for notifying state authorities include Idaho, Michigan, and Texas. States with low regulation include Alabama, Kentucky, and Mississippi. Most other states in the Southeast moderately regulate home schooling, whereas most states in New England regulate more intensively.[70]

Critics fear that home-schooled students miss important opportunities for social development and that many parents are not qualified to teach. They also worry that some parents isolate their children and instill in them religious prejudice. Some state and local officials consider home schooling an inconvenience. It forces them to come up with policies on home visits, gauge assessments that may be out of sync with conventional report-card grades, and wrestle with dilemmas such as whether a home-schooled student can play in the public high school band.

Can't Tell the Players without a Program: Groups That Influence Public Education

When the Texas Supreme Court struck down school-funding disparities in *Edgewood Independent School District v. Kirby* (1989), it declined to specify a precise solution to the problem. Instead, it opted to launch a dialogue with legislators and education officials. In Kentucky, the state supreme court was even more an activist. As previously discussed, in that same year it declared the state's school system unconstitutional and not adequate as "an efficient system of public schools." The court went on to lay out a set of goals and ability standards to be pursued.[71]

In both cases, judges knew that no legal ruling on the subject of education would hold sway without public support and buy-in from key stakeholders. That meant going far beyond a small elite of education officials. In Texas, for example, the Mexican-American Legal Defense and Education Fund (MALDEF) played an influential role in developing and supporting the state's new education reforms.

In Kentucky, the legislation and landmark school reform program that resulted from the state court's ruling gained ground largely because of support from such players as newspaper editorialists and a group of education and business leaders called the Prichard Committee for Academic

Excellence. Such groups as these are common participants in the educational debate and are part of the following roster of the familiar players in the education dramas that unfold across the country.

Teachers' Unions

For decades, the major **teachers' unions** have been the National Education Association (NEA), which boasts 3.2 million members, and the American Federation of Teachers (AFT), which reports more than 1.4 million members as of 2010.[72] These groups organize employees from the preschool level to the K–12 level to the university level to form state and local affiliates. They engage in collective bargaining, lobby for resources, and seek to upgrade teacher professionalism through training and publications.

For years, these two unions, both headquartered in Washington, D.C., have flirted with a merger, but style differences always intervene. The AFT was quicker than the NEA to join the school reform parade, for example, by participating in the creation of standards and charter schools. By the late 1990s, however, both had turned sour on the school choice movement, which they consider a threat to public education and their members' livelihoods. They have been critical, too, of NCLB, with the NEA leading the charge in lawsuits challenging the federal government's administration of the law. Both unions align themselves with the Democratic Party, one reason most Republicans blame them for obstructing school reform.

Parents' Groups

The **National PTA**, with 5 million members, bills itself as the "largest volunteer child advocacy organization in the United States."[73] For decades, this umbrella group for local parent-teacher associations and organizations was stereotyped as a klatch of moms putting on bake sales. Today, however, the PTA has school-based state and national organizations that combine to form a sophisticated lobbying and policy force. For the most part, the organization works to boost parent involvement and to encourage parent-teacher cooperation.

The PTA has strict rules about remaining nonpartisan. Despite this, the occasional endorsement of state legislative candidates based on school-funding commitments has gotten some locals in hot water. Other parent groups have emerged over the years to focus on narrower issues, such as the school desegregation efforts of the Mississippi-based Parents for Public Schools.

National Political Parties

For much of the latter part of the twentieth century, education was Democratic Party turf, mostly because of the Great Society legislation pushed through in the mid-1960s. The Democrats traditionally wanted to expand government spending to close the gap between affluent and low-income

TEACHERS' UNIONS

Public-sector unions that organize employees at all educational levels to form state and local affiliates. In the United States, primarily the National Education Association and the American Federation of Teachers, both headquartered in Washington, D.C.

NATIONAL PTA

Umbrella organization founded in 1897 consisting of state-based and school-based parent-teacher associations of volunteers who work to improve and support schools.

schools. Republicans, on the other hand, emphasized local control and social issues, such as efforts to overturn the ban on school prayer. During the Reagan administration, Republicans vowed to abolish the federal Department of Education set up by President Jimmy Carter. Many of them opposed proposals made during the mid-1990s to introduce a national standardized test. They based their protests on the need to preserve local control of schools.

By 2000, however, Texas governor George W. Bush moved the Republicans dramatically to the center of the education debate while campaigning for the Oval Office. His eventual victory in enacting NCLB, which is modeled in part on the system used since the early 1990s in Texas and borrows its name from the liberal Children's Defense Fund, was attributable to support from key Democratic lawmakers.

> Republican efforts to woo Democrats on the more controversial proposals for school vouchers have been less successful, due to the strong support that Democrats depend on from anti-voucher teachers' unions and their general skepticism about market-based alternatives to government programs.

Polls soon after showed that Republicans had caught up with Democrats in the competition to be the "education party." Republican efforts to woo Democrats on the more controversial proposals for school vouchers have been less successful, due to the strong support that Democrats depend on from anti-voucher teachers' unions and their general skepticism about market-based alternatives to government programs. More conservative lawmakers responded positively, however, to some of President Obama's reform proposals, including greater support for charter schools.

Business Groups

Corporations and small businesses have been among the most vocal in pushing for school reform. They cite what they perceive as a decline in the writing and math skills of young job applicants as industry has become more complex technologically. Business leaders, such as Intel chairman Craig Barrett, have joined with business groups, such as the Business Roundtable and the National Alliance of Business, to meet with governors, educators, and school reform activists to press for higher standards for students and teachers. The Business Coalition for Student Achievement, led by the Business Roundtable and the U.S. Chamber of Commerce, issued recommendations to improve NCLB, including a call to improve teacher quality; to focus on college and workplace readiness; and to strengthen science, math, and technology curriculums.[74]

Professional and Advocacy Groups

Within the education "establishment," each of the managerial groups—administrators, principals at the elementary and secondary levels, and school boards—have their own associations. These official decision makers usually win their jobs through a prerequisite set of academic credentials, years of experience in the classroom, and dues paid on the front lines of management.

In addition, there are research groups, such as the Education Trust, which is based in Washington, D.C., and performs research to encourage higher education to help with elementary and secondary school reforms. And there are the advocacy groups, such as the Center for Education Reform, which promotes school choice, and the Public Education Network, which organizes local funds to improve public engagement in school reform.

Issues to Watch

As if the battles over instruction, school choice, and testing weren't enough, debates on social policy and changes in the nation's demographics are playing out in the American classroom.

Evolution and Instruction

American students' achievement in science—or lack thereof—has long been central to U.S. competition with other countries, as seen in the TIMSS results. But the average American science classroom is also the center of a domestic dispute—the debate over the teaching of **intelligent design**, the idea that the universe is so complex that it must be explained by more than evolution.

Almost nowhere has the debate raged more fiercely than in Kansas, where the state board of education rewrote the science standards around evolution and intelligent design five times in eight years. After the board approved standards in 2005 that opened the door once again to intelligent design, the 2006 elections moved the majority of the board toward the pro-evolution members. In 2007, that group flipped the state's curriculum again, approving evolution-friendly standards. Regardless of future election results, that will not be the end of the debate in Kansas; state law requires another review of the curriculum by 2014.[75]

In 2006, in Pennsylvania a federal judge struck down the teaching of intelligent design in the Dover, Pennsylvania, school system, saying that the curriculum violated the separation of church and state. That ruling led Ohio's Board of Education in early 2006 to remove its direction that high school biology classes include a critical analysis of evolution.[76] The debate over evolution continues, although it's manifesting itself more in semantics than in the outright fights of Kansas and Dover. In 2009, the Texas Board of Education voted to eliminate its requirement that students learn the strengths and weaknesses of the theory of evolution, but critics said the

INTELLIGENT DESIGN
The theory that certain features of the universe and of living things are best explained by an intelligent cause, not an undirected process such as evolution.

In Michigan's Detroit school district in 2004, children of color constituted 97 percent of the enrollments.

States under Stress: The Vacation Days No One Wanted

A two-week vacation in Hawaii sounds like a dream to many people. It has been anything but for the state's teachers, however, who were forced to accept seventeen furlough days in the 2009–2010 school year as a cost-saving measure. While most states work off a 180-day school year, plus days for teacher planning and training, Hawaii actually rolled its school calendar back in 2009, to 163 days.[a]

The drastic measure is an indication of just how dire schools' budget problems grew during the Great Recession. Historically, teacher positions had been spared when other state employees were furloughed to save money, but not this time. Other states, including California and Georgia, also forced teachers to take days off without pay, and the same happened in many individual school districts across the country.

Policymakers defended the furloughs as one way to avoid teacher layoffs, but as the fiscal crisis wore on, furlough days appeared to be insufficient. Although one study estimated that the American Recovery and Reinvestment Act saved some 342,000 school jobs, that funding would be largely used up by fiscal year 2011.

In calling on the Congress to appropriate additional stimulus funds for schools, U.S. Secretary of Education Arne Duncan described the ongoing budget crisis as a potential "education catastrophe" and estimated that state budget cuts could imperil as many as 300,000 public school employees.[b]

Two thousand of those jobs are in Detroit, where officials released a plan to close forty-five schools at the end of the 2009–2010 academic year as part of its strategy for closing a projected $317 million budget gap. The troubled school system had already shuttered more than 100 schools between 2004 and 2009, but was still left with more than 50,000 excess seats in the system. "I think you can say that Detroit has hit bottom," said Jack Jennings, president of the Center on Education Policy, an education research group.[c]

Just as Detroit started to plan its turnaround, Hawaii lawmakers decided they had cut enough and voted to use $67 million from a hurricane relief fund to restore the seventeen furlough days planned for the 2010–2011 school year.[d]

[a]Associated Press, "Hawaii Lawmakers OK Funding to Restore School Days," *Education Week,* April 26, 2010, available at www.edweek.org/ew/articles/2010/04/24/349545hixgrhawaiischoolyear_ap.html.

[b]Tamar Lewin and Sam Dillon, "Districts Warn of Deeper Teacher Cuts," *New York Times,* April 20, 2010, available at www.nytimes.com/2010/04/21/education/21teachers.html.

[c]Susan Saulny, "Detroit Plan Would Close 45 Schools," *New York Times,* March 17, 2010, available at www.nytimes.com/2010/03/18/education/18detroit.html.

[d]Associated Press, "Hawaii Lawmakers."

language adopted by the board failed to adequately clarify if and how students would be taught about intelligent design.[77]

A Growing Minority

White students consistently score better than minority students on the nation's standardized tests. In 2009, 78 percent of white fourth graders scored at or above the basic level in reading on the NAEP, compared to just 49 percent of Hispanic fourth graders. Those numbers represented gains for both groups—fifteen years earlier, 70 percent of white students

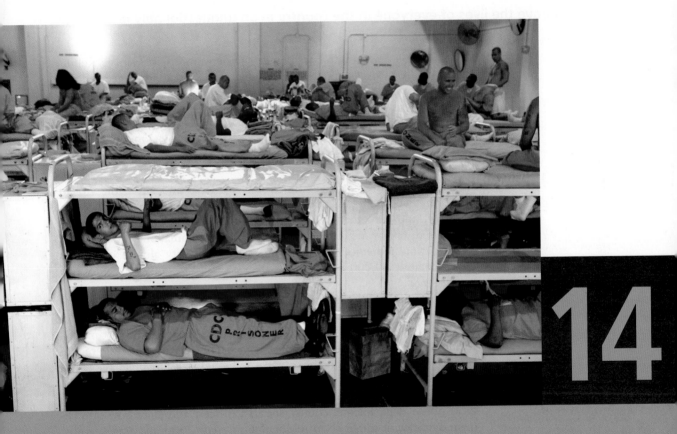

14

Why did different types of policing develop in the United States?

Why has creative problem solving become so important to law enforcement?

How does political culture affect law enforcement in the different states and localities?

Think back for a moment and consider this question: Over the past decade or two, did state or local governments do anything really notable? Something to improve the lives of everyone in the country in an unquestionably good way?

Anything come to mind? No? If not, then criminologist George Kelling thinks you're missing something pretty big. "The most impressive achievement of city governance during the urban renewal of the 1990s," writes Kelling, "was the enormous decline in crime."[1] The numbers speak for themselves. In 1990 alone, 23,438 people were murdered in the United States. By 2008, that number had fallen to 16,272—and this at a time when the population of the country as a whole grew by 55 million people.[2]

Overall, in just a decade's time, between 1990 and 2000, the violent crime rate declined to less than half that of 1973. Property crimes, robbery, burglary, and auto theft, which make up 75 percent of the total crimes committed, fell by a similar amount. The lives, trauma, and money saved by this crime reduction are immense. New York City alone experienced approximately 60,000 fewer crimes than it would have if crime rates had not declined.[3]

This crime drop of the mid- to late 1990s was a welcome development, and state and local officials and law enforcement were quick to take the credit. But was it really their accomplishment to boast about? To many, including Kelling, the answer is clearly yes. They credit the crime reduction to a revolution in policing. Further reductions are possible, advocates believe, as more police departments adopt the new methods. Given that the vast majority of law enforcement officers in the United States work for local police departments, county sheriff's offices, and state law enforcement agencies, it might seem reasonable to credit local and state governments with this improvement.

However, not all criminologists are applauding. Many doubt that improved law enforcement had much at all to do with the crime decline. University of Cincinnati criminologist John Eck sums up the resurgent conventional wisdom, "The bottom line is that one can't really give a lot of credence to the strong statement about the police having a huge *independent* role in reducing crime, particularly homicide."[4] In the view of Eck and other criminologists, crime rates are primarily the function of larger societal trends like the changing nature of the drug market, changing demographics, improved economic conditions, and increased incarceration rates. Still other researchers attribute the crime drop to such factors as improved trauma procedures in hospital emergency rooms and even legalized abortion.[5]

For anyone new to the field, the wide divergence in opinions about what happened, what works, and what is likely to occur in law enforcement may be startling. Welcome to the fractious world of the criminal justice system. This chapter is about the U.S. criminal justice system, which for most Americans translates to their local police departments and their state prison systems. It explores not just how the system works but also whether it works. Can police reduce crime? Do tougher penalties and longer jail terms deter criminals? Do Americans as a society have or want to have a penal system that emphasizes punishment? Or do we want a system that stresses rehabilitation?

This chapter also explores how states and localities approach solutions to crime differently. Should we be concerned that 13 percent of African American males currently cannot vote because of state laws that penalize criminal activity? Is capital punishment fair or racially biased? Are anti-drug laws too tough? Why is crime so much higher in some cities and states than in others? How can successful crime reduction strategies be replicated in other areas? These questions not only are the basis for a tour of the criminal justice system but also help us explore the causes of crime in a world where the connections between crime and punishment are often uncertain and unclear.

Gangs, guns, murder, drugs, and hard time are just some of what this chapter examines. The exploration of the criminal justice system also offers an opportunity to investigate our society's most basic values. After all, crime is about the transgression of a society's ethical norms, and punishment is about the enforced adherence to them. Understanding how a society disciplines itself and punishes people also provides insights into the nature and limits of state power, into the society's conception of justice, and, ultimately, into the nature of democracy itself.

Private Wrongs, Public Justice

Americans are fascinated with crime. Books about private eyes, detectives, and the courts regularly top the best-seller lists. Television shows about cops top the Nielsen charts. In fact, anyone who watches TV has a pretty good idea of how the criminal justice system in the United States works—the police enforce the law and make arrests.

However, they do not have the power to punish. That authority rests with the state. District attorneys initiate the prosecutions. Elected at the county level—except in Alaska, Connecticut, and New Jersey, where they are appointed by the governor—these individuals represent the state's interests in a case. Most of the time, the defendant is represented by either a defense attorney or a public defender and agrees to a plea bargain without ever going to trial.

The local news is often filled with stories of unexpected crimes happening in unexpected places and involving unexpected individuals. Pure sensationalism? Not quite. Although alarming, those reports reflect the rise of crime in suburban areas. In 2009, four police officers were shot and killed while sitting in a coffee shop in the Tacoma, Washington, suburb of Parkland.

If a case does go to trial, a jury decides the guilt or innocence of the accused. If the accused is found guilty—and most are—then a circuit judge metes out a penalty in accordance with relevant law. Judges may be appointed or elected, depending on the state, but their responsibilities are the same in this situation. Defendants who believe they received an unfair trial may file an appeal request with an appeals court or even with the state supreme court.

That is the U.S. criminal justice system—as seen on *CSI* or *Law and Order*. It's a pretty accurate picture, as far as it goes. The problem is, it doesn't go very far. In fact, Americans' very familiarity with the system obscures some basic facts about it. Take, for instance, the fact that punishment is a public function at all.

One of the most (pardon the pun) arresting features of the U.S. criminal justice system is that the state initiates and dispenses punishment for such crimes as homicide, assault, robbery, and burglary. To Americans, this seems entirely natural. People in the United States instinctively note the differences between civil and criminal affairs. Civil disputes are private. Your neighbors knock down your fence and then refuse to put it back up or pay to repair it. You've never much liked them, so you decide to sue. The state offers a forum for the dispute—the court—and carries out the penalty, but the dispute is between two private individuals and their lawyers, and the penalty is a fine. No one expects the county district attorney to initiate criminal proceedings against your neighbors. No matter how precious your fence or how guilty your neighbors, you cannot lock them away. In short, a civil offense is an offense against an individual.

Criminal offenses are thought of in an entirely different way. These are offenses not just against an individual but also against society itself. As a result, the state initiates the punishment—and the punishment can be severe. It can take the form of imprisonment or **probation**. Cruel and unusual punishment, such as torture, is not allowed, but for the most serious offenses, death is still an option.

When you stop to think about it, however, the distinction between civil and criminal cases is not really an obvious one at all. It's all well and good to say that the guy who pulls a gun on you, takes your wallet, and whacks you upside the head has committed a crime against "the public order." Yet you might be forgiven for thinking that what he really has done is commit a crime against *you*. If you happen to actually know the guy who mugged you, it might seem natural, just, and appropriate for you to try to punish him. If he hurts you, you might want to hurt him. As it says in the Book of Deuteronomy, "An eye for an eye, a tooth for a tooth, a hand for a hand, a foot for a foot."

A look at the historical record reveals something interesting—the distinctions that Americans see as natural are, in fact, not natural at all. For most of human history, from ancient Greece to monarchical Europe, private prosecution was the norm.[6] In medieval Britain, the attorney general initiated cases only for the king. Justices of the peace began prosecutions only when there was no private individual to initiate punishment.

Until comparatively recently, the governments of most nations simply set the rules for how offended parties should pursue justice. Their role was essentially that of umpire. Governments had to fight long and hard to establish that they had the *exclusive* right to punish wrongdoers.[7] A key figure in this transference of the right of retaliation from the wronged party to the state was the public prosecutor. For reasons that historians still do not fully understand, public prosecutors first appeared in North America—in Great Britain's Atlantic colonies.

On the whole, the state's successful monopoly on punishment has brought enormous benefits to the United States. Conflicts like the famous one between the Hatfields and McCoys notwithstanding, the nation is essentially free of ongoing feuds or vendettas. However, there are also drawbacks to such efforts to monopolize authority. Today, for instance, state and local governments in forty-eight states actively conceal what may be the greatest power enjoyed by U.S. citizens.

Common Law, Sovereign Power

The criminal justice system in the United States is rooted in the tradition of English **common law**. Forty-nine states operate within this common law tradition. (The exception is Louisiana. As a former French colony, the state instead operates under the Napoleonic code, which Emperor Napoleon I put forth in the early nineteenth century.) The common law tradition makes the U.S. system quite unlike the legal systems of most other

PROBATION

Supervised punishment in the community.

The feud between the Hatfields of West Virginia and the McCoys of Kentucky came to involve the U.S. Supreme Court and the National Guard before the families agreed to end the conflict in 1891.

COMMON LAW

Law composed of judges' legal opinions that reflects community practices and evolves over time.

> Americans are governed by a mixture of formal (statutory) law and case (or common) law. The common law is made up of legal opinions written by judges that recognize commonly accepted community practices and evolves gradually over time as a community's ideas change.

countries. In most of the world, law is enacted by a single sovereign power: a legislature, a monarch, or some combination.

This is partially true in the United States as well, of course. The nation is a federation in which the federal government and the state governments are both sovereign. Congress and the state legislatures both make laws—as do county and city governments at the discretion of the state. Citizens must obey these laws or risk punishment. However, lawmakers are not the only source of laws. Americans are governed by a mixture of formal (statutory) law and case (or common) law. The common law is made up of legal opinions written by judges that recognize commonly accepted community practices and evolves gradually over time as a community's ideas change.

One of American society's most important inheritances from the common law tradition is the institution of the jury. Serving on a jury is *the* defining act of citizenship. It is just about the only thing every citizen must do. (Men between the ages of eighteen and twenty-five must also register with the Selective Service in the event that the government needs to reinstitute the draft.) In most states, ignoring a jury summons is a crime. Failing to appear for jury duty without being properly exempted constitutes contempt of court and may present a somewhat less appealing opportunity to experience the criminal justice system, such as fines or even imprisonment. Unless you commit a crime or have the misfortune of being one of the roughly 5 million people who fall victim to a crime every year, serving on a jury probably will be your primary mode of interaction with the criminal justice system.[8]

As discussed in chapter 8, there are two types of juries. In most states east of the Mississippi River, a grand jury determines whether there is sufficient evidence for the state to prosecute someone for a crime. In states west of the Mississippi, district attorneys usually have the authority to take someone to trial on their own. Presented with a less clear instance of wrongdoing, a prosecutor also may impanel an investigative grand jury to study the evidence and determine exactly who should be targeted for prosecution. Once a grand jury or the district attorney has indicted an individual, another trial begins and another jury is formed to hear the case.

So what is the role of a juror? Most jurors are given clear instructions by the presiding judge. The word **verdict** comes from the Latin phrase *vera dicere*, "to speak the truth." Jurors usually are told that their role is to determine exactly what the truth of a case is. They are to apply the law, regardless of whether they personally agree with it or not. As a result, the role of the juror often is that of a cog—albeit a very important one—in the criminal justice machine.

VERDICT

A jury's finding in a trial.

This official story conceals the fact that the role of jurors historically has not been limited to deciding whether the prosecutor's charges are true or not and then delivering a verdict. Since the seventeenth century, jurors, like judges, also have enjoyed the legal right to set aside laws. (See box on page 536.) The effort to limit juries to mere fact-finding bodies is part of an ongoing and largely hidden struggle between the state and the citizenry over who should wield the power to punish.

The jury system is not the only inheritance left to the United States by the British legal system. Many of the other institutions that characterize the U.S. criminal justice system have their roots in the English justice system as well. County sheriffs are the most notable example. More than one thousand years old, the office of sheriff is the oldest law enforcement office within the common law system. The King of England appointed a representative called a reeve to act on behalf of the king in each shire or county. The *shire reeve*, or king's representative, became the *sheriff* as the English language changed. These days, the sheriff remains the primary law enforcement official in most communities.

Together with state law enforcement agencies like the highway patrol, county sheriffs make up the vast bulk of the law enforcement capacity in the United States. In most states, each law enforcement agency focuses on maintaining order in a specific geographical area, although agencies frequently do cooperate.

The Texas Rangers are the nation's oldest law enforcement agency, unofficially organized in 1823 and formally created in 1835.

The Purpose of Punishment

The criminal justice system of nearly every state comes from the same English common law tradition. As a result, most states share an idea of what is permitted and what is a crime. The ancient Greeks may have tolerated slavery while harshly cracking down on the crime of hubris (not knowing your place in society), but even Minnesota and Mississippi more or less agree on what constitutes a crime these days.

This is much less true of punishment, however. Here the differences among the states become more evident. The Deep South, for instance, imprisons people at a much higher rate than do other parts of the country. (See Map 14-1.) In one sense, this is not surprising. Different states and localities do have very different political cultures. It should come as no shock that they define some crimes differently and punish them differently.

Still, efforts to better understand this dynamic have produced some interesting findings. Studies have shown that the percentage of African American residents in a state's population correlates closely with the severity of penalties. The more black residents a state has, the tougher its laws tend to be.[9] Social scientists question the degree to which what is supposed to be an objective, color-blind criminal justice system—one that is administered largely by whites—systematically disadvantages blacks.[10]

MAP 14-1 **Incarceration Rates per 100,000 Population, 2008**

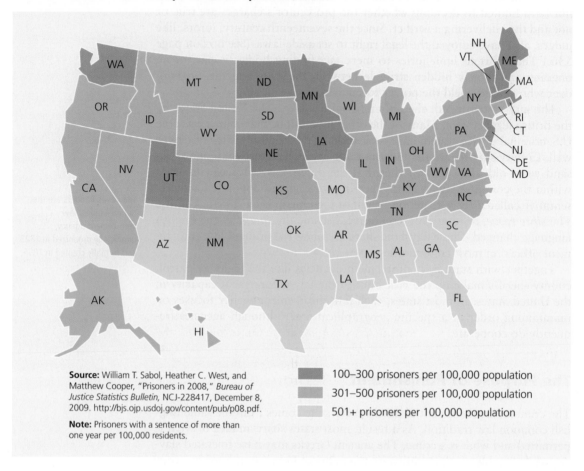

Source: William T. Sabol, Heather C. West, and Matthew Cooper, "Prisoners in 2008," *Bureau of Justice Statistics Bulletin*, NCJ-228417, December 8, 2009. http://bjs.ojp.usdoj.gov/content/pub/p08.pdf.

Note: Prisoners with a sentence of more than one year per 100,000 residents.

100–300 prisoners per 100,000 population

301–500 prisoners per 100,000 population

501+ prisoners per 100,000 population

The severity of punishment also is tied closely to the political parties. States with more Democratic legislators tend to have less severe penalties than states with more Republican legislators. Not surprisingly, election years tend to produce calls for tough new penalties as well.[11] The fairness and effectiveness of these penalties are hotly debated issues (see discussion later in this chapter).

Cultural differences cannot be dismissed when studying criminal justice at the state and local levels. They play an important role in explaining why states approach crime differently. New England, with its Puritan heritage, has always been a region that took a strong interest in saving people's souls, whether they wanted to be saved or not. During the nineteenth century, it was the center of the national abolitionist movement. The region exported missionaries, built universities, and fostered the temperance movement. It also sent hundreds of thousands of emigrants west, where they settled much of the Upper Midwest and Pacific Northwest. As a result, these regions share many cultural similarities. To use the typology of the political scientist Daniel Elazar, they all have a strong moralistic streak.[12]

Given this cultural background, it should be evident why New Englanders and their descendants and other moralistic groups, such as Quakers, view punishment as they do. By the early nineteenth century, a growing number of people in the Northeast were turning against the view that painful punishments deterred crime and were the fitting "just desserts" for criminal activity. Instead, they embraced a new idea—protecting society while rehabilitating criminals.

A new kind of institution soon spread across the landscape—the penitentiary. Unlike prisons, penitentiaries were designed for correction, not for punishment. The most famous penitentiary in early America was located in Philadelphia. Eastern State Penitentiary was designed to force criminals to face their consciences. It operated under a system of maximum solitary confinement. The facility went to extremes to achieve its goal. For example, until 1903, inmates were required to wear face masks when they left their cells. An unfortunate side effect of this "reform" was that many inmates, faced with such extreme isolation, suffered mental breakdowns.[13] This was not the last well-intentioned but ultimately unsuccessful criminological reform.

Of course, correction and penance are not the only purposes that a criminal justice system serves. There is also deterrence, incapacitation, and even vengeance. The debate over the proper purpose of punishment is very old. Different societies have addressed it in different ways at different times. Three centuries before the birth of Christ, in ancient Athens, public punishment was administered to salve the wounds and ease the anger of the injured party. The philosopher Socrates was the first Athenian to argue that public punishment should aim at correcting the deficiencies of the criminal and not just at revenge. For his efforts, Socrates eventually was tried and sentenced to die by drinking poison hemlock for "corrupting youths" and for heresy.

Here in the United States, punishments also have changed to reflect the evolving political cultures. To Pennsylvania Quakers, accustomed to silent contemplation, forcing inmates to confront their misdeeds in silent isolation was a natural idea. In the traditionalistic Deep South, governments chose another model of correction. Facilities like Parchman Farms in Mississippi and Angola Prison in Louisiana were organized as working plantations until well into the twentieth century. For their overwhelmingly African American inmate populations, the similarities to antebellum slavery were unmistakable.[14] Different histories and cultures produced very different institutions. Nonetheless, reformers believed that correction, not punishment, was the future. Then came the 1960s.

Jury Power: What the Courts Don't Want You to Know

The origins of the modern jury go back to the early 1200s, when the English crown enlisted the most notable men in local communities across England into administrative divisions called "hundreds." Twice a year, the king's circuit court judges would meet with these hundreds of notable individuals and ask them to identify all the miscreants in each village who had violated the king's peace. Fines and other forms of punishment were allotted accordingly.

By the fourteenth century, it had become clear that this approach was subject to abuse. As a result, it was decided that jury verdicts had to be unanimous. The presiding judge could punish juries that could not come to an agreement. Despite this strong-arming, the right to issue a verdict remained firmly in the hands of the local juries.[a]

In the mid-sixteenth century, the criminal justice system took a big step toward law and order as it is known today when Queen Mary decreed that henceforth justices of the peace had the power to investigate accusations, take statements from the accused and the accuser, and indict potential criminals. Justices of the peace were then to present their findings to the jury. They even could instruct the jury on how to proceed. In short, the state was asserting ever more control over the way the criminal justice system worked.

But, sometimes, juries refused to play along. This was particularly true when it came to enforcing laws about religion. In 1670, William Penn, a Quaker, was brought to trial for illegally preaching to the public. Under English law, only state-sanctioned Anglican priests could preach in public. Penn admitted that he had broken the law, but he argued that the law itself was illegal. He asked the jury to acquit him. It did, despite instructions from the presiding judge to enforce the law.

The Crown was profoundly displeased because, in a sense, the jury's challenge raised a very fundamental issue: Who really held sovereign power? When a jury could set aside laws made by the queen in Parliament, the clear implication was that the jury, not the government, was the ultimate power in society. To demonstrate where power really lay, all twelve jury members were fined.

Juryman Bushel, however, refused to pay. His appeal went to the court of Chief Justice Robert Vaughan, who ruled in favor of the stubborn juror. He rejected the practice of penalizing jurors for ruling in defiance of the law, and his opinion established something remarkable. Juries truly became the final authority in English society. This had been rather vague until that moment, and so Vaughan's ruling marked a turning point in judicial history. Today, the practice whereby juries set aside laws or penalties that they disagree with is known as jury

New Freedoms, New Fears

The 1960s was a decade of extremes. Its early years saw the birth of arguably the two most significant social movements of recent times—the civil rights movement and the modern feminist movement. Congress started to dismantle the Jim Crow laws that states had erected during the 1890s. Federal monitors were placed at polling stations throughout the South. Housing and real estate discrimination were outlawed. Women, who identified themselves as feminists, persuaded both Congress and most state legislatures to outlaw the practice of paying women less than men who performed the same job.[15]

Despite these accomplishments, the decade ended in a social inferno. A wave of riots nearly snuffed the life out of several inner-city neighborhoods, nullification. The right to a trial by jury is one of a citizen's basic constitutional rights, enshrined in the Sixth Amendment of the U.S. Constitution.

William Penn went on to establish the colony of Pennsylvania in North America. Like Penn, jury nullification also quickly jumped across the Atlantic. In the tumultuous years leading up to the Revolutionary War, American juries repeatedly refused to convict John Hancock and other agitators who were brought to trial on charges of smuggling. Their activities were viewed as principled acts of defiance rather than as crimes. During the 1850s, juries in the North regularly refused to enforce the Fugitive Slave Act, which had been passed at the insistence of the South in 1850 and made it illegal for anyone to assist a runaway slave.[b] Southern anger at Northern "lawlessness" and Northern anger at Southern "overreach" became major issues of contention in the years leading up to the Civil War.

The practice of jury nullification and the spirit of civil disobedience that inspired it also inspired other, less savory actions. For instance, in the 1950s and 1960s, many white juries in the South would not convict citizens who assaulted and sometimes killed civil rights workers. The federal government responded by enacting new guidelines for jury selection that made juries more representative of the community as a whole. Women, minorities, and poor whites began to sit on juries after centuries of nonrepresentation.

Despite the important role that jury nullification has played, no government in the United States is keen on letting folks know about it. Forty-eight states bar defense lawyers and judges from even mentioning that jurors may set aside a law. Indiana and Maryland are the exceptions. As in the days of Juryman Bushel, the state remains uneasy about the discretion that juries enjoy.

Does the fact that jurors can find whatever they want mean that they should? Not necessarily. Chief Justice Vaughan upheld the right of an English jury to reject laws promulgated by a thoroughly undemocratic monarchical government. In contrast, the United States today is a democracy in which nearly every adult citizen has the right to vote. Today, jury nullification can be seen as a profoundly undemocratic act. After all, laws are passed by democratically elected bodies. However, it is also a right that jurors can continue to enjoy. It may be a secret, but under the U.S. system of law, the jury is still sovereign.

[a]Danielle S. Allen, *The World of Prometheus: The Politics of Punishing in Democratic Athens* (Princeton, N.J.: Princeton University Press, 1999), 7.
[b]Ibid., 5–6.

jump-started the move to the suburbs, and ushered in a new era focused largely on public safety issues.

The first such urban disturbance occurred in summer 1964 in the historically African American neighborhood of Harlem in New York City. The event that triggered it all was the police shooting of a fifteen-year-old African American boy. The shooting confirmed a widespread belief that law enforcement in minority neighborhoods was arbitrary, ineffective, and sometimes brutal. One year later, a police stop in the Los Angeles neighborhood of Watts set off riots that lasted six days, cost thirty-nine people their lives, and caused hundreds of millions of dollars in damages. In summer 1967, large swaths of Newark, New Jersey, and Detroit, Michigan, went up in flames.

The riots that swept the Watts neighborhood of Los Angeles in August 1965 confirmed the beliefs of many nationwide that the law enforcement system needed an overhaul. In a spiral of violence, a police action started a retaliatory backlash from blacks that caused further violence on the part of law enforcement. Nearly four thousand people, like the young man in this picture, were arrested for looting and destruction of property.

Then, on April 4, 1968, Martin Luther King Jr. was assassinated in Memphis, Tennessee. Within days of King's death, Washington, D.C.; Chicago, Illinois; and many other cities were torn apart by riots. By one estimate, 329 "important" racial disturbances took place in 257 cities between 1965 and 1968. The result was nearly 300 deaths, 8,000 injuries, 60,000 arrests, and hundreds of millions of dollars in property losses.[16] The decade-long increase in crime showed no sign of stopping.

Confronted by the specter of race riots, most social scientists concluded that racism and inequality were the real fuel behind violence in urban America. These experts argued that, far from solving the problem, the police actually inflamed it on occasion with discriminatory and sometimes violent misconduct. The idea that better policing might be an appropriate response to the riots and rising crime rates was largely dismissed.

To support the belief that the police had little to do with the crime rate, researchers pointed to a decade of studies that documented what police actually did on the job. These seemed to show that the answer was, well, not much. Police officers spent most of their time walking around, talking to people, and occasionally mediating disputes. They did little actual crime fighting. Social scientists suggested that cities should look for other solutions that did not involve law enforcement. Programs to address inner-city poverty and a society-wide effort to reduce income inequality were the solutions.

Federal money began to flow to neighborhood community groups, with few apparent results. One possible reason for this is that all this funding was going to sometimes erratic community groups that were primarily interested in advocacy. This "me first" attitude did not accomplish much. Another reason for the lack of success was that many mayors resented the fact that federal money was flowing to someone other than them. The result was dissension and not much else.

No massive redistribution of income from wealthy Americans to poor Americans was ever tried. It is impossible to know if such a large-scale

Governing States and Localities

FIGURE 14-1 **The Rise and Fall of Crime Rates: Aggravated Assault, Robbery, and Homicide Rates per 100,000 Residents, 1960–2008**

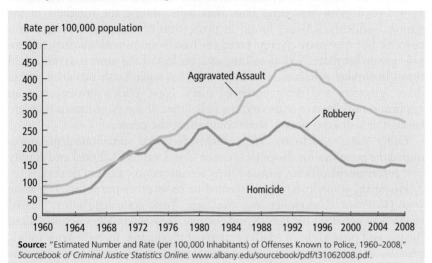

Source: "Estimated Number and Rate (per 100,000 Inhabitants) of Offenses Known to Police, 1960–2008," *Sourcebook of Criminal Justice Statistics Online*. www.albany.edu/sourcebook/pdf/t31062008.pdf.

move would have worked. Empowering neighborhood groups did not. Crime continued to rise throughout the 1970s. (See Figure 14-1.) In many U.S. cities, there was a belief that authority was collapsing and anarchy was at hand. Nowhere was this sense of imminent disaster more apparent than in New York.

On the evening of July 13, 1977, lightning strikes, coupled with a Con Edison repair mistake, plunged the city into darkness. In many neighborhoods, riots and looting broke out. Thousands of fires were set. Although the police ultimately arrested more than three thousand people, much of the city experienced what *Time* magazine described as "a night of terror."[17] The country was entering a world of fear that would last for several decades.

The War on Drugs

As policymakers cast about for a way to make sense of the growing crime problem in the United States, one problem in particular stood out—illegal drugs. By 1978, one-third of all kids ages twelve to seventeen admitted to having tried an illegal drug.[18] In the country's inner cities, heroin use was a particular problem. Many government officials first viewed the upsurge in drug use as a public health issue. However, as a strong link between illegal drug use and crime became clear, most turned to the criminal justice system for solutions.

Faced with a seemingly unstoppable rise in violence, more and more cities responded by increasing the penalties for dealing and possessing drugs. Nelson Rockefeller, the liberal Republican governor of New York state, led the way. In 1973, Rockefeller and the New York state legislature agreed to impose new drug laws that were among the toughest in the nation. Suddenly, anyone found in possession of 4 or more ounces of a narcotic like heroin or cocaine faced the likelihood of a *mandatory* fifteen-year prison sentence. Selling as little as 2 ounces of the same narcotic could result in similar penalties. The hope was that such harsh penalties would drive up prices and deter potential users. New York's strategy was an application of **deterrence theory,** the belief that, if the punishment is severe enough, it will keep people from committing the crime.

Other states and many cities quickly followed suit. State legislatures upped the penalties for the possession of illegal narcotics. Local and county law enforcement officers focused their resources on catching dealers.[19]

However, sometimes efforts seemed to be at cross-purposes. The same year Governor Rockefeller and the New York state legislature created tough new penalties for heroin and cocaine, they essentially decriminalized the use and possession of small portions of marijuana. In New York today, possession of less than 8 ounces of marijuana typically leads to a small fine for a first-time offender.[20]

By contrast, in the state of Arkansas, possession of more than 1 ounce of marijuana can open you up to prosecution on felony charges. Penalties can range from four to ten years in prison. In Montana, first-time offenders can face a life sentence for selling 1 pound of marijuana. But in New Mexico, the maximum penalty for selling 10,000 pounds of marijuana is three years.[21] Why is there such a wide variation in penalties? At least part of the answer can be traced back to the differing political cultures of these states.

Unfortunately, toughening the laws did not work as well as policymakers hoped. Efforts to deter drug use and dealing by setting draconian penalties probably did drive up prices somewhat, and the higher prices probably stopped at least some casual users from experimenting with illegal drugs. However, for the hard-core user, the high of heroin or the rush of cocaine was worth the fairly long-shot chance of a stint in prison.[22]

All in all, the tough new penalties directed against drug users had a minor effect at best on drug use. What they did succeed in doing is putting a lot more people in jail. In 1973, New York State incarcerated approximately 10,000 people. By 1980, that number had reached 20,000. To many, it seemed that things could hardly get worse. But by the mid-1980s, they were.

Crack Cocaine

In the early 1980s, intrepid drug dealers discovered that they could add baking soda and water to high-quality powder cocaine and bake up small

DETERRENCE THEORY

A theory advanced by criminologists that harsh penalties will deter people from committing crimes.

Policy in Practice: Is It Time to Admit Defeat in the War on Drugs?

Listen to the nightly news or read the daily paper and it's easy to conclude that the "war on drugs" has been something of a disaster. Billions of dollars spent and tens of thousands of Americans in prison, and yet drug use remains constant. The price of drugs actually has gone down. So, is it time to raise the white flag and do something different?

Most criminologists would say, yes, it is time to do something different. However, few see the most commonly proposed solution—legalization—as a good answer. The problem with legalizing drugs is who uses them. Basically, it is a disproportionate number of young people who do. The number of eighth-grade students who reported using marijuana within the previous year more than doubled between 1991 and 1996 before beginning to fall; almost 40 percent of high school seniors reported using the drug within the previous year during that same period.

Even if drugs were legalized, these would not be the people society wants using drugs, just as it currently does not want teenagers to smoke cigarettes. So most likely, even if most narcotics were legalized, say, for people twenty-one years old and older, there would still be a serious illegal drug problem. This leads University of California, Los Angeles, criminologist Mark Kleiman to this opinion about legalizing marijuana:

My view is that the risks [related to cannabis use] are substantially greater than most of my well-educated boomer friends believe. Taking the entire population of people who have used cannabis at least five times, the risk in that group of becoming a heavy daily cannabis user for a period of at least months is something like one in nine. . . .

That seems a strong enough reason to oppose the legalization of marijuana on any commercial basis. Think about how aggressively tobacco and alcohol already are marketed. Imagine what big business could do with legalized marijuana.

The federal government's stance aligns with Kleiman's opinion. It hasn't moved toward legalization; instead, it uses the Office of National Drug Control Policy to aggressively market an antidrug message through print advertising and television and radio spots. The effect of the ad campaigns is unclear. After almost a decade of decline, marijuana use among adolescents began an upward trend in 2008 and 2009.

Yet states have continued to take steps toward legalizing pot. Marijuana is now legal for medicinal purposes in fourteen states, and voters in California will decide in 2010 on a ballot question to legalize, regulate, and tax the drug—which proponents claim could raise as much as $1.4 billion annually in new revenues for the state.

Sources: Mark Kleiman, "Revenge of the Killer Weed," September 8, 2002, available at www.markarkleiman.com; Lloyd D. Johnston, Patrick M. O'Malley, Jerald G. Bachman, and John E. Schulenberg, "Teen Marijuana Use Tilts Up, While Some Drugs Decline in Use," University of Michigan News Service, December 14, 2009, available at www.monitoringthefuture.org; Jesse McKinley, "Latest Legal-Marijuana Push Is All about the Tax Revenue," *New York Times*, March 26, 2010, A1.

rocks. These rocks could be smoked in homemade pipes. Nicknamed "crack," for the crackling sound the rocks made when broken, it could be bagged and sold for as little as $5. Before, cocaine had been a yuppie drug, available only to those with the right connections and the right amount of cash. Now it could be bought for a week's allowance.

Crack delivered a potent high at a bargain price. As a result, it quickly found users—with devastating results. Many heroin addicts had managed to maintain functioning lives while also indulging their habit; that drug provides a comparatively gentle high. Crack was different. Highly concentrated, the craving it created in most users was so intense that they would do almost anything to get more. Children were abandoned. Prostitution was embraced. Condemned buildings were broken into and stripped of their contents, even of their plumbing pipes, just so users could make some extra money.

A new urban type was born—the "crackhead" or "fiend." On their best days, crack addicts resembled urban zombies; in particularly hard-hit neighborhoods, police recount seeing dozens of addicts wandering the streets in search of their next "fix." At their worst, they could be very violent; hard-core crack users would rob the grandmother next door or do much worse.

To serve this new market, open-air drug markets sprang up on street corners across urban America. In drug-infested neighborhoods, teenagers often occupied the perfect dealing niche. Many were juveniles and thus were hard to arrest. But dealing drugs on a street corner could be a violent business. Because these open-air drug markets were profitable, the street-level dealers became popular robbery targets. So they started carrying handguns. Neighborhood fistfights and gang brawls turned into running gun battles. Homicides, which had been rising slowly for years, skyrocketed.

Harsher Punishments and Penalties: Prison Nation

State and local government officials responded to this frightening surge in violence and crime in much the same way that legislators had responded to drug use concerns a decade earlier. They imposed tough new penalties for the use and possession of crack. Many states also made fundamental changes to their sentencing practices. For most of the post–Second World War era, U.S. courts had enjoyed considerable leeway in determining the severity of punishments they delivered. In academic-speak, this was known as indeterminate sentencing (see chapter 9).

By the 1980s, however, the public's rising fears led to more strident demands to get tough on crime. Most judges obliged, if only to placate voters. Federal judges are nominated by the president and approved by the Senate for life service. However, most states rely at least in part on elections to select judges—even state supreme court justices.[23]

Stories of judges releasing hardened criminals with little more than a slap on the wrist resulted in a growing number of states' moving toward determinate sentencing. "Truth in sentencing" laws were passed. These restricted a judge's ability to set penalties and curtailed a parole board's freedom to release prisoners early. Some states went even further. Fourteen states abolished discretionary parole and parole boards altogether. In 1994, California voters approved a "three strikes" law. Individuals arrested and convicted of three felony crimes must be imprisoned for a minimum of twenty-five years, if not for the rest of their lives. In 2004, the U.S. Supreme Court further constrained judges' sentencing flexibility but also set the stage for potentially shorter sentences when it ruled that only juries, not judges, can increase sentences beyond the maximums suggested by sentencing laws.

Nevertheless, the increased reliance on incarceration had a big effect on state budgets. In 1978, state governments spent about $5 billion on maintaining prisons and jails. By 2007, prison spending had risen to $44 billion. More than one in every one hundred U.S. adults were under lock and key.[24] States now spend an average of 7 percent of total general revenue funds—$1 out of every $14—on prisons.[25]

Not everyone felt the weight of determinate sentencing equally. By 2006, 5 percent of all black males in the United States were serving time either in a state prison or in a city or county jail. That stood in sharp contrast to the 1 percent of white males jailed during the same period.[26] Nearly one-third of all black males ages twenty to twenty-nine were either in prison or under some form of supervision, such as probation or **parole**. One study estimated that in 1997 black males had a 32 percent chance of going to prison at some point in their life. In contrast, Hispanic males had a 17 percent chance of being imprisoned, and white males had a 5.9 percent chance.[27]

Statistics like these have experts taking a closer look at mandatory minimums, such as those established in the late 1980s for crack and powder cocaine. Offenders receive the same minimum sentence in federal

PAROLE

Supervised early release from prison.

FIGURE 14-2 U.S. Incarceration Rate, 1920–2008

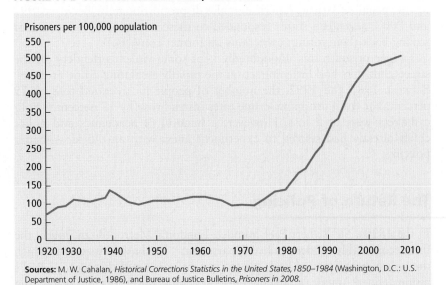

Sources: M. W. Cahalan, *Historical Corrections Statistics in the United States, 1850–1984* (Washington, D.C.: U.S. Department of Justice, 1986), and Bureau of Justice Bulletins, *Prisoners in 2008.*

prison for 5 grams of crack and for 500 grams of powder cocaine. African Americans make up 80 percent of the offenders in prison for crack, and they serve longer prison sentences than if they had been caught with the equivalent amount of powder cocaine. In 2007, the U.S. Sentencing Commission recommended equalizing crack and powder cocaine sentences,[28] and bills to end the disparities were pending in Congress in spring 2010.

Many of those men have a good chance of repeating their time, too. For too many, prison now functions as a kind of criminal finishing school. It is an educational facility whose graduates usually return to a life of crime. Roughly two-thirds of the people who leave prison after serving time for a felony return within three years. Unless state and local governments figure out an effective strategy to reverse this recidivism, millions of those locked away during the "tough on crime" 1980s and 1990s will almost certainly commit crimes again.

The high incarceration rate for black males has meant that many no longer can vote. Forty-eight states—Maine and Vermont being the exceptions—have laws that prohibit prisoners from voting. Felons on probation or out on parole are barred from voting in thirty states. Kentucky and Virginia deny convicted felons the right to vote *ever* again unless the governor restores the right on a case-by-case basis. As a result, 5.3 million Americans can no longer vote. This means that an estimated 13 percent of all black men cannot vote.[29] In Kentucky alone in 2004, the disenfranchisement rate for African Americans was 23.7 percent; in comparison the disenfranchisement rate for all potential Kentucky voters was 5.97 percent.[30]

States recently have embraced a restoration of voting rights for convicted criminals. Most of the impetus for this effort has come from civil rights organizations, which argue that state laws that deny felons the right to vote penalize African American males disproportionately. Between 1997 and 2007, seventeen states responded to these concerns by removing or scaling back their voting restrictions on former convicts.[31]

Longer prison terms undoubtedly kept some violent offenders off the streets, but they had little impact on the rapidly escalating crime problem. Between 1985 and 1992, the number of people incarcerated rose by 79 percent. Far from dropping, crime rates instead rose by 17 percent.[32] Policymakers were at a loss. However, a handful of academics and police chiefs already had started to experiment anew with an old idea—better policing.

The Return of Policing

In the 1820s, Sir Robert Peel founded London's Metropolitan Police, the first recognizably modern police department. "The basic mission for which the police exist," wrote Peel, "is to prevent crime and disorder."[33] Peel's vision defined American policing until the 1960s. Race riots and rising drug abuse then convinced criminologists and many police departments that there was little they could do to reduce crime in the face of shifting demographic trends.[34] By the 1970s, however, a handful of people began to rethink the role that law enforcement agencies should play. In time, these ideas would revolutionize the practice of policing.

The first big idea came in the late 1970s. Put forward by Herman Goldstein, a professor at the University of Wisconsin Law School in Madison, the idea was that the proper role of the police was not to enforce the law but to solve problems. Goldstein's work encouraged police chiefs in cities such as Madison, Wisconsin, and Newport News, Virginia, to think in more creative ways about how to deal with such issues as street-level drug problems. He urged local officials to search for ways to solve underlying societal problems. This philosophy came to be known as problem-oriented policing. Although it was more than a decade before Goldstein's theory began to take root in police departments, the idea that police ought to function as creative problem solvers eventually transformed the way in which many departments thought about policing.

The second breakthrough came in the early 1980s. Political scientist James Q. Wilson and criminologist George Kelling hatched an idea that changed the future of policing in the United States. Arguably, it changed the future of urban America. Their basic premise was simple: minor disorders, such as shoplifting and vandalism, often give rise to much more serious types of disorder and crime, such as robbery and arson.

To support this claim, Wilson and Kelling pointed to a famous experiment conducted by Stanford University psychologist Philip Zimbardo in the 1960s. Zimbardo took two identical cars, popped their hoods, and then abandoned them on two very different streets. One car was left on a high-crime street in the Bronx neighborhood of New York City; the other car was parked in Stanford's hometown of Palo Alto, California. The two cars met with very different fates. Within ten minutes of its being abandoned, vandals—most of whom were respectably dressed, clean-cut whites—began to strip the car left in the Bronx. One day later, virtually everything of value had been removed. In contrast, the car in Palo Alto sat untouched, hood up, for an entire week.

Then Zimbardo changed the equation. He smashed out the windshield of the car in Palo Alto. Within hours, the car had been turned upside down and essentially destroyed. Once again, most of the perpetrators were whites. He concluded that untended property—particularly property that looks as if it actually has been neglected—sends the signal that disorder is tolerated. This quickly gives rise to more serious forms of disorder.

Wilson and Kelling extended this idea to neighborhoods as a whole. They theorized that seemingly minor signs of neglect, such as graffiti, trash, or broken windows, signal that authority is absent and give rise to much more serious problems such as violent crime. The two social scientists went on to make a larger point about policing. Those police officers whom researcher in the 1950s observed walking around and resolving disputes actually might have been doing something important. By their very presence, they had been maintaining order. It was time, Wilson and Kelling wrote, to go back to the future.[35]

Community Policing versus the Professional Model

The first police car went on patrol in Akron, Ohio, in 1899. It was electric-powered and could reach a speed of 16 miles per hour.

Wilson and Kelling argued for a dramatic break from the **professional model of policing**. This approach to fighting crime emphasizes squad cars and quick response times; police departments across the country embraced it during the 1970s. The reason for this was an important new innovation—the 911 emergency number. Cops who had once walked the beat and played the role of friendly neighborhood supervisor now were put into squad cars. Response time—how quickly the police responded to a call for assistance—became the criterion by which departments were judged as successes or failures. It was an all-or-nothing situation because there simply were not enough police officers available to both monitor neighborhoods *and* answer emergency calls.

The professional model originated on the fast-growing West Coast. Long before the advent of 911, many West Coast police departments emphasized technology. They prided themselves on their small, highly mobile forces. The influence of the Los Angeles Police Department (LAPD) in particular on police technique nationwide cannot be understated. For many years, it was seen as the prototype for effective police departments. Its cool professionalism ("Just the facts, ma'am.") was captured in the TV show *Dragnet*. The department was the first to buy helicopters; it also pioneered the use of the now ubiquitous Special Weapons and Tactics (SWAT) teams.

When widespread use of 911 pushed policing nationwide even further toward the professional model, the East Coast departments changed the most because they had been most unlike the professional model in the first place. West Coast officials long had thought of East Coast police departments as dinosaurs with troubling opportunities for corruption. With many more police officers per capita than West Coast police departments, East Coast departments were portrayed as sources of patronage jobs, not as effective law enforcement agencies. A beat cop walking past the same gambling den or house of ill repute every day could be tempted all too easily to accept payoffs and look the other way.

West Coast police departments were convinced that they could do the same job better—or at least as well. Good tactics and high-tech equipment would prevail. And, for a while, departments such as the LAPD did maintain order, although at a cost. Their smaller forces used aggressive tactics—sometimes in a very arbitrary fashion. Senseless stops by the police became an all too familiar experience for residents of many predominantly minority areas. Consequently, a considerable number of Los Angeles African Americans and Hispanics came to mistrust the police department.

This state of affairs was underscored by the violence that broke out following the 1992 acquittal of the police officers involved in the beating of Rodney King.[36] Earlier that year, a bystander had videotaped LAPD officers violently subduing King, a black motorist who had led them on a high-speed chase and then resisted arrest.[37] When an all-white jury found the officers not guilty, riots erupted throughout the city. For six days, the police force, caught unprepared in part because of political maneuvering at its top levels, struggled to regain control.

A Return to Community Policing

By the early 1990s, it was obvious that a different model was needed. That model was **community policing**. In a sense, this represented a return to one of Sir Robert Peel's earliest ideas—that police officers should walk a beat and get to know their neighborhoods. Community policing emphasizes the importance of good relations with local neighborhoods and the need for residents and police officers to solve problems jointly. Isolated experiments with community policing began to appear in a handful of police departments, including that of San Francisco, California, as early as the late 1960s.

COMMUNITY POLICING
An approach that emphasizes police forming relationships with neighborhoods and engaging in collaborative problem solving.

The momentum for this change did not begin to build, however, until the late 1980s and early 1990s. Departments like those in Madison, Wisconsin, and Houston, Texas, embraced and developed the model during this period.[38] Then the Rodney King riots spotlighted the problems of the professional model, pushing other departments toward the community policing model. The most significant variation on community policing appeared in New York. During the early 1990s, Mayor David Dinkins introduced its precepts into the nation's largest police department, the New York Police Department (NYPD).

At the same time that the NYPD was experimenting with community policing, the city's transit police were attempting to test James Q. Wilson and George Kelling's belief that disorder left unattended bred crime. **Broken windows policing**, which emphasizes the maintenance of public order, was instituted. The result was immediate and dramatic. The transit police discovered that many of the vandals and turnstile jumpers they arrested were ex-felons who also were carrying guns or skipping out on warrants. By getting to these people early, the police were, in effect, disarming them. After crime underground increased by 48 percent between 1988 and 1990, the transit police under the leadership of Chief Bill Bratton in 1990–1991 managed to bring robberies down by 40 percent.[39]

BROKEN WINDOWS POLICING
Policing that emphasizes maintaining public order.

The community policing model is based on the idea of building good relationships with neighborhoods. Bensalem, Pennsylvania, police officer Theresa Nelson is doing exactly that by stopping to chat with Victoria McDaniel.

Bratton's successes caught the attention of an equally ambitious U.S. attorney, Rudolph Giuliani. Two years later, Giuliani won a close race to become mayor of New York. Reducing crime was one of his major priorities. The young chief who had done so much with the transit police immediately went to the top of Giuliani's list to head the NYPD. What secured the job offer for Bratton was his promise to Giuliani that, if he offered Bratton the job, Bratton would deliver a 40 percent crime reduction for the whole of New York City within three years.

It was an unprecedented and—in the eyes of most criminologists—outlandish commitment. Most experts believed that other factors, such as demographics, were far more important than any type of policing. And the demographics were bad. The problem was young people. People between the ages of eighteen and twenty-five commit crimes at disproportionate rates—more than five times the rate committed by people ages thirty-five and older. (See Figure 14-3.) During the 1990s, the proportion of young people in the population as a whole was growing fast. Demographers saw it as the echo of the baby boom in that a large number of the children of people born between 1946 and 1964 were reaching their teen years. Criminologists saw it in different terms—they predicted the coming of juvenile **superpredators**.

Fortunately for New York City, Mayor Giuliani was not much interested in criminology's conventional wisdom. Bratton's bold offer and the promise that broken windows policing had shown underground in the subway system appealed to the new mayor. Bratton got the nod. By the time he resigned two years later, homicides in New York had fallen by 39 percent.

So what happened? Officials in the NYPD say the answer is simple—better policing. The key innovation was a new computerized crime-mapping system known as Compstat. This system allowed the police to

SUPERPREDATORS

Ultra-violent youth whom experts predicted would further drive up the nation's crime rate.

FIGURE 14-3a Violent Crime, Arrests by Age, 1993–2005

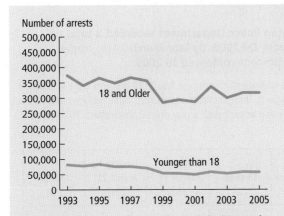

Source: *Crime in the United States 1993–2005,* Federal Bureau of Investigation.

Note: Gun violence is a frequent topic of discussion in the United States, with good reason: arrests for gun-related murders rose 40 percent among people aged eighteen to twenty-four between 1976 and 2004. More encouraging, though, is that all violent crime, including gun-related murders, committed by people younger than eighteen years of age has dropped significantly.

FIGURE 14-3b Homicide, Arrests by Age and Weapon, 1976–2004

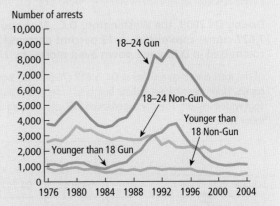

Sources: Jeffrey A. Butts and Jeremy Travis, *The Rise and Fall of American Youth Violence: 1980 to 2000* (Washington, D.C.: Urban Institute, 2000); and James Alan Fox and Marianne W. Zawitz, "Homicide trends in the U.S.," U.S. Department of Justice, Bureau of Justice Statistics, www.ojp.usdoj.gov/bjs/homicide/homtrnd.htm.

map crime in virtual real time, identify patterns or problems, and then shift resources and devise solutions accordingly. Before the creation of Compstat, the NYPD compiled crime statistics every quarter. Compstat provided fresh numbers every week and allowed police commanders to look for crime patterns and "hot spots." It also encouraged officers to try new tactics and introduced an element of accountability into policing.[40] Today, nearly 70 percent of large police departments in the United States use some version of this system. More police officers and a focus on broken windows, or quality-of-life offenses, rounded off the prescription for success.

In the mid-1990s and late 1990s, these concepts were exported to other cities nationwide. Former NYPD officials were hired as consultants in such cities as New Orleans, Louisiana; Newark, New Jersey; Philadelphia, Pennsylvania; and Baltimore, Maryland; and they put NYPD-style techniques into place. Many of these transplanted consultants generated dramatic results, especially at first. However, another dynamic soon became evident that caught public officials off-guard. Many cities that had done nothing to improve their police departments were also enjoying dramatically falling crime rates. (See Figure 14-4.)

Los Angeles was a case in point. Once one of the most admired police forces in the country, by the early 1990s, the LAPD had fallen on hard

CapStat

Departmental Performance Indicators: Citywide Crime

During Q4 2009, the Washington, D.C., Metropolitan Police Department recorded a total of 7,627 crimes committed—a 13 percent decrease from Q4 2008. By late March 2010, crimes committed in D.C. were down even more—by 26 percent compared to 2009.

Of the total crimes committed in Q4, 5,817 (76 percent) were nonviolent crimes and 1,810 (24 percent) were violent crimes. Nonviolent crimes include burglary, larceny, and auto theft. Violent crimes are murder, rape, robbery, and aggravated assault. The city experienced increases in burglary and assault with a gun only. By mid-March 2010, even those were down.

Crime Type	Q4 2008	Q4 2009	Change (%)	January 1–March 21, 2009	January 1–March 21, 2010	Change (%)
Homicide	45	43	−4	25	17	−32
Sex abuse	91	82	−10	77	54	−30
Robbery (excluding gun)	730	636	−13	562	435	−23
Robbery (with gun)	447	438	−2	328	210	−36
Assault with deadly weapon (excluding gun)	444	441	−1	351	374	+7
Assault with deadly weapon (with gun)	169	170	+1	118	95	−19
Total violent crime	**1,926**	**1,810**	**−6**	**1,461**	**1,185**	**−19**
Burglary	837	936	+12	671	633	−6
Theft	2,335	1,959	−16	1,898	1,322	−30
Theft from auto	2,340	1,846	−21	1,732	1,087	−37
Stolen auto	1,264	1,062	−16	902	686	−24
Arson	15	14	−1	14	7	−50
Total property crime	**6,791**	**5,817**	**−14**	**5,217**	**3,735**	**−28**
Total crimes	**8,717**	**7,627**	**−13**	**6,678**	**4,920**	**−26**

Like Compstat, CapStat is a computer-based mapping system that provides up-to-date citywide information, including which crimes are being committed and where they are being committed. This allows police departments to quickly identify trends and target law enforcement efforts to the hot spots of criminal activity.

FIGURE 14-4 Homicides in Large U.S. Cities, 1995, 2000, 2005

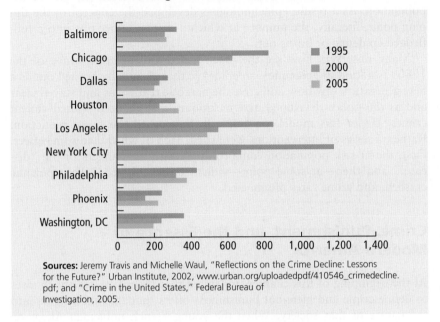

Sources: Jeremy Travis and Michelle Waul, "Reflections on the Crime Decline: Lessons for the Future?" Urban Institute, 2002, www.urban.org/uploadedpdf/410546_crimedecline. pdf; and "Crime in the United States," Federal Bureau of Investigation, 2005.

times. In the years that followed the Rodney King riots, the department went through two chiefs and struggled with sagging officer morale. Yet, despite all this, homicides in Los Angeles fell from 983 in 1990 to 425 in 1999.

As crime rates fell almost everywhere, regardless of policing techniques, questions about Bratton's accomplishment in New York and his philosophy of crime reduction reappeared. Criminologists began to look for factors other than improvements in policing. They explored such areas as changes in the structure of urban drug markets, demographics, the economic boom of the 1990s, and the high rates of incarceration during the 1980s and 1990s.[41]

The dispute between those who give the police most of the credit for the crime reduction of the 1990s and those who do not continues. There is, however, a more subtle and widely accepted explanation for what happened in New York and across the country that both sides more or less agree with. It's called the "tipping point." This concept comes from epidemiology, the study of diseases. Early in the history of the discipline, epidemiologists noted that diseases do not tend to spread in a linear fashion. Rather, a handful of people come down with a disease, then a few more, and then BOOM!, doctors are dealing with a full-fledged epidemic.

Moreover, the scientists noted that epidemics often end suddenly too. Some diseases spread too fast and then "burn out" or, if checked by quarantine, die out as infected people are isolated from the rest of the population. As a result, epidemiologists developed the concept of the tipping point, literally, the number at which a disease either tips into a full-fledged epidemic or burns out.

Many observers now see the crack-fueled violent crime wave of the 1980s as a kind of epidemic—an epidemic that eventually burned out as a new generation saw how addictive the narcotic really was and stayed clear and as the police developed new techniques that reduced related violent crimes. Under this model, no single factor caused the crime reduction. Rather, a series of interventions were tried, each of which had some effect. First, the at-risk population came to appreciate the dangers of the "disease," and then—at some point—violent crime "tipped." The epidemic crashed, and crime rates plummeted.

Crime, Punishment, and the Essence of Modern America

At the beginning of this chapter, we stated that the way a society chooses to define crime and mete out punishment offers fundamental insights into the nature of that society. When the young French nobleman Alexis de Tocqueville decided in the early 1830s to visit and investigate the fledgling democracy of the United States, his first stop was the prisons. When British author Charles Dickens visited in 1842, he too sought out the prisons and asylums.

Today, many Europeans view punishments like the death penalty as evidence of American cruelty and racism. They use the death penalty to argue against American "justice" in much the same way that critics of U.S. actions in the Middle East seized on the abuses at Abu Ghraib to criticize the U.S. occupation of Iraq. Most U.S. citizens these days are shielded from the reality of the nation's criminal justice system. It operates largely out of sight. Only a small percentage of Americans see what modern punishment looks like in this country. A tour of its state prisons and county and city jails may prove enlightening.

First, the system is rife with violence. A 2003 report by Human Rights Watch estimated that approximately 20 percent of all inmates are sexually assaulted in some way and at least 7 percent are raped. That equals approximately 1 million assaulted individuals over a twenty-year period. For many of these prisoners, rape may be just the beginning. Prisoners who are passive or effeminate may end up as slaves, forced to do menial jobs and sometimes "rented out" to other inmates to satisfy their sexual needs.[42]

Second, the prison population is a sick population. In the 1960s, most states disbanded the psychiatric hospitals that held many of society's mentally ill. At the time, the goal was to replace the old, often cruel networks of state mental hospitals with more humane, community-based clinics.

Unfortunately, the states did away with the hospitals without building the clinics. An estimated 56 percent of state prisoners and 64 percent of local jail inmates suffer from a mental health disorder, including serious illnesses like schizophrenia, bipolar disorder, and depression. That's more than 1 million mentally ill prisoners and inmates—far more than there are patients in mental hospitals. What's more, about three-quarters of those inmates with mental illnesses also are addicted to drugs or alcohol.[43]

Once in prison, do people with mental illnesses receive adequate treatment? Although more than a quarter of state prisoners report having taken medications prescribed to treat mental illnesses since entering prison, for the most part, the answer is no. In the words of another report by Human Rights Watch, across the nation, many prison mental health services are woefully deficient, crippled by understaffing, insufficient facilities, and limited programs. All too often, seriously ill prisoners receive little or no meaningful treatment. They are neglected, accused of malingering, and treated as disciplinary problems.[44]

A century and a half ago, many visitors to the United States praised the prisons and asylums. Today, they do not. A recent study by the international human rights group Amnesty International stated, "There were reports of ill-treatment by police and prison officers . . . often involving cruel use of restraints, or electro-shock weapons. . . . Thousands of prisoners continued to be confined in long-term isolation in high security units where conditions sometimes amounted to cruel, inhuman or degrading treatment."[45]

The organization found that more than 20,000 prisoners continued to be held in conditions of extreme isolation in **supermax security prisons**. In addition, between 1976 and 2009, 1,188 people have been executed in the United States. Roughly 35 percent of those executed have been black.[46]

What most shocks the rest of the developed world, however, is this country's treatment of children. According to Amnesty International, the United States is in violation of international law—and treaties it has ratified—when it sentences defendants who were under eighteen at the time of their crimes to life without the possibility of parole.[47] Amnesty International estimates that between 1995 and 2003, the United States executed roughly two-thirds of the total children ages seventeen and under who were put to death worldwide. Until the U.S. Supreme Court ruled the practice unconstitutional in 2005, the United States was the only developed country that made child execution a regular part of its criminal justice system.[48] The nation also leads the world in the execution of people with mental impairments.

> An estimated 56 percent of state prisoners and 64 percent of local jail inmates suffer from a mental health disorder, including serious illnesses like schizophrenia, bipolar disorder, and depression. That's more than 1 million mentally ill prisoners and inmates—far more than there are patients in mental hospitals.

SUPERMAX SECURITY PRISONS

High-security prisons designed for violent criminals.

Issues to Watch

After the long crime decline of the 1990s, many experts are uncertain about what to expect in the future. Crime rates in the United States still are well above the post–Second World War rate. Granted, the world has changed a lot since the 1950s; it may seem unrealistic and idealist to think that such an old benchmark is relevant anymore. Crime rates do remain remarkably lower than the dark days of the early 1990s. After a brief increase in violent crime in the middle of the last decade—illustrated by the police chief of Washington, D.C., declaring a crime emergency after thirteen people were killed in an eleven-day span—rates have headed south once again.

But if the 1990s showed anything, it was that making predictions about the direction of crime rates is an uncertain thing. Radical improvement is still the goal in cities such as Los Angeles. Today, the city has one of the country's highest homicide rates. The LAPD estimates that approximately 41,000 Los Angeles residents are gang members, one of the largest populations in the nation.[49] Yet despite these daunting numbers, Los Angeles's elected leadership insists that it is committed to making the city the nation's safest. With enough law enforcement personnel and creative problem solving, it just might happen. Even with the inherent uncertainty of predicting the future, some important trends already are evident in Los Angeles and nationwide.

Policing

Experts predict that the retreat from the professional model of policing will continue. The belief that the professional model was a misguided reform is now conventional wisdom. Even the West Coast, the one-time citadel of the professional model, now is trying to revamp its departments. Given its commitment to improved safety, it should be no surprise that the biggest change is taking place in Los Angeles. In fall 2002, Mayor James Hahn hired Bill Bratton of New York City fame to head the Los Angeles police force. After taking over, Bratton introduced his Compstat to the city and pushed hard to put an additional three thousand officers on the payroll.

Yet, despite Bratton's seven years of efforts—he left the LAPD in 2009—the legacies of the professional model linger. Even now, residents of East Coast cities continue to enjoy a far higher level of protection than residents of West Coast cities. To police a city of nearly 4 million people, the LAPD relies on approximately 10,000 officers. In contrast, New York City has a population of 8 million and 37,000 police officers. That is more than twice the number of police officers per capita for New York than for Los Angeles. Granted, Los Angeles and New York are extreme examples of (comparatively) small and large police forces, but such differences are visible among other cities as well. Cities in the Upper Midwest, including Chicago, Illinois; Milwaukee, Wisconsin; and Detroit, Michigan, tend to have larger police departments, in line with the size of East Coast forces. Cities in the Southwest and the Southeast, such as Dallas and El Paso, Texas; Phoenix, Arizona; Charlotte, North Carolina; and Memphis, Tennessee, often have smaller departments, comparable to West Coast cities like Los Angeles and Las Vegas.[50]

The End of Federal Support

This chapter has discussed crime and punishment as almost an entirely local matter. Basically, this is true. According to the Bureau of Justice Statistics, there are roughly 732,000 state and local law enforcement officers nationwide and only 105,000 federal law enforcement officers. This does not mean that the federal contribution to law enforcement is insignificant. Federal agencies take the lead in responding to crimes that cross state boundaries. They also are in charge of certain categories of crime, including counterfeiting, and, to a lesser extent, gun trafficking. Sometimes the division of responsibility between federal law enforcement, such as the Drug Enforcement Agency or the FBI, and state and local agencies can be quite unclear.

The most significant federal contribution to state and local law enforcement, however, has been financial. During the late 1960s, the federal government created the Law Enforcement Assistance Administration. This agency funneled hundreds of millions of dollars to local law enforcement agencies before its elimination in 1982. In the mid-1990s, President Bill Clinton and Republicans in Congress passed legislation that provided nearly $20 billion to states and localities to build more prisons and helped localities add about 70,000 police officers to their forces.

More recently, the Great Recession has drained state and local police department budgets. The ARRA made $1 billion in grants available to the agencies in 2009, helping them create or preserve about five thousand law enforcement positions for three years.[51] Additional state budget stabilization funds in the stimulus package helped cities fill gaps in their police budgets.

The New Criminal Frontier

There is a sense that the locus of crime is shifting. During the 1960s, 1970s, and 1980s, the notion of the city as a dangerous place established a powerful hold on the American mind. *Law and Order* is not set in Oklahoma City, Oklahoma, or suburban Indianapolis, Indiana; it is set in New York City. These days, more and more of these images of danger are just that—creations of the imagination. Today, New York is one of the safest cities, not just in the country but also in the world. Although gun crimes are still much, much rarer in European cities, London residents are more than twice as likely to be the victims of crime than New Yorkers.

WE NEED IT.

TaKe THe BaiT. GeT HooKeD. TeLLiNG STöRieS. SHaRiNG THe CaTCH.
FiSHiNG KeePs ouR CuLTuRe aLiVe. NaTiVe PRiDe.
WE NEED THE OUTDOORS. WE DON'T NEED METH.
THERE ARE LOTS OF COOL THINGS ABOUT BEING NATIVE. METH ISN'T ONE OF THEM.

ABOVETHEINFLUENCE.COM

Methamphetamine, or meth, is among the top drug problems facing law enforcement in rural areas and on reservations across America. Governments have turned to advertising campaigns to dissuade people from trying the drug.

In fact, a new dynamic is now at play in cities that reduced their rates of violent crime dramatically during the 1990s. These communities have exported much of their crime to their surrounding suburbs. Guns, gangs, and drug problems are no longer limited to large cities. In 2008, more than a quarter of all violent crime occurred in suburban areas.[52]

The countryside is not as quiet as the stereotype portrays it, either. Police departments in small towns increasingly fight the same battles against drugs and gangs as their urban neighbors. However, those departments lack many of the resources of their city counterparts. A survey conducted for the National Institute of Justice found that fewer than a quarter of small and rural police departments had the capability to use computers to aid their criminal investigations and that they underutilized other technologies, such as digital fingerprint imaging and global positioning systems.[53]

Many rural areas connect a rise in crime to the rise in the use of methamphetamine, a drug often made at home using the same ingredients found in cold medicine. Meth's popularity exploded in such states as Montana, Nebraska, and Oklahoma in the late 1990s. Surveys by the National Association of Counties consistently rank it as counties' top drug problem—higher than cocaine and marijuana combined—leading the association to develop a Meth Action Clearinghouse for its members.[54] By 2005, states across the country had attempted to curtail the drug's availability by moving over-the-counter medicines containing pseudoephedrine, meth's main ingredient, behind the pharmacy counter. In October 2005, Oregon passed a law requiring a prescription for these previously over-the-counter drugs. The states were ahead of the federal government, which passed a law limiting the distribution and sales of pseudoephedrine in March 2006.

There is some evidence that these laws have helped reduce the number of meth labs. In Oregon, the number of labs dropped from 192 found in 2005 to just 10 in 2009, and monthly meth lab seizures are down 96 percent statewide.[55] But, hard-core meth addicts may now be looking

Governing States and Localities

elsewhere for their fix. One Oklahoma sheriff reported an increase in the imports of "ice," a meth product from Mexico and labs in southern California. "Ice" is vastly more expensive than homemade meth, leading to an increase in crimes committed by addicts, who need money to pay for the drug, similar to those once committed by crack addicts.[56]

Moreover, suburban communities are dealing with these problems without the resources or the experience of big city police departments. In the next decade, we may witness an explosion of suburban public safety creativity that matches the urban innovations of the 1990s.

The Uncertain Future of the Death Penalty

In 1972, the U.S. Supreme Court found that the application of the death penalty in many states had been cruel, arbitrary, and unconstitutional. A moratorium, or indefinite delay, was placed on all executions. Four years later, the Court lifted the moratorium. By then, the states had passed sentencing guidelines that addressed the Court's concern that the death penalty was being applied in an arbitrary fashion. Today, the statutes of thirty-five states allow prosecutors to request the death penalty. More than 1,100 prisoners have been executed since capital punishment was reinstated, and another 3,279 people were on death row in 2009.[57]

The fact that most states sanction capital punishment does not mean that they use it in similar ways. Some counties and states are much more enthusiastic in its use than others. For example, suburban counties tend to apply the death penalty with more zeal than urban counties. In 2009, San Mateo County, a suburb of San Francisco, had seventeen people on California's death row; in contrast, San Francisco itself, a larger city with twice as many murders, had sentenced only four people to death. Richard Willing and Gary Fields found in 1999 that "fifteen counties account for nearly a third of all prisoners sentenced to death but only one-ninth of the population of the states with capital punishment."[58] One reason for this may be the rising crime rates in suburban areas and a "fight back" reflex felt by residents who have seen their safe communities become danger zones.

During the 1990s, a scientific breakthrough—DNA testing—shook up the capital punishment systems of most states. In state after state, lawyers and public interest groups convinced courts and prosecutors to reexamine forensic evidence. What they found was that many people had been convicted of crimes they had not committed. By December 2009, postconviction DNA testing had cleared 248 Americans. Seventeen of these people had been sentenced to death; 149 of them were African Americans.[59] The impact of this new research has been felt. In January 2000, Illinois

> During the 1990s, a scientific breakthrough—DNA testing—shook up the capital punishment systems of most states. In state after state, lawyers and public interest groups convinced courts and prosecutors to reexamine forensic evidence.

governor George Ryan, a Republican and an avowed supporter of capital punishment, became the first governor in the nation to halt executions.

Other states began examining the most widely used method of execution—lethal injection—after the U.S. Supreme Court ruled in June 2006 that lower courts must consider the possibility that the process can be cruel and painful, a finding that would make the procedure unconstitutional. Several states proposed adding an anesthesiologist to monitor executions and confirm that the three-drug process, intended to sedate, paralyze, and finally kill the prisoner, was working properly. There was just one problem—anesthesiologists balked at presiding over executions because that would go against their Hippocratic Oath "to do no harm." When California could not find a workable solution, the death penalty went on trial. In December 2006, a federal judge found California's method of lethal injection unconstitutional, but said the system could be fixed.[60]

In 2007, New Jersey became the first state in forty years to repeal capital punishment, and all states participated in a seven-month national death penalty moratorium, until the U.S. Supreme Court in April 2008 upheld Kentucky's lethal injection process. Many states have since resumed executions, although at least three states—California, Maryland, and North Carolina—continue to suspend their systems while they review their administration of lethal injection,[61] and New Mexico followed New Jersey's repeal with its own in 2009. Other states continue to struggle with their systems, including Ohio, where at least three executions were delayed when the needles necessary for the lethal injection could not be placed correctly. In light of these challenges, some experts are calling for a return to other execution methods, including the electric chair and the firing squad. "We've known for a long time that there are better methods, but states don't want to look bad and horrifying," says Deborah Denno, a law professor at Fordham University who has written about the death penalty.[62]

A New Interest in Alternative Punishments

An end to executions seems unlikely, but other changes to state criminal justice systems are becoming evident. Cost pressures are driving some of the changes as states search for savings amid their worst fiscal crisis since World War II. For instance, during the less severe 2001–2002 economic recession, many states concluded that they could no longer afford to warehouse ever-growing numbers of prisoners. Some states, notably Oregon and Alabama, responded with a simple but perhaps shortsighted solution—they released inmates early. Given the high recidivism rates, law enforcement officials may soon place many of these individuals back behind bars for other crimes.

Since then, a number of other states have approached early release in a more methodical way, by revising their sentencing and corrections policies with the goal of returning to society those prisoners less likely to reoffend. Mississippi, for example, tweaked its "truth in sentencing" law in 2008 to make nonviolent offenders eligible for parole after serving just one-quarter—not the previous 85 percent—of their sentences. That change resulted in more than three thousand inmates being released an average of thirteen months earlier than they otherwise would have been and contributed to a decrease in Mississippi's prison population of 5.4 percent between the end of 2008 and early 2010. What's more, just 0.2 percent of those released early reoffended during their first post-release year, a far cry from the national average of 10.4 percent.[63] California officials hope to have similar results to report in coming years. The state, under court order to reduce overcrowding in its prison system and stressed by prison system costs that eat 11 percent of the annual statewide budget, is cutting its prison population by 6,500. Along with additional changes to its parole policies, California is looking to save $100 million per year.[64]

Over the years, states have tried a number of alternative approaches, some more successful than others. During the late 1980s and early 1990s, states such as Arizona and Georgia pioneered the use of military-style boot camps for juvenile offenders. But boot camp seemed to have no impact on future criminal activities. The recidivism rates for juveniles who had gone through the boot camps were no lower than recidivism among juveniles who had not. The number of juvenile boot camps declined precipitously after the mid-1990s.[65]

Another alternative strategy has demonstrated greater success. **Drug courts**, special tribunals that offer nonviolent drug offenders a chance at reduced or dismissed charges in exchange for undergoing treatment or other rehabilitation, are an initiative that got underway during the Clinton administration. As of December 2008, about 1,950 drug courts were operating in all fifty states. National Institute of Justice researchers found evidence that the programs are successful in both reducing recidivism and lowering long-term costs. The researchers report that enrolling a participant in a drug court program saves more than $12,000 in criminal justice and victimization costs.[66]

Drug courts are closely connected to the **community, or restorative, justice movement**. The movement's basic goal is to give neighborhoods a voice in determining which kinds of criminals prosecutors should pursue. In practice, community justice initiatives range from the modest (placing prosecutors in local police stations where they can see the neighborhood needs firsthand) to the ambitious (alternative courts that may require juvenile offenders to apologize to the people they have harmed and perform community service in an attempt to rectify the harm done by the crime committed).

More Young People, More Crime?

For the past twenty years, the proportion of eighteen- to twenty-four-year-olds in the overall population has declined. However, that trend is now beginning to reverse. During the first decade of the twenty-first century, the

DRUG COURTS
Special tribunals that offer nonviolent drug offenders a chance at reduced or dismissed charges in exchange for undergoing treatment or other rehabilitation; an alternative forum for sentencing nonviolent drug offenders.

COMMUNITY, OR RESTORATIVE, JUSTICE MOVEMENT
A movement that emphasizes nontraditional punishment, such as community service.

Policy in Practice: Does Gun Control Work?

The late 1980s and early 1990s witnessed a huge surge in homicide rates. The rising numbers can be attributed to just one thing—the rise in the use of handguns by people twenty-five years of age and younger. Between 1985 and 1993, firearm homicides rose by 53 percent. Other homicides actually declined slightly.[a] Handgun homicides committed by juveniles eighteen years of age and younger *quadrupled*.[b]

The huge surge in juvenile gun violence in the mid-1980s raises an obvious question: Would tougher gun control laws have saved lives? For some people, the answer is obvious. In 1992, the United States suffered 13,200 gun-related homicides. Countries with strict gun control laws, such as Great Britain and Japan, suffered thirty-three and sixty gun-related deaths, respectively.

For others, the very suggestion of outlawing handguns is outrageous. Many gun owners view firearms ownership as a basic constitutional right. The Second Amendment proclaims, "A well-regulated militia being necessary for the security of a free state, the right to keep and bear arms shall not be infringed." Some have even attempted to argue that allowing citizens to carry concealed weapons would improve overall public safety. They claim that the country would be safer if more Americans carried guns, although the research supporting these claims has largely been undermined.

In general, the courts have not agreed with this more expansive interpretation of the Constitution. States and individual cities enjoy considerable discretion to restrict gun laws as they see fit—or not at all. As a result, the right to bear arms depends very much on where you live. Thirty-seven states essentially require law enforcement agencies to provide a concealed weapon license to any law-abiding citizen who applies. Eleven states—Alabama, California, Connecticut, Delaware, Hawaii, Iowa, Maryland, Massachusetts, New Jersey, New York, and Rhode Island—give law enforcement agencies the discretion to issue or deny weapons based on a variety of factors. Only Illinois and Wisconsin ban concealed weapons altogether.[c] In Alaska and Vermont, no permit is needed to carry a concealed weapon. Many cities also have passed laws banning concealed firearms, although in gun-friendly states, state preemption laws typically mean that people with concealed weapon licenses do not have to disarm before entering otherwise "firearm-free" cities.

Both sides believe that their position will increase public safety. The advocates of gun ownership point out that localities with strict gun control laws often have very high crime rates and that all bans on handguns do is ensure that only criminals have guns. The advocates of gun control acknowledge the problems

proportion of that same age group increased. The proportion of young African American males, a group that commits and suffers from crimes at a much higher rate than the population as a whole, will continue to increase through 2020.

From the traditional standpoint of a criminologist, this is bad news. As mentioned earlier, young people, particularly young men, commit crimes at a much higher rate than older people.[67] Young people are also much more likely to be the victims of crime than older people. According to the U.S. Centers for Disease Control and Prevention, homicide is the second leading cause of death among young people ages fifteen to twenty-four.[68] As a result, more young people usually means more crime.

Of course, demography is not destiny. During the mid-1990s, society dodged the dreaded juvenile superpredator and managed to actually reduce but counter that the real problem is that borders are porous and other surrounding jurisdictions often have very weak gun control laws. In fact, according to criminologist Garen Wintemute at the University of California–Davis, a dispassionate look at the evidence seems to support the key claims of both sides. Studies have shown that certain types of gun restrictions—waiting periods, background checks, and some level of screening for gun buyers—work. In Wintemute's words, "they reduce rates of criminal activity involving guns and violence among people who are screened out and denied purchase of a gun—about 25 percent to 30 percent of those who are screened." Other types of restrictions, such as gun "buy-backs," do not. They often encourage people to turn in only old, sometimes inoperable guns.

Some measures, such as requiring gun manufacturers to install trigger-locks on new handguns, are still too new to fully evaluate. However, the argument for treating gun violence as a public health problem is a strong one. Gun wounds, mainly accidental, are among the leading causes of death in the United States.[d] At the same time, there is no evidence to suggest that gun control laws reduce violent crime. This raises an intriguing question: How can gun control laws work and yet not work at the same time?[e]

Sources: Adapted from John Buntin, *Assertive Policing, Plummeting Crime: The NYPD Takes On Crime* (1530.0), case study written for use by the John F. Kennedy School of Government, Harvard University (0799). Copyright © 1999 by the Presidency and Fellowes of Harvard College.

[a]Jeremy Travis and Michelle Waul, "Reflections on the Crime Decline: Lessons for the Future?" Proceedings from the Urban Institute Crime Decline Forum, Washington, D.C., August 2002, 2.

[b]Alfred Blumstein, "Why Is Crime Falling—or Is It?" presentation, Washington, D.C., February 14, 2001.

[c]Data from "Compendium of State Laws Governing Firearms 2008," National Rifle Association Institute for Legislative Action, available at www.nraila.org/media/PDFs/Compendium.pdf.

[d]See David Hemenway, *Private Guns, Public Health* (Ann Arbor: University of Michigan Press, 2004), for a discussion of the public health approach to gun violence. See the U.S. Centers for Disease Control and Prevention's National Center for Injury Prevention and Control for statistics related to injuries and fatalities by year, www.cdc.gov/ncipc.

[e]Wintemute's answer: "The resolution of the apparent paradox is that under current criteria so few people are denied the purchase of a firearm under Brady and its state level analogs relative to the number of people who purchase guns every year that an impact on that select group is too small at the population level to be noticed." Travis and Waul, "Reflections on the Crime Decline," 16.

crime during the echo of the baby boom. In Boston, an interagency team of police, probation officers, corrections officers, social workers, and others targeted a rapidly growing juvenile violence epidemic fed by gangs with guns. Probation officers inspected the homes of gang members with police officers at the ready. Corrections officials and cops kept track of who was being released when. Social workers talked with gang members and warned them that gun play would result in constant police attention. The result was a dramatic reduction in juvenile gun violence. In 1990, seventy-three people under the age of twenty-four were murdered in Boston. By 1997, that number had fallen to fifteen.[69]

But soon after the turn of the century, complacency set in, the number of teens living in the city grew, and Boston's collaboration crumbled. Crime rates involving juveniles began heading north—but only briefly.

Then they fell again toward the end of the last decade. Overall juvenile arrests fell 3 percent between 2007 and 2008, and 2.11 million juveniles were arrested in 2008—16 percent less than in 1999.[70] According to Howard Snyder, director of systems research for the National Center for Juvenile Justice, the data show "no evidence of an upcoming crime wave or beginning of a new era of juvenile superpredator."[71]

Conclusion

Crime is one of the most complex—and contentious—issues in public policy. Its causes are not well understood, and the fairness of the criminal justice system and the best strategies for responding to crime are hotly debated. Nevertheless, the past fifteen years have brought remarkable progress. Such innovations as community policing, broken windows policing, and Compstat have given law enforcement agencies new tools and a new sense of purpose. Contrary to some alarmist predictions, crime rates have fallen sharply and youth violence also has declined. However, serious issues, notably the high incarceration and victimization rates of African American men, remain. Moreover, the future remains uncertain. Will new innovations continue to push crime down, or is the crime decline over? The data look promising, but only time will tell.

Key Concepts

broken windows
   policing (p. 547)
common law (p. 531)
community, or restorative,
   justice movement (p. 559)
community policing (p. 547)
deterrence theory (p. 540)
drug courts (p. 559)
parole (p. 543)
probation (p. 531)
professional model of policing
   (p. 546)

Suggested Readings

Blumstein, Alfred, and Joel Wallman. *The Crime Drop in America.* New York: Cambridge University Press, 2000. A comprehensive overview of current thinking on a wide range of issues.

Gladwell, Malcolm. *The Tipping Point: How Little Things Can Make a Big Difference.* New York: Little, Brown and Co., 2000. Details examples of tipping points in society.

Goldstein, Herman. *Problem-Oriented Policing.* New York: McGraw-Hill, 1990. One of the classics on modern policing.

"One in 100: Behind Bars in America in 2008." Pew Center on the States, Washington, D.C., December 2008. A first-of-its-kind analysis of incarceration in America.

making sure an ambulance or fire truck responds to a 911 call and responses as complex as managing an epidemic. A century ago, the latter might have involved yellow fever, cholera, or influenza. In 1918, it involved a flu pandemic that killed an estimated 600,000 Americans and 100 million people worldwide.[5] Such diseases pose continued threats. As a result, state and local governments spend an increasing amount of time planning for such crises and carrying out drills intended to simulate public health emergencies.

Just how active state and local governments should be on these issues is often a source of heated debate. Terrorism experts warn that the United States has far too few hospital beds in the event of a real emergency.[6] Many communities cannot even keep an adequate blood supply available to healthcare facilities when things are quiet and uneventful. Despite the dangers posed by illnesses like swine flu, most counties maintain only skeletal public health departments.

Pandemic flu, anthrax, and the specter of bioterrorism are frightening new developments in the field of public health. But they are not the only threats to the public. Sometimes the public is its own worst enemy. The impact of recent "outside" health threats pales beside more long-standing public health concerns. According to the CDC, smoking tobacco causes more than 400,000 deaths a year in the United States.[7]

In addition, a growing percentage of Americans are overweight or suffer from **obesity**. Some state and local officials have made combating obesity a major priority. They have pushed for educational programs for parents, and for children have restored physical education classes in and removed soft drink machines from schools. But others resist the idea that obesity is a problem that should be addressed through government policy.

OBESITY

The medical condition of being excessively overweight; defined as having a body mass index of more than 25.

The scope of public health varies from state to state. Some states are generous providers of assistance to their low-income citizens to cover the expenses associated with illness and hospitalization. Other states are much more restrictive. The explanations for these differences are explored in this chapter.

For all the variation among state and local governments, it is clear that over the course of the past decade governments have become much more assertive concerning public health. During the economic boom of the mid- and late 1990s, the states worked with the federal government to find new ways to extend health insurance to low-income parents and children. When the economy slipped into recession, states led the effort to find ways to reduce the cost of medical care and to improve the quality of care.

The decade that started in 2010 may prove to be a momentous realignment of the United States' system of federalism. Forty years ago, most states were minor players in the nation's healthcare system. The proponents of expanded health coverage and healthcare reform looked to the federal government for solutions. Today, the situation is different. A decade of inaction and partisan division in Washington in the 1990s shifted some of the most important—and most difficult—healthcare issues to the state and local governments. Since then, the lawmakers tackling tough issues like the rising rate of obesity, lack of health insurance for the uninsured, rising prescription drug costs, providing long-term care, controlling human immunodeficiency virus (HIV) and other sexually transmitted diseases, and addressing the problem of illicit drug use have been more likely to be sitting in the state capitols than under the Capitol dome in Washington, D.C. The federal government acted on decades of debate over healthcare reform in early 2010 with the passage of the Patient Protection and Affordable Care Act, but questions linger about what this legislation's implementation will mean for states—and their bottom lines.

In addition, states have taken the lead in rethinking such safety net programs as welfare. In 1996, Congress abolished the existing **Aid to Families with Dependent Children (AFDC)**, or welfare, program and replaced it with a system of block grants to the states, called **Temporary Assistance to Needy Families (TANF)**. These grants gave state governments the leeway to design their own personalized, work-oriented, time-limited welfare programs. The result has been a profusion of sometimes very different welfare-to-work programs.

For instance, Oklahoma, a traditionalistic state, used TANF funds to train government workers and religious volunteers to administer a program developed by the U.S. military and designed to strengthen the marriages of people moving from welfare to work. In contrast, states like New York have downplayed these so-called family formation policies. Part of this difference in emphasis reflects states' different political cultures; however, the structure of the state government also plays an important role. New York's welfare system is decentralized. It relies on the county governments to administer programs. So does Colorado. Despite having a political culture that would seem to be supportive of family formation, Colorado has made few efforts in that direction, largely because its decentralized structure makes the system unresponsive to directives of any sort.[8]

The Influence of Culture

How state governments define *public health* has a lot to do with a given region's distinctive political culture. All public health officials would agree that certain issues, such as terrorism and acquired immunodeficiency syndrome (AIDS), are important public health issues. No one would argue that a flu epidemic or the contamination of a major watershed would not also qualify.

568

Other topics are not so easily categorized. Is gun violence a public health issue? Researchers at the CDC think so. They point out that gun-related deaths, most of which are accidental, are the country's second leading cause of death. The AMA now advises doctors to talk with patients about the proper handling and storage of any guns they may own. Many gun owners, however, vehemently reject the idea that guns are a public health issue.

On other health fronts, some cities have attempted to reduce the transmission of dangerous blood-borne illnesses like HIV and hepatitis C by providing drug addicts with clean needles. Others have rejected these needle exchange programs. They charge that such programs give rise to disorder and crime and that they send the message that intravenous drug use is okay.

Then there is the always controversial question of sexual health and education. Should parents, educators, and other adult role models emphasize **abstinence** to teenagers or teach them to use condoms? Or is instruction in a variety of options that include both abstinence and birth control the answer? What role should government play in providing access to contraception?

As these examples demonstrate, state and local governments are being asked to respond to a variety of public health challenges, and they are doing so in very different ways. As we have seen before, often these different positions reflect very different political cultures. Oregon has granted terminally ill patients the right to physician-assisted suicide. Most other states continue to classify such an action as a felony, even if it is rarely prosecuted. Nebraska passed legislation to ban late-term abortions, and even though the U.S. Supreme Court later struck down the law, the Nebraska voters had made their preferences known.

Different states have very different notions about the roles state governments should fill. Wisconsin's innovative early attempts at welfare reform in the late 1980s and early 1990s laid the groundwork for the

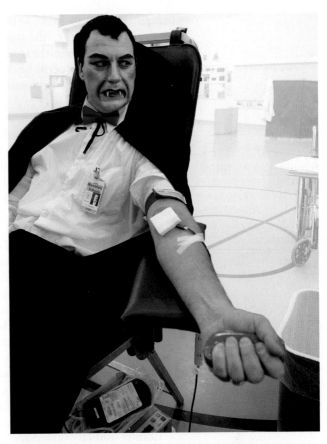

Vampires usually take blood rather than give it. Yet even Count Dracula (actually Marshfield, Wisconsin, American government teacher Troy Schmitt) is willing to donate a pint for a worthy cause. Local community blood drives are a central source of blood supplies and an important element of the nation's healthcare system. Marshfield High School does two such drives a year, each collecting between eighty and ninety pints of blood.

ABSTINENCE
Refraining from sexual activity, usually intercourse.

federal decision to junk AFDC altogether in 1996 and return most welfare responsibilities to the states. States such as Massachusetts and Maine sought to expand healthcare coverage to nearly every resident in advance of the passage of federal healthcare reform in 2010, whereas other states have shown no great enthusiasm for providing healthcare to low-income citizens.

Yet even states that have shown little interest in taking on new responsibilities have found that healthcare is *the* unavoidable issue. This is due largely to **Medicaid**, the joint state-federal health insurance program for low-income mothers and children, the elderly, and people with disabilities. When Congress created the program in 1965, it was supposed to be a modest program that served only a small number of extremely poor people. But it hasn't worked out that way.

As soon as it was created, Medicaid's expenditures started growing quickly—and never stopped. Today, it provides health insurance and services to approximately 45 million Americans—an all-time high. This includes 29.4 million low-income families, children, and pregnant women, and 11.5 million elderly and disabled.[9] States now devote an average of about 16 percent of their general revenue funds to Medicaid.[10]

The continuing growth of Medicaid has huge implications for the future of state governments, which fell into a deep recession in 2008 from which economists forecast they may not recover fully for years. Temporary stimulus funding helped buoy state Medicaid programs in 2009 and 2010, but it was just that—temporary. That means that as healthcare costs grow, states will either have to raise taxes or cut funding for other state priorities like education, transportation, and criminal justice.

County and city governments spend significant amounts on healthcare as well. In many parts of the country, hospitals and clinics funded by counties and cities continue to function as a critical social safety net for people without health insurance. These are people who earn too much to qualify for Medicaid but too little to be able to pay for private health insurance. Cities and counties also run the facilities that were tested during the 2009 H1N1 influenza pandemic, and if the United States ever experiences a large-scale biological attack, such facilities will determine how well this society survives.

How Government Got into the Healthcare Biz

Any serious discussion of healthcare soon arrives at a basic question: Who should pay for what? Over the past two decades, the answer has varied widely. During the early 1990s, the solution offered by many Democrats was that the federal government should provide health insurance to everyone who does not have it.

MEDICAID

A joint state and federal health insurance program that serves low-income mothers and children, the elderly, and people with disabilities.

But, by the early twenty-first century, a lot of those same Democrats were arguing that the state governments, not the federal government, should lead the way. Universal—or nearly universal—coverage, they stated, should be created by gradually extending existing health insurance programs, notably Medicaid. Such programs should be expanded to encompass various populations not currently eligible for it. In contrast, some Republicans argued that health insurance should be extended via federal tax credits. How much health insurance should be provided has been another hotly contested topic.

It wasn't always so complicated. For most of the nation's history, elected officials believed that the government should serve as the health and welfare provider of last resort for society's poorest and sickest members. The level of government that officials had in mind, however, was not the federal government and not even state governments. It was local government.

The role of local governments in health and welfare goes back to the very beginning of U.S. history. In colonial America, local communities maintained almshouses to feed and clothe people who could not care for themselves and who had no families to care for them. Back then few distinctions were made among the sick, the mentally ill, and people without a means of support. As sociologist Paul Starr has noted, almshouses "received dependent persons of all kinds, mixing together promiscuously the aged, the orphaned, the insane, the ill, the debilitated."[11] Those with infectious diseases, such as typhoid fever and cholera, were sent to pesthouses to survive as best they could.

That began to change in the nineteenth century. By the middle of the century, elected officials, social reformers, and physicians—who were just beginning to establish themselves as a respectable profession—came to believe that mixing juveniles, beggars, the mentally ill, widows, and others in almshouses was no longer the best course of action. In effect, physicians and public officials began to distinguish between the sick and the destitute. A new institution was needed—the hospital.

From the early to mid-1800s, cities like Philadelphia and New York transformed some of their almshouses into hospitals.[12] Privately organized charitable hospitals, many run by religious groups, appeared in many cities too. Even state governments made a modest foray into healthcare. By 1860, most states had established mental hospitals and homes for the blind and the deaf.

Like almshouses, the first hospitals were institutions for unfortunates without money or family. For people with families or money, a house call from the doctor was the preferred form of medical care. According to Starr, "[a]lmost no one who had a choice sought hospital care."[13] Hospitals were regarded with dread, and rightly so. They were dangerous places, in part because of the medical and hygienic practices of the time. Sick people were safer at home. The few who became patients went into hospitals because of special circumstances. They might be seamen in a strange port, travelers, the homeless, or the solitary aged, individuals who, whether traveling or destitute, were unlucky enough to fall sick without family, friends, or servants to care for them.[14]

Hospitals and physicians made a spirited effort to improve their image. Hospitals moved their sickest residents—as well as patients who were dissolute or morally objectionable—to other institutions. In 1847, for instance, Bellevue Hospital in New York decided to move the penitentiary and almshouse off its grounds and concentrate on medical care.[15] The hospital was beginning to emerge as a distinct institution.

As hospitals sought more respectable clientele, almshouses took on a harder edge. During the seventeenth and eighteenth centuries, many almshouses were patterned on conventional homes and sought to serve as a kind of surrogate family for their residents. During the nineteenth century, however, local governments refashioned almshouse to serve a different purpose. Such facilities now were used to illustrate the consequences of idleness, sinfulness, and poverty and to shame their residents. Shabby facilities and neglect became commonplace.[16]

The Idea of a Social Safety Net

This arrangement continued in the United States until well into the twentieth century. The duty of providing healthcare and welfare remained firmly in the hands of local governments. States assisted those with mental illnesses and people with disabilities. The federal government ran a compulsory health insurance system for the merchant marine, so that sick sailors could get care in any port, and provided pensions and healthcare to military veterans.

By the end of the nineteenth century, a new idea was percolating in progressive circles. Many social reformers came to believe that the federal government should take a much larger role in securing healthcare and pensions for the working class.

The idea first arose in Germany. In 1883, the conservative government of German chancellor Otto von Bismarck created the world's first compulsory sickness and unemployment insurance fund, which required employees and employers to set aside money to cover the costs of medical treatment for workers. Bismarck later created a compulsory retirement program, whose cost was divided among employees, employers, and the national government, in much the same way that it is done in the United States today. These innovations were momentous in the development of the state. Before Bismarck, talk of healthcare, unemployment insurance, and pensions had been done largely by socialists and communists. He showed that conservative capitalist countries could enact such programs too. Indeed, they could take the lead in developing a generous social safety net. Over the course of the next thirty years, other European countries followed Germany's lead.

The United States, however, did not. During the heyday of the Progressive movement in the early twentieth century, discussions about national health insurance were widespread. Eventually, opposition from physicians and from the country's largest labor union, the American Federation of Labor (the forebearer of today's AFL-CIO), fearful of government control of the healthcare system, effectively derailed the idea. During the 1920s, many states took the first small steps toward creating a social safety net by setting up workers' compensation funds for injured workers. However, amid the affluence of the times, there was little support for a more ambitious social safety net.[17] That changed with the start of the Great Depression.

The Birth of the American Safety Net

On Thursday, October 24, 1929, the stock market in New York City collapsed in what the *New York Times* called "the most disastrous trading day in the stock market's history."[18] By spring 1933, it was clear that the United States had entered an unprecedented economic slump—the Great Depression.

In response to this economic disaster, the federal government for the first time took on some of the social safety net functions that European governments had pioneered decades earlier.[19] In 1935, President Franklin Delano Roosevelt and Congress teamed up to pass the Social Security Act. This act established two social safety net programs. The first was a joint federal-state program of unemployment compensation. The second was a federally run program of retirement benefits for senior citizens, which soon would be known simply as Social Security.

The federal government also created the AFDC. AFDC's purpose was to provide monetary assistance to widowed women with children, women who had been abandoned by their husbands, and women who were in some way incapacitated. Funded by the federal government, the program was administered by the states.

The Roosevelt administration briefly considered adding a compulsory health insurance program to the Social Security Act as well. However, given the medical industry's continued vehement opposition due to fear of too much government control, the proposal was eventually dropped as too controversial. Instead, the Social Security Act provided federal grants to help states pay for programs for the disabled and the aged and to provide child welfare services, public health services, and vocational rehabilitation.[20] As a result, responsibility for providing a healthcare safety net remained in the hands of state and local governments.

A Multibillion-Dollar Afterthought

State governments became major participants in the U.S. safety net system almost by accident. After the assassination of President John F. Kennedy in 1963, Lyndon B. Johnson ascended to the Oval Office. Johnson and congressional Democrats were determined to pass legislation that would cover hospital costs for senior citizens. Congressional Republicans, however, had a different proposal in mind. They supported a voluntary health insurance program that would cover the cost of physician visits for seniors. So in 1965, the two parties decided to compromise in classic Washington fashion—by doing both. The result was **Medicare**, the federal health insurance program for the elderly.

But Congress didn't stop there. While it was on a roll, it also created Medicaid. Despite their very similar names, Medicare and Medicaid are very different programs. Medicare is run and paid for entirely by the federal government. As with Social Security, every senior who worked for ten years and paid taxes—or whose spouse worked for ten years and

With the strong backing of President Lyndon Johnson, Congress created Medicare in 1965. The federal health insurance program for the elderly has proven to be wildly popular, but also has proven to be incredibly expensive for state governments. Pictured here is John Gardner, Johnson's Secretary of Health, Education, and Welfare. His outline for implementing Medicare notably says nothing about who is covering the costs.

paid taxes—is eligible to participate, as are people with certain types of disabilities. The program is financed in part by a small payroll tax. Most retirees, however, take far more out of Medicare than they contributed.[21] Understandably, Medicare almost immediately became a popular program.

Medicaid, on the other hand, is a joint state-federal program that is paid for in part by the general revenue funds of state and local governments. The federal government does pick up most of the cost, however. On average, it covers 56 percent of Medicaid expenditures;[22] for poorer areas, the percentage is higher. Arkansas, Mississippi, Montana, New Mexico, Utah, and West Virginia all receive more than 70 percent of their Medicaid expenditures from the federal government.[23] Wealthier states split the cost 50-50. States do not have to participate; however, since 1982—when Arizona finally signed on—all states do.

Therefore, Medicaid is not an unfunded mandate; the federal government does not force states to participate in it. It is, however, an **entitlement program**; that is, it does create legally enforceable rights. In fact, it is a double entitlement program. First, states have a right to a certain amount of federal money every year; and also, individuals who meet its eligibility thresholds are entitled to its services, regardless of the cost. States are required to provide coverage to certain populations, including children in families with income below the **poverty line**, or **poverty threshold**, and parents who qualify for TANF.[24]

Beyond these basics, the states enjoy considerable leeway when setting those eligibility standards. (See Table 15-1.) They have created healthcare safety nets with very different levels of generosity. As of January 2009, Arkansas was the least generous state in the country. It allowed only those earning less than 17 percent of the federal poverty level—the threshold set by the U.S. Bureau of the Census to measure poverty—to receive Medicaid. That means that a working parent with two children who earned more than $249 a month—slightly less than $3,000 a year—earned too much to qualify. Few states want to be stingy when it comes to health coverage. But they need to balance their budgets, and paring back eligibility levels is one way to make the numbers work, especially when Medicaid expenditures increase by double-digit percentages every year.

The most generous state was Minnesota. It allowed families earning up to 275 percent of the federal poverty level to receive Medicaid benefits. In other words, a working parent with two children could earn up to $4,033 a month—more than $48,000 a year—and still qualify for Medicaid.[25] Even controlling for the fact that most parts of Arkansas have considerably lower costs of living than Minnesota, that is a dramatic difference. The United States may have one safety net for seniors, but for everyone else, it is a country with fifty-one safety nets.

In 2008 Medicaid expenditures accounted for 8.4 percent of Alaska's total budget, but 34.5 percent of Missouri's.

TABLE 15-1

Amount a Working Parent with Two Children Applying for Publicly Funded Coverage May Earn and Still Be Eligible for Medicaid (as of January 2009)

State	Monthly Income-Eligibility Threshold (dollars)	Annual Income-Eligibility Threshold (dollars)	Percentage of 2009 Federal Poverty Line
Alabama	367	4,400	25
Alaska	1,558	18,700	85
Arizona	2,933	35,200	200
Arkansas	249	2,992	17
California	1,555	18,656	106
Colorado	968	11,616	66
Connecticut	2,801	33,616	191
Delaware	1,775	21,296	121
District of Columbia	3,036	36,432	207
Florida	807	9,680	55
Georgia	763	9,152	52
Hawaii	1,687	20,240	100
Idaho	411	4,928	28
Illinois	2,713	32,560	185
Indiana	381	4,576	26
Iowa	1,261	15,136	86
Kansas	499	5,984	34
Kentucky	909	10,912	62
Louisiana	381	4,576	26
Maine	3,021	36,256	206
Maryland	1,701	20,416	116
Massachusetts	1,951	23,408	133
Michigan	968	11,616	66
Minnesota	4,033	48,400	275
Mississippi	675	8,096	46
Missouri	381	4,576	26

TABLE 15-1, continued

State	Monthly Income-Eligibility Threshold (dollars)	Annual Income-Eligibility Threshold (dollars)	Percentage of 2009 Federal Poverty Line
Montana	851	10,208	58
Nebraska	851	10,208	58
Nevada	1,335	16,016	91
New Hampshire	748	8,976	51
New Jersey	2,933	35,200	200
New Mexico	1,012	12,144	69
New York	2,200	26,400	150
North Carolina	748	8,976	51
North Dakota	909	10,912	62
Ohio	1,320	15,840	90
Oklahoma	704	8,448	48
Oregon	616	7,392	42
Pennsylvania	528	6,336	36
Rhode Island	2,655	31,856	181
South Carolina	1,320	15,840	90
South Dakota	792	9,504	54
Tennessee	1,965	23,584	134
Texas	396	4,752	27
Utah	997	11,968	68
Vermont	2,801	33,616	191
Virginia	440	5,280	30
Washington	1,129	13,552	77
West Virginia	499	5,984	34
Wisconsin	2,933	35,200	200
Wyoming	792	9,504	54
U.S. Median	968	11,616	66

Source: Adapted from "Income Eligibility for Parents Applying for Medicaid by Annual Income as a Percent of Federal Poverty Level, 2009," Kaiser Family Foundation, January 2009, available at http://statehealthfacts.org/comparetable.jsp?ind=205&rat=4.

Note: The federal poverty level for a family of three was $17,600 for the forty-eight contiguous states and Washington, D.C., $20,240 for Hawaii, and $22,000 for Alaska. Monthly and annual income thresholds rounded to the nearest dollar.

Oops!: The Unexpected Cost of Health Insurance

Medicare and Medicaid were structured very differently, but the two programs soon revealed a common trait. They both quickly proved to be fantastically expensive. From 1965 to 1970, the annual rate of increase in state and federal health expenditures was 20.8 percent.[26] By fiscal year 2009, the federal government and state governments spent more than $335 billion annually on Medicaid alone.[27]

As Medicaid spending soared, another disturbing trend was becoming evident. The number of women with children receiving financial assistance under the AFDC program was soaring too. After two decades of slow growth, the number of AFDC beneficiaries took off in the late 1960s, rising from slightly more than 2 million recipients in 1960 to more than 10 million recipients by 1972.

The composition of AFDC recipients also was changing. The widows of the 1940s were being replaced by divorced and separated women with children as well as single mothers who had never been married. By 1979, single mothers made up nearly 80 percent of all AFDC recipients.[28]

As the group benefiting from welfare changed, the program became increasingly unpopular with the public. During the late 1970s and early 1980s, Ronald Reagan and other conservative politicians railed against what they saw as the excesses of the welfare state. They evoked images of "welfare queens" who drove Cadillacs and paid for steak dinners with fat rolls of food stamps.[29] Reagan's welfare queen proved to be more of a myth than reality, but it was arguably true that the United States had created a set of permanent dependents of the sort that Roosevelt had warned against when he called government relief "a narcotic, a subtle destroyer of the human spirit."[30]

The 1970s were difficult for proponents of expanding the nation's social safety net. As the boom of the 1960s gave way to the stagflation of the 1970s, cities such as New York ran into serious problems. These were urban centers that had long prided themselves on generous housing subsidies and social programs. However, as manufacturing jobs vanished and businesses and middle-class residents abandoned many urban downtowns, cities were forced to radically scale back their efforts. In 1976, after years of lavish overspending and declining federal subsidies, New York City was forced to declare bankruptcy. Even state and local governments that had not attempted to forge comprehensive social safety nets were forced to dramatically reduce their social welfare programs.

The Devolution Revolution

The supporters of Ronald Reagan weren't the only people who were fed up. State and local officials were too. Many were frustrated by the high-handed

The Feds Falter

When Bill Clinton took office in 1993, he and his administration were prepared to let states take the lead on welfare reform. After all, the president's previous job had been governor of Arkansas. However, the president and his wife, Hillary, did see the problem of the uninsured as primarily a federal one. In early 1994, Clinton introduced the Health Security Act. This was legislation that would have provided universal health insurance to all Americans.

Senate Republicans initially countered with a proposal that would have extended health insurance coverage dramatically but would still have fallen short of universal health insurance. Clinton rejected this counterproposal, vowing to veto any measure that failed to provide 100 percent coverage.[37] Politics being politics, the two major parties were unable to find common ground. Nine months later, the Clinton health insurance proposal went down in defeat.[38]

Fast forward a decade. In 2008, more than 46 million Americans sixty-five years of age and younger lacked health insurance—fully 17 percent of the population.[39] (See Map 15-2.) The Kaiser Commission on Medicaid

MAP 15-2 Rates of Uninsurance among Non-Elderly, 2008

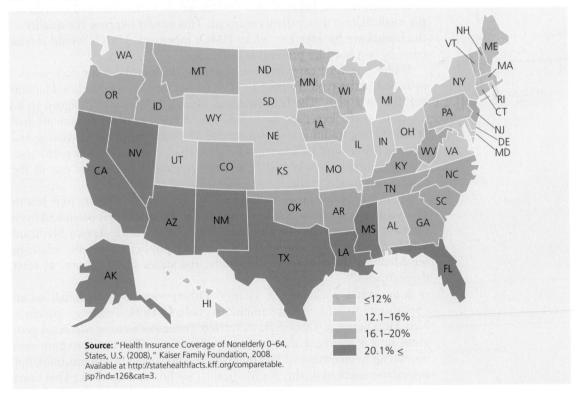

Source: "Health Insurance Coverage of Nonelderly 0–64, States, U.S. (2008)," Kaiser Family Foundation, 2008. Available at http://statehealthfacts.kff.org/comparetable. jsp?ind=126&cat=3.

≤12%
12.1–16%
16.1–20%
20.1% ≤

and the Uninsured estimates that some 20 percent of uninsured residents are noncitizens, who often work in low-wage jobs that do not include health coverage.[40]

The Rise of the Healthcare State

The collapse of healthcare reform efforts in the 1990s at the federal level left states in a tricky position. They were being squeezed between the pincers of the rising costs of state Medicaid programs and the rising demands for assistance from citizens struggling with prescription drug costs and a lack of health insurance. Finally, in the mid-1990s, states found what looked like a good way to both contain costs and expand coverage—**managed care**.

Proponents of managed care originally saw health maintenance organizations (HMOs) as a way to improve the quality of care that patients received. Most medical care that patients receive in the United States is poorly coordinated. Different doctors often cannot easily share a patient's medical records. In addition, physicians have little incentive to offer preventive services because they get paid for dealing with sickness. Paul Ellwood, the physician who coined the phrase *health maintenance organization* in the early 1970s, believed that HMOs would rationalize and coordinate the medical care that patients received. This would improve the quality of the healthcare for members of an HMO; moreover, HMOs would reduce costs by emphasizing preventive healthcare.

Under managed care, instead of paying doctors a fee for each service provided, states typically paid an HMO a flat fee for each Medicaid patient enrolled in a plan. The fee that states offered HMOs was designed to be lower than the expenses the states would have incurred if patients had remained in a traditional fee-for-service Medicaid program. HMOs agreed to these lower rates because they believed that, even with lower reimbursement rates, they would still be able to squeeze inefficiencies out of the system and turn a profit.

Medicaid beneficiaries benefited too. They were able to join health plans that gave them access to physicians and services that often had been unavailable under the old program. Traditional fee-for-service Medicaid reimbursement rates are so low that many physicians simply refuse to see Medicaid beneficiaries. Ultimately, the states saved money, at least theoretically.[41]

Some states pocketed the savings. Others viewed the windfall as an opportunity to achieve more ambitious goals. In 1994, Tennessee governor Ned McWherter, a Democrat, converted Tennessee's entire Medicaid program into a managed care program—TennCare. The new program was opened up to an estimated 400,000 people who lacked health insurance but earned too much to qualify for Medicaid. (See box on page 580.) That same year Oregon governor John Kitzhaber received permission from the U.S. Department of Health and Human Services to try an even more radical approach. Oregon was allowed to explicitly ration its healthcare dollars to cover as many people as possible in the most cost-effective fashion possible.

A Promising Beginning

For a while, the HMO approach seemed to work. By 1998, approximately half of all Medicaid recipients nationwide were in managed care programs.[42] As enrollment increased, health costs slowed. Between 1995 and 1999, Medicaid expenditures grew at the relatively modest rate of 4.3 percent annually. This was dramatically lower than the unprecedented 27 percent growth of the early 1990s.[43] In addition, as the economic expansion that began in the early 1990s gained momentum and swelled state coffers, a growing number of state officials and healthcare advocates began to think about addressing other problems of the uninsured. Advocates set their sights on a new state-federal partnership. The first goal—to extend health insurance to uninsured children in families that earned too much to qualify for Medicaid but too little to pay for healthcare on their own.

In August 1997, Congress created the **State Children's Health Insurance Program (CHIP)** at the behest of President Clinton. CHIP was designed to provide health insurance to roughly 6.5 million children in low-income families without health insurance.[44] As with Medicaid, CHIP would be designed and administered by the states and paid for primarily by the federal government. The federal government would spring for about 80 percent of total costs.

The states were given considerable flexibility in designing their child health programs. They were free to fold CHIP into their Medicaid programs or create stand-alone CHIP programs. As with Medicaid, they determined the eligibility levels. They also could cap CHIP enrollments and force recipients to pay some of the costs for the health insurance they received.[45]

Not surprisingly, states have taken advantage of this flexibility. Eighteen states allow children living in families earning up to 200 percent of the federal poverty level to qualify for CHIP. Another twenty states cover children in families with even higher incomes—sometimes significantly higher. Alabama, Connecticut, Iowa, Massachusetts, Missouri, New Hampshire, New Jersey, Oregon, Pennsylvania, Vermont, and Washington all set their eligibility levels from 300 to 350 percent of the federal level. Just two states, Idaho and North Dakota, cap coverage at less than 200 percent of the poverty level.[46]

Congress reauthorized the program in 2009 with an additional $33 billion in federal funds, and the Patient Protection and Affordable Care Act (the federal healthcare reform bill) further bolstered CHIP by extending program funding through 2015 and establishing the program itself until at

STATE CHILDREN'S HEALTH INSURANCE PROGRAM (CHIP)

A joint federal-state program designed to expand healthcare coverage to children whose parents earned income above the poverty line but still were too poor to afford insurance.

least 2019. There's just one catch: the legislation mandates that states maintain their CHIP eligibility standards as they existed on March 23, 2010. The rule came just a week after Arizona policymakers had agreed to eliminate the state's CHIP program, which covers 38,000 children, as part of its budget-balancing moves. Because the Arizona program was not due to end until June 2010, the state was forced to find the funds to reinstate it.[47]

Does It Work?

By the late 1990s, many health policy experts and advocates had come to see the gradual expansion of Medicaid and CHIP and of the state-federal partnership as the best way to address the widespread lack of health insurance in the United States. The Robert Wood Johnson Foundation reported in 2006 that the number of uninsured children had dropped by 20 percent since CHIP's introduction.[48]

That is clearly a significant accomplishment. Unfortunately, the CHIP approach has not reached everyone that it is supposed to reach. The Urban Institute estimated that in 2002 more than a quarter of all poor children—those whose families earn incomes below 100 percent of the federal poverty level—continued to lack insurance.[49] Indeed, data from 2008 show that 10 percent of children in the United States are not covered by insurance.[50] Among poor children—who make up about one-fifth of all children—that figure is significantly higher. This is despite the fact that almost all of this population qualifies for CHIP.[51]

In the early 2000s, officials saw promise in CHIP as a vehicle for covering adults as well as children. But as Medicaid spending accelerated and state revenues shriveled in 2002 and 2003, states retreated from plans to expand their CHIP programs and shifted their emphasis to containing costs as best they could. Caught in the budgetary crossfire were federal waivers allowing states to cover adults through CHIP who didn't qualify for Medicaid. Federal officials had expected the program to cover 2.7 million uninsured adults, but states simply couldn't afford to expand the coverage. By 2009, programs under the waivers covered just about 270,000 adults.[52]

The Safety Net Widens

What effect do these different policies have on the residents of these states? It's hard to say. Not having health insurance does not necessarily translate into no healthcare. Government-supported community health centers provide healthcare to more than 20 million uninsured Americans in thousands of communities across the country every year. These clinics treat people regardless of their ability or inability to pay.[53] (See box on page 588.) In addition, hospitals are required to provide treatment to people who come into their emergency rooms whether these people can pay or not.

Along with community health centers, public hospitals have long assumed a particularly important role in providing services to the uninsured. For many low-income individuals, the emergency room of a public hospital is their first and only way to access medical care. Many public hospitals border high-crime neighborhoods and provide essential advanced emergency and trauma services, as well as outpatient clinics for these same communities.

These are critically important functions. They are not, however, very profitable ones. The Urban Institute estimates uncompensated care—medical care provided to the uninsured that they do not pay for themselves—costs the medical system $64 billion annually.[54] In 2008, 16 percent of public hospitals' costs were uncompensated, compared to 5.8 percent for hospitals nationwide, according to the National Association of Public Hospitals and Health Systems.[55]

> Many public hospitals border high-crime neighborhoods and provide essential advanced emergency and trauma services, as well as outpatient clinics for these same communities. These are critically important functions. They are not, however, very profitable ones.

The result is that public hospitals have a tough time staying open. Between 1996 and 2002, the number of public hospitals in the 100 largest cities fell from 730 to 645.[56] The recent recession crunched them even further; public hospital systems across the country cut back on programs, including mental health services, pharmacies, and oncology clinics. New York cut four hundred positions from its public hospitals in 2009.[57]

Lack of access to care is not an issue limited to cities and suburbs. Rural areas long have been plagued by fragmented healthcare systems and shortages of doctors and nurses. Even worse, rural residents tend to be older and poorer than their urban and suburban counterparts, factors that often translate into a greater need for healthcare services.[58] It's not a formula for a healthy population.

The problem has not gone unnoticed. In partnership with the federal government, all fifty states have established offices of rural health. For instance, the Appalachian Regional Commission is a federal-state partnership that addresses economic and social issues in West Virginia and parts of twelve other states. This partnership advocates telemedicine as a strategy for residents to gain access to specialists and for doctors in rural areas to gain needed continuing education. In one instance, eleven sites in northeastern New York state have been equipped with computers and other technology to create a virtual pediatric center serving three counties where poverty is high, transportation is difficult, and healthcare is insufficient.[59]

Researchers have found a strong correlation between having health insurance and access to and use of healthcare.[60] In addition, giving more people more access to public healthcare is one direct way to increase their healthcare use.

But expanding eligibility for health insurance does not necessarily mean that fewer people are uninsured. Connecticut and Vermont are two states

States under Stress: Community Health Centers Step Up

Three California community health centers closed in August 2009. In an ironic twist, they shut their doors just as more people were lining up at them in search of healthcare after losing their jobs—and related insurance coverage—during the worst recession since World War II. The American Recovery and Reinvestment Act (ARRA) pumped $2 billion into the centers nationwide,[a] but the funds weren't enough in some cases to make up for the losses in the state revenue necessary to keep them open.

States provide just 10 percent of the centers' funding, but the governments have slashed funding as they search for any way to close their budget gaps. The National Association of Community Health Centers reported a drop in state funding of 23 percent between 2008 and 2010. Idaho and South Dakota eliminated funding for their states' centers entirely in 2010.

Community health centers have become a key piece of America's patchwork healthcare system, providing quality care to a large segment of low-income and uninsured people. More than 1,200 clinics across the country now serve about 20 million patients each year—an increase of 60 percent from a decade ago.[b] More than half of the patients fall below the federal poverty line, and more than one-third lack health insurance. As unemployment rose in 2008 and 2009, so did the centers' cases. Nationwide, their number of uninsured patients grew 21 percent from June 2008 to June 2009.[c]

Stimulus funds enabled the centers to bridge some of the gap left by state budget cuts. The $2 billion was designed to extend treatment to an additional 2.1 million people and to establish more than one hundred new centers across the country.[d]

Economists are forecasting a slow recovery from the recession, and states are notorious for emerging from recessions at a particularly slow pace. That could have set the stage for continued stress for community health centers, but the federal healthcare reform bill probably prevented that scenario. The bill will provide $9.5 billion annually to establish a new Community Health Centers Trust Fund. The National Association of Community Health Centers estimates the funds will enable the clinics to serve an additional 20 million people each year.[e]

[a]Colleen Boselli and Nicole Spoelma, *Weathering the Storm: State Funding for Health Centers during an Economic Crisis* (Bethesda, Md.: National Association of Community Health Centers, 2009).

[b]Josh Goodman, "Primary Care Looks to States for a Booster Shot," *Governing* magazine, September 2009, available at www.governing.com/article/primary-care-looks-states-booster-shot.

[c]Kristen Gerencher, "Community Health Centers Tested by Newly Uninsured," *MarketWatch,* February 11, 2010, available at www.marketwatch.com/story/story/print?guid=C31C8941–7602–4455–9E3F-FE0A7ED511E5.

[d]Boselli and Spoelma, *Weathering the Storm.*

[e]"Health Center Related Provisions in Health Reform Legislation," National Association of Community Health Centers, 2010, available at www.nachc.com/client/summary%200f%20health%20reform%20package_final_0420101.pdf.

that have made major efforts to expand eligibility for public health insurance; consequently, they have lower numbers of uninsured children than states like Idaho or Montana. However, that is not universally the case. During the 2007–2008 fiscal year, 12.2 percent of children were uninsured in "generous" New Jersey, while only 8 percent were uninsured in "stingy" North Dakota.[61] Such a paradox can be caused by a combination of factors: the availability of jobs offering health insurance, parents' awareness of programs for which their children qualify, and the cost of insurance for those just beyond the eligibility thresholds.

The Decline of Managed Care

After their initial surge of success mentioned earlier, many HMOs failed to meet the high hopes of their boosters. Consumers were dismayed by the ways in which HMOs limited their choices of doctors to a small group of physicians who had agreed to lower reimbursement rates. In some cases, the programs demanded that doctors receive preapproval before performing certain procedures. By the late 1990s, many consumers had turned against HMOs.

Eager to separate themselves from the HMOs they had initially supported, state legislators acted on their constituents' desires. Many states passed "patients' bill of rights" legislation. These laws made it easier for patients to sue HMOs and generally made it more difficult for managed care plans to restrict healthcare. Such acts may have curbed some of the HMOs' more egregious practices, but they also came with a cost of their own. By making it harder for HMOs to limit care and access to physicians, lawmakers also deprived HMOs of negotiating leverage and reduced their ability to hold down costs. Costs were again on the rise by the late 1990s.

TennCare, Tennessee's innovative program that used managed care to expand insurance coverage to 25 percent of the state's population, crumbled due to its reliance on unstable HMOs and due to rapidly escalating costs. One study projected that funding TennCare would require 91 percent of Tennessee's tax appropriations by 2008. In 2005, eligibility was scaled back dramatically, and more than 300,000 adults fell off the rolls. TennCare as the state had known it was dead.[62]

Time for Reform

Meanwhile, healthcare costs were on the rise again. In fiscal year 2000, Medicaid expenditure grew by 9 percent. By 2002, it was growing at 12.8 percent. What was behind this surge in healthcare spending? Several factors stand out: jumps in prescription drug costs; increasing unemployment, which left more Americans relying on the healthcare safety net; and the growing elderly population, which left greater numbers of people in need of long-term care, such as nursing homes, assisted living, or at-home care. The budget pressures were enough to push states toward ever more creative experiments to control costs while expanding coverage.

> What was behind this surge in healthcare spending? Several factors stand out: jumps in prescription drug costs; increasing unemployment, which left more Americans relying on the healthcare safety net; and the growing elderly population, which left greater numbers of people in need of long-term care, such as nursing homes, assisted living, or at-home care.

Lofty Goals

The defeat of federal healthcare reform in the 1990s left the states in charge of efforts to expand health insurance coverage. As we've already learned, Tennessee and several other states used Medicaid waivers to expand their programs with varying degrees of success. More recently, Maine and Massachusetts unveiled universal (or near-universal) healthcare plans that served as precursors to the federal healthcare reform bill passed in 2010.

When Dirigo, Maine's plan, began in 2004, 14 percent of the state's residents lacked health insurance, and 80 percent of the uninsured worked for small businesses that could not afford to provide coverage. Private insurers agreed to provide coverage, which the state would administer and, for the first year, subsidize. In the first phase of enrollment, geared toward small businesses and self-employed workers, 250 businesses and 1,000 individuals signed up.[63] But by late 2006, researchers found that, even though the program had enrolled more than 16,000 Mainers, it had reduced the state's uninsured population by less than 10 percent. They also reported that the state had raised insufficient funds to support Dirigo.[64] The plan ultimately ran into financial problems and capped enrollment well below its original goal.[65] "The time has passed for states to go it alone; DirigoChoice helps prove that," Maine representative Sharon Anglin Treat, chair of the state's Joint Standing Committee on Insurance and Financial Services, wrote in a letter to the editor of the *Wall Street Journal* in 2009.[66]

Maine's experience did not stop Massachusetts from launching an even more ambitious plan of its own. The plan required every resident of the state to have health insurance by July 2007 or face tax penalties. Under the law, every resident below the federal poverty line can receive insurance fully subsidized by the state; subsidies are extended on a sliding scale to those earning between 100 and 300 percent over the established federal poverty line. Businesses that do not provide health insurance are required to pay the state $295 per employee per year, which will be used to fund the coverage subsidies. However, calling this "universal healthcare" isn't exactly accurate. State officials estimated the law would extend health insurance coverage to as much as 95 percent of the state's population. They expected that the remaining residents would accept the tax penalties rather than pay for insurance that may still be too expensive, despite the government subsidies.[67]

By 2008, just 6.1 percent of Massachusetts' population was uninsured, the lowest rate in the nation. But the state was beginning to suffer under the strains of its initiative's expense. The Massachusetts Taxpayers Foundation estimated that the program added more than $700 million per year in annual costs, which the state splits 50-50 with the federal government. The state cut its payments to hospitals for uncompensated care and raised its cigarette tax by $1 a pack, but coupled with declining revenues, its efforts haven't been sufficient to close the gap.[68]

Shortly after taking office, President Barack Obama declared that the federal government would, once again, take on healthcare reform. Members of Congress invoked the Massachusetts program often during their debates; those in favor of reform pointed to its successes in reducing the uninsured population, while those opposed singled out its costs.

Ultimately, after nearly a year of hearings and speeches, President Obama signed the Patient Protection and Affordable Care Act into law on March 23, 2010. Some provisions have already been implemented, but the bulk of the legislation takes effect in 2014. The bill is structured similarly to the Massachusetts program, in mandating individual coverage, subsidizing insurance for low-income Americans, and assessing a tax penalty for those who go without coverage.[69]

Blood pressures ran high in summer 2009 as lawmakers and the public debated options for national healthcare reform. After months of rancor, the U.S. Congress passed a wide-ranging bill that will expand health insurance to millions of Americans.

The reforms rely heavily on an expansion of Medicaid to accomplish their goals. States will be required to set Medicaid eligibility at 133 percent of the poverty line or higher for *all* legal residents, including childless adults. For some states, such as Arkansas and Texas, which currently set their eligibility levels at 17 and 27 percent, respectively, this rule will mean substantial additions to their Medicaid rolls. The Congressional Budget Office estimates the enhanced coverage will cost states $20 billion—and the federal government hundreds of billions—by 2020.[70]

The fact that under the law the federal government will pick up the states' full cost of the expansion to 133 percent between 2014 and 2016 has been of little comfort to many states. Lawmakers in some states are opposed to the legislation on philosophical grounds, while others are simply worried about picking up any additional costs. "It's an unfunded, long-term mandate on our Medicaid program," Virginia governor Bob McDonnell said just before his state attorney general, Ken Cuccinelli, filed a federal lawsuit challenging the healthcare reform law.[71] By April 2010, Cuccinelli had been joined by eighteen of his peers in fighting the constitutionality of the new law.[72] Federal healthcare reform had finally been accomplished, but the debate was far from over. "It'll probably be 10 years before it all shakes out," said Chris Whatley, Washington director of the Council of State Governments. "This will push the fabric of the state-federal relationship in new directions, and we don't know how it will all come out."[73]

Issues to Watch

Passing federal healthcare reform legislation was just the first step. States will continue to grapple with its effects inside their borders, and they must continue to address a number of other burgeoning challenges.

Health Information Technology

In an age when laptops and smart phones are becoming ubiquitous, anyone who has had to fill out identical paperwork for each doctor they visit has probably wondered why those documents couldn't be saved electronically and shared. The federal government and states are working with private providers to do just that, through a number of health information technology (IT) initiatives. The initiatives integrate electronic medical records, prescription ordering, and other critical patient documents and facilitate the sharing of files among doctors and hospitals. A 2005 study by the RAND Corporation found that health IT could save the country as much as $77 billion annually in efficiencies.[74]

Most of the technology that the initiatives need already exists. But the states and the federal government must still convince private practitioners to participate, identify national standards to match technologies across state lines, address patient privacy concerns, and find a way to pay for it all—at a cost of as much as $400 million to build the nationwide network.[75]

The ARRA is making a small fraction of that money—about $560 million—available in competitive grants to states to help them pay for the development of health information exchanges, the backbone of the nationwide network. Those funds will provide some seed money, but they're temporary, which means states that use them to put a new or expanded system in place will need a revenue stream to keep them operational when the stimulus money runs out after 2011. Vermont is generating its funds through a fee the state is charging insurance companies. The fee has already pumped enough money into the state to pay for an electronic medical records system for physicians who are not affiliated with hospitals (independent practitioners often cannot afford the average $44,000 start-up costs). Florida is an example of a state that has been less successful in finding a financially viable way to sustain its health information exchanges. In 2004, the state used $5.5 million to fund ten pilot health information exchange projects—all of which failed to operate by the end of the projects.[76]

Progress is being made locally through regional health information organizations, described by the federal government as the building blocks to a national health information network. The organizations are being built, however, to work with industry within the state, not necessarily outside it. Such designs could make a national link up problematic.

Long-Term Care

Unlike private-sector health insurance plans, state Medicaid programs have an additional responsibility. Medicaid provides long-term care to the elderly and other services to people with disabilities. These services can range from providing nursing home care for low-income Medicaid recipients to developing rehabilitation plans for people with disabilities. All these services are extremely expensive. Although the elderly and disabled make up only about 0.25 percent of the people enrolled in Medicaid, they account for two-thirds of the total Medicaid spending.[77] More than 10 million Americans now use some form of long-term care.[78]

Moreover, the cost of long-term care is growing fast. According to the Congressional Budget Office, caring for elderly and disabled Medicaid beneficiaries accounted for more than 72 percent of the program's cost increases between 1975 and 2002. States' long-term care bills hit $147 billion in 2009 and may reach as much as $346 billion by 2040.[79]

Demographics are largely driving those cost increases. According to the Census Bureau, the number of people eighty-five years of age and older will grow by 40 percent by 2020. By 2040, that population is expected to grow by more than 250 percent, to 15.4 million people.[80] As it does, the number of people with serious disabilities will almost certainly increase. Many of these people will be unable—or unwilling—to pay for long-term care on their own.

Some states, such as Oregon, have kept costs down by shifting the elderly away from expensive care in nursing homes and toward less expensive at-home care and assisted-living centers. Seniors overwhelmingly support such alternatives to nursing homes. The federal government has encouraged the efforts despite opposition from the strong nursing home lobby. The percentage of Medicaid spending on noninstitutional care more than doubled between 1995 and 2007.[81] The federal healthcare reform bill will use financial incentives to move states more aggressively toward the provision of home-based services. The bill also creates the first national long-term care insurance plan, a voluntary program that will be financed through payroll deductions.[82] The Congressional Budget Office estimates that plan could reduce the federal budget deficit by about $74 billion by 2019.[83]

The Return of Public Health

The states have become major players in the field of healthcare. However, local governments at both the county and city levels continue to play important roles as well. In many parts of the country, local governments, unlike state governments, are direct healthcare providers.

In the wake of September 11, 2001, many government officials have come to view the public health system in a new light. Individuals in this field now are seen as the first responders to possible biological terrorism, pandemics, and natural disasters such as Hurricane Katrina. "Any community that fails to prepare and expects the federal government will come to the rescue is tragically wrong. It's not because we don't care, don't want to, or don't have the money, but because it's logistically impossible," Mike Leavitt, the U.S. secretary of health and human services under President George W. Bush, told state and local officials in 2006.[84] Some experts now believe that, instead of downsizing public hospitals, governments should look for ways to keep them available in case a crisis generates a high number of casualties.[85]

State and local governments had begun drawing up emergency response plans before swine flu emerged in 2009. The National Association of City and County Health Officials, anticipating as much as one-third of the population falling ill in such an epidemic, issued a guide to planning for local governments. Overall, experts thought the systems worked reasonably well during the height of the H1N1 pandemic. "[C]apacities were stretched but not broken by this pandemic," said William Schaffner, chair of the Department of Preventive Medicine at the Vanderbilt University School of Medicine.[86] Another test may come when, as experts expect, H1N1 returns for another round.

Another controversial issue in many communities involves sexual health and education. One in nine girls between the ages of sixteen and nineteen becomes pregnant outside of marriage, yet a considerable number of parents remain opposed to their children learning about sexuality in the classroom. These parents helped to resurrect abstinence-only sex education programs, which have received $1 billion in federal funding since 1998, when only 2 percent of schools offered such programs. By 2002, the number of schools teaching abstinence as the only way to avoid sexually transmitted diseases and pregnancy had risen to 23 percent.[87] Congressional Democrats allowed the program to expire in June 2009, but it was partially revived as part of a federal healthcare reform compromise. The bill will provide $250 million over five years for abstinence education—if states can provide 75 percent matching funds. It also allocates $375 million for comprehensive sex education.[88]

Evaluations of the programs report conflicting findings and are often used by both proponents and opponents of abstinence-only education to advance their positions. One recent study conducted by a Pennsylvania State University researcher found that fewer middle school students who were enrolled in an abstinence education program engaged in sexual activity within two years than those who had taken comprehensive sex education—but that more students in both groups remained sexually inactive than those who had no sex education at all.[89] Regardless of the teaching method, the statistics seemed headed in the wrong direction in recent years. The rates of teenage pregnancy, HIV, and syphilis increased between 2005 and 2007.[90]

The states are also the battlegrounds in the debate over access to contraception. At least twenty-five states have passed laws that require insurers that cover prescription drugs to include coverage of contraceptives. Twenty-one of the states, however, allow an exemption for employers who oppose such coverage for religious reasons.[91] The U.S. Food and Drug Administration (FDA) approved sales of emergency contraception to women ages eighteen and older without a prescription in September 2006, but nine states had allowed pharmacists to sell the drugs on their own in advance of the FDA's ruling. Access to these drugs is not universal, however; at least four states, Arkansas, Georgia, Mississippi, and South Dakota, passed conscience clauses that protect pharmacists who refuse to dispense the medication.[92]

What Is Good Health Anyway?

As if these issues were not enough, local health officials are increasingly wrestling with another question that has not been touched on in this chapter: What exactly constitutes a health issue anyway?

Consider obesity. Media attention has turned to this issue more and more as an ever-growing list of health studies proclaim just how out of shape Americans are. The films *Super Size Me!* and *Fast Food Nation* address people's obsession with fast food. The latest figures show that two-thirds of all adults in the United States are overweight or obese;[93] in 2008, Colorado was the only state where less than 20 percent of the population was classified as obese.[94] (See Map 15-3.) Kids are getting heavier too. In the past two decades, the number of overweight and obese children has nearly tripled. Today, according to the CDC, roughly 15 percent of children between the ages of six and eleven are overweight—up from just 4 percent thirty years ago. That number climbs to 18 percent for adolescents between the ages of twelve and nineteen; that too is a significant change from three decades ago, when just 6 percent of teens weighed too much.[95]

> The latest figures show that two-thirds of all adults in the United States are overweight or obese; in 2008, Colorado was the only state where less than 20 percent of the population was classified as obese.

Obesity contributes to a variety of ailments, among them heart disease, certain types of cancer, diabetes, stroke, arthritis, breathing problems, and psychological disorders such as depression. Overweight individuals suffer from these and other related conditions at a much higher rate than people who are not overweight. Indeed, researchers attribute about 112,000 deaths each year to obesity in the United States alone.[96] In 2003, obesity in the United States cost about $92.6 billion.[97] Researchers at Emory University estimate that, if the United States could curb the rate of increase of obesity, the nation could save $821 per adult by 2018.[98]

In 2006, New York City reignited the debate over government's role in promoting healthy eating habits when it banned the use of transfats (some of the most dangerous fats) in city restaurants. Soon after, other cities and states began to consider similar legislation. Parent groups and health

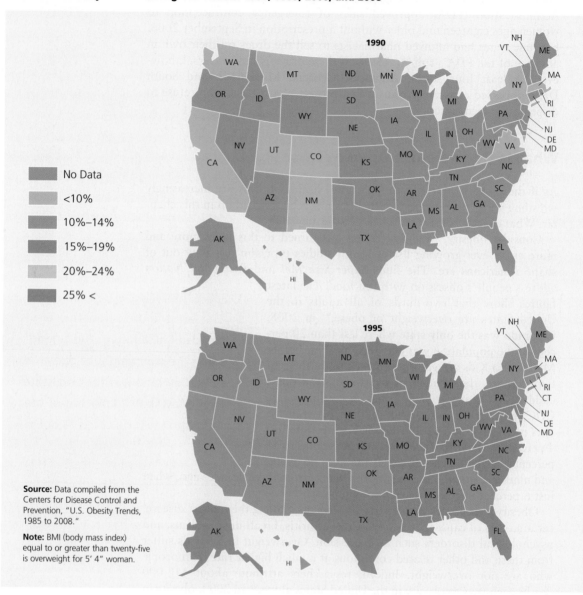

Source: Data compiled from the Centers for Disease Control and Prevention, "U.S. Obesity Trends, 1985 to 2008."

Note: BMI (body mass index) equal to or greater than twenty-five is overweight for 5' 4" woman.

Legend:
- No Data
- <10%
- 10%–14%
- 15%–19%
- 20%–24%
- 25% <

organizations demanded better, healthier fast-food options. And the fast-food restaurants quickly took notice. McDonald's, the world's largest fast-food chain, received such a negative rap for its unhealthy products that it was under strong pressure to take immediate action. It began expanding its "healthy" meal options with great fanfare, began shooting Ronald McDonald commercials showing Ronald with children rollerblading and exercising

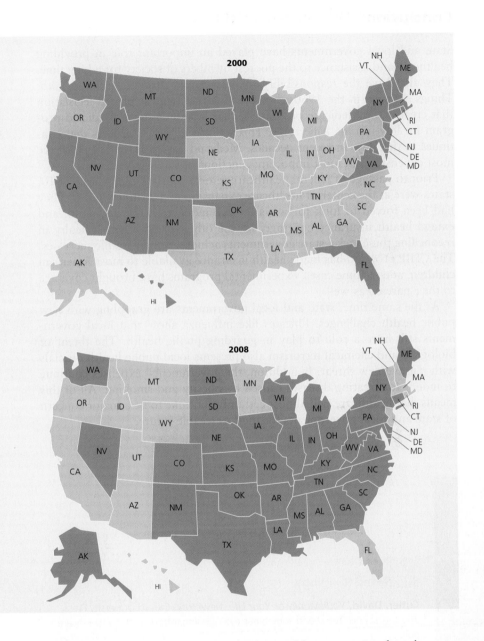

2000

2008

instead of sitting in the restaurant eating, and began posting fact sheets on its Web site announcing how much healthy food it had sold worldwide. Wendy's, KFC, Chili's, and other chains began frying their products in oils free of transfats. Ultimately, however, transfats-free does not equal health food, and doctors continue to advocate eating less drive-through fast food, and more fruits and vegetables, in the battle against obesity.

Conclusion

State and local governments have played an important role in providing healthcare and assistance to the poorest members of society for a long time. They also have the responsibility to protect and promote public health. Things changed in the 1960s, however, when Congress passed legislation that created the Medicare program for the elderly and the Medicaid program for low-income Americans. This set into motion a process that continues to this day. In recent decades, Medicaid has emerged as one of the most expensive and most important functions of state government.

Prior to passage of federal healthcare reform legislation in March 2010, states were at the center of healthcare expansion in the United States. They had been forced to look for ways to save money, on the one hand, and extend health insurance coverage, on the other. Despite the difficulty in reconciling these tasks, state governments achieved some notable successes. The CHIP program has made health insurance available to most American children, and in some cases, experimental programs have brought coverage to their parents as well.

At the same time, state and local governments are grappling with new public health challenges. Illnesses like influenza show that local governments still have a role to play in guarding public health. The threat of biological and chemical terrorism also presents local public health officials with a grave new threat. In addition, the governments' expenses continue to mount for treating diseases caused by obesity and smoking. All of this means that healthcare will almost certainly continue to be a major concern of state and local governments for the foreseeable future.

Key Concepts

abstinence (p. 569)

Aid to Families with Dependent Children (AFDC) (p. 568)

entitlement program (p. 575)

managed care (p. 584)

Medicaid (p. 570)

Medicare (p. 574)

Suggested Readings

Cutler, David. *Your Money or Your Life.* New York: Oxford University Press, 2003. A sophisticated and sometimes eye-opening introduction to healthcare policy.

Gawande, Atul. "The Cost Conundrum." *New Yorker,* June 1, 2009, available at www.newyorker.com/reporting/2009/06/01/090601fa_fact_gawande. An examination of McAllen, Texas, one of the costliest healthcare markets in the country; the study became required reading among Obama administration staff members working on federal healthcare reform.

Gingrich, Newt. *Saving Lives, Saving Money.* Washington, D.C.: Alexis de Tocqueville Institution, 2003. Former House Speaker Gingrich provides a spirited, conservative review of healthcare and possible future innovations.

Starr, Paul. *The Social Transformation of American Medicine.* New York: Basic Books, 1992. A wonderful account of the evolution of American healthcare.

Weil, Alan. "Ten Things Everyone Should Know about Welfare Reform," Urban Institute, May 9, 2002, available at www.urban.org/url.cfm?ID=31048. A concise yet thorough overview of welfare reform.

Suggested Web Sites

www.americashealthrankings.org. Home page of America's Health Rankings, a twenty-year project tracking health indicators at the state level.

www.astho.org. Web site of the Association of State and Territorial Health Officials.

www.familiesusa.org. Web site of FamiliesUSA, a liberal advocacy group that promotes a more activist government policy.

www.healthyamericans.org. Web site of Trust for America's Health, a nonprofit organization dedicated to protecting public health.

www.kaiserhealthnews.org. Home page of Kaiser Health News, a nonprofit news organization covering state and federal healthcare issues, funded by the Kaiser Family Foundation.

www.kff.org. Web site of the Henry J. Kaiser Family Foundation that offers a wealth of detail on state healthcare initiatives in general and Medicaid in particular.

www.naccho.org. Home page of the National Association of County and City Health Officials.

www.statehealthfacts.kff.org. A Kaiser Family Foundation Web site that provides detailed information on state healthcare policies.

CHAPTER 16

Environment and Climate Change

Thinking Globally, Acting Locally

California state senator Fran Pavley announces that the new Obama administration will reconsider the state's request to mandate strict environmental standards on vehicles, which the Bush administration had turned down. Gov. Arnold Schwarzenegger looks on at the January 26, 2009, news conference.

How did states become important voices on a global problem?

Why has climate change become a partisan issue?

16

Fran Pavley's journey to the White House took seven years. In 2002, Pavley, who was then a freshman state legislator in California, wrote a landmark law to regulate the tailpipe emissions of vehicles to cut down on greenhouse gases. Although the law was soon emulated by thirteen other states, it was tied up for years by court challenges and never received the federal sign-off necessary for it to take effect.

But a few months into his presidency, President Barack Obama fulfilled a campaign promise by supporting Pavley's initiative. Obama summoned Pavley and other political leaders from California to a White House Rose Garden ceremony in May 2009 where he announced that the federal government would regulate carbon emissions from vehicles, proposing standards that closely mirrored the Pavley bill's requirements. The federal government would also speed up rules to require higher gas mileage. "There were a lot of high-fives and hugs," Pavley said of the ceremony. "It was a seven-year journey. I equated it to a cat with nine lives. We went through a [U.S.] Supreme Court decision, several federal court decisions, two presidents, and a recalled governor."[1]

It's easy to forget that just a few years ago many state officials were skeptics about global warming issues. A decade ago, sixteen states passed legislation rejecting the Kyoto Protocol, the 1997 international treaty that sought to limit the emissions of carbon and other gases that contribute to global warming. Most of these pieces of legislation were resolutions expressing nonbinding opinions, but some states expressly forbade their agencies from taking any unilateral steps to reduce greenhouse gases.

But states have long since found the political will to address climate change. In 2006, Pavley was a sponsor of another California law, one aiming to reduce industrial carbon dioxide emissions by 25 percent by 2020, that represented the first imposition of statewide enforceable limits on greenhouse gas emissions that included penalties for noncompliance. More than half the states have adopted renewable energy portfolio standards requiring utilities to rely on renewable sources such as wind and solar energy to generate a significant share of their electricity (25 percent in most states) in future years. And groups of states in the Northeast, Upper Midwest, and interior West have formed regional compacts to create cap-and-trade systems to reduce industrial emissions. "They're committed to moving forward on various measures that they've already started in the absence of federal action," says Jessica Shipley, a fellow at the Pew Center on Climate Change. "Definitely, states are still working hard on climate, in conjunction with federal action."[2]

All this represents an important new role for states, which traditionally have taken a back seat to federal efforts when it comes to environmental issues. The major environmental laws of the early 1970s, such as the Clean Air and Clean Water acts, set out strict federal guidelines that states had to follow. In contrast to this command and control model, in which the federal government called all the shots, in the area of climate change the American states are leading, influencing not only federal policy under Obama but efforts in many other countries through state partnerships with regions and provinces in other nations.

Climate change, then, has become a particularly interesting exercise in federalism. States have sought to fill the vacuum left by the absence of federal leadership on an issue that state leaders themselves realize calls for a national—indeed, international—set of solutions. "States have been tripping all over themselves to show national leadership on this issue," said Barry G. Rabe, a professor of public policy at the University of Michigan. "California, I would argue, has made as heavy an investment in time and treasury into climate change as any government on Earth, including the European Union."[3]

Not all the states are on board with the program of seeking to address greenhouse gas emissions. Roughly half the states have taken little action, either because they are concerned that the price of addressing the issue, through limiting energy use, is simply too high, or because their leaders and political cultures remain skeptical that global warming is anthropogenic (that is, caused largely by human activity).

Skepticism is growing among all groups but particularly among Republicans. And that shift is having an effect on the policy debate. Just a few years ago, Republican governors were among those calling most loudly for concerted efforts against climate change. Some of them are now passing from the scene—or changing their minds. Yet even as climate change becomes more of a partisan issue than it has been, the regional divide among states remains in force, with many in the South and the industrial Midwest much more resistant to climate change efforts than those on the West Coast or the Northeast.

In short, inaction by the federal government and differences across states and localities have resulted in significant obstacles to a coordinated response to environmental problems, especially problems associated with global warming. Climate change is certain to remain an important issue among states and localities. It may remain, as it has been for the past decade, a central concern and focus for policy innovation. But whether a subset of the subnational governmental units of the United States can make a significant impact on greenhouse gas emissions in the absence of further action at the national and international levels remains very much in question.

In this chapter, we consider some of the specific environmental policy challenges facing states and localities. These include substantive policy topics such as regulating tailpipe emissions and promoting renewable energy, but they also include the problems that the federal system itself poses to comprehensive action on climate change, as well as the widening partisan divide that further fragments state and local government action on the environment.

States Get Serious about the Environment

New Jersey has 116 Superfund sites—the most of any state.

U.S. ENVIRONMENTAL PROTECTION AGENCY (EPA)

The federal agency charged with protecting the environment.

CLIMATE CHANGE

A shift in global temperatures.

GLOBAL WARMING

Rising average temperatures worldwide.

KYOTO PROTOCOL

A 1997 treaty that sought to reduce emissions of greenhouse gases.

Unlike education, crime, taxes, and budgets, the environment is a relatively modern policy concern for state and local governments. Indeed, it is a relatively modern policy concern for the federal government. The modern environmental movement can be traced to the 1960s, which in turn led to a concerted federal response in the early 1970s. This included the passage of landmark laws regarding air and water quality and the creation of the **U.S. Environmental Protection Agency (EPA)**. Enforcing and expanding those responsibilities has made environmental policy one of the central responsibilities of the federal and, increasingly, state and local governments. "Today, after nearly four decades, environmental protection is the most heavily funded regulatory responsibility in the United States," writes Marc Allen Eisner, a political scientist at Wesleyan University.[4]

At the heart of contemporary environmental debates is **climate change**, which has become a hot issue not just among national (and international) policymakers but also for state and local officials. It's worth remembering, however, that policymakers at all levels have taken this issue seriously for a relatively short time. "We're still very much at the embryonic stage of dealing with climate change in this country," said John Cahill, who worked on environmental legislation as an aide to former New York governor George Pataki.[5]

The federal government has, to put it mildly, a mixed record in dealing with the climate change challenge. Environmentalists derided President George W. Bush for not seriously addressing **global warming**, but Bush's predecessor's record was not notably better. Congress rejected President Bill Clinton's 1993 proposal to impose a tax on energy, and the Senate passed a unanimous resolution in 1997 that it would reject the **Kyoto Protocol** if it harmed the U.S. economy.

At least initially, states followed the skeptical approach of the federal government. It soon became clear, however, that many states were eager to address the problem of global warming, particularly after Bush's formal rejection of the Kyoto Protocol in 2001. "Ironically . . . American states may be emerging as international leaders at the very time the national government continues to be portrayed as an international laggard on global climate change," Rabe wrote in 2004.[6]

Most of these initial state-level efforts were largely symbolic, lacking specific mandates or resources. Unlike the federal government, however, some states actually put teeth into their efforts. As early as 1989, New Jersey governor Thomas Kean, a Republican, signed an executive order instructing all state agencies to take the lead in reducing **greenhouse gases**. In 2001, Massachusetts governor Jane Swift, also a Republican, issued a rule limiting a variety of pollutants from six major power plants, including the nation's first **carbon dioxide** standards. "The new, tough standards will help ensure older power plants in Massachusetts do not contribute to regional air pollution, acid rain and global warming," Swift said.[7] Her action was soon copied in New Hampshire.

Indeed, it was actually a state government—California—rather than the federal government that emerged as the leader in addressing climate change–related policies. California emerged as a leader in this policy arena not simply because of its green-leaning political constituencies or its large economy or its role as a national cultural trend-setter, although all these factors certainly played a role. As the only state allowed to set air pollution controls stricter than those mandated by federal law (thanks to a provision in the **Clean Air Act**), California occupies a unique policymaking niche in the federal system. There was strong pressure from environmental forces to move on the issue of greenhouse gases following the 1998 elections, with both the legislature and the governor's mansion in Democratic hands for the first time in two decades. And so on a series of important environmental issues, California began to act. Other states, following California's lead, began experimenting with innovative environmental policies. One of the biggest obstacles that the states faced in these efforts was the federal government.

Regulating Vehicles

In 2002, California lawmakers enacted a measure to regulate **tailpipe emissions,** or greenhouse gases released from vehicles, which in 1999 accounted for 37 percent of carbon dioxide emissions in the state.[8] The idea came from Bluewater Network, a San Francisco environmental group that has since become part of Friends of the Earth, a global organization. They found their sponsor in state representative Fran Pavley, a Democratic freshman willing to take on the fight when more prominent legislators were avoiding it. "We were happy at that point to find any progressive author, because we knew it would be a difficult bill," said Bluewater executive director Russell Long.[9]

The legislation survived a committee challenge and was ready to reach the floor by the middle of 2001, but Pavley held off on a vote until 2002 so she could broaden her backing. Carmakers and oil companies spent an estimated $5 million attempting to sink it, and she was ardently attacked by talk-radio hosts for impinging on the freedom of Californians to drive SUVs and other large vehicles.

GREENHOUSE GASES

Emissions—primarily carbon dioxide but also other gases such as methane—that are believed to contribute to global warming.

CARBON DIOXIDE

A naturally occurring gas, the prevalence of which is increased by the burning of fossil fuels.

CLEAN AIR ACT

The law, initially enacted in 1970, that provides authority for federal regulation of air pollution.

TAILPIPE EMISSIONS

Greenhouse gases released by cars and other vehicles.

Seattle mayor Greg Nickels fills a car with a blend of biodiesel fuel at a west Seattle Safeway gas station in 2007. The station was the first of Safeway's nearly three hundred fuel stations to offer biodiesel products.

Pavley responded with polls demonstrating overwhelming popular support for the bill, even among SUV owners. She also got help from water-quality districts; religious leaders; technology executives from Silicon Valley; and celebrities such as Paul Newman, Tom Hanks, and former president Bill Clinton, who called wavering lawmakers. Her bill's progress was also helped immeasurably by legislative leaders, who showed the former civics teacher some parliamentary tricks to ensure its passage.

One was to put language into the bill all in capital letters highlighting the fact that the California Air Resources Board would not have the power to ban SUVs or other specific types of vehicles, as bill opponents were warning would be the case in their advertisements. One of Pavley's colleagues called these the "We Really Mean It" amendments. The substance of the bill was not changed but the amendments were "put in to clarify it for the public," Pavley said. "Admittedly, in all the years I taught 'how a bill becomes law,' we didn't talk about that possibility."[10]

But her law did require the air resources board to adopt "cost-effective" and "reasonable" restrictions on carbon dioxide emissions from cars and light trucks by 2005, with automakers having until 2009 to comply. Not surprisingly, carmakers fought the law through numerous court challenges.

More than a dozen other states enacted laws saying they would abide by California's rules once they are approved and several others pledged to do so, but the Bush administration refused to grant California the necessary waiver. "All we asked for was permission to enforce, because the rules were all in place," California Air Resources Board spokesman Stanley Young said in a 2008 interview. "We've been ready for two years on Pavley. The rules were fully fleshed out. They were formally adopted back in 2005, and we're ready to move on them as soon as we get the green light."[11]

Challenging the Environmental Protection Agency

In the face of federal reluctance to regulate greenhouse gas emissions, several environmental groups as early as 1999 had petitioned the EPA to use its authority under the Clean Air Act to regulate the gases. The agency denied it had such authority and also argued that the link between greenhouse gases and climate change was not firmly established.

Massachusetts and eleven other states appealed the EPA's denial. In April 2007, the Supreme Court ruled 5–4 in the states' favor, noting that they had standing to bring such a case due to the "risk of catastrophic harm" they faced as sovereign entities. Justice John Paul Stevens wrote that the EPA had provided "no reasonable explanation for its refusal to decide whether greenhouse gases cause or contribute to climate change." In his dissent, Chief Justice John G. Roberts Jr. argued that it was an issue better decided by Congress and the executive branch.[12]

But the Court's majority had determined that carbon dioxide was indeed an air pollutant under the federal Clean Air Act, and that law—written at a time during the early 1970s when southern California was notorious for its **smog**—gives California the authority to regulate any such pollutant, as long as the state can get a waiver from the EPA. Other states are then allowed to follow California's rules.

The 2007 Supreme Court decision set the political stage for Congress to set a new mileage standard for cars and light trucks. In December 2007, President Bush signed into law requirements that a car manufacturer's entire fleet average thirty-five miles per gallon by 2020.

But just hours after that bill was signed, EPA administrator Stephen L. Johnson dashed hopes that the *Massachusetts v. EPA* decision would lead the agency to approve California's waiver application for enforcement of the Pavley bill. "The Bush administration is moving forward

SMOG

A type of air pollution; the word was constructed by combining *smoke* and *fog*.

with a clear national solution, not a confusing patchwork of state rules, to reduce America's climate footprint from vehicles," Johnson said in a statement.[13]

California had been granted more than fifty waivers under the Clean Air Act, which allowed it to develop such innovations as the catalytic converter, which reduces tailpipe emissions; tighter fuel caps to reduce gasoline evaporation; and computerized detectors to warn when a car's smog controls were not working. California's standards have often been adopted by other states and, thus, by carmakers. "If not for California's leadership, I think it's fair to say that cars wouldn't be as clean as they are today," said Ron Burke, Midwest climate change director for the Union of Concerned Scientists. "We would have suffered through more bad air days over the last thirty years."[14]

The *Los Angeles Times* reported that EPA staff had urged Johnson to grant the waiver. "California met every criteria . . . on the merits. The same criteria we have used for the last forty years on all the other waivers," one EPA staffer told the *Times*. "We told him [Johnson] that."[15] Technical and legal staff of the EPA also reportedly advised Johnson he would likely lose a legal challenge. The *St. Petersburg Times* reported that during the late summer and fall, Secretary of Transportation Mary Peters had quietly urged members of Congress and some governors to let the EPA know they opposed the waiver request.[16]

As noted earlier, the waiver had to wait until President Obama granted it—representing the federal government's first step toward regulating greenhouse gases. Under rules finalized in April 2010 by EPA and the Department of Transportation, emission and mileage standards for new vehicles would require an average performance of 35.5 miles per gallon by 2016. "The rules are expected to cut emissions of carbon dioxide and other heat-trapping gases about 30 percent from 2012 to 2016," the *New York Times* reported.[17] The Obama administration estimated that the new standards would add $985 to the price of a car but would save consumers $4,000 in fuel costs over the life of the vehicle.

Canada adopted identical standards the same day. The federal rules were largely based on the California law, but they also reflected an agreement hammered out with carmakers.

Vehicle Miles Traveled

VEHICLE MILES
TRAVELED (VMT)

How many miles each individual car is driven; an increasingly important measure of auto use.

One of the grails for environmentalists is to cut down on **vehicle miles traveled (VMT)**. Their notion is that limiting the amount that each car is driven will help cut back on greenhouse gas emissions. Toward that end, there has been a lot of talk in recent years about taxing VMT to get motorists to drive less. VMT has also attracted increasing attention from state and federal policymakers, not just for environmental reasons but for practical reasons associated with finding the money to build and maintain roads.

Surface transportation projects are primarily funded by per-gallon taxes on motor vehicle fuels. This gas tax has become the transportation finance equivalent of Churchill's famous remark about democracy: It's the worst system there is, except for all the others.

The National Governors Association complained in a 2008 report that federal and state gas taxes are "not producing adequate revenue to meet system needs."[18] The federal gas tax has not been raised since 1993, leading to a deficit in the Highway Trust Fund. Not only has the value of the 18.4-cent-per-gallon gas tax decreased over time due to inflation, but the amount of gas that people are buying has not kept pace with the wear and tear they put on the roads because of increased fuel efficiency. "For years, it worked pretty well because we had all these vehicles and they all got about the same lousy mileage," said Richard G. Little, director of the Keston Institute for Public Finance and Infrastructure Policy at the University of Southern California. "Now, we've gone from 7 or 8 miles per gallon to 50 for a hybrid," he continued. "It may be good for the environment, but someone driving at 50 miles per gallon is not really paying for the mileage—they're not paying for the value of the mobility."[19] Little's comments reflect the view among transportation officials that what's crucial is not the consumption of gasoline but the distance driven. What's needed, he and others suggest, is a move from a tax on gas to a tax on the use of the roads.

That's a difficult switch to pull off. New York City failed in its efforts to win state approval in 2008 for "congestion pricing," a plan to charge drivers a fee for entering parts of Manhattan during peak hours. The leasing of major roadways in Illinois and Indiana to private vendors that have raised tolls has proven controversial, and other tolling initiatives in Pennsylvania, New Jersey, and Texas have not gotten off the ground.

Several states have therefore been exploring the idea of taxing drivers directly on mileage. Oregon led the way with a 2007 pilot study in the Portland area. State transportation officials kept a close watch on individual drivers' mileage through use of global positioning system (GPS) devices. When cars pulled up to the pump, drivers were charged a tax of 1.2 cents per mile, instead of the state's gasoline tax of 24 cents per gallon, based on the distance driven since their last fill-up. The Oregon experiment is considered an important field test of how revenue might be generated based on VMT. Gov. Theodore R. Kulongoski, a Democrat, proposed expanding the experiment in his 2009 budget request.

But working out the technological kinks, suggests Jim Whitty, director of the Oregon Department of Transportation's Office of Innovative Partnerships, will still take seven to eight more years. Even then, the main challenge in implementing a broad-scale mileage tax will not be technological but political. Rural residents, for example, may feel unfairly penalized under a

Drivers in the Los Angeles metropolitan area waste more time in traffic than commuters anywhere else in the United States—approximately 5 days a year.

system that charges them more for the longer distances they have to drive. And taxing based solely on distance would not address the goal of congestion pricing—charging more for driving on the busiest streets at the most crowded times.

It's conceivable that a system could be created that taxes people based on where, when, and how much they drive—and even what they drive. It might cost a lot more, for example, to tool through downtown Los Angeles during rush hour in a Hummer than to coast across a desolate South Dakota back road in a Prius at midnight. But such a system would only exacerbate the privacy concerns that have already been part of the debate surrounding a simple mileage-based tax. "Privacy concerns were right there from the start," Whitty said. "The public doesn't like to be tracked."[20]

Early in 2009, U.S. Secretary of Transportation Ray LaHood sounded receptive to the idea of taxing VMT, but he was quickly shot down by the White House. President Obama has ruled out imposing a VMT tax. Nonetheless, Little predicts that a mileage tax based on the Oregon model is "where we're going to be. It's not going to be two years, and it's not going to be five years, but within ten years we're going to start seeing some fairly widespread rollouts on that."[21]

Cap and Trade

Cars are not the only source of greenhouse gas emissions. In 2006, Fran Pavley and other California lawmakers were promoting a piece of legislation, known as AB 32, which sought to address the stationary sources of pollution, such as power plants, oil refineries, and cement plants. The bill aims to reduce industrial carbon dioxide emissions by 25 percent by 2020. AB 32 represented the first imposition of statewide enforceable limits on greenhouse gas emissions that include penalties for noncompliance. The legislation was the first in the nation to require a cap-and-trade system to address greenhouse gases.

CAP AND TRADE

A system for limiting pollution by assigning allowances to polluters, which can sell their excess permits if they succeed in reducing their emissions.

Cap-and-trade systems put an overall limit—or cap—on the emission of a pollutant, such as carbon dioxide. Once the limit is set, polluters are given or sold some number of emissions allowances, in essence, permits to pollute. The amount of pollution they can release—say, 1,000 tons of carbon dioxide at a power plant—is slowly reduced over time. If they come in underneath their limits, they can sell or trade their excess permits; if not, they have to pay fines or buy extra permits from other polluters. That's the trade part.

Cap-and-trade systems have been used by the federal government and by other states to address environmental concerns. Congress created such a system to address acid rain in the 1990 Clean Air Act. (Acid rain is rain that contains a high concentration of sulfur dioxide; it is blamed for polluting lakes and streams.)

Ten states in the Northeast and Mid-Atlantic—Connecticut, Delaware, Maine, Maryland, Massachusetts, New Hampshire, New Jersey, New York, Rhode Island, and Vermont—have signed on to a cooperative effort known as the Regional Greenhouse Gas Initiative (RGGI), which uses cap and trade. These states have capped carbon dioxide emissions from their power sectors, requiring gradual reductions that will bring emissions down 10 percent by 2018.

Governors from seven states began RGGI negotiations in 2003, reached a formal agreement in 2006 (with the last three states, Maryland, Massachusetts, and Rhode Island, signing on the following year), and began auctioning pollution permits to power companies in 2009. The history of RGGI includes many touch-and-go moments when states dropped out of or rejoined the program. But the effort has stayed afloat based on the hope that, once carbon emissions carry a price, utilities will burn less coal, oil, and natural gas because it's in their economic interest, making carbon-free alternatives comparatively more attractive.

The early auctions have been considered a success, but not everyone is convinced that the most optimistic scenarios about reducing emissions will play out as intended. The region-by-region approach that's now in place leaves plenty of opportunities open for undermining the system.

In the Northeast, for example, it would be easy enough for a big industrial customer in New York, which is part of RGGI, to look for cheaper power generated by coal plants in Pennsylvania or Ohio, which are not part of the initiative. If that occurs, said Kenneth Pokalsky, a regulatory analyst for the Business Council of New York State, "We'll have the worst of both worlds: higher energy costs in New York to implement a program that has no discernible impact on worldwide greenhouse gas emissions."[22]

Nevertheless, other regional initiatives in the West and Midwest—and later Florida—began pursuing their own cap-and-trade schemes in 2007. The Midwestern group has outlined its cap-and-trade system, with an advisory group releasing its final recommendations and model rules in May 2010. The Western Climate Initiative (WCI), comprising seven states and four Canadian provinces, is bolder in its approach than RGGI, targeting not just carbon dioxide but other greenhouse gases as well. And the WCI isn't limiting its scope to power plants. Instead, it's trying to bring all major industries; transportation fuels; and residential furnaces, stoves, and hot water heaters into its system.

But the regional efforts are continuing to run into snags. After Democratic governor Janet Napolitano left Arizona to join the Obama cabinet in 2009, her replacement, Republican Jan Brewer, removed the state from the WCI's cap-and-trade negotiations—only the most notable sign that the pact may lack sufficient political and institutional support to carry out its ambitious goals.

With its 2007 Next Generation Energy Act, the Minnesota state legislature adopted the strategic goal of reducing the state's greenhouse gas emissions by at least 80 percent of 2005 levels by 2050.

In addition, newly elected Republican governor Chris Christie of New Jersey announced in 2010 that he intended to use that year's proceeds from RGGI allowance auctions to help balance the state budget rather than funding energy efficiency efforts and renewable energy research, as intended by the pact. "Next year, we plan on getting back to RGGI," Christie said.[23]

A cap-and-trade proposal was central to the approach taken by the 2009 bill passed by the U.S. House, but the concept itself became highly charged over the course of congressional debate. Critics derided the idea, calling it "cap and tax" and claiming that it would add billions to the nation's energy cost.

As White House counsel under President George H.W. Bush, C. Boyden Gray was an architect of the 1990 Clean Air Act cap-and-trade program designed to address acid rain. Nevertheless, he added his voice to the chorus of complaints about the cap-and-trade model proposed by federal climate change legislation. "The proponents always say they're copying the highly successful cap-and-trade program of the Clean Air Act and they're most decidedly not, because they've thrown in this auction function," Gray said. "It's purely a revenue function, and that becomes a tax. You pull $2 or 3 trillion out of the economy and that's what people are objecting to."[24]

In March 2010, in a move seen largely as a response to complaints that a cap-and-trade bill would hurt the economy by raising energy prices, Obama outlined a plan to open up much of the East Coast to offshore oil drilling. His proposal would have ended a long-time moratorium on offshore oil exploration. The West Coast would remain closed to drilling and exploration, as would the East Coast from New Jersey northward. But opening up oil exploration from Delaware down to the central coast of Florida covered 167 million acres of ocean.[25] Obama's move, which included more environmental protections than a similar idea floated by President George W. Bush, was mainly cheered by oil companies and supporters of increased domestic energy production— as well as by state officials, who welcomed the chance to share in oil-extraction tax revenues.

But within three weeks, an offshore oil rig exploded forty miles off the Louisiana coast. (This occurred in the Gulf of Mexico, an area that had long been open to oil drilling, not in the newly designated area.) The resulting catastrophic oil spill effectively ended any chance for an expansion of offshore drilling for the foreseeable future.

Promoting Renewable Energy

Meanwhile, more than half the states are pushing forward on another front intended to reduce greenhouse gas emissions and reduce U.S.

environmental concerns. Florida governor Charlie Crist, a Republican, asked a utility company to cancel two projects in his state. The Texas energy giant TXU Corp. shelved eight out of eleven planned coal plants, investing heavily in wind energy instead. Only three of ten plants that were once planned for southern Illinois remained active.[33]

Nowadays, wherever a coal-fired plant is proposed, the Sierra Club or an allied group steps forward with a lawsuit to block it.[34] Environmentalists believe that delays, and their concomitant costs, can only serve to move power generation away from coal. "Each time you step back and reassess the politics and economics of coal," said Bob Eye, a Sierra Club attorney and former counsel to the Kansas Department of Health and Environment (KDHE), "things are more difficult for the coal-plant proponents."[35]

But the case that got the most attention and drew the most political and legal heat came in Kansas. In 2007, Rod Bremby, KDHE secretary, blocked a pair of massive coal-fired power plants. Citing that year's *Massachusetts v. EPA* Supreme Court decision (which sought to force the EPA to regulate greenhouse gases), Bremby overruled his own staff and rejected Sunflower Electric Power Corp.'s application to build its $3.6 billion power plant project outside Holcomb.

Bremby was the first regulator to block a power plant strictly out of concern for climate change and without getting specific statutory cover from the legislature. "To approve the permit didn't seem a reasonable option, given that carbon dioxide is a pollutant and we're talking about 11 million tons of carbon," he said.[36] According to Robert Glicksman, a University of Kansas law professor, "There have been other decisions in which state public utility commissions or environmental regulators have blocked construction or operation of coal-fired plants on the basis of climate change, but those have been based on legislation designed to minimize pollution or used climate change coupled with other factors."[37] In Washington State, for instance, the legislature in 2007 limited the amount of greenhouse gases that coal plants could emit. To obtain construction permits, energy companies must show they can capture or sequester any carbon dioxide above strict limits.

Because Kansas lacks such legislation, and despite the state attorney general's opinion clarifying his authority, many critics complained that Bremby had overstepped his purview. Kansas law gives the KDHE secretary the authority to block emissions found to endanger health or the environment. However, according to Jay Emler, who chaired the state Senate Utilities Committee, that power applies only to emergencies. "His decision, which I say is nothing but a political decision, has had a disastrous effect on the economy of Kansas," Emler complained in 2008, "and will until it's rectified."[38]

Bremby and his allies pointed out that Sunflower was the only applicant not to receive a clean-air permit out of more than 3,100 applications during the six years that Democrat Kathleen Sebelius had been governor. But legislators—their attention captured by a million-dollar lobbying campaign by Sunflower and its allies—voted three times to ban Bremby's department from regulating greenhouse gases. Each time, Sebelius sided with Bremby and vetoed their efforts. The legislature came close to overriding her, but fell short. The issue appeared to be left to the courts, with a half-dozen state and federal lawsuits filed regarding the matter.

Things changed, however, in 2009, when Sebelius left Kansas to join the Obama cabinet. Within a week of taking office, her successor, Democrat Mark Parkinson, crafted a compromise that let Sunflower proceed. It was a deal of Solomon-like simplicity. Sunflower wanted two plants; Parkinson offered them one, an 895-megawatt facility, down from the 1,400 megawatts that the two plants would have created. Sunflower immediately went for the idea, and the legislature approved it.

The new governor's breakthrough blindsided environmentalists, who felt that he had snatched defeat from the jaws of victory. "It really does put Kansas out of sync with what's happening nationally," says Stephanie Cole, a regional representative of the Sierra Club.[39] Since Bremby's original decision, about ninety-five power plants around the country had seen their permits denied, delayed, or withdrawn for reasons similar to the ones he cited. Moreover, the deal allows Sunflower to come back and ask for a second plant in 2011.

But Parkinson thought it also was important for Kansas to move ahead with wind power generation and make progress toward a requirement that Sunflower and other utilities generate 20 percent of their power from renewable sources by 2020. That mandate was included in the final legislative package, and it would have been held up as long as Sunflower's permits were in limbo.

Parkinson had bought his state some peace on the legal and political fronts, but he also ended Kansas's brief, unexpected stature as a leader in the fight against climate change. In addition to compromising on the power plant, the new agreement blocks the KDHE from issuing air-quality standards that are any more stringent than the ones that Washington, D.C., requires.

Limiting Land Use

In addition to addressing the consumption of energy directly, states are looking at ways to cut back on individuals' use of fuel. Many environmentalists blame **sprawl**—the growth of suburban and exurban communities far from central cities and existing transit and transportation infrastructure—for contributing to the greater consumption of natural resources.

Tom Adams, president of the California League of Conservation Voters, argues that his state must cut down on sprawl to meet its long-term environmental goals. In 2008, the state took a big step in the direction that Adams favored by enacting a major new land-use law.

SPRAWL

The rapid growth of a metropolitan area, typically as a result of specific types of zoning and development.

Typically, land-use policies are decided at the local level, with cities or counties passing **zoning laws,** or ordinances, that, for instance, keep industrial sites separate from residential areas or require that no more than one house be built on each quarter acre of land. Some areas impose only loose zoning restrictions—or none at all, as in Houston. But state governments often do influence land-use policy, if only through their transportation programs. Numerous states, led by Maryland, have enacted policies in recent years to cut down on sprawl—by saying that the state will not build infrastructure outside of approved development areas, for instance. Most such laws have proved to be largely toothless.

California's 2008 law, known as SB 375, goes further than most. SB 375 directs the California Air Resources Board to come up with targets for reducing emissions from cars and trucks. Regional planning boards will then rewrite their master growth plans in ways that seek to meet those targets—for instance, by planning more housing near existing mass transit lines. The regions that come closest to the goals will be rewarded with extra federal and state transportation dollars.

It's no surprise that SB 375 was backed by environmentalists, but it also had the support of California's home builders, who liked the prospect of more predictability in the zoning process. One of the main goals of the bill is to induce localities to coordinate their major planning tasks: transportation, land use, and housing. Few had been doing that. In addition, SB 375 provides relief from certain air-quality standards that had, perversely, discouraged developers from undertaking infill projects. "Builders thrive on certainty, knowing what the rules are," says Tim Coyle, of the California Building Industry Association.[40] Local governments also supported the law; it provides incentives and creates a policymaking framework, but it doesn't create specific mandates for any individual region.

The new law will take years to implement, but it already has received lots of attention from other states. "It's really a very important piece of legislation," says Peter Kasabach, of New Jersey Future, a smart-growth group. "How we develop our land is going to impact our greenhouse gas targets. A lot of folks think that if we drive hybrids or change our lightbulbs, we'll be okay. But a significant amount of our greenhouse gas targets will be met by how we get around and reduce vehicle miles traveled."[41]

The notion that sprawl is bad both for the environment and for the health of communities has become fashionable over the past decade—perhaps nowhere more so than in Miami. That's surprising because, when it comes to building and construction, Miami has always been a wide-open town, home to endless rows of towering condo buildings.

But, in late 2009, the city council approved a new zoning code that is likely to have a profound effect on development. Ardently promoted by Miami mayor Manny Diaz but drafted in large part by architect Elizabeth Plater-Zyberk, the code embraces the **New Urbanist** principles that made her and Andres Duany (her husband and professional partner) famous.

ZONING LAWS

Regulations that control how land can be used.

NEW URBANISM

A design movement that seeks to promote walkable communities through transit-oriented, mixed-use development.

The new code, known as Miami 21, seeks to encourage street-level pedestrian activity and reduce automobile dependence. The hope is that neighborhoods will fit within a comfortable scale, with plenty of shops out front and buildings that conform to fixed height limits with upper-story setbacks from the street. At the same time, the goal is to create corridors with enough density that public transit will be viable. But the most important idea may be the decision to focus on entire neighborhoods rather than individual projects.

New Urbanist codes have been adopted in various places around the country for new projects in previously unbuilt areas (greenfields) and for specific areas undergoing redevelopment, such as riverfronts. But Miami became the first city of any size to attempt to apply these principles throughout its borders.

Advocates of the approach are making grand claims about its potential to transform much of the landscape and have explicitly promised that it will make Miami far more environmentally friendly as well. "A whole city is changing its strategy consistent with this idea of preventing climate change," says Armando Carbonell, chair of the Department of Planning and Urban Form at the Lincoln Institute of Land Policy.[42]

Many builders and architects support Miami 21, recognizing that the city's old plans are badly out of date. But not everyone is happy. Some developers warn that, despite its laudable goals, the scheme's new restrictions could hamper construction. They charge that it is inflexible in some ways and inconsistent in others. "Everything they say about it is absolutely fantastic," says one of the critics, Miami architect Kricket Snow. "But in many cases, the code doesn't actually do what they claim it will do."[43]

There's one more major problem. Miami was horrendously overbuilt during the overheated housing market that collapsed in 2007. It is home to thousands of foreclosed condos. "Our economic condition stinks down here," Truly Burton, a lobbyist for the Builders Association of South Florida, said bluntly after the code had passed.[44] So the fact that there are essentially no projects on the drawing board means it's going to take a particularly long time to find out whether the proponents or the doubters are right about Miami 21's merits.

BUILDING CODES

Rules regarding the standards for structures; they mainly have to do with safety issues, but sometimes also include requirements for things like exterior pedestrian walkways.

Green Building

Some states and localities have tried to change not only the way buildings are laid out in relation to one another but their interior efficiency as well. In 2008, Chicago mayor Richard Daley unveiled what the *New York Times* described as "perhaps the most aggressive plan of any major American city to reduce heat-trapping gases."[45] The plan, which aimed to cut Chicago's carbon output by 25 percent by 2020, focuses on tougher **building codes**.

"Green" building codes have drawn significant attention among local governments seeking to cut back on carbon emissions. Buildings account for 40 to 50 percent of a city's energy demands. They use 25 percent of the drinking water and produce 35 percent of the solid waste, mostly in the form of construction materials. And buildings produce anywhere from 30 to 70 percent of municipal carbon emissions, according to the American Institute of Architects (AIA). Many cities have received grants from former president Bill Clinton's foundation to rewrite their codes, but far more are pursuing such strategies on their own. In 2008, more than twenty-five thousand local officials attended the Greenbuild conference in Boston sponsored by the U.S. Green Building Council.[46]

Ron Sims, then the King County (Seattle), Washington, county executive, greets former Seattle mayor Norm Rice at an election event in 2004. Sims, now a top official with the U.S. Department of Housing and Urban Development, was a pioneer among local officials in planning how to cope with specific effects climate change was having on his community.

The trend has exploded in recent years. From 2003 to 2007, the number of cities with green building programs grew by 418 percent, from 22 to 92, according to the AIA. By mid-2008, 14 percent of municipalities with populations of more than fifty thousand had adopted such programs, with many more cities planning to implement programs soon.

By and large, cities' green building programs are based on the standards of the council's rating system, known as LEED (Leader in Energy and Environmental Design). To encourage developers to build green, cities are offering tax incentives, reductions in permit fees, and access to grants for projects that meet certain environmental benchmarks. Some cities offer bonus density allowances; a green building project might be exempt from height restrictions, for example. But the most popular incentive by far is expedited permitting for green projects. Cities can implement such a policy at virtually no cost to themselves, which has proven extremely attractive.

Some cities are going further and actually requiring energy-efficient construction through their building codes. In 2006, Washington, D.C., became the first major U.S. city to mandate green construction for all private buildings of at least fifty thousand square feet, beginning in 2012.

And in 2007, Boston became the first city actually to implement a green requirement for private construction and renovation projects.

Since then, a handful of other cities have adopted similar mandates. In 2009, the New York City Council began requiring the owners of its largest buildings to perform energy audits and upgrade lighting, and the council is considering more rules regarding the heating and insulation of individual apartments. In 2008, San Francisco adopted the strictest codes of any U.S. city so far, requiring green standards for any residential building taller than seventy-five feet and commercial buildings of more than five thousand square feet. That same year, California became the first state to require green environmental standards, such as recycling of construction waste, lowering the use of polluting materials, and mandating greater energy efficiency in new structures, in its statewide building code; these rules took effect in 2010.

Builders routinely have said that they support the goals of such regulations, but have often complained that they are too costly. Nevertheless, increased energy efficiency of new and existing structures has become a primary goal for all levels of government. In 2007, in response to requests from the U.S. Conference of Mayors and other groups, Congress authorized up to $2 billion annually in block grants for state and local programs designed to save energy. That authorization went unfunded until the 2009 enactment of the American Recovery and Reinvestment Act (ARRA), the federal stimulus bill. ARRA included $3.2 billion for energy efficiency block grants for states and localities and an additional $5 billion in funding for Department of Energy **weatherization** efforts, much of which also amounted to grants for the states.

Weatherization, at least for the first year after ARRA passed, became a case study in the difficulties of quickly ramping up an entirely new program within the federal system. Neither the states nor the federal government had ever devoted much money to weatherization, and suddenly both were spending billions. In addition, because the work relied on lots of local providers—such as nonprofit groups and individual contractors—many states were slow out of the gate in getting projects underway.

For example, by November 2009—nine months after ARRA's passage—Texas had spent just $1.8 million of the $163 million available weatherizing a grand total of seven homes statewide. Weatherization efforts began to pick up in 2010, but slowly. By the end of March, work had finished on 2,450 homes or apartments with plans in place for 2,200 more. Still, that was only 14 percent of the housing units that had been expected to be completed, and the state still had spent only 4 percent of its total funding with one-third of the program's limited lifespan already expired.[47]

Washington State also fell badly behind schedule during the first year of its stepped-up weatherization efforts. At summer's end, local agencies had weatherized just 10 percent of the units the state had planned. The problem drew the attention of Democratic governor Christine Gregoire's office,

WEATHERIZATION

Protecting buildings from the elements (for example, by installing insulation); also designed to cut down on energy use.

emissions amounted to Palin-style denials that human activity causes global warming. They also felt that planning for the effects brought about by climate change was defeatist. "It was seen as a potential smokescreen behind which high-emission countries could hide so they wouldn't have to make binding agreements to reduce," said Nathan Hultman, a professor of science, technology, and international affairs at Georgetown University.[61]

There are still advocates who argue that discussion about how to adapt to climate shifts amounts to a distraction from the larger project of reducing emissions. "There are people out there working on adaptation, but I have to say the overwhelming effort is to try to reduce our emissions," said Tom Adams, president of the California League of Conservation Voters. "At this point, some fairly significant climate impacts are inevitable, but a lot of us feel that this is a genuine planetary emergency, and it's imperative that we cut emissions."[62]

But the notion that talking about adaptation is just a smokescreen to conceal the lack of effort to reduce greenhouse gases seems to be fading away. There's a growing recognition among those concerned about global warming that even if carbon emissions were reduced to zero tomorrow—which clearly isn't going to happen—there is already enough carbon dioxide in the air to guarantee more changes to come. The Intergovernmental Panel on Climate Change, which shared the 2007 Nobel Peace Prize with former vice president Al Gore, has stressed the importance of adaptation in its recent reports, and in 2007 a group of scientists published an article in *Nature* called "Lifting the Taboo on Adaptation."[63]

On January 1, 2010, stores selling food or beverages in the District of Columbia began charging a 5-cent user fee on every paper or plastic bag. The money collected goes to cleaning the Anacostia River, and the law is meant to encourage use of reusable bags.

As a practical matter, policymakers are increasingly concerned about how to plan for the changes their communities are facing. Not surprisingly, the issue has drawn the most attention in areas along coastlines, such as Maryland and Oregon. But because climate change will manifest itself differently in different locales, adaptation questions are drawing attention all over. For instance, Republican governor James Douglas of Vermont has been working with the state university to begin crafting plans to help the forestry and farming industries cope with the local effects of climate change.

In parts of the nearby Cascade Range in Washington State, snowpack has declined by as much as 60 percent. In response, King County, which includes Seattle, has begun planning backward from 2050, formulating plans to adapt to the climate change effects that are seen as likely to occur even if carbon emissions are significantly cut between now and then. For example, officials expect coastal-erosion problems associated with rising sea levels, health effects such as new infectious diseases and heat stroke, increasing numbers of forest fires, and ecological issues affecting salmon. In 2007 the county council agreed to a tax inspired by such looming dangers, part of county executive Ron Sims's $335 million plan to bolster river levees and reduce flood risks.

The county is now building climate change risks into all its long-term planning and policy development. "We're learning to define ourselves not

This worker is shown arranging LED lights into bottles on a wall made of recycled plastic bottles. Part of the 2010 Taipei International Flora Expo, it was the world's first green building made from plastic bottles.

in 2009 terms but in 2050 terms," said Sims, who is now an official with the federal Department of Housing and Urban Development. "We're making decisions based on something that has not occurred yet."[64]

Like most environmentalists, Ron Burke, the Midwest climate change director for the Union of Concerned Scientists, says that both responses to climate change—reduction of carbon emissions, or **mitigation**, and adaptation—are important. Still, he says, "If you had to argue one versus the other, which I don't think is really helpful, I think mitigation is a higher priority given the urgency with which we need to create these reductions. You see that reflected in how most cities and states are going about their planning. They're definitely doing the mitigation piece first and then moving onto adaptation."[65]

One of the biggest adaptation efforts is taking place in the Netherlands. The Dutch are spending billions to create "floating communities" that can rise with flood waters and to otherwise reengineer their long coastline. They expect to spend $100 per year per person on climate-proofing over

MITIGATION

Reducing emissions of greenhouse gases and other steps taken to curb the forces that cause climate change.

Governing States and Localities

the next century, according to the *Washington Post*. Although some say their efforts are excessive, according to the *Post*, U.S. officials have consulted with the Dutch about how to protect New Orleans and other low-lying coastal areas.[66]

Relatively few jurisdictions in the United States have turned their full attention to adaptation and planning questions. Even normally proactive California has barely paid attention to adaptation issues and is unprepared for the flooding, coastal erosion, and loss of wildlife habitat predicted to occur in coming decades due to higher temperatures.[67] Only in 2008 did Gov. Arnold Schwarzenegger issue an executive order to identify the state's biggest vulnerabilities to rising sea levels and draft an "adaptation strategy."[68]

States and local governments face a practical challenge when it comes to crafting adaptation plans. Much of the science in this area has been, not surprisingly, global in scope. Thus, planning for climate change's local impacts will require experts to downscale the large-scale data to make them applicable and useful for communities. But, according to Sims, it's imperative for states, cities, and counties to accept the need to make decisions based on scientific modeling rather than historical experience. "With all the discussion we've had on global warming, I am stunned that people haven't realized that it's actually going to occur," he said in 2007. "The ice caps are melting now. They're not going to refreeze next year because we reduce our emissions. We're going to live in that world. So plan for it."[69]

> States and local governments face a practical challenge when it comes to crafting adaptation plans. Much of the science in this area has been, not surprisingly, global in scope. Thus, planning for climate change's local impacts will require experts to downscale the large-scale data to make them applicable and useful for communities.

Issues to Watch

Growing Partisanship and Skepticism

Of course, not everyone believes we are going to be living in a world forever altered by climate change. Public opinion polls in 2009 and 2010, in fact, showed that Americans are increasingly skeptical about the alarm bells that have been sounding about climate change. A Gallup Poll in March 2010 found that nearly half of Americans—48 percent—believed that fears about global warming were "generally exaggerated." That percentage had been in the low 30s for most of the previous decade.[70] Polling by Gallup and other groups consistently found that global warming in particular and the environment in general were not considered nearly as important to the public as other issues such as the economy.

A series of small controversies helped shift opinions on the issue, including a mistake about glacier loss in the Himalayas in an Intergovernmental Panel on Climate Change report and a scandal involving European scientists whose e-mails, suggesting they had withheld contradictory data, were hacked into and released (although official inquiries cleared them of serious wrongdoing).[71]

Just as a series of mild winters in the Northern Hemisphere and a batch of devastating hurricanes had contributed to fears about global warming in earlier years, an unusually cold and snowy winter in 2010 eased such concerns for some. Sen. Jim DeMint, R-S.C., an opponent of climate change legislation, tweeted in the midst of a series of large snowfalls in the Washington, D.C., region, "It's going to keep snowing until Al Gore cries 'uncle.'"[72]

Media attention devoted to the climate change issue turned largely into disquisitions about whether all these points raised by skeptics had been blown out of proportion and why climate scientists, who appeared to have won the argument about whether global warming was real, now appeared to be on the defensive on the public relations front.

But advocates for measures addressing climate change were losing ground in Congress, as well. A cap-and-trade system that was the centerpiece of the climate change bill passed by the U.S. House in June 2009 appeared dead even before the major Senate climate change bill was introduced in April 2010. Interior Secretary Ken Salazar said during a March 2010 CNBC interview, "I think the term 'cap and trade' is not in the lexicon anymore."[73]

At the state level in 2010, a number of state legislatures debated legislation that highlighted the skepticism about global warming—notably a resolution adopted in South Dakota urging schools to offer "balanced teaching" about global warming, saying that it "is a scientific theory rather than a proven fact."

What is most striking for political scientists, as opposed to climate scientists, is not only how much the ground is shifting on this issue but how partisan it is becoming. As climate change began to emerge as an issue of pressing concern a few years ago, it was associated with Democrats such as Al Gore, and many of the leading doubters were Republicans, such as James Inhofe of Oklahoma, who chaired the Senate Environment and Public Works Committee when the GOP held the majority.

Yet many of the voices calling loudest for a policy response were Republicans. Sen. John McCain, R-Ariz., the GOP presidential nominee in 2008, had sponsored cap-and-trade legislation. Some of the most prominent governors cheerleading for action on the issue were Republicans, including Arnold Schwarzenegger of California, George E. Pataki of New York, Charlie Crist of Florida, Jon Huntsman Jr. of Utah, and Tim Pawlenty of Minnesota. It was still easier to muster support for climate change legislation among Democrats than Republicans at all levels of government, but the issue was far less partisan in nature than, say, healthcare or taxes.

By the 2010 midterm election season, however, it was hard to find a Republican who was raising climate change as an issue—unless it was to denounce it. Some Republicans who had advocated tough environmental measures are leaving the scene, such as Schwarzenegger, who signed a landmark California law capping carbon emissions in 2006 but was term-limited out of office as governor in 2010. Others have switched their position, now advocating more of a market response and shying away from strict governmental controls. That's especially true of Republicans reaching for higher office—including the presidency. Insisting on caps on energy use has become something of a nonstarter for GOP candidates. The March 2010 Gallup Poll showed that more than twice as many Republicans as Democrats say the seriousness of global warming is "greatly exaggerated."

"You see growing sentiment that climate change has been exaggerated," said Karlyn Bowman, a polling expert at the American Enterprise Institute, a conservative think tank. Still, she added, she is struck by the growing partisan divide on the issue: "The Republican-Democrat and conservative-liberal differences are quite large."[74]

Opposition to cap-and-trade legislation nearly became official Republican Party dogma. It was one of ten items on a list that some members of the Republican National Committee wanted candidates to be required to take a stand on; candidates would only receive party backing if they agreed to at least eight. The Republican National Committee rejected the idea of such a "purity test" in January. But party candidates have needed no such official sanction to express their disapproval of cap and trade. Sarah Palin had always expressed skepticism that climate change was human-made, but as governor of Alaska, she thought her state should prepare for its effects. In late 2010, she tweeted that climate science was "bogus."[75]

Also, in 2008 Republican governor Pawlenty of Minnesota appeared with Janet Napolitano, then the Democratic governor of Arizona, in a nationwide radio advertisement criticizing Congress for not addressing climate change. But appearing on NBC's *Meet the Press* in February 2010, Pawlenty, considered a likely presidential hopeful in 2012, said, "Cap and trade . . . would be a disaster." "With Tim Pawlenty, I guess he sees that there's a need to talk about climate change in a more skeptical frame to make himself more appealing in a Republican primary," said Jim DiPeso, vice president for policy and communications at Republicans for Environmental Protection.[76]

Moreover, climate change turned into a point of attack in several GOP Senate primary races in 2010. In Arizona, former representative John D. Hayworth has frequently castigated McCain for his past climate change efforts. McCain, once a cap-and-trade champion, kept mum on the issue, both at home and in Washington.

Other GOP politicians also seem to have experienced their own changes of heart. As a state senator, Scott Brown voted in 2008 in support of Massachusetts's participation in RGGI (Regional Greenhouse Gas Initiative).

During his successful campaign in a special U.S. Senate election in 2010, however, Brown expressed doubts about the science underpinning global warming theories. He explained his new position by saying that RGGI hadn't worked.

Similarly, Marco Rubio, as Speaker of the Florida House, declared in 2007 that "this nation—and ultimately the world—is headed toward emission caps."[77] He backed the idea of creating a state cap-and-trade program the following year. In his 2010 campaign for the U.S. Senate, however, Rubio has blasted Crist, his primary opponent, for having pushed the cap-and-trade idea. Rubio said that he doesn't believe the scientific evidence for human-influenced climate change.

It's true that Sen. Lindsey Graham, R-S.C., worked on drafting the main Senate climate change bill in 2010 with John Kerry, D-Mass., and Joseph Lieberman, an independent from Conn. But Graham attracted no other Republicans to the effort and was widely castigated back home in South Carolina for his work. The Charleston County GOP passed a resolution condemning Graham for undermining "Republican leadership and party solidarity for his own benefit."[78] Graham withdrew his support from the bill just before it was introduced because, he said, he was angry about Democratic plans to move immigration legislation onto the Senate floor ahead of it.

This leads straight to a chicken-and-egg question. Are many Republican leaders growing more skeptical about climate change legislation due to concerns raised by their political base? Or are GOP voters following a shift among top officials and the conservative media? "Many ordinary citizens take their cues on complex political issues from leaders of the political party that they identify with," said DiPeso, from the GOP environmental group.[79]

But Daniel J. Weiss, senior fellow and director of climate strategy at the Center for American Progress Action Fund, a Democratic-leaning group, thinks that it is public opinion that is leading the leaders in this case. He cites the frequent attacks against global-warming legislation efforts launched by Rush Limbaugh and commentators on Fox News Channel. "That has really riled up their highly conservative base," Weiss said.[80]

He also notes that elected officials are well aware of the opposition to congressional climate change legislation led by energy companies and the U.S. Chamber of Commerce—a group that announced it would spend $50 million seeking to influence the 2010 elections. "If you're a Republican, would you really stand up to them and risk getting on their wrong side," Weiss said, "when they have so much money to spend?"[81]

International Agreements

Just a couple of weeks after he was elected president in November 2008, Barack Obama offered a videotaped address to state leaders gathered at a climate change policy summit in California. "When I am president, any governor who's willing to promote clean energy will have a partner in the White House," he said.[82] When Obama came into office, he made it clear that climate change was among his highest priorities.

That was welcome news to those assembled, an audience of policymakers that had felt frustrated by the lack of attention that global warming had received under President George W. Bush. Some were openly emotional, believing Obama's remarks signaled a new day. Many state and local leaders had gotten involved in climate change policy only because of the lack of federal action—a state of affairs they felt certain was at its end.

But by the time of Obama's election, it was clear that many states and localities were already too invested in the issue simply to cede the ground to Washington. They became highly vocal lobbyists during deliberations in Congress, as well as in international forums. In contrast to the general run of environmental issues, where policies have largely been set by the federal government even though responsibilities are carried out by the states, climate change had become an issue in which states and localities had already claimed their ground. In large part because its effects are felt differently in different locales, many states and cities had become convinced of the need to formulate their own strategies and plans, even if the logjam in Washington looked like it was ready to be broken.

As it turned out, state leaders that believed greenhouse gas emissions needed to be lowered were still acting on their own, at least in the first eighteen months of the Obama presidency. Obama and other world leaders failed to reach any serious agreement at a summit in Copenhagen in December 2009, which had been designed to revamp and update the international treaty that had been written in Kyoto a dozen years earlier. And, despite White House lobbying, it seemed certain that the Senate would not pass a global warming bill with anything like the ambition of the version passed by the House in 2009.

That meant that, ultimately, the more significant news out of the California climate change policy summit in 2008 was not Obama's statement but agreements reached between American states and provinces in other countries. At that meeting, governors from thirteen states and regional leaders from four other nations signed a declaration to work together to combat global warming. Under a separate agreement, California, Illinois, and Wisconsin pledged to work with the governors of six provinces within Indonesia and Brazil to help slow tropical deforestation and land degradation through joint projects and incentive programs. "When California passed its global warming law two years ago, we were out there on an island, so we started forming partnerships everywhere we could," Gov. Arnold Schwarzenegger said.[83]

In 2009, Schwarzenegger and subnational leaders from Canada, Nigeria, France, and Algeria announced that they had formed the Club of 20 Regions (R20) to lobby their respective national governments on

Local Focus: On Global Issue, Acting Locally

In 2008, Seattle mayor Greg Nickels recalled his concern as he looked out over the Cascade Mountains during the winter 2005. The snowpack that his city relies on for both drinking water and hydroelectric power had almost failed to materialize.

"At that point, it was sort of an 'Aha' moment," he says. "Climate change went from being an esoteric issue affecting someone else in the near future to hitting us here, now."

Nickels went on to spearhead an effort among local officials to abide by the Kyoto Protocol, even though it hasn't been ratified by the U.S. Senate. More than one thousand mayors have signed on from cities that are home to a total of more than 81 million Americans, according to the U.S. Conference of Mayors. "We as mayors recognize the threat of hurricanes, drought and the lack of snowpacks" that have been linked to global warming, says Nickels, who lost his reelection bid in 2009. "It's our obligation to take action."

But there are limits on what local officials can do. They lack the authority to regulate the dominant sources of greenhouse gas emissions—power plants and vehicles. The mayors' efforts, as a result, have mostly been small-scale affairs. Many local officials lack the ability even to measure their cities' total emission levels, let alone reduce them.

In many instances, their actions appear more symbolic than substantive. Critics say that it's going to take more than the door-to-door promotion of new lightbulbs (to cite one Minneapolis initiative) or replacing inefficient streetlights to prevent global warming. "Virtually all of the actions that have been taken at the local level are symbolic," said Myron Ebell, director of energy and global warming policy at the Competitive Enterprise Institute, a business-backed advocacy group. "They are meant to gain immediate public approval for the current incumbent and put all the responsibility for achieving those future goals on some future officeholder."

Even some environmentalists concede that the mayors' efforts, although obviously well-intentioned, aren't enough to put a serious dent in carbon emissions. "It's a mixed bag," said Teri Shore, a campaign director with Friends of the Earth, an environmental group in San Francisco. "You've got a lot of cities and counties that have signed up and set goals, but the harder part comes with actually implementing those goals."

Barry G. Rabe, a University of Michigan political scientist, notes that, because of the lack of standardized emissions reporting, it's hard to know which efforts have been successful and which haven't. For example, it was only in 2008 that Chicago put forward models of the first city-specific climate change projections. At that time, Chicago mayor Richard M. Daley announced a plan to reduce the city's greenhouse gas emissions by 25 percent in 2020, compared to 1990 levels, through tougher building codes, improved transportation, reduced industrial pollution, and use of clean and renewable energy sources. "We can't solve the world's climate change problem in Chicago," Daley said, "but we can do our part."

Chicago had already drawn praise for its green rooftops program, which boasts plantings on more than two hundred buildings, including City Hall and the Target and Apple stores. But not even the cities that have been most ambitious about trying to meet climate change policies and to implement those policies and any international agreements more quickly. The group, which has received the blessing of the United Nations, was set to launch officially in 2010.

"When Obama got elected, there was a bit of a pause because we thought we'll have federal legislation and an international agreement," said Terry Tamminen, Schwarzenegger's former state EPA secretary. "But the lack of agreement in Copenhagen and, so far, the lack of an agreement in Washington has inspired states to keep going. The frustration level by

Notes

Chapter 1

1. California State University, Public Affairs, "State Budget Cuts to Impact System's Ability to Serve Students," February 20, 2009, available at www.calstate.edu/PA/News/2009/budget_feb .shtml.

2. Gale Holland, "Cal State Trustees Approve 20% Fee Hike, Faculty and Staff Furloughs," *Los Angeles Times*, July 21, 2009, available at http://latimesblogs.latimes.com/lanow/2009/07/ cal-state-trustees-approves-20-fee-hike-faculty- and-staff-furloughs.html.

3. Vincent Del Casino Jr., "California College Crunch," *Los Angeles Times*, July 16, 2009, available at http://articles.latimes.com/2009/ jul/16/opinion/oe-delcasino16.

4. Cyndee Fontana, "Students Scrape to Meet Rising State College Costs," *Fresno Bee*, July 31, 2009, available at www.fresnobee.com/local/ story/1567725.html.

5. "Total Fall Enrollment in Degree-Granting Institutions, by Attendance Status, Sex of Student, and Control of Institution: Selected Years, 1947 to 2002," *Digest of Education Statistics*, October 2008, available at http:// nces.ed.gov/programs/digest/d08/tables/ dt08_188.asp.

6. "Current-Fund Revenue of Public Degree-Granting Institutions, by Source of Funds: Selected Years, 1980–81 to 2000–01," *Digest of Education Statistics*, October 2003, available at http://nces.ed.gov/programs/digest/d04/tables/ dt04_332.asp.

7. "Appropriations from State and Local Governments for Public Degree-Granting Institutions, by State or Jurisdiction: Selected Years, 1990–91 through 2005–06," *Digest of Education Statistics*, May 2008, available at http://nces.ed.gov/programs/digest/d08/tables/ dt08_352.asp.

8. "Undergraduates Enrolled Full-Time and Part-Time, by Aid Status, Source of Aid, and Control and Type of Institution: 1999–2000," *Digest of Education Statistics*, August 2002, available at http://nces.ed.gov/programs/digest/d03/tables/ dt322.asp.

9. National Center for Education Statistics, "Average Amounts of Federal, Institutional, or State Aid Received by Undergraduates: 1999– 2000," 2000, available at www.nces.ed.gov/ surveys/npsas/table_library/tables/npsas .04.asp.

10. "Enrollment in Grades 9 to 12 in Public and Private Schools Compared with Population 14 to 17 Years of Age: Selected Years, 1889–90 to Fall 2005," *Digest of Education Statistics*, April 2005, available at http://nces.ed.gov/programs/ digest/d04/tables/dt04_056.asp.

11. National Center for Education Statistics, "Enrollment in Educational Institutions, by Level and by Control of Institution: 1869–70 to Fall 2008," 2009, available at http://nces.ed.gov/ programs/digest/d09/tables/dt09_003.asp.

12. Kenneth J. Meier, *Politics and the Bureaucracy* (Pacific Grove, Calif.: Brooks/Cole, 1993), 2.

13. Christopher Z. Mooney, "Why Do They Tax Dogs in West Virginia?: Teaching Political

Science through Comparative State Politics," *PS: Political Science & Politics* 31 (June 1998): 199–203.

14. Federation of Tax Administrators, "Comparison of State and Local Retail Sales Taxes, July 2004," available at www.taxadmin.org/fta/rate/sl_sales.html.

15. Based on a standard ordinary least squares (OLS) regression analysis in which average tuition bills at public four-year universities are the dependent variable and state appropriations as thousands of dollars per enrolled student is the dependent variable. Data taken from the National Center for Education Statistics, *Digest of Education Statistics*, available at http://nces.ed.gov/programs/digest/d04_tf.asp.

16. U.S. Bureau of the Census, "State and County Quick Facts," n.d., available at http://quickfacts.census.gov/qfd/index.html.

17. U.S. Bureau of the Census, "100 Fastest Growing Counties," March 18, 2009, available at www.census.gov/popest/housing/HU-EST2005-top100.html.

18. Helen Huntley, "Florida Population Rate Tumbles," *St. Petersburg Times*, March 28, 2008, available at www.tampabay.com/news/business/article434356.ece.

19. Daniel Elazar, *American Federalism: A View from the States* (New York: Crowell, 1966). This book has gone through three editions, the most recent of which was published in 1984.

20. Ibid., 88.

21. Maureen Moakley, "New Jersey," in *The Political Life of the American States*, ed. Alan Rosenthal and Maureen Moakley (New York: Praeger, 1984), 222.

22. Associated Press, "Many in N.J. Don't Know Enough about Politics to Complain," *Daily Journal* (Vineland, N.J.), June 3, 2003, 4A.

23. Quoted in Robert D. Putnam, *Bowling Alone* (New York: Simon & Schuster, 2000), 293.

24. Russell Hanson, "Political Culture Variations in State Economic Development Policy," *Publius* 21, no. 2 (spring 1991): 63–81; Kevin B. Smith, *The Ideology of Education* (Albany: SUNY Press, 2003).

25. Calculated by author using state rankings in 2004 and 2005 data from the U.S. Bureau of the Census, www.census.gov/statab/www/ranks.html.

26. Phillip W. Roeder, *Public Opinion and Policy Leadership in the American States* (Tuscaloosa: University of Alabama Press, 1994).

27. Bruce Wallin, "State and Local Governments Are American Too," *Political Science Teacher* 1 (1988): 1–3.

28. U.S. Bureau of the Census, "Government Employment and Payroll," n.d., available at www.census.gov/govs/apes.

29. U.S. Bureau of the Census, "State and Local Government Finances by Level of Government and by State, 2005–06," January 11, 2010, available at http://ftp2.census.gov/govs/estimate/06slsstab1a.xls.

30. Evan J. Ringquist and James C. Garand, "Policy Change in the American States," in *State and Local Politics*, ed. Ronald E. Weber and Paul Brace (New York: Chatham House, 1999).

31. David Osborne and Ted Gaebler, *Reinventing Government: How the Entrepreneurial Spirit Is Transforming the Public Sector* (New York: Plume, 1993).

Chapter 2

1. Quoted in Michael Grunwald, "The New Action Heroes," *Time*, June 25, 2007, available at www.time.com/time/nation/article/0,8599,1632736,00.html.

2. "Who Needs Washington?" *Time*, June 25, 2007.

3. Dennis Cauchon, "Federal Aid Is Top Revenue for States," *USA Today*, May 4, 2009, available at www.usatoday.com/news/nation/2009-05-04-fed-states-revenue_N.htm.

4. South Carolina Office of the Governor, "Governor to Ask White House for Waiver to Pay Down State Liabilities," March 11, 2009, available at www.scgovernor.com/news/releases/3-11-09.htm.

5. Office of the Governor of the State of Louisiana, "Governor Jindal Declines Stimulus Provision

That Would Result in an Unemployment Tax Increase on Business," February 20, 2009, available at www.gov.state.la.us/index.cfm?md=newsroom&tmp=detail&catID=2&articleID=1016&navID=12.

6. Cass Sunstein, "The Return of States' Rights," *American Prospect,* November 30, 2002, available at www.prospect.org/cs/articles?article=the_return_of_states_rights.

7. James Collier and Christopher Collier, *Decision in Philadelphia* (New York: Random House, 1986).

8. Quoted in ibid., 3.

9. Ellen Perlman, "The Preemption Beast: The Gorilla That Swallows State Laws," *Governing* magazine, August 1994, 46–51.

10. Quoted in Harry Scheiber, "The Condition of American Federalism: An Historian's View," in *American Intergovernmental Relations,* ed. Laurence J. O'Toole Jr. (Washington, D.C.: CQ Press, 2000), 71.

11. Ibid.

12. Kala Ladenheim, "History of U.S. Federalism," March 16, 1999, available at www.cas.sc.edu/poli/courses/scgov/History_of_Federalism.htm.

13. Scheiber, "Condition of American Federalism."

14. Ellis Katz, "American Federalism, Past, Present and Future," *Issues of Democracy* 2, no. 2 (1997), available at www.doge.us/govecon/AmericanFederalismPast.pdf.

15. Paul L. Posner, *The Politics of Unfunded Mandates: Whither Federalism?* (Washington, D.C.: Georgetown University Press, 1998), 13.

16. David S. Broder, "President's Unfunded Mandates Criticized," *Washington Post,* March 11, 2004, A25.

17. Timothy Conlon, "Federalism and Competing Values in the Reagan Administration," *Publius: The Journal of Federalism* 16, no. 4 (1986): 29–47.

18. Thomas J. Anton, "New Federalism and Intergovernmental Fiscal Relationships: The Implications for Health Policy," *Journal of Health Politics, Policy and Law* 22, no. 3 (1997): 691–720.

19. Richard L. Cole and John Kincaid, "Public Opinion and American Federalism: Perspectives on Taxes, Spending and Trust," *Spectrum: The Journal of State Government* 74, no. 3 (2000): 14–18.

20. "Same-Sex Marriage: Federal and State Authority," *Congressional Digest* 75 (November 1996): 263.

21. Peter Harkness, "Potomac Chronicle: Obama and the States," *Governing* magazine, January 1, 2009, 18.

22. Bardon Aronson, "The Rising Tide of Federalism," CNN.com, February 1, 2001, available at www.cnn.com/2001/LAW/02/columns/fl.aronson.federalism.02.01.

23. Alan Ehrenhalt, "Devolution in Reverse," *Governing* magazine, December 1, 2008, 8.

24. Peter Harkness, "Potomac Chronicle: Devolution? What's That?" *Governing* magazine, July 2009, 14.

25. Michael S. Greve, *Real Federalism: Why It Matters, How It Could Happen* (Washington, D.C.: AEI Press, 1999), 17.

26. Jeffrey G. Homrig, "*Alden v. Maine:* A New Genre of Federalism Shifts the Balance of Power," *California Law Review* 89, no. 1 (2001): 183–205.

27. David G. Savage, "Justices Rule U.S. Can Ban Medical Pot," *Los Angeles Times,* June 7, 2005.

28. John Dinan, "The State of American Federalism 2007–2008: Resurgent State Influence in the National Policy Process and Continued State Policy Innovation," *Publius* (May 2008): 381–415.

29. Brady Baybeck and William Lowry, "Federalism Outcomes and Ideological Preferences: The U.S. Supreme Court and Preemption Cases," *Publius: The Journal of Federalism* 30, no. 1 (2000): 73–96.

Chapter 3

1. Bill Rufty, "High-Speed Rail Authority Still Exists," *The Ledger* (Lakeland, Fla.), May 13, 2005.

2. Tom Blackburn, "Hogging the Constitution," *Palm Beach Post,* November 10, 2002.

3. In 2006, Floridians made it more difficult to approve new constitutional amendments, voting in favor for yet another amendment that requires 60 percent approval for an amendment to pass.

4. See chapter 1 for a discussion of Elazar's typology.

5. Donald Kettl, "Governor Rehnquist," *Governing* magazine, July 1999.

6. Christopher Hammons, "Was James Madison Wrong?: Rethinking the American Preference for Short, Framework-Oriented Constitutions," *American Political Science Review* 93, no. 4 (1999): 837.

7. Ibid., 840.

8. Ibid. See also John G. Kester, "Amendment Time," *Washingtonian,* March 1995.

9. Janice C. May, "Trends in State Constitutional Amendment and Revision," in *The Book of the States 2003* (Lexington, Ky.: Council of State Governments, 2003), 8.

10. Robert J. Taylor, ed., *Massachusetts, Colony to Commonwealth* (New York: Norton, 1961).

11. Quoted in Willi Paul Adams, *The First American Constitutions: Republican Ideology and the Making of the State Constitutions in the Revolutionary Era* (Chapel Hill: University of North Carolina Press, 1980), 53.

12. Quoted in ibid., 61.

13. Quoted in ibid., 207

14. Alan Tarr, *Understanding State Constitutions* (Princeton, N.J.: Princeton University Press, 1998), 121.

15. W. B. Stouffer, Cynthia Opheim, and Susan Bland Day, eds., *State and Local Politics: The Individual and the Governments* (New York: HarperCollins College Publishers, 1996).

16. Bruce Sundlun, "R.I.'s Martyr for Democracy," *Providence Journal-Bulletin,* August 11, 2002.

17. Delaware is the only state that does not refer constitutional amendments to the electorate as a whole. The legislature may enact constitutional amendments on its own if a measure receives support in two consecutive legislative sessions.

18. *The Book of the States 2001* (Lexington, Ky.: Council of State Governments, 2001), 5. In South Carolina, a majority of both houses of the legislature must vote to approve a constitutional amendment a second time, after it has passed a popular referendum, before it can go into effect.

19. Initiative and Referendum Institute, www .iandrinstitute.org. The institute's Web site includes detailed time lines of initiative and referendum activity in each state.

20. Juan B. Elizondo Jr., "Ratliff: Time to Rewrite Constitution; Lawmaker Joined by Watchdog," *Austin American-Statesman,* October 28, 1999.

21. *The Book of the States 2003* (Lexington, Ky.: Council of State Governments, 2003), 3–4.

22. Warren Richey, "Unique Law Lets Florida Voters Make Changes to Constitution," *Christian Science Monitor,* May 8, 1998.

23. Quoted in Alan Ehrenhalt, "Vermont's Judicial Distillery," *Governing* magazine, February 2000, available at www.governing.com/archive/ archive/2000/feb/assess.txt.

24. Hammons, "Was James Madison Wrong?" 839.

25. Joni James, "Voters Hold Key to Big Shake-Up in State Cabinet: The Revision Would Eliminate Three Posts, Give the Governor More Power, and Shift Control of Education Policy," *Orlando Sentinel,* October 20, 1998, D1.

26. Stuart MacCorkle and Dick Smith, *Texas Government* (New York: McGraw-Hill, 1960).

27. Daniel Elazar, *American Federalism: A View from the States,* 3rd ed. (New York: Harper & Row, 1984), 115.

28. Hammons, "Was James Madison Wrong?" 846.

29. See ibid. for a more complete argument along these lines.

30. Melinda Gann Hall, "State Judicial Politics: Rules, Structures, and the Political Game," in *American State and Local Politics,* ed. Ronald Weber and Paul Brace (New York: Chatham House, 1999).

31. Ibid., 136.

32. "Gubernatorial Veto Authority with Respect to Major Budget Bill(s)," National Conference of State Legislatures, December 2008, available at www.ncsl.org/IssuesResearch/BudgetTax/

GubernatorialVetoAuthoritywithRespectto Major/tabid/12640/Default.aspx.

33. Andrew Taylor, "Line Item Budget Barely Trims Spending at State Level," *Denver Rocky Mountain News,* January 15, 1995.

34. Scott Milfred, "Some Want to Clip Gubernatorial Wings: A Resolution in the Legislature Would Curtail Wisconsin Governor's Exceptionally Broad Veto Power," *Wisconsin State Journal,* September 23, 2001, A1.

35. Virginia Gray, Herbert Jacob, and Kenneth N. Vines, eds., *Politics in the American States: A Comparative Analysis* (Boston: Little, Brown, 1983).

36. In 2003, the U.S. Supreme Court invalidated laws prohibiting sodomy. Until that time, Alabama, Florida, Idaho, Louisiana, Massachusetts, Mississippi, North Carolina, South Carolina, Utah, and Virginia had laws that explicitly prohibited sodomy. Kansas, Oklahoma, and Texas prohibited same-sex sodomy only. Lambda Legal Defense and Education Fund Web site, www .lambda.org.

37. Alexander Hamilton, James Madison, and John Jay, *The Federalist Papers,* ed. Charles Kesler and Clinton Rossiter (New York: Penguin Putnam, 1961), 76.

38. Ibid. Hamilton, Madison, and Jay envisioned other safeguards as well. One was the well-known principle of the separation of powers among the three branches of government. The other was the large size of the republic itself. Previous theorists of democracy had worried about republics that became too large to govern. In *The Federalist,* No. 10, Madison makes the novel claim that a more extensive republic would be less likely to succumb to factionalism than the smaller republics of old.

39. Quoted in David Broder, *Democracy Derailed: Initiative Campaigns and the Power of Money* (New York: Harcourt, 2000), 27.

40. Ibid.

41. "The History of Initiative and Referendum in the United States," Initiative and Referendum Institute, available at www.iandrinstitute.org.

42. Richard Ellis, *Democratic Delusions: The Initiative Process in America* (Lawrence, Kans.: University Press of Kansas, 2002).

43. Broder, *Democracy Derailed.*

44. Keon S. Chi, "Emerging Trends Shaping State Governments: 2005 and Beyond," in *The Book of the States 2005* (Lexington, Ky.: Council of State Governments, 2005).

45. Broder, *Democracy Derailed,* 1.

46. Lawrence F. Keller, "Municipal Charters," *National Civic Review* 91, no. 1 (spring 2002): 57.

Chapter 4

1. Anya Sostek, "Vallejo's Fiscal Freefall," *Governing* magazine, November 2008, available at www.governing.com/print/article/vallejos-fiscal-freefall.

2. Lucy Dadayan and Donald J. Boyd, "Recession or No Recession, State Tax Revenues Remain Negative," Rockefeller Institute of Government, Albany, N.Y., January 2010, 3.

3. Council of State Governments, "Federal Assistance," 2010, available at www.statereco very.org/federal-assistance.

4. Elizabeth McNichol and Nicholas Johnson, "Recession Continues to Batter State Budgets; State Responses Could Slow Recovery," Center on Budget and Policy Priorities, January 28, 2010, available at www.cbpp.org/cms/?fa= view&id=711.

5. "State-Local Tax Burdens, All States, 2008," Tax Foundation, 2010, available at www .taxfoundation.org/files/sl_ burden_1977–2008– 200808073.pdf.

6. These figures and many that follow come from U.S. Department of Commerce, *Statistical Abstract of the United States, 2010* (Washington, D.C.: U.S. Census Bureau, 2010), and refer to the fiscal year that concluded in 2006, one of the last years for which such data are available. This figure is derived from Table 424.

7. Ibid.

8. *The Fiscal Survey of States* (Washington, D.C.: National Governors Association and National Association of State Budget Officers, fall 2009), vii.

9. U.S. Department of Commerce, *Statistical Abstract of the United States,* Table 424.

10. "State Cigarette Excise Tax Rates and Rankings," Campaign for Tobacco-Free Kids, January 26, 2010, available at www.tobaccofreekids.org/research/factsheets/pdf/0097.pdf.

11. U.S. Department of Commerce, *Statistical Abstract of the United States,* Table 435.

12. Estimated sales tax calculated at Minnesota online sales tax calculator for Bloomington, Minnesota, www.taxes.state.mn.us/taxcalc/index.shtml.

13. Katherine Barrett, Richard Greene, Michele Mariani, and Anya Sostek, "The Way We Tax: A 50-State Report," *Governing* magazine, February 2003, available at www.governing.com/gpp/2003/gp3intro.htm.

14. Donald Bruce, William F. Fox, and LeAnn Luna, "State and Local Sales Tax Revenue Losses from E-Commerce," Center for Business and Economic Research, University of Tennessee, Knoxville, April 13, 2009, available at http://cber.bus.utk.edu/ecomm/ecom0409.pdf.

15. Cited in Penelope Lemov, "The Untaxables," *Governing* magazine, July 2002.

16. Alan Greenblatt, "The Sales Tax Goes Online," *Governing* magazine, December 2005.

17. "Frequently Asked Questions," Streamlined Sales Tax Governing Board, available at www.streamlinedsalestax.org/index.php?page=faqs.

18. Saul Hansell, "Court to Amazon: Keep Paying Sales Tax," Bits Blog, January 13, 2009, available at http://bits.blogs.nytimes.com/2009/01/13/court-to-amazon-keep-collecting-sales-tax-to-new-yorkers.

19. U.S. Department of Commerce, *Statistical Abstract of the United States,* Table 424.

20. The effective tax rate information for the nation and New Hampshire can be found in ibid., Table 436.

21. Ibid., Table 443.

22. "2004 State Expenditure Report," National Association of State Budget Officers, Washington, D.C., 14.

23. *Funding Gaps 2006* (Washington, D.C.: Education Trust, 2006). Based on 2003–2004 U.S. Department of Education and U.S. Census Bureau data.

24. Ibid.

25. Alan Greenblatt, "The Loathsome Local Levy," *Governing* magazine, October 2001.

26. U.S. Department of Commerce, *Statistical Abstract of the United States,* Table 424. Corporate income taxes account for an additional 4 percent of state and local tax revenues.

27. Fifteen states allow certain localities to impose income taxes as well, but for the most part, income tax receipts are a minor source of funds for cities and counties.

28. U.S. Department of Commerce, *Statistical Abstract of the United States,* Table 430.

29. "State Individual Income Tax Collections, 2007," Tax Foundation, February 5, 2009, available at www.taxfoundation.org/taxdata/show/282.html.

30. U.S. Department of Commerce, *Statistical Abstract of the United States,* Table 424.

31. Ibid.

32. *Fiscal Survey of States*, 18.

33. U.S. Department of Commerce, *Statistical Abstract of the United States,* Table 424.

34. Ibid., Table 419.

35. "2008 State Expenditure Report," National Association of State Budget Officers, Washington, D.C., 2.

36. Ibid., 9.

37. U.S. Department of Commerce, *Statistical Abstract of the United States,* Table 424.

38. Alan Greenblatt, "Enemies of the State," *Governing* magazine, June 2002.

39. "State-Local Tax Burdens, All States, 2008."

40. U.S. Department of Commerce, *Statistical Abstract of the United States,* Table 441.

41. "Personal Income Per Capita, 2007," *State and Local Sourcebook*, online supplement to *Governing* magazine, 2010, available at http://sourcebook.governing.com/subtopicresults.jsp?ind=677.

42. "State-Local Tax Burdens, All States, 2008."

43. See the Mayflower Compact for further insights into the mindset of the founders of the Massachusetts Bay Colony, available at www.pilgrimhall.org/compact.htm.

44. "Total State & Local Spending Per Capita, 2006," *State and Local Sourcebook*, online supplement to *Governing* magazine, 2010, available at http://sourcebook.governing.com/subtopicresults.jsp?ind=697; "State-Local Tax Burdens, All States, 2008."

45. John E. Petersen, "Guide to Municipal Finance: Credit Raters Make Their Mark," *Governing* magazine, June 2005.

46. U.S. Department of Commerce, *Statistical Abstract of the United States*, Table 423.

47. See "Budget Processes in the States," National Association of State Budget Officers, Washington, D.C., January 2002, for a detailed discussion of the state budget process.

48. These states are Arizona, Arkansas, Connecticut, Hawaii, Indiana, Kentucky, Maine, Minnesota, Montana, Nebraska, Nevada, New Hampshire, North Carolina, North Dakota, Ohio, Oregon, Texas, Virginia, Washington, Wisconsin, and Wyoming. "Budget Processes in the States," National Association of State Budget Officers, Washington, D.C., summer 2008, 1.

49. For a detailed discussion of state balanced budget requirements, see "Legislative Budget Procedures: A Guide to Appropriations and Budget Processes in the States, Commonwealths and Territories," National Conference of State Legislatures, November 2008, available at www.ncsl.org/?TabID=12669.

50. Robert Zahradnik, "Rainy Day Funds: Opportunities for Reform," Center on Budget and Policy Priorities, March 9, 2005, available at www.cbpp.org/3–9-05sfp.htm.

51. "Total State & Local Spending Per Capita, 2006."

52. *State and Local Sourcebook*, online supplement to *Governing* magazine, 2010, available at http://sourcebook.governing.com/topicmain.jsp?cat=20#20.

53. Ibid.

54. U.S. Department of Commerce, *Statistical Abstract of the United States*, Table 444.

55. "2008 State Expenditure Report," 13.

56. Ibid., 4.

57. "State Higher Education Finance Early Release 2008," State Higher Education Executive Officers, February 9, 2009, available at www.sheeo.org/finance/shef/SHEF%20FY08%20Early%20Release%202.pdf.

58. *Fiscal Survey of States*, 6.

59. "2008 State Expenditure Report," 47.

60. Ibid., 44.

61. Donna Cohen Ross, Marian Jarlenski, Samantha Artiga, and Caryn Marks, "A Foundation for Health Reform: Findings of a 50 State Survey of Eligibility Rules, Enrollment and Renewal Procedures, and Cost-Sharing Practices in Medicaid and CHIP for Children and Parents during 2009," Center on Budget and Policy Priorities and Kaiser Commission on Medicaid and the Uninsured, Washington, D.C., December 2009.

62. U.S. Department of Commerce, *Statistical Abstract of the United States*, Table 8.

63. Ibid., Table 424.

64. Cynthia Miller, "Leavers, Stayers, and Cyclers: An Analysis of the Welfare Caseload," Manpower Demonstration Research Corporation, New York, November 2002. For a full discussion of the effects of welfare reform, see also Alan Weil, "Ten Things Everyone Should Know about Welfare Reform," no. A-52, Urban Institute, Washington, D.C., May 9, 2002.

65. "2008 State Expenditure Report," 33.

66. U.S. Department of Commerce, *Statistical Abstract of the United States*, Table 424.

67. "2008 State Expenditure Report," 66.

68. "Total State & Local Highway Spending (in millions), 2006," *State and Local Sourcebook*,

online supplement to *Governing* magazine, available at http://sourcebook.governing.com/subtopicresults.jsp?ind=627.

69. "2007 State Expenditure Report," National Association of State Budget Officers, Washington, D.C., 66.

70. "2008 State Expenditure Report," 67.

71. "The Trillion Dollar Gap: Underfunded State Retirement Systems and the Road to Reform," Pew Center on the States, Washington, D.C., February 18, 2010, available at www.pewcenteronthestates.org/report_detail.aspx?id=56695.

72. Greenblatt, "Enemies of the State."

73. Bill Piper, *A Brief Analysis of Voter Behavior Regarding Tax Initiatives* (Washington, D.C.: Citizen Lawmaker Press).

74. This section is adapted from the February 2003 *Governing* magazine special issue on state tax systems; see Barrett et al., "Way We Tax."

Chapter 5

1. E-mail correspondence with Larry J. Sabato, October 10, 2008.

2. E-mail correspondence with Larry J. Sabato, March 15, 2010.

3. Quoted in Alan Greenblatt, "Changing U.S. Electorate," *CQ Researcher*, May 30, 2008, 461.

4. Quoted in Thomas B. Edsall, "Census a Clarion Call for Democrats, GOP," *Washington Post*, July 8, 2001, 1A.

5. Earl Black and Merle Black, *Divided America* (New York: Simon and Schuster, 2007), 10.

6. Mark Hugo Lopez and Paul Taylor, "Dissecting the U.S. Electorate: Most Diverse in U.S. History," Pew Research Center, April 30, 2009, available at http://pewresearch.org/assets/pdf/dissecting-2008-electorate.pdf.

7. Steven Hill, *Fixing Elections* (New York: Routledge, 2002), 119.

8. Quoted in Alan Greenblatt, "Blueburbs," *Governing* magazine, October 2008, 22.

9. Ibid.

10. Caroline J. Tolbert, John A. Grummel, and Daniel A. Smith, "The Effects of Ballot Initiatives on Voter Turnout in the American States," *American Politics Research* 29, no. 6 (2001): 625–648.

11. Interview with Rhodes Cook, December 11, 2006.

12. "Q&A with Bob Levey," *Washington Post*, September 16, 2003, available at http://discuss.washingtonpost.com/wp-srv/zforum/03/r_metro_levey091603.htm.

13. Kevin J. Coleman, Thomas H. Neale, and Joseph E. Cantor, "The Election Process in the United States," Congressional Research Service, Washington, D.C., July 6, 1995, 69.

14. National Conference of State Legislatures, "Straight-Ticket Voting," available at www.ncsl.org/programs/legismgt/elect/straight_ticket.htm.

15. Election Data Services, *The Election Data Book: A Statistical Portrait of Voting in America* (Lanham, Md.: Bernan Press, 1992), App.

16. Kay Lawson, "How State Laws Undermine Parties," in *Elections American Style*, ed. A. James Reichley (Washington, D.C.: Brookings Institution, 1987), 241.

17. Cited in William C. Binning, Larry E. Esterly, and Paul A. Sracic, *Encyclopedia of American Parties, Campaigns, and Elections* (Westport, Conn.: Greenwood Press, 1999), 95.

18. Phone interview with Richard Winger, September 11, 2003.

19. "Jimmy Carter Supports Ballot Access Reform," *Ballot Access News*, August 1, 2003, 3, available at www.ballot-access.org/2003/0801.html.

20. Lawson, "How State Laws Undermine Parties," 246.

21. Binning, Esterly, and Sracic, *Encyclopedia of American Parties*, 95.

22. Dan Eggen and Amy Goldstein, "Voter-Fraud Complaints by GOP Drove Dismissals," *Washington Post*, May 14, 2007, A4.

23. Andrew Hacker, "Obama: The Price of Being Black," *New York Review of Books*, September 25, 2008, available at www.nybooks.com/articles/21771.

24. Phone interview with Curtis Gans, September 4, 2003.

25. Phone interview with Steven Hill, September 11, 2003.

26. Interview with Ruy Teixeira, April 2006.

27. Alan Greenblatt, "Slow March to the Polls," *Governing* magazine, June 2006, 17.

28. Barbara G. Salmore and Stephen A. Salmore, *New Jersey Politics and Government*, 2nd ed. (Lincoln: University of Nebraska Press, 1998), 128.

29. See "Texas Politics," Liberal Arts Instructional Technology Services, University of Texas at Austin, available at http://texaspolitics.lamc .utexas.edu/html/exec/index.html.

30. Associated Press, "The Decatur Daily on Windom Candidacy," October 4, 2001.

31. Rob Gurwitt, "The Lone Comptroller," *Governing* magazine, October 2003, 68.

32. Quoted in Alan Greenblatt, "Where Campaign Money Flows," *Governing* magazine, November 2002, 44.

33. Alan Greenblatt, "The Avengers General," *Governing* magazine, May 2003, 54.

34. Zach Patton, "Robe Warriors," *Governing* magazine, March 2006, 34.

35. Initiative and Referendum Institute Web site, www.iandrinstitute.org.

36. John F. Camobreco, "Preferences, Fiscal Policy, and the Initiative Process," *Journal of Politics* 60, no. 3 (August 1998): 822.

37. Quoted in James Dao, "Same-Sex Marriage Key to Some G.O.P. Races," *New York Times*, November 4, 2004, P4.

38. Simon Jackman, "Same-Sex Marriage Ballot Initiatives and Conservative Mobilization in the 2004 Election," presentation, available at http://jackman.stanford.edu/papers/RISS Presentation.pdf.

39. Quoted in Alan Greenblatt, "Some Presidential Politics Is Local," *New York Times*, October 10, 2004, Sec. 4, 5.

40. Alan Greenblatt, "Total Recall," *Governing* magazine, September 2003, 27.

41. Phone interview with Randall Gnant, August 7, 2003.

42. V. O. Key, *Public Opinion and American Democracy* (New York: Knopf, 1964), 7.

43. Interview with Doug Duncan, November 15, 2006.

44. See especially Robert S. Erikson, Gerald C. Wright, and John D. McIver, *Statehouse Democracy: Public Opinion and Policy in the American States* (New York: Cambridge University Press, 1993).

45. Paul Brace, Kellie Sims-Butler, Kevin Arceneaux, and Martin Johnson, "Public Opinion in the American States: New Perspectives Using National Survey Data," *American Journal of Political Science* 46, no. 1 (January 2002): 173–189.

46. Susan Herbst, "How State-Level Policy Managers 'Read' Public Opinion," in *Navigating Public Opinion: Polls, Policy, and the Future of American Democracy,* ed. Jeff Manza, Fay Lomax Cook, and Benjamin I. Page (New York: Oxford University Press, 2002), 176.

47. Phone interview with Greg Shaw, September 3, 2003.

48. Phone interview with Paul Brace, September 10, 2003.

Chapter 6

1. Gabriel García Márquez, *One Hundred Years of Solitude,* trans. Gregory Rabassa (New York: Everyman's Library, 1995), 171.

2. Karen Tumulty, "The End of a Revolution," *Time,* October 16, 2006, 30.

3. Alan Greenblatt, "The Disengaging Voter," *CQ Weekly,* October 24, 1998, 2880.

4. Ed Kilgore, "Diagnosing Dems," *Blueprint*, May 17, 2006, available at www.ndol.org/ndol_ci .cfm?kaid=127&subid=171&contentid=253867.

5. Quoted in Mark Leibovich, "The Tea-Party Primary," *New York Times Magazine,* January 10, 2010, 29.

6. Quoted in Alan Greenblatt, "Wired to Win," *Governing* magazine, October 2006, 26.

7. Quoted in Alan Greenblatt, "Politics and Marketing Merge in Parties' Bid for Relevance," *Congressional Quarterly Weekly Report,* August 16, 1997, 1967.

8. Jeff Greenfield, "Hayes's Ride," *Washington Monthly,* March 2003.

9. Alvin Kess, *Politics in New York State* (Syracuse, N.Y.: Syracuse University Press, 1965), 29.

10. David R. Mayhew, *Placing Parties in American Politics: Organization, Electoral Settings and Government Activity in the 20th Century* (Princeton, N.J.: Princeton University Press, 1986), esp. 24.

11. Quoted in Bertil L. Hanson, "County Commissioners of Oklahoma," *Midwest Journal of Political Science* 9 (1965): 396.

12. Joel H. Sibley, "The Rise and Fall of American Political Parties, 1790–1990," in *The Parties Respond: Changes in the American Party System,* ed. L. Sandy Maisel (Boulder, Colo.: Westview Press, 1990), 9.

13. Mayhew, *Placing Parties in American Politics,* 105.

14. Ibid., 185.

15. John F. Bibby and Thomas M. Holbrook, "Parties and Elections," in *Politics in the American States: A Comparative Analysis,* 7th ed., ed. Virginia Gray, Russell L. Hanson, and Herbert Jacobs (Washington, D.C.: CQ Press, 1999), 71.

16. John F. Bibby, "State and Local Parties in a Candidate-Centered Age," in *American State and Local Politics: Directions for the 21st Century,* ed. Ronald E. Weber and Paul Brace (New York: Chatham House, 1999), 198.

17. Rhodes Cook, "Republican Brawls through the Century Helped Define Party for Years to Come," *Congressional Quarterly Weekly Report,* April 6, 1996, 942.

18. John R. Schmidt and Wayne W. Whalen, "Credentials Contests at the 1968—and 1972—Democratic National Conventions," *Harvard Law Review* 82 (May 1969): 1456.

19. Alan Greenblatt, "History: Winds of War Blew through Chicago," *Congressional Quarterly Weekly Report,* August 17, 1996, 23.

20. Bibby "State and Local Parties," 199.

21. Peter W. Wielhower and Brad Lockerbie, "Party Contacting and Political Participation, 1952–90," *American Journal of Political Science* 38 (February 1994): 213.

22. See John H. Kessel, "Ray Bliss and the Development of the Ohio Republican Party during the 1950s," in *Politics, Professionalism and Power: Modern Party Organization and the Legacy of Ray C. Bliss,* ed. John C. Green (Lanham, Md.: University Press of America, 1994), 49–50.

23. Interview with Lee Herrington, September 2002.

24. Leon D. Epstein, *Political Parties in the American Mold* (Madison: University of Wisconsin Press, 1986), 155.

25. Michael McDonald, "2008 General Election Voter Registration Statistics," United States Election Project, March 3, 2009, available at http://elections.gmu.edu/Registration_2008G.html.

26. Malcolm E. Jewell and Sarah M. Morehouse, *Political Parties and Elections in American States,* 4th ed. (Washington, D.C.: CQ Press, 2001), 76.

27. Bibby, "State and Local Parties," 198.

28. Bibby and Holbrook, "Parties and Elections," 70.

29. Ibid., 71.

30. Quoted in Ruth Marcus, "Party Spending Unleashed; Justices Say Independence from Candidate Is Key," *Washington Post,* June 27, 1996, A1.

31. Alan Greenblatt, "Soft Money: The Root of All Evil or a Party-Building Necessity?" *Congressional Quarterly Weekly Report,* September 26, 1997, 2064.

32. Don Van Natta Jr. and Richard A. Oppel Jr., "Parties Set Up Groups to Elude Soft Money Ban," *New York Times,* November 2, 2002, A1.

33. Agustín Armendariz and Aron Pilhofer, "McCain-Feingold Changes State Party Spending," Center for Public Integrity, May 26, 2005, available at www.publicintegrity.org/partylines/report.aspx?aid=690.

34. Interview with Larry J. Sabato, May 2002.

35. Tim Storey and Gene Rose, "GOP #1 First Time in 50 Years," *State Legislatures* 12 (December 2002): 12–17.

36. Alan Greenblatt, "Undoing the Split," *Governing* magazine, February 2009.

37. Jewell and Morehouse, *Political Parties and Elections,* 22–23.

38. "Changing Hands," *Governing* magazine, January 2003, 24.

39. Mayhew, *Placing Parties in American Politics,* 291.

40. "New Hampshire District Opposes Kindergarten Mandate," *Penton Insight,* January 8, 2009. A 2007 state law mandated public kindergarten, but a number of school districts sued the state, challenging the law was an unfunded mandate.

41. Mayhew, *Placing Parties in American Politics,* 292–293.

42. Jason Szep, "Youth Turnout in Election Biggest in 20 Years," Reuters, November 8, 2006.

43. Emily Hoban Kirby and Kei Kawashima-Ginsberg, "The Youth Vote in 2008," The Center for Information and Research on Civic Learning and Engagement, August 17, 2009, available at www.civicyouth.org/PopUps/ FactSheets/FS_youth_Voting_2008_ updated_6.22.pdf.

44. Jim Reagen, "Scozzafava: Race Became 'Referendum on Issues Far from Here,'" *Watertown Daily Times,* November 1, 2009, available at www.watertowndailytimes.com/ article/20091101/NEWS05/311019896.

45. Alan Ehrenhalt, "Political Pawns," *Governing* magazine, July 2000, 20.

46. Alan Greenblatt, "'Big Tent' Advocates Look Likely to Defeat Abortion Measure," *Congressional Quarterly Weekly Report,* January 10, 1998, 89.

47. Martin P. Wattenberg, *The Decline of American Political Parties, 1952–1992* (Cambridge, Mass.: Harvard University Press, 1994), x.

48. Quoted in Cathy Newman and Ben White, "States Left to Pick Reform Ticket," *Washington Post,* August 27, 2000, A5.

49. Quoted in Joel Siegel, "Party's over for Liberals," *Daily News,* February 24, 2003, 20.

50. Greenblatt, "Politics and Marketing," 1967.

51. "Independents Take Center Stage in Obama Era," Pew Research Center for People and the Press, May 21, 2009, available at http:// people-press.org/report/517/political-values-and-core-attitudes.

52. Larry M. Bartels, "Partisanship and Voting Behavior, 1952–1996," *American Journal of Political Science* 44 (January 2000): 35.

53. Ibid., 36–37.

54. Quoted in Greenblatt, "Politics and Marketing," 1967.

55. Phone interview with Daniel Millenson, July 2006.

56. "State Divestment Legislation," National Conference of State Legislatures, April 9, 2008, available at www.ncsl.org/default.aspx?tabid= 13297.

57. Paul S. Herrnson, Ronald G. Shaiko, and Clyde Wilcox, *The Interest Group Connection: Electioneering, Lobbying and Policymaking in Washington,* 2nd ed. (Washington, D.C.: CQ Press, 2004), xiii.

58. Frank J. Sorauf, *Political Parties in the American System* (Boston: Little, Brown, 1964), 13.

59. Clive S. Thomas and Ronald J. Hrebenar, "Interest Groups in the States," in *Politics in the American States: A Comparative Analysis,* 8th ed., ed. Virginia Gray and Russell L. Hanson (Washington, D.C.: CQ Press, 2004), 114–115.

60. Leah Rush, "Hired Guns," The Center for Public Integrity, December 20, 2007, available at http://projects.publicintegrity.org/hiredguns/ report.aspx?aid=957.

61. Virginia Gray and David Lowery, "Interest Representation in the States," in *American State and Local Politics,* 267.

62. Quoted in Alan Rosenthal, *The Third House: Lobbyists and Lobbying in the States,* 2nd ed. (Washington, D.C.: CQ Press, 2001), 17.

63. Quoted in Alan Greenblatt, "Squeezing the Federal Turnip," *Governing* magazine, March 2003, 28.

64. Quoted in Matt Canham, "Utah Cities Are Shelling Out for D.C. Lobbyists," *Salt Lake Tribune,* June 8, 2008.

65. Christopher Swope, "Winning without Steaks and Cigars," *Governing* magazine, November 2000. See also Rob Gurwitt, "Cookie-Jar Clampdown," *Governing* magazine, April 2007.

66. Rosenthal, *Third House,* 78.

67. Ibid., 45.

68. Quoted in Alan Greenblatt, "Secondhand Spokesmen," *Governing* magazine, April 2002, available at www.governing.com/archive/archive/2002/apr/tobacco.txt.

69. Quoted in Rosenthal, *Third House,* 61.

70. Clive S. Thomas and Ronald J. Hrebenar, "Lobby Clout," *State Legislatures* (April 1999).

71. Thomas and Hrebenar, "Interest Groups in the States," 121–122.

72. Alan Greenblatt, "Real Power," *Governing* magazine, June 2006, 46.

73. Phone interview with Alan Rosenthal, February 6, 2007.

Chapter 7

1. Quoted in Philp D. Duncan and Christine C. Lawrence, *Congressional Quarterly's Politics in America 1998* (Washington, D.C.: CQ Press, 1997), 755.

2. William M. Bulger, *While the Music Lasts: My Life in Politics* (Boston: Houghton Mifflin, 1996), 71.

3. Alexander Hamilton, *Federalist* No. 73, available at http://thomas.loc.gov/home/fedpapers/fed_73.html.

4. Bob Bergren, presentation at the Council of State Governments western regional meeting, October 7, 2009.

5. Phone interview with Jim Abeler, April 2, 2008.

6. Quoted in Alan Greenblatt, "Renegade Retribution," *Governing* magazine, May 2008, 22.

7. Quoted in Rob Gurwitt, "The Riskiest Business," *Governing* magazine, March 2001, 21.

8. Phone interview with bill clerk, New York state legislature, October 26, 2009.

9. Phone interview with bill clerk with Montana Legislative Services Division, March 13, 2007.

10. Associated Press, "Wisconsin Governor Signs Bill to Increase Efforts to Kill Deer to Fight Fatal Disease," May 20, 2002.

11. Alan Greenblatt, "Fit to Be Tied," *Governing* magazine, August 2001, 20.

12. Quoted in Alan Greenblatt, "The Date-Checking Game," *Governing* magazine, October 2006, 17.

13. Quoted in Jennifer Steinhauer, "At State Level, More Attempts to Limit Guns," *New York Times,* April 15, 2008, A1.

14. Judith C. Meredith, *Lobbying on a Shoestring,* 2nd ed. (Dover, Mass.: Auburn House Publishing, 1989), 4.

15. Alan Greenblatt, "Health Crusader," *Governing* magazine, November 2001, 33.

16. Greenblatt, "Fit to Be Tied," 20.

17. Quoted in Andy Sher, "GOP Claims Strides on Issues," *Chattanooga Times Free Press,* June 21, 2009, A1.

18. Alan Rosenthal, *Engines of Democracy* (Washington, D.C.: CQ Press, 2009), 310.

19. Quoted in Josh Goodman, "Smoked Out," *Governing* magazine, October 2009, 17.

20. Quoted in ibid.

21. Virginia Gray and David Lowery, "Where Do Policy Ideas Come From? A Study of Minnesota Legislators and Staffers," *Journal of Public Administration Research and Theory* 10 (January 2000): 573–597.

22. See Gary F. Moncrief, Joel A. Thompson, and Karl T. Kurtz, "Old Statehouse Ain't What It Used to Be," *Legislative Studies Quarterly* 21, no. 1 (February 1996): 57–72.

23. MSNBC interview with Amy Klobuchar, July 1, 2009.

24. Rosenthal, *Engines of Democracy*, 84.

25. Interview with Rosalind Kurita, October 7, 2002.

26. Alan Rosenthal, *Governors and Legislatures: Contending Powers* (Washington, D.C.: CQ Press, 1990), 187.

27. Diane D. Blair, *Arkansas Politics and Government* (Lincoln: University of Nebraska Press, 1988), 182, cited in Rosenthal, *Governors and Legislatures*.

28. Katherine Barrett and Richard Greene, "B&G Interview: Questions for John Turcotte," February 1, 2008, available at www.governing .com/column/bg-interview-questions-john-turcotte.

29. John Turcotte, presentation at the annual meeting of the National Conference of State Legislatures, July 21, 2009.

30. Alan Rosenthal, Burdett Loomis, John Hibbing, and Karl Kurtz, *Republic on Trial: The Case for Representative Democracy* (Washington, D.C.: CQ Press, 2003), 26.

31. Wes Clarke, "The Divided Government and Budget Conflict in the U.S. States," *Legislative Studies Quarterly* 23, no. 1 (February 1998): 5.

32. Greenblatt, "Fit to Be Tied."

33. Quoted in Alan Greenblatt, "Reformer in Power," *Governing* magazine, January 2009, 20.

34. Meredith, *Lobbying on a Shoestring*, 34.

35. Edmund Burke, "The English Constitutional System," in *Representation*, ed. Hannah Pitkin (New York: Atherton Press, 1969).

36. Quoted in Christopher Swope, "Winning without Steak and Cigars," *Governing* magazine, November 2000, 40.

37. Quoted in Alan Ehrenhalt, "Putting Practice into Theory," *Governing* magazine, November 2000, 6.

38. Quoted in Rosenthal, *Engines of Democracy*, 237.

39. Alan Ehrenhalt, *The United States of Ambition: Politicians, Power and the Pursuit of Office*

(New York: Times Books/Random House, 1991), 158.

40. Foster Church, "Just like a Woman," *Governing* magazine, September 1990, 26.

41. Richard A. Clucas, "Principal-Agent Theory and the Power of State House Speakers," *Legislative Studies Quarterly* 26, no. 2 (May 2001): 319–338.

42. Quoted in Alan Greenblatt, "The Mapmaking Mess," *Governing* magazine, January 2001, 23.

43. Ibid., 22.

44. David Rosenbaum, "Campaign Season," *New York Times*, October 3, 2002, 24.

45. Rosenthal et al., *Republic on Trial*, 69.

46. Howard Troxler, "Choice for Attorney General Not So Easy," *St. Petersburg Times*, October 18, 2002, 1B.

47. Quoted in Alan Greenblatt, "Real Power," *Governing* magazine, June 2006, 46.

48. Otis White, "Making Laws Is No Job for Lawyers These Days," *Governing* magazine, June 1994, 27.

49. Kathleen Dolan and Lynne E. Ford, "Change and Continuity among Women Legislators: Evidence from Three Decades," *Political Research Quarterly* 50 (March 1997): 137–152.

50. "Women in State Legislatures 2007," Center for American Women and Politics, January 2007, available at www.cawp.rutgers.edu/Facts/ Officeholders/stleg.pdf.

51. Renee Loth, "The Matriarchy Up North," *Boston Globe*, April 30, 2009, 15.

52. Interview with Barbara Lee, October 8, 2002.

53. Thomas H. Little, Dana Dunn, and Rebecca E. Dean, "A View from the Top: Gender Differences in Legislative Priorities among State Legislative Leaders," *Women and Politics* 22, no. 4 (2001): 29–50.

54. Donald E. Whistler and Mark C. Ellickson, "The Incorporation of Women in State Legislatures: A Description," *Women and Politics* 22, no. 2 (1999): 84.

55. Ibid.

56. Michael B. Berkman and Robert E. O'Connor, "Do Women Legislators Matter: Female Legislators and State Abortion Policy," *American Politics Quarterly* 21, no. 1 (January 1993): 105.

57. Kerry L. Haynie, *African American Legislators in the American States* (New York: Columbia University Press, 2001), 19.

58. Ibid., 2.

59. Ibid., 25.

60. Bernard Grofman and Lisa Handley, "Impact of the Voting Rights Act on Black Representation in Southern State Legislatures," *Legislative Studies Quarterly* 16 (1991): 111–128.

61. Malcolm E. Jewell and Samuel C. Patterson, *The Legislative Process in the States* (New York: Random House, 1966), 138.

62. William Pound, "State Legislative Careers: Twenty-Five Years of Reform," in *Changing Patterns in State Legislative Careers,* ed. Gary F. Moncrief and Joel A. Thompson (Ann Arbor: University of Michigan Press, 1992).

63. James D. King, "Changes in Professionalism in U.S. State Legislatures," *Legislative Studies Quarterly* 25, no. 3 (May 2000): 327–343.

64. Wade Rawlins, "Lawmakers Adjourn," *News and Observer* (Raleigh), October 4, 2002.

65. Ellen Perlman, "The 'Gold-Plated' Legislature," *Governing* magazine, February 1998, 37.

66. Bob Mahlburg, "Special Session to Cost Taxpayers $25,000 a Day," *Orlando Sentinel,* April 30, 2002, A1.

67. Alan Ehrenhalt, "An Embattled Institution," *Governing* magazine, January 1992, 30.

68. "Broadcasts and Webcasts of Legislative Floor Proceedings and Committee Hearings," National Conference of State Legislatures, February 18, 2010, available at www.ncsl.org/IssuesResearch/TelecommunicationsInformationTechnology/LegislativeWebcasts/tabid/13479/Default.aspx.

69. Rosenthal, *Engines of Democracy,* 19.

70. Interview with John Hibbing, October 15, 2002.

71. Quoted in Nicholas Confessore, "Perception of Being Slighted Stoked Revolt by Lawmakers," *New York Times,* February 9, 2007, B7.

72. William Powers, "The Saturation Fallacy," *National Journal,* September 7, 2002, 2565.

73. Jonathan Walters, "How to Tame the Press," *Governing* magazine, January 1994, 30.

74. Steve Parker, "Fewer Reporters Are Covering This Year's Super Bowl," *St. Louis Post-Dispatch,* January 27, 2009, available at http://stltoday.com.

75. Jennifer Dorroh, "Statehouse Exodus," *American Journalism Review* (April–May 2009): 20.

76. Peverill Squire, "Professionalization and Public Opinion of State Legislatures," *Journal of Politics* 55, no. 2 (1993): 479–491.

77. Interview with Gary Moncrief, October 2, 2002.

78. Christopher Swope, "Instant Influence," *Governing* magazine, July 2005, 23.

79. Christopher Swope, "13th Floor: Queen of the State Blogs," Governing.com, April 24, 2007, available at http://governing.typepad.com/13thfloor/2007/04/queen_of_the_st.html#more.

80. Rob Gurwitt, "Death and Life in the Pressroom," *Governing* magazine, January 2009, 32.

81. Anita Chadha and Robert A. Bernstein, "Why Incumbents Are Treated So Harshly: Term Limits for State Legislators," *American Politics Quarterly* 24 (1996): 363–376.

82. Patricia Lopez, "Coleman's Journey Crosses Typical Divide," *Minneapolis Star Tribune,* October 16, 2002, available at www.startribune.com/stories/462/3367928.html.

83. Quoted in Rob Gurwitt, "Southern Discomfort," *Governing* magazine, October 2002, 32.

84. Ibid.

Chapter 8

1. Quoted in Alan Greenblatt, "The Job of a Lifetime," *Governing* magazine, June 2009, 24.

2. Quoted in ibid.

3. Quoted in Larry J. Sabato, *Goodbye to Good-Time Charlie,* 2nd ed. (Washington, D.C.: CQ Press, 1983), 4.

4. Lynn R. Muchmore, "The Governor as Manager," in *Being Governor: The View from the Office,* ed. Thad Beyle and Lynn R. Muchmore (Durham, N.C.: Duke University Press, 1983), 83.

5. Terry Sanford, *Storm over the States* (New York: McGraw-Hill, 1967), 185–188, quoted in Eric B. Herzik and Brent W. Brown, "Symposium on Governors and Public Policy," *Policy Studies Journal* 17 (1989): 761.

6. David Nitkin, "Maryland's Governor Ranks Second to None in Chief Budget Power," *Baltimore Sun,* January 21, 2004, 4B.

7. E. Lee Bernick, "Gubernatorial Tools: Formal vs. Informal," *Journal of Politics* 42 (1979): 661.

8. Quoted in Alan Rosenthal, *Governors & Legislatures: Contending Powers* (Washington, D.C.: CQ Press, 1990), 14.

9. Muchmore, "Governor as Manager," 13.

10. Ethan G. Sribnick, ed., *A Legacy of Innovation: Governors and Public Policy* (Philadelphia: University of Pennsylvania Press, 2008), 8.

11. Quoted in H. Edward Flentje, "The Political Nature of the Governor as Manager," in *Being Governor,* 89.

12. Alan Greenblatt, "Steady in a Storm," *Governing* magazine, November 2006, 28.

13. Sribnick, *Legacy of Innovation,* 113.

14. Quoted in Alan Greenblatt, "Governing in the Fast Lane," *Governing* magazine, January 2004, 28.

15. Bill Ritter, veto message to Colorado House, February 9, 2007, available at www.colorado.gov/governor/press/february07/HB1072-veto-message.html.

16. "Gov. Ehrlich, Pitchman," *Washington Post,* May 21, 2006, B6.

17. Alan Ehrenhalt, "Myths and Realities of Statehouse Power," *Governing* magazine, December 2002, 6.

18. Sabato, *Goodbye to Good-Time Charlie,* 4.

19. See Muchmore, "Governor as Manager."

20. Alan Greenblatt, "Tug of War," *Governing* magazine, August 2004, 32.

21. Quoted in Alan Greenblatt, "Posse Politics," *Governing* magazine, December 2006, 18.

22. Rob Gurwitt, "The Governor's People," *Governing* magazine, March 1991, 28.

23. Daniel C. Vock, "Govs Enjoy Quirky Veto Power," Stateline.org, April 24, 2007, available at www.stateline.org/live/details/story?contentId=201710.

24. Alan Greenblatt, "Killing Frankenstein," *Governing* magazine, June 2008, 17.

25. Alan Greenblatt, "Why Are We Meeting Like This?" *Governing* magazine, August 2002, 40.

26. Ibid.

27. Rosenthal, *Governors & Legislatures,* 28.

28. Garry Young and Vicky M. Wilkins, "The Influence of Governors on Veto Override Attempts: A Test of Pivotal Politics," *Legislative Studies Quarterly* 27, no. 4 (2002): 557.

29. Laura A. Van Assendelft, *Governors, Agenda Setting and Divided Government* (Lanham, Md.: University Press of America, 1997), 1.

30. Wes Clarke, "Divided Government and Budget Conflict in the U.S. States," *Legislative Studies Quarterly* 23, no. 1 (1998): 5.

31. Quoted in Alan Greenblatt, "States of Frustration," *Governing* magazine, January 2004, 26.

32. Quoted in Alan Greenblatt, "Rod Reeling," *Governing* magazine, September 2007, 18.

33. Lynda Gledhill, "Taxes—or Fees—in New Health Plan Raise Critics' Ire," *San Francisco Chronicle,* January 22, 2007, B1.

34. Quoted in Van Assendelft, *Governors, Agenda Setting and Divided Government,* 71.

35. Clayton McClure Brooks, ed., *A Legacy of Leadership: Governors and American History* (Philadelphia: University of Pennsylvania Press, 2008), 185.

36. Raphael J. Sonenshein, "Can Black Candidates Win Statewide Elections?" *Political Science Quarterly* 105 (1990): 219.

37. We are indebted for these figures to Professor Thad Beyle of the University of North Carolina, who compiled them for Council of State

Governments, *The Book of States* (Lexington, Ky.: Council of State Governments, 2009).

38. Quoted in Thomas Clouse, "Kempthorne at the Helm," *Idaho Statesman,* January 5, 1999, 1A.

39. Quoted in Brian Friel, "For Governors in Congress, No More King of the Hill," *National Journal,* June 27, 2009.

40. Quoted in Brooks, *Legacy of Leadership,* 219.

41. Interview with Julia Hurst, January 5, 2004.

42. Quoted in Josh Goodman, "The Second Best Job in the State," *Governing* magazine, April 2009, 34.

43. Quoted in Alan Greenblatt, "Where Campaign Money Flows," *Governing* magazine, November 2002, 44.

Chapter 9

1. Orrin Hatch and Jim Talent, "The Bench vs. People," *Washington Times,* May 16, 2004, available at www.washingtontimes.com/news/2004/may/16/20040516–102448–7686r.

2. Sandra Day O'Connor, "The Threat to Judicial Independence," *Wall Street Journal,* September 27, 2006, A18.

3. The full text of Senator Kennedy's speech is available at http://tedkennedy.com/journal/72/senator-kennedys-floor-speech-onthe-nuclear-option.

4. George F. Will, "In Florida, 'Uniform' Foolishness," *Washington Post,* March 23, 2006, A23.

5. Quoted in Scott Shane, "Ideology Serves as a Wild Card on Court Pick," *New York Times,* November 4, 2005, A1.

6. O'Connor, "Threat to Judicial Independence," A18.

7. National Center for State Courts Online, *Examining the Work of State Courts, 2003,* available at www.ncsconline.org/D_Research/CSP/2005_files/3-EWOverview_final_1.pdf.

8. National Center for State Courts Online, *Examining the Work of State Courts, 2007,* available at www.ncsconline.org/D_Research/csp/2007B_files/EWSC-2007-v21-online.pdf.

9. David Rottman and Shauna M. Strickland, *State Court Organization, 2004* (Washington, D.C.: Bureau of Justice Statistics, 2004), available at www.ojp.usdoj.gov/bjs/pub/pdf/sc004.pdf.

10. Diana Penner, "Judge: Jurors Antics Harmless," *Indianapolis Star,* November 30, 2006, 1.

11. Rottman and Strickland, *State Court Organization, 2004,* Table 2.

12. R. Leflar, *Internal Operating Procedures of Appellate Courts* (Chicago: American Bar Foundation, 1976), cited in Victor Flango and Carol Flango, "A Taxonomy of Appellate Court Organization," *Caseload Highlights: Examining the Work of the State Courts,* Vol. 3, no. 1 (July 1997).

13. Sari S. Escovitz, *Judicial Selection and Tenure 4* (Chicago: American Judicature Society, 1975).

14. Caleb Nelson, "A Re-Evaluation of Scholarly Explanations for the Rise of the Elected Judiciary in Antebellum America," *American Journal of Legal History* 37 (April 1993): 190–224.

15. Larry C. Berkson, "Judicial Selection in the United States: A Special Report," *Judicature* 64, no. 4 (1980, updated in 1999 by Seth Andersen): 176–193, available at www.ajs.org/selection/berkson.pdf.

16. G. Alan Tarr, "Rethinking the Selection of State Supreme Court Justices," *Willamette Law Review* 39, no. 4 (2003): 1445.

17. Ibid.

18. February 2007 Pennsylvania Keystone Poll, produced by Franklin & Marshall College in Lancaster, Pennsylvania. Polls and other analysis available at http://politics.fandm.edu.

19. Ciara Torres-Spelliscy, Monique Chase, and Emma Greenman, "Improving Judicial Diversity," Brennan Center for Justice, January 12, 2009, available at http://brennan.3cdn.net/96d16b62f331bb13ac_kfm6bplue.pdf.

20. Mark S. Hurwitz and Drew Noble Lanier, "Diversity in State and Federal Appellate Courts: Change and Continuity across 20 Years," *Justice System Journal* 29, no. 1 (2008): 47–70.

21. Molly McDonough and Debra Cassens Weiss, "Huge Defeat for 'Jail 4 Judges'; Female Judicial Candidates Win Big," ABAJournal.Com, November 9, 2006, available at www.abanet.org/journal/redesign/n8elect.html.

22. American Judicature Society, "Judicial Selection in the States: Appellate and General Jurisdiction Courts" (1986, revised October 2002), available at www.ajs.org/js/judicialselectioncharts.pdf.

23. Ibid.

24. David B. Rottman, Anthony Champagne, and Roy A. Schotland, *Call to Action: Statement of the National Summit on Improving Judicial Selection* (Williamsburg, Va.: National Center for State Courts, 2002).

25. Frontline, "Justice for Sale: Interview with Justices Stephen Breyer and Anthony Kennedy," available at www.pbs.org/wgbh/pages/frontline/shows/justice/interviews/supremo.html.

26. Ibid.

27. Paul Brace and Melinda Gann Hall, "Studying Courts Comparatively: The View from the American States," *Political Research Quarterly* 48 (1995): 5–29. See also Paul Brace and Brent D. Boyea, "State Public Opinion, the Death Penalty, and the Practice of Electing Judges," *American Journal of Political Science* 52, no. 2 (2008): 360–372.

28. Brace and Hall, "Studying Courts Comparatively."

29. Gerald F. Uelmen, "Crocodiles in the Bathtub: Maintaining the Independence of State Supreme Courts in an Era of Judicial Politicization," *Notre Dame Law Review* 72 (1997): 1133, 1135–1142.

30. Ibid., 1133, 1137.

31. Stephen J. Ware, "Money, Politics and Judicial Decisions: A Case Study of Arbitration Law in Alabama," *Journal of Law and Politics* 15 (1999): 645.

32. Adam Liptak and Janet Roberts, "Campaign Cash Mirrors a High Court's Rulings," *New York Times,* October 1, 2006.

33. Quoted in ibid, Sec. 1, 1.

34. "*Caperton v. Massey,*" Brennan Center for Justice, June 8, 2009, available at www.brennancenter.org/content/resource/caperton_v_massey.

35. "Money and Elections," Justice at Stake, available at www.justiceatstake.org/issues/state_court_issues/money_elections.cfm.

36. Sheila Kaplan, "Justice for Sale," *Common Cause Magazine,* May–June 1987, 29–30.

37. Stan Greenberg and Linda A. DiVall, "National Surveys of American Voters and State Judges," Greenberg Quinlan Rosner Research, February 14, 2002, available at www.gavelgrab.org/wp-content/resources/polls/Pollingsummary FINAL.pdf.

38. Uelmen, "Crocodiles in the Bathtub."

39. Quoted in Mark A. Behrens and Cary Silverman, "The Case for Adopting Appointive Judicial Selection Systems for State Court Judges," *Cornell Journal of Law and Public Policy* 11, no. 2 (2002): 275.

40. Zach Patton, "Robe Warriors," *Governing* magazine, March 2006.

41. Charles H. Sheldon and Linda S. Maule, *Choosing Justice: The Recruitment of State and Federal Judges* (Pullman: Washington State University Press, 1997).

42. Rottman, Champagne, and Schotland, *Call to Action.*

43. Quoted in Behrens and Silverman, "Case for Adopting," 282.

44. "Judicial Selection in the States: Appellate and General Jurisdiction Courts," *American Judicature Society,* 1986 (updated January 2004), available at www.ajs.org/js/judicialselectioncharts.pdf.

45. Behrens and Silverman, "Case for Adopting."

46. Berkson, "Judicial Selection in the United States."

47. Ibid.

48. Behrens and Silverman, "Case for Adopting," 303.

49. Ibid.

50. Rottman, Champagne, and Schotland, *Call to Action.*

51. "Methods of Judicial Selection," American Judicature Society, 2010, available at http://

judicialselection.us/judicial_selection/methods/selection_of_judges.cfm?state.

52. Luke Bierman, "Beyond Merit Selection," *Fordham Urban Law Journal* 29 (2002): 851, 864–865.

53. American Bar Association, "An Independent Judiciary, Report of the Commission on Separation of Powers and Judicial Independence" (1997), 48–49, and Henry J. Abraham, *The Judicial Process: An Introductory Analysis of the Courts of the United States, England, and France,* 6th ed. (New York: Oxford University Press, 1993), 42, cited in ibid.

54. "Methods of Judicial Selection."

55. Brace and Hall, "Studying Courts Comparatively," 24.

56. Drew Noble Lanier and Roger Handberg, "In the Eye of the Hurricane: Florida Courts, Judicial Independence, and Politics," *Fordham Urban Law Journal* 29 (2002): 1033.

57. "Judicial Compensation FAQs," National Center for State Courts, last modified July 7, 2009, www.ncsconline.org/WC/CourTopics/FAQs.asp?topic=JudCom.

58. Robert L. Misner, "Recasting Prosecutorial Discretion," *Journal of Criminal Law and Criminology* 86 (1996): 717, 741.

59. Steve Weinberg, "Inside an Office: An Elected Prosecutor Explains," *The Center for Public Integrity,* available at www.publicintegrity.org/pm/default.aspx?act=sidebarsa&aid=28.

60. Steven W. Perry, "Prosecutors in State Courts 2005," Bureau of Justice Statistics Bulletin, no. NCJ-213799, Washington, D.C., July 2006.

61. Ibid.

62. Misner, "Recasting Prosecutorial Discretion."

63. Carol J. DeFrances, "State Court Prosecutors in Large Districts 2001," Bureau of Justice Statistics Special Report, no. NCJ-191206, Washington, D.C., December 2001.

64. Ibid. "About two-thirds of Part I Uniform Crime Report (UCR) offenses reported to the police in 1998 occurred in the prosecutorial district served by these offices" (2).

65. Los Angeles County District Attorney's Office Web site, http://da.co.la.ca.us.

66. Shelby A. Dickerson Moore, "Questioning the Autonomy of Prosecutorial Charging Decisions: Recognizing the Need to Exercise Discretion— Knowing There Will Be Consequences for Crossing the Line," *Louisiana Law Review* 60 (winter 2000): 371, 374.

67. Wayne R. LaFave, "The Prosecutor's Discretion in the United States," *American Journal of Comparative Law* 18 (1970): 532, 533.

68. Misner, "Recasting Prosecutorial Discretion."

69. Telephone interview with Kenneth Noto, the deputy chief of the narcotics section at the U.S. Attorney's Office for the Southern District of Florida, in William T. Pizzi, "Understanding Prosecutorial Discretion in the United States: The Limits of Comparative Criminal Procedure as an Instrument of Reform," *Ohio State Law Journal* 54 (1993): 1325 n88.

70. Perry, "Prosecutors in State Courts 2005."

71. Moore, "Questioning."

72. Floyd D. Weatherspoon, "The Devastating Impact of the Justice System on the Status of African-American Males: An Overview Perspective," *Capital University Law Review* 23 (1994): 23, 43.

73. Steven K. Smith and Carol J. DeFrances, "Indigent Defense," Bureau of Justice Statistics Selected Findings, no. NCJ-158909, Washington, D.C., February 1996.

74. Ibid.

75. Lynn Langton and Donald J. Farole Jr., "Public Defender Offices, 2007—Statistical Tables," Bureau of Justice Statistics Selected Findings, no. NCJ-228538, Washington, D.C., November 2009, available at http://bjs.ojp.usdoj.gov/content/pub/pdf/pd007st.pdf.

76. Carol J. DeFrances and Marika F. X. Litras, "Indigent Defense Services in Large Counties 1999," Bureau of Justice Statistics Bulletin, no. NCJ-184932, Washington, D.C., November 2000.

77. Ibid. Public defenders' offices in the largest one hundred counties employed more than 12,700 individuals during 1999, including more than 6,300 assistant public defenders, 1,200 investigators, 300 social workers, 21,700 support staffers, and nearly 400 paralegals.

78. Criminal Justice Standards Committee, *Standards for Criminal Justice: Providing Defense Services,* 3rd ed. (Chicago: American Bar Association, 1992).

79. Carol Lundberg, "Justice for All," *Michigan Lawyers Weekly,* June 22, 2009.

80. Smith and DeFrances, "Indigent Defense."

81. Adele Bernhard, "Take Courage: What the Courts Can Do to Improve the Delivery of Criminal Defense Services," *University of Pittsburgh Law Review* 63 (2002): 293, 305.

82. DeFrances and Litras, "Indigent Defense Services in Large Counties."

83. Brian Ostrom, Robert LaFountain, and Neal Kauder, "Profiling Felony Cases in the NACM Network," *Caseload Highlights: Examining the Work of State Courts* 7, no. 1 (2001). In seventeen courts surveyed, nearly three-quarters of all felony cases resulted in pleas of guilty by the defendant.

84. "Improving Criminal Justice Systems through Expanded Strategies and Innovative Collaborations: Report of the National Symposium on Indigent Defense," no. NCJ-181344, U.S. Department of Justice, Office of Justice Programs, Washington, D.C., 2000; Richard Klein and Robert Spangenberg, *The Indigent Defense Crisis* (Washington, D.C.: ABA Section of Crime Justice 1993), 25.

85. David Cole, *No Equal Justice: Race and Class in the American Justice System* (New York: New Press, 1999), 92.

86. David Cole, "Commentary: Still No Equal Justice for Poor," National Association of Criminal Defense Lawyers, March 17, 2003, available at www.nacdl.org/public.nsf/GideonAnniversary/news04?opendocument.

87. Andrew Rachlin, "Rights of Defense," *Governing* magazine, January 2007, available at www.governing.com/archive/archive/2007/jan/defense.txt.

88. "ACLU Files Class-Action Lawsuit against Montana's Indigent Defense Program," ACLU press release, February 14, 2002.

89. Kevin Clermont and Theodore Eisenberg, "Trial by Jury or Judge: Transcending Empiricism," *Cornell Law Review* 77 (1992): 1124.

90. See *Williams v. Florida,* 399 U.S. 78 (1970), approving six-member juries, and *Apodaca v. Oregon,* 406 U.S. 404 (1972), allowing nonunanimous verdicts.

91. Rottman and Strickland, *State Court Organization, 2004.*

92. "New Directions from the Field: Victims' Rights and Services for the 21st Century," Executive Summary U.S. Department of Justice, Office of Justice Programs, Office for Victims of Crime, Washington, D.C., 1998.

93. Wayne A. Logan, "Through the Past Darkly: A Survey of the Uses and Abuses of Victim Impact Evidence in Capital Trials," *Arizona Law Review* 41 (1999): 143, 177–178.

94. See *Payne v. Tennessee,* 501 U.S. 808 (1991), which reversed *Booth v. Maryland,* 482 U.S. 496 (1987).

95. "1 in 31: The Long Reach of American Corrections," Pew Center on the States, March 2009.

96. "2008 State Expenditure Report," National Association of State Budget Officers, Washington, D.C., 66.

97. In *Ring v. Arizona,* 536 U.S. 584 (2002), the Supreme Court invalidated Arizona's capital sentencing procedures, holding that the jury, not the judge, must find the aggravating factors necessary to impose the death penalty. Similar procedures in Colorado, Idaho, Montana, and Nebraska also were ruled unconstitutional.

98. Melissa T. Cantrell, Carol R. Flango, Randall Hansen, Neil LaFountain, and David B. Rottman, *State Court Organization 1998* (Washington, D.C.: U.S. Department of Justice, June 2000).

99. Michael M. O'Hear, "National Uniformity/Local Uniformity: Reconsidering the Use of Departures to Reduce Federal-State Sentencing Disparities," *Iowa Law Review* 87 (2002): 721, 756.

100. Ibid., 749.

101. Robert Mosteller, "New Dimensions in Sentencing Reform in the Twenty-First Century," *Oregon Law Review* 92 (2003): 1, 16–17.

102. Arizona, California, Delaware, Florida, Illinois, Maine, Minnesota, Mississippi, New Mexico, North Carolina, Ohio, Virginia, and Washington have adopted determinate sentencing laws. "1996 National Survey of State Sentencing Structures," no. NCJ-169270, Bureau of Justice Assistance, Washington, D.C., 1998, 4–5.

103. Marguerite A. Driessen and W. Cole Durham Jr., "Sentencing Dissonances in the United States: The Shrinking Distance between Punishment Proposed and Sanction Served," *American Journal of Comparative Law* 50 (2002): 623, 635.

104. Bureau of Justice Statistics, National Corrections Reporting Program 2005, Table 9, "First Releases From State Prison," available at http://bjs.ojp.usdoj.gov/index.cfm?ty=pbdetail&iid=2045.

105. "1996 National Survey," Exhibit 1-1.

106. Rottman and Strickland, *State Court Organization, 2004.*

107. Driessen and Durham, "Sentencing Dissonances in the United States."

108. Patrick Marshall, "Three-Strikes Laws," *CQ Researcher,* May 10, 2002.

109. Rottman and Strickland, *State Court Organization, 2004.*

110. Glenn Dubin, Kamala Mallik Kane, David Kirk, Katherine J. Rosich, and William J. Sabol, "Influences of Truth-in-Sentencing Reforms on Changes in States' Sentencing Practices and Prison Populations," Urban Institute, Justice Policy Center, July 3, 2002.

111. Rottman and Strickland, *State Court Organization, 2004.*

112. Ibid., Table 47.

113. O'Hear, "National Uniformity/ Local Uniformity."

114. Ralph Ranalli, "Crack Sentence Debate Reopened: Proof Whites, Blacks Treated Equally Asked," *Boston Globe,* September 26, 1999, B1, cited in ibid., 733n.113.

115. Brian Ostrom, Neal Kauder, and Robert LaFountain, *Examining the Work of the State Courts, 1999–2000: A National Perspective from the Court Statistics Project* (Williamsburg, Va.: National Center for State Courts, 2000).

116. Judith S. Kaye, "The State of the Judiciary, 2003: Confronting Today's Challenge," annual address, Albany, N.Y., January 13, 2003, 4.

117. Quoted in Alan Greenblatt, "Docket Science," *Governing* magazine, June 2001, 40, available at www.governing.com/archive/archive/2001/jun/civil.txt.

118. Ibid.

119. Quoted in ibid. For more on his reforms to the Hennepin County courts, see also the profile of Kevin Burke in "Court Reform," *Governing* magazine, November 2004.

120. Todd Ruger, "Two Minutes, and Home Goes Away," *Sarasota Herald-Tribune,* May 14, 2009, A1; Todd Ruger, "'Rocket Docket' Can Be Slowed," *Sarasota Herald-Tribune,* September 27, 2009, BN1.

121. Greenblatt, "Docket Science."

122. Rebecca A. Koppes Conway, Timothy M. Tymkovich, Troy A. Eid, Britt Weygandt, and Anthony van Westrum, "Report of the Committee on Magistrates in the Civil Justice System," October 1, 2000, available at www.state.co.us/cjrtf/report/report2.htm.

123. Rottman, Champagne, and Schotland, *Call to Action.*

124. "Supreme Court Will Not Hear Challenge to North Carolina Courts' Public Finance System," Press Release, Brennan Center for Justice, November 3, 2008, available at www.ncvce.org/index.php?page=brennan_release.

Chapter 10

1. Larry Hannan, "Police Shut Down Girl's Lemonade Stand: City Later Offers Free Permit," *Naples Daily News,* available at www.bonitanews.com/03/06/naples/d945350a.htm.

2. H. H. Gerth and C. Wright Mills, *Max Weber: Essays in Sociology* (New York: Oxford University Press, 1943).

3. Ronald C. Moe and Robert S. Gilmour, "Rediscovering Principles of Public

Administration: The Neglected Foundation of Public Law," *Public Administration Review* 55, no. 2 (March–April 1995): 135–146.

4. John J. Gargan, "Introduction and Overview of State Government Administration," in *Handbook of State Government Administration*, ed. John J. Gargan (New York: Marcel-Dekker, 2000).

5. Jerrell D. Coggburn and Saundra K. Schneider, "The Quality of Management and Government Performance: An Empirical Analysis of the American States," *Public Administration Review* 63, no. 2 (March–April 2003): 206–213.

6. Le Zhou and Frank Johnson, "Revenues and Expenditures for Public Elementary and Secondary Education: School Year 2006–07," National Center for Education Statistics, March 2009, available at http://nces.ed.gov/pubs2009/2009337.pdf.

7. Charles Barrilleaux, "Statehouse Bureaucracy: Institutional Consistency in a Changing Environment," in *American State and Local Politics,* ed. Ronald E. Weber and Paul Brace (New York: Chatham House, 1999).

8. Michael Lipsky, *Street-Level Bureaucracy* (New York: Russell Sage Foundation, 1980).

9. Cornelius Kerwin, *Rulemaking: How Government Agencies Write Law and Make Policy,* 3rd ed. (Washington, D.C.: CQ Press, 2003).

10. Deil S. Wright, Chung-Lae Cho, and Yoo-Sun Choi, "Top-Level State Administrators: Changing Characteristics and Qualities," *The Book of the States 2002* (Lexington, Ky.: Council of State Governments, 2002).

11. Charles T. Goodsell, *The Case for Bureaucracy: A Public Administration Polemic,* 4th ed. (Washington, D.C.: CQ Press, 2003).

12. U.S. Census Bureau, *Statistical Abstract of the United States: 2009* Table 443, "Governmental Employment and Payrolls (1982–2006)," available at www.census.gov/compendia/statab/tables/09s0443.pdf.

13. Goodsell, *Case for Bureaucracy.*

14. George W. Downs and Patrick D. Larkey, *The Search for Government Efficiency* (Philadelphia: Temple University Press, 1986).

15. Elliott Sclar, *You Don't Always Get What You Pay For* (Ithaca, N.Y.: Cornell University Press, 2000).

16. J. Norman Baldwin, "Public versus Private Employees: Debunking Stereotypes," *Review of Public Personnel Administration* 12 (winter 1991): 1–27.

17. Barrilleaux, "Statehouse Bureaucracy," 106–107.

18. John J. DiIulio Jr., Gerald Garvey, and Donald F. Kettl, *Improving Government: An Owner's Manual* (Washington, D.C.: Brookings Institution, 1993).

19. "The Government Performance Project," Pew Center on the States, available at http://pewcenteronthestates.org/initiatives_detail.aspx?initiativeID=36072.

20. Coggburn and Schneider, "Quality of Management," 206–213.

21. Dennis Cauchon, "Bad Moves, Not Economy behind Busted State Budgets," *USA Today,* June 23, 2003, P1A.

22. Kenneth J. Meier, "Bureaucracy and Democracy: The Case for More Bureaucracy and Less Democracy," *Public Administration Review* 57, no. 3 (May–June 1997): 193–199.

23. Quoted in Katherine Barrett and Richard Greene, "Time for a Check Up," *Governing* magazine, November 2005, www.governing.com/archive/archive/2005/nov/manage.txt.

24. Elizabeth G. Hill, "California Legislative Analyst's Office: An Isle of Independence," *Spectrum: The Journal of State Government* 6, no. 4 (2003): 26–29.

25. Barrett and Greene, "Time for a Check Up."

26. Barbara Romzek and Melvin Dubnick, "Accountability in the Public Sector: Lessons from the Challenger Tragedy," *Public Administration Review* 47, no. 3 (May–June 1987): 227–238.

27. Alfred Steinberg, *The Bosses* (New York: Macmillan, 1972).

28. Dwight Waldo, *The Administrative State* (New York: Holmes and Meier, 1948).

29. "Union Membership Edges Up, but Share Continues to Fall," *Monthly Labor Review,* January 1999, 1–2.

30. WEAC's legislative goals are available on its Web site, www.weac.org/capitol/2005-06/legagenda/main.htm.

31. "2007–08 Committee Contributions to Candidates and LCCs," Wisconsin Education Association Council, available at www.wisdc.org/WEB_PAC_Amt2007-08.php.

32. Charles J. Sykes, *Profscam: Professors and the Demise of Higher Education* (New York: St. Martin's Press, 1989).

33. U.S. Census Bureau, *Statistical Abstract of the United States: 2009*, Table 446, "State and Local Government, Full-Time Employment and Salary by Sex and Race/Ethnic Group: 1980–2005," available at www.census.gov/compendia/statab/tables/09s0446.pdf.

34. Jennifer 8. Lee, "In Police Class, Blue Comes in Many Colors," *New York Times*, July 8, 2005.

35. C. J. Chivers, "For Black Officers, Diversity Has Its Limits," *New York Times*, April 2, 2001.

36. Sally Selden, *The Promise of Representative Bureaucracy: Diversity and Responsiveness in a Government Agency* (Armonk, N.Y.: M. E. Sharpe, 1997).

37. Adam Liptak, "Supreme Court Finds Bias against White Firefighters," *New York Times*, June 29, 2009; Steven Greenhouse, "Supreme Court Ruling Offers Little Guidance on Hiring," *New York Times*, June 29, 2009.

38. Donald F. Kettl, *The Global Public Management Revolution: A Report on the Transformation of Governance* (Washington, D.C.: Brookings Institution, 2000).

39. H. George Frederickson and Kevin B. Smith, *The Public Administration Theory Primer* (Boulder, Colo.: Westview Press, 2003), 215.

40. Darrell M. West, "Assessing E-Government: The Internet, Democracy and Service Delivery by State and Federal Governments," World Bank, 2000, available at www1.worldbank.org/publicsector/egov/EgovReportUs00.htm.

41. Ramona McNeal, Caroline J. Tolbert, Karen Mossberger, and Lisa J. Dotterweich, "Innovating in Digital Government in the American States," *Social Science Quarterly* 84, no. 1 (March 2003): 52–70.

42. "Digital States Survey 2008," Center for Digital Government, available at www.centerdigitalgov.com/survey/61/2008.

43. Ellen Perlman, "eGovernment Special Report," *Governing* magazine, September 2002, available at www.governing.com/archive/2002/sep/eg2c.txt.

44. Darrell West, "State and Federal Electronic Government in the United States," Brookings Institution, 2008, available at www.brookings.edu/~/media/Files/rc/reports/2008/0826_egovernment_west/0826_egovernment_west.pdf.

45. Karen Mossberger, Caroline Tolbert, and Ramona McNeal, "Developing E-Government in the Fifty States 2000–2004," paper presented at the 2005 State Politics and Policy Conference, East Lansing, Mich., May 14, 2005, available at http://polisci.msu.edu/sppc2005/papers/satam/MossbergerTolbertMcNealSPPC.doc.

46. West, "State and Federal Electronic Government"; "Digital States Survey 2008."

Chapter 11

1. National League of Cities Web site, www.nlc.org/about_cities/cities_101/146.cfm.

2. Richard Cole and John Kincaid, "Public Opinion on U.S. Federal and Intergovernmental Issues in 2006," *Publius: The Journal of Federalism* 36, no. 3 (2006): 443–459.

3. This figure is based on an estimated total population of 300 million.

4. City-Data.com, Web site, www.city-data.com/city/Hove-Mobile-Park-North-Dakota.html.

5. David Miller, *The Regional Government of Metropolitan America* (Boulder, Colo.: Westview Press, 2002).

6. Quoted in Jonathan Walters, "Cry, the Beleaguered County," *Governing* magazine, August 1996, available at www.governing.com/archive/archive/1996/aug/counties.txt.

7. See the National Association of Counties Web site, www.naco.org/Template.cfm?Section=About_Counties. See also Roger L. Kemp, ed., *Model Government Charters: A City, County,*

Regional, State, and Federal Handbook (Jefferson, N.C.: McFarland, 2003), 55.

8. National Association of Counties, "NACo Leaders, Administration Officials, Grapple with Recovery Act Implementation," 2009, available at www.naco.org/CountyNewsTemplate .cfm?template=/ContentManagement/ ContentDisplay.cfm&ContentID=30352.

9. "A Brief Overview of County Government," National Association of Counties, August 2003, available at www.naco.org/Content/ NavigationMenu/About_Counties/County_ Government/Default271.htm.

10. Ibid.

11. Miller, *Regional Government of Metropolitan America*, 26.

12. U.S. Conference of Mayors Web site, www .usmayors.org.

13. Penelope Lemov, "Infrastructure Conference Report: Building It Smarter, Managing It Better," *Governing* magazine, October 1996.

14. Rob Gurwitt, "Are City Councils a Relic of the Past?" *Governing* magazine, April 2003.

15. National League of Cities, "Serving on City Councils," *Research Brief on America's Cities*, no. 2003-5, Washington, D.C., September 2003.

16. Kemp, *Model Government Charters*, 10.

17. William Hansell, "Evolution and Change Characterize Council-Manager Government," *Public Management* 82 (August 2000): 17–21.

18. Michael Zuckerman, *Peaceable Kingdoms: The New England Towns of the 18th Century* (New York: Knopf, 1970).

19. Miller, *Regional Government of Metropolitan America*, 41.

20. Quoted in Anwar Syed, *The Political Theory of the American Local Government* (New York: Random House, 1966), 40.

21. Alexis De Tocqueville, *Democracy in America: A New Translation*, trans. George Lawrence, ed. J. P. Mayer (New York: HarperCollins, 2000), 33.

22. Lemov, "Infrastructure Conference Report," 40

23. Ann O. Bowman, "Urban Government," in *Handbook of Research on Urban Politics*

and Policy in the United States, ed. Ronald K. Vogel (Westport, Conn.: Greenwood Press, 1997), 133.

24. Kemp, *Model Government Charters*, 59.

25. League of Women Voters of California Web site, http://smartvoter.org.

26. Elaine B. Sharpe, "Political Participation in Cities," in *Cities, Politics, and Policy: A Comparative Analysis*, ed. John P. Pelissero (Washington, D.C.: CQ Press, 2003), 81.

27. Lana Stein, "Mayoral Politics," in *Cities, Politics, and Policy*, 162.

28. Sharpe, "Political Participation in Cities," 71.

29. "Compensation and Workload for Local Elected Officials," National League of Cities, available at www.nlc.org/About_Cities/cities_101/147 .cfm.

30. Ibid.

31. Center for State & Local Government Excellence, *The Great Recession and State and Local Government Work Force* (Washington, D.C.: Center for State & Local Excellence, 2010).

32. Quoted in International City/County Management Association, *How It Plays in Peoria: The Fiscal Crisis on Local Governments* (Washington, D.C.: ICMA, 2010), 7.

33. Robert O'Neill, "An Opportunity for Creative Destruction" *Governing* magazine, October 2009, available at www.governing.com/column/ opportunity-creative-destruction.

34. De Tocqueville, *Democracy in America*, 63.

Chapter 12

1. Christopher Briem, "A Primer on Local Government Fragmentation and Regionalism in the Pittsburgh Region," available at www.pitt .edu/~cbriem/ pittsburghindex.htm.

2. Figures calculated by author from U.S. Census Bureau data, 2003, http://quickfacts.census.gov/ qfd/states/42/42003.html.

3. Advisory Commission on Intergovernmental Relations, "Metropolitan Organization: The

Allegheny County Case," Washington, D.C., February 1992, available at www.briem.com/files/ACIRAlleghenyCounty.pdf.

4. Allegheny County, Pa., map, www.alleghenycounty.us/munimap/index.asp.

5. Anthony Downs, "The Devolution Revolution: Why Congress Is Shifting a Lot of Power to the Wrong Levels," Policy Brief no. 3, Brookings Institution, 1996, available at www.brookings.edu/index/scholarwork.htm?scholar=Downs*Anthony**.

6. Alan Greenblatt, "In Memphis, a Plea for Regionalism," *Governing* magazine, September 2009.

7. U.S. Census Bureau, "Metropolitan Statistical Area," 2008, available at http://quickfacts.census.gov/qfd/meta/long_metro.htm.

8. U.S. Census Bureau, "Metropolitan and Micropolitan Statistical Areas," 2008, available at www.census.gov/population/www/metroareas/metrodef.html.

9. Bruce Katz, "A Nation in Transition: What the Urban Age Means for the United States," Brookings Institute, 2007, available at www.brookings.edu/speeches/2007/0504community development_katz.aspx.

10. Ann O. Bowman, "Urban Government," in *Handbook of Research on Urban Politics and Policy in the United States,* ed. Ronald K. Vogel (Westport, Conn.: Greenwood Press, 1997), 133.

11. David Miller, *The Regional Governing of Metropolitan America* (Boulder, Colo.: Westview Press, 2002), 1.

12. David Cieslewits, "The Environmental Impacts of Sprawl," in *Urban Sprawl: Causes, Consequences, and Policy Responses,* ed. Gregory D. Squires (Washington, D.C.: Urban Institute Press, 2002).

13. Ibid.

14. See, for example, Myron Orfield, *American Metropolitics: The New Suburban Reality* (Washington, D.C.: Brookings Institution, 2002).

15. Ibid., 41.

16. Peter Dreier, John Mollenkopf, and Todd Swanstrom, *Place Matters: Metropolitics for the*

Twenty-First Century (Lawrence: University of Kansas Press, 2001).

17. Ibid., 67.

18. Orfield, *American Metropolitics,* 10.

19. G. Ross Stephens and Nelson Wikstrom, *Metropolitan Government and Governance: Theoretical Perspectives, Empirical Analysis, and the Future* (New York: Oxford University Press, 1999).

20. "About Metro," available at www.oregonmetro.gov/index.cfm/go/by.web/id=24201/level=1.

21. Heike Mayor and John Provo, "The Portland Edge in Context," *The Portland Edge: Challenges and Successes in Growing Communities,* ed. Connie P. Ozawa (Washington, D.C.: Island Press, 2004).

22. National Association of Regional Councils, "What Is a Regional Council?" available at http://narc.org/regional-councils-mpos/what-is-a-regional-council.html.

23. Ibid.

24. Miller, *Regional Governing of Metropolitan America,* 103.

25. James F. Wolf and Tara Kolar Bryan, "Identifying the Capacities of Regional Councils of Government," *State and Local Government Review* 41 (2010): 61–68, quotation on 61.

26. Ibid., 67.

27. Simon Andrew, "Recent Development in the Study of Interjurisdictional Agreements: An Overview and Assessment," *State and Local Government Review* 41 (2010): 133–142.

28. National Association of Counties Web site, www.naco.org/Content/ContentGroups/Publications1/County_News1/20035/6-2-03/Successful_City-County_Consolidations.htm.

29. Quoted in Jeffrey Cohan, "Reports Outline Options in Merging Pittsburgh-Allegheny County Services," *Pittsburgh Post-Gazette,* April 2, 2004.

30. Lara Brenckle, "City, County Study Merger . . . Again," *Pittsburgh Tribune-Review,* October 20, 2006, available at www.pittsburghlive.com/x/pittsburghtrib/news/cityregion/s_475861.htm.

31. National League of Cities, "Serving on City Councils," Research Brief on America's Cities, no. 2003-5, Washington, D.C., September 2003.

32. David Rusk, *Cities without Suburbs*, 2nd ed. (Washington, D.C.: Woodrow Wilson Center Press, 1995).

33. Bowman, "Urban Government," 139.

34. Rob Gurwitt, "Annexation: Not So Smart Growth," *Governing* magazine, October 2000.

35. Barbara Kelly, *Expanding the American Dream: Building and Rebuilding Levittown* (Albany, N.Y.: SUNY Press, 1993).

36. Charles Tiebout, "A Pure Theory of Local Expenditures," *Journal of Political Economy* 64, no. 5 (October 1956): 416–424, quotation on 422.

37. William Lyons, David Lowery, and Ruth Hoogland DeHoog, *The Politics of Dissatisfaction: Citizens, Services, and Urban Institutions* (Armonk, N.Y.: M.E. Sharpe, 1992).

38. Paul Teske, Mark Schneider, Michael Mintrom, and Samuel Best, "Establishing the Micro Foundations of a Macro Theory: Information, Movers and the Competitive Local Market for Public Goods," *American Political Science Review* 87, no. 3 (September 1993): 702–713.

39. Paul Teske, Mark Schneider, Michael Mintrom, and Samuel Best, "The Empirical Evidence for Citizen Information and a Local Market for Public Goods," *American Political Science Review* 89, no. 3 (September 1995): 707–709.

40. Dave Ranney, "State's Rural Population Continues to Shrink," *Lawrence Journal-World,* available at www2.1jworld.com/news/2005/dec/13/states_rural_population_continues_shrink.

41. Alan Greenblatt, "Little Mergers on the Prairie," *Governing* magazine, July 2006, 48–54.

42. Nebraska Department of Education, Education Support Services, "2009–2010 Number of Districts/Systems," available at http://ess.nde.state.ne.us/DataCenter/DataInformation/Downloads/0910/Districts.pdf.

43. Greenblatt, "Little Mergers on the Prairie," 49–50.

44. Ibid, 54.

Chapter 13

1. U.S. Department of Education, "Race to the Top Program Guidance and Frequently Asked Questions," Washington, D.C., January 13, 2010, 3.

2. Michele McNeil, "Why Delaware and Tennessee Won Race to the Top," *Education Week* blog, March 29, 2010, available at blogs.edweek.org/edweek/campaign-k-12/2010/03/why_delaware_and_tennessee_won.html?print=1.

3. "More States Drop Out of 'Race,'" Stateline.org, April 23, 2010, available at www.stateline.org/live/details/story?contentId=479647.

4. David Tyack and Larry Cuban, *Tinkering toward Utopia: A Century of Public School Reform* (Cambridge, Mass.: Harvard University Press, 1995), 2.

5. Lyndon B. Johnson, speech on the Great Society given at University of Michigan, May 22, 1964; the full sentence is "The Great Society rests on abundance and liberty for all." Read more about LBJ's Great Society initiatives at the Web site of the LBJ Presidential Library, available at www.lbjlib.utexas.edu/johnson/archives.hom/biographys.hom/lbj_bio.asp.

6. National Association of State Budget Officers, "2008 State Expenditure Report," Washington, D.C., December 2009, 3.

7. Michael A. Rebell, "Fiscal Equity Litigation and the Democratic Imperative," *Journal of Education Finance* 24, no. 1 (1998): 23–50.

8. Elissa Gootman, "Debate on New York Schools Pivots on One Man at the Top," *New York Times,* March 6, 2009, A24.

9. Amanda Ripley, "Rhee Tackles Classroom Challenge," *Time,* November 26, 2008, available at www.time.com/time/magazine/article/0,9171,1862444-1,00.html.

10. Bill Turque, "D.C. Teachers Contract Settled," D.C. Schools Insider blog for the *Washington Post,* April 6, 2010, available at http://voices.washingtonpost.com/dcschools/2010/04/dc_teachers_contract_settled.html.

11. Charles Mahtesian, "Too Much Democracy," *Governing* magazine, January 24, 2000,

available at www.governing.com/view/vu01 2400.htm.

12. Lei Zhou and Frank Johnson, *Revenues and Expenditures for Public Elementary and Secondary Education: School Year 2006–07 (Fiscal Year 2007)* (Washington, D.C.: U.S. Department of Education, 2009), 4.

13. Education Commission of the States Web site, February 2006, www.ecs.org/clearinghouse/57/32/5732.htm.

14. Rebell, "Fiscal Equity."

15. Tyack and Cuban, *Tinkering toward Utopia,* 47.

16. William Duncombe, John Ruggiero, and John Yinger, "Alternative Approaches to Measuring the Cost of Education," in *Holding Schools Accountable: Performance-Based Reform in Education,* ed. Helen F. Ladd (Washington, D.C.: Brookings Institution, 1996), 338. See also Christopher B. Swanson, "Ten Questions (and Answers) about Graduates, Dropouts, and NCLB Accountability," Urban Institute, October 21, 2003, available at www.urban.org/publications/310873.html.

17. Harold Wenglinsky, "School District Expenditures, School Resources and Student Achievement: Modeling the Production Function," in *Developments in School Finance, 1997—Does Money Matter?* ed. William J. Fowler Jr. (Washington, D.C.: National Center for Education Statistics, 1998).

18. Allan Odden, "Equity and Adequacy in School Finance Today," *Phi Delta Kappan* 85 (October 2003): 120–125.

19. Margaret Ritsch, ed. *Money Matters: A Reporter's Guide to School Finance* (Washington, D.C.: Education Writers Association, 2003), 5.

20. "Funding Gaps 2006," Education Trust, Washington, D.C., 2006. Based on 2003–2004 U.S. Department of Education and U.S. Census Bureau data.

21. "Total and Current Expenditures per Pupil in Fall Enrollment in Public Elementary and Secondary Education, by Function and State or Jurisdiction: 2005–06," in *Digest of Education Statistics, 2008* (Washington, D.C.: U.S. Department of Education, 2009), Table 182.

22. Tamar Lewin and Sam Dillon, "Districts Warn of Deeper Teacher Cuts," *New York Times,* April 20, 2010, available at www.nytimes.com/2010/04/21/education/21teachers.

23. "Quality Counts 2003," *Education Week,* January 9, 2003, 22.

24. Richard Rothstein, *The Way We Were: The Myths and Realities of America's Student Achievement* (New York: Century Foundation, 1998), 19.

25. William J. Bushaw and John A. McNee, "Americans Speak Out: Are Educators and Policy Makers Listening?" *Phi Delta Kappan* 91 (September 2009): 8–23.

26. Jennifer McMurrer, "Instructional Time in Elementary Schools: A Closer Look at Changes for Specific Subjects," Center on Education Policy, Washington, D.C., February 20, 2008.

27. Robert Rothman, *Measuring Up: Standards, Assessment, and School Reform* (San Francisco: Jossey-Bass, 1995), 53.

28. "Trends in International Mathematics and Science Study," National Center for Education Statistics, available at http://nces.ed.gov/timss/index.asp.

29. "2009 College-Bound Seniors Are Most Diverse Group Ever to Take SAT as More Minority Students Prepare for Higher Education," The College Board, August 25, 2009, available at www.collegeboard.com/press/releases/206201.html.

30. "The Texas Miracle," CBSNEWS.com, January 6, 2004, available at www.cbsnews.com/stories/2004/01/06/60II/main591676.shtml.

31. Sam Dillon, "U.S. to Require States to Use a Single School Dropout Formula," *New York Times,* April 1, 2008.

32. "Quality Counts 2001," *Education Week,* January 2001.

33. Kevin Smith, *The Ideology of Education: The Commonwealth, the Market, and America's Schools* (Albany, N.Y.: SUNY Press, 2003), 59.

34. "States Weight National Ed Standards," Stateline.org, March 15, 2010, available at www.stateline.org/live/printable/story?contentId+468942.

35. Ying Zhang, "State High School Exit Exams: Trends in Test Programs, Alternate Pathways and Pass Rates," Center on Education Policy, November 5, 2009, available at www.cep-dc .org/document/docWindow.cfm?fuseaction= document.viewDocument&documentid=297& documentFormatId=4558.

36. Nancy Kober et al., "States High School Exit Exams: A Challenging Year," Center on Education Policy, Washington, D.C., August 16, 2006.

37. Ying Zhang, "State High School Exit Exams."

38. Kati Haycock, "Good Teaching Matters: How Well-Qualified Teachers Can Close the Gap," *Thinking K–16* 3, no. 2 (1998).

39. Economists Steven G. Givkin and Eric A. Hanushek, cited (along with researcher William Sanders) in "Quality Counts 2003," 10.

40. John Wirt, Susan Choy, Patrick Rooney, Stephen Provasnik, Anindita Sen, and Richard Tobin, *The Condition of Education 2004: Out-of-Field Teacher in Middle and High School Grades* (Washington, D.C.: National Center for Education Statistics, 2004).

41. Bess Keller, "Most States Pass Federal Review on Highly Qualified Teachers," *Education Week,* August 17, 2006.

42. Diane Stark Rentner et al., "From the Capital to the Classroom: Year 4 of the No Child Left Behind Act," Center on Educational Policy, Washington, D.C., 2006.

43. Michael Allen, "Eight Questions on Teacher Preparation: What Does the Research Say?" Education Commission of the States, Denver, Colo., July 2003.

44. Jerry Johnson and Marty Strange, "Why Rural Matters 2009: State and Regional Challenges and Opportunities," Rural School and Community Trust, Arlington, Va., 2009; Vicki Hobbs, "The Promise and the Power of Distance Learning in Rural Education," Rural School and Community Trust, Arlington, Va., 2004.

45. Thomas D. Snyder and Sally A. Dillow, "Digest of Education Statistics 2009" (Washington, D.C.: U.S. Department of Education, 2010), Tables 84 and 86.

46. See studies such as Erin McHenry-Sorber, "School Consolidation in Pennsylvania: An Analysis of Governor Rendell's Policy Proposal," *Beacon,* summer 2009. One study of school consolidation in New York State between 1985 and 1997 by researchers at Syracuse University found substantially reduced operating costs but only by consolidating the smallest districts. See William Duncombe and John Yinger, "Does School District Consolidation Cut Costs?" Center for Policy Research Working Paper no. 33, January 2001, available at www-cpr .maxwell.syr.edu/cprwps/pdf/wp33.pdf.

47. Joe Bard, Clark Gardener, and Regi Wieland, "Rural School Consolidation Report," prepared for the National Rural Education Association Executive Board, University of Oklahoma, Norman, Okla., April 1–2, 2005.

48. Melissa Maynard, "Still Too Many Schools?" Stateline.org, March 22, 2010, available at www.stateline.org/live/details/story?contentId= 470554.

49. Hobbs, "Promise and the Power."

50. Lowell C. Rose and Alec M. Gallup, "38th Annual Phi Delta Kappa/Gallup Poll," 2006, available at www.pdkintl.org/kappan/kpoll pdf.htm.

51. Sarah Grady, Stacey Bielick, and Susan Aud, *Trends in the Use of School Choice: 1993 to 2007* (Washington, D.C.: U.S. Department of Education, 2010).

52. Lee Hoffman, *Numbers and Types of Public Elementary and Secondary Schools from the Common Core of Data: School Year 2006–07— First Look* (Washington, D.C.: U.S. Department of Education, 2008). See also USCharterSchools. org, a Web site run by a consortium of educational associations with an interest in providing information and promising practices about charter schools, for more statistics about charter schools.

53. "State Profiles," U.S. Charter Schools, available at www.uscharterschools.org/pub/uscs_docs/sp/ index.htm.

54. Erika Hayasaki, "Charter Academy Shuts 60 Schools," *Los Angeles Times,* August 16, 2004,

available at http://articles.latimes.com/2004/
aug/16/local/me-charter16.

55. Brian P. Gill, P. Michael Timpane, Karen E. Ross, and Dominic J. Brewer, *Rhetoric versus Reality: What We Know and What We Need to Know about Vouchers and Charter Schools* (Santa Monica, Calif.: RAND Corporation, 2001), xviii; Charles S. Clark, "Charter Schools," *CQ Researcher,* December 20, 2002.

56. U.S. Department of Education, Institute of Education Sciences, National Center for Education Statistics, National Assessment of Educational Progress (NAEP), 2003 Reading Charter School Pilot Study, Washington, D.C., December 2004.

57. Dan Keating and Theola Labbé-DeBose, "Charter Schools Make Gains on Tests," *Washington Post,* December 15, 2008. This article and a variety of multimedia resources about the Washington, D.C., charter schools are available at www.washingtonpost.com/wp-srv/metro/specials/charter/index.html.

58. Diana Jean Schemo, "Nation's Charter Schools Lagging Behind, U.S. Test Scores Reveal," *New York Times,* August 17, 2003, available at www.nytimes.com/2004/08/17/education/17charter.html?hp.

59. "Multiple Choice: Charter School Performance in 16 States," Center for Research on Education Outcomes, June 2009, available at http://credo.stanford.edu/reports/MULTIPLE_CHOICE_CREDO.pdf.

60. Kenneth Jost, "School Vouchers Showdown," *CQ Researcher*, February 15, 2002.

61. See William A. Fischel, "Why Voters Veto Vouchers: Public Schools and Community-Specific Social Capital," *Economics of Governance* 7, no. 2 (2006): 109–132.

62. Josh Hafenbrack, "UPDATE: Florida Supreme Court Strikes Voucher, Property Tax Amendments from the Ballot," Central Florida Political Pulse, a blog of the *Orlando Sentinel,* September 3, 2008, available at http://blogs.orlandosentinel.com/news_politics/2008/09/florida-supreme.html.

63. Angela Townsend, "More than 2,500 in Ohio Apply for School Vouchers," *Cleveland Plain Dealer,* July 4, 2006. Also see the Ohio Department of Education's Web site on Ohio EdChoice, www.scohio.org, for more information on the program.

64. Amanda Paulson, "Milwaukee's Lessons on School Vouchers," *Christian Science Monitor,* May 23, 2006.

65. John Robert Warren, "Graduation Rates for Choice and Public School Students in Milwaukee, 2003–2008," School Choice Wisconsin, February 2010, available at www.schoolchoicewi.org/data/currdev_links/2010-Grad-Study-1–31–2010.pdf.

66. See the work of Paul Peterson at Harvard University School of Education, for example, Paul E. Peterson and David E. Campbell, eds., *Charters, Vouchers, and Public Education* (Washington, D.C.: Brookings Institution Press, 2001).

67. Government Accounting Office, "School Vouchers: Publicly Funded Programs in Cleveland and Milwaukee," GAO 01–914, Washington, D.C., 2001, 4; Zachary M. Seward, "Long-Delayed Education Study Casts Doubt on Value of Vouchers," *Wall Street Journal,* July 15–16, 2006.

68. Grady, Bielick, and Aud, *Trends.*

69. National Center for Education Statistics, *The Condition of Education* (Washington, D.C.: U.S. Department of Education, 2005).

70. "State Laws," Home School Legal Defense Association, available at www.hslda.org/laws/default.asp.

71. Matthew H. Boswell, *Courts as Catalysts: State Supreme Courts and Public School Finance Equity* (Albany, N.Y.: SUNY Press, 2001), 125.

72. See the NEA and AFT Web sites, www.nea.org and www.aft.org.

73. "About PTA," PTA, available at www.pta.org/about_pta.asp.

74. "Position Statement," Business Coalition for Student Achievement, 2007, available at www.biz4achievement.org/about_the_coalition/position_statement.html.

75. "Kansas Board Backs Teaching of Evolution," *Education Week,* February 21, 2007, 24.

76. "One More Victory for Evolutionary Science," *Star Tribune,* February 16, 2006; Jodi Rudoren, "Ohio Board Undoes Stand on Evolution," *New York Times,* February 15, 2006; and Patrick Cain, "Science Theories May Face Scrutiny," *Beacon Journal,* September 7, 2006.

77. Sean Cavanagh, "Evolution Debate Remains Vexing for Texas Board," *Education Week,* April 1, 2009, 4.

78. National Center for Education Statistics, *The Nation's Report Card: Reading 2009* (Washington, D.C.: U.S. Department of Education, 2010).

79. "Percentage Distribution of Public School Students, by Sex, Race/Ethnicity, Percentage Minority, and State: 2007–08," *Schools and Staffing Survey 2007–08* (Washington, D.C.: U.S. Department of Education, 2009), Table 3.

80. "Five Shoes Waiting to Drop on Arizona's Future" and "Beat the Odds," Morrison Institute for Public Policy, Arizona State University, 2001, both available at http://morrisoninstitute.asu.edu.

Chapter 14

1. George Kelling and Ronald Corbett, "This Works: Preventing and Reducing Crime," *Civic Bulletin* 32 (March 2003), 1.

2. "Crime in the United States by Volume and Rate per 100,000 Inhabitants, 1989–2009," *Uniform Crime Report 2008* (Washington, D.C.: Federal Bureau of Investigation), Table 1.

3. Kelling and Corbett, "This Works," 3.

4. Quoted in Jeremy Travis and Michelle Waul, "Reflections on the Crime Decline: Lessons for the Future?" Proceedings from the Urban Institute Crime Decline Forum, Washington, D.C., August 2002, 18.

5. See John Donohue and Steven Levitt, "The Impact of Legalized Abortion on Crime," National Bureau of Economic Research working paper, November 2000, available at www.nber.org/papers.

6. Danielle S. Allen, *The World of Prometheus: The Politics of Punishing in Democratic Athens* (Princeton, N.J.: Princeton University Press, 1999), 3.

7. For a brilliant discussion of how this transformation came to pass, see Sir Frederick Pollock and F. W. Maitland, *History of English Law before the Time of Edward I* (Cambridge, UK: Cambridge University Press, 1969).

8. Marc Mauer, "The Crisis of the Young African American Male and the Criminal Justice System," presentation to the U.S. Commission on Civil Rights, Washington, D.C., April 15–16, 1999, 6.

9. Kevin Smith, "The Politics of Punishment: Evaluating Political Explanations of Incarceration Rates," *Journal of Politics* 66, no. 3 (2004): 925.

10. Katherine Beckett, *Making Crime Pay: Law and Order in Contemporary Politics* (New York: Oxford University Press, 1997).

11. Smith, "Politics of Punishment."

12. Daniel J. Elazar, *American Federalism: A View from the States* (New York: Crowell, 1972), 106–107.

13. For more details on nineteenth-century views of incarceration and on the Quakers' long-standing opposition to corporal punishment, see Norman Johnston, *The Crucible of Good Intentions* (Philadelphia: Philadelphia Museum of Art, 1994)..

14. See David Oshinsky's *Worse than Slavery: Parchman Farm and the Ordeal of Jim Crow Justice* (New York: Free Press, 1996). As Oshinsky's title makes clear, the author is no fan of Parchman Farm. It is therefore interesting that he concludes in the book's final chapter that the modern penal institution that replaced the farm in the 1970s is in many ways worse.

15. The discrimination, however, persists. Women continue to earn only three-quarters of what men with similar backgrounds and experience earn. Francine Blau and Lawrence Kah, "The Gender Pay Gap," in the National Bureau of Economic Research Report, summer 2001, available at www.nber.org/reporter/summer01/blaukahn.html

16. Stephan Thernstrom, remarks made at the Heritage Foundation symposium on the Kerner

Commission, March 13, 1998, available at www.heritage.org/Research/PoliticalPhilosophy/h1619.cfm.

17. "Night of Terror," *Time,* July 25, 1977.

18. This figure—from the Office of National Drug Control Policy—does not include alcohol, which is considered the most popular drug of all.

19. See Robert MacCoun and Peter Reuter's *Drug War Heresies: Learning from Other Vices, Times, and Places* (New York: Cambridge University Press, 2001), 26, 29.

20. See the National Organization for the Reform of Marijuana Laws Web site for state-by-state drug laws, www.norml.org.

21. Eric Schlosser, *Reefer Madness: Sex, Drugs, and Cheap Labor in the American Black Market* (Boston: Houghton Mifflin, 2003), 26.

22. For an exploration the drug culture in one inner-city Baltimore neighborhood, see David Simon and Edward Burns, *The Corner: A Year in the Life of an Inner-City Neighborhood* (New York: Broadway Books, 1998). This was later made into an HBO mini-series.

23. Kathleen Hunger, "Money Mattering More in Judicial Elections," Stateline.org, May 12, 2004, available at www.stateline.org/live/ViewPage.action?siteNodeId=136&languageId=1&contentId=15646.

24. "One in 100: Behind Bars in America 2008," Pew Center on the States, Washington, D.C., December 2008, available at www.pewcenteronthestates.org/uploadedFiles/8015PCTS_Prison08_FINAL_2-1-1_FORWEB.pdf.

25. "State Expenditure Report, 2008," National Association of State Budget Officers, Washington, D.C., 58.

26. "One in 100."

27. Allen J. Beck and Thomas P. Bonczar, "Lifetime Likelihood of Going to State or Federal Prison," Bureau of Justice Statistics, Criminal Offenders Statistics, 1997, available at www.ojp.usdoj.gov/bjs/crimoff.htm.

28. Josh Meyer, "Obama Administration Urges Equal Penalties for Crack, Powder Cocaine Dealers," *Los Angeles Times,* April 30, 2009,

available at Articles.latimes.com/2009/apr/30/nation/na-crack30; "Bad Science and Bad Policy," *New York Times,* March 2, 2010, available at www.nytimes.com/2010/03/03/opinion/03wed3.html.

29. Sentencing Project, including "A Decade of Reform: Felony Disenfranchisement Laws in the United States," available at www.sentencing project.org.

30. Ryan S. King, "Expanding the Vote: State Felony Disenfranchisement Reform, 1997–2008, Sentencing Project, September 2008, available at www.sentencingproject.org/doc/publications/fd_statedisenfranchisement.pdf.

31. Sentencing Project, "Decade of Reform."

32. Mauer, "Crisis."

33. The first of Peel's Nine Principles; quoted, for example, in Sandra Nazemi, "Sir Robert Peel's Nine Principals of Policing," Los Angeles Community Policing, available at www.lacp.org/2009-Articles-Main/062609-Peels9Principals-SandyNazemi.htm.

34. For an account of how well-intentioned policies went horribly wrong, see Fred Siegel's *The Future Once Happened Here: New York, D.C., LA, and the Future of America's Big Cities* (New York: Free Press, 1997).

35. James Q. Wilson and George L. Kelling, "Broken Windows: The Police and Neighborhood Safety," *Atlantic Monthly,* March 1982.

36. For an account of the Rodney King beating and the LAPD, see Lou Cannon's, *Official Negligence: How Rodney King and the Riots Changed Los Angeles and the LAPD* (New York: Westview Press, 1999).

37. Ibid.

38. For a detailed account of early experiments with community policing and problem-oriented policing, see George L. Kelling and Mary A. Wycoff, "Evolving Strategy of Policing: Case Studies of Strategic Change," National Criminal Justice Reference Center Document no. 198029, Washington, D.C., May 2001.

39. William Bratton, *Turnaround: How America's Top Cop Reversed the Crime Epidemic* (New York: Random House, 1998), 143, 180.

40. For an account of how Compstat was created and how it is used, see John Buntin, "Assertive Policing, Plummeting Crime: The NYPD Takes on Crime in New York City," Kennedy School of Government Case Study, Harvard University, Cambridge, Mass., August 1999.

41. This section is drawn from an August 2002 seminar at the Urban Institute, "Reflections on the Crime Decline: Lessons for the Future," Washington, D.C., 12–19.

42. Robert Weisberg and David Mills, "Violence Silence: Why No One Really Cares about Prison Rape," Slate, October 1, 2003, available at www.slate.com/id/2089095. See also "No Escape: Male Rape in U.S. Prisons," Human Rights Watch, 2001, available at www.hrw.org/reports/2001/prison/report.html.

43. Doris J. James and Lauren E. Glaze, "Mental Health Problems of Prison and Jail Inmates," U.S. Department of Justice, Bureau of Justice Statistics, Washington, D.C., September 2006.

44. "Ill-Equipped: U.S. Prisons and Offenders with Mental Illnesses," Human Rights Watch, 2003, available at www.hrw.org/reports/2003/usa1003.

45. "Amnesty International Report 2009: State of the World's Human Rights," Amnesty International, London, May 28, 2009, available at http://thereport.amnesty.org/en/regions/americas/usa.

46. "Facts about the Death Penalty," Death Penalty Information Center, April 2010, available at http://deathpenaltyinfo.org/documents/FactSheet.pdf.

47. "Rights of Children Must Be Respected," Amnesty International, London, April 25, 2003.

48. Ibid. Currently, eighty child offenders await execution in the United States for crimes committed when they were sixteen or seventeen years old. Nineteen children were executed in the United States between 1995 and 2003.

49. Los Angeles Police Department Web site, www.lapdonline.org.

50. Brian A. Reaves and Matthew J. Hickman, "Police Departments in Large Cities, 1990–2000," Bureau of Justice Statistics Special Report, NCJ-175703, Washington, D.C., May 2002.

51. "COPS Hiring Recovery Program (CHRP)," U.S. Department of Justice, July 29, 2009, available at www.cops.usdoj.gov/default.asp?item=2108.

52. "Crime Trends by Population Group 2008," Uniform Crime Report 2008 (Washington, D.C.: Federal Bureau of Investigation), Table 16.

53. "Law Enforcement Technology—Are Small and Rural Agencies Equipped and Trained?" U.S. Department of Justice, Office of Justice Programs, Washington, D.C., June 2004.

54. For research and survey findings and other resources, see Meth Action Clearinghouse, National Association of Counties, available at www.naco.org.

55. John Gramlich, "New Script for Sudafed?" Stateline.org, March 15, 2010, available at www.stateline.org/live/printable/story?contentId=468500.

56. Jim Barnett, "Bush Signs Legislation to Fight the Spread of Meth across U.S.," Oregonian, March 10, 2006; Chris Casteel, "Meth Imports Rising, Sheriff Says," Oklahoman, July 19, 2006.

57. "Facts about the Death Penalty."

58. Richard Willing and Gary Fields, "Geography of the Death Penalty," USA Today, December 20, 1999, A1.

59. "Facts on Post-Conviction DNA Exonerations," The Innocence Project, available at www.innocenceproject.org/Content/351.php.

60. Denny Walsh, "Judge: Rethink Lethal Injection," Sacramento Bee, December 16, 2006.

61. John Gramlich, "No End in Sight to Death Penalty Wrangling," Stateline.org, July 31, 2008, available at www.stateline.org/live/details/story?contentId=529997.

62. Quoted in Nathan Koppel and Chris Herring, "Lethal Injection Draws Scrutiny in Some States," Wall Street Journal, October 15, 2009, A13.

63. "Prison Count 2010," Pew Center on the States, March 2010, available at www.pewcenteronthestates.org/uploadedFiles/Prison_Count_2010.pdf?n=880.

64. Randal C. Archibold, "Driven to the Financial Brink, a State Opens the Prison Doors," New York Times, March 24, 2010, A14.

65. "Correctional Boot Camps: Lessons from a Decade of Research," National Institute of Justice, U.S. Department of Justice, Washington, D.C., June 2003.

66. "Do Drug Courts Work?: Findings From Drug Court Research," U.S. Department of Justice, Office of Justice Programs, National Institute of Justice, May 12, 2008, available at www.ojp.usdoj.gov/nij/topics/courts/drug-courts/work.htm.

67. In 2000, 44 percent of the 625,243 people arrested nationwide were ages twenty-four or younger. Jeremy Travis and Jeffrey Butts, "The Rise and Fall of Youth Violence," Urban Institute, Washington, D.C., March 2002, 9.

68. See "Leading Cause of Death Reports," National Institute of Injury Prevention and Control, U.S. Centers for Disease Control and Prevention, available at http://webappa.cdc.gov/sasweb/ncipc/leadcaus10.html.

69. John Buntin, "A Community Responds: Boston Confronts an Upsurge of Youth Violence," Kennedy School of Government Case Study, Harvard University, Cambridge, Mass., June 1998.

70. Charles Puzzanchera, "Juvenile Arrests 2008," Juvenile Justice Bulletin, Office of Justice Programs, December 2009, available at www.ncjrs.gov/pdffiles1/ojjdp/228479.pdf.

71. Howard N. Snyder, "Not This Time: A Response to the Warnings of the Juvenile Superpredator," *Corrections Today,* April 2007, 116.

Chapter 15

1. Robert Roos, "Pandemic Underscored Influenza's Unpredictability," CIDRAP News, April 23, 2010, available at www.cidrap.umn.edu/cidrap/content/influenza/swineflu/news/apr2310pandemic-jw.html.

2. Carol E. Lee and Amie Parnes, "Biden Would Avoid Subways, Planes after Swine Flu Outbreak," Politico, April 30, 2009, available at www.politico.com/news/stories/0409/21925.html.

3. Maryn McKenna, "Vaccine Production Foiled, Confirmed Experts' Predictions," CIDRAP News, April 27, 2010, available at www.cidrap.umn.edu/cidrap/content/influenza/swineflu/news/apr2610h1n1vax.html.

4. "CDC 2009 H1N1 Flu," U.S. Centers for Disease Control and Prevention, April 11, 2010, available at www.cdc.gov/h1n1flu.

5. John Barry, *The Great Influenza: The Epic Story of the Deadliest Plague in History* (New York: Viking Penguin, 2004).

6. "Third Annual Report to the President and Congress of the Advisory Panel to Assess Domestic Response Capabilities for Terrorism Involving Weapons of Mass Destruction," RAND Corporation, Washington, D.C., December 15, 2001, 44.

7. "Tobacco and Mortality," U.S. Centers for Disease Control and Prevention, last updated September 16, 2009, available at http://cdc.gov/tobacco/data_statistics/fact_sheets/health_effects/tobacco_related_mortality.

8. Gary Bryner, "Welfare Reform in Utah," Report no. 14, Nelson A. Rockefeller Institute of Government, Albany, N.Y., August 2002. See also Deborah A. Orth and Malcolm L. Goggin, "How States and Counties Have Responded to the Family Policy Goals of Welfare Reform," Report to the U.S. Department of Health and Human Services, Administration for Children and Families (Grant No. 90XP0028/01), Nelson A. Rockefeller Institute of Government, Albany, N.Y., 2003.

9. Eileen Ellis, Dennis Roberts, Tanya Schwartz, and David M. Rousseau, *Medicaid Enrollment in 50 States* (Washington, D.C.: The Kaiser Commission on Medicaid and the Uninsured, Kaiser Family Foundation, 2010). The Kaiser Family Foundation Web site has a host of Medicaid-related facts and statistics, www.kff.org.

10. "2008 State Expenditure Report," National Association of State Budget Officers, Washington, D.C., 3.

11. Paul Starr, *The Social Transformation of American Medicine* (New York: Basic Books, 1992), 149.

12. Ibid., 72.

13. Ibid.

14. Ibid.

15. NYU Medical Center Web site, www.med.nyu.edu/Bellevue.

16. Starr, *Social Transformation of American Medicine,* 150.

17. Samuel Gompers, the head of the AFL, viewed compulsory health insurance as "paternalistic" and worried that it might weaken the labor movement by causing workers to look to employers instead of to unions for benefits. Starr, *Social Transformation of American Medicine,* 254–255.

18. "Stocks Collapse in 16,410,030-Share Day, but Rally at Close Cheers Brokers," *New York Times,* October 30, 1929.

19. Scholars such as Theda Skocpol have argued that the federal government's first major foray into safety net programs actually came much earlier in the form of lavish pensions for Union veterans of the Civil War. Theda Skocpol, "America's First Social Security System: The Expansion of Benefits for Civil War Veterans," *Political Science Quarterly* 108 (spring 1993): 85–86.

20. "Social Security," in *Columbia Encyclopedia,* 6th ed. (New York: Columbia University Press, 2001).

21. Jay Bhattacharya and Darius Lakdawalla, "Does Medicare Benefit the Poor?: New Answers to an Old Question," Working Paper w9280, National Bureau of Economic Research, Cambridge, Mass., October 2002.

22. "2008 State Expenditure Report," 45.

23. Ibid, 47.

24. "An Introduction to Medicaid," Center for Budget and Policy Priorities, October 2, 2006, available at www.cbpp.org/10–2-06health.htm.

25. All Medicaid eligibility figures calculated from "Income Thresholds for Jobless and Working Parents Applying for Medicaid by Annual Income as a Percent of Federal Poverty Level (FPL), 2009," Kaiser Family Foundation, January 2009, available at http://statehealthfacts.org/comparetable.jsp?ind=205&rat=4.

26. John Klemm, "Medicaid Spending: A Brief History," *Health Care Financing Review* 22, no. 1 (2000). For more recent data, see the Kaiser Family Foundation Statehealthfacts Web site, http://Statehealthfacts.org.

27. "2008 State Expenditure Report," 44.

28. By 1983, the number of single mothers had fallen back to about 50 percent of AFDC recipients. By 1992, that number had crept back up to 55 percent of AFDC recipients. National Research Council, *Evaluating Welfare Reform in an Era of Transition,* ed. Robert A. Moffitt and Michele Ver Ploeg (Washington, D.C.: National Press, 2001), 17.

29. Steven Roberts, "Food Stamps Program: How It Grew and How Reagan Wants to Cut It Back," *New York Times,* April 4, 1981.

30. Quoted in Lou Cannon, *Governor Reagan: His Rise to Power* (New York: Public Affairs, 2003), 349. Of course, Roosevelt made this statement to argue for government-funded work programs—a measure that Reagan never supported as president.

31. Andy Schneider, *Medicaid Resource Book* (Washington, D.C.: Kaiser Commission on Medicaid and the Uninsured, July 2002), 97–98.

32. "Public Officials of the Year: Leading in Good Times and in Bad," *Governing* magazine, December 1997.

33. Charles Mahtesian, "Captains of Conservatism," *Governing* magazine, February 1995.

34. National Research Council, *Evaluating Welfare Reform,* 19.

35. Quoted in Mickey Kaus, "Has Welfare Reform Worked? Yes, Smashingly," *Blueprint Magazine,* January–February 2002, available at www.dlc.org/ndol_ci.cfm?kaid=114&subid=143&contentid=250083.

36. "TANF: Total Number of Recipients, Fiscal Year 2009," Administration for Children and Families, U.S. Department of Health and Human Services, Washington, D.C., January 28, 2010. Caseload data available at www.acf.hhs.gov/programs/ofa/data-reports/caseload/caseload_current.htm.

37. For a comprehensive account of the healthcare debate, see Haynes Johnson and David Broder's

The System: The Way of American Politics at the Breaking Point (New York: Little, Brown 1996).

38. Ibid.

39. "Health Insurance Coverage in America, 2008," Kaiser Commission on Medicaid and the Uninsured, Washington, D.C., 2009.

40. "The Uninsured: A Primer," Kaiser Commission on Medicaid and the Uninsured, October 2009, available at www.kff.org/uninsured/upload/7451-05.pdf.

41. In practice, states might not save money if HMOs managed to enroll the healthiest Medicaid recipients, who would not have used many medical services anyway, a practice known as risk selection.

42. Christopher Swope, "The Medicaid Windfall: Enjoy It While It Lasts," *Governing* magazine, September 1998.

43. Medicaid expenditures grew at an annual rate of 27.1 percent between 1990 and 1992. "Medicaid 101 Briefing Charts," Kaiser Commission on Medicaid and the Uninsured/Alliance for Health Care Reform, Washington, D.C., February 28, 2003.

44. "Enrolling Uninsured Low Income Children In Medicaid and SCHIP," Kaiser Commission on Medicaid and the Uninsured, Washington, D.C., May 2002.

45. National Conference of State Legislatures, "NCSL Resources—SCHIP General Information," 2009, Washington, D.C.

46. "Income Eligibility Levels for Children's Separate CHIP Programs by Annual Incomes and as a Percent of Federal Poverty Level, December 2009," Kaiser Family Foundation, December 2009, available at http://state healthfacts.org/comparemaptable.jsp?ind=204 &cat=4.

47. "Children's Health Insurance Program Overview," National Conference of State Legislatures, March 2010, available at http://ncsl.org/default.aspx?tabid=14510.

48. State Health Access Data Assistance Center, "The State of Kids' Coverage," Robert Wood Johnson Foundation, University of Minnesota, Minneapolis, August 9, 2006.

49. Lisa Dubay, Ian Hill, and Genevieve Kenney, "Five Things Everyone Should Know about SCHIP," Urban Institute, Washington, D.C., October 2002.

50. "Health Insurance Coverage of Children 0–18," Kaiser Family Foundation, 2008, available at http://statehealthfacts.org/comparetable.jsp?ind=127&cat=3.

51. "Health Insurance Coverage of Children 0–18 Living in Poverty (under 100% FPL), States (2007–2008), U.S. (2008)," Kaiser Family Foundation, 2008, available at www.stat ehealthfacts.org/comparebar.jsp?ind=128 &cat=3.

52. Vernon Smith, Dennis Roberts, David Rousseau, and Tanya Schwartz, "CHIP Enrollment: June 2009," Kaiser Commission on Medicaid and the Uninsured, April 2010, available at http://kff .org/medicaid/upload/7642–04.pdf.

53. "United States at a Glance," National Association of Community Health Centers, Bethesda, Md., 2009.

54. Bowen Garrett, Matthew Buettgens, Lan Doan, Irene Headen, and John Holahan, *The Cost of Failure to Enact Health Reform: 2010–2020* (Washington, D.C.: Urban Institute, 2010).

55. Obaid S. Zaman, Linda C. Cummings, and Sari Siegel Spieler, *America's Public Hospitals and Health Systems, 2008* (Washington, D.C.: National Public Health and Hospital Institute, 2010).

56. Katherine Vogt, "Public Hospitals Seen Slipping Away, Changing into Other Entities," Amednews.com, September 12, 2005.

57. Kevin Sack, "Immigrants Cling to Fragile Lifeline at Safety-Net Hospital," *New York Times,* September 24, 2009, A16.

58. "Rural Health Care," Agency for Healthcare Research and Quality, U.S. Department of Health and Human Services, available at www.ahrq.gov/news/focus/focrural.htm.

59. "How Technology Is Being Used to Enhance the Delivery of Healthcare Services," Appalachian Regional Commission, www.arc.gov/index .do?nodeID=2043.

60. John Holahan and Brend Spillman, "A Strong Safety Net Is Not the Same as Insurance," Urban

Institute, January 15, 2002, available at www .urban.org/url.cfm?ID=31041.

61. "Health Insurance Coverage of Children 0–18."

62. Katherine Barrett, Richard Greene, and Michele Mariani, "Insurance Coverage: Access Denied," *Governing* magazine, February 2004; Penelope Lemov, "Setting Limits on Medicaid," *Governing* magazine, March 2005.

63. Barrett, Greene, and Mariani, "Insurance Coverage"; Penelope Lemov, "Maine's Medical Gamble," *Governing* magazine, November 2004; "Dirigo Agency Reaches Deal with Anthem to Extend Dirigo Choice," Associated Press, September 22, 2006.

64. Debra J. Lipson, James M. Verdier, and Lynn Quincy, "Leading the Way?: Maine's Initial Experience in Expanding Coverage through Dirigo Health Reforms," Mathematica Policy Research, December 2007, available at www .commonwealthfund.org/usr_doc/Lipson_leading thewayMaineexpDirigo_1079.pdf?section=4039.

65. "No Maine Miracle Cure," *Wall Street Journal,* August 21, 2009, available at http://online.wsj .com/article/SB1000142405297020461900457 4322401816501182.html.

66. Sharon Anglin Treat, "Competing Lessons from Maine's Health Insurance Plan," *Wall Street Journal,* August 25, 2009, A14.

67. Anna C. Spencer, "Massachusetts Going for Full Coverage," *State Health Notes,* April 17, 2006, available at www.ncsl.org/programs/health/ shn/2006/sn465.htm.

68. Richard Wolf, "Mass. Has Lessons for Health Care Debate," *USA Today,* July 23, 2009.

69. "Summary of New Health Reform Law," Kaiser Family Foundation, April 8, 2010, available at http://kff.org/healthreform/upload/8061.pdf.

70. Jake Grovum, "Confusion in the Capitols," Stateline.org, April 8, 2010, available at www.stateline.org/live/printable/story?content Id=475804.

71. Quoted in Rosalind Helderman, "McDonnell: Health Care Overhaul to Cost Virginia $1 Billion over 12 Years," Washingtonpost.com, March 22, 2010, available at http://voices .washingtonpost.com/virginiapolitics/2010/03/ health_care_to_cost_virginia_1.html.

72. Robbie Brown, "Georgia Insurance Commissioner Balks at Request on New Health Law," *New York Times,* April 13, 2010, available at www.nytimes.com/2010/04/14/ health/policy/14georgia.html.

73. Quoted in Grovum, "Confusion in the Capitols."

74. "Health Information Technology," RAND Health Research Highlights, 2005, available at www.rand.org/pubs/research_briefs/2005/ RAND_RB9136.pdf.

75. Ellen Perlman, "Digitally Dazed," *Governing* magazine, June 2007, available at www .governing.com/archive/archive/2007/jun/ healthit.txt.

76. Ellen Perlman, "Finding the Money for Health IT," *Governing* magazine, October 6, 2009, available at www.governing.com/print/column/ finding-money-health-it.

77. "Medicare and Medicaid: An Overview," Congressional Budget Office, November 2007, available at www.cbo.gov/ftpdocs/87xx/ doc8758/AppendixA.4.1.shtml.

78. Molly O'Malley Watts, "The Community Living Assistance Services and Supports (CLASS) Act," Kaiser Commission on Medicaid and the Uninsured, Kaiser Family Foundation, October 2009, available at kff.org/healthreform/ upload/7996.pdf.

79. Christine Vestal, "Hope for the Long Term," Stateline.org, April 15, 2010, available at www .stateline.org/live/details/story?contentId=477299.

80. Ibid.

81. "Medicaid Home and Community-Based Service Programs: Data Update," Kaiser Commission on Medicaid and the Uninsured, Kaiser Family Foundation, November 2009, available at http://kff.org/medicaid/upload/ 7720–03.pdf.

82. Vestal, "Hope for the Long Term."

83. "Medicaid Home and Community-Based Service Programs."

84. Quoted in Aimee Curl, "Bracing for Bird Flu," *Federal Times,* April 10, 2006.

85. Janet Heinrich "Public Health and Medical Preparedness. Testimony before the Subcommittee on Public Health, Committee on Health,

Education, Labor, and Pensions, U.S. Senate," Washington, D.C., October 9, 2001.

86. Quoted in Roos, "Pandemic Underscored Influenza's Unpredictability."

87. Nicholas Kristof, "Shaming Young Mothers," *New York Times,* August 23, 2002; Jane Brody, "Abstinence-Only: Does It Work?" *New York Times,* June 1, 2004.

88. Erik W. Robelen, "Program Promoting Sexual Abstinence Gets Resurrected; Instructional Approach Winds Up in Health-Care Law," *Education Week,* April 7, 2010, 6.

89. Faye Flam, "Study Offers Nuanced View of Abstinence Education: Penn's Sex-Education Study," McClatchy-Tribune Business News, February 16, 2010.

90. Lorrie Gavin, et al., "Sexual and Reproductive Health of Persons Aged 10–24 Years—United States, 2002–2007," *Morbidity and Mortality Weekly Report* 58, no. SS-6 (July 17, 2009).

91. "Insurance Coverage for Contraception Laws," National Conference of State Legislatures, February 2010, available at http://ncsl.org/default.aspx?tabid=14384.

92. Daniel C. Vock, "FDA Ruling Puts Pharmacists in Crossfire," Stateline.org, September 6, 2006, available at www.stateline.org/live/details/story?contentId=139338.

93. "Obesity and Overweight," U.S. Centers for Disease Control and Prevention, January 18, 2010, available at www.cdc.gov/nchs/fastats/overwt.htm.

94. "U.S. Obesity Trends, Trends by State, 1985–2008," U.S. Centers for Disease Control and Prevention, November 20, 2009, available at www.cdc.gov/obesity/data/trends.html#State.

95. "Obesity and Overweight."

96. Todd Zwillich, "CDC: Obesity Is Still an Epidemic," WebMD Health News, June 2, 2005, available at www.webmd.com/diet/news/20050602/cdc-obesity-is-still-epidemic.

97. Eric A. Finkelstein, Ian C. Fiebelkorn, and Guijing Wang, "National Medical Spending Attributable to Overweight and Obesity: How Much, and Who's Paying?" *Health Affairs,* May 14, 2003.

98. "The Future Costs of Obesity: National and State Estimates of the Impact of Obesity on Direct Health Care Expenses," United Health Foundation, American Public Health Association, and Partnership for Prevention, November 2009, available at www.americashealthrankings.org/2009/report/Cost%20Obesity%20Report-final.pdf.

Chapter 16

1. Phone interview with Fran Pavley, October 23, 2009.

2. Phone interview with Jessica Shipley, November 18, 2009.

3. Phone interview with Barry Rabe, December 8, 2008.

4. Marc Allen Eisner, *Governing the Environment: The Transformation of Environmental Regulation* (Boulder, Colo.: Lynne Rienner Publishers, 2007), 1.

5. Phone interview with John Cahill, December 5, 2008.

6. Barry G. Rabe, *Statehouse and Greenhouse: The Emerging Politics of American Climate Change Policy* (Washington, D.C.: Brookings Institution Press, 2004), xiv.

7. Ibid., 77.

8. Alan Greenblatt, "Fran Pavley: Legislative Prodigy," *Governing* magazine, September 2002, 80.

9. Quoted in ibid.

10. Phone interview with Fran Pavley, September 3, 2002.

11. Phone interview with Stanley Young, November 21, 2008.

12. Quoted in Linda Greenhouse, "Justices Say EPA Has Power to Act on Harmful Gases," *New York Times,* April 8, 2007, A1.

13. Quoted in John M. Broder and Felicity Barringer, "EPA Says 17 States Can't Set Greenhouse Gas Rules for Cars," *New York Times,* December 20, 2007, A1.

14. Phone interview with Ron Burke, November 20, 2008.

15. Quoted in Janet Wilson, "EPA Chief Is Said to Have Ignored Staff," *Los Angeles Times,* December 21, 2007, A30.

16. Craig Pittman, "Crist Blasts EPA's Ruling," *St. Petersburg Times,* December 21, 2007, 1A.

17. John M. Broder, "Limits Set on Pollution from Autos," *New York Times,* April 2, 2010, B1.

18. David Burwell and Robert Puentes, "Innovative State Transportation Financing and Funding: Policy Options for States," National Governors Association Center for Best Practices, June 2008, available at www.nga.org/Files/pdf/0901 transportationfunding.pdf.

19. Quoted in Alan Greenblatt, "Fuel Tax: The Devil We Know," *CQ Weekly,* February 23, 2009, 417.

20. Quoted in ibid.

21. Quoted in ibid.

22. Quoted in Tom Arrandale, "Carbon Goes to Market," *Governing* magazine, September 2008, 26.

23. Quoted in Abby Gruen, "Battle Brewing over Cap-and-Trade Funds," (Newark) *Star-Ledger,* March 19, 2010, 32.

24. Phone interview with C. Boyden Gray, April 5, 2010.

25. John M. Broder, "Obama to Open Offshore Areas to Drilling," *New York Times*, March 31, 2010, A1.

26. Quoted in Chelsea Waugaman, "Voltage Charge," *Governing* magazine, November 2005, 76.

27. Quoted in Mannix Porterfield, "Manchin Wants Aggressive Renewable Energy Policy," (Beckley) *Register-Herald,* October 20, 2008.

28. Dirk Lammers, "US Wind Energy Adds 1,400 MW of Capacity," Associated Press, October 22, 2008.

29. Michael Burnham, "Public Spending Drives Robust Growth in U.S. Geothermal Industry, Report Says," NYTimes.com, April 13, 2010, available at www.nytimes.com/gwire/2010/04/13/13greenwire-public-spending-drives-robust-growth-in-us-geo-72049.html.

30. Phone interview with Margo Thorning, November 13, 2008.

31. Interview with Rabe.

32. Phone interview with Terry Tamminen, October 22, 2009.

33. Michael Hawthorne, "How Coal Got a Dirty Name," *Chicago Tribune,* July 9, 2008, 1.

34. Judy Pasternak, "Coal at Heart of Climate Battle," *Los Angeles Times,* April 14, 2008, A1.

35. Phone interview with Bob Eye, May 15, 2008.

36. Quoted in Alan Greenblatt, "Guarding the Greenhouse," *Governing* magazine, July 2008, 21.

37. Phone interview with Robert Glicksman, May 15, 2008.

38. Phone interview with Jay Emler, May 13, 2008.

39. Quoted in Alan Greenblatt, "Coal-Fired Compromise," *Governing* magazine, July 2009, 12.

40. Quoted in Alan Greenblatt, "Confronting Carbon," *Governing* magazine, December 2008, 14.

41. Quoted in ibid.

42. Quoted in Alan Greenblatt, "Miami's Vision," *Governing* magazine, November 2009, 15.

43. Quoted in ibid.

44. Quoted in ibid.

45. Dirk Johnson, "Chicago Unveils Multifaceted Plan to Curb Emissions of Heat-Trapping Gases," *New York Times,* September 19, 2008, A13.

46. David Beard, "At Least 25,000 at Greenbuild Conference in Boston," Boston Globe Greenblog, November 19, 2008, available at www.boston.com/lifestyle/green/greenblog/2008/11/at_least_25000_at_greenbuild_c.html.

47. Randy Lee Loftis, "Weatherization Picking Up—Slowly," *Dallas Morning News,* March 31, 2010, B1.

48. Christopher Swope, "Lofty Goals," *Governing* magazine, March 2009, 22.

49. Phone interview with R. T. Rybak, 2008.

50. "The New Apollo Program: Clean Energy, Good Jobs," The Apollo Alliance, September 2008, available at www.apolloalliance.org/downloads/fullreportfinal.pdf.

51. "Current and Potential Green Jobs in the U.S. Economy," *Global Insight,* October 2008.

52. Phone interview with Pavley, 2009.

53. Phone interview with Eric Crawford, November 20, 2008.

54. Quoted in Anthony DePalma, "New Jersey Dealing with Solar Policy's Success," *New York Times,* June 25, 2008, B1.

55. Phone interview with Myron Ebell, November 19, 2008.

56. Quoted in Rana Foroohar, "The Real Green Revolution," *Newsweek,* April 12, 2010, 25.

57. Al Gore, "The Climate for Change," *New York Times,* November 9, 2008, WK10.

58. Michael Shellenberger and Ted Nordhaus, "A New Inconvenient Truth," New Republic Online, November 17, 2008, available at www.tnr.com/politics/story.html?id=971eed4b-1dc8–4afd-a8fe-193c373286ac.

59. Quoted in Alec MacGillis, "Palin Gives Beliefs, Demurs on Policies," *Washington Post,* October 1, 2008, A7.

60. Quoted in Alan Greenblatt, "Confronting Warming," *CQ Researcher,* January 9, 2009, 9.

61. Quoted in Alan Zarembo and Thomas H. Maugh II, "U.N. Says It's Time to Adapt to Warming," *Los Angeles Times,* November 17, 2007, A1.

62. Phone interview with Tom Adams, November 18, 2008.

63. Roger Pielke Jr., Gwyn Prins, Steve Rayner, and Daniel Sarewitz, "Lifting the Taboo on Adaptation," *Nature,* February 8, 2007, 445.

64. Quoted in Christopher Swope, "Local Warming," *Governing* magazine, December 2007, 25.

65. Quoted in Greenblatt, "Confronting Warming," 10.

66. Anthony Faiola and Juliet Eilperin, "Dutch Defense against Climate Change: Adapt," *Washington Post,* December 6, 2009, A1.

67. Louise Bedsworth and Ellen Hanak, "Preparing California for a Changing Climate," Public Policy Institute of California, San Francisco, November 2008.

68. Chris Bowman, "California Bulks Up Defenses against Tide of Global Warming," *Sacramento Bee,* November 24, 2008, A1.

69. Quoted in Swope, "Local Warming," 25.

70. Frank Newport, "Americans' Global Warming Concerns Continue to Drop," March 11, 2010, available at www.gallup.com/poll/126560/Americans-Global-Warming-Concerns-Continue-Drop.aspx.

71. Karla Adam and Juliet Eilperin, "Panel Clears 'Climate-Gate' Scientists," *Washington Post,* April 15, 2010, A6.

72. Quoted in Bill McKibben, "Record Snows on a Warming Planet," *Washington Post,* February 14, 2010, B1.

73. Quoted in Rachel Slajda, "Salazar: 'Cap and Trade' Not in the Lexicon Anymore," TalkingPointsMemo.com, March 31, 2010, available at http://tpmdc.talkingpointsmemo.com/2010/03/salazar-cap-and-trade-not-in-the-lexicon-anymore.php.

74. Phone interview with Karlyn Bowman, March 23, 2010.

75. Quoted in Alan Greenblatt, "How Republicans Learned to Reject Climate Change," NPR.org, March 25, 2010, available at www.npr.org/templates/story/story.php?storyId=125075282.

76. Phone interview with Jim DiPeso, March 23, 2010.

77. Quoted in William March, "Rubio Questions Climate Change," *Tampa Tribune,* February 13, 2010, 7.

78. Quoted in Andy Barr, "S.C. GOP Castigates Lindsey Graham," *Politico,* November 13, 2009, available at www.politico.com/news/stories/1109/29476.html.

79. Phone interview with DiPeso.

80. Phone interview with Daniel J. Weiss, March 19, 2010.

81. Ibid.

82. Quoted in Samantha Young, "Schwarzenegger Opens Climate Summit with Obama," Associated Press, November 19, 2008.

83. Quoted in John M. Broder, "Obama Affirms Climate Change Goals," *New York Times,* November 19, 2008, A4.

84. Phone interview with Terry Tamminen, March 29, 2010.

Glossary

abstinence. Refraining from sexual activity, usually intercourse. (Chapter 15)

accreditation. Certification process in which outside experts visit and evaluate a school or college to vouch for minimum quality standards. (Chapter 13)

activist judge. A judge who is said to act as an independent policymaker by creatively interpreting constitutions and statutes. (Chapter 9)

adaptation. Taking steps to prepare for and deal with the effects of climate change. (Chapter 16)

ad hoc federalism. The process of choosing a state-centered or nation-centered view of federalism on the basis of political or partisan convenience. (Chapter 2)

affirmative action. Policies designed to help recruit and promote disadvantaged groups. (Chapter 10)

Aid to Families with Dependent Children (AFDC). The original federal assistance program for women and their children, started under Roosevelt's New Deal. (Chapter 15)

alternative dispute resolution. A way to end a disagreement by means other than litigation. It usually involves the appointment of a mediator to preside over a meeting between the parties. (Chapter 9)

American Recovery and Reinvestment Act (ARRA). A $787 billion federal government package intended to stimulate economic growth during the recession of 2008–2009. (Chapter 4)

annexation. The legal incorporation of one jurisdiction or territory into another. (Chapter 12)

appeal. A request to have a lower court's decision in a case reviewed by a higher court. (Chapter 9)

appointment powers. A governor's ability to pick individuals to run state government, such as appointing cabinet secretaries. (Chapter 8)

apportionment. The allotting of districts according to population shifts. The number of congressional districts that a state has may be reapportioned every ten years. (Chapter 7)

appropriations bills. Laws passed by legislatures authorizing the transfer of money to the executive branch. (Chapter 3)

assigned counsel. Private lawyers selected by the courts to handle particular cases and paid from public funds. (Chapter 9)

at-large elections. Elections in which city or county voters vote for council or commission members. (Chapter 11)

back to basics. A movement against modern education "fads" advocating a return to an emphasis on traditional core subjects such as reading, writing, and arithmetic. (Chapter 13)

balanced budget. A budget in which current expenditures are equal to or less than income. (Chapter 4)

ballot initiative. Process through which voters directly convey instructions to the legislature, approve a law, or amend the constitution. (Chapter 3)

bench trials. Trials in which no jury is present and a judge decides the facts. (Chapter 9)

bicameral legislatures. Legislatures that possess two chambers, typically a house of representatives, or assembly, and a senate. (Chapter 3)

Bill of Rights. The first ten amendments to the Constitution, which set limits on the power of the federal government and set out the rights of individuals and the states. (Chapter 2)

block grants. Federal grants-in-aid given for general policy areas that leave states and localities with wide discretion on how to spend the money within the designated policy area. (Chapter 2)

bonds. Certificates that are evidence of a debt on which the issuer promises to pay the holder a specified amount of interest for a specified length of time and to repay the loans on their maturity. (Chapter 4)

broken windows policing. Policing that emphasizes maintaining public order. (Chapter 14)

budget deficit, or shortfall. When the money coming into the government falls below the money being spent. (Chapter 4)

budget process. The procedure by which state and local governments assess revenues and set budgets. (Chapter 4)

building codes. Rules regarding the standards for structures; they mainly have to do with safety issues, but sometimes also include requirements for things like exterior pedestrian walkways. (Chapter 16)

bureaucracy. Public agencies and the programs and services that they implement and manage. (Chapter 10)

bureaucrats. Employees of public agencies. (Chapter 10)

candidate-centered politics. Politics in which candidates promote themselves and their own campaigns rather than relying on party organizations. (Chapter 6)

cap and trade. A system for limiting pollution by assigning allowances to polluters, which can sell their excess permits if they succeed in reducing their emissions. (Chapter 16)

capital investments. Investments in infrastructure, such as roads. (Chapter 4)

capital outlays. A category of school funding that focuses on long-term improvements to physical assets. (Chapter 13)

carbon dioxide. A naturally occurring gas, the prevalence of which is increased by the burning of fossil fuels. (Chapter 16)

car-dependent living. Owning a car for transportation becoming a necessity; an outcome of low-density development. (Chapter 12)

casework. The work undertaken by legislators and their staffs in response to requests for help from constituents. (Chapter 7)

categorical grants. Federal grants-in-aid given for specific programs that leave states and localities with little discretion on how to spend the money. (Chapter 2)

caucus. All the members of a party—Republican or Democrat—within a legislative chamber. Also refers to meetings of members of a political party in a chamber. (Chapter 7)

cause lobbyist. A person who works for an organization that tracks and promotes an issue, for example, environmental issues for the Sierra Club or gun regulation for the National Rifle Association. (Chapter 6)

centralized federalism. The notion that the federal government should take the leading role in setting national policy, with state and local governments helping to implement the policies. (Chapter 2)

charter. A document that outlines the powers, organization, and responsibilities of a local government. (Chapter 11)

charter schools. Public schools, often with unique themes, managed by teachers, principals, social workers, or nonprofit groups. The movement was launched in the early 1990s. (Chapter 13)

cities. Incorporated political jurisdictions formed to provide self-governance to a locality. (Chapter 11)

city commission system. A form of municipal governance in which executive, legislative, and administrative powers are vested in elected city commissioners. (Chapter 11)

city council. A municipality's legislature. (Chapter 11)

city-county consolidation. The merger of separate local governments in an effort to reduce bureaucratic redundancy and service inefficiencies. (Chapter 12)

city manager. An official appointed to be the chief administrator of a municipality. (Chapter 11)

civil cases. Cases that involve disputes between private parties. (Chapter 9)

Clean Air Act. The law, initially enacted in 1970, that provides authority for federal regulation of air pollution. (Chapter 16)

climate change. A shift in global temperatures. (Chapter 16)

closed primaries. Nominating elections in which only voters belonging to that party may participate. Only registered Democrats can vote in a closed Democratic primary, for example. (Chapter 6)

coalition building. The assembling of an alliance of groups to pursue a common goal or interest. (Chapter 7)

collective bargaining. A process in which representatives of labor and management meet to negotiate pay and benefits, job responsibilities, and working conditions. (Chapter 10)

colonial charters. Legal documents drawn up by the British crown that spelled out how the colonies were to be governed. (Chapter 3)

commission-administrator system. A form of county governance where executive and legislative powers reside with an elected commission, which hires a professional executive to manage the day-to-day operations of government. (Chapter 11)

committee. A group of legislators who have the formal task of considering and writing bills in a particular issue area. (Chapter 7)

common law. Law composed of judges' legal opinions that reflects community practices and evolves over time. (Chapter 14)

common school. In a democratic society, a school in which children of all income levels attend at taxpayer expense. (Chapter 13)

community, or restorative, justice movement. A movement that emphasizes nontraditional punishment, such as community service. (Chapter 14)

community policing. An approach that emphasizes police forming relationships with neighborhoods and engaging in collaborative problem solving. (Chapter 14)

compact theory. The idea that the Constitution represents an agreement among sovereign states to form a common government. (Chapter 2)

comparative method. A learning approach based on studying the differences and similarities among similar units of analysis (such as states). (Chapter 1)

compromise. The result when there is no consensus on a policy change or spending amount but legislators find a central point on which a majority can agree. (Chapter 7)

concurrent powers. Powers that both federal and state government can exercise. These include the right to tax, borrow, and spend. (Chapter 2)

confederacy. A political system in which power is concentrated in regional governments. (Chapter 2)

constituents. Residents of a district. (Chapter 7)

constituent service. The work done by legislators to help residents in their voting districts. (Chapter 7)

constitutional amendments. Proposals to change the constitution, typically enacted by a supermajority of the legislature or through a statewide referendum. (Chapter 3)

constitutional convention. An assembly convened for the express purpose of amending or replacing a constitution. (Chapter 3)

constitutional revision commissions. Expert committees formed to assess a constitution and suggest changes. (Chapter 3)

contract attorneys. Private attorneys who enter into agreements with a state, a county, or a judicial district to work on a fixed-fee basis per case or for a specific length of time. (Chapter 9)

contract lobbyist. A person who works for different causes for different clients in the same way that a lawyer represents more than one client. (Chapter 6)

cooperative federalism. The notion that it is impossible for state and national governments to have separate and distinct jurisdictions and that both levels of government must work together. (Chapter 2)

council-executive system. A form of county governance where legislative powers are vested in a county commission and executive powers are vested in an independently elected executive. (Chapter 11)

council-manager system. A form of municipal governance in which the day-to-day administration of government is carried out by a professional administrator. (Chapter 11)

counties. Geographical subdivisions of state government. (Chapter 11)

county commission system. A form of county governance in which executive, legislative, and administrative powers are vested in elected commissioners. (Chapter 11)

court of first instance. The court in which a case is introduced and nothing has been determined yet. (Chapter 9)

criminal cases. Cases that involve violations of the law. (Chapter 9)

criterion referenced tests. Standardized tests designed to gauge a student's level of mastery of a given set of materials. (Chapter 13)

crosscutting requirements. Constraints that apply to all federal grants. (Chapter 2)

crossover sanctions. Federal requirements mandating that grant recipients pass and enforce certain laws or regulations as a condition of receiving funds. (Chapter 2)

crossover voting. Members of one party voting in another party's primary. This practice is not allowed in all states. (Chapter 6)

dealignment. When no one party can be said to dominate politics in this country. (Chapter 6)

delegates. Legislators who primarily see their role as voting according to their constituents' beliefs as they understand them. (Chapter 7)

departments of education. State-level agencies responsible for overseeing public education. (Chapter 13)

determinate sentencing. The judge sentences an offender to serve a specific amount of time in prison depending on the crime. (Chapter 9)

deterrence theory. A theory advanced by criminologists that harsh penalties will deter people from committing crimes. (Chapter 14)

devolution. The process of taking power and responsibility away from the federal government and giving it to state and local governments. (Chapter 1)

Dillon's Rule. The legal principle that says local governments can exercise only the powers granted to them by state government. (Chapter 11)

direct democracy. A system in which citizens make laws themselves rather than relying on elected representatives. (Chapters 3 and 5)

direct lobbying. A form of lobbying in which lobbyists deal directly with legislators to gain their support. (Chapter 6)

discretionary jurisdiction. The court has the power to decide whether or not to grant review of a case. (Chapter 9)

discretionary spending. Spending controlled in annual appropriations acts. (Chapter 4)

districts. Geographical areas represented by members of a legislature. (Chapter 7)

dividend. A payment made to stockholders, or in Alaska's case, residents, from the interest generated from an investment. (Chapter 4)

drug courts. Special tribunals that offer nonviolent drug offenders a chance at reduced or dismissed charges in exchange for undergoing treatment or other rehabilitation; an alternative forum for sentencing nonviolent drug offenders. (Chapter 14)

dual constitutionalism. A system of government in which people live under two sovereign powers. In the United States, these are the government of their state of residence and the federal government. (Chapter 3)

dual federalism. The idea that state and federal governments have separate and distinct jurisdictions and responsibilities. (Chapter 2)

edgeless cities. Office and retail complexes without clear boundaries. (Chapter 12)

e-government. The delivery of public services and programs via the Internet or other digital means. (Chapter 10)

electorate. Individuals who can vote. (Chapter 3)

Elementary and Secondary Education Act. Federal law passed in 1965 as part of President Johnson's Great Society initiative; steered federal funds to improve local schools, particularly those attended primarily by low-income and minority students. (Chapter 13)

en banc. Appeals court sessions in which all the judges hear a case together. (Chapter 9)

entitlement. Service that government must provide, regardless of the cost. (Chapter 4)

entitlement program. A government-run program that guarantees unlimited assistance to those who meet its eligibility requirements, no matter how high the cost. (Chapter 15)

enumerated powers. Grants of authority explicitly given by the Constitution. (Chapter 2)

estate taxes. Taxes levied on a person's estate or total holdings after that person's death. (Chapter 4)

excise, or sin, taxes. Taxes on alcohol, tobacco, and other similar products that are designed to raise revenues and reduce use. (Chapter 4)

exclusive powers. Powers given by the Constitution solely to the federal government. (Chapter 2)

executive orders. Rules or regulations with the force of law that governors can create directly under the statutory authority given them. (Chapter 8)

expenditures. Money spent by government. (Chapter 4)

exurbs. Municipalities in rural areas that ring suburbs. They typically serve as bedroom communities for the prosperous, providing rural homes with easy access to urban areas. (Chapter 12)

factional splits, or factions. Groups that struggle to control the message within a party; for example, a party may be split into competing regional factions. (Chapter 6)

federalism. Political system in which national and regional governments share powers and are considered independent equals. (Chapter 2)

felony. A serious crime, such as murder or arson. (Chapter 9)

filibusters. Debates that under Senate rules can drag on, blocking final action on the bill under consideration and preventing other bills from being debated. (Chapter 7)

fiscal federalism. The system by which federal grants are used to fund programs and services provided by state and local governments. (Chapter 4)

fiscal year. The accounting period used by a government. (Chapter 4)

focused consumption taxes. Taxes that do not alter spending habits or behavior patterns and therefore do not distort the distribution of resources. (Chapter 4)

for cause challenge. A lawyer's asking the judge to excuse a potential juror because the individual appears to be biased or unable to be fair. (Chapter 9)

formal powers. The powers explicitly granted to a governor according to state law, such as vetoing legislation or appointing heads of state agencies. (Chapter 8)

Fourteenth Amendment. Constitutional amendment that prohibits states from depriving individuals of the rights and privileges of citizenship and requires states to provide due process and equal protection guarantees. (Chapter 2)

franchise. The right to vote. (Chapter 3)

full faith and credit clause. Clause requiring states to recognize each other's public records and acts as valid. (Chapter 2)

general act charters. Charters that grant powers, such as home rule, to all municipal governments within a state. (Chapter 11)

general elections. The decisive elections in which all registered voters cast ballots for their preferred candidates for a political office. (Chapter 6)

general equivalency degree (GED) program. Series of tests that can be taken to qualify for a high school equivalency certificate or diploma. (Chapter 13)

general jurisdiction trial courts. Courts that hear any civil or criminal cases that have not been assigned to a special court. (Chapter 9)

general obligation bonds. Investments secured by the taxing power of the jurisdiction that issues them. (Chapter 4)

general revenue sharing grants. Federal grants-in-aid given with few constraints, leaving states and localities almost complete discretion over how to spend the money. (Chapter 2)

general welfare clause. An implied power giving Congress the authority to provide for the "general welfare." (Chapter 2)

gentrification. The physical rehabilitation of urban areas, which attracts investment from developers and drives up property values. (Chapter 12)

gerrymanders. Districts clearly drawn with the intent of pressing partisan advantage at the expense of other considerations. (Chapter 7)

gift taxes. Taxes imposed on money transfers made during an individual's lifetime. (Chapter 4)

global warming. Rising average temperatures worldwide. (Chapter 16)

Goals 2000. The Educate America Act, signed into law in March 1994, which provided resources to states and communities to ensure that all students reached their full potential. (Chapter 13)

grand jury. A group of between sixteen and twenty-three citizens that decides if a case should go to trial; if it decides yes, an indictment is issued. (Chapter 9)

grants-in-aid. Cash appropriations given by the federal government to the states. (Chapter 2)

greenhouse gases. Emissions—primarily carbon dioxide but also other gases such as methane—that are believed to contribute to global warming. (Chapter 16)

green jobs. Occupations that contribute to environmental sustainability. (Chapter 16)

habitual offender laws. Statutes imposing harsher sentences on offenders who previously have been sentenced for crimes. (Chapter 9)

high-stakes standardized testing. Testing of elementary and secondary students in which poor results can mean either that the student fails to be promoted or that the school loses its accreditation. (Chapter 13)

home rule. A form of self-governance granted to towns and cities by the state. (Chapter 3) The right of localities to self-government, usually granted through a charter. (Chapter 11)

home schooling. The education of children in the home; a movement to grant waivers from state truancy laws to permit parents to teach their own children. (Chapter 13)

impact fees. Fees that municipalities charge builders of new housing or commercial developments to help offset the costs of extending services. (Chapter 12)

impeachment. A process by which the legislature can remove executive branch officials, such as the governor, or judges from offices for corruption or other reasons. (Chapter 8)

implied powers. Broad, but undefined, powers given to the federal government by the Constitution. (Chapter 2)

income taxes. Taxes on income. (Chapter 4)

incumbent. A person holding office. (Chapter 7)

independent expenditures. Ad campaigns or other political activities that are run by a party or an outside group without the direct knowledge or approval of a particular candidate for office. (Chapter 6)

indeterminate sentencing. The judge sentences an offender to a minimum and a maximum time in prison, and a parole board decides how long the offender actually will remain in prison. (Chapter 9)

indictment. A formal criminal charge. (Chapter 9)

indirect lobbying. A form of lobbying in which lobbyists build support for their cause through the media, rallies, and other ways of influencing public opinion with the ultimate goal of swaying legislators to support their cause. (Chapter 6)

individualistic culture. A political culture that views politics and government as just another way to achieve individual goals. (Chapter 1)

informal powers. The things a governor is able to do, such as command media attention or persuade party members, based on personality or position, not on formal authority. (Chapter 8)

insurance trust funds. Money collected from contributions, assessments, insurance premiums, or payroll taxes. (Chapter 4)

intelligent design. The theory that certain features of the universe and of living things are best explained by an intelligent cause, not an undirected process such as evolution. (Chapter 13)

interest groups. Individuals, corporations, or associations that seek to influence the actions of elected and appointed public officials on behalf of specific companies or causes. (Chapter 6)

intergovernmental transfers. Funds provided by the federal government to state governments and by state governments to local governments. (Chapter 4)

interjurisdictional agreement (IJA). A formal or informal agreement between two or more local governments to cooperate on a program or policy. (Chapter 12)

intermediate appellate court. A court that reviews court cases to find possible errors in their proceedings. (Chapter 9)

interstate commerce clause. The constitutional clause that gives Congress the right to regulate interstate commerce. This clause has been broadly interpreted to give Congress a number of implied powers. (Chapter 2)

Jim Crow laws. Measures passed in the last decade of the nineteenth century that sought to legally and systematically separate blacks and whites. (Chapter 3)

judicial federalism. The idea that the courts determine the boundaries of state-federal relations. (Chapter 3)

judicial review. The power of courts to assess whether a law is in compliance with the constitution. (Chapter 3)

jury nullification. A jury's returning a verdict of "not guilty" even though jurists believe the defendant is guilty. By doing so, the jury cancels out a law that it believes is immoral or was wrongly applied to the defendant. (Chapter 9)

Kentucky Education Reform Act. The 1990 law passed in response to court findings of unacceptable disparities among schools in Kentucky and considered the most comprehensive state school reform act to date. (Chapter 13)

Kyoto Protocol. A 1997 treaty that sought to reduce emissions of greenhouse gases. (Chapter 16)

laboratories of democracy. A term used for the states that emphasizes their ability to engage in different policy experiments without interference from the federal government. (Chapter 1)

leapfrog development. Developments that jump—or leapfrog—over established developments, leaving undeveloped or underdeveloped land between developments. (Chapter 12)

legislative overcriminalization. The tendency of government to make a crime out of anything the public does not like. (Chapter 9)

liability. A legal obligation or responsibility. (Chapter 9)

limited, or special jurisdiction, trial courts. Courts that hear cases that are statutorily limited by either the degree of seriousness or the types of parties involved. (Chapter 9)

line-item veto. The power to reject a portion of a bill while the rest remains intact. (Chapter 3)

local education agencies (LEAs). School districts, some of which may be cities, counties, or subsets thereof. (Chapter 13)

logrolling. The practice in which a legislator will give a colleague a vote on a particular bill in return for that colleague's vote on another bill to be considered later. (Chapter 7)

low-density development. Development practices that spread (rather than concentrate) populations across the land. (Chapter 12)

magistrates. Local officials or attorneys granted limited judicial powers. (Chapter 9)

majority-minority districts. Districts in which a minority group, such as African Americans or Hispanics, make up a majority of the population or electorate. (Chapter 7)

majority rule. The process in which the decision of a numerical majority is made binding on a group. (Chapter 7)

malapportionment. A situation in which the principle of equal representation is violated. (Chapter 7)

managed care. An arrangement for the provision of healthcare whereby an agency acts as an intermediary between consumers and healthcare providers. (Chapter 15)

mandatory jurisdiction. The court is required to hear every case presented before it. (Chapter 9)

mandatory minimum sentences. The shortest sentences that offenders may receive upon conviction for certain offenses. The court has no authority to impose a shorter sentence. (Chapter 9)

mayor. The elected chief executive of a municipality. (Chapter 11)

mayor-council system. A form of municipal governance in which there is an elected executive and an elected legislature. (Chapter 11)

Medicaid. A joint state and federal health insurance program that serves low-income mothers and children, the elderly, and people with disabilities. (Chapter 15)

Medicare. The federal health insurance program for elderly citizens. (Chapter 15)

megalopolis. An urban area made up of several large cities and their surrounding urban areas. (Chapter 12)

merit systems. Systems in which employment and promotion in public agencies are based on qualifications and demonstrated ability; this blends very well with the organizational characteristics of bureaucracy. (Chapter 10)

metropolitan area. A populous region typically comprising a city and surrounding communities that have a high degree of social and economic integration. (Chapter 12)

metropolitan planning organization (MPO). A regional organization that decides how federal transportation funds are allocated within a regional area. (Chapter 12)

metropolitan statistical area (MSA). An area with a city of 50,000 or more people, together with adjacent urban communities that have strong ties to the central city. (Chapter 12)

misdemeanor. A less serious crime, such as shoplifting. (Chapter 9)

mitigation. Reducing emissions of greenhouse gases and other steps taken to curb the forces that cause climate change. (Chapter 16)

model constitution. An expert-approved generic or "ideal" constitution that is sometimes used by states as a yardstick against which they can measure their existing constitutions. (Chapter 3)

moralistic culture. A political culture that views politics and government as the means to achieve the collective good. (Chapter 1)

municipal bonds. Bonds issued by states, counties, cities, and towns to fund large projects as well as operating budgets. They are exempt from federal taxes and from state and local taxes for the investors who live in the state where they are issued. (Chapter 4)

municipal charter. A document that establishes operating procedures for local governments. (Chapter 3)

municipalities. Political jurisdictions, such as cities, villages, or towns, incorporated under state law to provide governance to a defined geographical area; more compact and more densely populated than counties. (Chapter 11)

National Assessment of Educational Progress (NAEP). The only regularly conducted, independent survey of what a nationally representative sample of students in grades four, eight, and twelve know and can do in various subjects; known as the "nation's report card." (Chapter 13)

National PTA. Umbrella organization founded in 1897 consisting of state-based and school-based parent-teacher associations of volunteers who work to improve and support schools. (Chapter 13)

national supremacy clause. The constitutional clause stating that federal law takes precedence over all other laws. (Chapter 2)

nation-centered federalism. The belief that the nation is the basis of the federal system and that the federal government should take precedence over the states. (Chapter 2)

natural law, or higher law. A set of moral and political rules based on divine law and binding on all people. (Chapter 3)

necessary and proper clause. An implied power giving Congress the right to pass all laws considered "necessary and proper" to carry out the federal government's responsibilities as defined by the Constitution. (Chapter 2)

neutral competence. The idea that public agencies should be the impartial implementers of democratic decisions. (Chapter 10)

New Federalism. The belief that states should receive more power and authority and less money from the federal government. (Chapter 2)

New Urbanism. A design movement that seeks to promote walkable communities through transit-oriented, mixed-use development. (Chapter 16)

No Child Left Behind Act (NCLB). Federal law enacted in January 2002 that introduced new accountability measures for elementary and secondary schools in all states that wish to receive federal aid. (Chapter 13)

nonpartisan ballots. Ballots that do not list candidates by political party; still often used in local elections. (Chapter 6)

nonpartisan elections. Elections in which candidates do not have to declare party affiliation or receive a party's nomination; local offices and elections are often nonpartisan. (Chapter 5)

norm referenced tests. Standardized tests designed to determine how a student's mastery of a set of materials compares with that of a specially designed sampling of students determined to be the national "norm" for their age group. (Chapter 13)

nullification. The process of a state's rejecting a federal law and making it invalid within state borders. (Chapter 2)

obesity. The medical condition of being excessively overweight; defined as having a body mass index of more than 25. (Chapter 15)

office group (Massachusetts) ballot. A ballot in which candidates are listed by name under the title of the office they are seeking. (Chapter 5)

open primaries. Election races that are open to all registered voters regardless of their party affiliation. (Chapter 6)

oversight. The role the legislature takes in making sure that the implementation of its laws by the executive branch is being done properly. (Chapter 7)

pandemic. An outbreak of a disease that spreads across a large geographical area and affects a high proportion of the population. (Chapter 15)

panels. Groups of (usually) three judges who sit to hear cases in state courts of appeals. (Chapter 9)

parole. Supervised early release from prison. (Chapter 14)

party column (Indiana) ballot. Ballot in which the names of candidates are divided into columns arranged according to political party. (Chapter 5)

party conventions. Meetings of party delegates called to nominate candidates for office and establish party agendas. (Chapter 6)

patronage. The ability of elected officials or party leaders to hand out jobs to their friends and supporters rather than hiring people based on merit. (Chapter 6) The process of giving government jobs to partisan loyalists. (Chapter 10)

peremptory challenges. Lawyers' dismissing potential jurors for any reason except race or gender. (Chapter 9)

plea bargain. An agreement in which the accused admits guilt, usually in exchange for a promise that a particular sentence will be imposed. (Chapter 9)

plural executive system. A state government system in which the governor is not the dominant figure in the executive branch but, instead, is more of a first among equals, serving alongside numerous other officials who were elected to their offices rather than being appointed by the governor. (Chapter 5)

plurality. The highest number of votes garnered by a candidate for a particular office but short of an outright majority. (Chapter 5)

policy implementation. The process of taking the expressed wishes of government and translating them into action. (Chapter 10)

political action committees. Groups formed for the purpose of raising money to elect or defeat political candidates. They usually represent business, union, or ideological interests. (Chapter 6)

political culture. The attitudes and beliefs broadly shared in a polity about the role and responsibility of government. (Chapter 1)

political machines. Political organizations controlled by a small number of people and run for partisan ends; they controlled party nominations for public office and rewarded supporters with government jobs and contracts. (Chapter 6)

political parties. Organizations that nominate and support candidates for elected offices. (Chapter 6)

poverty line, or poverty threshold. An annual income level, set by the federal government, below which families cannot afford basic necessities. (Chapter 15)

precedent. In law, the use of the past to determine current interpretation and decision making. (Chapter 9)

preemption. The process of the federal government overriding areas regulated by state law. (Chapter 2)

prejudicial error. An error that affects the outcome of a case. (Chapter 9)

primary elections. Elections that determine a party's nominees for offices in general elections against other parties' nominees. Participation in primary elections is sometimes limited to voters registered as members of that particular party. (Chapter 6)

privileges and immunities clause. Clause prohibiting states from discriminating against citizens of other states. (Chapter 2)

probation. Supervised punishment in the community. (Chapter 14)

professionalization. The process of providing legislators with the resources to make politics their main career, such as making their positions full time or providing them with full-time staff. (Chapter 7) Bureaucratic employees earn their jobs based on qualifications and merit. (Chapter 10)

professional model of policing. An approach to policing that emphasizes professional relations with citizens, police independence, police in cars, and rapid responses to calls for service. (Chapter 14)

progressive tax system. System in which the tax rate paid reflects the ability to pay. (Chapter 4)

prosecutor. A government official and lawyer who conducts criminal cases on behalf of the people. (Chapter 9)

public choice model. A model of politics that views governments and public services in market terms; governments are seen as producers of public services and citizens are seen as consumers. (Chapter 12)

public defender. A government lawyer who provides free legal services to those accused of a crime who cannot afford to hire a lawyer. (Chapter 9)

public health. Government agencies' protection and improvement of citizen health and hygiene. (Chapter 15)

pure appointive systems. Judicial selection systems in which the governor appoints judges alone without a nominating commission. (Chapter 9)

rank-and-file members. Legislators who do not hold leadership positions or senior committee posts. (Chapter 7)

ratification. A vote of the entire electorate to approve a constitutional change, referendum, or ballot initiative. (Chapter 3)

realignment. When popular support switches from one party to another. (Chapter 6)

recall. A way for voters to oust an incumbent politician prior to the next regularly scheduled election; they collect signatures and then vote on the ouster of the politician. (Chapter 5)

recall election. A special election allowing voters to remove an elected official from office before the end of his or her term. (Chapter 8)

recidivism. A return to, or relapse into, criminal behavior. (Chapter 9)

Reconstruction. The period following the Civil War when the southern states were governed under the direction of the Union Army. (Chapter 3)

redistricting. The drawing of new boundaries for congressional and state legislative districts, usually following a decennial census. (Chapters 5 and 7)

referendums. Procedures that allow the electorate to either accept or reject laws passed by the legislature. (Chapter 3)

reform perspective. An approach to filling gaps in service and reducing redundancies in local governments that calls for regional-level solutions. (Chapter 12)

regional council. A planning and advisory organization whose members include multiple local governments. Regional councils often are used to administer state and federal programs that target regions. (Chapter 12)

regressive taxes. Taxes levied on all taxpayers, regardless of income or ability to pay; they tend to place proportionately more of a burden on those with lower incomes. (Chapter 4)

renewable energy. Power generated by natural sources that can be replenished, such as wind and solar energy, as opposed to nonrenewable fossil fuels. (Chapter 16)

representation. Individual legislators acting as the voices of their constituencies within the house of representatives or senate. (Chapter 7)

representative bureaucracy. The idea that public agencies that reflect the diversity of the communities they serve will be more effective. (Chapter 10)

representative government. A form of government in which citizens exercise power indirectly by choosing representatives to legislate on their behalf. (Chapter 2)

responsible party model. The theory that political parties offer clear policy choices to voters, try to deliver on those policies when they take office, and are held accountable by voters for the success or failure of those policies. (Chapter 6)

retention elections. Elections in which judges run uncontested and voters are asked to vote "yes" if they wish to retain a judge in office for another term or "no" if they do not. (Chapter 9)

revenue bonds. Investments secured by the revenue generated by a state or municipal project. (Chapter 4)

revenues. The money governments bring in, mainly from taxes. (Chapter 4)

riders. Amendments to a bill that are not central to its intent. (Chapter 7)

rocket docket. Fast-tracked cases that often have limited, specific deadlines for specific court procedures. (Chapter 9)

rulemaking. The process of translating laws into written instructions on what public agencies will or will not do. (Chapter 10)

runoff primary. An election held if no candidate receives a majority of the vote during the regular primary. The two top finishers face off again in a runoff to determine the nominee for the general election. Such elections are held in some states, primarily in the South. (Chapter 6)

rural flight. The movement of rural youth and the middle class to more urban areas. (Chapter 12)

sales taxes. Taxes levied by state and local governments on purchases. (Chapter 4)

school boards. Elected or appointed bodies that determine major policies and budgets for each of the nation's school districts. (Chapter 13)

school districts. Local administrative jurisdictions that hire staff and report to school boards on the management of area public schools. (Chapter 13)

school vouchers. Movement dating to the 1950s to allow taxpayer dollars to be given to families to use at whatever public, private, or parochial schools they choose. (Chapter 13)

secession. The process of a government or political jurisdiction withdrawing from a political system or alliance. (Chapter 2)

secret (Australian) ballot. A ballot printed by the states that allows voters to pick and choose among different candidates and party preferences in private. (Chapter 5)

seniority. The length of time a worker has spent in a position. (Chapter 10)

separation of powers. The principle that government should be divided into separate legislative, executive, and judicial branches, each with its own powers and responsibilities. (Chapter 3)

settlement. A mutual agreement between parties to end a case before going to trial. (Chapter 9)

severance taxes. Taxes on natural resources. (Chapter 4)

site-based management. A movement to increase freedom for building administrators such as school principals to determine how district funds are spent at a given school. (Chapter 13)

smart growth. Environmentally friendly development practices, particularly those that emphasize more efficient infrastructure and less dependence on automobiles. (Chapter 12)

smog. A type of air pollution; the word was constructed by combining smoke and fog. (Chapter 16)

sociodemographics. The characteristics of a population, including size, age, and ethnicity. (Chapter 1)

soft money. Money not subject to federal regulation that can be raised and spent by state parties. A 2002 law banned the use of soft money in federal elections. (Chapter 6)

sovereign immunity. The right of a government to not be sued without its consent. (Chapter 2)

special act charters. Charters that grant powers, such as home rule, to a single municipal government. (Chapter 11)

special districts. Local governmental units created for a single purpose, such as water distribution. (Chapter 11)

spoils system. The right of an electoral winner to decide who works for public agencies. (Chapter 10)

sprawl. The rapid growth of a metropolitan area, typically as a result of specific types of zoning and development. (Chapters 12 and 16)

standards. In education, fixed criteria for learning that students are expected to reach in specific subjects by specific grade years. (Chapter 13)

standards movement. Effort to create benchmarks of adequate learning in each subject for each grade level so that students and teachers can be evaluated on the mastery of this predetermined material. (Chapter 13)

state board of education. Top policymaking body in each of the fifty states, usually consisting of appointees selected by governors. (Chapter 13)

state-centered federalism. The belief that states are the basis of the federal system and that state governments should take precedence over the federal government. (Chapter 2)

State Children's Health Insurance Program (CHIP). A joint federal-state program designed to expand healthcare coverage to children whose parents earned income above the poverty line but still were too poor to afford insurance. (Chapter 15)

states' rights. The belief that states should be free to make their own decisions with little interference from the federal government. (Chapter 2)

state supreme court. The highest level of appeals court in a state. (Chapter 9)

straight ticket. Originally, ballots that allowed voters to pick all of one party's candidates at once; today, voting for all of one party's candidates for various offices—for instance, voting for all Democrats or all Republicans. (Chapter 5)

street-level bureaucrats. Lower-level public agency employees who actually take the actions that represent law or policy. (Chapter 10)

strong mayor system. A municipal government in which the mayor has the power to perform the executive functions of government. (Chapter 11)

successful schools model. Education model that uses observed spending levels in the highest-performing schools as the model from which to calculate necessary spending in other, lower-performing schools. (Chapter 13)

supermajority vote. A legislative vote of much more than a simple majority, for instance, two-thirds of a legislative chamber's voting to override a governor's veto. (Chapter 8)

supermax security prisons. High-security prisons designed for violent criminals. (Chapter 14)

superpredators. Ultra-violent youth whom experts predicted would further drive up the nation's crime rate. (Chapter 14)

swing voters. Individuals who are not consistently loyal to candidates of any one party. They are true independents whose allegiance is fought for in every election. (Chapter 6)

tailpipe emissions. Greenhouse gases released by cars and other vehicles. (Chapter 16)

tax burden. A measurement of taxes paid. (Chapter 4)

tax capacity. Measurement of the ability to pay taxes. (Chapter 4)

tax effort. A measure of taxes paid relative to the ability to pay taxes. (Chapter 4)

teacher licensure procedures. The academic degrees, work experience, and performance on adult standardized tests that a state requires before a teacher candidate can be certified to work in a school district. (Chapter 13)

teachers' unions. Public-sector unions that organize employees at all educational levels to form state and local affiliates. In the United States, primarily the National Education Association and the American Federation of Teachers, both headquartered in Washington, D.C. (Chapter 13)

Temporary Assistance to Needy Families (TANF). The next-generation welfare program (passed in 1996) that provides federal assistance in the form of block grants to states, which have great flexibility in designing the program. (Chapter 15)

Tenth Amendment. Constitutional amendment that guarantees a broad, but undefined, set of powers be reserved for the states and the people. (Chapter 2)

ticket splitting. Voters' or districts' voting for different parties' nominees for different offices—for instance, supporting a Republican for president while supporting a Democrat for Congress. (Chapter 6)

Tiebout model. A model of local government based on market principles wherein a metro area is made up of a series of micropolitical jurisdictions that, on the basis of their services and costs, attract or repel certain citizens. (Chapter 12)

town meeting form of government. A form of governance in which legislative powers are held by the local citizens. (Chapter 11)

townships. Local governments whose powers, governance structure, and legal status vary considerably from state to state. In some states, townships function as general purpose municipalities; in others, they are geographical subdivisions of counties with few responsibilities and little power. (Chapter 11)

traditionalistic culture. A political culture that views politics and government as dominated by elites. (Chapter 1)

Trends in International Mathematics and Science Study (TIMSS). A regularly updated study launched by the United States in 1995 that compares the performance in science and mathematics of students in forty-six countries. (Chapter 13)

trial court. The first level of the court system. (Chapter 9)

trustees. Legislators who believe they were elected to exercise their own judgment and to approach issues accordingly. (Chapter 7)

truth-in-sentencing laws. Laws that give parole boards less authority to shorten sentences for good behavior by specifying the proportion of a sentence an offender must serve before becoming eligible for parole. (Chapter 9)

unfunded mandates. Federal laws that direct state action but provide no financial support for that action. (Chapter 2)

unicameral legislatures. Legislatures that possess only one chamber. Nebraska is currently the only state with a unicameral legislature. (Chapter 3)

unitary systems. Political systems in which power is concentrated in a central government. (Chapter 2)

urban growth boundary (UGB). The border established around urban areas that is intended to control the density and type of development. (Chapter 12)

U.S. Environmental Protection Agency (EPA). The federal agency charged with protecting the environment. (Chapter 16)

user fees. Charges levied by governments in exchange for services; a type of hidden tax. (Chapter 4)

variance. The difference between units of analysis on a particular measure. (Chapter 1)

vehicle miles traveled (VMT). How many miles each individual car is driven; an increasingly important measure of auto use. (Chapter 16)

verdict. A jury's finding in a trial. (Chapter 14)

veto. The power to reject a proposed law. (Chapter 8)

voir dire. The interviewing and examination of potential jurors. (Chapter 9)

voter identification. When a voter consistently identifies strongly with one of the parties and can be considered, for example, a Democrat or Republican. (Chapter 6)

voter turnout. The percentage of eligible citizens who register to vote and do vote. (Chapter 5)

ward, or district, elections. Elections in which voters in a municipal ward vote for a candidate to represent them on a council or commission. (Chapter 11)

wards. Divisions of municipalities, usually representing electoral districts of the city council. (Chapter 11)

weak mayor system. A municipal government in which the mayor lacks true executive powers, such as the ability to veto council decisions or appoint department heads. (Chapter 11)

weatherization. Protecting buildings from the elements (for example, by installing insulation); also designed to cut down on energy use. (Chapter 16)

white flight. A demographic trend in which the middle and upper classes leave central cities for predominantly white suburbs. (Chapter 12)

zoning laws. Regulations that control how land can be used. (Chapters 12 and 16)

growth in, 371–373, 528, 539, 539f, 551
juries, 363–365
rights of criminally accused, 365–367
sentencing, 367–370
victims' rights, 365–367
Crist, Charlie, 296–297
Criterion referenced tests, 505
Crosscutting requirements for federal grants, 54
Crossover sanctions, 54
Crossover voting, 190
Cuccinelli, Ken, 591
Culture. *See also* Political cultures
public health and, 568–570
of states and localities, 10–17, 15m, 16t
Cuomo, Andrew, 319
Curb, Mike, 318
Cypress, California, and eminent domain, 439

D
The Daily Show, 317
Daley, Richard J., 399, 434
Dallas, Texas
council-manager system in, 435
elections in, 446
police departments in, size of, 555
school districts in, 494
Daniels, Mitch, 130
Darby Lumber Company; United States v. (1941), 60
Darfur, Sudan, genocide in, 210
Databases, political uses of, 193
Data privacy, bills on, 234
Davis, Gray, 168, 169, 312, 313
Dayton, Ohio
council-manager system in, 433
school board election in, 497
Dealignment, 194
Dean, Howard, 315
Death penalty
ban lifted, 7
elected judges and, 342
flat fees for contract defense attorneys and, 363
future trends, 557–558
political culture and, 557

Death taxes as revenue, 104, 112
Deeds, Creigh, 142
Defendants' rights, 365–367
Defense attorneys, 359–363, 529. *See also* Public defenders
Defense of Marriage Act (1996), 57
DeHoog, Ruth Hoogland, 482
Delaware
acquisition by Penn, 77
appellate courts in, 334
constitutional amendment process in, 79, 83
gubernatorial elections in, 308
gun-control laws in, 560
judicial selection in, 346
local governments in, 421
per capita gross state product of, 17
Race to the Top funds to, 490
ratification in, 79, 83
tax system in, 109
Del Casino, Vincent, 4
Delegates, 247
Democratic Farmer Labor Party, 208
Democratic Party
attorneys general and, 159–161, 319
characterization of supporters, 181–184
early history of, 179–180
elections (2002), 198
elections (2006), 184
elections (2008), 180
factions in, 181
gubernatorial elections and, 312
handling of domestic issues in U.S. Congress by, 263
local elections and, 447–448
periods of dominance of, 193
political cultures and, 199, 201
Republican Party compared to, 178
Southern voters and, 180, 200
state and local organization of, 182f, 193
state legislative leadership and, 242
teachers' unions and, 519

voter identification with, 208–209
voters in cities vs. in suburbs and, 142
Democratic Republicans, 179
Demographic factors. *See also* Age factors in voting
taxing variations and, 117
voter turnout and, 141, 151, 153
Demonstration waivers, for welfare, 579
Denno, Deborah, 558
Denver, Colorado, 2006 election in, 146
Des Moines and Polk County, Iowa, consolidating operations of, 474
Determinate sentencing, 368, 542
Deterrence theory, 540
Detroit, Michigan
megalopolis with Windsor, Ontario, 461
police departments in, 554
riots (1967), 537
school boards in, 495
school closings in, 522
school funding priorities in, 502
Detroit Free Press on Democratic Party ads, 344
Devolution
Bush and, 64
Clinton and, 57
Obama and, 56
promotion of, 22–25
public health and, 578–579
DeVos, Dick, 312–313
Dewhurst, David, 158, 286
Dickens, Charles, 552
Dillon, John F., 440
Dillon's Rule, 439, 440–442, 451–452
Dinkins, David, 547
Dionne, E. J., Jr., 165
Direct democracy
ballot initiatives and, 93–94
in California, 69
defined, 68, 161
elections and, 161–169, 162–163t
referendums and, 93–94

F

Facebook, 170
Factional splits, or factions, 179
Fairfax County, Virginia, revenue sources in, 425
Family courts, integrated, 372
Farmer, Rick, 266
Farmer-Labor Party, 208
Farris, Michael, 518
Fast Food Nation (film), 595
Favoritism, 405
Federal Bureau of Investigation (FBI), 39, 295, 555
Federal Cigarette Labeling and Advertising Act (1965), 63
Federal Emergency Management Agency (FEMA), 40
  Bush (G.W.) and, 41
  Clinton and, 41
  federalism and, 40, 41
  Hurricane Hugo and, 40
  Hurricane Katrina and, 40, 41
  National Guard and, 41
Federal employees' labor unions, 402
Federal government. *See also* Constitution, U.S.
  centralization and, 50
  devolution of power and policy from, 22, 64
  fiscal year, 120
  funding tied to regional cooperation, 473
  as revenue source for state and local governments, 112
  state and local government vs., 19–22, 46*f*
  Washington, D.C., government and, 24
Federal grants. *See* Grants-in-aid
Federalism, 28–65
  ad hoc, 57–59
    Tenth Amendment vs., 61–63
  advantages and disadvantages of, 36–39, 37*t*
  California and, 56
  centralized, 50–54, 51–52*f*
  collaborative, 56
  compact theory of, 47
  constitutional provisions for, 39–45, 42–43*t*

cooperative, 48–50
defined, 31
development of, 46–59
Disaster Relief Act and, 40
dual, 47–48
FEMA and, 40, 41
fiscal, 124
missing level in, 458–463
National Response Plan and, 40
nation-centered, 59–61
NCLB and, 491
New Federalism. *See* New Federalism
New Judicial, 331
Obama and, 56
origins of, 34–36
as political system, 31
power, systems of, 32–34, 33*f*
Supreme Court as umpire of, 59–63, 62*f*, 62*t*
systems of power, 32–34, 33*f*
Tenth Amendment vs., 61–63
The Federalist
  No. 10, 92–93, 96
  No. 73, 225
Federalists, 35–36, 179
Federal Trade Commission (FTC), 38–39
Fees, as revenue, 112, 112*t*
Felonies, 359
Felons
  credits toward parole and, 369–370
  jury service by, 365
  voting disenfranchisement of, 544
FEMA. *See* Federal Emergency Management Agency
Feminist movement, 536
Fenty, Adrian, 494
Fields, Gary, 557
Fifteenth Amendment, 150
Fifth Amendment, 439
Files and records maintenance, 381, 395
Filibusters, 225
Finance, 100–133. *See also* Taxes
  ballot initiatives and, 166, 167
  bonds, 118
  budget process, 119–131
  budget restraints, 128–131

expenditures, 121–128, 122–123*t*
fees and charges, 112, 112*t*
healthcare costs for current and retired public employees, 128
insurance trust funds, 114
intergovernmental transfers, 114–115
lessons learned, 131–132
rainy day funds, 121, 130
revenues, 104–131, 122–123*t*
unfunded mandates, 54, 128–129
Financial industry
  federal government and, 58
  near-collapse of, 260
Finkbeiner, Carleton S., 429–430, 443
Fire protection, budgetary expenditures for, 126–128
Fire-safe cigarettes mandate, 234–235
First Amendment, 374
Fiscal federalism, 124
Fiscal year, 119–120
Fishel, Jeff, 209
Fisher, Deb, 172
Fitch Ratings, 118
Fletcher, Ernie, 202
Florida
  ballot initiatives in, 94, 166
  ballots used in, 145
  city-county consolidations in, 475, 476*t*
  constitution, on judicial compensation, 354
  constitutional revision commissions in, 82, 83
  courts, budget impacts on, 374
  death penalty in, 342
  drug prosecution in, 358
  election (2007), 146
  electronic voting in, 146
  geography of, 18, 19
  governor's power in, 280
  health information technology in, 592
  House and Senate Republican conflicts, 269

prison sentences in, 370
professional and personal
    services taxes in, 105
school funding in, 501
state capitol reporters in, 265
Supreme Court rulings on
    political party regulations,
    195
Immigrants
    as elected city officials, 447
    illegal, ballot initiatives on
        services for, 95
    state immigration laws, 58
Impact fees, 464
Impact statement, 367
Impeachment, 313, 346
Implied powers, 42. *See also*
    Reserved powers
Incarceration rates. *See* Prisons
Income and voting, 156
Income taxes
    as revenue source, 104,
        109–111, 110–111*t*
    school funds from, 496
    Sixteenth Amendment and, 50
Incumbents, 216, 238, 496
Independence Party (Minnesota),
    207
Independent candidates, 149,
    206–209
Independent expenditures, 196
Indeterminate sentencing,
    367–368, 542
Indiana
    attorney general's election in,
        160
    ballots in, 144, 145*f*
    constitutional amendment
        process in, 79
    constitutional convention
        provisions in, 81
    economic cycle and, 117
    gubernatorial elections in, 78,
        308
    judicial elections in, 337, 341
    judicial review of voting law
        (2005), 150
    judicial selection in, 340
    jury nullification in, 537
    legislators in, 253
    lieutenant governors in, 318

professional and personal
    services taxes in, 105
    ratification in, 79
Indianapolis, city council in, 430
Indictments, 358, 532
Indirect lobbying, 214
Individualistic cultures
    characteristics of, 12, 13, 16*t*
    defined, 13
    scrutiny of politician's record
        in, 173
    states with, 15*m*
    voter participation by, 151
Individual lobbyists, 211
Information technology (IT), 105,
    170, 268, 592
Informed citizens, in Tiebout
    model, 479–483
Initiative and referendum.
    See Ballot initiatives;
    Referendums
Instant-runoff voting (IRV), 147
Institute for Women's Policy
    Research (IWPR), 14
Insurance commissioners,
    elections of, 158, 321
Insurance companies. *See
    also* Health maintenance
    organizations (HMOs)
    homeowners insurance against
        natural disasters, 296–297
    state regulation of, 217, 228
Insurance trust funds, 114
Integrated family courts, 372
Intelligent design theory, 521
Intensive probation, 370
Interagency Working Group on
    Federalism, 57
Interest groups. *See also* Business
    groups; Lobbyists
    characteristics, 209–219
    defined, 179
    educational, 518–521
    environmental, 212–213
    ideology and, 181
    judicial elections and, 327, 340,
        341, 343, 375
    most influential in states
        (2007), 216*t*
    political parties and, 184, 201,
        202–203, 215

public opinion shaping
    by, 172
state and local decision-making
    authority and, 22–23
voter preferences and, 138
Intergovernmental transfers,
    114–115
Interjurisdictional agreements
    (IJAs), 474
Intermediate appellate courts
    associate justices' salaries, by
        rank, 2006, 354, 355*t*
    initial judicial selection for,
        336–338, 339*m*
    role in state court system,
        329–330, 334–336
    terms of office and
        reappointment methods
        by state (2010), 346,
        349–351*t*
Intermodal Surface
    Transportation Efficiency Act
    (ISTEA, 1991), 470
International City/County
    Management Association
    (ICMA), 429, 433, 435, 445,
    448–449
Internet
    interface with constituents by,
        170
    as news source, 268
    sales tax on shopping on, 105
Interracial marriage, 87
Investigative grand juries, 532
Iowa
    chief state school officer
        in, 493
    CHIP program in, 585
    constitutional amendment
        process in, 79
    constitutional convention
        provisions in, 81
    government consolidation in,
        474, 485
    gun-control laws in, 560
    partisan control of legislature
        in, 251
    ratification in, 79
    redistricting in, 250
    rural flight in, 483–484, 484*m*
    same-sex unions in, 69, 87

universal healthcare in, 590
voting by felons in, 544
Majority leader in state
legislature, 242
Majority-minority districts, 252
Majority rule, 224
Major Party Support, 208–209
Malapportionment, 250
Mall of America, Bloomington,
Minnesota, sales tax and,
105
Managed care, 584–585, 589.
See also Health maintenance
organizations (HMOs)
Management by Objectives
(MBO), 407
Managerial judges, 372
Mandates
financial, 73
on fire-safe cigarettes, 234–235
funded, 445
on greenhouse gas emissions,
213
unfunded, 54, 128–129
Mandatory jurisdiction, 335
Mandatory minimum sentences,
368, 369
Mann, Horace, 491, 493, 511
Mansell, Al, 253
Marble cake federalism, 51*f*
Maricopa County, Arizona
death penalty, 363
role in Phoenix's government,
294, 424
Marijuana, 63, 166, 540, 541
Markham, William, 77
Marriage. *See also* Same-sex
unions
defined
by federal government, 57
by Proposition 8 (California),
87
licenses for, local governments
and, 419
Marshall, John, 47, 48, 59
Maryland
constitution of, 72
environmental lobbyists in,
212–213
EPA's enforcement of clean air
rule and, 212

governor
election of, 200, 312
influence on state budget,
157, 279
veto power, 293
greenhouse gas emissions
mandate in, 213
gun-control laws in, 560
high-stakes standardized tests
in, 509
individualistic culture in, 13
judicial selection in, 345
jury nullification and, 537
lethal injection process in, 558
one-party dominance in, 173
political party allegiances in,
173
Smart Growth Act in, 287
state colleges, tuition and cost-
cutting measures in, 113
tax system in, 109
women as legislators in, 254
*Maryland ex. rel. Washington
County v. Baltimore & Ohio
Railroad Co.* (1845), 421
Massachusetts
ballot initiatives in, 167–168
CHIP program in, 585
compulsory testing results in,
509
constitutional amendment
process in, 79
constitutional changes by
Supreme Court of, 86
constitutional convention
provisions in, 81
county government corruption
in, 426
election of U.S. senator in 2010,
159
governor's power in, 280
gun-control laws in, 560
healthcare coverage in, 570
judicial terms of office in, 346
legislature of
introducing bills to, 230
sessions in, 230, 244
voting in, 248
lobbying regulations in, 214
party competition in, 8
Proposition 2½, 108

ratification in, 79
royal charter of, 75
same-sex unions in, 69, 86, 87,
167–168, 230, 327
Senate leadership powers in,
244
shortage of court officers in,
374
state board of education in, 491
tax system in, 109, 116
tobacco products advertising
in, 63
universal healthcare in, 590
U.S. Senate special election
(2010), 164
Massachusetts ballots, 144
Massachusetts Bay Colony, 74, 77
Massachusetts Supreme Judicial
Court, 327
Massachusetts Taxpayers
Foundation, 590
Masset, Royal, 178
Mayhew, David R., 302
Mayor-council system, 157,
429–432, 431*f*
Mayors, 157, 429, 447–448
McAdams, Don, 496
McCain, John, 184
McCain-Feingold campaign
finance law, 196, 198
McCarthy, Eugene, 192
McCulloch v. Maryland (1819),
47, 60
McDonald's, 596–597
McDonnell, Robert, 142, 159,
591
McDonough, John, 248
McGovern, George, 192
McGreevey, Jim, 314
McLaughlin, Ed, 197
McWherter, Ned, 299, 584
Mecham, Evan, 168, 313
Media. *See also* Newspapers;
Television
complaints about, 186
governors' use of, 302–304
legislative process and, 229,
235, 264
lobbying coverage by, 213, 214
public opinion shaping and,
172

legislators' responses to public opinion in, 173
lobbying regulations in, 214
minor parties in, 207, 208
political culture in, 202
political party regulation in, 195, 196
sales tax waivers in, 106
same-day registration and voting in, 150, 155
transportation package in, 227
voting in, 150, 151, 154, 155
women as legislators in, 254
Minnesota Democrats Exposed blog, 268
Minorities. *See also* African Americans; Hispanics
as jurors, 537
as state supreme court justices, 340
student achievement by, 522–523
voter turnout by, 151, 153
Minority leader in state legislature, 242
Minor parties. *See also* Third parties
ballot access regulations and, 148–149
candidates, 207
state government role for, 194
Misdemeanors, 359
Mississippi
African American legislators in, 255
ballot initiatives in, 80
budget process in, 121
constitutional convention provisions in, 81
economic cycle and taxes in, 117
emergency contraceptives law in, 595
gambling operations and economy of, 117
gubernatorial elections in, 78, 308
home schooling in, 518
judicial elections in, 90, 341
jury selection regulations in, 365

lieutenant governor's power in, 318
Medicaid program in, 575
per capita gross state product of, 17
politics and women's status in, 14
rainy day funds, 130
Reconstruction and, 86
school desegregation in, 519
school funding in, 501
sentencing and early prison release in, 558–559
TANF spending in, 582
tort laws in, 233
traditionalistic political culture in, 13, 118
unions in, 233
voting ease in, 154
Missouri
CHIP program in, 585
criminal sentencing in, 367
gubernatorial elections in, 308
judicial elections in, 90, 338, 340
jury selection regulations in, 365
legislators in, 242
Medicaid programs in, 575
political parties in, 142
Missouri Compromise (1820), 48
Missouri Plan for judicial selections, 90, 338
Moakley, Maureen, 13
Mobility of citizens. *See* Migration patterns
Model constitutions, 89
Molnau, Carol, 316
Moncrief, Gary, 265
Monocentric metropolitan areas, 482
Montana
appellate courts in, 334
constitutional convention provisions in, 82
drug laws in, 540
election (2004) ruling in, 207
geography of, 18
gubernatorial elections in, 308
judicial elections in, 341
legislature of, bills before, 230

Medicaid program in, 575
methamphetamines in, 556
privacy rights in, 92
public health services in, 588
state superintendent of education in, 321
tax system in, 109, 130
term limits in, 266
transportation spending in, 128
Montessori schools, 513
Moody's Investors Service, 118
Moore, Roy S., 330
Moralistic cultures
characteristics of, 12, 16*t*
civic engagement in, 157
scrutiny of politician's record in, 173
states with, 15*m*
voter turnout in, 151
voting ease in, 154
Morrison; United States v. (2000), 61, 62*t*
Morse, Steven, 236*f*
Motor vehicle taxes, 104
Motor voter registration, 150, 151, 154–155
Mountain West, political leanings in, 139–141, 180, 200
Moynihan, Daniel Patrick, 582
Muchmore, Lynn, 277
Multnomah County, Oregon, and regional government, 469
Munger, Willard, 236*f*
Municipal bonds, 118
Municipal charters, 97, 443–444
Municipalities, 428–438. *See also* Cities; Local governments; Metropolitics
annexation, 478–479
commission system, 435–436
council-manager system, 432–435, 433*f*, 436
county government vs., 424
defined, 419
jurisdiction of, 419
mayor-council system, 157, 429–432, 431*f*
most common government forms, 434–435, 434*t*
regional councils and, 470

Simon, Len, 213, 214
Simpson, O. J., 329
Sims, Ron, 473
Single-use zoning, 463
Sin taxes, 104
Site-based management for schools, 507
Sixteenth Amendment, 39–42, 43t, 50
Sixth Amendment, 359, 364
Smart growth, 287, 472
Smart Growth Act (Maryland, 1998), 287
Smith, Bob, 184
Smith, David, 363
Smith, Rich, 233
Smith, Rick, 450
Smog, 464–465
Smoking bans, 167
Snyder, Howard, 562
Socialist Party, 207
Social safety net, 572–573. *See also* Medicaid; Medicare; Public health and welfare
Social Security Act (1935), 60, 401, 573
Social services and political parties, 186
Social status and indeterminate sentencing, 368
Sociodemographics, 9–10
Socrates, 535
Soft money, 196
Softshells, 179
Sorauf, Frank J., 210
Sotomayor, Sonia, 406
South (region). *See also* Traditionalistic cultures
council-manager systems in, 435
county's importance in, 416, 421–424
criminal justice systems in, 533
Democratic Party and, 180, 200
literacy tests in, 150
police departments in, size of, 555
political culture evolution in, 139, 200
public schools' administration in, 493

punishment conventions in, 535
Republican Party and, 180, 200
school board elections in, 494
secretaries of agriculture in, 321
traditionalistic culture in, 13, 15
trial lawyers in, 233
voter turnout in, 153
South Carolina
ARRA and, 30
budget process in, 121
constitutional amendment process in, 79, 83
constitutional convention provisions in, 81
governor
election of, 78, 159
powers of, 304
judicial selection in, 345
jury selection regulations in, 365
legislative sessions in, 256
ratification in, 79, 83
traditionalistic culture in, 13
South Dakota
appellate courts in, 334
appropriations bills in, 73
ballot initiatives in, 80, 327
community health centers in, 588
constitutional convention provisions in, 81
constitution of, 72, 73
emergency contraceptives law in, 595
judicial compensation in, 354
judicial elections in, 341
professional and personal services taxes in, 105
school funding in, 500, 502
state capitol reporters in, 265
supermajorities in, 73
tax system in, 109
transportation spending in, 128
Southeast (region) and home schooling, 518
Southwest (region) police departments, 555
Sovereign immunity, 62
Sovereign power and juries, 536–537

Spain, Mississippi, and shipping, 35
Speaker of the House, 226, 242, 254
Special act charters, 444
Special districts, 96, 419–420, 437–438, 456
Special jurisdiction trial courts, 332
Spellings, Margaret, 507
Spitzer, Eliot, 307, 314, 319
Spoils system, 399
Spokane and Spokane County, Washington, city-county consolidation, 475
Sprawl, 463–465, 478
Springfield, Oregon, and effects from Great Recession, 450
Sputnik satellite, 504
Standard and Poor's, 118
Standardized testing movement, high-stakes, 492, 505–507
Standards movement in education, 492, 507–508, 509
Stanford Achievement Test (SAT), 505, 506
Stanford University study on charter schools, 514
Stark, Lloyd, 338
Starr, Paul, 571
State agencies, 280, 384. *See also* Bureaucracies
State boards of education, 491. *See also* School boards
State-centered federalism, 48
State Children's Health Insurance Program (CHIP), 124–125, 294, 585–586
State governments. *See also* *specific branches*
common law and, 531–533
elections, supervision of, 144–147
employment by, 20–21, 21*m*, 449
federal government vs., 8, 19–22, 45, 46*f*
federalism and, 36–37
fiscal year of, 120

funded mandates and, 445
GASB 45 effect on, 128
healthcare spending by,
124–126
hiring freezes, 449
as laboratories of democracy,
22–25
local governments and, 114,
438–445
New Federalism and, 54
partisan control in 1954,
245–246m
political parties and, 147–149,
185
preemption and, 40
public health role for, 571
taxing variations among,
115–116
State political parties
campaign finance, 196–198
campaign reform (late
twentieth century) and,
192–194
governor as chief of, 282–283
national parties and, 180–181
regulation of, 147–149,
195–196
suburban vs. city voters and,
142
State politics
comparative method of
studying, 7–19
daily impact of, 5–7
States' rights, 47, 54–57, 61–63
State supreme courts. *See* Supreme
courts, state
Statutory law, 532
Stem-cell research, 95, 142, 143,
168, 263
Stern, Howard, 240
Stimulus package (2009). *See*
American Recovery and
Reinvestment Act of 2009
(ARRA)
Stimulus plan by Bush (G.W.),
164
Stolberg, Irving, 249
Straight tickets, 147, 209
Straus, Eric, 231
Strayhorn, Caroline Keeton,
158–159

Streamlined Sales Tax
Project, 106
Street-level bureaucrats, 383
Strong mayor system, 429, 431f
Subnational governments, 31.
See also Local governments;
Metropolitics; State
governments
Subprime mortgages, 119
Suburbs. *See also* City-county
consolidation
demographic trends in, 142
rise of crime in, 556
Successful schools model, 501
Sudan Divestment Task Force,
210, 211, 214
Suffolk County, New York, and
Tiebout model, 483
Suffrage Movement, 77
Suicide, physician-assisted, 63,
166
Sunshine Amendment (Florida),
68
Sunstein, Cass, 31
Superintendents, school, 496–497
Supermajority votes, 71, 79, 130,
278
Supermax security prisons, 553
Superpredators, 548
Supremacy clause, national,
39–42, 43t, 45, 59
Supreme Court, U.S.
activism on, 326
on affirmative action and New
Haven firefighters, 406
on California's anti-political
law, 189, 195
on death penalty, 557
on equal school funding, 498
federalism, key rulings on,
59–63, 62t
grand jury role, key rulings on,
358
as highest court, 330
on jury verdicts, 364
on late-term abortions, 569
on lethal injection, 558
on majority-minority districts,
252
on National Guard deployment
policies, 283

on party affiliation as basis for
state government hiring,
202
on political party regulation,
195, 196
on presidential election (2000),
63, 146, 190, 327
on right to an attorney, 359
on sales taxes for Internet
shopping, 105
on school vouchers, 516,
517
on sentencing, 543
Supreme courts, state. *See also*
Courts of last resort
activism on, 326–328
assertiveness of, 69, 71
definition, 330
education reforms and, 518
role in court system,
330–331
state constitutional changes by,
83–86
on states' rights, 63
Swine flu, 566, 594
Swing voters, 184
Symington, Fife, 313

T
Taft, William Howard, 190
Takoma Park, Maryland, mayor-
council system, 432
Talk radio, 186
Talmadge, Gene, 399
Taney, Roger B., 48, 60, 421
TANF. *See* Temporary Assistance
to Needy Families
Tax capacity, 116
Tax Day protests, 164
Tax effort or burden, 104, 116,
117
Taxes. *See also* Revenues
on alcohol, 104
ballot initiatives on, 167
car taxes, 104, 112
death taxes, 104, 112
on dogs, 7
estate taxes, 104, 112
excise taxes, 104
gasoline taxes, 104
gift taxes, 104

income taxes, 109–111,
110–111*t*
on Internet shopping, 105
local, 424, 425, 441
oil taxes, 112
paid by U.S. residents
(2008), 103
property taxes, 106–109
regressive taxes, 104–105
sales taxes, 9, 104–105
sin taxes, 104
taxing variations, 115–118
Tax revolts, 94. *See also*
Proposition 13
Teachers
furlough days, 522
as legislators, 253
licensure procedures for, 493
recruitment of, 509–511
unions, 253, 519
Teach for America, 494, 511
Teamsters, 203
Tea Party movement, 164–165,
184
Technology, government uses of,
171
Teixeira, Ruy, 153
Television. *See also* Media
depictions of state party
preferences on, 137
government issues and political
advertising on, 192, 344
Temporary Assistance to Needy
Families (TANF)
benefit variations among states,
582
defined, 568
eligibility for, 575
income eligibility thresholds
(2005), 582*m*
as replacement for AFDC, 126,
568, 581
Ten Commandments display in
Alabama Supreme Court,
330
TennCare, 580, 584, 589
Tennessee
constitutional amendment
process in, 79
elected county executives in,
426

Internet shopping and sales tax
revenues in, 105
judicial selection in, 340, 346
jury selection regulations in,
365
lieutenant governor of, 318
managed care in, 589
Medicaid program in, 580, 585
Medicaid waivers in, 590
privacy rights in, 92
Race to the Top funds to, 490
rainy day funds, 130
ratification in, 79
Reconstruction and, 86
Republican control of both
chambers in, 234
tax system in, 105, 109
urban growth boundaries
in, 469
voter turnout in, 151
Tenth Amendment
ad hoc federalism vs., 61–63
defined, 45
Dillon's Rule on, 440
enumerated powers and, 49
local governments and, 440
national supremacy and,
59, 60
public education and, 492
reserved (state) powers under,
39–42, 43*t*, 44, 45, 59, 74,
242
Term limits, 95, 167, 266–267,
269, 314
Terribile, Mike, 363
Terrorism preparedness, 58, 567.
See also Bioterrorism
Texas
attorney general's election
(2002) in, 160
ballot access in, 148
bilingual government Web sites
in, 409
blogging corps in, 265
civil and criminal appeals, 335
commission system in, 435
constitutional convention
provisions in, 81
counties in, 421, 424
criminal sentencing in, 367
cultural influences in, 10–11

death penalty in, 342
economic cycle in, 117
en banc appellate court
hearings in, 335
executions in, 7
executive power in, 92, 278
fiscal year in, 120
franchise and, 87
geography of, 18
governor's powers in, 157–158,
280, 286
gubernatorial campaign
spending in, 308
home schooling in, 518
income taxes and, 259
interest groups and education
reforms in, 518
Internet shopping and sales tax
revenues in, 105
judicial elections in, 90, 340,
342, 344
legislative sessions in, 259
legislators in, 256
lieutenant governor's power in,
92, 157, 244, 318
Medicaid eligibility in,
232, 591
non-enforcement of laws as
informal constitutional
change in, 87
petition restrictions in, 148
plural executive system in,
157–158
political culture in, 16
political parties in, 188
power distribution in, 91–92
rainy day funds, 130
Reconstruction and, 86, 88
redistricting in, 252
Republican Party in, 201
school districts in, 494
Senate leadership powers in,
244
state politics, college course
requirements in, 6
statewide officials in, 316
tax system in, 109, 116
traditionalistic culture
in, 16
Texas Rangers, 533
Textbooks, 508

War on Drugs, 539–540
Warrants, 436
Warren, Earl, 326
Washington (state)
    ballot initiatives and budget
        process in, 129
    CHIP program in, 585
    city-county consolidations in, 475
    direct democracy in, 166
    economic priorities in, 17
    judicial elections in, 90, 341
    performance audits in, 395
    Seattle, ballot initiative for
        football stadium in, 96
    tax system in, 109, 112
    transportation project funding
        in, 230–231
    urban growth boundaries in, 469
Washington, Booker T., 70
Washington, D.C. *See* District of
    Columbia
Washington, George, 34, 35, 178
Washington County, Oregon, and
    regional government, 469
Watergate scandal, 174, 264
Watertown, New York, special
    election (2009), 204
Wattenberg, Martin, 206
Watts. *See* Los Angeles (city)
Weak mayor system, 429, 430,
    431*f*
Wealth and voting, 151, 153
Web sites, 170, 409
Weicker, Lowell, 207
Welfare. *See* Aid to Families with
    Dependent Children (AFDC);
    Public health and welfare;
    Temporary Assistance to
    Needy Families (TANF)
Wendy's restaurants, 597
West (region). *See also* Mountain
    West; Pacific Northwest
    council-manager systems in,
        435
    Democratic Party and, 180
    police departments in, 554, 555
    professional model of policing
        in, 546–547
    special water districts in, 438
    states with direct democracy in,
        94, 166

West Mifflin Sanitary Sewer
    Municipal Authority, special
    district of, 456
West Virginia
    Appalachian Regional
        Commission and, 587
    appeals process in, 336
    ballot access in, 149
    corrections in, 128
    interest groups in, 218
    judicial elections in, 90, 340
    Medicaid program in, 575, 580
    party machine in, 187
    schools consolidation in, 512
    taxation in, 7
    tort laws in, 233
West Virginia University Medicaid
    study, 580
Wharton, A. C., Jr., 459
Whatley, Chris, 591
Whigs, 179, 180
Whistle-blower laws, 400
White, Mark, 158
White flight, 466
Whitman, Christine Todd, 205
Wickard v. Filburn (1942), 60
Wikis, government use of, 171
Wilder, Doug, 307
Will, George, 326
Williams v. Rhodes (1968), 148
Willing, Richard, 557
Wilson, James Q., 545, 547
Wilson, Pete, 430
Wilson, Woodrow, 192
Windham, Jeanne, 328
Windom, Steve, 158
Windsor, Ontario, megalopolis
    with Detroit, Michigan, 461
Winger, Richard, 148
Winner-takes-all-system, 206
Wintemute, Garen, 561
Winthrop, John, 74, 77
Wisconsin
    constitutional amendment
        process in, 79
    constitution and political
        culture of, 88
    geography of, 18, 19
    gun-control laws in, 560
    judicial elections in,
        341, 375

legislative process in, 230
minor parties in, 208
party competition for governor
    in, 200
political culture in, 12, 16
power distribution in, 91
professional legislators in, 259
Progressive Party in, 93
public campaign financing in,
    197
ratification in, 79
traditionalistic culture in, 16
veto authority of governor in,
    295
voter turnout in, 151
welfare reform in, 569, 579
Wisconsin Education Association
    Council (WEAC), 204, 403
Wisconsin Manufacturers and
    Commerce, 204
Wisconsin State Journal on state
    legislative process, 295
Wisconsin Territory and Missouri
    Compromise (1820), 48
Wisconsin Works, 287
Wolfinger, Raymond E., 154
Women
    as elected city officials, 447
    franchise for, 77, 149
    as governors, 307
    as jurors, 537
    as state legislators, 242,
        254–255, 257–258*t*
    as state supreme court justices,
        340
    status of, 14, 14*t*
Working Families Party, 208
Works Progress Administration
    (WPA), 443
World War I and federal
    government centralization,
    50
World War II and federal
    government centralization,
    50
Wright, Ralph, 249
Write-in candidates, 147
Wyoming
    appellate courts in, 334
    ballot initiatives in, 81, 94
    economic cycle and, 117